W9-BCS-004

A Writer's Workshop

Crafting Sentences, Building Paragraphs, Designing Essays

Brannan ▪ Finlay-Clark ▪ Bradley-St-Cyr

McGraw-Hill
Ryerson

A Writer's Workshop
Second Canadian Edition

The Internet addresses listed in the text were accurate at the time of publication. The inclusion of a Web site does not indicate an endorsement by the authors or McGraw-Hill Ryerson, and McGraw-Hill Ryerson does not guarantee the accuracy of the information presented at these sites.

ISBN-13: 978-0-07-059394-7
ISBN-10: 0-07-059394-9

4 5 6 7 8 9 WEB 1 9 8 7 6 5

Printed and bound in Canada

Care has been taken to trace ownership of copyright material contained in this text; however, the publisher will welcome any information that enables them to rectify any reference or credit for subsequent editions.

Director of Product Management: Rhondda McNabb
Group Product Manager: Kim Brewster
Product Manager: Karen Fozard
Marketing Manager: Margaret Janzen
Senior Product Developer: Sara Braithwaite
Senior Product Team Associate: Marina Seguin
Supervising Editor: Graeme Powell
Permissions Editor: Monika Shurmann
Copy Editor/Proofreader: Ashley Rayner
Plant Production Coordinator: Michelle Saddler
Manufacturing Production Coordinator: Lena Keating
Cover and Interior Design: Ellissa Glad
Cover Image: Thinkstock.com (RF)/istockphoto.com (RF)
Page Layout: Laserwords Private Limited
Printer: Webcom Inc.

Library and Archives Canada Cataloguing in Publication

Brannan, Bob, author
  A writer's workshop: crafting sentences, building paragraphs, designing essays/Brannan, Finlay-Clark, Bradley-St-Cyr.—Second Canadian edition.

Includes bibliographical references and index.
ISBN 978-0-07-059394-7 (pbk.)

  1. English language—Sentences—Problems, exercises, etc. 2. English language—Paragraphs—Problems, exercises, etc. 3. English language—Rhetoric—Problems, exercises, etc. 4. English language—Grammar—Problems, exercises, etc. 5. Report writing—Problems, exercises, etc. I. Bradley-St-Cyr, Ruth, 1962–, author II. Finlay-Clark, Jan, author III. Title.

PE1441.B73 2014   808'.042   C2013-906334-X

Contents

UNIT ONE: PREPARING FOR SUCCESS 1

Chapter 1

Chapter 2

UNIT TWO: CRAFTING SENTENCES: UNDERSTANDING HOW THEY WORK 29

Chapter 3

Chapter 4

Chapter 7

Chapter 5

Chapter 8

Chapter 6

Chapter 9

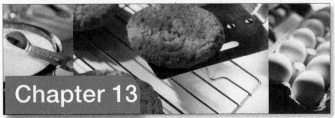

Chapter 18

Varying Sentences 221

Chapter 17

Spelling and Sound-alike Words 208

Chapter 19

Choosing Effective Words 231

UNIT THREE: BUILDING PARAGRAPHS 241

Chapter 20

Introducing the Paragraph 242

Chapter 21

Revising Paragraphs 261

UNIT FOUR: DESIGNING ESSAYS 273

Chapter 22

Chapter 23

Chapter 24

Chapter 25

Writing with Examples (Illustration) 327

Chapter 26

Explaining Processes 343

Chapter 27

Discovering Cause and Effect 359

Chapter 28

Exploring Similarities and Differences (Comparison and Contrast) 374

Chapter 29

Creating and Explaining Groups (Classification) 391

Chapter 30

Defining Terms (Definition) 406

Chapter 31

Writing Persuasively (Argument) 423

Chapter 32

About this Book

OVERVIEW

A Writer's Workshop: Crafting Sentences, Building Paragraphs, Designing Essays engages developing writers with a **hands-on, process-oriented, collaborative,** and **practical** approach to writing.

Hands On . . .

A Writer's Workshop advocates that the best way to learn to write well is by writing. This book offers a wealth of opportunities for students to write sentences, paragraphs, and essays about topics in a variety of disciplines, encouraging writers to draw on their own experiences and other courses. Along the way, it provides both instruction and practice opportunities for using essential grammar, punctuation, and sentence skills that will help student writers clearly express their ideas.

Process-Oriented . . .

The text's central focus and user-friendly design ensure that "process" is more than a buzzword in writing *and* reading. The writing-assignment chapters offer thorough process breakdowns, revision strategies, and **Journal/Blog** prompts in the context of actual assignments. Inclusion of student work provides a variety of prewriting approaches and annotations that examine multiple drafts and stages of revision.

Collaborative . . .

Most chapters offer **Working Together** activities, opportunities for collaborative learning and practice. **Peer review** prompts in writing-assignment chapters encourage workshopping at the revision stage of the writing process. In this way, student writers have an opportunity to share work with fellow students. This provides a constant affirmation of the complexity of the writing process and the opportunity to realize that peer readers can be extremely helpful in refining one's work.

Instructors are encouraged to combine Units 4 and 5 with Units 2 and 3 in order to develop the details of crafting good sentences with writing effective paragraphs and essays. For example, a good partner for Chapter 20, *Introducing the Paragraph,* would be Chapter 3, *Subjects, Verbs, and Other Sentence Parts.* A good partner for Chapter 23, *Describing a Person, Place, or Object (Description),* would be Chapters 6, *Nouns,* or 8, *Adjectives and Adverbs.* Writing instructors are encouraged to be creative in combining chapters to most effectively help students develop writing skills according to their course outlines.

Practical . . .

In select chapters, **Linking to Previous Experience** sections help developing writers connect what they already know to lessons in the book. **Linking to Future Experience** sections summarize main points and tie writing skills to future applications, giving long-range purpose to what students are practising.

Alternate Assignments in Unit 4 offer students practice opportunities in a variety of programs—business, culture, education, health care, science, and technology—helping students apply their skills in context.

Shortly after leaving this course, students may find themselves wrestling with a researched argument in an ethics course, a term paper in business marketing, or perhaps a process description in a health sciences course. This textbook will help students to develop solid foundational skills for all their future writing projects.

NEW TO THIS EDITION

Unit 1

Preparing for Success engages students with the reading and writing process: outlining reading strategies useful in any course and focusing on the steps most writers use to discover, focus, and organize ideas, as well as strategies for revising and editing. New features include:

- Expanded discussion of pre-writing strategies.
- Consideration of writing for different purposes and audiences.
- Updated activities.
- Expanded section on annotating, note taking, and summarizing.
- Discussion of critical reading and reading for different purposes.

Unit 2

Crafting Sentences: Understanding How They Work explains and illustrates the parts of speech, showing how they combine to form phrases and clauses and how these sentence parts can be ordered through coordination and subordination. Grammar study is applied directly to students' own writing with examples drawn from their daily lives. New features include:

- Greater diversity of examples including more academic examples and more examples from a variety of disciplines, programs, and vocations (police foundations, early childhood education, business, design, hospitality, health, arts, and science).

Unit 3

Building Paragraphs introduces students to the paragraph as the building block of composition, including an overview of paragraphs and detailed instruction for revising paragraphs. New features include:

- Reorganized chapter 20 that begins with creating topic sentences, then moves to a focus on body paragraph development and the organization of the body paragraph, and ends with concluding sentences and finding the right title.

- Greater variety of examples and topics introduced.
- Expanded discussion of the difference between editing and proofreading.
- Additional revision exercises that require students to revise the sample of student writing.

Unit 4

Designing Essays helps students make a smooth transition from writing paragraphs to writing essays and introduces the nine patterns of development. New features include:
- Discussion of moving beyond the 5 paragraph essay.
- Expanded discussion in each chapter of writing paragraphs in the featured rhetorical mode.
- New Canadian readings.
- Discussion of narration beyond first-person context.
- New content on directional versus informational processes.
- Updated and expanded examples and activities.
- Clarification of the difference between argument and persuasion.

Unit 5

Researching and Documenting provides information about how to research and document a research essay using the two most common documentation styles: MLA (Modern Language Association) style and APA (American Psychological Association).

KEY FEATURES OF *A WRITER'S WORKSHOP*

- **Linking to Previous Experience, Linking to Future Experience.** All major chapters open with an overview asking students to link prior knowledge to recently acquired knowledge. Each paragraph- or essay-writing chapter (Units 3 and 4) calls upon this familiar ground as a point of entry through the **Linking to Previous Experience** feature, then closes with **Linking to Future Experience,** which explores the usefulness of chapter content beyond the course. In other chapters (Units 2 and 5), the relevance of acquiring various skills is explored under the heading **What Are We Trying to Achieve and Why?**
- **Activities.** Each chapter offers an array of practice opportunities, including collaborative and online exercises, which are an integral part of each writing assignment.
- **Working Together Activities** suggest collaborative work, both within textbook exercises and online.
- **Feedback/Peer Review** prompts encourage working in pairs or small groups at all stages of the writing process.
- **More than 100 possible writing topics for key assignments, including additional alternate assignments.** The opening assignment for each writing chapter is linked to an image or images, encouraging visual literacy to provide inspiration and a helpful bridge for visual learners. You will notice a multicultural theme in many of the photos, a reminder to celebrate—and write about—the varied people who are in our lives.

- **Journal and Blog Entries.** These prompts help students make the connection between the chapter assignment and their lives, calling for specific, detailed examples and reinforcing the integration of a writer's aims.
- **Hints.** Useful marginal suggestions and cross-references connect the paragraph- and essay-writing process to sentence skills and reading strategies.
- **English Review Notes.** In the textbook's margins, these tips provide in-context, helpful guidance for non-native speakers. Selected grammar chapters feature end sections entitled **For English as a Second Language Learners,** which include in-depth explanations of grammar difficulties specific to ESL and multilingual students.

Supplements Package

McGraw-Hill Connect™ is a web-based assignment and assessment platform that gives students the means to better connect with their coursework, with their instructors, and with the important concepts that they will need to know for success now and in the future.

With Connect, instructors can deliver assignments, quizzes and tests online and integrate grade reports easily with Learning Management Systems (LMS) such as WebCT and Blackboard. By choosing Connect, instructors are providing their students with a powerful tool for improving academic performance and truly mastering course material. Connect allows students to practice important skills at their own pace and on their own schedule. Importantly, students' assessment results and instructors' feedback are all saved online—so students can continually review their progress and plot their course to success.

Connect Composition helps students improve their writing and grammar skills through comprehensive and reliable instruction, practice material, and more!

For Instructors

- An Instructor's Manual that offers sample syllabi, teaching strategies, and an answer key.
- Microsoft® PowerPoint® slides that can be downloaded and adapted to meet course needs.

SUPERIOR LEARNING SOLUTIONS AND SUPPORT

The McGraw-Hill Ryerson team is ready to help you assess and integrate any of our products, technology, and services into your course for optimal teaching and learning performance. Whether it's helping your students improve their grades, or putting your entire course online, the McGraw-Hill Ryerson team is here to help you do it. Contact your *Learning Solutions Consultant* today to learn how to maximize all of McGraw-Hill Ryerson's resources!

For more information on the latest technology and Learning Solutions offered by McGraw-Hill Ryerson and its partners, please visit us online: *www.mcgrawhill.ca/he/solutions*.

Acknowledgments

Many thanks, first of all, go to the reviewers who took the time to offer valuable suggestions for improving *A Writer's Workshop*. It is great to have such valuable colleagues to help with such a big project:

Carolyn Ambrose	Niagara College	Teresa MacVicar	Conestoga College
Lorraine Argatoff	Capilano University	Melanie Mahadeva	Seneca College
Trevor Arkell	Humber College	Mary Ann Pruyser	North Island College
Maria Berrafati	Mohawk College	Curtis Runions	St Lawrence College
Adrian Bond	George Brown College	Stephanie Samboo	Sheridan College
Katharine Ferguson	Seneca College	Mavis Smith	Camosun College-Landsdowne

To my colleagues at McGraw-Hill Ryerson, thank you for all your help and for providing such great material to work with. I was an Associate Editor at McGraw-Hill Ryerson from 1993 to 1994 so I know how hard you all have to work to make it look so easy:

Karen Fozard, Product Manager
Sara Braithwaite, Senior Developmental Editor
Graeme Powell, Supervising Editor
Ashley Rayner, Copy Editor

Besides being my main contact for this book project, Sara also facilitated my research into the books of the Ryerson Press, which are lovingly preserved in the McGraw-Hill Ryerson library, and she took me to lunch. Many thanks, Sara! You finally feel like a real author when your publisher takes you to lunch.

To Steven Heighton, who is always a pleasure to work with as well as a pleasure to read, thank you for Vimy Ridge.

To my colleagues in the English Department of the University of Ottawa, especially my stalwart teaching assistant Amanda Montague, a million thanks. To our students in the Winter 2013 class of English 1100U, both the House of Montague and the House of Bradley, thank you for making teaching fun, even at 8:30 a.m. on Monday mornings, and for field-testing this textbook. A particular thank you goes to the anonymous student whose evaluation form dubbed me "the magical unicorn of the English department." What more could I desire to be?

To my family—Bau, Nicole, Emily, and Daniel—thanks for all the dinners, chores, hugs, distractions, and especially for telling me when something I've written is too "lame" to go into a textbook or an English course. To Miley, my fabulous office cat and writing associate, thank you for providing companionship while never stepping on my keyboard.

And most of all, my everlasting gratitude and respect goes to Jan Finlay-Clark, the author of the first Canadian edition, who left such a rock-solid base upon which to revise the second Canadian edition.

Ruth Bradley-St-Cyr

Preparing for Success

The Reading Process

Describe a pleasurable or frustrating reading experience you had in high school or college. Be specific: what was particularly interesting and/or challenging about the reading assignment?

What Is the Link Between Reading and Writing?

LO1.1

You may be wondering why a writing textbook would begin with a chapter on reading. You've been reading for years, so why bother with a chapter like this? Of course, at the post-secondary level, some reading material is complex and requires a sophisticated reading strategy. Reading a textbook is not like reading a novel; you aren't reading for pleasure, although hopefully you enjoy your classes. Instead, you are reading to learn and to retain the important points, some of which you might want to quote or paraphrase in your own writing. This sort of critical reading requires different techniques.

As well as using different reading strategies in order to learn more, you must also read in order to understand how writers write. You cannot become a better writer yourself without becoming a more observant, more critical reader. You must read to recognize all the elements that writers use to communicate. When you make observations and ask questions about a text reading, you are interacting with the text; this is a step toward interacting with your own writing. Just as you would not aim to become a writer of children's picture books without being an avid reader of them, so too must you read essays in order to be able to write them.

Is There a More Effective Way to Read?

LO1.2

Although most of us are competent readers, not many of us regularly read and interact with complex, information-heavy texts, such as college textbooks. This type of reading may include learning concepts, showing how they interrelate, memorizing facts and other detailed examples, and evaluating ideas and issues. While critical reading is challenging, learning the few simple methods listed below can make it easier. The rest of this chapter expands on these three stages in the reading process— pre-reading, reading, and post-reading—to help you become a more effective reader.

STAGES IN THE READING PROCESS

1. Pre-reading: Preparing to understand
2. Reading:
   - Focusing on and recording main ideas
   - Getting into the details
3. Post-reading: Retaining ideas

Pre-reading: Preparing to Understand

LO1.3

Reading, like writing, is best understood as a process. Just as you spend time planning before writing a first draft, so too should you spend some time sizing up a text before you begin to read it. Here are three useful approaches:

1. **Skim** by reading rapidly all *signposts* for a quick overview of the shape of the content. Signposts include the following: titles; headings; subheadings; highlighted, boldfaced, and italicized print; chapter previews; summaries; analytical questions; text boxes; and marginal notes.

2. **Scan** by reading selectively for *key ideas* and then *detail*. Do this by reading the introduction, the concluding paragraph, and the first sentence of each

paragraph between the introduction and the conclusion. Then look for detail by noting where there are proper (capitalized) nouns and numbers.

3. **Link** *new* information to *previous* knowledge. Developmental psychologists call this *scaffolding* because building knowledge is like building a house; you need foundations before you can build higher.

Skimming the Signposts

HINT

Signposts create a chapter outline.

All textbooks use visual aids to help students focus on the main points in each chapter. The title itself usually contains the main idea of the chapter. After the title, headings and subheadings will help you understand how the material is organized. Highlighted, **boldfaced,** and *italicized* words and passages emphasize a point. Chapter previews often appear as bulleted lists or brief summaries (like the Learning Objectives list under the photo on page 2). Brief summaries or numbered lists of essential points often appear at the end of main sections, and many chapters conclude with a summary or questions on the primary ideas of the chapter. Text boxes and marginal notes highlight significant points and ask questions to help readers reflect on the material. You may skim through a chapter noting one kind of visual aid distributed throughout (like subheadings), or you may do a linear skim and take in the transitions from one type of visual aid to another. Skimming through a chapter and noting these reading aids may take a few minutes, but it is time well spent.

Scanning for Key Ideas and Detail

Each chapter has a central focus (this chapter's focus is *reading effectively*), which divides into several key topics (such as *pre-reading*, *reading*, and *post-reading*). Before reading the body of a chapter, quickly read the chapter's introduction and the concluding paragraph (this may be the chapter summary). Then scan the body paragraphs, focusing on the *first* and *last* sentences of each one. This is where you should find the unifying idea, as a topic sentence at the beginning of the paragraph, and/or as a summary sentence at the end. The key topics, in turn, are divided into subtopics, all of which are then developed through examples, details, and explanations. You can often recognize them by the use of proper (capitalized) nouns indicating details about people, places, and things. Numbers provide details about when an event occurs (e.g., a date), or how many and how much of something we are discussing. This is not key information; this is detail. Just being aware of proper names and numbers as you scan will provide a good foundation for comprehension when you begin to read through the text.

Linking New Knowledge to Previous Knowledge

After previewing a chapter, pause for a moment to reflect. What have you just read? What does it mean to you at this point? How do the terms and ideas fit into your previous experience? We each have a large store of experience and knowledge to draw from. When we link new knowledge to what we already know, we understand and remember it better. For example, the concept of global climate change might seem difficult to understand at first, but if we compare the buildup of carbon dioxide and other gases in the atmosphere to adding extra insulation to the walls of a house, we can see how the earth, like that house, would hold in more heat.

Within almost all new material, we can identify something familiar. If we have little actual experience with a topic, we can still make associations and useful comparisons that will help us engage with it. In each chapter in Unit Four of this text, the **Linking to Previous Experience** feature emphasizes ways that concepts might be familiar to you already. Similarly, the **Linking to Future Experience** feature explores how skills and processes discussed could be useful to you in future classes and in the world beyond formal education.

ACTIVITY 1.1   Active Pre-reading Technique: Previewing a Chapter

HINT

Turn ahead to Chapter 2 in order to skim and scan its signposts and key ideas. For now, don't read the body of the text, just sample the chapter's key topics. After five minutes of skimming and scanning, answer the questions below on a separate sheet of paper. Feel free to continue scanning the chapter as you answer the questions.

1. What is the central focus of Chapter 2?

2. What five questions should a writer ask at the start of a writing project?

3. What are five ways to discover ideas for writing?

4. To what can you compare a rough outline?

5. What are six solutions for *writer's block*?

6. What are four revision priorities?

Active reading is a deliberate, often slow process. Active readers interact with the text.

Reading

L01.4

Focusing On and Recording Main Ideas

Knowing a few common patterns for organizing and developing ideas will make your reading easier and more efficient the first time through. Using a pencil and a highlighter will also make the material easier to review. The following guidelines will help focus your reading and your methods for recording the information you have located:

1. **Look** for thesis, topic, and summary sentences

2. **Focus** on main examples

3. **Notice** repeated material

4. **Recognize** patterns of development

5. **Learn** to annotate, outline, paraphrase, and summarize

LOOK FOR THESIS, TOPIC, AND SUMMARY SENTENCES

Thesis sentences contain the main idea of an essay; topic sentences contain the main idea of a paragraph. Both sentences state, "This is my topic, and this is what I'm going to say about it." Essays and textbook chapters usually have a thesis statement in the opening paragraphs. Within body paragraphs, the first or second sentence is often a topic sentence; at the end of the paragraph, a summary sentence often reiterates the main idea or connects it to ideas in the next paragraph. Look for these sentences when you preview a text, and then concentrate on them while reading. In the following paragraph, the topic and summary sentences are highlighted. (The meaning of the boldfacing and the boxing is explained in the sections following the paragraph.)

Preparing a Workspace

Before drafting, why not set up a workspace that will help you write? Some people are comfortable working around **noise** and activity, but many aren't. If you need **quiet**, find a quiet spot (a library?). Give yourself enough **time** to get something done. If thirty minutes is enough, great, but keep yourself **on task** the whole time. Decide **what else** might help you **to be productive:** food, water, coffee, music? Do you work best curled up in bed with a pencil, paper, and clipboard; or do you like to be in front of your computer? Make your work easier by creating a space that encourages you to write.

FOCUS ON MAIN EXAMPLES

Paragraphs are built from detailed examples and explanations. However, not all of these are critical to a reader's understanding of the paragraph's main idea. When reading for information, you should concentrate on the primary examples and most important explanations. Try not to be distracted by the less important ones. In the paragraph above, the main points that support the topic sentence are in **bold type**. The other supporting examples—library, thirty minutes, food, etc.— are secondary.

NOTICE REPEATED MATERIAL

Academic articles in particular repeat and elaborate important ideas, providing many examples and explanations. When you notice repeated material within a paragraph or chapter section (often highlighted in lists, charts, summaries, headings, and text boxes), pay special attention; repeated material is probably important. In the example paragraph above, notice that the idea of a workspace that encourages writing is repeated in the <u>boxed phrases</u>.

RECOGNIZE PATTERNS OF DEVELOPMENT

Writers use common patterns of development to expand and clarify their ideas. Body paragraphs are usually developed with detailed examples, and writers use those examples in predictable ways. For example, the paragraph above on preparing a workspace focuses on process instructions, explaining how to create a productive writing environment. It could be further developed with a brief story, or a comparison, or any of the other patterns of development that will be expanded upon in Unit Four. When we begin to recognize these patterns, the ideas and information contained within them become easier to understand and to recall.

LEARN TO ANNOTATE, OUTLINE, PARAPHRASE, AND SUMMARIZE

The note-taking processes of annotating, outlining, paraphrasing, and summarizing can be done in different ways and are somewhat similar to taking notes in class. There are many different methods of note taking, such as the Cornell method, and you can find out more online at http://lsc.cornell.edu/LSC_Resources/cornellsystem.pdf. Unlike with a lecture, though, when you are taking notes while reading, you have the freedom to stop, re-read, fast forward by skimming, and so on, which you certainly cannot do with your professor. The skills of paraphrasing and summarizing, in particular, are important to learn properly because in academic essays, you will be expected to cite your sources, accurately convey their messages, and not inadvertently plagiarize by sticking too closely to the original choice and order of words.

Annotate

After discovering the main points in a text, active readers often **annotate**—that is, they underline or highlight important points and then write marginal notes to record their reactions to the material. It is common for readers to write questions, agree/disagree with a point, express surprise, link an idea with one found elsewhere in the text, and so on. You might number examples, star (asterisk) passages, circle prominent facts, and connect information with arrows. There is no one correct way to annotate, but in general, highlight selectively. Highlighting three-fourths of the text will not help you focus on its critical parts. Less is better.

English Review Note

Focus on main ideas and supporting details; resist focusing on unfamiliar words.

SAMPLE ANNOTATION
PREPARING A WORKSPACE

Here's the main point.
Before drafting, why not set up a workspace that will help you write? Some people

are comfortable working around noise and activity, but many aren't. If you need quiet,

Go with noisy or quiet, whatever works.
find a quiet spot (a library?). Give yourself enough time to get something done. If

How can anyone stay focused all the time?
30 minutes is enough, great, but keep yourself on task the whole time. Decide what

else might help you to be productive: food, water, coffee, music? Do you work best

curled up in bed with a pencil, paper, and clipboard; or do you like to be in front of your

computer? Make your work easier by creating a space that encourages you to write.

Outline

Informal "scratch" outlines can also be useful for retaining information. Here is how we might outline the preceding paragraph:

SAMPLE "SCRATCH"
OUTLINE

Topic sentence: Before drafting, why not set up a workspace that will help you write?

Supporting details:

1. Go with a quiet or noisy space, whatever works best for you.
2. Set a time limit for work, stick to it, and stay focused.
3. Have food, drink, music, or whatever helps you to write.
4. Use a computer or pencil and paper.

Paraphrase and Summarize

Paraphrasing and summarizing material that you read helps you remember it because these activities require you to put the text's ideas into your own words. In a paraphrase, you keep both primary and secondary examples. Therefore, a **paraphrase** is longer than a summary. You change the words and rearrange them into phrases and sentences that are different from the original text. Because you keep most of the main ideas from your source, a paraphrase is about the same length as the original.

The main point of this paragraph is to set up a comfortable writing workspace. Some people need noise; others need quiet. Some work best with a computer, others with paper and pencil. It's good to write for a set time and stay focused. Writers should give themselves whatever treats they need to be comfortable.

HOW TO PARAPHRASE

1. Rephrase or reword the main ideas of the text.
2. Include both the primary ideas and the supporting detail.
3. Supporting detail may include statistics, anecdotes, and explanations.
4. Use numerical facts without changing them.
5. Do not add your own opinions.
6. The length of the original text and the paraphrase may be similar.

A **summary**, on the other hand, consists only of the main idea and significant examples. When you summarize, you reword the commentary and most examples. Summaries are usually much shorter than the original. They focus on presenting *key ideas*, but not supporting detail.

This paragraph advises people to create a workspace that helps them write and then to work for a set time and stay focused until they are finished.

Three problems often occur when attempting to paraphrase or to summarize:

1. Misinterpreting the source's ideas,
2. Omitting an idea or adding one that should not be there, and
3. Using too many of the author's words and a word arrangement that is too similar to the original.

HOW TO SUMMARIZE

1. Use your own words to convey only the main ideas of the text.
2. Focus on presenting an overview.
3. Do not interpret the meaning of the text.
4. Do not include your opinions.
5. Do not include details (statistics, anecdotes, or examples) or repeat ideas.
6. Use the present tense.

For examples and more details about a paraphrased or summarized text, see Chapter 32, "Writing a Research Essay."

Read the paragraph below, underlining the topic sentence and any main examples. (Remember that topic sentences are usually the first or second sentence but can be located elsewhere in a paragraph.) Next, annotate in the margins to show your reactions. Finally, write a brief scratch outline and a one-sentence summary of the paragraph.

Moving Ahead

Good writing is not usually easy and challenges all writers to overcome problems in their way. If it is a time problem, time must be found. If you are a fast writer whose work seems unfocused, you may need to slow down. Alternately, you may write so slowly that you can't meet deadlines and so need to speed up. If you usually write on paper but aren't making much progress, you might try drafting on a computer. Sometimes we have difficulties resuming work on a draft we have left for a while. Starting again can be easier if we jot a few notes to remind us of where we want the draft to go, and sometimes simply stopping mid-sentence can be a solution. Despite the problems that all writers must deal with, we should resist the impulse to be overly critical of our rough drafts. They are just that—works in progress. We will be more critical as we begin to revise.

Getting into the Details

Once you are reading the details in a chapter, it is helpful to try to **understand words in context**. It will speed up your reading if you do not have to check the dictionary for every unfamiliar word; however, if you have the time, using a dictionary as you read will improve your vocabulary and help ensure that you are using words correctly. It is also helpful to work at **distinguishing fact from opinion**. The two can be confused, especially in a paragraph or essay developed by narration or persuasion. Often a textbook will aid your understanding of a reading by providing comprehension questions, encouraging you to **reflect critically**.

UNDERSTANDING WORDS IN CONTEXT

Often you can figure out the meaning of an unknown word by considering its context within the sentence in which it appears. The sentences that come before and after the one in which the unknown word appears provide clues. Consider the italicized word in the following text:

Squirrels climb trees better than any other animal. A metre away from the trunk, a female squirrel *catapults* from the ground onto a tree. Then she runs quickly along a branch.

Even if you do not know the meaning of the word *catapults*, the context helps you realize that it has to do with movement. However, if you are still confused, definitely consult a dictionary.

DISTINGUISHING FACT FROM OPINION

Daily we express our opinions: "That fish dinner had no taste." "My English professor is the best teacher I have ever had." "We need more doctors in Emergency at the hospital." When we express our thoughts orally, we don't always provide reasons for our opinions. However, when we write essays, we must include reasons to support our points of view. These reasons provide evidence for the readers, who will then come to their own conclusions.

> **ACTIVITY 1.3** Active Reading Technique: Distinguishing Fact from Opinion
>
> Look at the essay "Ambition" by Perri Klass in Chapter 30. Read the first paragraph and distinguish between the opinions of the author's friends and the facts on which they base their opinions. For example, it is a **fact** that Beth "was interested in foreign relations, in travel, in going to law school." However, it is Beth's **opinion** that she will "be secretary of state someday." Read the rest of the paragraph and make distinctions between other facts and opinions.

REFLECTING WITH COMPREHENSION QUESTIONS

The readings in this textbook are followed by comprehension questions, titled as *Thinking About the Model*. These questions are intended to guide you into thoughtful reflection on what you have read. For example, no one reads a passage and instantly comprehends why the author has used particular vocabulary, sentence structure patterns, and supporting details to illustrate the main ideas, or a specific essay development pattern, such as definition, argument, or comparison. When you read an essay in this textbook, don't wait for your instructor to prompt your understanding of the material by asking the comprehension questions. You can be a step ahead if you use these questions on your own to reflect on the reading before coming to class.

> **ACTIVITY 1.4** Active Reading Technique: A Timed Reading
>
> Read "Back to the Garden" by student Michael Wolfe in Chapter 23. Give yourself five minutes to read the essay. Then answer the following comprehension questions:
>
> WORDS IN CONTEXT:
>
> 1. After reading the first sentence, write your own definition for "swarming."
>
> SUMMARIZE:
>
> 2. Summarize in one sentence the main idea of this essay.
>
> MAIN IDEA:
>
> 3. List three main concerns of the writer, as outlined in the introduction.
>
> LINKING TO PREVIOUS KNOWLEDGE:
>
> 4. What do you do to escape from the pressures of your own life?

L01.5 Post-reading: Retaining Ideas

To get the most from your reading, it is important to review the material after you have finished. Take a few minutes to keep interacting with the text by asking questions like these: What do I think of this reading? How does it fit with my experience? Are there points that I agree or disagree with, an idea or suggestion that I will use from now on, or is there an idea that I think is useless?

There are many ways to review effectively, and you have probably tried some of them: silently scanning main points, stating them aloud, or organizing your thoughts on paper. Here are some suggestions that will help you review any reading assignment:

1. **Repeat the pre-reading step,** focusing especially on signposts (chapter previews and summaries, headings, etc.).

2. **Summarize or outline the main points.** This may only require pulling together the paragraph summaries you have already written or listing the main points you underlined when you annotated.

3. **Quiz yourself** on the material as if your instructor were asking the questions. The comprehension questions will help. And if you can't answer your own questions, you know you have to reread.

4. **Try to define any important term or idea** in a sentence of fewer than 20 words. Can you remember (or come up with) an example that helps to define the term or support the idea?

5. **List** what you feel are the three most important points from your reading.

TAKING GREEN NOTES

When taking notes on a reading, use both sides of each piece of notebook paper. Or consider taking notes on your laptop or a classroom computer. You will save money—and trees—and you will have easy access to your notes anytime. Resist the urge to browse online and remember to turn off your cellphone or iPod. Always be sure to back up your files on a network or flash drive—or email the notes to yourself. If the computer fails, you won't lose your work.

ACTIVITY 1.5 Active Post-reading Technique: Creating This Chapter's Summary

By using any of the five suggestions for reviewing reading assignments, review Chapter 1, and then list the essential points about reading that you need to remember. Limit your list to ten (or fewer) points.

Chapter Summary

1. _____
   _____
   _____

2. _____
   _____
   _____

3. _____
   _____
   _____

4. _____
   _____
   _____

5. _____
   _____
   _____
6. _____
   _____
   _____
7. _____
   _____
   _____
8. _____
   _____
   _____
9. _____
   _____
   _____
10. _____
    _____
    _____

The Writing Process

Imagine you are jumping from this airplane as it flies from Vancouver towards Powell River in British Columbia. Even if it's your first time, you took steps to prepare for this jump. This preparation process parallels the pre-writing procedure for a writer. Just as there is a pre-jump checklist, there are a series of steps to take before and as you are writing. As the ground gets closer and the vista below comes into focus, the parachutist is confident because she is well prepared. So, too, before you navigate your way through a writing assignment, you as the writer require advanced training skills. And just like the parachutist in this photo, you are not making the jump alone.

LEARNING OBJECTIVES

2.1 How do we begin to write?

2.2 What do we ask at the start of a writing project?

2.3 What are the steps in the writing process?

LO2.1 How Do We Begin to Write?

One answer to the question "How do I begin to write?" is that you *continue* rather than *begin*. Unlike the pilot in the scenario described above, you have been writing in various ways for many years: school papers and exams, letters and emails to friends, text messages, invitations and cards, directions, instructions for completing projects, and more. Not long after you could speak fluently, you began acquiring a writing "vocabulary." As you grew, this vocabulary expanded, and you learned to organize these new words in different ways, forming sentences that no longer simply mirrored your spoken words. To some degree, we are all competent speakers, and we can all write with varying degrees of proficiency. Our task, in this and the following chapters, is to build on skills that we already have in order to discover ideas more effectively, and then focus, organize, develop, and edit them.

Many students believe that essay writing is just an academic pursuit that has no application in the real world. Nothing could be further from the truth. Essay writing teaches you to think and write critically, to form opinions, to look for evidence, to construct an argument, to master research—all skills required in other courses and in any workplace. Police officers, nurses, and early childhood educators all must write reports. Lawyers must be able to construct coherent and supported arguments. Marketing people must know how to do proper research. No matter what profession you choose, critical thinking and writing will be necessary in one form or another.

LO2.2 What Do We Ask at the Start of a Writing Project?

What Is My Purpose?

You always write for a reason, whether you are conscious of it or not. However, knowing the reason up front will help you to stay focused. In academic writing, people primarily write to inform or persuade a reader, but there are other reasons: to explore an idea, to encourage critical reflection, and to research a topic for more in-depth understanding, for example.

Who Is My Audience?

Knowing your audience as specifically as possible, right down to a single person, will help you to discover, focus, and develop your ideas. Consider, for example:

- A particular age group (children, teens, adults)
- A particular professional group (professors, fellow students, field supervisors, bosses)
- A particular personal group (friends, spouse, parents, children)
- A reader's knowledge or experience with the subject

Knowing your audience determines your tone, your vocabulary, the amount of detail included, and the organizational structure of the work.

What Is the Point of View?

FIRST PERSON—*I, WE*

In the singular first person, the writer is "present" through expressing an opinion and first-hand experience (i.e., *I*).

I've always liked ambitious people, and many of my closest friends have had grandiose dreams. I like such people, not because I am desperate to be buddies with a future Minister of Foreign Affairs but because I find ambitious people entertaining, interesting to talk to, fun to watch.—from "Ambition," Ch. 30.

In the plural first person, the writer includes herself in the same category as the reader (i.e., *we*).

SECOND PERSON—*YOU*

Second person is an unusual point of view. While at some times the writer is speaking *to* the reader, at other times the writer is presuming to speak *for* the reader. Nevertheless, it is a helpful viewpoint for placing the reader within the article.

So before you load the cooler with pricey vitamin-enhanced waters, consider filling up empties at the tap instead. There are better ways to relax, get refreshed and boost your immunity than by downing the enhanced waters.—from "A Healthy Drink? Try Plain Water," Ch. 29.

THIRD PERSON—*HE, SHE, IT, THEY*

In the third person, the writer is *not* present. This is a more formal way of writing than when first person—"I" or "we"—is used.

The early Earth was a vision of hell, all scalding rock and choking fumes. Since then, its surface has cooled, continents have drifted, mountains have risen and eroded, and life has emerged, benign and green.—from "Earth in the Beginning," Ch. 26.

NOTE: Be careful *not* to shift your point of view within a paragraph as you write. For example, do not start out with "I" and then write about "he" or "they" or "you." When reading someone's work, ask yourself these questions: Are the pronouns consistent throughout a paragraph, or does the writer change the point of view? Is this helpful or confusing?

What, Exactly, Is the Project?

When you have an assigned writing task, it is essential to learn all you can about how to approach and complete it. Your instructor may give you written instructions, or you may follow the directions in the chapter assignments of this book. In either case, learn the assignment's purpose, audience, point of view, expected overall organization, length, and due date (including for drafts before the final copy).

How Can I Develop a Real Interest in the Project?

The truth is that writing is work, and most of us don't want extra work. We're busy enough. However, much of what we do requires work, even our leisure activities: planning a vacation to Quebec City, swimming at Manipogo Beach on Lake Manitoba, or dancing at the Vancouver FanClub. It's not so much the work as the *attitude* we have toward it. Think about that friend who practises her guitar for two hours daily or the one who carries his 20-kilogram pack in Banff National Park for a week and calls that fun!

If you can find something to care about in each topic you choose this semester, you will enjoy your writing more, learn more, create work that is more interesting, and probably end up with a better grade.

What Are the Steps in the Writing Process?

L02.3

As writers, we need a process in order to carry out our writing projects successfully, just as builders need a step-by-step process to put up a house. It makes sense to lay down a foundation before trying to put up walls or a roof, right? The following box outlines the steps required in a standard **writing process**. The order of the steps, however, is not rigid: for example, you may need to create more material as you revise, and you may edit as you draft.

THE WRITING PROCESS

1. Discovering Ideas: Pre-writing
2. Organizing Ideas
3. Drafting
4. Revising
5. Editing
6. Proofreading

HINT

Remember that you may continue to discover ideas even during revision; the order of steps is not fixed.

This chapter walks you through each step of the writing process. We'll examine a student model paragraph—"The Trail of Blood" by Kyle Burnett—in stages to illustrate the progression from discovering ideas to proofreading. The final draft of this model paragraph is on page 26.

Discovering Ideas: Pre-writing

If you have ever sat in front of a blank sheet of paper or stared at the blinking cursor on an empty screen, you know how frustrating it can be to find and then develop a writing topic. To get past the blank page, we need methods to help shake loose some ideas. **Pre-writing** is a method of getting started, and there are various techniques that you can use. The common purpose of all pre-writing exercises is just to get ideas out of your head and onto paper, the step that many people find the most difficult part of writing. It is important to find a technique that will get your writing flowing since you can't succeed by trying to write your essay the night before it is due. You need to start working on ideas as soon as possible so that you don't run out of time. You will find five **pre-writing** methods within Connect all used to develop the paragraph "The Trail of Blood."

1. Freewriting
2. Clustering
3. Brainstorming (or listing)
4. Asking a journalist's questions
5. Using patterns of development

Organizing Ideas

After you have found a topic and have some sense of direction for it, you should focus it further so that you can develop it within one paragraph. An effective way to do this is to write a **topic sentence**, a sentence that names the topic and limits it with a statement. (See Chapter 20 for more on topic sentences.) Here is the topic sentence from "The Trail of Blood," with the <u>topic</u> underlined once and the <u>limiting statement</u> underlined twice:

The night <u>a sanding disk exploded at the automotive shop</u> where I work, I <u>learned how dangerous</u> the job could be.

The limiting, or focusing, statement will help you decide what examples and details to keep and what additional details you might need. Once you have a topic sentence, the next step is to try an outline.

ROUGH OUTLINES

A **rough outline** is usually just a simple list of ideas. Narrative writing, for example, organizes its details chronologically (by time), as you can see below for "The Trail of Blood":

ROUGH OUTLINE

1. Working late with Jeff
2. Rushing the job
3. Being uncomfortably hot
4. Being razzed by Jeff
5. Hearing the disk explode
6. Seeing Jeff's injured arm
7. Taking him to the hospital

These points give us a place to start writing. From here, we can cut or add necessary material and consider further ideas that an audience might be interested in.

FORMAL OUTLINES

Formal outlines are useful for both short projects, such as a paragraph, and longer writing projects, such as an essay. Note the patterns of a formal outline:

FORMAL OUTLINE FOR A PARAGRAPH
Topic sentence (controlling idea of paragraph)
Supporting details (sentences with specific information to develop the key ideas introduced in the topic sentence)
Concluding sentence (summary of the main ideas within the paragraph with reference back to the topic sentence)

Below is an example of the formal paragraph outline format applied to a student-written paragraph by Meagan McGraw. She defines the concept of fetal alcohol syndrome.

FORMAL OUTLINE FOR A MODEL STUDENT PARAGRAPH

Topic sentence (controlling idea of paragraph):
Fetal alcohol syndrome (FAS) is a birth defect caused by drinking alcohol during pregnancy.

Supporting details (sentences with specific information to develop the key ideas introduced in the topic sentence):
-symptom of defect is low birth weight
-infants unable to take in, retain, or use the calories needed to gain weight and grow as expected
-FAS babies characteristically have small heads, facial abnormalities, undeveloped bones, and possible heart murmur
-children with defect most likely to have socialization problems, learning problems, and behavioural problems

Concluding sentence (summary of the main ideas within the paragraph with reference back to the topic sentence):
In conclusion, FAS is a birth defect that causes abnormalities in birth weight, physical disabilities, and developmental problems, which can be prevented by women not drinking any alcohol during pregnancy.

Later in this textbook, we will focus on developing full essays. In order to compare the formal paragraph and the essay outline, a preview glance for an essay with a student example follows:

FORMAL OUTLINE FOR AN ESSAY	
Introduction	Thesis statement (controlling idea of essay)—often three main points introduced to be developed with supporting details in the body of the essay)
Body Paragraph 1	I. A. First topic sentence (first main point) B. Supporting detail—examples, statistics, illustrations, evidence C. Concluding sentence (summary of main ideas within paragraph—could explain their significance)
Body Paragraph 2	II. A. Second topic sentence (second main point) B. Supporting detail—examples, statistics, illustrations, evidence C. Concluding sentence (summary of main ideas within paragraph—could explain their significance)
Body Paragraph 3	III. A. Third topic sentence (third main point) B. Supporting detail—examples, statistics, illustrations, evidence C. Concluding sentence (summary of main ideas within paragraph—could explain their significance)
Conclusion	Concluding topic sentence (restatement of thesis statement) Summary of main points in the body of the essay Concluding sentence (final statement which could introduce a new point of view)

An example of a student essay following the formal outline above is Marc Doucett's "The Gift of Music: A Blessing and a Curse," which argues two sides of a topic. Here is the outline for that essay:

FORMAL OUTLINE FOR A
MODEL STUDENT ESSAY

Introduction	**Thesis statement:** Music is a gift that allows the musician to express emotions, but is also a curse because of the deviant and antisocial behaviour often associated with a musician's career. Dedication and perseverance in practising provides positive results. This leads to emotional expressiveness that deeply satisfies the musician as well as the audience, but the high of emotional release can lead to a destructive lifestyle.
Body Paragraph 1	**I. A. First topic sentence (first main point):** -started with mother's old guitar which she taught me to play **B. Supporting detail—examples, statistics, illustrations, evidence:** -first chords -"one hundred repetitions to commit to memory" -blisters on fingertips -calluses led to smooth consistency **C. Concluding sentence (summary of main ideas within paragraph—could explain their significance):** -dedication and perseverance strengthened my determination to keep practising

Body Paragraph 2   **II. A. Second topic sentence (second main point):**

-deep, personal, expressive nature of creating music leads to emotional bonding

     B. Supporting detail—examples, statistics, illustrations, evidence:

-playing guitar acts as catalyst for emotional expression

-reserved feelings turn into audible tones

-during live performance, musician notices emotional effect on audience

-emotional charge is a gift

     C. Concluding sentence (summary of main ideas within paragraph—could explain their significance):

-but music as an emotional release can be taxing experience when shared with others

Body Paragraph 3   **III. A. Third topic sentence (third main point):**

-rock 'n' roll lifestyle can also be curse of the bard

     B. Supporting detail—examples, statistics, illustrations, evidence:

-destructive lifestyle thought to be result of fame, fortune, desire to rebel

-argue that destructive lifestyle comes from desire to escape

-drug and alcohol abuse used to cope with stress

     C. Concluding sentence (summary of main ideas within paragraph—could explain their significance):

-musician's nature involves embracing intense emotions on continuous basis

Conclusion   **Concluding topic sentence (restatement of thesis statement):**

Playing music has helped me become well rounded and balanced, despite the "curse of the bard."

Summary of main points in the body of the essay:

-guitar is now an old friend

-playing has taught me dedication and perseverance

-I've learned how to express great joy and come to terms with profound sorrow

-privilege to share music with an audience

Concluding sentence (final statement which could introduce a new point of view):

-fortunate to have embraced life of an artist

Drafting

With your material in hand and the overall shape of your paper determined, you can confidently begin the *first* draft. More drafts will follow.

MOVING AHEAD

As you write, focus on your main idea, purpose, and audience. Try to keep writing, even when you know a sentence isn't quite right. Reread your sentences as you go to keep yourself from drifting too far off course; but at this point, focus your review of sentences on ideas, not grammar. Are the ideas flowing one to the next, and are they explained so that a reader can understand them? Feel free to edit a bit as you write, but don't lose the thread of your ideas over a misspelled word. Thorough editing will be important later.

Good writing is not usually easy. The writing process challenges us all to overcome problems in our own ways. If you are a fast writer whose work seems unfocused, you may need to slow down. Alternately, if you write so slowly that you can't meet deadlines, you need to speed up.

Sometimes it's difficult to resume writing a draft we haven't worked on for a few days. Make starting again easier: before you put a draft aside, leave yourself some notes about where you want it to go. Or try stopping the draft mid-sentence.

Resist the impulse to be overly critical of **rough drafts**. They are just rough drafts—works in progress. You will have the chance to be more critical during revision.

SOLUTIONS FOR WRITER'S BLOCK

1. **Write out your topic sentence** at the top of the page and review it often. It will keep you from drifting.

2. Try any of the **pre-writing methods** listed online (freewriting, clustering, and so forth).

3. **Talk to yourself** by writing about the problems holding you back.

4. **Talk to yourself aloud or to another person.** Just having someone else listen can help clarify a fuzzy idea or give you a new direction.

5. **Try some throwaway writing.** Allow yourself to write awkward, incomplete, messy sentences. Move ahead with these sentences knowing that you will throw most or all of them away. The point here is just to get you writing again.

6. **Take a break.** Sometimes a 10-minute trip to the kitchen is just what you need; at other times, it may take a day or two, thinking about the paper only occasionally.

ACTIVITY 2.1 Drafting

Following the guidelines above, select a topic, do some pre-writing to generate ideas, write a topic sentence, and then write a rough draft of around 200 words. Remember not to be overly concerned with grammar, spelling, or punctuation at this point in the process. Read below to see how Kyle Burnett, the student author of "The Trail of Blood," managed his first draft.

The Trail of Blood

<u>I had a terrible night at work a while back, and I hope I never have to go thru another night like that even if I live to be a hundred.</u> My friend, and I were working late and I was welding and he was sanding an old car. There were shadows around the shop. I was sweating in my gloves but being careful because welding is hot! Jeff was racing along at his job. He called over to me, "You'll be here till midnight if you don't get on it." I nodded, through he couldn't see me, and kept welding. "You just keep it up, hot-dog," I said to him, "see if you don't burn through that fender." I heard the sanding disk catch on the metal. I though, "Serves him right." The shop was almost quiet with the sander off, accept for the hum of my welder. Jeff call my name. The tone said trouble. Raising my hood I walked toward him. His back was to me and, he was looking down. Just behind him was the grinder, on its side. Then I saw blood drops leading to Jeff. "Jeff, what the hell." But I stopped when I saw the damage. Blood was all over his shirt and his wrist was sliced open. There was also a black mark on his arm. I grabbed him by the other arm and said, "We need to get to a hospital." We left all the shop stuff lying where we had dropped it, and got out to my truck in a hurry. I didn't even lock up. And I was luck that no one decided to stop off for some expensive power tools because there are thousands of dollars worth lying around for the taking. I made it to the hospital fast, and the doctor's and nurses' took took care of him their. Jeff was lucky, he always seemed to be. He was only out of work for three weeks, and their was no lasting damage. But that night we both learned to slow down when messing around with dangrous machines.

Kyle's topic sentence introduces the subject of the paragraph (a terrible night at work) and makes an emotional connection.

Revising

Going easy on yourself is important while drafting, but revising requires a different approach. To revise effectively requires a critical (but not negative) frame of mind and a willingness to look closely at your work, knowing that you can improve it. When you revise, you look for opportunities to add, shift, and cut material. Remember that revising is not easy. It takes time to learn what to look for, gain insight into what you want to say, and let go of words and sentences—sometimes even whole drafts—that aren't working. However, if you invest the time and view your work critically, your writing will improve.

After you have finished your first draft, take some time away from it (a day or more). Think again about your main idea, purpose, audience, and point of view. Then reread your draft critically using the following Revision Priority Checklist.

As you practise revising, you will get better at it. Moving slowly through your drafts and focusing on one category to revise at a time will make this process more manageable.

COLLABORATIVE REVISING

In the past, have you tried to revise by yourself without much luck? Fortunately, in your writing class, you will have the help of fellow students and your instructor.

1. **Content: The content of your work is the most important feature.**

   ☐ Check your ideas for clarity: Can you and other readers understand your point?

   ☐ Be sure you have enough examples and details to convey your meaning and satisfy the reader's curiosity.

   ☐ Check for unnecessary points, examples, or details—anything that is repetitive or will distract readers from the central idea.

2. **Organization: Make sure your readers can follow your ideas.**

   ☐ Check your topic or thesis sentence to see if it still clearly guides your reader.

   ☐ Review the overall organizational pattern. Have you expanded on the topic sentence of the paragraph with details?

   ☐ Look closely at how your sentences and paragraphs flow together. If transitions or other connectors are needed, use them.

   ☐ Check your ending. Does it link to the main point of your paper and leave the reader with something to reflect on?

   ☐ Check the pronouns. Is your point of view consistent?

3. **Style: Word choice and arrangement can make writing easy or difficult to follow.**

   ☐ What words are not working well?

   ☐ Is your meaning unclear?

   ☐ Do you repeat words unnecessarily?

   ☐ Do you have enough variety in the length, type, and beginnings of your sentences?

   ☐ Where can you tighten sentences, eliminating words that serve no purpose?

4. **Mechanics: The last elements to check in your paper are grammar, spelling, and punctuation.**

   ☐ When you move into more polished drafts, edit out important errors that keep you from communicating clearly. Note this chapter's sections on Editing and Proofreading.

HINT

Use constructive criticism when revising the work of fellow students. You don't have to be an English whiz to help others improve their writing.

To profit most from collaborative work, you should be open to constructive criticism. Although none of the students in your class is an English teacher, you don't have to be an expert to respond to each other's drafts. Just letting a student author know that an idea is unclear or that a paragraph seems to be drifting can be important help.

In this textbook's unit on Designing Essays (Unit Four), you will find Peer Review checklists at the end of each chapter, which will help you and your fellow students to read each other's work. They will also serve as checklists when you revise your own work.

Each writing assignment chapter in this book gives advice on discovering ideas, organizing, drafting, and beginning to revise. Also, Chapter 21 offers thorough, step-by-step suggestions for improving your drafts. However, for some general suggestions to make peer reviews productive, consult the following lists:

HOW THE WRITER CAN HELP THE READER

1. In a sentence or two at the top of your draft, **identify your audience and purpose.**

2. Tell the reader **your main point.**

3. Direct the reader to any part of the paper you have **specific concerns** about. For example, "I'm not sure about my topic sentence. Does it tell you what I think the main point is?" Or "Do you think I might have too many details in the first half of the paragraph?"

4. After the reader has finished your paper, listen carefully to the reader's responses, and then **ask for clarification** of any points you didn't understand.

5. **Do not let a reader overwhelm you.** Be selective in the advice you follow. Ask other readers to respond to suggestions for revision, especially if a suggestion feels wrong for your paper.

HOW THE READER CAN HELP THE WRITER

1. **Ask about the audience, purpose, main point, and point of view.**

2. **Read** the draft quickly.

3. Tell **what you liked** or thought the author did well.

4. **Answer any questions** the author has about the draft.

5. Answer the remaining questions in the **Peer Review Guideline,** provided for each chapter on a writing pattern of development in Unit Four.

6. **Reread** the draft again slowly. **Jot notes** in the margin of the paper. A helpful shorthand is to draw a <u>straight line under words, phrases, and sentences that you particularly like</u> and <u>a wavy line under any parts that seem questionable.</u>

7. **Talk to the writer.** Share your reactions honestly. Remember, neither of you should expect the other to be the "teacher." Your job is just to give the best response you can according to the assignment instructions.

KYLE'S REVISED DRAFT:
A MODEL

The Trail of Blood

The night a sanding disk exploded at the automotive shop where I work, I learned how dangerous the job can be. My friend Jeff and I were working late Friday night and he especially was in a hurry, since he was two hour's late to meet his girlfriend. I was welding an axle and he was sanding a '75 Corvette. The electric lights hanging from cords spotlighted us and cast deep shadows around the rest of the shop. I was sweating in my heavy welding gloves and hood but being careful, 1000 degrees is a lot of heat to make a mistake with. Jeff, though, was racing along. He called over to

Revise the topic and concluding sentences for clarity and interest.

Add sentence connectors for smoother time transitions.

Editing for content . . .

Add useful detail to increase the suspense and clarify the auto workshop setting.

Cut (cross out) ~~unneeded blocks of information.~~

Editing for style . . .

Replace general words with specific ones.

Use more active verbs and –ing words (gerunds).

Cut ~~redundant words.~~

me, "Kyle, you're a slug. You'll be here till midnight if you don't get on it." I nodded, through he couldn't see me, and kept the arc on the bead. "You just keep it up, hot-dog," I said to him, "see if you don't burn through that fender." That's when, over the sizzle of the Miller welder and the roar of the grinder. I heard the sanding disk catch on the metal and explode. I though to myself, "Serves him right. As soon as I'm done with this, I'll razz him." The shop was almost quiet with the sander off, accept for the hum of my welder. Then I heard Jeff, in a weak, tight voice, call my name. The tone said trouble. Raising my hood, not knowing what to expect, I walked toward him. His back was to me, his white T-shirt plastered to it with sweat his elbows tight against his sides, as he looked down at his hands. Just behind him was the grinder lying on its side on the concrete floor, with the sanding pad torn to shreds. Then I saw a trail of blood leading to Jeff. "Jeff, what the hell—" I said but broke off when I saw the damage. Blood was trickling steadily out of Jeffs right arm, and the bones and tendons in his wrist were exposed. The hard rubber backing of the sander had left a black streak across his flesh. Grabbing him by the other arm, I said, "We need to get you to a hospital." ~~We left all the shop stuff lying where we had dropped it, and got out to my truck in a hurry. I didn't even lock up. And I was luck that no one decided to stop off for some expensive power tools because there are thousands of dollars worth lying around for the taking.~~ I made it to Saint Luke's in minutes, and they took care of him their. ~~the doctor's and nurses' took took care of him their.~~ Jeff was lucky. ~~he always seemed to be.~~ He was only out of work for three weeks, and their was no lasting damage. But that night we both learned that in this job their is no safe way to rush.

—*Kyle Burnett*

English Review Note

Try editing from the last sentence, moving backward.

Editing

After you have revised your paper several times for material, organization, and style, it's time to focus on mechanics: grammar, spelling, and punctuation. The object of editing is to make your writing more readable, which you will do by controlling *most* of your errors. Do keep in mind that few people write 100 percent error-free prose; however, you will learn this semester what you need to know to edit effectively.

EFFECTIVE EDITING

1. **Review slowly.** When you edit, you will tend to see whole word groups as you are used to seeing them, rather than how they actually appear on the page. Your mind will fill in the blanks for missing words, register "there" as "their," or create or eliminate pauses for commas unpredictably.

   To help you concentrate, try putting your finger on each word of your printed draft. Move line by line, stopping frequently at the end of completed thoughts. If you are not sure about a possible mistake, write a question mark and continue. But don't just ignore it, hoping the question will go away. It won't.

2. **Review repeatedly.** Read through your paper many times, each time focusing on just one or a few kinds of errors. One popular course given by the Editors' Association of Canada is called "Eight-Step Editing," showing

that even professional editors can't catch every mistake with one edit, but have to go through the text many times looking for different things each time.

3. **Track your error types.** Begin an Improvement Chart after your instructor returns your first in-class writing sample (often called a **diagnostic writing sample**). On your Improvement Chart, list your most common errors—perhaps using the apostrophe or forming complex sentences—so that you can track and then correct them. Find the chapters in this textbook that will help with these faults and drill yourself until they are corrected. Does it make more sense to memorize all the rules in a 500-page textbook or to figure out the handful of mistakes that cause *you* the most problems?

4. **Consult instructional materials.** Unit Two (Chapters 3 to 19) deals with all sorts of common writing errors. Use it along with a supplemental handbook, if your instructor requires one. As you write papers, your instructor will mark errors, including **pattern errors**, also known as recurring mistakes of the same type. This text gives examples of common pattern errors and shows how to correct them.

5. **Take advantage of others' input.** Allow enough time for others to review your work with you: classmates, friends, family members, writing centre tutors, and your writing instructor.

6. **Use a computer.** Type your draft. Errors are more noticeable on a cleanly word-processed page than on a handwritten one, especially since you can see wavy lines underneath your mistakes when your spelling, grammar, and style checkers are turned on.

Proofreading

Proofreading is the last step in the writing process. After you have closely edited your last draft and caught all the mechanical errors possible, print out the copy you plan to turn in for a grade. As careful as you have been, chances are that this draft still has a few mistakes you can catch and correct before your instructor does.

English Review Note

After submitting your first paper, ask your instructor which specific errors you should focus on (articles, subject–verb agreement, etc.). You will likely be able to tell by how the paper has been marked.

THE FINAL STEP: PROOFREADING

1. Check for **typographical errors** such as misspelled, run-together, and omitted words. Often when fixing errors at the editing stage, writers slip up in small ways on the keyboard. *Be sure to spell-check once again.*

2. Check the following items carefully: **font size** (12 point), **line spacing** (double space), **margins** (1 inch), and **title.**

3. **Staple** your pages in the top left-hand corner. Do not hand in an assignment unstapled—or expect the instructor to staple it! Avoid putting your paper in a plastic sleeve, which most instructors consider a nuisance.

Proofread your paper before giving it to your instructor. Then be sure to read your teacher's comments and corrections carefully when he or she returns your paper. Note how Kyle Burnett polished "The Trail of Blood" at the editing and proofreading stages.

KYLE'S EDITED DRAFT:
A MODEL

The Trail of Blood

The night a sanding disk exploded at the automotive shop where I work, I

learned how dangerous the job can be. My friend Jeff and I were working late Friday
(comma added)   (comma deleted)   (apostrophe deleted)
night, and he especially was in a hurry, since he was two hour's late to meet his
(comma added)
girlfriend. I was welding an axle, and he was sanding a '75 Corvette. The electric

lights hanging from cords spotlighted us and cast deep shadows around the rest of
(semicolon fixes comma splice)
the shop. I was sweating in my heavy welding gloves and hood but being careful;

1000 degrees is a lot of heat to make a mistake with. Jeff, though, was racing

along. He called over to me, "Kyle, you're a slug. You'll be here till midnight if you don't
(spelling error corrected)
get on it." I nodded, through he couldn't see me, and kept the arc on the bead. "You
(comma splice corrected)
just keep it up, hotdog," I said to him,. "See if you don't burn through that fender."
(comma fixes fragment)
That's when, over the sizzle of the Miller welder and the roar of the grinder, I heard

the sanding disk catch on the metal and explode. I thought to myself, "Serves him

right. As soon as I'm done with this, I'll razz him." The shop was almost quiet with
(spelling error corrected)
the sander off, accept except for the hum of my welder. Then I heard Jeff, in a weak,

tight voice, call my name. The tone said trouble. Raising my hood, not knowing

what to expect, I walked toward him. His back was to me, his white T-shirt plastered
(comma added)   (comma deleted)
to it with sweat, his elbows tight against his sides, as he looked down at his hands.

Just behind him was the grinder lying on its side on the concrete floor, with the

sanding pad torn to shreds. Then I saw a trail of blood leading to Jeff. "Jeff, what

the hell—" I said but broke off when I saw the damage. Blood was steadily trickling
(apostrophe added)
out of Jeff's right arm, and the bones and tendons in his wrist were exposed. The

hard rubber backing of the sander had left a black streak across his flesh. Grabbing

him by the arm, I said, "We need to get you to a hospital." I made it to Saint Luke's
(spelling error corrected)
in minutes, and they took care of him their there. Jeff was lucky. He was only out

of work for three weeks, and there was no lasting damage. But that night we both
(spelling error corrected)
learned that in this job, their there is no safe way to rush.

—*Kyle Burnett*

Before you begin any of the assignments below, review this chapter's advice on discovering ideas, organizing, and drafting. Try at least one pre-writing method, and aim to write a single paragraph of around 200 to 250 words (one typed page, double-spaced). After you have revised your draft, be sure to edit and proofread it carefully. Because your instructor may ask for them, save your pre-writing and organizing notes so that you can turn them in along with your draft. For each assignment, your **audience** is your instructor, and your **purpose** is to practise the writing process and demonstrate writing skills.

1. How is this chapter's advice about writing the same as, or different from what you were taught in high school? How well do you feel your high school prepared you for the written assignments expected at the post-secondary level?

2. What writing experiences have you had in your life up to now? Do you keep a journal or blog? What do you use writing for in your daily life? Do you expect the importance of writing to change in your life over the years, and if so, how?

3. Why are you in college or university? What do you hope to gain from this experience? Is post-secondary education a form of job training or a form of brain training?

Crafting Sentences: Understanding How They Work

2

UNIT

Subjects, Verbs, and Other Sentence Parts

In a few sentences, describe yourself or someone else actively participating in a sport. Try to use interesting, exciting action words.

What Are We Trying to Achieve and Why?

Describing this chapter's opening picture, we could say, "The <u>snowboarder</u> <u>flies</u> downhill, enjoying every second." The athlete is the **subject** of our attention, but what he is doing as he "flies" downhill—the action, or **verb**—makes the picture especially interesting. This chapter provides a brief overview of the words we use when we speak and write, and then it helps you find verbs and subjects in sentences. As you become more familiar with how words function in sentences, you will become more confident when you write—and speak. The points you are trying to make will become clearer, and errors that get in the way of what you want to express will gradually decrease.

Identifying the Parts of Speech   LO3.1

All words in sentences fall into the following eight traditional categories, known as the **parts of speech**; the categories indicate how the words function within the sentence.

THE PARTS OF SPEECH

1. Verbs
2. Nouns
3. Pronouns
4. Adjectives
5. Adverbs
6. Prepositions
7. Conjunctions
8. Interjections

We will cover each of these parts of speech briefly in the next few pages so that you can better understand how to distinguish verbs and subjects—the essential elements in a sentence—from surrounding words. Later chapters will explore particular parts of speech in greater detail.

Verbs

Verbs, along with nouns, are the core of sentences. The verb expresses an action or a state of being, and nouns (or pronouns) are doers of the action or the focus of the being verb. There are several types of verbs, such as those italicized and underlined in the examples below:

1. **Action verbs** show something happening—physically, mentally, or emotionally. Sarah *plays* on the University Quidditch team.

2. **Being (or linking) verbs** tell about a state of being. The verb *be* in its various forms (*am, are, is, was, were, been, being*) is the most common of these. Alexander *is* a strong man.

3. **Helping verbs** help the main verb of a sentence express meaning. With the main verb, they create a unit called a **verb phrase** (see p. 35). Common helping verbs include *be, have, do, may, might, must, can, should*, and *would*.

   Dale <u>*should be* editing</u> his term paper before he hands it in.

Nouns

Nouns, along with verbs, form the core of our sentences, telling who or what is doing the action or is the focus of the verb. Nouns name a person (*Maria*), place (*plaza*), thing (*hammer*), concept (*evolution*), or quality (*loyalty*).

Pronouns

Pronouns are words that stand in place of nouns. Like nouns, they can perform the action in a sentence (*He* lost the scholarship) or receive the action (He lost *it* [the scholarship]).

COMMONLY USED PRONOUNS											
I	you	he	she	it	we	they	all	everyone	many	someone	
who	this	that	my	your	his	hers	its	their			

Adjectives

Adjectives are words that describe nouns or pronouns by answering questions like the following: what size? (*tall* vase), what kind? (*loud* child), how many? (*three* apples). Adjectives in English usually come directly before the word they describe.

Adverbs

Adverbs are words that describe verbs, adjectives, or other adverbs by answering questions like these: when? (he went *early*), how? (she spoke *softly*), and *how* often? (he *frequently* comes to class unprepared).

Prepositions

Prepositions are words that come before nouns and pronouns in sentences to form prepositional phrases (*on* the table, *in* the box, *by* the stream), which are phrases of description and never serve as the subject of a sentence. Prepositions often—but not always—show location. It is helpful to bracket prepositional phrases as an exercise in omitting the confusion about where to find the subject of a sentence (i.e., outside the prepositional phrase).

Conjunctions

Conjunctions are words that link sentence parts. The main types are the coordinating conjunctions (*and, but, or, so, yet, for, nor*) and the subordinating conjunctions (*because, if, when, although*).

Interjections

Interjections are words used to express emotion (*oh, no!, hey!, hurray!*).

We seldom use all of the parts of speech in any one sentence, but we often use many in our most common expressions, as in the following sentence:

CONJ N V PRO N N ADV V ADJ N
After Portia handed her the wrench, Ellen firmly tightened the last bolt

PREP N CONJ V INTERJ
on the garage door opener and exclaimed, "Hallelujah!"

In this chapter, we will focus on the verbs and subjects (nouns and pronouns) in simple sentences.

Recognizing Verbs in Simple Sentences

The sentence is one of the most important word groups in writing. When we are sure about where our sentences begin and end, we stand a better chance of making our ideas understood, which is the whole point of writing. Most sentences require a **subject**, a **verb**, and a **complete thought**. The rest of this chapter will give you experience in recognizing subjects (the doers of action or focus of a verb) and verbs (the action or being words).

First, to help spot subjects and verbs, keep in mind that most sentences in English are ordered with the subject (S) coming in front of the verb (V), followed by the word receiving the action, the **object** (O), as in this example:

> S   V   O
> **Sasha jumped the fence.**

Identifying Verbs

When trying to decide whether a sentence is complete, writers often try to find the subject first, which can be confusing if there are several words that look like subjects. It can be more useful to look for the verb first. One test for a verb is to see if it has a **tense**: present, past, or future. Using the words *today, yesterday,* and *tomorrow* can help, as in the examples below:

> **Today, Jan *registers* the hotel guests.**
>
> **Yesterday, Jan *registered* the hotel guests.**
>
> **Tomorrow, Jan *will register* the hotel guests.**

Because the word *register* changes form, it is a verb.

To find verbs, you can also eliminate some words that may look like verbs but are not. Three of these are called **verbals**, and they may begin with the word *to* (as in *to drive*) or end in an *-ing* (as in *rushing*). (See pp. 68–71 for more on verbals.) Here are three examples with the <u>subjects</u> and <u>verbs</u> underlined and the *verbals* italicized:

1. <u>Clara</u> <u>learned</u> *to drive* at the age of 17.

2. <u>Jack</u> <u>paddled</u> upstream against the *rushing* water.

3. <u>Gloria</u> <u>enjoys</u> <u>swimming</u>.

ACTION VERBS

Another test for verbs is whether the word shows **action**. This action can be physical, mental, or emotional, as in the following examples:

Physical action: Shania Twain *sings* country music.

Mental action: Twain *thinks* deeply about her performances.

Emotional action: Shania *hopes* for continued success.

ACTIVITY 3.1   Working together: *Creating Action Verbs*

Fill in the blanks below with any action verb that makes sense to you. As a variation, you can do this exercise in pairs and come up with two possible words for each blank.

1. Many talented people _____ on the reality show *Canadian Idol.*

2. Barbara often _____ about the children she taught in her preschool.

3. Max _____ in a new pair of running shoes.

4. Police officers _____ criminals.

5. Mountain goats on the Canadian west coast _____ very steep slopes.

6. The airboat _____ through Georgian Bay.

ACTIVITY 3.2   Finding Action Verbs

In the paragraph below, underline all the <u>action verbs.</u>

Although being lean helps manufacturers hold down costs by keeping stockpiles of components and finished goods low, it can leave them high and dry if production supplies don't arrive as expected, a risk highlighted by the parts shortages caused by the earthquake and tsunami in Japan. The March 11, 2011, disaster that killed thousands, damaged factories, and hobbled ports in Japan has thrown the situation into sharp relief. The disruptions quickly radiated out, putting kinks in the global supply chains of several industries. Auto plants in the U.S. Midwest and Ontario, and electronics factories across Asia, scrambled to find substitutes for Japanese-made parts. Many other industries had to assess how the disruptions would filter back to them. Clearly, lean supply chains require improved risk management by the organizations that choose to implement them.

BEING (OR LINKING) VERBS

While action verbs are essential to understanding sentences, being or linking verbs are equally important. These verbs tell about a state of being, a quality, or important characteristics of the subject they are describing. The verb *to be*, in its many forms, is the most common linking verb. The chart below lists each of these forms, as well as several other common linking verbs:

BEING OR LINKING VERBS					
Forms of *To Be*			**Other Linking Verbs**		
am are is was			act appear become feel get grow		
were been being			look remain seem smell sound taste		

In a sense, linking verbs act as an equal sign between the subject and the word or words that follow the verb to describe the subject, as in the following examples:

The T. Rex *was* a savage predator.   T. Rex = savage predator

Roxanne *is* a genius.   Roxanne = genius

That tiger kitten *looks* sick.   Tiger kitten = sick

Finding Linking Verbs

Referring to the chart of linking verbs above, underline each <u>linking verb</u> in the following sentences.

1. Shane is a great quarterback. It looks like the team will have a great season.

2. Pad Thai smells delicious. I love it when the cafeteria is having Asian food night.

3. In the tree branches overhead, the stream of windswept toilet paper was a mess. Frosh week, thank goodness, was over at last.

4. After facing many family problems in his life, Art remained a good person.

5. Coffee tastes bitter to many people but people get addicted to the caffeine.

6. After a year of repeated arguments, Carol grew tired of working with her supervisor.

ACTIVITY 3.4 Choosing Linking Verbs

Referring to the chart of linking verbs on page 34, fill in the blanks below with any linking verb that makes sense to you. Use a variety of verbs.

1. Danny _____ hungry for the honey-baked ham served on Friday nights in the residence cafeteria.

2. My friend Heather _____ disappointed by the faculty of music's concert.

3. Nunavut _____ created from part of the Northwest Territories on April 1, 1999.

4. After the spring flood, the farms along the Red River _____ devastated.

5. All of the children _____ happy at the thought of Kwanzaa.

6. The leak in the Alberta pipeline _____ a major problem for Pioneer gas stations.

HELPING VERBS

Another type of verb is the **helping verb**. These kinds of verbs, as the name states, help a main verb complete its meaning. So instead of a single action or linking verb, now we have two or more verbs working together in a unit (called a **verb phrase**). Following is a list of common helping verbs:

HELPING VERBS					
be	could	has	may	must	will
can	do	have	might	should	would

Remember that these verbs can appear in various forms (for example, the verb *to be* appears as *is, am, are,* and so forth).

Here are some sentences with the <u>verb phrase</u> underlined and the *helping verbs* italicized. Note that **sentences 2 and 3** have forms of the helping verb *be* in them. Also, you can see that the verb phrase in **sentence 3** has the word *not* in it.

Sometimes verb phrases have extra words in them that are not verb parts (for example, *only, often, always, never, not,* and *already*).

1. **Hannah *should have* <u>arrived</u> on time for class.**
2. **Harinder *might be* <u>flying</u> overhead in the traffic helicopter.**
3. **I *am* <u>not working</u> hard in the lab today.**
4. **Kyle *can* <u>jog</u> a 6-minute mile.**

Notice that in the example sentences above, the main verb is at the end of the verb phrase. When forms of *be* are followed by another verb, *be* is a helping verb. But *be* can stand by itself as a being (or linking) verb (as we saw in Activities 3.3 and 3.4) or *be* can take a helping verb.

English Review Note

Let your instructor know if you'd like more clarification about these terms: *verb forms, tenses.*

ACTIVITY 3.5   Finding Helping Verbs

In the following sentences, underline the <u>main verb</u> and box or circle the ⟨helping verbs⟩. Refer to the chart of helping verbs above.

1. Cody could win the gold medal for downhill skiing.
2. The police have been stopping cars in their R.I.D.E. program.
3. Humpback whales can travel thousands of kilometres in a year.
4. Marc must have been excited about the success of his experiment.
5. With a better early warning system, more people should survive tsunamis.
6. Yuan is cooking dinner for the whole team.

ACTIVITY 3.6   Choosing Helping Verbs

Referring to the preceding chart of helping verbs, fill in the blanks with any helping verb(s) that make(s) sense to you. Use a variety of helping verbs.

1. The Athletic Centre _____ reopen early in the spring.
2. Even in the winter, Harold _____ swim in the lake.
3. Marge _____ singing professionally for three years.
4. All adult citizens _____ vote in the next election.
5. The hospital interns _____ finished their first rotation in surgery.
6. Sophie _____ qualify for the honour roll this year.

COMPOUND VERBS

Another way to build sentences is with several verbs separated by other words. When a sentence has two or more verbs for the same subject—connected by *and, but,* or any other coordinate conjunction—we say they are **compound verbs**. These compounds can be action, linking, or helping verbs.

COMPOUND ACTION VERBS:

The professor *laughed* and *reached* for the chalk.

The cashier at the campus bookstore *smiled* at me, *totalled* my purchases, and *wished* me a good day.

COMPOUND LINKING VERBS:

Samantha *looked* tired and *felt* sick.

COMPOUND VERB PHRASES:

Yuan *will cook* dinner for us tonight and *will wash* the dishes, too.

In the last sentence, note that the helping verb *will* could be left out before *wash*; the second part of a compound verb phrase sometimes omits the helping verb.

ACTIVITY 3.7 Finding Compound Verbs

Underline the compound verbs and verb phrases in the sentences below.

1. Jason swung at the pitch, yet missed the ball.

2. The students gathered in the hall, talked about the exam, and prayed for luck.

3. The cost of tuition may rise even higher and make it even harder for students to afford university.

4. Bad weather is rocking the boat but not endangering it.

5. Road construction will be blocking traffic today but will close the street tomorrow.

6. Madison will be playing soccer this morning or, if it rains, doing math homework.

English Review Note

Remember that compound verbs must be in the same form.

Recognizing Subjects in Simple Sentences

LO3.3

After locating the verb in a sentence, we next look for the subject. Subjects can be a single word or several words as a unit, called the **simple subject**. (Ann runs for the bus. The air conditioner is blowing cool air.) Subjects can also include just their immediate describing words or additional word groups attached to the simple subject, in which case we have a **complete subject**. (An MPP from Windsor ran for prime minister in 2008.) The subject either does the action or is linked by a verb to a describing word, as in the following sentences:

Simple Subjects

1. Subject with action verb: Canadian Justin Morneau launches home runs for the Minnesota Twins.

2. Subject with helping and linking verbs: Morneau may be the best run producer in baseball.

In **sentence 1**, we ask, "Who launches?" and we answer, "Justin Morneau." We have found the subject. In **sentence 2**, we ask, "Who may be the best run producer?" and we answer, "Morneau." Again, we have found the subject. In most cases, we can find the subject in a sentence by asking who or what is doing the action or being linked to a describing word.

Subjects can be nouns (people, places, things, concepts, qualities: *Justin, Parliament Hill, convocation, happiness, compassion*) or pronouns (words standing in place of nouns: *I, you, he, she, we, they, it*).

Two other kinds of words that can be subjects are called **gerunds** (verb forms with an *-ing* on the end that act as nouns) and **infinitives** (verb forms that begin with *to* and can be nouns). Here are two examples:

Gerund subject:	Laughing is good for the spirit.
Infinitive subject:	To succeed requires hard work.

English Review Note

The agreement with gerund or infinitive subjects is always singular.

ACTIVITY 3.8 Finding Simple Subjects

Find the simple subject in each sentence below by asking who or what is doing the action, or who or what is linked by a verb to a describing word. Next, underline the verb and box or circle the subject. Remember that subjects can be pronouns and nouns (including gerunds and infinitives).

1. Walking can be good aerobic exercise.

2. NASA's Mars rover Curiosity has discovered sulfur, nitrogen, hydrogen, oxygen, phosphorus, and carbon so far.

3. At the skating rink, I rented a pair of hockey skates.

4. Climate change is putting polar bears at risk of starvation.

5. "Life's but a walking shadow, a poor player that struts and frets his hour upon the stage and then is heard no more."

6. Shakespeare died at the age of 52.

Complete Subjects

As we have noted under "Recognizing Subjects," a complete subject contains the simple subject along with its describing words; for example, "Four great blue herons circled the kayaks." Because there are often many words in the complete subject, it can be difficult to locate the simple subject. This problem becomes more confusing because of word groups called **prepositional phrases** (see Chapter 11). These word groups begin with a preposition (*in, on, near, etc.*) and end with a noun or pronoun (*me, him, her, them*). Here are several examples of prepositional phrases:

in the store   on the bus   near him   by the car   through the door   beside Jason

Because in English the simple subject of a sentence **is never found** within a prepositional phrase, learning how to spot these phrases will make it easier for you to pick out simple subjects. Notice how crossing out the prepositional phrases from the complete subjects, in the example sentences below, makes the simple subjects clearer:

1. Loud noises in a house at night frighten most people.

2. The problem of too much credit for my best friend, Alex, has grown out of control.

A brief list of common prepositions follows:

COMMON PREPOSITIONS				
about	at	down	of	through
above	behind	during	off	to
across	below	for	on	under
along	beneath	in	onto	with

In the following sentences, underline the <u>verbs</u> or <u>verb phrases</u>. Then cross out the prepositional phrases. Now box or circle the simple subjects.

1. Two of my aunts from my mother's side of the family are going to the reunion.

2. A large group of students from the department of archeology go to Turkey for a dig every fall.

3. One of these mistakes in a game plan by team members throws off the whole defence.

4. The elm tree by the roses on the west side of Frank's house leans danger- ously over the roof.

5. The fans in the parking lot of the Edmonton Commonwealth Stadium jump at the chance for players' autographs.

6. Across the street, a young red-bellied woodpecker with a cicada in its beak settled onto a branch for a snack.

Compound Subjects

Similar to compound verbs, subjects can be linked when two or more are performing the same action or being described by the same verb. These **compound subjects** usually use the words *and* or *or*. Notice the example sentences below with the <u>simple subjects</u> underlined once and the <u>verbs</u> and <u>verb phrases</u> twice:

<u>Airplanes and cars</u> <u>carry</u> the most passengers these days.

<u>My Ford Fiesta, Dodge Caliber, and Honda Civic</u> <u>have been</u> terrific vehicles.

<u>Hurricanes or earthquakes</u> <u>will be featured</u> on the Weather Channel tonight.

ACTIVITY 3.10 Finding Compound Subjects

In the following sentences, underline the <u>verbs</u> and box or circle the compound subjects.

1. Pens, pencils, and computers are the instruments for writing these days.

2. Apple or Dell makes the best computers for the money.

3. During the graphic design competition, prizes were given to everything from books to websites.

4. At the Air Canada ticket counter, a passenger and an agent discussed the weight restriction on luggage.

5. Apples, potatoes, onions, and beans have a fairly long shelf life.

6. In Canada, hockey, baseball, and football are the three most popular sports.

ACTIVITY 3.11 Subjects and Verbs in Context—A Review

In the following paragraphs, underline all <u>simple subjects</u> once and box or circle all verbs and verb phrases. Be alert to compound subjects and verbs, and remember that the verbals (examples: *to learn* and *learning*) are not verbs. The first two sentences are done as an example.

Reproductive Health

My underline(interest) in reproductive health (dates) back to when I (worked) in a small clinic in East Africa. underline(Basic medical services) (are very limited) and the reproductive health underline(situation) (is very challenging) in this region. At the clinic, I examined one pregnant mother infected with tuberculosis and at risk of premature birth. Her serious condition required immediate attention. Unfortunately, I could do nothing for her except transfer her to another hospital because of my lack of obstetric knowledge.

I am an experienced general clinician and have been devoted to community health for a decade but know almost nothing about reproductive health care. It is almost impossible for general practitioners to learn about reproductive health in Canada because it is the exclusive domain of obstetricians and midwives. Because Canada has one of the lowest mortality rates in the world and a rapidly declining birth rate, the reproductive situation is far different from that of developing countries where I work for Doctors Without Borders. My experience with this woman showed me the importance of learning comprehensive skills to deal with maternal and perinatal health problems in order to promote community health in developing countries.

ACTIVITY 3.12 *WORKING TOGETHER*: Using Subjects and Verbs in Examples

In almost any writing assignment, you will use subjects and verbs to form examples of your main point. For instance, to illustrate a roommate's odd habits, you would describe both the person (subject) and his or her actions (verbs). With a partner, choose a writing topic from Chapter 25 (see "Alternative Assignments" in the section *Writing an Illustration Essay*), and together draft a paragraph using examples. Use at least one of each of the following: a compound verb, a simple subject, a complete subject, a compound subject. Go back and underline all the underline(subjects), double underlining all the underline(main verbs). (Remember that a verbal cannot serve as a main verb.)

Chapter Summary

1. All words in sentences can be categorized into eight parts of speech: verbs, nouns, pronouns, adjectives, adverbs, prepositions, conjunctions, and interjections.

2. A sentence requires a verb and a subject that work together to convey a complete thought.

3. When trying to decide whether a sentence is complete, look for the verb first. Both action and being (or linking) verbs can work as complete verbs in a sentence.

4. Verbals (gerunds, participles, and infinitives) cannot function as complete verbs in a sentence. Helping verbs can work with—but not without—a main verb.

5. Two or more verbs sharing the same subject are called compound verbs; they are separated by *and, or,* or one of the other five coordinating conjunctions.

6. A simple subject can be one noun or several functioning together as a unit. Gerunds and infinitives can function as subjects.

7. A complete subject includes the words (such as articles, adjectives, and prepositional phrases) that describe the noun. Crossing out prepositional phrases is one helpful way to isolate the simple subject.

8. A compound subject is two or more nouns that perform the same action or are described by the same verb.

Verbs: Forms and Tenses

*Below, the first description of this photograph uses only **being verbs**, while the second uses mostly **action verbs**. How is the effect different? Why are action verbs more effective in many writing situations? When might being verbs be more appropriate?*

Being Verbs

These **are** broadswords. The broadsword, a popular choice in beginning stage-fighting classes, **is** not sharp-edged. Generally, one sword **will be** between 900 grams and 1.4 kilograms in weight.

Action Verbs

Two student actors **practise** the art of stage combat. In this scene, the performers **will play** enemies duelling to a violent death, so they **must rehearse** each beat of the fight carefully. Here, one student **lunges** as the other one **blocks**.

LEARNING OBJECTIVES

4.1   Simple tenses

4.2   Helping verbs

4.3   Perfect tenses

4.4   Progressive tenses

4.5   Irregular verbs

4.6   Verb tense sequences and unneeded tense shifts

4.7   Verb challenges for English as a second language learners

What Are We Trying to Achieve and Why?

Verbs are one of the most important types of words in our language. In Chapter 3, we saw how verbs work with subjects and we learned that without verbs, we cannot form sentences. However, verbs can pose challenges because they take so many different forms and can serve a variety of functions in a sentence. In this chapter, we will look at the several forms verbs take, paying special attention to **tense** (time change).

Simple Tenses

LO4.1

Present Tense

The **present tense** has several uses, in general showing **action happening either right now or continuously**: "Jamie's heart *beats* rapidly." Here are four other uses:

To show habitual action:	Roxanne *bathes* every morning.
To express general truths:	Tulips *bloom* on Parliament Hill in the spring.
To discuss works of art:	<u>Harry Potter and the Deathly Hallows</u> *completes* the series.
To refer to future events (sometimes):	The plane *arrives* in an hour.

Notice that only one form in the present tense differs from the others, the *-s* ending used with *he, she, it* (all third person singular in number), and many indefinite pronouns in the same position (for example, *each, no one, everyone*):

	SINGULAR	PLURAL
FIRST	I *study*	we *study*
SECOND	you *study*	you (plural) *study*
THIRD	he, she, it, everyone *studies*	they *study*

ACTIVITY 4.1   Finding Present Tense Verbs

In the following sentences, underline the <u>present tense verbs</u> once. Note that infinitives (*to run*), participles (*sleeping* baby/ *broken* toy), and gerunds (*recycling* is useful) cannot be present tense verbs (see Chapter 5).

EXAMPLE: **On clear nights, I <u>watch</u> for satellites and shooting stars.**

1. Jan uses herbs from the college greenhouse to bake savoury cakes.

2. Some insects in the tundra of northern Canada drink water droplets from their own bodies.

3. In Edmonton, roses grow well only in full sun.

4. Eleven hydraulic cylinders work together to lower the convertible Mercedes top.

5. Four-hundred-pound jellyfish swim in the Sea of Japan.

6. Peter Ramos creates photographs capturing the magnificent west coast of Vancouver Island.

Past Tense

The simple **past tense** tells about actions occurring in the past that do not continue into the present. Regular verbs form their past by adding -*d* and -*ed* to the base:

Laurie *hauled* the AV equipment to her oral presentation.

The action occurred one time and was finished. Notice that unlike the third person singular present (-*s*), there is no ending change in the third person singular past tense.

	SINGULAR	PLURAL
FIRST	I *hauled*	we *hauled*
SECOND	you *hauled*	you (plural) *hauled*
THIRD	he, she, it *hauled*	they *hauled*

Irregular verbs, however, change their spellings in the past tense, sometimes radically; for example, *eat/ate, kneel/knelt, keep/kept, choose/chose*. We will discuss irregular verbs later in this chapter.

ACTIVITY 4.2 Finding Past Tense Verbs

The following paragraph uses both present and past tense verbs. Locate and underline the <u>past tense verbs</u> once (there are 16 of them). Note that infinitives (*to run*), participles (*sleeping* baby), and gerunds (*recycling* is useful) cannot be past tense verbs (see Chapter 5).

For people who know its history, Niagara Falls, Canada, excites a great deal of curiosity. Even one hundred years ago, newlyweds often chose Niagara Falls as the ideal honeymoon spot. As far back as 1846, families visited Niagara Falls to ride the *Maid of the Mist*. The most recent boat, *Maid of the Mist VII*, replaced *Maid of the Mist III*. This latest boat at its final stage was 24 metres long, weighed 145 tons, and had a capacity to carry 582 passengers. It launched into service on Friday, July 11, 1997.

The name of the many versions of the boat came from a First Nations legend in which Lelawalo, the daughter of a Chief, was sacrificed to the spirit of the Falls. A son of the god Hinum supposedly caught Lelawalo in his arms. She agreed to take one of the god's sons as her husband with one condition—she asked to return to her tribe one more time. She warned her people of a poisonous snake living at the bottom of the river. They killed the snake and its body took the shape of a horseshoe. That is how Niagara Falls, Canada, got its shape. To this day, the gods are believed to be protecting the nearby First Nations' tribes against evil spirits.

Source: Based on www.niagarafrontier.com/maidmist.html

Future Tense

The final simple tense is the **future**, which we use to show anticipated action. We usually form this tense by adding the helping verb *will* to the base verb: "Alicia *will* compete in the district spelling contest this month." Notice that unlike the third person singular present (-*s*), there is no ending change in the third person singular future tense.

English Review Note

Be careful to use the correct verb form after *will*. Correct: "He will *compete*." Incorrect: "He will *competes*."

	SINGULAR	PLURAL
FIRST	I *will compete*	we *will compete*
SECOND	you *will compete*	you (plural) *will compete*
THIRD	he, she, it *will compete*	they *will compete*

ACTIVITY 4.3 Finding Future Tense Verbs

In the following sentences, underline the future tense verbs once. Note that infinitives (*to run*), participles (*sleeping* baby), and gerunds (*recycling* is useful) cannot be future tense verbs (see Chapter 5).

EXAMPLE: **Isobel will climb to the alpine meadows above Lake Louise this summer.**

1. The Canadian Museum of Nature will reopen to the public soon.
2. Paul Haggis will return to his hometown of London, Ontario, after directing another film in Hollywood.
3. Vancouver will renovate Stanley Park after the destruction of this summer's storm.
4. As climate change continues, snowstorms will grow even heavier.
5. Hiro will teach me a little about website design this weekend.
6. Lake Ontario will become shallower as its water evaporates.

Helping Verbs

L04.2

To form verb tenses, English often uses helping verbs with main verbs in a combination known as a **verb phrase**.

Common Helping Verbs

The most common helpers are forms of the verbs *be, do,* and *have,* listed in the chart below. By themselves, they do not express the action or condition in a sentence. Their function is to help establish the tense of the main verb.

COMMON HELPING VERBS		
To Be	**To Do**	**To Have**
am	do	have
is	does	has
are	did	had
was		having
were		

When combined with main verbs, helpers create phrases like the following:

The whole team *was* hoping for a miracle.

After eating the whole pizza, Anna *did* feel a little sick.

I found out that my son was the one who *had* borrowed my car.

I *am* going to the seminar later.

ACTIVITY 4.4 Finding Helping Verbs

Underline the helping verbs once (there are 12 of them) in the paragraphs below. Use the preceding chart as a reference.

It has taken less than a quarter-century for electronic mail to emerge as the heart and soul of corporate communication. Yet while email has made it faster and easier for people to exchange words and data, it also has given us inbox overload and an endless stream of spam. Future email systems will need to remedy today's problems—but also add new capabilities.

Some senders already have matched a predetermined list—either by name, company, or IP (Internet provider) address—or they have found themselves blocked. In addition, better anti-spam programs have helped sift out the junk.

More powerful information-management and collaboration tools likely are emerging. We already are linking associated messages and are tracking message streams more efficiently. Also, unified messaging is allowing workers to check email, voice mail, mobile messaging, and fax machines from a single cellphone. Perhaps automatic language translation is taking hold on a universal basis.

Source: Based on "Fast Forward: 25 Trends That Will Change the Way You Do Business" at www.workforce.com/

Modals

Aside from *be, do,* and *have,* there is another common group of helpers often called **modals:** *may/might, can/could, will/would, should, must.* In this group, the modals *can* and *will* express a sense of the present or future, while *could* and *would* generally express a sense of the future. Modals are used to express requests, doubt, capability, willingness, necessity, and advisability, as in the following sentences:

Request:	*Will (would, could, can)* you lend me the book?
Doubt:	I *might (may, could)* go to *The PhD Movie* with you.
Capability:	I *can (could)* still make it to the top of the class.
Willingness:	I *will (would)* help you with studying.
Necessity:	To do well, we *must* study for the final exam.
Advisability:	Whenever possible, we *should* avoid foods that use hydrogenated oils.

Modals help refine the meaning of main verbs and are especially useful in softening requests. For example, while eating dinner, we might say, "Pass me the butter" as a command. Or we could reduce the command to a request, using one of the modals: *Would* you please pass me the butter.

HINT

The base form of a verb always follows the modal.

MODALS			
may	can	will	should
might	could	would	must

ACTIVITY 4.5 Finding Modal Verbs

Review the preceding chart; then underline the <u>modal helping verbs</u> in the following sentences.

EXAMPLE: The government <u>must</u> invest in raising the riverbanks because future storms <u>could</u> wreak even greater damage.

1. Rivers can be things of beauty and the historic lifeblood of a community.

2. So it may seem hard to believe that a small, slow-flowing stream or gentle river could cause serious damage to people and places in which people live and work.

3. Flooding could turn even the most harmless-looking watercourse into a raging torrent of large-scale destruction.

4. Buildings might prove to be no obstacle to the power of the flooding.

5. Food crops can be ruined leading to food shortages and even starvation.

6. People's lives may be lost through drowning, disease, and homelessness.

Source: Based on "River Flooding" at www.sln.org.uk/geography/enquiry/we30.htm #Why%20do%20Rivers%20Flood?

Perfect Tenses

LO4.3

The three main tenses of present, past, and future help express many essential time relationships, but they do not cover them all. To discuss **an action finished earlier in time than another**, we use the **perfect tenses**, present, past, and future. To form a perfect tense, we put *has, have,* or *had* in front of a **past participle**. The past participle for regular verbs is the same as the simple past tense (base verb usually ending in *-d* or *-ed*). However, irregular verbs often—but not always— change forms in their past participle (often ending with a *-t* or an *-n*). (There is further discussion of irregular verb forms later in this chapter.) Notice the similarities and differences between the simple past and the past participle for the regular and irregular verbs listed below.

VERB FORMS			
	Base Form	**Simple Past**	**Past Participle**
Regular verb	talk	talked	talked
Irregular verbs	speak	spoke	spoken
	begin	began	begun
	catch	caught	caught

Present Perfect

The **present perfect** is the tense that describes actions **begun in the past and finished at some unknown time** or actions begun in the past that **continue into the present**. With this tense, we use either *has* or *have* before the past participle. However, **if we mention a specific time, we use the simple past** rather than the present perfect. Compare the examples of present perfect and simple past below:

1a. Present perfect: Janice *has* talked to her mother about the problem.

1b. Simple past: Janice talked to her mother about the problem yesterday.

2a. Present perfect: I *have* flown to Calgary many times on business.

2b. Simple past: I flew to Calgary last Monday for a meeting.

Sentence **1a** tells us that Janice has spoken with her mother at some point in the past, but we cannot say when, so we use the present perfect tense. Because **sentence 1b** tells us when Janice spoke with her mother, "yesterday," we use the simple past.

Sentence 2a says that the speaker has flown many times, and we can assume that he or she will continue to fly; therefore, we use the present perfect tense. However, **sentence 2b** tells us that the speaker flew to Calgary on Monday, an act started and finished in the past, so we use the simple past.

ACTIVITY 4.6   Choosing Simple Past and Present Perfect

In the following sentences, look at the base verb form in parentheses, decide on simple past or present perfect, and then write your answer in the space provided.

EXAMPLE: **Computers** *have evolved* **(to evolve) faster than anyone could have imagined.**

1. Television _____ (to change) a great deal over the past 60 years.

2. One major change that _____ (to amaze) audiences of the forties _____ (to be) the switch from black-and-white to colour.

3. When, for example, *The Wizard of Oz* _____ (to change) from black-and-white to colour after Dorothy _____ (to land) in Oz, people in audiences _____ (to gasp) and could scarcely believe their eyes.

4. Another milestone in TV viewing _____ (to occur) when the number of channels_____ (to increase).

5. The arrival of cable television _____ (to increase) the number of channels available to viewers from three to hundreds.

6. As technology _____ (to advance), satellites _____ (to provide) even greater viewing options.

Past Perfect

The **past perfect** is the verb tense that allows us to show **one action happening further back in time than another past action.** We form this tense with the helper verb *had* and the past participle. If we are simply referring to **one past act** (rather than showing different actions begun at different times in the past), we use the **simple past tense.** Notice how the <u>simple past</u> (underlined once) and the <u>past perfect</u> (underlined twice) work together in the sentences below:

1. Roselyn <u>*had finished*</u> her report just before the phone <u>*rang*</u>.

2. Brandon <u>*was*</u> late picking up his grandmother, who <u>*had arrived*</u> at the airport an hour earlier.

In **sentence 1,** Roselyn completed her report in the past, and then, still in the past, the phone rang. Since completing the report is farther back in time, we use the past perfect tense. The phone ringing is in the simple past.

In **sentence 2,** Brandon's grandmother arrived at the airport further back in time than when Brandon came to pick her up. Therefore, we use the past perfect for the arrival and the simple past for the picking up. Notice that the past perfect tense can appear in the sentence either before the simple past, as in sentence 1, or after, as in sentence 2.

ACTIVITY 4.7   Finding Verbs in the Past Perfect and Simple Past

In the following paragraph, underline the <u>simple past tense verbs</u> once (there are 18) and box or circle the past perfect verbs (there are 12). Notice that the helper verb *had* can also be a main verb, as it is in the first sentence below.

In that case, it is in the simple past. Watch for split verbs, both past perfect and simple past.

Crashing down the Lachine Rapids

On our trip through the Lachine Rapids this past summer, we had many exciting moments. Nick, the river guide, explained how dangerous this class-5 white-water rapids could be. For several years, this site of the only rapids on the St. Lawrence River, near Montreal, had been a source of adventure for people of all ages. Then Nick told us about a rafter who had drowned last year, and how this event had caused raft guides to increase the number of crewmembers for each ride. Even so, a few moments after we had put the eight-person raft into the swift current, we lost our first paddler overboard. We quickly picked her up and found that she had only bruised a leg. She was mostly just wet, cold, and embarrassed. A mile downstream, the current increased because the river had narrowed. The water got rougher, and we remembered the story we had heard about the drowned rafter. We raced past boulders large and small. Several paddlers shifted to the bottom of the raft, one crushing the litre water bottle I had brought. Sunglasses and hats were repositioned as huge waves splashed over the side. Although it was a hot day, the waves were icy. At one point, our raft was hung up on a submerged rock, and we found ourselves spinning out of control, bouncing off boulders near the cliff side of the river. Somehow, Nick reorganized the crew just before we headed into the Brain Wash, an icy rapid so loud that I recommend wearing earplugs! By the time we reached the take-out point, we were exhausted and chilled but happy that we had experienced this exciting part of the river.

Source: Based on www.tripadvisor.com/ShowUserReviews-g155032-d649517-r34687 721Saute_Moutons_Lachine_Rapids_Jet_Boat_Tours-Montreal_Quebec.html *(accessed Apr. 11, 2010).*

Future Perfect

The **future perfect** is the verb tense that lets us show **one action being completed before another future act.** We almost always begin this tense with the helper verb *will,* though *shall* is sometimes used instead (for first person singular and plural: *I* and *we*). *Will* is followed by the helper verb *have,* plus a past participle. Note the example sentences below:

1. Lauren *will have* practised her spelling words 20 times before the test on Thursday.

2. By the end of July, Jan almost certainly *will have* hit 300 revision hours on this textbook.

In **sentence 1**, Lauren will keep studying those spelling words as the week progresses until the more distant future event of the test.

Sentence 2 predicts that Jan will put in more revision hours in the future, but she will do so before the later future date of the end of July.

English Review Note

Learn the difference between the future and the future perfect tenses. Be careful to use future perfect in a specific time clause.

ACTIVITY 4.8   Deciding on Future Perfect Verbs

In the following sentences, fill in the blanks with the proper future perfect form of the verb.

EXAMPLE: **Many happy high school seniors** *will have crossed* **(to cross) the stage before graduation is over.**

1. Margaret _____ (to save) $1500 toward next year's college expenses by her graduation date in June.

2. Before the end of her short summer, she _____ (to work) as many as 500 hours at the bookstore.

3. When she reaches the fifteenth of August, she _____ (to pay) $3000 for tuition.

4. Margaret says that she _____ (to complete) the two quilts for her cousins by the time she leaves for college.

5. Some think that before they enter the work force in five years' time, 10 000 high school students in Ontario _____ (to leave) the province to find more suitable college programs elsewhere.

6. Before classes begin at her chosen college in September, Margaret _____ (to sign) a lease for an apartment that can accommodate all her art supplies.

LO4.4 Progressive Tenses

Whereas the perfect tenses express when acts are completed, the **progressive tenses** show **ongoing action within tenses—present, past, or future.** While we use the past participle (*-d* or *-ed*) to form the perfect tenses, we use the **present participle** for the progressive tenses. The present participle consists of an *-ing* attached to the base form of a verb, regular or irregular (*talk/talking* or *speak/speaking*). When we add a form of the helper verb *to be* (*is, am, are, was, were, been*) before the present participle, we have a progressive tense (*is talking* or *was speaking*), as shown in the chart below:

PROGRESSIVE VERB FORMS				
	Present Participle	**Present Progressive**	**Past Progressive**	**Future Progressive**
Regular verb	talking	I am talking	I was talking	I will be talking
	planting	you are planting	you were planting	you will be planting
Irregular verbs	speaking	he is speaking	he was speaking	he will be speaking
	beginning	we are beginning	we were beginning	we will be beginning
	catching	they are catching	they were catching	they will be catching

Present Progressive

The **present progressive** tells of **ongoing action in the present** and uses the helping verbs *am, is,* or *are* before a present participle. Sentences using this tense imply or sometimes use phrases like *right now* or *at this moment*. In the following sentences, you can contrast this usage with the simple present, which suggests repeated or habitual action.

1a. Present progressive: Presently, Rajiv *is watching* the cardinals and chickadees at his feeder. [at this moment]

1b. Simple present: Every morning, Rajiv watches the cardinals and chickadees at his feeder. [repeatedly—every day]

2a. Present progressive: The Blue Jays' first baseman *is sliding* into home. [at this moment]

2b. Simple present: The Jays' first baseman slides into home when the throw is close. [repeatedly—every game]

Sentence 1a states that Rajiv is watching the birds at that moment, whereas sentence 1b suggests a habitual act.

Sentence 2a implies that the base runner is sliding now, while sentence 2b tells what the player does habitually under a certain circumstance.

ACTIVITY 4.9   Switching to Present Progressive from Simple Present

In the following sentences, change the simple present tense verbs in parentheses to the present progressive. Use the helper verbs *am, is,* or *are*.

EXAMPLE: **The project requirements (spins)** *are spinning* **out of control.**

1. I (skate) _____ with my roommate at Bell Arena.

2. My boyfriend (drives) _____ to meet us despite the weather advisory.

3. At home games, the team (play) _____ especially well together.

4. Larry (gazes) _____ anxiously at the sky because it (thunders) _____.

5. Isabel and Olivia, who are best friends, (text message) _____ back and forth.

6. The girls (decide) _____ which library to study in.

Past Progressive

The **past progressive** describes **ongoing action in the past** and uses the helping verbs *was* and *were* before a present participle. Like the past perfect, it can indicate one action occurring before another, but the past progressive describes **ongoing action that may immediately lead to another past action.** As with the present progressive, the past progressive sometimes uses phrases like *right then* or *at that moment.* In the following examples, you can contrast use of the past progressive with the simple past, which shows an action starting and finishing in the past.

1a. Past progressive: Elaine *was* dusting the living room when Stephanie walked in.

1b. Simple past: Yesterday Elaine dusted the living room, and Stephanie spilled the vacuum cleaner bag.

2a. Past progressive: As they *were* walking through the Vancouver Aquarium, Gregor and Katrina saw an octopus squirt ink.

2b. Simple past: Gregor and Katrina walked through the Vancouver Aquarium and saw an octopus squirt ink.

3. Past progressive: As I *was* cleaning the plates, Ben *was* putting them in the dishwasher.

Sentence 1a tells us that Elaine was in the process of dusting the room before the other past action of Stephanie walking in. **Sentence 1b** describes two completed past acts without indicating which happened first.

In **sentence 2a,** Gregor and Katrina saw the octopus while they were in the process of walking through the aquarium (an event that occurred in the past). In **sentence 2b,** the couple might have seen the octopus at the start of their walk, during it, or just before they left.

Sentence 3 describes two past actions occurring at the same time.

In the following sentences, fill in the blanks with the past progressive form of the verb listed in parentheses. Remember to use a helper verb, either *was* or *were*.

> EXAMPLE: Yesterday, Byron *was driving* (to drive) to the bank when his car broke down.

1. I _____ (to hope) that Margot would arrive on time when she ran up the stairs.

2. We _____ (to drive) to avoid the storm when the sleeting rain began.

3. After arriving at the cottage, Margot _____ (to search) for her favourite brand of green tea as I was taking the cups from the cupboard.

4. Waves _____ (to hiss) up onto the pebble beach when the wind blew away the towels.

5. Nobody _____ (to deny) the need for immediate action when the lightning hit the porch.

6. The new plasma TV _____ (to flicker) when the electricity died.

Future Progressive

The **future progressive** describes **ongoing action in the future** and, like the simple future, uses the helper verb *will*. However, the future progressive also requires the helper verb *be* in front of a present participle. Often there is little difference between the future progressive and the simple future, as you might notice in the following sentences.

1a. Future progressive: Mark *will be* playing lead guitar at the concert this afternoon.

1b. Simple future: Mark *will play* lead guitar at the concert this afternoon.

2a. Future progressive: The geese *will be* flying south soon.

2b. Simple future: The geese *will fly* south soon.

In the following sentences, fill in the blanks with the future progressive form of the verb in parentheses. Remember to use the helper verbs *will be* before a present participle.

> EXAMPLE: By the end of the county tour, your mind *will be reeling* (to reel).

1. Soon we _____ (to use) wind turbines throughout Ontario as a plentiful source of energy.

2. The wind turbines being erected in Amherstburg _____ (to create) pollution-free power for many years to come.

3. Home owners, farms, and small businesses _____ (to install) small wind turbines to reduce electricity bills.

4. I _____ (to try) to convince my neighbours to accept this alternative form of energy.

5. Boat owners _____ (to charge) batteries for sailboats with very small wind turbines.

6. It will not be long before everyone _____ (to adapt) to this practical and cost-effective energy source.

Irregular Verbs

LO4.5

The most important irregular verb in English is *to be*. Because it is used so often both as a helper (*is* running) and on its own as a linking verb (Jonathan *is* a kind man), you should learn its various forms: *am, are, is, was, were, been, being*.

FORMS OF TO BE		
	Singular	**Plural**
Present	I am	we are
	you are	you are
	he, she, it is	they are
Past	I was	we were
	you were	you were
	he, she, it was	they were
Past perfect	I had been	we had been
	you had been	you had been
	he, she, it had been	they had been

Regular verbs in English form their past tense by adding *-d* or *-ed* to the base or dictionary form (*walk/walked*), but **irregular verbs** do not follow that pattern. The past tense and past participle of irregular verbs are usually spelled differently from the base form; sometimes a vowel changes, sometimes consonants change, but sometimes there is no change at all. The best approach to handling these forms is to memorize them and, when in doubt, to consult a dictionary. A list of the principal parts of some common irregular verbs follows.

COMMON IRREGULAR VERBS					
Present Tense	**Past Tense**	**Past Participle**	**Present Tense**	**Past Tense**	**Past Participle**
arise	arose	arisen	cast	cast	cast
awake	awoke	awoken	catch	caught	caught
become	became	become	choose	chose	chosen
begin	began	begun	come	came	come
bend	bent	bent	cost	cost	cost
bite	bit	bitten	creep	crept	crept
bleed	bled	bled	cut	cut	cut
blow	blew	blown	deal	dealt	dealt
break	broke	broken	dig	dug	dug
bring	brought	brought	dive	dived/dove	dived
build	built	built	do	did	done
burst	burst	burst	draw	drew	drawn
buy	bought	bought	drink	drank	drunk

COMMON IRREGULAR VERBS

Present Tense	Past Tense	Past Participle	Present Tense	Past Tense	Past Participle
drive	drove	driven	rise	rose	risen
eat	ate	eaten	run	ran	run
fall	fell	fallen	say	said	said
feed	fed	fed	see	saw	seen
feel	felt	felt	sell	sold	sold
fight	fought	fought	send	sent	sent
find	found	found	set	set	set
fit	fit	fit	sew	sewed	sown/sowed
fly	flew	flown	shake	shook	shaken
forget	forgot	forgotten	shine	shone/shined	shone/shined
forgive	forgave	forgiven	shoot	shot	shot
freeze	froze	frozen	show	showed	shown
get	got	got/gotten	shrink	shrank	shrunk
give	gave	given	shut	shut	shut
go	went	gone	sing	sang	sung
grow	grew	grown	sit	sat	sat
hang (a picture)	hung	hung	sleep	slept	slept
hang (a person)	hanged	hanged	slide	slid	slid
have	had	had	speak	spoke	spoken
hear	heard	heard	spin	spun	spun
hide	hid	hidden	spend	spent	spent
hit	hit	hit	spring	sprang	sprung
hold	held	held	stand	stood	stood
hurt	hurt	hurt	steal	stole	stolen
keep	kept	kept	stick	stuck	stuck
kneel	knelt	knelt	sting	stung	stung
know	knew	known	strike	struck	struck
lay (put)	laid	laid	swear	swore	sworn
lead	led	led	sweep	swept	swept
leave	left	left	swell	swelled	swelled/swollen
lend	lent	lent	swim	swam	swum
let	let	let	swing	swung	swung
lie (recline)	lay	lain	take	took	taken
light	lit/lighted	lit/lighted	teach	taught	taught
lose	lost	lost	tear	tore	torn
make	made	made	tell	told	told
mean	meant	meant	think	thought	thought
meet	met	met	throw	threw	thrown
pay	paid	paid	upset	upset	upset
prove	proved	proven	understand	understood	understood
put	put	put	wake	woke/waked	woken/waked
quit	quit	quit	wear	wore	worn
read	read	read	win	won	won
ride	rode	ridden	wind	wound	wound
ring	rang	rung	write	wrote	written

The following sentences are written with present tense irregular verbs. In the blanks provided, work with a partner to change these verbs to past participles using the helper verbs *has* and *have*.

EXAMPLE: **Winter (brings) <u>has brought</u> cold weather, snow, and icy streets to the east coast.**

1. Craig (leaves) _____ the bread in the oven too long.

2. Fortunately, I (buy) _____ enough flour to make more.

3. I (find) _____ that making bread is an activity that requires practice.

4. We (become) _____ fond of eating freshly baked bread.

5. So Craig (makes) _____ progress in perfecting bread making to an art form.

6. Frequent practice (leads) _____ Craig to master many of the skills required.

Problem Verbs

Among the irregular verbs listed above, several can cause additional problems because they are each easily confused with another verb. These problem pairs are *lie/lay*, *sit/set*, and *rise/raise*.

PROBLEM VERBS				
Base Form	**Past Tense**	**Past Participle**	**Present Participle**	**-s Ending**
lie	lay	lain	lying	lies
lay	laid	laid	laying	lays
sit	sat	sat	sitting	sits
set	set	set	setting	sets
rise	rose	risen	rising	rises
raise	raised	raised	raising	raises

LIE VERSUS *LAY*

- *Lie* means to rest or recline, as in: I'm tired. I think I <u>will</u> *lie* down now.
- *Lay* means to place something, as in: I <u>will</u> *lay* the book on the table.

SIT VERSUS *SET*

- *Sit* means to be seated, as in: I <u>will</u> *sit* in the chair.
  It also means to be situated, as in: The glass <u>is</u> *sitting* on the table.
- *Set* means to place something, as in: I <u>will</u> *set* the cup on the counter.

RISE VERSUS *RAISE*

- *Rise* means to go up, as in: The balloon <u>is</u> *rising* in the sky.
- *Raise* means to lift, as in: I <u>will</u> *raise* the window to get some air.

In the following sentences, underline the correct form in the verb pairs in parentheses.

EXAMPLE: Working on her tan, Francine decided to (lay/<u>lie</u>) by the pool.

1. Marybeth said to her son, "(Sit/Set) the groceries on the table, and we'll (set/sit) for a while."

2. Angelo (lay/laid) the flashlight on the table.

3. Some people must use a sleep aid at night or (lay/lie) awake for hours.

4. The harp seal had been (laying/lying) on the ice most of the morning.

5. I found the iPod (sitting/setting) on the floor.

6. The attorney said, "My client never (laid/lay) a finger on the plaintiff."

Phrasal Verbs

When you are trying to link subjects with verbs in sentences, **phrasal verbs**—also known as **two-part verbs**—can be confusing. Phrasal verbs use a main verb or verb phrase followed by a preposition or an adverb.

VERB + **ADVERB** = PHRASAL VERB   VERB PHRASE + **ADVERB** = PHRASAL VERB

<u>figure</u> **out**   to <u>figure</u> **out**

VERB + **PREPOSITION** = PHRASAL VERB VERB PHRASE + **PREPOSITION** = PHRASAL VERB

<u>hand</u> **in**   to <u>hand</u> **in**

If you come across verbs in your own sentences that seem incomplete without another word attached, you may be using a phrasal verb. They are common in our language, especially in informal usage. Some phrasal verbs can be separated (for example, *to ask* a friend *out*); others cannot be (for example, *to get in* a car). The following are brief lists of common phrasal verbs:

SEPARABLE PHRASAL (TWO-PART) VERBS		
Verb	**Meaning**	**Example**
ask out	invite on a date	Gabriele *asked* Sergei *out* to a movie.
ask over	invite to a place	Michael *asked* Marta *over* to his home.
back up	support	I hope my friends will *back* me *up*.
blow up	destroy	The construction crew had to *blow* the bridge *up*.
break down	disassemble	Sonia *broke* her tent *down* in the morning.
bring back	return	Frank had to *bring* the videos *back*.
call off	cancel	The promoters *called* the concert *off*.
call up	telephone	Hans was too nervous to *call* Elena *up*.
carry out	do	The Canadian soldiers *carried* their mission *out*.
cover up	hide	Politicians are often trying to *cover* something *up*.
drag out	prolong	The professor *dragged* the lecture *out* for an hour.

INSEPARABLE PHRASAL (TWO-PART) VERBS		
Verb	**Meaning**	**Example**
call on	visit, ask	Professor Finlay-Clark *called on* Amy to answer.
catch up (with)	reach	I *caught up* with the bus at the corner.
come across	discover	Jay *came across* a great DVD sale.
drop by	visit	My cousin *dropped by* unexpectedly.
drop out	leave	Too many teenagers are *dropping out* of school.
get along (with)	coexist	Everyone *gets along* with Alex.
get into	enter	Thomas *got into* the car.
get off	leave	The passengers *got off* the plane.
get on	enter	The passengers *got on* the plane.
get out (of)	leave, avoid	Peter *got out* of the final exam.
get over	recover from	Marco *got over* the reprimand from his boss.

English Review Note

Two-word verbs are idiomatic and may cause difficulty. It can be challenging to figure out which verbs are separable. Don't hesitate to look them up in a dictionary or handbook.

ACTIVITY 4.14 Finding Phrasal Verbs

In the following sentences, underline the underlined phrasal verbs and box or circle their subjects. Refer to the lists above for help, and remember that sometimes the verb parts will be separated.

EXAMPLES: Tina checked out ten books from the library on Wednesday.

Dad said, "You kids clean that mess up!"

1. The lieutenant carried his orders out.

2. While searching the victim's files, the detective came across a clue to the murder.

3. After a six-month investigation, Rick brought the criminal in.

4. After waving to her friends on the beach, Kate said she would catch up with them after work.

5. Dora's boss dropped by her office and found her working hard.

6. The financial adviser covered his criminal actions up for years before finally being caught.

Verb Tense Sequences and Unneeded Tense Shifts

LO4.6

When writing, we often combine verb tenses, speaking of actions in the present, past, and future. As we move from a subordinate clause to a main clause, however, we should be sure that the verb tenses indicate a logical time relationship so that we do not confuse the reader. We can show many time relationships by combining tenses, including the following:

1. **Present/present:** Muhammad *wins* the scholarship because he *is* a hard worker.

2. **Past/past:** Muhammad *won* the scholarship because he *worked* hard every day in high school.

3. **Past/present:** Muhammad *won* the scholarship because he *works* hard every day in school.

4. **Future/present perfect/present progressive:** Muhammad *will win* the scholarship because he *has worked* hard every day in school and *is spending* weekends studying.

Sentence 1 tells us that Muhammad gets the award in the present because he is always so diligent.

Sentence 2 says that he won in the past because of his past efforts.

Sentence 3 states that Muhammad earned the prize in the past because of his habitual, ongoing efforts.

Sentence 4 speculates that he will win in the future because of his ongoing efforts in the past that are still ongoing in the present and because he is currently in the process of preparing even more.

However, there are also illogical tense relationships that we want to avoid, as in the following:

Muhammad *wins/has won* the scholarship because he *will work* hard every day in high school.

Logically, Muhammad's hard work should lead to his winning the scholarship, and not the reverse situation of the scholarship leading to hard work.

One of the most common ways that writers confuse their readers is to shift needlessly from present to past (and sometimes back again). Notice how the tenses shift in the following passage:

> Sadly, my uncle *died* at the age of 50 from a heart attack. He *was* a humorous man, and he *liked* to play with children. In particular, he *loves* his 12-year-old grandson, who often *sleeps* at his house. In the summer, my uncle, his grandson, and I *went* fishing. My uncle always *jokes* around with people and *called* me by my nickname, Simmi.

Since this passage describes a person who has passed away, the writer should stick with the past tense all the way through.

> Sadly, my uncle *died* at the age of 50 from a heart attack. He *was* a humorous man, and he *liked* to play with children. In particular, he *loved* his 12-year-old grandson, who often *slept* at his house. In the summer, my uncle, his grandson, and I *went* fishing. My uncle always *joked* around with people and *called* me by my nickname, Simmi.

ACTIVITY 4.15 Choosing Consistent Verb Tenses

In the following sentences, underline the correct <u>verb tense</u> (in parentheses).

EXAMPLE: **Most of the time when I visited his house, he (jokes/joked) with me.**

1. My uncle also helped me with my math, and now whenever I (study/studied) math, I (miss/missed) him.

2. Once my uncle gave me a gold wristwatch for Christmas, and that watch (reminds/reminded) me of him.

3. I (remember/remembered) my aunt and uncle fondly, and I think of them often.

4. Because they lived so far away, I only (visit/visited) them once a year, during summer break.

5. My aunt once gave me a pair of tiny diamond earrings, a gift that I still (treasure/treasured).

6. Whenever I visited her, we (cook/cooked) dinner together.

Verb Challenges for English as a Second Language Learners

LO4.7

Verbs are the heart of writing, combining with subjects (nouns or pronouns) to create grammatical sentences. All sentences in English require a verb and a subject (though the subject may only be implied in a command, as in "Shut the door, please"). Verbs have three simple tenses—past, present, and future—and must agree in person and number with their subject:

Abdul is studying, but his brothers are watching TV.

Here are some common verb challenges when English is not your first language.

Word Order

Verbs generally come after subjects in sentences:
Sam works hard.
However, remember that for **questions**, word order may change:
Will you come to dinner?
Inverted sentences move the subject close to or all the way to the end of the sentence:
Into the operating room walked the surgeon.
Helping verbs precede action verbs in a verb phrase:
Sam will *work* today.
A **verb phrase** may be separated by other words:
Sam will not work today.

Three Irregular Verbs: To Do, To Have, and To Be

Two irregular verbs that can work as either helper verbs or action verbs are *to do* (forms: *do, does, did,* and *done*) and *to have* (forms: *have, has, had*).

Action verb:	Joaquim *did* the bills for the month. (meaning "completed the job")
Helping verb:	Alek *did* go home for Christmas. (emphasizes *go*)
Action verb:	Ivan *had* only $50 to live on until Friday. (meaning "possessed")
Helping verb:	He *had* hoped to have $150. (past perfect tense of *hope*)

USING TO DO

When used as a helping verb, *to do,* in all its forms, can help with questions, express a negative, and emphasize an action verb:

Question:	Where *do* you think you will go?
Negative:	I *do* not like cooked spinach.
Emphasizer:	Amil *does* plan on graduating this semester.

The irregular verb *to be* (forms: *am, are, is, was, were, been, being*) can work as either a verb that expresses a state of being (a linking verb) or a helping verb:

State of being:	Stephen *is* a neurosurgeon. (links the subject, *Stephen*, to the noun complement, *neurosurgeon*)
	Stephen *is* intelligent. (links Stephen to the adjective complement, *intelligent*)
Helping verb:	Emily *is* painting her home office today. (present progressive tense of *paint*)

ACTIVITY 4.16 Choosing Forms of To Be, To Do, and To Have

In the spaces below, write the correct form of the verbs *to be, to do,* and *to have.*

EXAMPLE: **Seth** *did* **(to do) the laundry but forgot to fold the clothes.**

1. The humidity _____ (to be) so high that we sweated standing still.

2. The phones _____ (to have) not been working since the windstorm.

3. Fatima _____ (to have) two hours of free time before the plane arrived.

4. Saltwater crocodiles _____ (to be) deadly predators.

5. The yellow Labrador _____ (to have) a problem with shedding.

6. All of Iryna's relatives _____ (to do) think that she will become a lawyer.

Modals

Modals create shades of meaning and so are useful in making requests. For example, while watching TV, we could demand, "Hand me the remote," or we could make a request by using a modal, "*Would* you please hand me the remote."

The base form of a verb always follows the modal, so be careful not to use the past tense or an infinitive:

Not this:	Yelena *should worked* out her problem with her friend.
But this:	Yelena *should work* out her problem with her friend.
Not this:	They *may to save* their relationship if they try.
But this:	They *may save* their relationship if they try.

ACTIVITY 4.17 Practising Modals

In the following sentences, write the modal that expresses the meaning in parentheses.

1. The stereo is too loud. _____ you please turn it down. (request)

2. If the ice storm does pass through, you _____ salt your driveway. (advisability)

3. Multinational corporations _____ stop paying workers less than the minimum wage set by the workers' governments. (necessity)

4. Someday Nigeria _____ insist on stricter pollution controls in the extraction of its oil. (doubt)

5. Canada _____ take a lead in caring for the health of the planet. (advisability)

6. Stavros _____ arrive on time for the concert. (doubt)

Stative Verbs

Stative verbs indicate that a subject will remain in a certain state for some time. For example, we might say, "Art knows that his family loves him." This sentence tells us that Art knows that his family cares deeply for him and is not likely to stop caring for him in the near future. Therefore, we call "to know" a stative verb. This class of verbs usually cannot use the present progressive, so it would be incorrect to write, "Art *is knowing* that his family loves him."

HINT

Stative verbs usually do not use the present progressive tense.

COMMON STATIVE VERBS			
be	hate	love	resemble
believe	have	mean	think
belong	know	need	understand
cost	like	own	weigh

Several verbs can be either stative or **active**, depending on their meaning. *Weigh* and *look* are two such verbs. When functioning as active verbs, these verbs can use the present progressive tense. For example:

Active use: Sarah *is looking* for her friend at the roller rink.

Stative use: Sarah *looks* as if she is lost.

ACTIVITY 4.18 Choosing Active vs. Stative Verbs

In the following sentences, underline the correct form in the verb pairs in parentheses. Refer to the preceding chart for help, and remember that some verbs can be either stative or active, depending on their meaning.

EXAMPLE: **The students (were hating/hated) the thought of more homework.**

1. Saiching (is liking/likes) the cool fall weather.

2. The next-door neighbours (were having/have) trouble getting their car started today.

3. The neighbours (are having/have) a 1970 Corvette with 250 000 kilometres on it.

4. There are many who (are arguing/argue) that China needs to take more steps to protect the environment.

5. Many also (are believing/believe) that Canada should do more to limit its global pollution.

6. Ahmad (is needing/needs) a ride to work this morning.

Phrasal (Two-Part) Verbs

Another potentially confusing verb is the **two-part** or **phrasal verb**, which follows a verb with a preposition or an adverb; some examples are *to call back, to check out,* or *to hang up.* These verbs usually express a different idea than they would without the attached preposition or adverb, so they can be difficult to understand if thought of literally, especially for those whose first language is not English. For example, if we said, "The English teacher *dragged out* his explanation for 30 minutes," we wouldn't mean that the explanation had literally been pulled around the room; we would mean that the teacher had prolonged his explanation.

Most phrasal verbs consisting of a main verb and an adverb can either be split or remain attached:

SPLIT: Paul will *pull* the weeds *up* from his garden today.

ATTACHED: Paul will *pull up* the weeds from his garden today.

However, when a pronoun is used as the object, it must be placed *between* the two verb parts, as in the example below:

CORRECT: Paul will pull *them* up today.

INCORRECT: Paul will *pull up* them today.

Many phrasal verbs consisting of a main verb and a preposition are non-separable, as in the following example:

CORRECT: After that, Paul will *get through* the rest of his chores.

INCORRECT: After that, Paul will *get* the rest of his chores *through.*

In informal conversation, we use many phrasal verbs that we would avoid in more formal writing. Often, a more concise substitute can be found. Here is an example:

PHRASAL VERB: The football coach was trying to *get across* the plays to his team.

SUBSTITUTE: The football coach was trying to *explain* the plays to his team.

ACTIVITY 4.19 Finding Phrasal Verbs

In the following sentences, underline the <u>phrasal verbs</u>.

EXAMPLE: **If people work together, they can *bring about* change.**

1. Selma said that she would get over the breakup soon.

2. The construction crew put the new building together almost overnight.

3. Majid's parents look after their children more carefully than do most parents.

4. Trying to save energy (and money), Natasha told her children, "Turn the lights off!"

5. After the fourth call in one day, I could not put up with the telemarketer.

6. If I had his home phone number, I would call him up ten times in a day to see how he would like it.

Chapter Summary

DEFINITION OF VERB TENSES AND FORMS	EXAMPLES
Past: shows action that happened in the past but is no longer happening • regular verbs add *-ed* or *-d* to base verb	Beth *planted* daffodil bulbs in her front garden. Chris *baked* pumpkin pies for Thanksgiving.
Present: shows action or state of being right now or continuously	Tomatoes *grow* well in southern Ontario. Jan *is* happy with her life.
Future: shows anticipated action • add the helping verb *will* to base verb	Luciano *will compete* in the Architectural Technology Department's concrete canoe competition this year.
Helping Verbs: cannot work alone but are added to a main verb to create verb phrases • common helping verbs are *be, do, did, have, will*	After eating all the malted Easter eggs, Greta *did* feel a little sick. Art *will* stop at the tavern for a beer on his way home from work.
Modals: express requests, doubt, capability, willingness, necessity, and advisability • useful in softening difficult requests • common modals are *may/might, can/could, will/would, should, must*	I *may* have time to visit you in Amherstburg tomorrow. There *should* be a prayer chapel in this school. You *must* visit Newfoundland sometime in your life.
Past perfect: shows something occurring in *past* related to something occurring in *more distant past* • *had* in front of a past participle using a *-d* or *-ed* ending	Roselyn *had finished* cleaning the bathroom just before the phone *rang*. David *was* late picking up his mother and father, who *had arrived* at the airport an hour earlier.
Present perfect: shows action beginning in the past and finishing at an unknown time *or* continuing into present *or* just recently ended • *has* or *have* in front of a past participle using a *-d* or *-ed* ending	Margaret *has talked* to the head nurse about her retirement from the hospital. Max and his family *have flown* to Germany from Montreal many times on business.
Future perfect: shows one action being completed before a future act • usually begins with *will* or *shall* followed by the helper verb *has* or *have* in front of a past participle	John believes that he *will have spent* $50 000 on home renovations before the end of the year. Joyce *will have practised* for 100 hours before playing her violin concert in Calgary next week.
Past progressive: shows ongoing action that may be connected to another past action • a helping verb (*was, were, been*) in front of a present participle (*-ing* ending)	I *was walking* into the drug store when my chiropractor left the parking lot. Bob and Jan *were finishing* lunch when their sister entered the restaurant.
Present progressive: shows ongoing action in the present • a helping verb (*is, am, are*) in front of a present participle (*-ing* ending)	Currently, our administrative assistant *is having* a baby at the hospital. Our boss *is looking* for a temporary replacement.
Future progressive: shows ongoing action in the future • helping verbs (*will* and *be*) in front of a present participle (*-ing* ending)	Marc *will be moving* to Halifax in the fall. He *will be continuing* his university nursing program there.
Irregular verbs: most important one is *to be,* which is used as a helper and as a linking verb • see chart on pages 53–54 for list of irregular verbs	She *is* on a very tight schedule every day. I *have broken* my own record for remaining calm and composed.

DEFINITION OF VERB TENSES AND FORMS	EXAMPLES
Phrasal verbs: two-part verbs • a main verb or verb phrase followed by a preposition or adverb • can be separable or inseparable	**Separable:** Matthew *asked* Maria *over* to his apartment. Her mother *dragged* the lecture *out* for an hour. **Inseparable:** Too many students are ***dropping out*** of class. Adam ***got over*** his love affair with Jane quickly.
FOR ESL: **Stative verbs:** indicate that a subject will remain in a certain state for some time	Samir *knows* that his family loves him. Howard *intends* to live in this house for the rest of his life.

Subject/Verb Agreement

5

Just as musicians must tune their instruments so the notes flow together, so too must writers "tune" the parts of their sentences, especially the subjects and verbs, to help the ideas flow smoothly. Write a brief paragraph that explores an image of harmony involving people or things getting along well together.

What Are We Trying to Achieve and Why?

Aside from understanding verb tense, writers also must know how verbs agree with their subjects. Singular verbs should be paired with singular subjects and plural verbs with plural subjects. Although it might seem confusing, the *-s* ending on a present tense verb marks it as **singular**, whereas the same ending on a subject marks it as **plural**. Ordinarily we don't think much about this distinction but observe it naturally in speaking and writing, as in the following two examples:

The <u>girl</u> <u>runs</u> home after school.

The <u>girls</u> <u>run</u> home after school.

However, as we write more complicated sentences than these, we sometimes have trouble finding subjects and verbs and then making them agree in number. Chapter 5 will help you with subject/verb agreement problems.

LO5.1 Intervening Words and Prepositional Phrases

Intervening Words

One common <u>trouble spot</u> in <u>sentences</u> <u>occurs</u> when dealing with a verb separated from its subject by a number of words—as in this sentence! We often try to connect the verb with the closest noun (in this case, <u>sentences</u>) instead of the actual subject (<u>trouble spot</u>). Here are several examples of sentences with the <u>subjects</u> underlined once and the <u>verbs</u> twice:

1. **<u>Cashew wine</u>, the national wine of Belize, <u>is fermented</u> from the cashew fruit.**

2. **<u>Kevin Bacon</u>, famous for the party game "Six Degrees of Kevin Bacon" that links him with other actors, <u>has appeared</u> in more than 50 films.**

3. **<u>Lasers</u>, which were thought of as sci-fi technology only 50 years ago, now <u>can be bought</u> for a few dollars in hardware stores throughout the nation, much to the delight of household cats.**

4. **A <u>chance</u> to listen to and perhaps see wild grey wolves <u>awaits</u> people visiting the forests of British Columbia.**

5. **<u>David Suzuki</u>, along with several other environmentalists who attempted to convince us about the seriousness of the planet's peril, <u>emphasized</u> that we're all in the same vehicle heading toward a brick wall.**

To find the subject, first look at the verb and ask who or what is doing the action (for an action verb) or what is the focus (of a being verb). For example, in **sentence 1,** what is fermented? *Cashew wine* is. In **sentence 2,** who has appeared? *Kevin Bacon* has. You might also notice in sentence 2 that there are several **prepositional phrases** (word groups starting with a preposition and ending with a noun or pronoun). As we learned in Chapter 3, subjects are *never* found within prepositional phrases; therefore, when you see these phrases, you can mentally (or on paper, as in the following examples) cross them out to help you find the real subject.

For sentence 2: <u>Kevin Bacon</u>, famous ~~for the party game "Six Degrees of Kevin Bacon" that links him with other actors,~~ <u>has appeared</u> ~~in more than fifty films.~~

For sentence 5: <u>David Suzuki</u>, ~~along with several other environmentalists who attempted to convince us about the seriousness of the planet's peril,~~ <u>emphasized</u> that we're all ~~in the same vehicle~~ heading ~~toward a brick wall.~~

Also note that sentence 5 uses the preposition *along with*, one of a small group of prepositions that do not affect the number of the subject. Other such prepositions include *in addition to, as well as, plus, including,* and *together with*.

Prepositional Phrases

Below are key prepositions that often begin prepositional phrases. Remember that subjects in sentences are never found within prepositional phrases.

PREPOSITIONS				
LOCATION			**OTHER USES**	
above	behind	off	about	in addition to
across	below	on	according to	in place of
after	beneath	onto	as	in spite of
against	beside	out (out of)	aside from	instead of
ahead of	between	outside	as well as	like
along	beyond	over	because of	of
amid	by	past	by way of	regarding
among	down	through	despite	since
around	from	toward	due to	till
at	in	under	during	until
atop	inside	up	except (except for)	with
before	into	upon	for	without

ACTIVITY 5.1 Intervening Words and Prepositional Phrases: Making Sure Separated Subjects and Verbs Agree

Being aware of intervening words and prepositional phrases that separate subjects and verbs, underline the correct <u>verb</u> in parentheses and circle the subject.

EXAMPLE: Researchers at the University of Saskatchewan, in Saskatchewan (has/have) found skunks to be timid creatures that try not to spray people.

1. The blue whale, like so many of its cousins, (travel/travels) in groups called pods.

2. My mother, one of Paul McCartney's many fans, (listen/listens) to *Memory Almost Full* at least twice a day.

3. Many of the liveliest peewee soccer games I have seen in this city (feature/features) parents shouting from the sidelines and getting more exercise than their children.

4. The girls in the red jerseys with the International Quiddich Association logo (play/plays) for the home team.

5. The police officer, whose children attend the same school as my little brother, (ticket/tickets) at least a dozen people a day for texting while driving.

6. Jogging 30 minutes every other day, along with cycling 50 kilometres a week, (make/makes) Danny feel he is ready to hike the length of the Cabot Trail.

L05.2 Verbals as Incomplete Verbs: Participles, Gerunds, and Infinitives

Another potential problem in establishing agreement between subject and verb is finding the main verb in the first place. In Chapter 3, we noted that certain words can look like verbs but are not (see page 35). These words, explained below, are called **verbals**. While they have a sense of action or being, they are not complete verbs; therefore, they can never be the main verb in a sentence. Because verbals are used so much in writing, they often cause agreement problems when writers mistake them for main verbs. In Chapter 11, we will study verbal phrases, but for now we will focus just on these incomplete verbs:

TYPES OF VERBALS

1. **Participles:** *-ing* or *-ed* form of a regular verb, *-ing* also for irregular verbs and often *-n* or *-t* (used as an adjective)
2. **Gerunds:** *-ing* form of a verb (used as a noun)
3. **Infinitives:** *to* + verb (used as an adjective, adverb, or noun)

Participles

Participles, as we have seen earlier in this unit (see Chapter 4), come in present and past tense. The present tense form for both regular and irregular verbs always ends in *-ing* (laugh*ing*, play*ing*, fly*ing*) and describes a noun (running *athletes*) or pronoun (I see *them* [the athletes] running). The past participle for regular verbs ends in *-ed* and for irregular verbs often ends in *-n* or *-t*. Participles function as **adjectives**, and they also **work with helper verbs to form main verbs**. Notice in the following sentences how we might use participles:

PRESENT PARTICIPLES   1.   A trumpeting elephant is *defending* his territory.

2.   Sophia was *telling* her boring friend that he needed a more exciting life.

The word *trumpeting* in **sentence 1** describes the subject elephant; though it conveys action, it is not the main verb. The phrase *is defending* is the main verb made up of a helper and the present participle *defending*.

Sentence 2 includes the participles *boring* and *exciting*, both of which describe the noun that follows them. The main verb (a helper verb plus a present participle) is the phrase *was telling*.

PAST PARTICIPLES   3.   The exhausted soldiers have *retreated* slowly toward a battered Humvee.

4.   Dejected, David has *shredded* carefully preserved love letters and faded pictures of his high school sweetheart.

In **sentence 3,** the past participle *exhausted* describes the subject, soldiers, while the participle *battered* tells about the Humvee. The main verb (a helper plus a past participle) is the phrase *have retreated*.

Sentence 4 has four past participles—*dejected, shredded, preserved,* and *faded*—three in front of the noun that each describes, and one as the main verb with its helper, both double-underlined.

Finding Participles Used as Describing Words
and Participles in Verb Phrases

The following sentences use both present and past participles as adjectives.
The participle plus a helper verb can also be used as a main verb phrase.
Circle all (participles) used as adjectives, then find and underline the <u>main verb</u>
or <u>verb phrase.</u> Once the participles and main verbs are identified, it should
be easy for you to recognize the subject.

Note: Several sentences have more than one participle used as an adjective.

EXAMPLE: (Streamlined) and visually (appealing), the new Apple Notebook <u>is winning</u> rave reviews.

1. The friendly, smiling gecko has made GEICO a lot of money.

2. Diana Krall, the kind and understanding mother of twins, is playing at
   Kemper Arena in Vancouver this weekend.

3. Finally identified, the virus was still leaving thousands of dying cows in
   its wake.

4. Pawing at the earth, the enraged bull was threatening the coyote trotting
   past the field.

5. Runoff water flowing from the homes along Indian Creek was polluting
   the stream.

6. A hard-working veterinarian was saving the lives of many infected horses.

Gerunds

Gerunds look a lot like present participles because they always end in *-ing*. However, gerunds do not describe words as participles do; instead, they *name* words.
Gerunds may look like verbs, but they are **nouns**. They can be used as subjects,
complements, or objects, as in the following example sentences:

1. Gerund subject: <u>Swimming</u> <u>requires</u> strength and confidence.

2. Gerund subject complement: In the summer, Chris's favourite <u>sport</u> <u>is</u>
water-skiing.

3. Gerund object: Many <u>people</u> <u>fear</u> *flying.*

4. Gerund object of a preposition: Many <u>people</u> <u>are</u> afraid of *flying.*

Sentence 1 uses the gerund *swimming* as a subject.
Sentence 2 uses the gerund *water-skiing* as a subject complement (a noun or
pronoun tied to the subject with a linking verb).
Sentence 3 uses the gerund *flying* as an object (a noun or pronoun that receives
the action of the main verb), while **Sentence 4** uses *flying* as object
of the preposition *of.*
When trying to locate the main verb or verb phrase in a sentence, consider
how each word functions. To decide if an *-ing* word is a gerund, try mentally
replacing it in a sentence with the pronoun *it*. Note the following two sentences:

1. Gerund: *Dancing* <u>has always been</u> a part of Mena's life.

2. Participle: When Mena was young, her <u>mother</u> <u>told</u> her that she had
"*dancing* feet."

We can mentally replace the word *dancing* in **sentence 1** with *it*, but we can't
do the same in **sentence 2** ("it feet" makes no sense).

> **HINT**
>
> For more about objects of the
> preposition, see Chapter 6.

In the following sentences, circle the gerunds, and underline the main verbs or verb phrases.

Note: Several sentences have more than one gerund. Which gerunds are also subjects?

EXAMPLE: Complaining will not solve the problem.

1. Surprising people with a practical joke can be funny or sometimes dangerous.

2. At first, Frodo and Sam looked forward to beginning the journey.

3. The blizzard stopped us from skiing in Collingwood today.

4. Danielle hates filling out her tax forms but loves getting the money back.

5. Many students stop studying when they are tired, unless working the extra hours is crucial.

6. Learning the basics early in life makes the rest of education much easier.

Infinitives

Infinitives, the final and most flexible type of verbal, can serve a number of functions within a sentence. Like gerunds, they can serve as nouns (subjects, complements, or objects); like participles, they can act as adjectives; and finally, they can function as modifiers for adjectives, verbs, and adverbs. If this seems like a lot for one class of words, it is! However, infinitives are fairly easy to recognize because they begin with the word *to* (though sometimes *to* is implied), followed by the base or dictionary form of the verb (*run, love, travel*). Note the following examples:

1. **Noun:**   To try is all anyone can ask.

2. **Adjective:** For novices, those are the right horses to ride.

3. **Adverb:**   At first, some trails seem easy to hike.

Sentence 1 uses the infinitive as a noun and as the subject.

In **sentence 2,** since *to ride* describes *horses,* a noun, the infinitive is an adjective.

In **sentence 3,** *to hike* describes the word *easy,* an adjective modifying the noun *trails.* Therefore, *to hike* is working as an adverb.

An important point to remember about identifying infinitives is that writers often drop the *to* before a pair or series of infinitives (to cut unneeded words), but the *to* is understood to be there, so the word is still an infinitive. In the example sentences below, the infinitives are italicized and the "understood" *tos* are in parentheses:

My friends and I were too old *to race* in the car and (*to*) *do* the jump ourselves.

So we decided *to put* my sister in the car, (*to*) *strap* her inside, and (*to*) *put* a pillow in for padding.

In the following sentences, circle all the infinitives first. Then find and underline the main verbs or verb phrases. Finally, underline the subjects with a wavy line. If the infinitive is a subject, you will underline with a wavy line *and* circle it.

Note: Several sentences have more than one infinitive.

EXAMPLE: Peter Jackson decided not to include the character of Glorfindel in his *Lord of the Rings* films.

1. Joe intended to finish his composition paper, but his friend wanted him to go to a party instead.

2. That hockey player cannot afford to spend any more time in the penalty box.

3. Sam begged Clarissa to forgive him for forgetting her birthday.

4. Canada promised to help Afghanistan become a peaceful nation.

5. To manage his web design business was becoming harder for Hector.

6. I tried to swim quietly past the fifteen Canada geese feeding on the shore.

Compound Subjects

L05.3

Compounds Using And, Both/And

Subject/verb agreement errors sometimes occur when we use a **compound subject** (a subject with two or more parts). Most often, compound subjects are plural, as you can see in the following examples:

> City **officials**, **residents**, and **visitors** all **think** that placing large directional decals on sidewalks outside subway stops could help to orient people.

> Both local **residents** and **visitors** to Toronto often **cannot tell** where they are when they get off at a subway stop.

However, some singular subjects may appear to be compound, as in the following example:

> **The coach and counsellor** Rick Stafford devoted his life to his team.

ACTIVITY 5.5   Finding Compound Subjects with *And* and *Both/And*

In the following sentences, underline the main verb, and then circle the compound subjects.

EXAMPLE: Staph and other secondary infections are becoming more dangerous as people arriving at hospitals with minor ailments contract killing infections.

1. Ralph Marvin Steinman and many other Canadian scientists have received the Nobel Prize for their work in physiology or medicine.

2. Both the community centre and the homeless shelter are open 24/7.

3. In the backyard, cardinals, blue jays, and mourning doves are swarming the feeder.

4. Both airbeds and memory foam mattresses can reduce back pain.

5. The travel agent and her assistants can help you with booking your trip to Nicaragua.

6. Diet and exercise can best help you control weight, diabetes, and other health problems.

Compounds Using Or, Either/Or, Neither/Nor

To keep compound subjects in agreement with verbs when using *or, either/or,* and *neither/nor,* we have three possibilities for subject/verb agreement:

1. When the subjects are both singular, the verb is singular.

   Either a plasma or an LCD TV is a good choice.

2. When the subjects are both plural, the verb is plural.

   Football games or basketball games are his favourite entertainment.

3. When the subjects are singular and plural, the verb agrees with the closest subject.

   Neither the minister nor the members of his congregation want the separation of the church from the diocese.

   Note: While it is grammatically correct to write a sentence with the singular subject closest to the verb, it often sounds awkward, as it does in the example below, and so should be avoided.

   AWKWARD: **Neither the members of his congregation nor the minister wants the separation of the church from the diocese.**

ACTIVITY 5.6 Choosing Singular or Plural Verbs with *Or, Either/Or, Neither/Nor*

In the following sentences, underline the correct verb, and circle the part or whole of the paired subjects with which the verb must agree.

   EXAMPLE: **Either Mark or his cousins (is/are) driving to Kingston this evening.**

1. Neither going to the movies nor dining out (seems/seem) like a good idea tonight.

2. Preston or Leonardo (is/are) picking us up after school.

3. Either Halloween or Thanksgiving (falls/fall) on the 31st of October.

4. Neither the police officer nor the firefighters (was/were) able to open the car door.

5. Either Honduras or Guatemala (has/have) the best-preserved Mayan ruins.

6. Either the in-school daycare or a private home daycare close to her apartment (was/were) the choices that Helen was left with once the early Montessori program was full.

LO5.4 Changing the Order of Subjects and Verbs

Remember that the most common word order in English sentences is subject, verb, object:

   S   V   O
   Ethan broke the window.

However, writers sometimes change this order for variety, emphasis, and clarity. When we change these standard word locations, especially by reversing subject and verb, we sometimes have trouble with subject/verb agreement. Three common ways that writers shift the order of sentence parts are by using the following:

1. There/Here
2. Questions
3. Passive Voice

There/Here

Writers sometimes begin sentences with the words *there is, there are, here is,* or *here are.* These constructions push the subject past the verb, so agreement can become a problem. Notice where the <u>subjects</u> are located in the following sentences:

1. **There <u>are</u> 30 <u>people</u> <u>coming</u> to the make-up seminar later.**
2. **There <u>is</u> a <u>flaw</u> evident in the design for this room.**
3. **<u>Here</u> <u>are</u> the <u>keys</u> for the chemistry lab.**

If the subject and verb are unclear to you in sentences like these, you can mentally rearrange them, putting the <u>subject</u> back into its front position, as in the following examples:

1. **Thirty <u>people</u> <u>are coming</u> to the make-up seminar later.**
2. **A <u>flaw</u> <u>is</u> evident in the design for this room.**
3. **The <u>keys</u> for the chemistry lab <u>are</u> here.**

> ### ACTIVITY 5.7 Locating Subjects and Verbs with *There Is/Are* and *Here Is/Are*
>
> In the following sentences, circle the (subjects) and underline the <u>verbs.</u>
>
> EXAMPLE: There <u>is</u> widening (income inequality) in Canada, with great wealth becoming concentrated in the hands of a few.
>
> 1. There are good reasons for choosing this college.
> 2. Here are the design plans for redecorating the student commons.
> 3. Here is the DVD with Arcade Fire in concert.
> 4. There are many peregrine falcons dining on pigeons in big cities.
> 5. Here are the notes from today's lecture.
> 6. There is a reasonable likelihood of snow today.

Questions

Questions can also cause subject/verb agreement problems. When we ask questions, the (subject) and <u>verb</u> usually change positions, as in the following examples:

1. **<u>Are</u> (you) <u>cancelling</u> our make-up seminar?**
2. **Why <u>are</u> those (people) <u>staring</u> at us?**
3. **How <u>is</u> that (frozen yogurt?)**
4. **Where <u>is</u> the (key) to the chemistry lab?**

In **sentences 1 and 2,** the subject has moved between two verb parts.
In **sentences 3 and 4,** the linking verb *is* simply precedes the subject.
You can often spot the verb and subject if you rewrite the question as a statement, as we might do with sentence 1: You <u>are cancelling</u> our make-up seminar.

Note: Questions can also appear in regular word order, as when a statement is spoken as a question: You <u>are going</u> on a date with *him*?

English Review Note

The words *here* and *there* announce the subject, so look ahead for correct subject/verb agreement.

English Review Note

Use *do/does* to form a question in the present.

In the following sentences, circle every (subject) and underline every verb or verb phrase.

> EXAMPLE: When <u>will</u> thoughtless (smokers) <u>stop</u> throwing their cigarette butts out of their car windows?

1. Why are you sending that patient for more tests?

2. How are we supposed to find our way through the legal system without a lawyer?

3. Do you know how to read a topographic map?

4. Will the garbage truck pick up that many bags of leaves?

5. Is Microsoft ever going to make a version of Word that doesn't undo all my favourite features?

6. Are any insurance companies willing to lower rates for teen drivers?

Passive Voice

Passive voice is a way of constructing a sentence to downplay or eliminate the active agent, the subject. Compare sentence 1, in **active voice,** to sentence 2, in **passive voice:**

   S   V   O   S   V   O

1. <u>Joe threw</u> the ball.   2. The <u>ball was thrown</u> (by Joe).

    Sentence 1 clearly has the intended subject, Joe, throwing the ball, the direct object. However, **sentence 2** shifts the direct object to the subject position, making the ball the subject and moving Joe, the actor in the sentence, to an object slot.

    When the doer of an action is relatively unimportant or unknown—such as in the sentence "Mira was taken to hospital"—the passive voice can be an effective choice. However, active voice works best when—as in most cases—you want the doer of the action to receive full attention. For instance, which of the next two sentences sounds best to you?

3. <u>Climbing</u> hills on her dirt bike <u>is loved</u> by Katie.

4. <u>Katie loves</u> climbing hills on her dirt bike.

If you chose **number 4,** it's because active voice sounds best when readers expect the subject of the sentence to be the actor.

    However, there are times when passive voice is the better choice. Here are two sentences that use passive voice to emphasize the words placed in the subject position:

Patrick's new Toyota <u>Prius</u> <u>was destroyed</u> today.

This sentence focuses on the destruction of the new car, rather than on who destroyed it.

On September 11, 2001, the <u>World Trade Centre</u> <u>was demolished.</u>

The writer of this sentence wants the reader to think about the tragedy, rather than the people who caused it.

English Review Note

Avoid overusing the passive voice, except in cases where it is expected, like lab reports.

ACTIVITY 5.9 Locating Subjects and Verbs in Passive Voice
Sentences

In the following sentences, circle every (subject) and underline every <u>verb</u> or
<u>verb phrase.</u> Next, decide which verbs are in the active and which are in the
passive voice, and write *A* or *P* over each.

                      A   P

     **EXAMPLE: When they <u>ran out</u> of gas, the (Johnsons) <u>were saved</u>
by CAA.**

1. I see that the dirty dishes were left in the sink again.

2. Bears, wolves, and cougars are feared by coyotes.

3. Some unfair accusations were made during the residence meeting, but no
   one objected to them.

4. Jack's house was robbed last night, but Jack was not hurt and the police
   found several leads at the scene.

5. The Toronto Stock Exchange's S&P/TSX composite index was down
   134.47 points, or 1.04 percent, closing at 12,744.11 by the end of trading.

6. The children were left unattended by the pool and the parents sued the
   daycare.

ACTIVITY 5.10 Locating Subjects and Verbs in Passive Voice
Sentences

In the following paragraph, circle every (subject) and underline every <u>verb</u> or
<u>verb phrase.</u> Then write a *P* over every verb phrase that is in the passive voice.
Look for a form of the verb to be (*am, is/are, was/were*) before a past participle
(*was <u>broken</u>*), and look for a word that should *receive* the action in the sentence
instead being used as the subject.

A stretch of the Rocky Mountains runs virtually unbroken for 400 kilometres
from central Montana into southern Canada with a skyline that exalts all
the land within eyeshot. Many call this the Crown of the Continent. Glacier
National Park, connected to wildernesses on the south and in both Alberta
and British Columbia on the north, is the centrepiece. Up to three kilometres
high, Glacier's peaks embrace a million Montana acres and 762 lakes to
reflect them in hues from milky turquoise strewn with ice floes so diamond
clear that you can see bottom stones 15 metres deep. One of the largest lakes
has its head in Glacier and its azure body in a 125,000-acre sister reserve,
Waterton Lakes National Park, set solely in Alberta. The adjoining protected
areas were proclaimed the world's first international peace park in 1932.
Both were designated international biosphere reserves during the 1970s, and
in 1995, Waterton-Glacier International Peace Park was further distinguished
as a World Heritage site. Although 95 percent of Glacier is managed as
wilderness, more than 1100 kilometres of interconnecting trails invite foot
traffic into the farthest contours.

         —from "Crown of the Continent" by Douglas H. Chadwick

L05.5 Collective, Plural, and "False" Plural Nouns with Verbs

Collective Nouns

English Review Note

Some collective nouns may be plural in other languages.

English usually views words that stand for groups as singular; for example, *audience, choir, class, committee, crowd, family, flock, gathering, group, herd, majority, minority, school, staff,* and *team.* Notice that the <u>subjects</u> (and <u>verbs</u>) in the following two sentences are singular:

1. **Our <u>team</u> <u>feels</u> that the coach is wrong.**

2. **Our <u>staff</u> <u>works</u> new employees hard in the probation period.**

However, if the members of the group are acting individually, it often sounds more natural to revise the sentence to reflect this, as, for example, in this modification of **sentence 1:**

> **<u>Most</u> of the players on the team <u>feel</u> that the coach is wrong, but some think he's right no matter what.**

Here's a modification of **sentence 2** to show "staff" as individuals rather than a unit:

> **<u>Each</u> staff member <u>can work</u> with the new employees for a period of one week to teach them the ropes.**

ACTIVITY 5.11 Making Collective Nouns Agree with Verbs

In the following sentences, underline the correct form of the <u>verb</u> and circle the (subject) of the verb.

> EXAMPLE: A (school) of blue-fin tuna (<u>brings</u>/bring) tens of thousands of dollars to the boat that catches it.

1. The comedian is so awful that the crowd (shouts/shout) him off the stage.

2. Because they surface so close to ice floes in the Arctic, a pod of narwhals (becomes/become) a target for Inuit hunters.

3. A herd of cattle generally (moves/move) slowly unless it is startled.

4. Flying low over the river, a flock of mallards (is/are) looking for food.

5. Chilliwack, a classic rock band, (continues/continue) to attract young fans.

6. Making its feelings known, the class (complains/complain) about the weekend homework.

Plural Nouns/Plural Verbs

While collectively singular nouns can cause agreement problems, so can nouns that are always plural. The following is a short list of common words that require plural verbs: *binoculars, clothes, fireworks, glasses, pants, pliers, scissors, shorts,* and *slacks.* Note the sentence below for plural agreement:

> **My <u>green pants</u> <u>are</u> in the closet.**

"False" Plural Nouns

Not all nouns that end in -s are plural; for example, *athletics, economics, mathematics, physics, statistics, measles, mumps, ethics, politics,* and *pediatrics.* Also, though titles may contain plural nouns—for example, *The Incredibles* or *The Ten Commandments*—they take singular verbs. Sums of money, distances, measurements, and time units may also look plural, but when they are being used as a unit, they too are grammatically singular.

1. **Physics** **explains** how the world works. (academic subject)

2. **Two hundred minutes** **makes** for a long movie. (time unit)

3. **Fifteen hundred dollars** **buys** a good 42-inch plasma TV these days. (sum of money)

ACTIVITY 5.12 Making Plural Nouns and "False" Plurals Agree

In the following sentences, underline the correct form of the <u>verb</u> or <u>verb phrase,</u> and circle the subject of the verb.

> EXAMPLE: Measles (is/are) a childhood disease that has been brought under control in North America.

1. Prescription sunglasses (costs/cost) a lot but may be worth the money.

2. While trying to tighten a table leg, Camille saw that her pliers (was/were) too small for the job.

3. Binoculars (is/are) a good way to begin exploring the moon.

4. Competitive athletics (teaches/teach) important life lessons.

5. Pediatrics (demands/demand) a great deal of patience and compassion from its practitioners.

6. Nylon shorts (dry/dries) quickly in the sun.

Chapter Summary

1. Singular verbs should be paired with singular subjects and plural verbs with plural subjects.

2. A verb may be separated from its subject by a number of intervening words.

3. Finding the main verb in a sentence is an important part of ensuring agreement; verbals (participles, gerunds, and infinitives) are not complete verbs and cannot function as the main verb.

4. Using a compound subject can sometimes cause confusion in subject/verb agreement. Remember that compound subjects are almost always plural.

5. The most common way to arrange an English sentence is subject-verb-object, but sentence parts can be reordered for variety, emphasis, or clarity.

6. Most collective nouns, which name groups, are treated as singular and should, therefore, be used with singular verbs.

Nouns

"What is that weird thing?" you might ask if you have never seen a stereoscope. This object was an early precursor to 3-D glasses. Placing a stereo card—showing two photographs of the same object taken at slightly different angles and viewed together—into the stereoscope would give the photo a three-dimensional appearance. This stereo card shows two photos of the Ice Castle from Mid-Winter Carnival in Montreal, 1932. When placed into the stereoscope, the ice structure and skaters in the foreground gave an impression of depth. Look closely at the ice castle stereo card—and make a list of nouns naming every person, place, object, or quality that you see.

LEARNING OBJECTIVES

What Are We Trying to Achieve and Why?

As we learned in Chapter 3, **nouns** name things. They are vital to our writing because they focus verbs. Without nouns (or pronouns standing in their place), sentences would have no subjects to say something about; a noun is the *someone* or *something* that acts or is acted upon. Learning to recognize nouns and their functions in sentences will give you more confidence as you write. You will be better able to determine sentence boundaries and avoid errors that make complex ideas difficult to understand.

What a Noun Looks Like

LO6.1

Nouns name things, yes, but more specifically, they name people (*David Johnston, boy*), objects (*computer, glass*), animals (*hummingbird, Pongo*), places (*Saskatoon, Moosonee*), emotional states (*joy, sadness*), qualities (*loyalty, stubbornness*), and concepts (*global warming, consumerism*). Most of us are comfortable thinking of nouns as people, places, things, and animals; but emotions, qualities, and concepts may seem a bit trickier. For example, can you identify and underline the nouns in this sentence? (The verbs are double-underlined.)

> **Hatred is a self-destructive emotional state that throws off people's balance and may destroy their happiness.**

Knowing what you do about verbs from Chapters 3, 4, and 5, you can spot *hatred* as the subject of the linking verb *is*. However, the other nouns in the sentence—*state, balance,* and *happiness*—are less obvious.

To pick out the nouns in a sentence, use this **three-point test** to ask the following questions of each word:

THREE-POINT TEST FOR IDENTIFYING NOUNS:

1. Can I put an article (*a, an, the*) or a word like *my, this, some,* or *one* in front of the word?
2. Can I make the word plural?
3. Can the word show possession?

In the preceding sentence about hatred, we can put the word *state* to the test. First, we notice that it has the article *a* in the sentence, and we can say *a state* or *one state*. We can also make the word plural, saying *states*. Trying the third test, we can show possession by saying *this emotional state's self-destructive force*. The word *state* meets all three tests and so must be a noun.

Another noun test that can help is noting suffixes (word endings) that often indicate nouns. Here are a few of these word endings: *-tion, -sion, -age, -ment, -al, -ant, -er, -ist, -ism, -ty, -ance, -ture, -dom, -ship,* and *-ness*. Note how these suffixes make the following words nouns:

NOUN-MARKING SUFFIXES		
atten*tion*	occup*ant*	govern*ance*
fu*sion*	rent*er*	depar*ture*
leak*age*	environmental*ist*	king*dom*
require*ment*	extrem*ism*	friend*ship*
arriv*al*	communi*ty*	happ*iness*

Using the Articles *the*, *a*, *and* an

The article *the* refers to something specific or already known by the reader (e.g., *the* dog next door that woke us up), whereas the articles *a* and *an* refer to a non-specific noun or one not already known by the reader (*a* dog woke us up).

Use *a* before nouns that begin with a consonant sound (*a* book) and *an* before nouns that start with a vowel sound (*an* apple). Notice that the sound rather than the letter determines the choice of *a* or *an*: *a* used backpack (*u* sounds like *y*); *an* hour, *an* honour (both *h*'s are silent); *a* historic site, *a* hospital waiting room (both *h*'s are pronounced).

English Review Note

Study this distinction between *the* and *a/an* closely. Articles often pose challenges for non-native speakers.

ACTIVITY 6.1   Finding Nouns with the Three-Point Test

In the following sentences, use the three-point test and the word endings listed above to find the <u>nouns,</u> and then underline them.
Note: Nouns sometimes describe other nouns, for example, *baby carriage, oven mitt, pastry chef,* and *deck chair.*

> EXAMPLE: <u>Katrina</u> was serving a <u>detention</u> after <u>school</u> for her <u>part</u> in the <u>prank.</u>

1. Both the buyer and the seller were pleased with the transaction.

2. Perfectionists spend much energy on tiny details.

3. As the plane's cabin pressure increased, Minissha could not clear her ears.

4. After deer-hunting season, Tom decided to try vegetarianism.

5. Self-discipline is a trait that often leads to success.

6. After completion of the kitchen work, the designer will begin on our living room.

LO6.2   Kinds of Nouns

We can begin to classify nouns based on how relatively *general* and *abstract* or how *specific* and *concrete* they are. People, objects, animals, and places tend to be relatively specific and concrete, forming an image in our minds. This makes them easier to spot as nouns than concepts, qualities, and emotions, which tend to be more general and abstract. But there are other useful categories of nouns, which are listed below:

1. **Common nouns** name things that are not unique, and English has a huge number of these nouns. They can name people (*musicians*), objects (*stethoscopes*), animals (*lizards*), places (*gardens*), concepts (*religions*), qualities (*patience*), or emotions (*love*).

2. **Proper nouns** name specific, unique things and are capitalized. They name people (*Norman Bethune*), objects (*Kleenex*), animals (*Northern Dancer*), places (*Port Coquitlam*), and concepts (*Hinduism*).

3. **Count nouns** name things that can be quantified or enumerated and generally form their plurals by adding an *-s* or *-es,* as in the following examples:

   tree/trees   book/books   dress/dresses   kiss/kisses   class/classes

4. **Non-count nouns** name things that cannot be counted and have no plural form, such as *coffee, milk, rice, flour, bread, furniture, luggage, sugar, gravel, earth, water,*

coal, aluminum, rain, air, sunshine, gasoline, luck, courage, pride. We can say, for example, "I like coffee in the morning" but not "I like coffees in the morning."

To express a quantity of a non-count noun, add other words in front of it, as in these examples:

two cups of <u>coffee</u>   **20 litres of <u>gasoline</u>**

English Review Note

Some non-count nouns may be countable in other languages. In English, food and drink words (*flour, sugar*), substances (*furniture, wood*), and abstract nouns (*courage, pride*) are non-count.

5. **Collective nouns** name a group that is considered a unit and so are grammatically singular. Examples include *group, team, family, herd, crowd, faculty, staff, committee, government, flock, audience, band, company, party, crew, league, association, bunch,* and *gang.*
   Note that a collective noun agrees with a singular verb:

   The basketball *team* is playing well tonight.

6. **Irregular plural nouns** do not follow the usual pattern of forming their plurals by adding *-s* (cat/cat*s*) or *-es* (brush/brush*es*). Here is a brief list:

HINT

For more on collective nouns and subject/verb agreement, refer to Chapter 5.

COMMON IRREGULAR NOUN PLURALS	
woman/women	man/men
child/children	mouse/mice
foot/feet	tooth/teeth
knife/knives	life/lives
hypothesis/hypotheses	criterion/criteria
fish/fish	sheep/sheep

ACTIVITY 6.2   WORKING TOGETHER: *Recognizing Nouns*

In pairs or small groups, identify and underline the <u>nouns</u> in the following sentences. For help with this activity, review the six noun categories above.

EXAMPLE: The <u>Sulphur Hot Springs</u>, <u>Alberta</u>, are in a beautiful mountain <u>setting</u> near <u>Banff</u>.

1. It takes courage to overcome irrational fears like arachnophobia.

2. Cat lovers have observed that the Serval cat is the most elite of all cat breeds.

3. Our family gathering at Thanksgiving seemed like a herd of cows stampeding toward the dining room table.

4. After mowing the yard, Teru had a glass of fruit juice and rested on his deck chair.

5. Moose Jaw requires all restaurants to list calorie information on their menus.

6. Rohana said, "I judge a truck by these criteria: cost, performance, and reliability."

Functions of Nouns

L06.3

Another way to determine if a word is a noun is by its function in the sentence. The following are various roles nouns can play:

Subjects: Nouns can act.

Objects: Nouns can receive action.

Complements:	Nouns can describe or rename subjects following linking verbs (such as *is*).
Appositives:	Nouns can describe or rename other nouns without linking verbs.

Subjects

Subjects are the doers of the action in a sentence or the focus of a linking verb. In the following example, what leaves the water? The Canada geese do, so they must be the subject.

Canada geese leave the water frequently to feed on land.

Objects

Objects receive the action of the verb: *direct* objects receive action directly, while *indirect* objects receive it indirectly. An *object of a preposition* is the last word in a prepositional phrase. We can see how each kind of object works in the following sentence:

Direct Object   Indirect Object

The government of Canada gave much *land and money* to *Maa-nulth First Nations*

Object of Prep.
in *June 2009*.

A **direct object** tells who or what receives the action of the verb. The subject in the preceding sentence, the government of Canada, gave what to Maa-nulth First Nations? The answer is *land and money*. These words receive the direct action of the verb, so they are the direct object.

An **indirect object** tells for or to whom or what the action of the verb is done. In the sentence above, the government of Canada gave *land and money* (the direct object) to whom? The answer, or indirect object, is *Maa-nulth First Nations*. An action is passed through the direct object to the indirect object.

Sometimes indirect objects appear without *to* or *for* and can come between the verb and the direct object, as in the following sentence:

Indirect Object   Direct Object

The government of Canada gave *Maa-nulth First Nations* much *land and money* in

Obj. of Prep.
June 2009.

The **object of a preposition** is the final word in a prepositional phrase (common prepositions: *in, on, of, by, over, to, around*). In the sentence above, the phrase *in June 2009* begins with the preposition *in* and ends with the number noun *2009*. *June 2009* is the object of the preposition.

Complements

A subject complement is a noun that follows a linking verb (*is, was, were*, for example). In the following sentence, we might consider the linking verb *is* to be an equal sign: *Jan = English professor*, a subject complement.

Jan is an *English professor*.

Note: A subject complement can also be an adjective, as in the following sentence:

Jan is *hard working*.

Appositives

Appositives are single words or phrases that rename or define another word, which usually comes before them in the sentence. The appositive noun works much like a synonym. In the following sentence, the word *radicals* is the appositive noun renaming the subject *eco-educators*.

Eco-educators, hopeful *radicals*, began organizing many practical online resources for improving the environment in 1992.

ACTIVITY 6.3 Practising How Nouns Function

In the following sentences, fill in the blanks to identify the boldface **nouns** as subjects (*S*), direct objects (*DO*), indirect objects (*IO*), objects of prepositions (*OP*), complements (*C*), or appositives (*A*).

> EXAMPLE: Fall <u>S</u> is gradually becoming less colourful on the West coast <u>OP</u>.

1. **Angela** _____ ordered a side **cup** _____ of hot **sauce** _____ with her **pizza** _____ .

2. For **fun** _____ , **Benjamin** _____ climbed the 15-metre-tall elm **tree** _____ near his **cottage** _____ .

3. The **matriarch** _____ , or ruling **female** _____ , of the **pride** _____ , gave a small **portion** _____ of her **kill** _____ to the hungry **male** _____ .

4. **Global warming** _____ is melting the **ice sheets** _____ of **Greenland** _____ at an accelerating **rate** _____ .

5. Some **car dealerships** _____ are now offering their **customers** _____ 100 000-kilometre **warranties** _____ .

6. Chilliwack's song, **"Fly at Night,"** _____ was a huge **hit** _____ in the **seventies** _____ and is still popular with young **people** _____ .

Verbals as Nouns: Gerunds and Infinitives

LO6.4

Abstract nouns—like *beauty* or *intelligence*—can be hard to spot in a sentence. Nouns that are derived from verbs are also difficult to spot; for example, *swimming* in the following sentence:

Swimming was her favourite sport.

In other sentences, *swimming* can be used as part of a main verb or as an adjective; but in the above sentence, it is the subject. We call these kinds of nouns **verbals**. There are two common verbal types that can function as nouns in sentences: **gerunds** and **infinitives**.

Gerunds

Gerunds are verb forms that always end in *-ing*; they function as nouns in sentences. Other examples, in addition to *swimming*, include *walking, skiing, running, riding, flying, drinking*. Because gerunds look like verbs, and imply action like verbs, they can be confusing.

As we learned earlier in this chapter, nouns can function in different ways in sentences—as subjects, complements, objects, and appositives—and so gerunds can appear in many places in a sentence. (For more on gerunds, revisit Chapter 5.)

TYPES OF GERUNDS:

Gerund subject:	<u>Flying</u> requires patience these days because of airport security procedures.
Gerund complement:	Rajiv's most relaxing pastime is <u>reading</u>.
Gerund object:	
• **Direct object:**	His Labrador finally quit <u>begging</u> for table scraps.
• **Object of a preposition:**	Genji is excited about <u>leaving</u> for his vacation.
Gerund appositive:	Aerobic sports, such as <u>jogging, cycling, and walking,</u> are important to everyone's health.

Infinitives

HINT

Remember that *to* + a base verb makes an infinitive, but *to* + a noun (*to the store*) or pronoun (*to it*) makes a prepositional phrase.

Infinitives are verb forms that usually begin with *to* before a base verb; they can function as nouns, adjectives, and adverbs. In this section, we will focus on infinitives working as nouns. Here are several examples: *to read, to think, to sleep, to lead*. As with gerunds, because infinitives can be nouns, they can appear in several places in a sentence. (For more on infinitives, revisit Chapter 5.)

Here are two types of infinitives:

Infinitive subject:	<u>To win</u> requires hard work and persistence.
Infinitive object:	Ramon intends <u>to visit</u> his cousin today.

ACTIVITY 6.4 — Spotting Verbal Nouns

In the following sentences, underline all *gerunds* and *infinitives*. Watch out for the *-ing* used as a progressive verb tense (e.g., is/was *thinking*) and as an adjective (e.g., *floating* logs). Also, remember that *to* can signal a prepositional phrase rather than an infinitive.

EXAMPLE: <u>Crying</u> is not the way <u>to solve</u> this problem.

1. Hatsu is interested in learning how to ice skate.

2. Crossing into the U.S. from Canada did not require a passport several years ago.

3. I avoided thinking about the website design test all day.

4. It is beginning to snow, and the biting wind is blowing hard.

5. To reach the final stage takes more effort than Abdul is willing to spend.

6. Cooking is an exciting career to some and a boring labour to others.

ACTIVITY 6.5 — Mixed Review: Finding Nouns

Review what you have learned in this chapter, and then underline every noun in the following paragraph. Remember the three-point noun test, the kinds and functions of nouns, and verbals as nouns—gerunds and infinitives.

Watch out for the *-ing* used as a progressive verb tense (e.g., is/was *celebrating*) and as an adjective (e.g., *sleeping* cats). Also, remember that *to* can signal a prepositional phrase rather than an infinitive.

Martial Arts and the Mastery of Body, Mind, and Spirit

When most people think of martial arts, the first thing that comes to mind is physical brutality, kicking, punching, and grappling. I can understand why, because of how the martial arts are portrayed in Hollywood movies, and by the popular MMA (Mixed Martial Arts) sporting events held worldwide. I was no exception to this misguided outlook, until I started training in the traditional Korean martial art of Tae Kwon Do. It was in my preparation for my first sparring (fighting) tournament that I that realized the essence of the martial arts is not self-defence and learning how to fight. I learned that the true purpose of martial arts is mastery of the body, mind, and spirit.

—Eric Chan

For English as a Second Language Learners

LO6.5

More about Count Nouns

As we read earlier in this chapter, count nouns can be quantified or enumerated; we can count two *trees, cellphones, songs,* or *shoes.* A determiner (see the following list) should be placed before count nouns when they are singular and often when they are plural.

DETERMINERS	
Articles	a, an, the
Possessive nouns	Ahmadi's, Marketta's, your brother's
Demonstrative pronouns	this, these, that, those
Possessive pronouns	his, her, my, your, its, our, their, whose
Indefinite pronouns	some, both, any, neither, either, every, each, no, enough
Numbers	one, two, three, . . .

> **English Review Note**
>
> One way to identify count nouns is to try the word *many* in front of them. Can you say *many tricycles*? Yes, so *tricycles* is a count noun. Can you say *many traffic*? No, so *traffic* is a non-count noun. You can also try the word *much* in front of a noun. If you can say *much traffic*, you have identified a non-count noun.

The following sentences show *a count noun* preceded by <u>determiners</u>:

1. <u>A</u> *dog* can be a good companion.
2. <u>Guishan's</u> *dog* is well behaved.
3. <u>The</u> *dogs* in my <u>neighbour's</u> yard are barking.
4. <u>His</u> *dogs* have become pests.

It would be incorrect to drop the determiners from **sentences 1 and 2**. In English, we can't say "Dog can be a good companion." We must include a determiner, in this case the article *a* or the possessive noun *Guishan's*. While **sentences 3 and 4** could be written without the determiners, these changes would alter the meaning of the sentences. As written, *the* and *his* refer to specific, known dogs.

More about Non-count Nouns

Remember that non-count nouns are usually difficult or impossible to count—*air, light, meat, water, dust*—and do not have a plural form.

Some words can be used as both count and non-count nouns, depending on context. For example, notice the difference in meaning between the *change* (non-count) in someone's pocket and the *changes* (count) you went through when you came to Canada.

You may also occasionally run into a non-count noun that is used with a countable meaning; for example, "The espresso bar offers a dozen exotic *coffees*." Non-count nouns may or may not be preceded by a <u>determiner.</u>

1. Rosa mixed honey (not *honeys*) in her tea.
2. Antonio spilled <u>some</u> *coffee* (not *coffees*) on the table.
3. Rosa mixed <u>two tablespoons</u> of *honey* in her tea.
4. Antonio spilled <u>some</u> hot *coffee* (not *coffees*) on the table.

Sentence 1 shows the noun *honey* without a determiner, whereas **sentence 2** uses the determiner *some*. In **sentence 3**, you can see how to show a plural with a non-count noun by adding quantifying words, in this case *two tablespoons* (which is a count noun with a determiner).

Sentence 4 shows that modifiers (*hot*) can come between a determiner (*some*) and a noun.

While count nouns can be enumerated and non-count nouns cannot, count nouns often form a more specific group contained within a non-count group, as in the following list:

COUNT	NON-COUNT
essays	homework
tricycles	traffic
loonies	money
mountains	scenery

ACTIVITY 6.6 Identifying Count and Non-count Nouns

Identify each of the following words as count or non-count nouns.

EXAMPLE: tulip: <u>Count</u>

1. tulip	2. economics
3. oil	4. backpack
5. wheat	6. pollution
7. flour	8. flower
9. couch	10. washroom
11. nail	12. snow

Articles: Choosing among *the, a, and an*

There are three *articles* in English that are often placed in front of nouns: the definite article *the* and the indefinite articles *a* and *an*. Although using articles in English can be tricky, there are guidelines that will help you in most instances. *The* is used to refer to a *specific* person, place, or thing; *a* or *an* is used when the noun's identity is *general* or unknown to the reader.

To determine which article to use, you need to know whether the noun is count or non-count, general or specific, and plural or singular. The following sentences illustrate the use of general versus specific articles:

1. **General:**   *A* game of soccer is a good workout.
2. **Specific:**   *The* game we played this afternoon wore me out.

Sentence 1 speaks about soccer games in general and so uses *a*, whereas **sentence 2** refers to a specific game and so uses *the*.

A noun is often introduced in writing or speaking using *a* or *an*. Then, after being identified for the reader or listener, it is referred to with *the*.

English Review Note

Non-count nouns never use *a* or *an*: We want cheese (not a cheese) on the hamburger.

3. We went to *a* good movie this afternoon, *Super 8* by J. J. Abrams.

4. *The* movie that we saw had a great plot and terrific special effects.

Sentence 4 uses *the* before *movie* because the writer mentioned *movie* in **sentence 3** and now expects the reader to know which movie is being referred to.

If a plural count or a non-count noun is general, do not use any article, for example:

General plural count noun: *Airplanes* often need to be de-iced in the winter.

General non-count noun: *Water* is necessary for life.

The articles *a* and *an* are used only before singular count nouns (*a* bus, not *a* busses).

RULES FOR ARTICLE USE		
Count/Non-count Noun	**General**	**Specific**
Singular count noun: car, bird, apple	Use *a* or *an*	Use *the*
Plural count noun: cars, birds, apples	Use no article	Use *the*
Non-count noun: weather, advice, luggage	Use no article	Use *the*

Chapter Summary

1. Nouns name things: people, animals, objects, places, emotional states, qualities, and concepts. As we learned in Chapter 5, every sentence needs a subject (which is or includes a noun or nouns) and a verb.

2. The three-point test and commonly used suffixes help determine whether or not a word is a noun.

3. Common nouns name things that are not unique, so they are lower case; proper nouns indicate specific names and are capitalized.

4. Count nouns, which name things that can be quantified, have plural forms; non-count nouns, which have no specific quantity, have only a singular form.

5. Collective nouns name things grouped together as a unit; they are grammatically singular.

6. Nouns can function in a sentence as subjects, objects (direct or indirect), objects of prepositions, complements, or appositives. Each serves a different purpose.

7. Nouns derived from verbs are called verbals. Verbals that function as nouns include gerunds (which end in *-ing*) and infinitives (which begin with *to*).

8. The three articles in English are *a, an,* and *the; a* and *an* illustrate the general and *the* illustrates the specific.

Pronouns

So who just won the prize? She did. Who is "she"? Unless we have a noun to refer back to—in the picture, Allison is the winner—we cannot know the person's identity. Write a brief paragraph that tells about a prize, game, or contest you have won. Referring to the pronoun chart on the next page, underline all the pronouns in your paragraph.

What Are We Trying to Achieve and Why?

Like verbs and nouns, **pronouns** are a common and important part of speech. Pronouns like *it, this, who, myself,* and *everyone* stand in the place of nouns and help create variety in writing. You will probably recognize most of the pronouns in the categories listed below.

PRONOUN TYPES	
Personal pronouns	I, you, he, she, it, we, they, me, her, him, us, them
Indefinite pronouns	all, any, anybody, anything, both, each, everybody, everyone, everything, few, many, more, most, much, nobody, none, no one, one, several, some, somebody, someone, something
Relative pronouns	who, which, that, what, whatever, whichever, whoever, whom, whomever, whose
Interrogative pronouns	what, who, which, whatever, whichever, whoever, whom, whomever, whose
Demonstrative pronouns	this, that, these, those
Reflexive and intensive pronouns	myself, yourself, herself, himself, itself, oneself, ourselves, yourselves, themselves
Reciprocal pronouns	each other, one another
Possessive pronouns	my, mine, your, yours, her, hers, his, its, our, ours, their, theirs

All of these pronouns have a place in our sentences, and if we were without them, we would end up with some fairly repetitive writing. Compare the following two paragraphs about Lydia's virtue from *Pride and Prejudice* by Jane Austen:

USES *NOUNS* ONLY
(NO *PRONOUNS*)

1. "This is a most unfortunate affair, and will probably be much talked of. But we must stem the tide of malice, and pour into the wounded bosoms of each other the balm of sisterly consolation." Then, perceiving in Elizabeth no inclination of replying, Mary added, "Unhappy as the event must be for Lydia, we may draw from it this useful lesson: that loss of virtue in a female is irretrievable; that one false step involves Lydia in endless ruin; that Lydia's reputation is no less brittle than it is beautiful; and that Lydia cannot be too much guarded in Lydia's behaviour towards the undeserving of the other sex."

USES A MIX OF
NOUNS AND
PRONOUNS

2. "This is a most unfortunate affair, and will probably be much talked of. But we must stem the tide of malice, and pour into the wounded bosoms of each other the balm of sisterly consolation." Then, perceiving in Elizabeth no inclination of replying, Mary added, "Unhappy as the event must be for Lydia, we may draw from it this useful lesson: that loss of virtue in a female is irretrievable; that one false step involves *her* in endless ruin; that *her* reputation is no less brittle than it is beautiful; and that *she* cannot be too much guarded in *her* behaviour towards the undeserving of the other sex."

HINT

For more on variety and coherence through pronouns, see Chapter 18.

Clearly, in **paragraph 1**, the repetition of *Lydia* becomes monotonous. To solve this problem, **paragraph 2** uses pronouns to replace her name. As a brilliant and gifted writer, Jane Austen, of course, wrote **paragraph 2**. Both paragraphs contain pronouns about people other than Lydia. Highlight these pronouns using the chart above as a guide.

As useful as pronouns are, however, they have a fundamental problem. Because they mean nothing by themselves, they must refer to a noun to have an identity. When Anil says, "He was not considerate," we ask, "Who was not considerate?" We cannot know until Anil clarifies by saying, "Alex Desjardins." Using a noun can tell the reader exactly what the writer means.

Whenever we use pronouns in our writing, we must be sure that the reader knows what we are referring to, and we must be careful to use the correct pronoun form. This chapter will help us explore both of these subjects.

LO7.1 Referring to the Antecedent

English Review Note

Some languages do not require subject pronouns. In your English writing, you must include them.

A pronoun refers to an **antecedent**, a word that the pronoun substitutes for—most often a noun, but occasionally another pronoun or phrase. The antecedent is usually located before the pronoun, either within the same sentence or within a nearby sentence, as in the following:

> <u>Darlene</u> succeeded in scaling <u>the Niagara Escarpment</u>. <u>She</u> reached the top of <u>it</u> in three hours.

The words *she* and *it* take the place of *Darlene* and *the Niagara Escarpment*.

The farther the pronoun is removed from its antecedent, the greater the chance for confusion. Consider the following sentences:

English Review Note

Take care not to use both a noun and a pronoun to serve the same purpose.

1. Fabio asked if Philippe would be taking *his* son to the soccer game on Saturday.

2. After checking *his* schedule, *he* told *him* that *he* could take *him*, but *he* would have to leave with *him* 30 minutes early.

Whose son might go to the game? **Sentence 1** doesn't clarify who *his* refers to. **Sentence 2** confuses things further with a string of pronouns that have no clear noun antecedents. To clarify meaning, we could recast the sentences this way:

1. Fabio asked if Philippe would be taking Fabio's son to the soccer game on Saturday.

2. After checking *his* schedule, Philippe told Fabio that *he* could take Fabio's son, but Philippe would have to leave with the boy 30 minutes early.

Now we can see that Fabio is asking a favour of his friend and that Philippe will probably give Fabio's son a ride to the game.

We can achieve even greater clarity, and less awkwardness, if we can add another specific noun, the name of Fabio's son:

1. Fabio asked if Philippe would be taking Fabio's son Bruno to the soccer game on Saturday.

2. After checking his schedule, Philippe told Fabio that he could take Bruno but would have to leave with the boy 30 minutes early.

Pronouns that can be particularly confusing to readers are *it, they, them, this, that, these, those,* and *which*. These words should usually refer to a specific noun rather than a general idea, and they should be close to the noun they represent to avoid unclear meanings, as in the following three examples:

EXAMPLE 1

DRAFT: *It* made the girls unhappy that *they* bought up all the tickets for the concert.

What made the girls unhappy, and who bought all the tickets? Was it the girls or someone else? Perhaps ticket scalpers were the source of the girls' unhappiness. We can clarify by recasting the sentence with a clear noun antecedent:

REVISED: The girls were unhappy because <u>ticket scalpers</u> had bought up all the concert tickets.

EXAMPLE 2

DRAFT: But *this* didn't trouble *them* at all because *they* knew there was always a good market for the right concert tickets.

What didn't trouble whom? Revising for clarity, we can clearly indicate what nouns these pronouns refer to.

REVISED: The <u>girls' unhappiness</u> didn't trouble the <u>ticket scalpers</u> because they knew there was always a good market for the right concert tickets.

EXAMPLE 3

DRAFT: The real problem, as *they* saw *it*, was that *they* were allowed to purchase as many of *them* as *they* wanted, *which* kept *them* from buying *them* at a reasonable price.

Example 3 begins with an unclear *they* reference and then goes from confusing to incomprehensible. None of the pronouns refers to a clear antecedent. The revision achieves clarity by replacing unclear pronouns with nouns and keeping several pronouns by linking them clearly to specific antecedents:

REVISED: The real problem, the <u>girls</u> thought, was that the <u>scalpers</u> were allowed to purchase as many <u>tickets</u> as *they* wanted, a <u>practice</u> that kept the <u>public</u> from buying <u>tickets</u> at a reasonable price.

English Review Note

Remember that pronouns *he/his, she/her,* and *it/its* agree with their antecedents and not with the words they modify.

As we can see from the preceding examples, pronouns are useful in writing, but we must be careful to link each pronoun clearly with its antecedent.

ACTIVITY 7.1   Recognizing Antecedents

In the following sentences, underline each <u>pronoun</u> and circle each (antecedent). Next, write the pronoun/antecedent pair at the end of each sentence. Some sentences have several pronoun/antecedent pairs (or groups).

EXAMPLE: **Banff is a friendly Alberta (town) that attracts many artists.**
town/that

1. Volunteer fire departments have saved their communities a great deal of money.

2. Dust mites are hard to eliminate because they are so tiny and plentiful.

3. When Katie arrived at school, she saw her sister, who was in the parking lot.

4. The members of the expedition rested their packs on boulders by the trailside.

5. Before submitting its plan, the company thoroughly researched its proposal.

6. Before Ming attempted her triple Axel, she smiled at the onlookers, who held their breath in anticipation.

In the space provided, revise the following sentences to correct unclear pronoun reference. You will often replace a pronoun with a noun and sometimes reword a sentence to make the reference clear.

EXAMPLE:

ORIGINAL: To prevent squirrels from destroying your roses, set out live traps for them.

REVISED: *To prevent squirrels from destroying your roses, set out live traps for the rodents.*

1. Clarissa saw a meadowlark on a fence post that was eating a grasshopper.

   _____

   _____

2. We broke the speed limit getting home from the concert, but we still drove carefully, which is why we got a speeding ticket.

   _____

   _____

3. Max told his brother that he was going to regret staying up so late.

   _____

   _____

4. If you can't get your daughter to remove the adhesive bandage from her own finger, just pull it off yourself.

   _____

   _____

5. To combat climate change, many people favour carbon credits. This problem requires intensive international cooperation.

   _____

   _____

6. Malik watched a creepy old *X-files* episode and then drank some hot chocolate before bed, but it kept him awake half the night.

   _____

   _____

LO7.2 Agreeing in Number with the Antecedent

Not only must pronouns be clearly linked to their antecedents, but they must also agree in **number**: singular nouns take *singular pronouns*; plural nouns take *plural pronouns*. Consider the following examples:

1. **Margarine keeps forever, but *It* has little nutritional value.**

2. **Hydrogenated oils in the margarine keep it fresh, but *they* also contribute to heart disease.**

Sentence 1 uses the singular pronoun *it* to refer to the singular noun *margarine*. **Sentence 2** links the plural pronoun *they* with the plural noun *hydrogenated oils*.

Most difficulties with pronoun/antecedent agreement fall into one of three categories: indefinite pronouns, collective nouns, or compound antecedents.

Indefinite Pronouns

Indefinite pronouns as antecedents can be a problem because they do not refer to a specific person or thing. Although most are singular, a few are plural, and several (*all, any, enough, more, most, none, some*) can be either singular *or* plural, depending on what noun they connect with. Note the following list:

INDEFINITE PRONOUNS			
SINGULAR		**PLURAL**	**SINGULAR OR PLURAL**
anybody	nobody	both	all
anyone	no one	few	any
anything	nothing	many	enough
each	one	others	more
either	somebody	several	most
everybody	someone		none
everyone	something		some
neither			

Notice how we might use indefinite pronouns in sentences:

1. **_Everyone_ on the staff <u>contributes</u> regularly.**

2. **_Someone_ <u>is holding</u> a lit candle.**

3. **_Several_ <u>were</u> happy to volunteer.**

Sentences 1 and 2 use singular indefinite pronouns, while **sentence 3** uses a plural pronoun. If the sentences above seem clear, here are several others that might be more puzzling:

4.   CORRECT: *Each* of the teams <u>hopes</u> that *it* will make the playoffs.

     INCORRECT: *Each* of the teams hope that *they* will make the playoffs.

Sentence 4 uses the singular pronoun *each* as the subject, which requires a singular verb, *hopes*. And even though the noun *teams* is plural, the singular pronoun *it* refers back to *each*. (The sentence is talking about one team at a time.)

5.   CORRECT: Neither of the *coaches* <u>believes</u> that *his* team can be beaten.

     INCORRECT: *Neither* of the *coaches* believe that their team can be beaten.

Sentence 5 uses the singular pronoun *neither* as its subject, requiring a singular verb, *believes*, and though the noun *coaches* is plural, the singular pronoun *his* refers back to *neither*. Here are several more examples illustrating correct pronoun agreement:

6. **_One_ of the officers was trying to find *his* pen to write a ticket.**

7. **_Anyone_ who knows about lightning will not pitch *his* or *her* tent under a lone tree.**

8. **We are having trouble with our water. _Some_ leaks out, and *it* forms a puddle on the bathroom floor every morning.**

English Review Note

Sentence 7 uses the construction *his or her* to overcome gender bias in pronoun usage. (See Chapter 19.)

Underline the <u>indefinite pronoun antecedent</u> in each of the following sentences, and then underline the appropriate <u>pronoun</u> in parentheses.

EXAMPLE: **<u>Anybody</u> who studies as much as the professor expects (them/<u>him or her</u>) to should do well in the course.**

1. Because of the drought, almost everybody in Saskatoon is worried about the shortage of water in (their/his or her) city.

2. Neither of the men could believe that (they/he) had found a 32-metre-long dinosaur.

3. Both of the CFL players thought (they/he) had gotten an unfair call.

4. Almost all of the ice cream had disappeared from (their/its) hiding place in the freezer.

5. Nobody at the accident thought that (they/he or she) was at fault.

6. Any animal that lives in the abyss of the ocean catches (their/its) prey without the use of eyesight or creates (their/its) own light.

Collective Nouns

English treats most groups of things, animals, and people as a single unit, that is, individuals acting together as one; for example, *jury, league, association, club, company, board, party, crew, bunch, gang, fleet, committee, team, band, class, audience, crowd, gathering, group, herd, school, swarm, pod, pack,* and *flock.* Pronouns referring to singular collective nouns are also singular:

COLLECTIVE NOUN	SINGULAR PRONOUN
The *jury* felt that	*it* had served justice.
Our *bowling league* opens	*its* membership to bowlers who can keep the ball out of the gutter.

However, if the members of the group are acting individually, the noun becomes plural and so does the pronoun, for example:

COLLECTIVE NOUN	PLURAL PRONOUNS	PLURAL PRONOUN

The *audience* lingered, *some* of *them* looking pleased and *some* just puzzled.

Underline the <u>antecedent</u> in each of the following sentences, and then underline the appropriate <u>pronoun</u> in parentheses.

EXAMPLE: **A <u>pack</u> of dogs can create much trouble if (they are /<u>it is</u>) not controlled.**

1. The Hidden Lake Homeowners' Association insists that (they have/it has) the right to keep fences in the development under two metres high.

2. A flock of robins descended on Staci's backyard, and (they/it) dug dozens of small craters in her mulch beds.

3. A large corporation usually serves the financial interests of (their/its) stockholders over any other consideration.

4. The clan came together to discuss (their/its) plans for dealing with the mining company.

5. A fleet of trawlers swept countless tons of cod into (their/its) nets in international waters until one day all the cod were gone.

6. A pod of dolphins seemed to be constantly checking on (their/its) youngest members.

Compound Antecedents

Compound antecedents are nouns of two or more words joined as a unit with the conjunctions *and, or,* and *nor.* They are often used as subjects but they also appear as other parts of a sentence. When the antecedent is linked by *and*, it is usually plural, requiring a plural pronoun, as in the following examples:

COMPOUND ANTECEDENT
Manitoba and Ontario's cottage country have been struck by massive flooding in recent

PLURAL PRONOUN
years, and *they* are *both* still recovering from the disasters.

COMPOUND ANTECEDENT
It is difficult to spot differences between *a house sparrow and a house finch* when

PLURAL PRONOUN
they are at a distance.

However, be careful when dealing with several nouns used as a unit (compound nouns). These nouns are usually singular and so require a singular pronoun when referenced:

COMPOUND NOUN
The *Therapeutic Products Directorate (TPD) of Health Canada* approves drugs sold in Canada,

SINGULAR PRONOUN
and in this way *it* contributes to safe health practices in Canada.

When the antecedent is linked by *or* or *nor*, if both parts are plural, use a plural pronoun to reference them. If both parts are singular, the pronoun referring to them should be singular. If one part of the antecedent is plural and the other singular, the pronoun should agree with the *nearer* part of the antecedent, as in the following examples:

1a. Plural:	Neither *grizzly bears* nor *mountain lions* usually view a human being as *their* natural prey.	
1b. Singular:	However, *a grizzly bear* or *a mountain lion* may attack people if *it* is provoked.	
2a. Plural:	Either the plant supervisor or *the shift workers* are responsible for the fire at *their* factory.	
2b. Singular:	Either the shift workers or *the plant supervisor* is responsible for the fire at *his* factory.	

For smoother-sounding sentences, when using a plural and a singular compound antecedent, write the plural word second, as in **sentence 2a.**

> **HINT**
>
> For more on compound subjects and agreement, review Chapters 5 and 6.

Underline the <u>antecedent</u> in each of the following sentences, and then underline the appropriate <u>pronoun</u> in parentheses.

> EXAMPLE: The <u>dentist and doctor</u> are vital for our health, but (he or she/<u>they</u>) can also cause much anxiety and pain.

1. Neither the art teacher nor any of her students thought that (she/they) would have the projects completed on time.

2. Fergus likes Thanksgiving and Christmas because (it/they) are a time for lots of food and presents.

3. Either Sheila or the boys should clean up the mess in the lab if (she/they) want to go out for pizza tonight.

4. My aunts, sisters, and mother have decided that (she/they) know what's best for me.

5. Either hockey skates or figure skates can be a good choice if (its/their) blades are sharp.

6. Neither the other daily newspapers nor the *Globe and Mail* was able to lower (its/their) price enough to make the subscribers happy.

L07.3 Choosing Proper Pronoun Case

Even after clarifying a pronoun's antecedent and checking for agreement in number, we can still have problems with **case**, one of the forms a pronoun takes to show how it works in a sentence: as subject, object, or possessor.

Subjective Case

Pronouns used as subjects or subject complements are in the **subjective case**.

1. **Pronoun as subject:**   <u>We</u> <u>went</u> to see Serena Ryder in concert.
2. **Pronoun as complement:**   The <u>winner</u> of the gold medal in freestyle competition <u>is</u> *she*.

Objective Case

Pronouns used as objects (receiving the action of verbs) or as objects of prepositional phrases (the pronoun at the end of the phrase) are in the **objective case**.

1. **Pronoun as direct object:** <u>Arthur</u> <u>saw</u> *them* at the pool.

   Who or what did Arthur see? He saw *them*. The pronoun *them* receives the action of the verb and so is a direct object and in the objective case.

2. **Pronoun as indirect object:** <u>Pascale</u> <u>threw</u> the book to *him*.

   The book receives the action in this sentence, and so it is the direct object. However, the book is passed along to *him*, so the action moves through the direct object to the indirect object. To identify indirect objects, ask to whom or for whom the action is happening.

   Sometimes the *to* is only implied, as in the following example:

   <u>She</u> threw *him* the book.

   The pronoun *him* remains an indirect object and so is in the objective case.

   <u>Denise</u> <u>asked</u> *her* to open the window.

In this sentence, we ask who will open the window, and we see that it is the pronoun *her*, the indirect object, which answers, "Asked (to) whom?" "To open the window" answers the question "asked what?" so it is the direct object. (For more on subjects, objects, and complements, review Chapter 6.)

3. **Pronoun as object of preposition:** <u>Barry</u> <u>smiled</u> at Elise and *me*.

The pronoun *me* is the final word in a prepositional phrase. Pronouns and nouns in this position are always in the objective case.

Possessive Case

Pronouns used to show ownership are in the **possessive case**:

Is that *your* coat? No, that one is not *mine*. *My* coat is the blue one.

The following chart will help you choose the correct pronoun case:

PRONOUN CASE CHART			
	Subjective	**Objective**	**Possessive**
First-person singular	I	me	my, mine
Second-person singular	you	you	your, yours
Third-person singular	he, she, it, who, whoever	him, her, it, whom, whomever	his, her, hers, its, whose
First-person plural	we	us	our, ours
Second-person plural	you	you	your, yours
Third-person plural	they, who	them, whom	their, theirs, whose

ACTIVITY 7.6 Choosing Pronoun Case

In the following sentences, fill in the blank with a pronoun in the correct case: subjective, objective, or possessive. Refer to the pronoun case chart above for help. Several pronouns may work in a given space.

EXAMPLE: **The Canpar driver delivered a package to** *me*.

1. Nobody knew _____ jacket was left lying on the floor.

2. Ron's mother always loved _____ best.

3. The sergeant told _____ squad that _____ would go on patrol in the morning.

4. Sati hopes that _____ will be on time for once.

5. The bank gave _____ free chequing for opening a student account.

6. The flooding is not _____ problem because we live on high ground.

Solving Common Problems with Pronoun Case

L07.4

Pronoun case often causes problems in four categories: compounds, comparisons, *who/whom*, and relative pronouns as subjects.

Compounds

Compound (two-part) case difficulties occur when two pronouns, two nouns, or a noun and a pronoun are linked by *and* or *or,* as in the following examples:

Subjects:	*Jenny and I/me* <u>talked</u> until 2 a.m.
Objects:	The <u>discussion</u> <u>affected</u> *her* and *I/me.*
Objects of preposition:	<u>It</u> <u>involved</u> our long friendship, which has always been important to *her* and *I/me.*

In each of these sentences, confusion sometimes results from the pairings. However, if we mentally cross out one of the pair, the remaining word will often guide us to the correct case. Look at the first sentence, for example:

~~Jenny and~~ I talked until 2 a.m.

It doesn't sound right to say, "*Me* talked until 2 a.m." So "*Jenny and I* talked until 2 a.m." is correct. "I" is in the subjective case.

The discussion affected ~~her and~~ me.

Again, it doesn't sound right to say, "The discussion affected *I.*" So the correct answer is "The discussion affected *her* and *me.*" Both "her" and "me" are in the objective case.

It involved our long friendship, which has always been important to *her* and *me.*

Most of us wouldn't say "which has always been important to *I.*" In these instances, your ear can lead you to the right grammatical choice: "It involved our long friendship, which has always been important to *her* and *me.*" Again, "her" and "me" are in the objective case.

ACTIVITY 7.7 Choosing Pronoun Case with Compounds

In the following sentences, underline the <u>pronoun</u> in the correct case: subjective, objective, or possessive.

EXAMPLE: **Between you and (I/<u>me</u>), there is no way to win this game.**

1. The clown offered Caitlyn and (I/me) a cone of pink cotton candy.

2. Is it true that (she/her) and Regina will be working backstage at the concert?

3. No one saw you and (I/me) entering the office.

4. You and (she/her) should start talking *to* rather than *at* one another.

5. There was too much confusion at the time to get the whole story from Frances and (they/them).

6. (They/Them) were embarrassed when the servers sang happy birthday to (they/them).

Comparisons

We often make noun/pronoun and pronoun/pronoun comparisons using the words *than* and *as.* These comparisons can be confusing because they may imply words left out of the sentence, as in the following examples:

Kyoko plays her electric bass more skillfully than *I/me.*

I am not yet quite as good as *she/her.*

HINT

When "me" is used in a compound construction, it is always mentioned last: e.g., *Jenny and me,* not *me and Jenny.*

If we add the implied verbs to sentences like these, it becomes easier to determine the correct pronoun case. With the verbs in place, we can see that the pronouns *I* and *she* are subjects and therefore must be in the subjective case:

Kyoko plays her electric bass more skillfully than I (*play*).

I am not yet quite as good as *she* (is).

Using this strategy of adding implied words, we can see that the pronouns *her* and *him* are the correct choices as direct objects in the following examples:

Michael always liked Jessie better than (he *liked*) ***her/she*.**

Polluted rivers distress Rosa as much as (polluted rivers distress) ***him/he*.**

Sometimes choosing pronoun case affects the meaning of your sentence, as in the following example:

Tyler focuses more on his studies than me. (than he focuses on *me*)

Tyler focuses more on his studies than I. (than *I* focus on my studies)

ACTIVITY 7.8   Choosing Pronoun Case with Comparisons

In the following sentences, underline the correct pronoun in parentheses. Next, in the blank at the end of the sentence, write in the words that were left out of the comparison.

> EXAMPLE: **David can't bench-press as much weight as (he/him)** *can bench-press*.

1. My friends from Montreal come to visit me more often than (he/him) _____.

2. The letter from Canada Revenue spelled as much trouble for me as _____ (her /she).

3. Even though Casey and his wife are both a little crazy, we think she needs more help than (he /him) _____.

4. Even after a failed exam, few people seem as genuinely miserable as (she/her) _____.

5. Of my four brothers, the oldest can go without sleep longer than the rest of (they/them) _____.

6. By the middle of the basketball game, it was clear that Art was more excited by the team's performance than (she/her) _____.

Who/Whom

The relative pronouns *who/whoever* and *whom/whomever* can also cause case problems. *Who/whoever* are used as subjects and *whom/whomever* have traditionally been used as objects. The case for these pronouns depends on how they are used in the clause in which they appear, rather than on how that clause is used in the sentence. For example:

Object: Kristi <u>was</u> *whom* **the court ordered to appear on Friday.**

Although the pronoun *whom* is a subject complement (Kristi = *whom*) and would ordinarily be in the subjective case, within the bold clause, *whom* is the direct object and so must be in the objective case.

Subject: The <u>kickoff goes</u> to *whoever* **wins the toss.**

Although the pronoun *whoever* is the object of the preposition *to,* in the bold clause, *whoever* is the subject and so must be in the subjective case.

Subject: *Who* <u>will pick up</u> the kids from school today?

The verb phrase is *will pick up* and the subject is *who,* so the relative pronoun must be in the subjective case.

Object: <u>You</u> <u>owe</u> your success to *whom?*

To *whom* do <u>you</u> <u>owe</u> your success?

Whom do <u>you</u> <u>owe</u> your success to?

In these versions of the same question, *owe* is the main verb with *you* as the subject and *whom* as the indirect object, so *whom* must be in the objective case.

Although the distinction between *who* and *whom* has been fading—*who* is often used in place of *whom*—you will indicate a note of formality when you observe the difference. If the objective use of *whom* seems awkward or contrary to the tone of your work, you can always recast the sentence so that the relative pronoun is unneeded; or you can sometimes just drop it, as in the following example:

The person ~~whom~~ Peter Parker admired most was his Uncle Ben.

ACTIVITY 7.9   **Choosing Pronoun Case with *Who/Whom***

In the main clauses of the following sentences, underline the <u>subject</u>. Next, circle the correct form of *who/whom.* In some cases, you will be underlining and circling the same word. If a verb immediately follows the relative pronoun, the pronoun is usually a subject, and therefore should be *who* or *whoever.* The verbs are indicated in **bold** to help you determine the subjective and objective cases.

EXAMPLE: (**Whoever**/Whomever) **gets** to the family room first gets the best seat.

1. (Who/Whom) **will meet** us at the movies?

2. We **will begin** our business letter with this greeting: To (who/whom) it may concern.

3. (Who/whom) **did** you **go** with to the skating party?

4. The glory **belongs** to (whoever/whomever) finishes the marathon.

5. People **should be able to work** for (whoever/whomever) they **want** to.

6. A boss (who/whom) Dan **respects** is working the late shift tonight.

Relative Pronouns as Subjects

We learned in Chapter 3 that pronouns must refer to nouns (or other pronouns) to have an identity. The same is true for the **relative pronouns** *who, which,* and *that* (among others), which are the subjects of relative clauses, as you can see in the examples below. These pronouns are singular or plural based on the noun to which they refer.

Singular: 1. A **politician** <u>*who*</u> <u>has</u> integrity is careful about where *his or her* money comes from.

Plural: 2. **Politicians** <u>*who*</u> <u>have</u> integrity are careful about where *their* money comes from.

Singular: 3. A **bear** *that* <u>bothers</u> people is generally relocated or killed.

Plural: 4. **Bears** *that* <u>bother</u> people are generally relocated or killed.

Sentences 1 and 2 use the *who* pronoun to refer to *politician*—singular in 1, plural in 2. Notice that the verb *to have* changes to agree with the singular and plural nouns.

This pattern holds for **sentences 3 and 4** as well. The verb *to bother* changes to agree with the singular and plural nouns.

ACTIVITY 7.10 Identifying Relative Pronouns as Subjects

In the following sentences, circle the relative pronoun, draw an arrow to show which noun it refers to, and then underline the correct verb form.

EXAMPLE: **Jack Sparrow, who (is/are) a captain in *Pirates of the Caribbean*, spends much of his time staggering around his ship.**

1. The weather for the last three nights—which (has/have) been unusual—has been freezing.

2. Dogs that bark too often (is/are) an awful nuisance.

3. Carter will give the money to those people who (needs/need) it the most.

4. Hayao Miyazaki is the only director who (has/have) been called the "father of Japanese animated cinema."

5. The fish in my aquarium, which (is/are) well fed, sometimes leap out of the water at me.

6. Rachel always shops in grocery stores that (sells/sell) organic food.

Remaining Consistent in Person

LO7.5

As we noticed in the Pronoun Case Chart (see page 97), pronouns have *number* (singular or plural) and *person* (first, second, or third). **Person** is the perspective the author assumes when he or she writes: first person (*I, we*), second person (*you*), and third person (*he, she, it,* or *they*). Writers should be consistent in both number and person.

The most frequent shift error is from the first person, *I*, or third person, *they*, to the second person, *you*, as in the following examples. Note how the writer corrects these mistakes.

EXAMPLE 1

I loved being out of doors when *I* was young. After a long, cold winter, when April finally came around, y~~ou~~ could see the daffodils and tulips pushing up out of the ground. And y~~ou~~ could see the grass turning green again and the leaves slowly unfolding. *I* waited every spring for the robins to return from their hiding places in the woods, pecking at unwary earthworms.

EXAMPLE 2

People who have nothing good to say about Canadian politics are often
the ones who don't vote in elections. ~~You~~ *One* should vote in order to have the
right to complain.

Writers often mix person in their work, but there should always be a good reason for doing so. The *I* of personal experience is sometimes used in introductions and conclusions but then avoided in the body paragraphs of an essay (except in a personal anecdote). To address the reader directly, we can use *you*, as we do occasionally in introductions and conclusions and often in process analysis instructions (as in textbooks like this one). *We, us,* and *our* are useful pronouns for connecting with an audience, especially in persuasive writing.

However, you should control shifts in person, especially avoiding the examples shown previously. When using the slightly more formal third person, there are several options for avoiding an inappropriate second-person *you*. We can use third-person pronouns *(he, she, they)* or nouns that stand in their place *(people, students, employees*—whatever noun describes the subject), or we can leave the pronoun out altogether. In the following example, note three possible fixes for the pronoun shift:

INAPPROPRIATE PRONOUN SHIFT: The Loyalists who came to Canada in 1783 endured many hardships and suffered many losses. <u>You</u> were lucky if <u>you</u> survived <u>your</u> first winter.

1. **Fixed (pronoun third person):** The Loyalists who came to Canada in 1783 endured many hardships and suffered many losses. *They* were lucky if *they* survived *their* first winter.

2. **Fixed (noun):** The Loyalists who came to Canada in 1783 endured many hardships and suffered many losses. These *settlers* were lucky if they survived their first winter.

3. **Fixed (pronoun deleted):** The Loyalists who came to Canada in 1783 endured many hardships, suffered many losses, and were lucky to survive the first winter.

ACTIVITY 7.11 Avoiding Shifts in Person

In the following paragraph, cross out incorrect pronouns and write the appropriate ones and other word substitutions in the space above the crossed-out word.

EXAMPLE: If children begin doing housework at an early age, ~~you~~ *they* will be
learning early how to live on ~~your~~ *their* own.

Earning an allowance has many benefits for young children. Having to work for your money makes you proud of your accomplishments. It helps them realize that they can contribute in a real way to the household. You can see that you are needed in the home. Although a child might not need the money, you might even do the work because it makes you feel good. The pride that children feel in cleaning a family room well or doing the dishes may even encourage you to do more housework. If you earn your allowance, you are working gradually toward independence from your parents.

Chapter Summary

1. Pronouns stand in the place of nouns and help create variety in our work.

2. Pronouns can be classified as one or more of the following types: personal, indefinite, relative, interrogative, demonstrative, reflexive and intensive, reciprocal, and possessive.

3. Pronouns must be clearly linked to their antecedents, and they must agree with them in number.

4. Most difficulties with pronoun/antecedent agreement fall into one of these categories: indefinite pronouns, collective nouns, or compound antecedents.

5. Some indefinite pronouns are singular, others plural, and others can be used in singular or plural constructions, depending on the nouns they refer to.

6. Pronouns can be in the subjective, objective, or possessive cases.

7. Pronoun case often causes problems in four categories: compounds, comparisons, *who/whom*, and relative pronouns as subjects.

8. One common pronoun error is shifting (without reason) from the first-person *I* or third-person *they* to the second-person *you*.

Adjectives and Adverbs

In a paragraph, describe the scene shown here, using specific, vivid details, especially noting the colours. (See Chapter 23 for more on description.) After reviewing this chapter on adjectives and adverbs, return to your paragraph. How many of each (adjectives and adverbs) did you use? If you were going to revise, would you use more or fewer of each? Why?

LEARNING OBJECTIVES

What Are We Trying to Achieve and Why?

Writers often add information to sentences by using adjectives and adverbs, words that *describe* or *modify*. **Adjectives** tell about *nouns* and *pronouns* (*yellow* mums, they were *yellow*). **Adverbs** tell about *verbs, adjectives,* and other *adverbs* (walks *gracefully, very* small dog, *not too* sleepy). Although we usually locate these modifiers close to the word they describe, adverbs in particular may be some distance from the words they modify.

The problems we generally have with adjectives and adverbs include choosing the right ones, using them selectively, and attaching them clearly to the words we intend them to describe. This chapter will help you to become more precise when using adjectives and adverbs.

Adjectives

L08.1

Adjectives describe nouns and pronouns, telling *how many; which;* or *what kind,* colour, shape, size, texture, or age a person or thing is. Many adjectives have endings like *-ish (foolish), -less (fearless), -able (agreeable), -al (traditional),* and *-y (pretty).* Adjectives are usually located in front of the word they describe, but they may follow it, and they may be more than one word. Note the following examples:

ADJECTIVES LOCATED DIRECTLY IN FRONT OF THE WORD THEY DESCRIBE

These two tell number and size:

In our pond lives *one large* **snapping turtle.**

ADJECTIVES CONNECTED TO A SUBJECT BY A LINKING VERB

These adjectives (telling colour and texture) are connected to *it* by the linking verb *is*:

It is *green* and *mossy.*

COMPOUND ADJECTIVES

These two tell colour as a unit and so are hyphenated as a **compound adjective:**

It has *yellow-brown* **markings** on the edges of its shell.

DEMONSTRATIVE PRONOUN

This adjective tells which one. Other demonstrative pronouns used as adjectives are *these, those*:

This **turtle** is wary.

POSSESSIVE PRONOUN

This adjective tells which one. Other **possessive pronouns** used as adjectives are *your, his, her, its, our, their, whose*:

My **dog** frightened it this morning.

POSSESSIVE NOUN

This adjective tells which one:

The *turtle's* **leap** from the rock it was sunning itself on was spectacular.

INDEFINITE PRONOUN

This adjective tells how many. Other **indefinite pronouns** used as adjectives are *several, both, many, few, other, all, each, every, no, either, neither, any*:

Some **children** at the pond applauded.

Participles and Infinitives

Adjectives can also be **participles** in the *-ing* or *-ed* form of a regular verb:

> *floating* **feather**   *tired* **taxi driver**

English Review Note

In English, adjectives usually come before the words they describe or modify.

HINT

Other **linking verbs** include *feel, appear, seem, act, smell, sound, taste, look, become, get, grow,* and *remain.*

HINT

See Chapter 4 for more information on participles.

HINT

Verbals are discussed in Chapters 3 and 11.

English Review Note

The *–ed* form is used for a person undergoing an experience, while the *–ing* form is used for a person who is causing experiences or feelings.

English Review Note

In English, adjectives do not change form to agree with the words they describe or modify.

They can also be participles in the *-n* or *-t* form of an irregular verb:

broken window   *burnt* marshmallow

Adjectives can be **infinitives** with *to* + base verb:

kiosk *to rent*

Each of these verbals tells what kind:

Present participle:	The *floating* feather drifted into my lap.
Past participle:	A *tired* taxi driver stopped for me.
Irregular past participle:	He looked through a *broken* window at the *burnt* marshmallow.
Infinitive:	The proprietor had one last kiosk *to rent* at the mall.

Nouns as Adjectives

Nouns are often used as adjectives to describe other nouns:

desk drawer   *laundry* hamper   *fruit* juice

In the following sentence, the noun *laundry* tells what kind of hamper and so it is used as an adjective:

Margot found the *laundry* hamper in the closet.

ACTIVITY 8.1 Recognizing Adjectives

In the following sentences, underline all the adjectives (including nouns used as adjectives). Remember to ask *how many; which;* or *what kind*, colour, shape, size, texture, or age the person or thing is.

EXAMPLE: This morning, Kaitlyn went for a 6-kilometre run.

1. Nobody thought a lazy person like Shaun could manage to write an A-plus essay.
2. Nasser Hassoun always constructs well-built homes at affordable prices.
3. Is your lab partner working on Friday night again?
4. Some people still prefer film cameras to digital.
5. Undiagnosed Crohn's disease can cause many problems in children, such as lack of growth.
6. City highways are filled with time-conscious, distracted drivers, who are changing CD selections and holding coffee cups in their laps.

Adjective Phrases

Single-word and compound adjectives are common in sentences, but so are certain phrases that function as adjectives. To review, prepositional phrases always begin with a preposition, often a short word that tells location (*in, on, at, by, under*). Participial phrases begin with a participle, either present, ending in *-ing* (sleep*ing* on the couch) or past, ending in *-ed* for regular verbs (excit*ed* by the idea). Infinitive phrases begin with the word *to* + a base verb (*to sleep* until noon).

In the following sentences, the underlined phrases all tell about the noun *person*, and so the phrases function as adjectives:

Prepositional: Hannah was the first person *at the seminar.*

Participial: Hannah was the first person *arriving* at the seminar.

Infinitive: Hannah was the first person *to arrive* at the seminar.

Adjective Clauses

Adjective clauses have a verb and a subject and usually begin with one of three relative pronouns, *who, which,* or *that* (*who* saw the accident). The relative pronoun is the subject in these clauses. The following example contains an adjective clause, which also works as an adjective, giving information about a noun:

Hannah was the first person *who* arrived at the seminar.

HINT

For more on phrases and clauses, see Chapters 10 and 11.

English Review Note

Do not repeat the subject in the clause. *Who* replaces the subject.

ACTIVITY 8.2 Recognizing Adjective Phrases and Adjective Clauses

In the following sentences, underline any adjective phrases (prepositional, participial, and infinitive) and adjective clauses that you see. Often you will find prepositional phrases inside other phrases and clauses (see the infinitive phrase in the example below), but be sure to include the participle or the infinitive when they begin the phrase. Some sentences have several phrases and clauses. Note that the part of the sentence not underlined is the main idea!

EXAMPLE: **Eileen wrote down the recipes to add to her cookbook.**

1. Those are the trees for the city to mark for removal.

2. Smiling in anticipation, the professor began the first class of the year.

3. Going too fast for the road conditions, Raina lost control of the car, sliding into a ditch.

4. The lime-green plastic portfolio is mine.

5. Juno drinks a mild tea that does not keep her awake at night.

6. Here are some suggestions to help with your insomnia.

Adverbs

L08.2

Adverbs describe verbs, adjectives, and other adverbs, telling *when, where, why, how,* and *to what degree or extent* something was done. Adverbs, like adjectives, can be single words, phrases, or clauses. Many adverbs are formed by adding *-ly* to the end of an adjective, so one way to identify adverbs is to look for this *-ly* ending:

bad ⟹ badly   happy ⟹ happily   sweet ⟹ sweetly

This method of identifying adverbs is not foolproof, however, because not all words ending in *-ly* are adverbs (e.g., *lovely*) and because many adverbs do not have the *-ly* ending, as in the following list:

English Review Note

Be careful not to confuse *then* (an adverb indicating time) with *than* (a word used to form a comparison).

ADVERBS THAT DO NOT END IN *-LY*				
already	awhile	now	quite	there
almost	forever	not	soon	too
always	here	often	then	very

Knowing how a word *functions* is the best way to determine what part of speech it is. Notice below how an adverb can function:

1. **Modifying a verb** (tells how):   Jessie Littleriver *patiently* addressed the crowd.

2. **Modifying an adjective** (tells to what degree):   She was *quite* determined to tell the whole story.

3. **Modifying an adverb** (tells to what degree):   Jessie *very* patiently endured another interruption.

Because adverbs are the easiest of the modifiers to manoeuvre, you may find them before or after the word they describe and sometimes separated by many words from the word they tell about. We could rewrite **sentence 1** in this way: "Jessie Littleriver addressed the crowd *patiently*."

ACTIVITY 8.3   Recognizing Adverbs

Underline the adverbs in the following sentences. Remember that not all adverbs have an *-ly* ending.

EXAMPLE: **The lightning flashed across the sky, <u>instantly</u> disappearing.**

1. After her mother started singing, Roxanne left the party quickly.

2. Too many people dispose of batteries carelessly.

3. "Already," thought Lauren, "the stupid alarm is buzzing."

4. The other students thought all the spelling bee words would be easily spelled by Francis Meriwether.

5. Greta climbed to her feet slowly, completely uncertain about how to spell "cyanide."

6. Julie creatively explained why her assignment was not ready.

Adverb Phrases and Clauses

Prepositional and infinitive phrases (discussed previously as adjectives) and the adverb phrase and clause can serve as adverbs in sentences. The adverb clause has a subject and a verb and begins with a subordinating conjunction (*after, although, as, because, if, since, so that, when, where, while,* for example; see Chapter 10). Like single adverbs, adverb phrases and clauses answer the questions *when, where, why, how,* and *to what degree or extent* something was done.

The following sentences use two types of **adverb phrases**, prepositional and infinitive, to tell *when* (**sentence 1**) or *why* (**sentence 2**) the people left. Both phrases (underlined in these examples) describe the main verb *left* and so are being used as adverbs:

1. **Prepositional phrase:**   We left for the class *on time.*

2. **Infinitive phrase:**   We left for the class early *to arrive* there on time.

In **sentence 3**, the underlined **adverb clause** functions as an adverb, telling *why* the people left:

3. **Adverb clause:**   We left for the class early *because* we wanted to arrive there on time.

HINT

For more on punctuating phrases and clauses, see Chapters 15 and 16.

Word groups used as adverbs can often be shifted in sentences to help with clarity and sentence variety. For example, we could rewrite **sentence 2** this way:

To arrive there on time, we left for the class early.

When you shift these word groups to the front of a sentence, be sure to set them off with a comma.

ACTIVITY 8.4 Recognizing Adverb Phrases and the Adverb Clause

In the following sentences, underline all the adverb phrases (prepositional and infinitive) and the adverb clause. Often you will find prepositional phrases inside other phrases and clauses, but be sure also to underline the infinitive at the front of the phrase. Some sentences have several phrases and clauses. Remember to ask *when, where, why, how,* and *to what degree.*

EXAMPLE: **Harry washes his car to keep it from rusting.**

1. To finish his thesis project, Sujay needed more money.

2. Although Raphael was not religious, he liked visiting cathedrals to admire the stained glass and to appreciate the sculpture and architecture.

3. Antoine shopped at a thrift store to find good buys on cookware.

4. The Venus flytrap must capture insects in order to survive in poor soil.

5. Justin left home an hour early to study at the college before class.

6. Because Victoria, British Columbia, is on Vancouver Island, to visit it, you must ride a ferry or fly from the mainland.

Comparative and Superlative Forms

LO8.3

Adjectives and adverbs often compare two things. Those that compare two things use an *-er* ending or the words *more* and *less*, forms known as **comparatives**. Those that compare three or more things use *-est* or the words *most* and *least*, forms called **superlatives**. Here are some examples:

COMPARATIVE AND SUPERLATIVE FORMS FOR ADJECTIVES		
Adjective	**Comparative**	**Superlative**
1. big	bigger	biggest
2. friendly	friendlier	friendliest
3. careful	more (less) careful	most (least) careful
4. intelligent	more (less) intelligent	most (least) intelligent

The Hamilton Botanical Gardens are *bigger* than Kew Gardens, but Edwards Gardens are the *biggest* of all.

My beagle is *less intelligent* than my terrier, but my boxer is the *least intelligent* of the three dogs.

COMPARATIVE AND SUPERLATIVE FORMS FOR ADVERBS		
Adverb	**Comparative**	**Superlative**
5. soon	sooner	soonest
6. patiently	more (less) patiently	most (least) patiently
7. creatively	more (less) creatively	most (least) creatively

English Review Note

In English, the comparative is formed using one word unless the adjective has multiple syllables and doesn't end in *y*. Avoid incorrect constructions like *more big* or *more bigger*.

HINT

For more on spelling with word endings, see Chapter 17.

The *sooner* we go the better, but the *soonest* we can leave is 6 o'clock.

Tony waited *less patiently* than his mother, but his youngest sister waited *least patiently* of all.

Notice that both adjectives and adverbs of only one syllable (as in **numbers 1 and 5** above) usually use *-er* and *-est* to form their comparatives and superlatives. Also note that some adjectives that end in *y*, as in **number 2** above, change the *y* to *i* before adding the *-er* and *-est* endings. However, most adjectives and adverbs of two or more syllables form their comparatives and superlatives by using *more* (*less*) and *most* (*least*), as in **numbers 3, 4, 6, and 7.**

ACTIVITY 8.5 Choosing Comparative and Superlative Forms

In the following sentences, fill in the blanks with the correct comparative or superlative form of the adjective or adverb in parentheses. Remember to use *more/most* or *less/least* for modifiers of more than one syllable.

EXAMPLE: **Sami runs (fast)** *faster* **than anyone on the team.**

1. Because we were in front of the stage, the band seemed (loud) _____ than the last time we were here.

2. George solved the algebraic equation (creatively) _____ than most.

3. The teaching assistant was hoping that this batch of essays would be (good) _____ than the last.

4. The anniversary of the Montreal Massacre is the (sad) _____ day in December.

5. The track team worked out (vigorously) _____ than the football team.

6. Sophie's mother said, "You should be (careful)_____ , Sophie. You will get in trouble because you are the (careful) _____ of all your friends."

L08.4 Irregular Adjective and Adverb Forms

Other adjectives and adverbs that can cause problems are the irregular ones, which do not follow the standard pattern of comparative and superlative forms. Therefore, these forms have to be memorized. Here are the most common comparatives and superlatives:

IRREGULAR ADJECTIVE FORMS		
Adjective	**Comparative**	**Superlative**
1. good	better	best
2. well	better	best
3. bad	worse	worst
4. little (amount)	less	least
5. many	more	most
6. far	farther, further	farthest (distance), furthest

IRREGULAR ADVERB FORMS		
Adverb	**Comparative**	**Superlative**
7. well	better	best
8. badly	worse	worst

The words *good, well,* and *bad* can be a special problem because we use them so frequently, and their forms overlap. If you test these words for their function in a sentence, you will find them easier to use correctly. The word *good* is always an adjective, whereas *well* is more often an adverb but sometimes an adjective. As an adverb, *well* means "properly" or "skilfully." As an adjective, *well* generally means "healthy." Note the following examples:

GOOD

Adjective: Ginny has a *good* cat.

WELL

Adverb (describes the verb *behaves*):   Ginny's cat behaves *well*.

Adjective (connects to the noun *cat*
through the linking verb *seem*):   Ginny's cat does not seem *well*.

BAD

The word *bad* can also be confusing. Keep in mind that *bad* is always an adjective and can only describe nouns. To describe verbs, adjectives, or other adverbs, use the adverb *badly* instead. Note the following examples:

Adjective (describes the noun *day*):   Paul was having a *bad* day.

Adjective (connects to the noun *Paul*
through the linking verb *looked*):   His friends even said that Paul looked *bad*.

BADLY

Adverb (describes the verb phrase   It seemed as if everything was going *badly*
was going):   for him.

ACTIVITY 8.6   Choosing Irregular Comparative and Superlative Forms

In the following sentences, underline the correct <u>comparative</u> or <u>superlative</u> form of the irregular adjectives or adverbs in parentheses.

EXAMPLE: **Because he partied too hard last night, Aaron was feeling (<u>bad</u>/badly), but by noon he felt (good/<u>well</u>) enough to get out of bed.**

1. Glenda could see that the car was (bad/badly) damaged and that (worse/worst) trouble was ahead.

2. It was (good/well) to know that (better/best) planning would keep Fang's GPA from falling (further/furthest).

3. Chantal claimed that she wrote (good/well) and (more/most) often than other students who only *thought* they were (good/well) writers.

4. As (more/most) people realize that global warming is humanity's (more/most) pressing problem, (less/little) fossil fuel will be used until people cut back to the (less/least) amount possible.

5. England did (bad/badly) on the first leg of the Tour de France, but the team hoped they would do (better/best) on the next leg.

6. The (farther/farthest) south you go in South America, the (closer/closest) you get to Antarctica.

Problems with Modifiers

Overuse of Modifiers

As helpful as adjectives and adverbs can be in explaining and building images, writers sometimes overuse them. A few common culprits are adverbs like the following: *very, really, extremely, awfully,* and *incredibly.* It is occasionally appropriate to use these intensifiers; but more often than not, they should be cut and the words they describe replaced with more specific words to achieve clarity, emphasis, and economy. For example, compare the following sentences:

DRAFT: The day was *really very* cold, and my toes were *extremely* frozen, and my fingers hurt *awfully* badly because the temperature was so *incredibly* low.

REVISION: It was minus 20 degrees, so my fingers and toes were frozen, and I was miserable.

If you think that this revised sentence has more force, then try to avoid most of the mushy intensifying adverbs of its draft version.

It is not uncommon in first drafts to cram too many modifiers into one sentence, often simply stacking them in front of a word. For example, compare the following sentences:

DRAFT: A huge, smelly, dim-witted, violent neighbourhood bully always dressed in a beat-up black leather jacket, Spud was feared by all the kids on my block.

REVISION: Spud, the neighbourhood bully, was huge, dim-witted, and smelly. When we saw that beat-up black leather jacket that he wore, all the kids on my block scattered.

Here, the draft sentence tries to stack too many adjectives in front of the noun *Spud.* The revision solves the problem by creating two sentences and redistributing the modifiers. Sometimes you will just cut modifiers, and other times you will weave them into your rewritten sentences.

ACTIVITY 8.7 Revising for Clarity and Economy

Revise the following paragraph by crossing through excessive modifiers. The first sentence has been done as an example.

In the ~~wired,~~ digital world, the Internet and the World Wide Web have created ~~multiple web-based~~ virtual museums. By late 1997, there were over 8000 museums and heritage sites on the Web; so many that some knowledgeable people began to ask the big, unanswerable question: "Will this virtual/digital museum domain take over the role of the physical/architectural museum domain?" Wireless, hand-held, mobile devices such as PDAs, 3G handsets, and Tablet PCs can better facilitate visitor interaction with the wonderful and varied museum exhibits and with other curious and interactive visitors. The museum can be a place to learn across the curriculum in an engaging and stimulating learning environment and there is ever-increasing current research into the use of mobile devices to support and facilitate school museum visits. New research shows that active support of this social, real-time interaction can help the museum continue to operate as an attractive, useful, educational leisure destination. Ubiquitous computer technology has been shown to stimulate active, enthusiastic, participatory learning by children visiting a museum.

Dangling Modifiers

When a single modifier or a word group at the beginning of a sentence describes the wrong following word or no word at all, it is said to *dangle*. Here are several examples:

1. Sledding down the snow-covered hill, **my eyes** were watering from the cold.
   (incorrectly implies that "my eyes" were sledding)

2. Awakened at 6:00 a.m., **the sound of hammering** annoyed Luke.
   (incorrectly implies that "the sound of hammering" was awakened)

3. To like them, **the marshmallows** must be toasted a golden brown for Larissa.
   (incorrectly implies that "the marshmallows" are the ones with a preference)

4. As a dedicated professor, **her students** filled most of Natasha's life.
   (incorrectly implies that "her students" are a dedicated professor)

As you can see, the leading phrase in each sentence seems to describe the first noun that follows it; but this arrangement distorts the intended meaning. To correct the dangling modifier, you can either insert a subject into the leading phrase, or place the intended noun directly after the phrase, at the beginning of the main clause. The following examples make the relationship between the phrase and its noun clear:

FIX BY ADDING SUBJECT:

1. As I was sledding down the snow-covered hill, my eyes were watering from the cold.

2. **Luke** was annoyed when he was awakened at 6:00 a.m. by the sound of hammering.

3. For **Larissa** to like them, the marshmallows must be toasted a golden brown.

4. **Natasha** is a dedicated professor whose students fill most of her life.

FIX BY MOVING SUBJECT:

1. Sledding down the snow-covered hill, **I** felt my eyes watering from the cold.

2. Awakened at 6:00 a.m., **Luke** was annoyed by the sound of hammering.

3. To like them, **Larissa** wanted the marshmallows toasted a golden brown.

4. As a dedicated professor, **Natasha** filled most of her life with her students.

Misplaced Modifiers

Misplaced modifiers also appear to modify an unintended word, creating confusion for the reader, as in the following examples:

1. Shelly sang a lullaby to her **daughter** in her nightgown.
   (confuses whose nightgown it is, Shelly's or her daughter's)

2. Gilberto's office was messy with books from the **libraries** stacked on every surface. (incorrectly implies that libraries are stacked on every surface)

3. Christian found a coin at a **flea market** that was 150 years old.
   (incorrectly implies that the flea market was 150 years old)

4. Carolyn enjoyed the **trampoline** <u>bouncing three metres in the air</u>.
(incorrectly implies that the trampoline was bouncing in the air)

5. The Humber River is usually fairly shallow and slow moving; **but now**

it is flooded, <u>which makes it safe for a family float</u>.
(means the opposite of what it intends, incorrectly implying that the flooded river makes it safe)

To correct the misplaced modifier, we move it closer to the word it should describe, sometimes adding a word or two. Note the following examples:

1. <u>In her nightgown,</u> **Shelly** sang a lullaby to her daughter.

2. Gilberto's office was messy with library **books** <u>stacked on every surface</u> .

3. At a flea market, Christian found a **coin** <u>that was 150 years old</u> .

4. <u>Bouncing three metres in the air,</u> **Carolyn** enjoyed the trampoline.

5. **The Humber River is usually fairly shallow and slow moving,** <u>which makes it safe for a family float;</u> but now it is flooded.

ACTIVITY 8.8 WORKING TOGETHER: Correcting Dangling and Misplaced Modifiers

Work alone or with a partner to rewrite the following sentences, adding or rearranging words to correct the dangling and misplaced modifiers. If you are working in pairs or groups, try fixing each modifier problem in two different ways.

EXAMPLE: **Snow covered the yard that was blowing in from the north.**
Snow that was blowing in from the north covered the yard. **Or,** *Blowing from the north, the snow covered the yard.*

1. There are many young people wearing strapless prom dresses and black tuxedos giggling as they cross the street.

2. Grazing and whipping around their tails to brush off the flies, I was surrounded by the horses.

3. Too tired for words, my head nodded as I fell asleep over my homework.

4. To teach the class properly about grammar, Amanda's notes had to be in order.

5. Excited by the sound of the street band, concentrating on the work was difficult for Mario.

6. You might win the lottery by buying that ticket or just fund someone else's winning, which would be terrific.

LO8.6 # For English as a Second Language Learners: Adjective Order

Adjectives describe nouns and pronouns and are generally placed before them in a sentence (*silly* boy, *green* trees). When you use more than one adjective, the resulting word group gathers meaning as it moves closer to the noun or pronoun it describes (*an interesting glass* bottle). There is a preferred order of adjectives, according to their type:

ORDER OF ADJECTIVES	
Determiners:	this, these, that, the, a, an, some, many, my, our, your, all, both, each, several, one, two, three
Judgment:	unusual, interesting, impressive, ugly, beautiful, inspiring, hopeful, smart, funny
Size:	large, massive, small, tiny, heavy, light, tall, short
Shape:	round, square, rectangular, wide, deep, thin, slim, fat
Age:	young, adolescent, teenage, middle-aged, old, senior, new, worn, antique
Colour:	white, black, blue, red, yellow, green
Proper noun derivatives:	Canadian, German, Arabic, Parisian, Gothic, Disneyesque, Seussian
Material:	wood, plastic, cloth, paper, cardboard, metal, stone, clay, glass, ceramic
Nouns used as adjectives:	*coffee* mug, *water* bottle, *pencil* sharpener, *garden* hose

Here are several combinations of adjectives:

DETERMINER/JUDGMENT/AGE/NOUN USED AS ADJECTIVE

The impressive new marine sanctuary northwest of Halifax offers habitat to thousands of species.

DETERMINER/JUDGMENT/SIZE

Many unusual small mushrooms appeared in David's yard overnight.

DETERMINER/SIZE/SHAPE/PROPER NOUN DERIVATIVE

One small square French pastry was left on the tray.

The adjectives above add meaning to each other as they move toward the noun they describe; therefore, we call these **cumulative** adjectives, and they *do not* need commas. On the other hand, adjectives that modify or describe a noun or pronoun equally are **coordinate** adjectives and *do* require a comma between them (*funny, inspiring* poetry).

In general, avoid "stacking" adjectives in front of nouns and pronouns. Using more than two or three modifiers at one time overloads the word you are describing. Try spreading the modifiers around within several sentences for better effect.

ACTIVITY 8.9 Ordering Adjectives

In each of the following sentences, rearrange the adjectives so their order is appropriate.

EXAMPLE: Jasmine wanted a ~~winter lightweight black~~ coat. (*lightweight black winter*)

1. Erica found a round tiny milky-white pebble.

2. In the museum, we admired a clay elegant Japanese sculpture.

3. These boutique-style modern beautiful hotels are all the rage in Europe.

4. Mohammed was interested in studying a class in Canadian nineteenth-century literature.

5. This French inspiring old watercolour, thought Kristy, belongs in my living room.

6. There are still some small unusual colonies of elk-horn coral left in the Caribbean.

Chapter Summary

1. Adjectives describe nouns and pronouns, telling *how many, which,* or *what kind.*

2. Adverbs describe verbs, adjectives, and other adverbs, telling *when, where, why, how,* and *to what degree or extent* something was done.

3. The comparative form of adjectives and adverbs compares two things using an *-er* ending or the words *more* and *less.*

4. The superlative form of adjectives and adverbs compares three or more things using *-est* or the words *most* and *least.*

5. There are several common irregular adjective and adverb forms that are best handled through memorizing; e.g., *good, well, bad, little, many,* and *far.*

6. Be careful not to stack too many modifiers before a noun.

7. Dangling and misplaced modifiers occur when single words and word groups are not positioned closely enough to the word they mean to describe.

8. Adjectives are generally placed before nouns in a sentence. Cumulative adjectives add meaning to each other as they move toward the noun. Adjectives that modify or describe a noun or pronoun equally are coordinate adjectives.

Prepositions

9

"*OVER the river and THROUGH the wood,*

TO Grandfather's house we go" *are the opening lines of a poem written in 1844 about children travelling to*

Thanksgiving dinner. What do you think these happy children might be celebrating or looking forward to?

Write a paragraph that describes the source of their happiness by using prepositional phrases.

Or write a paragraph that describes your own celebration.

LEARNING OBJECTIVES

9.1   Identifying prepositions

9.2   For English as a second language learners

What Are We Trying to Achieve and Why?

Prepositions can be considered sentence connectors; but more importantly, they introduce the phrases that add the descriptive colour to a sentence. As such, they never introduce a phrase that holds the main idea of a sentence. In other words, the subject of the sentence is never in the prepositional phrase. This chapter will look at not only the linking function of prepositions in sentences, but also their descriptive function.

L09.1 Identifying Prepositions

Prepositions are an important type <u>of</u> sentence connector. We use prepositions even <u>in</u> fairly short sentences. Notice the underlined prepositions <u>in</u> this sentence and <u>in</u> the two <u>before</u> it. **Prepositions** (such as *in, on,* and *near)* are short words that often (but not always) show location; they connect nouns and pronouns in word groups called **prepositional phrases** (such as *on the floor*). These phrases give information that embellishes the main part of the sentence, so they work as adjectives or adverbs, as in the following example:

She saw the DVD case *with* the bright blue cover lying *on* the floor.

The following chart lists many common prepositions. Some are composed of more than one word. Notice that some prepositions can work as other parts of speech. For example, *for* can also be a coordinating conjunction (see Chapter 10). *Since, until,* and *because (of)* are often used as subordinating conjunctions. The preposition *like* is commonly misused as a subordinating conjunction (to mean *as* or *as if*). While many of the following prepositions do show location, notice that others show relationships like time (*when*), addition (*in addition to*), cause (*due to*), and exception (*except*). Also, some prepositions of location can be used to show time (*in, by, at, on, before, after*).

PREPOSITIONS					
Location			**Other Uses**		
above	behind	off	about	in addition to	
across	below	on	according to	in place of	
after	beneath	onto	as	in spite of	
against	beside	out (out of)	aside from	instead of	
ahead of	between	outside	as well as	like	
along	beyond	over	because of	of	
amid	by	past	by way of	regarding	
among	down	through	despite	since	
around	from	toward	due to	till	
at	in	under	during	until	
atop	inside	up	except (except for)	with	
before	into	upon	for	without	

Here are several examples showing how prepositions are used:

1. **Tom put his soft drink <u>on the table</u>.**

2. **Anna handed her coat <u>to him</u>.**

3. **Laureen (picked up) her daughter's toys <u>from the floor</u>.**

Idiomatic Phrases

sh Review Note

continue to keep a
matic phrases that
o you.

Customary practice has established that certain prepositions follow adjectives and verbs. When we substitute a different preposition, the phrase becomes non-standard English. The only way to become fluent with idiomatic phrases is to listen carefully to native speakers, read extensively, and memorize the phrases that are new to you or that your instructor marks on your papers.

COMMON PREPOSITIONAL PHRASES		
abide *by* a decision	apologize *for* an accident	concerned *about* illness
abide *in* Quebec	argue *with* a professor	connected *to* business
absent *from* work	arrive *at* school	count *on* family
accuse *of* stealing	aware *of* a mistake	decide *on* a new life
acquainted *with* him	believe *in* yourself	independent *of* parents
addicted *to* cigarettes	blame *for* a bad joke	interested *in* issues
afraid *of* spiders	bored *with (by)* the lecture	proud *of* a daughter
agree *with* a friend	capable *of* speaking	responsible *for* a cat
agree *to* a proposal	charge *for* dinner	rewarded *by* a boss
angry *with* a pet	comply *with* demands	rewarded *for* responsibility

ACTIVITY 9.5 Choosing Idiomatic Prepositions

In each of the following sentences, determine whether the idiomatic prepositions are used correctly. If the sentence contains no preposition errors, mark C (for "correct") in the space provided. Otherwise, cross out the incorrect preposition, and write the correct one above it. Refer to the list above for help.

EXAMPLE: We promised to abide ~~with~~ *by* the judge's decision.

1. _____ Hopefully being addicted with cigarettes is becoming a thing of the past.

2. _____ Pat did not agree with the company's hiring policies.

3. _____ He was capable of dealing with any computer problem but had trouble with finding matching socks in the morning.

4. _____ By the time most teens finish high school, they want to be independent with their parents.

5. _____ Isabel knew that she could always count in her study group for help.

6. _____ No one was more afraid with snakes than Amir.

Chapter Summary

1. Prepositions introduce phrases that add descriptive detail to sentences.

2. Prepositions never introduce a phrase that holds the main idea (that is, the subject and main verb) of a sentence.

3. Prepositions are usually one word, but they can also be multi-word.

4. Prepositions often show location and introduce nouns and pronouns in word groups called prepositional phrases.

5. Prepositions of place and time can be confusing and often must be memorized.

6. Idiomatic phrases can be confusing and often must be memorized.

Sentences 1 and 2 use prepositional phrases that show location: "*on* the table" ends in a noun, while "*to* him" ends with a pronoun. **Sentence 3** has another prepositional phrase of location, "*from* the floor," but note that the circled verb, *picked up*, is a phrasal verb with *up* attached. *Up* is part of the verb and does not function as the beginning of a prepositional phrase.

4. **Salvador was excited *about* learning guitar.**

5. **_During_ the train ride, Yvette began ⟨to read⟩ quietly *to herself*.**

Sentence 4 illustrates a prepositional phrase that tells *what* rather than location. **Sentence 5** shows when ("*during* the train ride"), but notice that the circled infinitive, *to read*, is not part of a prepositional phrase. *To* in front of a base verb form like *read* indicates an infinitive, not a prepositional phrase. On the other hand, *to* in front of *herself* in "to herself" is a prepositional phrase.

6. **_In addition to_ the new Toyota Prius, you have won a week's vacation *in Vancouver*.**

Sentence 6 shows three words working at the beginning as a prepositional unit.

HINT

For more on phrasal verbs, review Chapter 4.

ACTIVITY 9.1 WORKING TOGETHER: Using Prepositions

Working with a partner, fill in the blanks in the following sentences with the appropriate preposition; more than one possibility may work in the same spot. Notice that a comma marks the end of prepositional phrases that begin a sentence.

EXAMPLE: *Ahead of* me *on* the highway, I saw a deer frozen *in* my headlights.

1. _____ the bridge, Jerry found an old bicycle _____ fix up and give _____ his brother.

2. The summons was _____ Katrina to appear _____ court _____ January 31.

3. Vanessa played stickball _____ the boys _____ the playground.

4. The daycare charged a dollar a minute _____ late fees _____ my explanation about the broken water main blocking the road.

5. Jake bought a hybrid _____ the gas-guzzling pickup his friends thought he wanted for his company car.

6. Some scientists are concerned _____ the ice breaking up _____ western Antarctica, an event that could raise worldwide ocean levels quickly.

ACTIVITY 9.2 Identifying Prepositions and Prepositional Phrases

Circle the ⟨prepositions⟩—including all parts of multi-word prepositions (*by way of*)—and underline each whole prepositional phrase in the following sentences. Be alert to phrasal verbs (*roll up* the window), and infinitives (*to leave* the store), which are *not* prepositional phrases. Notice too that gerunds (*-ing* verb forms) can be the objects of prepositions and so are part of the phrase ("upon *leaving*"). Remember that a comma marks the end of a prepositional phrase that begins a sentence.

EXAMPLE: The autumn leaves floated down to blanket the yard ⟨with⟩ a deep layer ⟨of⟩ red and gold.

1. Because of his baking skills, Alex was responsible for bringing the pies.

2. The painter bid on the job without carefully thinking about it.

3. Instead of cleaning up the mess, officials decided to employ volunteers who were working on addressing the oil spill themselves.

4. In spite of all the tests, the doctor could not figure out what was wrong with my mother, except for the fact that she was not feeling well.

5. In addition to the strike at the factory, the local morale was low due to the layoffs at the dairy.

6. Jared pitched his first minor league game like a major league contender.

L09.2 For English as a Second Language Learners

Prepositions of Place

There are many prepositions of place, but the ones that can most often cause us problems are *on, in, by,* and *at.*

On tells us where something rests or is positioned:

> **The beaker is *on* the counter.**
>
> **The hat is *on* her head.**
>
> **Anil's apartment is *on* Metcalf Street.**

In tells us that something is contained, surrounded, or enveloped:

> **The three friends were together *in* class.**
>
> **Marko was training *in* the swimming pool.**
>
> **Aleksandra is *in* a great mood today.**

By tells us that one person or thing is next to another:

> **Mansa is sitting *by* the library.**
>
> **Boys race their skateboards in the street *by* my house.**

At tells about one person or thing in relation to another:

> **We found powdered milk *at* the grocery store.**
>
> **Cesar left his Mercedes *at* a shop for an oil change.**

ACTIVITY 9.3 | Choosing Prepositions of Place

In the following sentences, determine whether the prepositions *on, in, by,* and *at* are used to show location correctly. If the sentence contains no preposition errors, mark *C (for "correct")* in the space provided. Otherwise, cross out the incorrect preposition, and write the correct one above it.

> EXAMPLE: Althea walked in from the hall, placed her keys ~~by~~ *on* the table, and said, "I'm happy to spend the evening ~~in~~ *at* home."

1. _____ Ravi looked by the clock on the wall and thought that he should be on bed.

2. _____ Rushing to arrive in the ballet, Yelena realized she was wearing a sweater two sizes too small.

3. _____ Patients arrive by Emergency scared and worried.

4. _____ The hotel was popular since it was by the airport.

5. _____ Hassan advised, "When by fog, focus your flashlight in the ground."

6. _____ Climbing on a loose scree slope is dangerous for mountain climbers.

Prepositions of Time

There are only a few prepositions that indicate time (including *until, till, during, for,* and *since*), but the ones that are particularly troublesome are those that overlap with location: *on, in, by,* and *at.*

On tells about a specific day or date:

> **The mortgage payment is due *on* November 1.**
>
> **Janet and Doug will be here *on* Saturday for lunch.**

In tells about relatively specific time periods, such as mornings, afternoons, evenings, minutes, hours, days, months, years, and seasons:

> **Nick's dad will help him with homework *in* the late afternoon.**
>
> ***In* 20 more minutes, you can watch the movie.**

By tells "at this point in time":

> **Mei Lin said she would leave the college *by* 2:00.**
>
> ***By* 2:30, she should be home.**

At tells about a specific time:

> **Jennifer took her daughter to dance class *at* 10:00 A.M.**
>
> **The latest class of the day starts *at* 6:00 P.M.**

ACTIVITY 9.4 | Choosing Prepositions of Time

In the following sentences, determine whether the prepositions *on, in, by,* and *at* are used to show time correctly. If the sentence contains no preposition errors, mark *C (for "correct")* in the space provided. Otherwise, cross out the incorrect preposition, and write the correct one above it.

> EXAMPLE: I left home ~~on~~ *at* 8:00 to reach the doctor's office ~~in~~ *by* 8:30, but the traffic ~~by~~ *at* rush hour made me late.

1. _____ In about 10 minutes, Adam must be at the bus stop.

2. _____ The website assignment is due by Tuesday on midnight.

3. _____ We are leaving by a little while; but in the meantime, why not read another chapter?

4. _____ Fatima was at her job early enough on the morning to have coffee in the cafeteria and still begin work on time.

5. _____ After exams, especially at night, people should drive very carefully to compensate for the fatigue.

6. _____ Peter was supposed to meet Valerie in 5:00, but he made it by 5:15.

Coordination and Subordination

10

Although you could go mountain climbing by yourself, the team effort shown here allows less experienced climbers to subordinate their efforts to the leaders who can ensure a coordinated success.

Write a paragraph giving several examples of situations when you have coordinated or subordinated your behaviour to that of others. What value do you see in having the ability to coordinate? What value do you see in having the ability to subordinate?

What Are We Trying to Achieve and Why?

Chapters 11 and 12 will focus on sentence parts: what they are and how they work. This chapter helps you understand the important role coordination and subordination play in ordering the ideas in a sentence. Not everything writers tell readers has equal weight, so writers need to signal when the audience should pay special attention to a particular point. Balance in sentences depends on the following relationships:

- **Coordination** gives roughly *equal weight* to ideas.
- **Subordination** *de-emphasizes one idea* while stressing another.

Chapter 10 shows you how to use each of these strategies in your writing. We will focus particularly on the usefulness of conjunctions.

LO10.1 Conjunctions

There are four kinds of conjunctions: **coordinating conjunctions, correlative conjunctions, conjunctive adverbs,** and **subordinating conjunctions.**

Coordinating Conjunctions

Of all the types of conjunctions, we use the coordinating ones most often. **Coordinating conjunctions** show that parts of a sentence are equal. They link similar grammatical units: verbs with verbs, nouns with nouns, phrases with phrases, clauses with clauses, and so on. There are only seven coordinating conjunctions; and of this group of seven, only five are used most of the time. Notice in the following chart that *but* and *yet* are placed together because they are virtually synonyms (you can use *yet* in place of *but* for variety). Also, while the word *for* is frequently used as a preposition (as in the clause "she cared *for* the girls"), it is rarely used as a coordinating conjunction.

HINT

Use the acronym FANBOYS (*for, and, nor, but, or, yet, so*) as a quick and helpful way to remember coordinating conjunctions.

COORDINATING CONJUNCTIONS					
and	but/yet	or	so	nor	for

For help in memorizing the coordinating conjunctions, you can use the acronym *FANBOYS*, as shown in the following chart. Also, remember that while *but* and *yet* can be used as synonyms, the other coordinating conjunctions express different relationships between ideas.

ACRONYM FOR COORDINATING CONJUNCTIONS		
Acronym	**Reason to Use**	**Example**
For	Explains why, meaning "because"	Michael was sad, *for* Marie-Claire had broken the date.
And	Shows agreement and addition, meaning "also"	Justin *and* Emon believe in democracy.
Nor	Excludes, meaning "neither" option	Kareem will not go to graduation, *nor* will he go to the party later.
But	Shows disagreement or contrast, meaning "however"	Daiyu believes in voting, *but* she doesn't like any of the candidates.
Or	Shows alternatives, meaning "either"	I am going to get up *or* go back to sleep.

Acronym	Reason to Use	Example
Yet	Shows disagreement or contrast, meaning "however"	Amir believes in sobriety, *yet* his best friend does not.
So	Shows cause/effect, meaning "therefore"	Michelle sat down next to me, *so* I left.

The following examples show how several parts of sentences can be linked with coordinating conjunctions.

1. **Verbs:** When the deer fly bit him, Charlie <u>jumped</u> from his seat *and* <u>dropped</u> his sandwich.

2. **Nouns:** Trying to swat the fly, <u>Charlie</u> *and* <u>Faith</u> almost tipped over the canoe.

3. **Pronouns:** After that, <u>Charlie</u> *and* <u>Faith</u> laughed, vowing to be more careful.

4. **Adjectives:** The next insect that buzzed them was a <u>black</u> *and* <u>yellow</u> hornet.

5. **Adverbs:** This time Faith and Charlie remained <u>quietly</u> *but* <u>nervously</u> seated.

6. **Conjunctions:** If *or* <u>when</u> the hornet returned, Faith was prepared to swat it.

7. **Prepositions:** Turkey vultures circled <u>above</u> *but* <u>near</u> the canoe.

8. **Phrases:** <u>Pointing to a sign along the river</u> *and* <u>reading it aloud</u>, Charlie said, "'Two kilometres to Niagara Falls. What do you suppose that means?'"

9. **Clauses:** <u>Faith joked that maybe the vultures knew something she and Charlie didn't</u>, *but* <u>she did wonder why the current seemed to be speeding up.</u>

> **English Review Note**
>
> Avoid using coordinating conjunctions with subordinating conjunctions.

ACTIVITY 10.1 Choosing Coordinating Conjunctions

Fill in the blanks in the following sentences with the appropriate coordinating conjunctions. Notice that a comma is used with a coordinating conjunction between two *main* clauses.

EXAMPLE: **After raking 50 bags of leaves** *and* **carrying them to the curb, Allen contemplated mulching and selling them for compost.**

1. Bumper sticker: "I used up all of my sick days, _____ I am calling in dead."

2. In the fall, Sadie is going to the University of British Columbia _____ Simon Fraser University.

3. Greg wanted to visit the bathroom, _____ he had just finished a 500-ml root beer, _____ the movie was too exciting to leave.

4. Driving from Toronto, Cameron wanted to vacation in Cape Breton _____ Newfoundland.

5. Jan couldn't get away from work that often, _____ when she did, she liked walking along the Bow River _____ hiking at Lake Louise.

6. Scientists have looked into the deep ocean beyond the Bay of Fundy _____ found many odd life forms.

Correlative Conjunctions

Correlative conjunctions should seem familiar because they have some coordinating conjunctions attached to them. However, correlatives come in *pairs* to link parts of sentences that are grammatically equivalent: nouns with nouns, noun phrases with noun phrases, clauses with clauses, and so forth. Note the following list:

CORRELATIVE CONJUNCTIONS		
both. . .and	just as. . .so	not only. . .but also
either. . .or	neither. . .nor	whether. . .or

Here are a few examples containing correlative conjunctions:

1. **Nouns:** *Either* Wayne *or* Bob will have to be the first speaker in our presentation.

2. **Noun phrases:** *Neither* Amanda's mother *nor* her father will agree to letting her travel more than five hours away for university.

3. **Clauses:** *Just as* nearly 4000 pets were sickened or killed by tainted pet food in 2007, *so* will other animals continue to suffer in Canada from improperly inspected food.

Use a comma with a correlative conjunction *only* if it separates two *clauses*, as in **sentence 3** and the following example:

Either Wayne will have to be the first speaker in our presentation, or Bob will have to do it.

ACTIVITY 10.2 Choosing Correlative Conjunctions

Fill in the blanks in the following sentences with the appropriate correlative conjunctions. Refer to the above list. Notice that a comma is used with a correlative conjunction between two *main* clauses.

EXAMPLE: **You will find the hammer** *either* **in the workroom** *or* **in the garage.**

1. The blizzard will strike _____ today _____ tomorrow but on the weekend.

2. _____ has government spending on domestic priorities decreased dramatically in the past seven years, _____ the national debt in Canada has risen to more than $800 billion.

3. Many skeptics do not believe that _____ the increase in violent storms _____ the melting of glaciers are evidence of climate change.

4. _____ is Toby studying philosophy, _____ he is studying political science.

5. _____ the Dumbo octopus _____ the vampire squid may qualify as the most unusual deepwater animal.

6. Many experts believe that today North America is _____ safer from terrorist threats _____ better able to care for its people than it was in 2001.

Conjunctive Adverbs

Unlike coordinating and correlative conjunctions—which can link words, phrases, and clauses—**conjunctive adverbs** link only main clauses. They hold together two separate but closely related ideas and are, therefore, punctuated with a semicolon before and a comma after. A list of common conjunctive adverbs follows:

English Review Note

Review this chart and memorize the meanings of these words.

CONJUNCTIVE ADVERBS				
also	further	likewise	nonetheless	then
anyway	furthermore	meanwhile	now	thereafter
besides	however	namely	otherwise	therefore
consequently	incidentally	nevertheless	similarly	thus
finally	instead	next	still	undoubtedly

Here are a few sentence examples using these conjunctions:

1. Adam used to study too late at night; *however,* he solved the problem by making use of the library between classes.

2. Our gas bill is too high this month; *therefore,* we will lower the thermostat next month.

3. Facebook has 27 million users; *furthermore,* it is the sixth most-accessed website in the world.

As you can see, each conjunctive adverb separates two main clauses that could be stand-alone sentences.

Conjunctive adverbs (like other adverbs) can, however, often be moved to various places in a sentence. When they are used simply as adverbs, they are not separating main clauses and, therefore, are not set off with a semicolon, as with *however* in the following sentence, which is a rewrite of **sentence 1** above:

1b. Adam used to study too late at night. He solved the problem, *however,* by making use of the library between classes.

When using conjunctive adverbs as simple adverbs, you set them off with commas.

ACTIVITY 10.3 Choosing Conjunctive Adverbs

English Review Note

The semicolon is often used differently in other languages, so take care that you are using it correctly. (See Chapter 16 for more on the semicolon.)

Fill in the blanks in the following sentences with the appropriate conjunctive adverbs; several may work in the same spot. Refer to the list above. Be sure to use a semicolon before and a comma after a conjunctive adverb to separate *main* clauses, but only commas or no punctuation when the conjunctive adverb is used as a simple adverb.

EXAMPLE: I'm going to swim laps now; *otherwise,* there is no reason for me to be at the pool today.

1. They wanted to go to a downtown theatre _____ they went to one north of the city.

2. Stephanie thinks that *Republic of Doyle* is the best crime show on TV; her mother _____ votes for *Murdoch Mysteries.*

3. Paul heard the dreaded news: "You now have to pay for your own tuition _____ you must pay for your own insurance."

4. The trail to the bottom of the Badlands Wall was long and steep _____ the hikers put padding in the toes of their boots to prevent blisters.

5. Michael said, "I love playing *MapleStory* _____ how else can I meet new people?"

6. Katrina should be at home until 6:00 _____ you will find her on her way to the Royal Winnipeg Ballet.

Subordinating Conjunctions

Subordinating conjunctions are the fourth type of conjunction and are used to introduce adverb clauses. Whereas coordination expresses an equal relationship between sentence parts, subordination shifts the focus away from the subordinated part. Words, phrases, and clauses are often subordinated in sentences. Below you will see a list of common subordinating conjunctions. Remember that some of these conjunctions can function as other parts of speech (for example, as prepositions: *before, after, until*).

SUBORDINATING CONJUNCTIONS				
after	because	in order that	though	whenever
although	before	now that	till (less formal than *until*)	where
as	even if	once	unless	whereas
as if	even though	rather than	until	wherever
as long as	if	since	when	while

Here are some example sentences using these conjunctions:

1. *After* **he did the CN Tower Climb, Caleb couldn't walk without pain for a week.**

2. *Although* **medicine pouches are worn by Native Americans for strength and courage during daily activities, they are also a reminder of the elements that will keep life in balance.**

3. *Because* **Emma enjoys playing chess, many of her friends think she's weird.**

Each of these sentences begins with a subordinating conjunction that helps to show an adverbial function (*when, where, why, how,* or *to what degree*). The adverb clause in **sentence 1** tells *when* Caleb couldn't walk without pain, and in **sentence 2** it tells *why* Native Americans wear medicine pouches. The *because* conjunction in **sentence 3** tells *why* Emma's friends think she's strange. Because adverbs are often movable parts in sentences, we could shift the subordinate clauses in our example sentences to follow the main clauses, like this:

3b. **Many of Emma's friends think she's weird** *because* **she enjoys playing chess.**

When adverb clauses begin sentences (as in **Sentences 1-3**), they usually require a comma, but when they follow a main clause (as in **Sentence 3b**), they usually do not. Note that subordinate clauses are always incomplete sentences and must be attached to a main clause to avoid creating a sentence fragment.

HINT

For more on punctuating subordinate clauses, see Chapters 12, 15, and 16.

ACTIVITY 10.4 Choosing Subordinating Conjunctions

Fill in the blanks in the following sentences with the appropriate subordinating conjunctions; several may work in the same spot. Refer to the list above. Notice that a comma marks the end of an adverb clause when it begins a sentence, but not when the adverb clause follows the main clause.

> EXAMPLE: *Until* **Andrea learns how to parallel park, she won't pass her driver's test.**

1. _____ Dan isn't feeling well, he stays home from school.

2. Evo Morales opposed the U.N. ban on products made from the coca plant _____ he became Bolivia's first indigenous president.

3. _____ many in the band weren't ready to play, Jason started warming up the crowd.

4. _____ more than a million people die from malaria each year, it is past time to commit more international resources to controlling the disease.

5. One child will continue to die of malaria in Africa every 30 seconds _____ more effort is spent on controlling the illness.

6. Tom saw two meteors flash across the horizon _____ he was admiring the night sky.

Coordination

LO10.2

Coordination in writing balances sentence parts through the use of coordinating conjunctions (*and, but, or, so, yet, for, nor*). Few of us have problems linking words or phrases; however, coordination of clauses can be more difficult.

The following examples show how clauses can be balanced with coordinating conjunctions:

1. **but** I will have to stay up late tonight, *but* I want to see Mars look as large as the full moon.

2. **yet** Right now, Mars looks like a bright star, *yet* it is only a fraction of the moon's size.

3. **nor** I cannot dispute the prediction that Mars will look as large as the moon, *nor* can I believe this until I see it with my own eyes.

Avoiding Excessive Coordination

Although coordination is an important method for communicating ideas, writers should be careful not to overuse coordinating conjunctions—*and*, in particular. Compare the following two paragraphs. Which seems more readable?

1. **Carbon dioxide levels are increasing in the Earth's atmosphere, *and* more of the sun's heat is trapped, *and* it is radiated back to the surface, *and* this is gradually raising the Earth's temperature, *and* there is little debate anymore about the rise in temperature, *and* there are some who still maintain that this rise is naturally occurring *and* not caused by people, *and* because it is a natural process, we shouldn't worry about it, *and* if we do forget about it, some people claim the planet will take care of itself as it has always done, *and* therefore we shouldn't feel guilty about the whole climate change issue.**

2. **Carbon dioxide levels are increasing in the Earth's atmosphere as more of the sun's heat is trapped. The heat is radiated back to the surface, gradually raising the Earth's temperature. There is little debate anymore about the rise in temperature. *But* there are some who still maintain that this rise is naturally occurring, not caused by people, *and* that because it is a natural process, we shouldn't worry about it. If we do forget about it, some people claim the planet will take care of itself as it has always done; therefore, we shouldn't feel guilty about the whole climate change issue.**

All the ideas in these paragraphs are the same. Granted, the use of *and* in **paragraph 1** is exaggerated. However, it clearly makes the point that **paragraph 2** is more readable when the nine *and*s have been trimmed to one, a *but* has been added to show a more accurate relationship between ideas, and several other methods of joining sentences have replaced the overused coordinating conjunction.

Read through the following paragraph, and fill in each blank with a coordinating conjunction that makes sense to you.

Requiescat in Pace

We should put aside for a moment the question of who or what is primarily responsible for climate change *and* instead focus on its results. It is clear that we are headed for a planet-wide disaster, _____ people must realize the urgency of the situation—and quickly. As the ice sheets melt worldwide, the ocean level will rise _____ creep up over the coastal plains, drowning some of the world's largest cities. Hurricanes will continue to worsen. Deserts will become swamps, _____ wetlands will become deserts. Arid areas around the world, such as the U.S. Southwest, will become unliveable, _____ animals unable to adapt to this rapid climate change will become extinct. People will migrate on a massive scale, _____ they will die as their homelands become uninhabitable. When the migrants try to move into territory controlled by others, there will be war. Resources needed to sustain life will become more limited, _____ people will still need them. Civilization as we know it will end, _____ this does not mean the end of the planet.

L010.3 Subordination

Coordination helps with clarity and sentence variety, but coordination alone is not enough to create readable prose. When writers add **subordination**, they not only add variety to their sentences, but also help the reader see which ideas they should pay the most attention to. By using adverb and adjective clauses, writers will develop more interesting and informative sentences.

Using Adverb Clauses

As well as words and phrases, which you have already practised in this chapter, we also subordinate whole clauses that function as nouns, adjectives, and adverbs. The **adverb clause** in particular (beginning with words like *because, if,* and *although*) helps to show how ideas relate within sentences. Notice how the example that follows leaves the reader to make a cause-and-effect connection:

Tammy is worried about childcare costs. Her daycare centre just raised its hourly rate.

If we subordinate the second sentence by adding the conjunction *because*, the cause-and-effect relationship becomes clear:

Tammy is worried about childcare costs *because* her daycare centre just raised its hourly rate.

Adverb clauses function like single adverbs, answering the questions *why, when, where, how,* and *to what extent or degree* something was done. *Why* is Tammy worried? Because her daycare centre raised its rates.

When beginning sentences with adverb clauses, unless they are very short, set each clause off with a comma. When the adverb clause follows the main clause, however, we usually do not use a comma (except with the subordinating conjunctions *although, though,* and *even though*). Here are several examples:

1. ***Because*** her daycare centre just raised its hourly rate, Tammy is worried about childcare costs.

2. ***If*** the bus does not arrive on time, Fabiola will be late.

HINT

For more on adverb clauses, see Chapter 12.

3. **_When_ we get to the used car lot, let me do the talking. (comma needed)**

4. **Let me do the talking _when_ we get to the used car lot. (no comma needed because the adverb clause follows the main clause)**

Refer to the Subordinating Conjunctions list on page 128 for words that begin adverb clauses. As with coordinating conjunctions, you should choose the subordinator that accurately conveys your meaning. Often, several choices will work equally well. For example, we could say, "_Because_ (_Since_ or _Now that_) everyone is here, we will begin."

ACTIVITY 10.6 Subordinating with Adverb Clauses

Fill in the blanks in the following sentences with clauses that work with the given subordinating conjunction. To be sure you have written a subordinate clause, underline the <u>verb</u> in each subordinate clause twice and the <u>subject</u> once.

EXAMPLE: **Wherever** _you decide to host the party,_ **be sure to let me know.**

1. When _____, it will be a shocker!

2. The offence was doing well until _____.

3. Although _____, Thiago still cares a great deal for her.

4. Dale bought an electric lawnmower so that _____.

5. After _____, the temperature drops rapidly.

6. If _____, its oil wealth will be exploited and its people will be left in poverty.

HINT

Remember to use a comma only to set off adverb clauses that _begin_ sentences—unless the clause uses _although, though,_ or _even though._

Using Adjective Clauses

Almost as useful as adverb clauses for subordinating ideas within sentences are **adjective clauses**, also known as relative clauses, which generally begin with the relative pronouns _who, which,_ or _that_. While adverb clauses work as adverbs (telling _when, why, where, how,_ and _to what degree or extent_), adjective clauses work as adjectives, meaning that they describe nouns and pronouns, answering the questions _which one; how many;_ and _what kind, shape, colour, texture,_ or _condition_. We use _who_ to refer to people and _which/that_ to refer to objects, ideas, and animals.

Adjective clauses help compress information, making sentences more economical and fluid. Adjective clauses may be _essential_ or _non-essential_ to the meaning of a sentence. Here are several examples:

HINT

For more on essential versus non-essential adjective clauses, see Chapter 12.

NON-ESSENTIAL ADJECTIVE CLAUSES

1. **Many Canadian citizens think of Africa as a single country. ~~Africa~~ is actually a continent with 53 nations.**

2. **Many Canadian citizens think of Africa, <u>which is actually a continent with 53 nations</u>, as a single country.**

Sentence 2 eliminates repetition of the word _Africa_ from **Sentence 1** and replaces it with the relative pronoun _which_ to create the non-essential adjective clause. The _which_ clause subordinates the information about Africa being a continent, shifting the writer's emphasis to the misperception by people that Africa is a single country.

HINT

Non-essential clauses are an excellent structure for _writing_ as in **Sentence 2**. However, when _speaking_, the repetition in **Sentence 1** is easier for the listener to comprehend.

ESSENTIAL ADJECTIVE CLAUSES

1. **The man is my father. ~~The man~~ is kneeling by the tree.**

2. **The man <u>who is kneeling by the tree</u> is my father.**

Sentence 2 replaces the words *the man* from **Sentence 1** with the relative pronoun *who*, which begins the adjective clause describing *the man*. If you imagine that there could be several men close by, then it is clear that the reader or listener needs the description of a "kneeling man" to identify who among the men is the father. The adjective clause is, therefore, essential.

3. **The hot air balloon is ahead in the race. ~~The hot air balloon~~ is covered with stars.**

4. **The hot air balloon *that is covered with stars* is ahead in the race.**

Sentence 4 replaces the second *hot air balloon* from **Sentence 3** with the relative pronoun *that*, which begins the adjective clause describing *hot air balloon*. Without the clause "that is covered with stars," we can't know which balloon is winning the race.

The underlined adjective clauses in both **Sentences 2 and 4** are essential to the meaning of the main part of the sentence, so they are *not* enclosed with commas.

ACTIVITY 10.7 Subordinating with Adjective Clauses

Fill in the blanks in the following sentences with an appropriate adjective clause. The subject of each of these clauses is the relative pronoun (*who/which/ that*) that begins it. Double-underline the <u>verb</u> in each clause.

EXAMPLE: **My parents,** *who moved to Stratford recently,* **are coming to visit.**

1. The Desmarais family has a charitable foundation _____.

2. In the twenty-first century, many people have come to rely on their computers, _____.

3. Cynthia Dale is one of the judges for a new TV talent show _____ _____

4. The light bulb, _____, has been both a blessing and a curse, allowing people to extend their day far into the night.

5. Peter Mansbridge, _____, has had a long and distinguished career as CBC's news anchor.

6. The iPhone has changed the cellphone market; now everyone wants a phone _____

HINT

That is the correct relative pronoun for an essential clause when you are referring to an object, and *which* is used for non-essential clauses.

HINT

Note that commas are used to set off non-essential clauses but not essential clauses.

Avoiding Excessive Subordination

As with over-coordination, over-subordination can be too much of a good thing. Sometimes we put more ideas into a sentence than the reader can sort out. When this happens, writing becomes overly dense and hard to understand. The easy solution to the problem is simply to "unpack" a few of the sentences, often by splitting them into two or even three parts. Here is an example of overly subordinated writing followed by a revision (subordinating words are italicized):

DRAFT

When people become concerned about their effect on the environment, *which* is happening more and more frequently, many of them begin to wonder about the cleaning products *that* they are using in their homes, products *that* include

commercial cleaners *that* are to a greater or lesser extent environmentally unfriendly and toxic to humans as well, *namely*, chlorine, ammonia, phosphates, and alkyphenol ethoxylates, *which* are harmful to people *as well as* animals *when* the chemicals run down the drain; but one solution to this problem is to use natural cleaning agents, such as white vinegar, lemon juice, and baking soda for surface cleaning, scouring tough stains, or cleaning windows *because* these substances are non-toxic substitutes, just a few of many *that* you can use in keeping your house clean.

REVISION

When people become concerned about their effect on the environment, many wonder about their home cleaning products. Most commercial cleaners are environmentally unfriendly and toxic to humans as well. For example, chlorine, ammonia, phosphates, and alkyphenol ethoxylates are all harmful to people. Animals also suffer *when* these chemicals run down the drain. One solution to this problem is to use natural cleaning agents for surface cleaning, scouring tough stains, or cleaning windows. White vinegar, lemon juice, and baking soda are just a few of the non-toxic substitutes *that* you can use to keep your house clean.

Notice that aside from being clearer, the revision is also shorter and more concise than the draft without having sacrificed any ideas from the original.

ACTIVITY 10.8 WORKING TOGETHER: Reducing Excessive Coordination and Subordination

Working as a group or in pairs, revise this paragraph on a separate sheet of paper to reduce—but not eliminate—both coordination and subordination; your goal is to make the paragraph more readable. As you rewrite sentences, you may have to cut unneeded words, but keep all main points from the original. Read the revised passage out loud.

Teaching Responsibility as the Ability to Respond

The Native American purpose in life is growth, understanding, and living in harmony, and taking responsibility for the Past, the Present, and the Future. Responding to the Past means honouring traditions of ancestors, and their wisdom, and honouring the Sacred Medicine Objects that have guarded and guided their collective path, and then passing the wisdom on to their children. Responding to the Present involves seeking beauty in every moment of the day, and using gifts, talents, and abilities for the greater good of all, and honouring all life forms can be achieved by having gratitude for every blessing of life and fostering joy in their hearts. To understand the Future, they strive to understand the Present and realize that the survival and well-being of the next seven generations depends upon every thought and action taken now, and looking to the future with hope, they know that we will all need to learn how to grow food, to use healing plants, and to care for each other.

> **HINT**
>
> Think about subordinating conjunctions (*because, if, when,* etc.), relative pronouns (*who, which, that*), and coordinating conjunctions (*and, but*) to signal which sentence parts to focus on.

ACTIVITY 10.9 Use Conjunctions—Coordinating and Subordinating

Choose your own topic and write a paragraph using what you have learned about coordinating and subordinating conjunctions. Try using five of each.

Chapter Summary

1. There are four types of conjunctions: coordinating conjunctions, correlative conjunctions, conjunctive adverbs, and subordinating conjunctions.

2. Coordinating conjunctions (*and, but, or, so, yet, for, nor*) show that parts of a sentence are equal. When placed between main clauses, coordinating conjunctions use a comma before them.

3. Correlative conjunctions (example: *both . . . and*) come in pairs to link parts of sentences that are grammatically equivalent.

4. Conjunctive adverbs (example: *therefore*) are words often used to link main clauses. When used between main clauses, conjunctive adverbs are preceded with a semicolon and followed by a comma.

5. Subordinating conjunctions (example: *because*) are words used to begin adverb clauses. When adverb clauses begin sentences, they require a comma; but a comma is not required when the adverb clause comes after a main clause.

6. Coordination in writing balances sentence parts using coordinating conjunctions (*and, but, or, so, yet, for, nor*).

7. Main clauses connected by a coordinating conjunction require a comma to separate the clauses.

8. Subordination de-emphasizes one sentence part in order to emphasize another.

9. Subordinating conjunctions (examples: *because, if, when*) usually signal adverb clauses, which are set off by a comma when the clause begins a sentence. A comma is not necessary when the adverb clause follows the main clause (except with the subordinating conjunctions *although, though,* and *even though*).

10. Adjective clauses are subordinate word groups and may be essential (requiring no comma) or non-essential (requiring a comma). They begin with the relative pronouns *who, which,* and *that*.

Phrases

11

When playing an instrument, a musician needs to indicate, through tempo, pauses, and emphasis, the phrasing of musical bars as they are written. A writer also needs to be aware of how to phrase, but rather than using musical notes, a writer groups words to clarify the relationship between sections of a sentence. In a paragraph, explain how phrases, either in music or in writing, help to construct a whole bar of music or a whole sentence, and, ultimately, help to construct the whole piece. Use examples from a favourite song or poem.

HINT

To review the parts of speech, see Chapters 3–10.

What Are We Trying to Achieve and Why?

Having worked with parts of speech in Chapter 3, you know how important verbs and nouns are to make meaning in a sentence. You also know that modifiers give colour and clarity to nouns and verbs to make sentences more interesting. In this chapter, we will look more closely at how words function in groups—as nouns, adjectives, and adverbs—to form **phrases**.

Whereas a **clause** must have both a subject and a verb, a **phrase** may have a subject or a verb form, but not both. Because phrases can work as nouns, adjectives, or adverbs, knowing these parts of speech will help you identify, construct, and punctuate phrases to make your writing more readable.

We have discussed the **noun phrase** (a noun with modifiers in front of it; for example, *a tired student, the red backpack*) and the **verb phrase** (a main verb with its helpers; for example, *will be going, should have gone*); but now we want to look more closely at several other phrases. In this chapter, we will further explore the six types of phrases that are fundamental to our writing: **prepositional, infinitive, participial, gerund, absolute,** and **appositive.**

L011.1

Prepositional Phrases

HINT

For more on prepositions, see Chapter 9.

A **prepositional phrase** begins with a preposition (*in, on, with, during*) and ends with a noun (or words working as a noun) or pronoun. Prepositional phrases function in a sentence as adjectives (adding description or telling *who, which one, what kind,* or *how many*) or adverbs (telling *when, where, why, how,* or *to what extent or degree*). We identify these phrases just as we did single adjectives and adverbs. Note the following examples:

ADJECTIVE PHRASES

1. The **backpack** *with* the lime green crest is Jim's. (tells which one)

2. The **man** *on* the plane told me my fortune. (tells which one)

3. Celia made a reservation for a **party** *of* three. (tells how many)

4. The **jalapeno** is Art's favourite *of* all peppers to add to a salad. (tells what kind)

ADVERB PHRASES

5. Richard accidentally **injured** a friend *in* his eye. (tells where)

6. The accident **happened** *during* rush hour. (tells when)

7. The victim **was transported** to the hospital *with* great speed. (tells how)

We use prepositional phrases more often than any other phrase. The adverb form is often easy to move, allowing greater sentence variety and increasing clarity and emphasis. For example, we could recast **sentence 7** like this:

7a. *With* great speed, the victim **was transported** to the hospital. (tells how)

The following chart lists many common prepositions; some consist of more than one word. Notice that some prepositions can work as other parts of speech. For example, *for* can also be a coordinating conjunction. *Since, until, after,* and *because* are often used as subordinating conjunctions.

English Review Note

Certain prepositions follow adjectives and verbs by convention, forming idiomatic phrases. When we substitute a different preposition, the phrase becomes non-standard English. Memorize phrases that are new to you or that your instructor marks on your papers.

PREPOSITIONS

LOCATION			OTHER USES	
above	behind	off	about	in addition to
across	below	on	according to	in place of
after	beneath	onto	as	in spite of
against	beside	out (out of)	aside from	instead of
ahead of	between	outside	as well as	like
along	beyond	over	because of	of
amid	by	past	by way of	regarding
among	down	through	despite	since
around	from	toward	due to	till
at	in	under	during	until
atop	inside	up	except (except for)	with
before	into	upon	for	without

Infinitives (*to* + a verb: *to jog*) can be mistakenly identified as prepositional phrases, and phrasal verbs——verbs with a preposition attached (*pick up, call on, check out*)—can also be mistaken for prepositional phrases.

ACTIVITY 11.1 Identifying Prepositional Phrases

Circle the prepositions that begin prepositional phrases and underline each entire prepositional phrase (there may be more than one) in the following sentences. Watch out for infinitives (always beginning with *to*), which are not prepositional phrases.

EXAMPLE: In a ditch along the roadside, we saw several broken beer bottles.

1. Instead of driving by the mess, we stopped to clean it up.

2. One way to remember that Lake Superior is the northernmost of the Great Lakes is to recall that on a map, it sits above the other lakes.

3. In the past ten years, malaria in Peru has grown from a handful of cases to more than 100 000.

4. When spring creeps in from the south, crocuses and daffodils are among the first flowers to emerge from the soil.

5. To complete the deal, Jeffrey had to go to the west end of town to pick up a black leather bag with a lock on it.

6. Because of their fighting, neither of the brothers was allowed to go to the game.

Infinitive Phrases

L011.2

Infinitives, along with gerund and participial phrases, are called **verbals**, meaning that they are a verb form with a sense of action, but they are incomplete verbs. Infinitives and **infinitive phrases** can <u>never</u> be the main verb in a sentence.

Infinitives are usually marked by the word *to* in front of any base verb—for instance, *to sleep, to live, to swim*—and so they are easy to spot in a sentence. To form an infinitive phrase, combine the infinitive with another word or phrase: *to sleep* for a week (a prepositional phrase following the infinitive), *to live* each day (a noun phrase after the infinitive), *to swim* bravely (an infinitive modified by an adverb). Infinitives work as adjectives, adverbs, or nouns, as in the examples that follow:

ADJECTIVE

1. Peter has several new **paintings** *to sell today.* (underlined phrase tells which paintings)

ADVERB

2. Hannah **joined** the group *to become* lead singer. (underlined phrase tells why she joined)

As with the adverb prepositional phrase, the infinitive adverb form can often be moved from one part of a sentence to another to add flexibility to your writing. For example, we could recast the previous sentence like this:

2b. *To become* lead singer, Hannah **joined** the group.

Introductory adverb infinitive phrases require a comma.

NOUN

3. *To succeed* at his profession is **Simon's primary focus.** (underlined phrase is the sentence subject)

When noun infinitive phrases follow verbs like *hear, let, see, help, make,* and *watch,* the *to,* even though it is part of the infinitive, is dropped:

We all saw him *(to) help* the elderly woman out of her car.

Also, the *to* may be dropped from infinitive phrases in a list, after the first one:

Jackie learned early in life *to be* polite to strangers, *(to)* care for her friends, and *(to)* love her family.

ACTIVITY 11.2 Identifying Infinitive Phrases

Circle the infinitives and underline the infinitive phrases in the following sentences. Watch out for prepositional phrases that begin with *to,* which are not infinitive phrases but may be *included* within the infinitive phrase.

EXAMPLE: To listen to all of Megan's complaints would take all day.

1. To avoid repeating past mistakes, we need to know history.
2. Malaria, once thought to be under control, now threatens half the planet.
3. To feel needed is psychologically important to all human beings.
4. To read David Suzuki is to be reminded that people are supposed to protest when they feel that politicians are not addressing long-term issues.
5. Many people want to visit Stanley Park to walk among giant red cedar trees that have been alive longer than Canada has been a nation.
6. The question is how to do the best job of managing our forests for everyone.

Participial Phrases

Participles, like infinitives, have a sense of action but are incomplete verbs, never able to stand as the main verb in a sentence. Like participles, **participial phrases** always function as adjectives.

As single-word modifiers, participles might look like this: *dancing* monkeys, *smiling* faces, *cooked* roast, or *worn* fleece. Here are several examples of participial phrases within sentences:

PRESENT PARTICIPIAL PHRASE

1. *Skating* across the pond, **Marquita** heard the ice crack beneath her.

2. **Ozzie** yelled, "Get off the ice!", *waving* for his sister to come back to shore.

3. Fortunately, **a couple** *jogging* past the pond saw the problem and headed out to rescue Marquita.

In **sentence 2**, note the prepositional phrases and the infinitive phrase within the participial phrase: waving (for his sister) (to come back) (to shore).

PAST PARTICIPIAL PHRASE

4. *Frightened* by the narrow escape, **Marquita** sat by her brother as she removed her skates.

5. **Ozzie,** *shaken* but acting unconcerned, laughed and said that it was no big deal.

6. Marquita made Ozzie promise not to tell their parents because she didn't want to be **a child** *punished* for her own bad judgment.

Participial phrases can be *essential* to the meaning of the word they are describing, as they are in **sentences 3 and 6**, or *non-essential*, as they are in the other sentences. When participial phrases are non-essential, they are set off with commas, and they can often be repositioned in a sentence. For example, we might recast **sentences 1 and 4** like this:

1b. **Marquita,** *skating* across the pond, heard the ice crack beneath her.

4b. **Marquita,** *frightened* by the narrow escape, sat by her brother as she removed her skates.

When shifting non-essential participial phrases, be careful that their placement and punctuation do not mislead your reader. Placing the participial phrase next to "her brother," as in the following example, would distort the intended meaning because Marquita (not Ozzie) is supposed to be frightened:

Frightened by the close call, her brother sat by Marquita as she removed her skates.

Be careful not to confuse gerunds (verbals ending in *-ing* but used as nouns) and the progressive verb tenses (*-ing* forms that show ongoing action/being) with participial phrases. Note that the following examples are **not** participial phrases:

Gerund phrase:	Skating on ponds in the winter is fun.
Progressive verb tense:	Marquita is (was) skating across the pond.

HINT

For more information on participles, refer to Chapter 5.

HINT

Non-essential phrases, as in sentences 1, 2, 4, and 5, require a comma. Sentence 2 uses an exclamation point as well as a comma, which is an exceptional combination.

HINT

Essential phrases, as in sentences 3 and 6, do not use a comma.

HINT

Gerund phrases are *nouns*. Progressive verb tenses are *verbs*. Neither of these can be participial phrases, which are used as *adjectives*.

Circle the present participles and underline the participial phrases in the following sentences. Remember that participial phrases are not part of the main verb and always function as adjectives.

> EXAMPLE: Whispering quietly to his friend, Jonathan told him what had happened.

1. Not knowing how to light a fire in the wild, Chris spent a cold night, shivering in his tent.

2. A sick feeling that he had missed the exam woke Ameen early in the morning.

3. Watching his roommate studying hard, David resolved to do the same, pausing only to find out where he had stacked his textbooks back in September.

4. Sophie loved sledding down hills in the winter, but walking home from the park, she usually felt cold and tired.

5. Snoring loudly, John alerted the entire class that he found the lecture dull.

6. Slithering on their bellies is how snakes get around, managing to glide, burrow, swim, and climb quite well.

7. Write three sentences that use a present participial phrase in each. Circle the participle, and underline the phrase. Set off all non-essential participial phrases with commas. Be sure that your phrases are describing the words that you intend.

   a. _____

   b. _____

   c. _____

Circle the past participles and underline the participial phrases in the following sentences. Look for regular past participles ending in -d or -ed and irregular past participles ending in -n or -t. Remember that participial phrases are not part of the main verb and always function as adjectives.

> EXAMPLE: Frustrated by the lack of service, Ella left the store, determined never to shop there again.

1. Irritated at getting a ticket, Ron said, "What, they call parking in a handicapped zone in a blizzard illegal?"

2. The circus once called The Greatest Show on Earth has shrunk to a remnant of its former glory.

3. Faced with a hostile minority in the legislature, the premier was unable to carry out many of her reforms.

4. The pioneer family faced the awful cold of their first Canadian winter, huddled together for warmth in a tight little group.

5. "I've been hit harder," the boxer declared, seemingly unconcerned with his rapidly swelling eye.

6. Gathered by our priest, we listened anxiously to the list of parish closings.

7. Write three sentences that use a past participial phrase in each. Circle the (participle) and underline the phrase. Set off all non-essential participial phrases with commas. Be sure that your phrases are describing the words that you intend.

    a. _____

    b. _____

    c. _____

Gerund Phrases

The **gerund** is a verb form ending in *-ing* that is used as a noun, for example, *bicycling, sailing,* or *leaving.* **Gerund phrases**, the third type of verbal phrase, begin with a gerund and are followed by other words (such as prepositional phrases). They may appear in several places in a sentence. Note the following examples:

1. **Gerund phrase as subject:** *Bicycling on Yonge Street* requires energy and caution.

2. **Gerund phrase as possessive subject:** *Cindy's bicycling in the summer* keeps her fit.

3. **Gerund phrase as subject complement:** One low-impact sport is *bicycling on a well-paved path.*

4. **Gerund phrase as direct object:** My sister loves *bicycling down large hills.*

5. **Gerund phrase as object of preposition:** But sometimes Cindy jogs alone instead *of bicycling with me.*

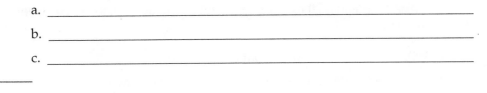

HINT

Try the pronoun replacement test to identify gerunds. If you can substitute a pronoun, the *-ing* word, or phrase, is a gerund.

While the gerund *-ing* looks like a participle, the gerund works as a *noun* rather than an adjective. One way to tell the difference between participles and gerunds is that gerunds can be mentally replaced with a pronoun. When we substitute pronouns for the five previous sentence examples, we have:

Sentence 1: *It* requires energy and caution.

Sentence 2: *It* keeps her fit.

Sentence 3: One low-impact sport is *this.*

Sentence 4: My sister loves *it.*

Sentence 5: But sometimes Cindy jogs alone instead of *this.*

You can see that pronoun replacement works with gerund phrases, but it does *not* work with participial phrases. Contrast the following examples:

Gerund phrase : *Bicycling* 135 kilometres in one day requires strength, persistence, and maybe a bit of craziness.

Participial phrase: *Bicycling* 135 kilometres, Cindy finished the first day of her ride across Essex county.

We can say, "*It* requires strength," but we can't say, "*It,* Cindy finished." The participial phrase tells *about* Cindy, the subject of the sentence, whereas the gerund phrase *is* the subject of the sentence. While the participial phrase requires a comma, the gerund phrase does not.

Watch for single participles, participial phrases, and verbs in the progressive tense, none of which is a gerund phrase. Using pronoun substitution will help you spot the gerund phrases. Remember that gerund phrases do not use commas.

Circle the (gerund) and underline the gerund phrase (there may be more than one) in the following sentences. Remember that the gerund phrase, functioning as a noun, can be replaced by a pronoun.

EXAMPLE: (Scanning) through email is not the most exciting task of Janet's morning.

1. Will you help with handing out the exam booklets?

2. Raising a family takes time, energy, patience, and love.

3. We all appreciated Maria's editing of the manuscript.

4. Megan misses owning her own business.

5. Antonio's dream was becoming an RCMP officer.

6. Keeping thermostats down in the winter and up in the summer is a good practice, saving consumers money and reducing greenhouse gas emissions.

7. Write three sentences that use a gerund phrase in each. Circle the (gerund) and underline the phrase.

a. _____

b. _____

c. _____

L011.5 Absolute Phrases

The **absolute phrase** resembles a participial phrase in that it uses a present (-ing) or past participle (- d/-ed, - n/-t), but it differs in one important respect: a noun or pronoun always precedes the participle. This noun or pronoun is called the subject of the phrase; combined with a participle, it can make the phrase appear to be a clause (which it is not).

Since absolute phrases **lack complete verbs**, they cannot stand on their own as complete sentences. Unless they are joined to an independent clause or rewritten as complete thoughts (e.g., through the addition of the verb *to be*), absolute phrases are sentence fragments.

Absolute phrases describe the rest of the sentence they are attached to, rather than modifying a single word; therefore, they can be in various positions within a sentence. Absolute phrases may also contain other word groups, such as prepositional phrases. Here are several examples with the subjects of the phrases underlined once, the *participles* in italics, and the [absolute phrases] in square brackets:

Absolute Phrases Using Present Participles

1. [His voice *growing* hoarse from the bitter cold,] the quarterback barked out the final play of the game.

2. Jordan listened to the officer's accusations, [her fingers *drumming* nervously on the desk.]

3. [The game (*being*) almost over,] we left early to avoid the crowd.

4. [With his reel *jamming* for the third time,] Ted swore he would give up fishing.

Sentence 1 begins with an absolute phrase that gives extra information about the main clause, describing the quarterback's voice as he calls the play. *The phrase is descriptive, but not necessary to understand the main idea in the sentence.* Note that by adding the helping verb *was* to the absolute phrase, we could rewrite the opening phrase as a stand-alone sentence.

Similarly, the absolute phrase in **sentence 2**, which is placed at the end of the sentence, could be made an independent clause by adding the helping verb *were*.

Sentence 3 shows that *to be* (*being*) can sometimes be omitted in an absolute phrase when its meaning is understood.

Sentence 4 is an example of an absolute phrase beginning with the word *with*, which usually signals a prepositional phrase.

Recognizing and Building Absolute Phrases

To help you recognize and write absolute phrases, remember that a form of *to be* is missing from a stand-alone sentence, thereby reducing the main clause to a phrase. The phrase is then attached with a comma to a main clause. Notice the following examples, which illustrate this change:

1a. His voice was *growing* hoarse from the bitter cold. The quarterback barked out the final play of the game.

1b. His voice was *growing* hoarse from the bitter cold, t The quarterback barked out the final play of the game.

1c. His voice *growing* hoarse from the bitter cold, the quarterback barked out the final play of the game.

Absolute phrases give writers a chance to vary the length and pattern of their sentences. These phrases are especially good at describing action and are often combined with participial phrases to make narrative, and other forms of writing, more interesting. Which of the following examples seems more readable?

2a. Jordan listened to the officer's accusations. She wondered what would happen next. Her fingers drummed nervously on the desk.

2b. Jordan listened to the officer's accusations, *wondering* what would happen

PARTICIPIAL PHRASE

ABSOLUTE PHRASE

next, [her fingers *drumming* nervously on the desk.]

Absolute Phrases Using Past Participles

Absolute phrases can also be formed using past participles by omitting a form of *to be* from a main clause. Past participles for regular verbs end in *-d* or *-ed* (*worked, laughed*) and often end in *-n* or *-t* for irregular verbs (*broken, bought*). Note the following examples (**sentences 1 and 2** with regular verbs and **sentences 3 and 4** with irregular verbs):

1. [The assignment *completed*,] Simone was able to finish watching her movie.

2. Simone relaxed into her recliner, [her legs *crossed* at the ankles and her arms *outstretched*.]

3. [His ID stuck in his wallet,] James apologized and told the cashier to take the next customer.

4. J.P. felt safe for the night, [his shelter in the trees hidden from view.]

ACTIVITY 11.6 Seeing and Writing Absolute Phrases with Present Participles

In the following sentences, underline the <u>absolute phrase,</u> and circle the subject of the absolute phrase. Remember that the absolute phrase is descriptive but not necessary to understand the main idea in the sentence.

EXAMPLE: His hands shaking, the novice wizard tried to recover the pieces of his shattered wand.

1. With his delivery owl missing, Ron Weasley had trouble sending mail.

2. The ship cruised through crystalline waters, three bottlenose dolphins riding the pressure waves off its bow.

3. After our professor broke down, the students sat silent and motionless, wondering what to do next.

4. Its compressor failing, the air conditioner merely blew hot air around the living room.

5. Clichés oozing from every page, Paul's novel proved impossible to read, let alone revise.

6. With flames shooting into the air and sirens wailing on all sides, the news crew pushed inward to question the survivors of the explosion.

7. Write three sentences, each using a present participle in an absolute phrase. Underline the <u>absolute phrase,</u> and circle its subject.

   a. _____

   b. _____

   c. _____

ACTIVITY 11.7 Seeing and Writing Absolute Phrases with Past Participles

In the following sentences, underline the <u>absolute phrase,</u> and circle the past participle. Remember that the absolute phrase is descriptive but not necessary to understand the main idea in the sentence.

EXAMPLE: With Toronto defeated, the Red Sox won another World Series.

1. Both boys were a mess, their hands and arms covered in sticky green melted popsicle.

2. With the bowl of whipped cream shattered on the floor, 5-year-old Nayda stared down at the mess and sobbed.

3. Their work nearly finished, the builders suddenly realized they had not put in a front door.

4. His guilt proven beyond a doubt, Bernie looked to Ken for salvation one last time.

5. With a challenging question finally asked, the candidate smiled charmingly and responded by shifting the blame.

6. The tub filled almost to the top, Roselyn sank down into the warm water with a sigh.

7. Write three sentences, each using a past participle in an absolute phrase. Underline the <u>absolute phrase</u>, and circle the (past participle)

a. _____

b. _____

c. _____

Appositive Phrases

L011.6

The last of the six phrases, the appositive phrase, does not function as an adjective or an adverb, but it does add useful information to a sentence. **Appositive phrases** are word groups that rename or explain a noun or pronoun; they may be thought of as containing a synonym, or "stand-in" word, for a noun or pronoun. Most appositives are non-essential, giving useful but not vital information. Therefore, they should be set off with commas.

Here are several examples with the appositive phrases underlined and the "stand-in" words italicized:

1.	**Noun appositive:**	Mahalia Jackson, <u>a *singer*,</u> began performing at the age of four.
2.	**Noun phrase appositive:**	Mahalia Jackson (<u>perhaps the best gospel *singer* of all time</u>) began performing at the age of four.
3.	**Noun phrase with clause appositive:**	Mahalia Jackson—<u>perhaps the best gospel *singer* of all time and one who was prominent in the civil rights movement in the fifties and sixties</u>—began performing at the age of four.

HINT

Non-essential appositives require commas before and after the phrase; all non-essential materials should be set off with commas.

Sentence 1 contains a single noun appositive, *singer.* This word stands in place of Jackson, giving a small bit of additional information about her. **Sentence 2** offers more information with the modifiers, including the prepositional phrase *of all time.* **Sentence 3** gives the most information.

Notice that non-essential appositives, seen above, can be set off by commas (or parentheses)—or dashes. Parentheses de-emphasize the appositive while dashes highlight it.

Appositives usually follow the word or word phrase they describe, but they can be useful, too, as sentence openers, as in this example:

4.	**Appositive as sentence opener:**	<u>A gospel *singer*,</u> Mahalia Jackson began performing at the age of four.

Because appositives usually contain nouns, they can also be gerunds and infinitives, as in the following examples:

5.	**Gerund appositive:**	Cesar Milan's life work, <u>*training* problem dogs,</u> has brought him international fame.
6.	**Infinitive appositive:**	One of humanity's worst tendencies—<u>*to forget* last year's, last month's, and even yesterday's lessons</u>—was displayed as the oil leak continued.

HINT

Remember that infinitives and gerunds can be (but are not necessarily) appositives. Test each word group by finding the word in the main clause that it expands on.

In **sentence 5**, the gerund *training* provides more specific information about *life work*, and the infinitive *to forget* provides more specific information about *tendencies* in **sentence 6**. Notice that dashes can take the place of paired commas, if the writer wants to emphasize the appositive.

ACTIVITY 11.8 Seeing and Writing Appositive Phrases

Circle the appositive words and underline the appositive phrases in the following sentences. Remember that most appositives are non-essential, giving useful but not vital information. They are *usually* set off by paired commas—or dashes.

> EXAMPLE: Fire ants, aggressive defenders of their colony, will attack intruders large or small.

1. Drake, a well-known Canadian rapper, was born as Aubrey Drake Graham.

2. The symptoms of menopause—hot flashes, night sweats, and mood swings—can be helped through exercise, diet, and relaxation techniques.

3. Antonio has adopted a new life motto—climb every *other* mountain.

4. Hanging on by her fingertips, Jasmine knew that if she achieved her goal—to reach the top of the climbing wall—she would win the bet, $500.

5. We wondered about the beat-up old car, an ancient VW bug with a huge peace sign decaled on the hood and bumper stickers that read "Tree-hugging dirt worshipper."

6. Serena Ryder's newest album, the long-awaited *Harmony*, features the hit single "Stompa."

7. Write three sentences, using an appositive phrase in each. Circle the appositive words, and underline the phrase, setting it off with the required commas.

   a. _____

   b. _____

   c. _____

Chapter Summary

1. Prepositional phrases begin with a preposition (often a word telling location—*in, on, near*) and end with a noun or pronoun. Prepositional phrases function as adjectives or adverbs.

2. Infinitive phrases are one of three types of verbal phrase. They begin with *to* before a base verb (*to sing*) and can function as nouns, adjectives, or adverbs.

3. Participial phrases are another type of verbal phrase. They are recognized by an *-ing* ending on a verb as a present participle (gallop*ing* horses) or a *-d/-ed* ending for the past participle of a regular verb (frighten*ed* children). Participial phrases always function as adjectives.

4. Gerund phrases are the third type of verbal phrase. They begin with a verb form ending in -*ing* (jogg*ing* three times weekly will keep a person in shape). Gerund phrases always function as nouns.

5. Absolute phrases are phrases that contain a participle, present or past, preceded by a noun (subject). These phrases describe the whole sentence to which they are attached.

6. Appositive phrases are word groups that usually follow a noun or pronoun and explain or rename it. Every appositive phrase has a word or word phrase that can take the place of the noun or pronoun that it follows.

Clauses and Sentence Types

People rely on one another to accomplish many tasks, one of which you can see in the accompanying photo. Write a brief paragraph telling either who supports you when you are faced with a challenge or who most relies on you in a difficult situation. In writing, clauses within a sentence help each other out just as people rely on one another.

What Are We Trying to Achieve and Why?

The six types of phrases we worked with in Chapter 11 are crucial sentence parts, adding great flexibility to our writing. However, because phrases do not contain both a subject and verb, they cannot form complete sentences. Phrases rely on **clauses**, which *do* have both a subject and a verb, to complete their meaning. Chapter 12 will help you recognize **main** and **subordinate clauses** and see how they work together to form various **sentence types**.

Clauses

LO12.1

Clauses are critical sentence parts. Without them, we could write only partial sentences, such as, "On our way to the bank." This would leave readers in suspense, wanting to know what happened next. However, when we add a clause to the above phrase, like "<u>we saw</u> a double rainbow," we satisfy the reader's curiosity, completing the thought:

On our way to the bank, we saw a double rainbow.

Main Clauses and Subordinate Clauses

Clauses are of two sorts, main and subordinate. The **main** (or independent) **clause** contains a subject, a verb, and a complete thought, so it can function as a stand-alone (simple) sentence.

A **subordinate** (or dependent) **clause** has a subject and a verb but lacks a complete thought and so cannot stand alone. Like a phrase, it depends on and must be attached to a main clause to form a sentence.

Notice how the main and subordinate clauses below can easily be combined:

1. **Subordinate clause**   If enough toxic <u>runoff</u> <u>enters</u> a stream

   +

   Main clause   <u>It</u> <u>will kill</u> the <u>river</u>.

   Combined clauses   If enough toxic runoff enters a stream, it will kill the river.

2. **Main clause**   <u>This</u> <u>is beginning</u> to happen in Alberta to the Bow River.

   +

   Subordinate clause   <u>Which</u> in the past <u>has provided</u> great fishing and good drinking water for nearby towns.

   Combined clauses   This is beginning to happen in Alberta to the Bow River, which in the past has provided great fishing and good drinking water for nearby towns.

We will focus next on three kinds of subordinate clauses——noun, adjective, and adverb——which work just as their names suggest.

Subordinate Noun Clauses

Noun clauses are subordinate clauses that work as single nouns and noun phrases do. They are often used as subjects, as in the following examples:

1. **Single-word subject:** Harold's <u>comment</u> <u>pleased</u> his sister.
2. **Noun clause subject:** *<u>What</u> Harold said about his wife* <u>pleased</u> his sister.

Noun clauses are useful because they give more information than single nouns. In **sentence 1**, we learn that the single-word subject (*comment*) pleased Harold's sister, but we don't know why. However, in **sentence 2**, we find out through the noun clause that it was "what Harold said *about his wife*" that pleased his sister.

> **HINT**
>
> Subordinate clauses standing alone are sentence fragments.

> **English Review Note**
>
> In some languages, a subordinate clause can stand alone; in English, it must combine with a main clause to form a complete sentence.

Here are some example sentences that use noun clauses in other ways:

1. **Direct object:**   The polls showed <u>that two-thirds of the country wanted to end the war.</u>

2. **Object of preposition:**   Sanjay hopes to protect the habitat for <u>whatever animals still live in the estuary.</u>

3. **Complement:**   The 1960s revolution in Chile was exactly <u>what economists were hoping for.</u>

HINT

Use the pronoun replacement test to identify noun clauses.

In each of the preceding sentences (just as with gerund phrases), notice that the noun clauses can be replaced with a pronoun. For example, in **sentence 1**, we could say, "The polls showed *it*." For **sentence 2**, "Sanjay hopes to protect the habitat for *them*."

However, this pronoun replacement method does not work with adjective clauses, which can be confused with noun clauses. Notice the difference between the following examples:

Noun clause: Some health experts say *that* <u>cold temperatures are perfectly safe to exercise in.</u>

Adjective clause: The researchers published studies *that* <u>back up this assertion.</u>

While we can say, "Some health experts say *it*," we cannot say, "The researchers published studies *it*." This replacement test will help you distinguish between noun and adjective clauses.

For **sentence 3**, the noun clause as a complement completes the sentence. Without it, the sentence would be impossible to understand.

When noun clauses used as direct objects begin with the word *that*, writers often omit *that*. Sometimes this can make it difficult to see where the noun clause begins.

Deleted *that*:   I thought (<u>that</u>) <u>the game was almost over.</u>

The following is a list of common cue words that begin noun clauses:

CUE WORDS FOR NOUN CLAUSES						
how	that	whatever	where	which	whoever	whose
if	what	when	whether	who	whom	why

ACTIVITY 12.1   Seeing and Writing Noun Clauses

Using the preceding chart, fill in the blanks with a cue word that makes sense to you, and then underline the entire <u>noun clause</u>.

EXAMPLE: Charlene insisted *that* <u>she was right,</u> even though everyone else argued *that* <u>she was wrong.</u>

1. Robert didn't want _____ his friends did from life, which is why he was studying forestry.

2. Emon explained _____ the rock came to break the kitchen window.

3. _____ John needed to switch his major was clear to him.

4. The whole class decided _____ locating noun clauses wasn't all that difficult.

5. _____ will bring the pies to Thanksgiving dinner has not yet been decided.

6. Justin wasn't responsible for _____ his friend's dog wandered.

7. Write three sentences that use a noun clause. Circle the (cue word), and underline the clause.

   a. _____

   b. _____

   c. _____

Subordinate Adjective Clauses

Adjective clauses (or relative clauses) work as single adjectives and adjective phrases do, describing nouns and pronouns.

1. **Single adjective:**   Kareem needs a *quiet* room to sleep well.

2. **Adjective clause:**   Kareem needs a room *that is quiet* to sleep well.

Both **sentences 1** and **2** tell what kind of room Kareem needs, a quiet one. Notice that the single adjective, *quiet*, is in front of the noun it describes, while the clause, *that is quiet*, follows the noun.

Usually adjective clauses begin with one of the following relative pronouns, using *who* to refer to people and *which/that* to refer to animals and things.

RELATIVE PRONOUNS: ADJECTIVE CLAUSE CUE WORDS		
who	which	that

Also, adjective clauses can begin with several other cue words, including *whose, whom, when, where,* and *why.*

To punctuate adjective clauses correctly, you need to determine whether they are *essential* to the meaning of the sentence.

ESSENTIAL ADJECTIVE CLAUSES

If a clause is **essential,** that is, if removing it would alter the main idea of the sentence, you do *not* use a comma, as in the following examples:

1. **Jack Freed is an entrepreneur <u>*who* established his clothing business in Windsor, Ontario.</u>**

2. **Windsor is a city <u>*that* offers friendly, loyal, hardworking people.</u>**

In **sentence 1**, we don't know why we should be interested in Freed until reading the adjective clause and finding out that he is the entrepreneur who brought a business to a small city. **Sentence 2** uses the adjective clause to tell something important about Windsor. Therefore, the clauses are essential and *not* set off with a comma. We often use the relative pronouns *who* and *that* to signal essential adjective clauses.

NON-ESSENTIAL ADJECTIVE CLAUSES

Non-essential adjective clauses can be cut from a sentence without significantly changing its meaning, so we set them off with commas, whether they appear in the middle of the main clause or at the end, as in the following examples:

1. **Karla Schonhardt, <u>*who* wanted to be an astronaut as a child,</u> is now a bank president.**

2. **In her teens, Karla began to develop vertigo, <u>*which* changed her mind about career options.</u>**

> **HINT**
>
> Essential clauses do not use commas.

> **HINT**
>
> Non-essential adjective clauses require commas.

Sentence 1 emphasizes that Schonhardt is a bank president but adds a less important comment about her childhood dream. *Who* and *which* clauses that immediately follow proper nouns are non-essential. **Sentence 2** uses the *which* clause to add interesting but non-essential information about Schonhardt's vertigo problem.

To avoid confusing adjective clauses with noun clauses, you can use the pronoun replacement test we practised in the preceding section on noun clauses, as in the following:

3. **Adjective clause:** Windsor is a city *that* attracts friendly, loyal, hardworking people.

4. **Noun clause:** Jack Freed says that Windsor is a city of friendly, loyal, hardworking people.

It makes no sense to say, "Windsor is a town *it*"; therefore, the clause in **sentence 3** is *not* a noun clause. However, *it* may be substituted for the underlined clause in **sentence 4**——"Jack Freed says *it*"——so this clause is a noun clause.

ACTIVITY 12.2 Seeing and Writing Adjective Clauses

In the following sentences, underline the adjective clauses and circle each relative pronoun (*who, which, that*). Indicate in the space following the sentence whether the adjective clause is *essential* or *non-essential*.

EXAMPLE: Barry Bonds, who broke Hank Aaron's home-run record, has been indicted on charges of perjury in relation to steroid use. *Non-essential*.

1. Some police officers who have served as soldiers in Afghanistan are now having difficulty adjusting to the use of force with civilian lawbreakers.

2. There are some passengers who have had to wait in their plane for up to eight hours.

3. Deric decided to return to college because he is no longer happy with his roofing job, which keeps him outside in extreme weather.

4. Cyclone Sidr is the one that killed 52 people in Bangladesh.

5. Rico saw that after paying for dinner he would have only five dollars left, which he hoped would cover the tip.

6. The young peregrine falcon that was following the mallards downriver looked hungry.

7. Write three sentences that use an adjective clause. Circle the cue word and underline the clause.

   a. _____

   b. _____

   c. _____

HINT

Use the *it* or *them (for noun clauses)* and *which (for adjective clauses)* replacement tests to be sure that you are writing adjective rather than noun clauses. Use commas with non-essential adjective clauses.

Subordinate Adverb Clauses

Adverb clauses function as single adverbs and adverb phrases do, describing verbs, adjectives, and other adverbs. They give information about a main clause, telling *when, why, where, how,* and *to what extent,* as in the following sentences:

1. **_When_ Gabrielle arrived, her friends shouted, "Happy birthday!"** (when)

2. **_Because_ Lauren had a cold, she could not focus well during the test.** (why)

3. **_Where_ birds of paradise gather, colourful plumage dazzles the eye.** (where)

4. **_Until_ the balloon almost popped, Ho San kept filling it with water.** (extent)

Adverb clauses, like other adverbs, can often be moved in a sentence. For example, we could reverse the subordinate and main clauses in any of the preceding examples:

3b. **Colourful plumage dazzles the eye where birds of paradise gather.**

COMMAS WITH ADVERB CLAUSES

When *beginning* a sentence with an adverb clause, set the clause off with a comma. (See the above **sentences 1–4.**)

However, if the adverb clause *follows* the main clause, a comma usually is not needed. (See **sentence 3b.**) Exceptions are *though, although,* and *even though,* which show concession; these words usually use a comma even when following a main clause. Here is an example:

> **Colourful plumage dazzles the eye where birds of paradise gather, _although_ the birds often take cover in thick rainforest.**

English Review Note

Be sure not to use the words *although* and *but* in the same sentence.

SUBORDINATING CONJUNCTIONS WITH ADVERB CLAUSES

Adverb clauses always begin with cue words called **subordinating conjunctions,** which you can see in the following list:

SUBORDINATING CONJUNCTIONS: ADVERB CLAUSE CUE WORDS				
after	because	in order that	till (less formal than *until*)	where
although	before	now that	unless	whereas
as	even if	once	until	wherever
as if	even though	since	when	whether
as long as	if	though	whenever	while

English Review Note

Review this chart and learn the differences between the adverb clause cue words, especially similar-sounding ones such as *even though* and *even if*.

Some of these words can also introduce prepositional phrases (*after, before, until*), noun clauses (*when* and *where*), and adjective clauses (*when* and *where*). Notice that the underlined word groups in the following sentences are *not* adverb clauses:

1. **Prepositional phrase:** After several minutes, the class decided that the professor was not coming.

2. **Noun clause:** Glenda is the one who saw where the accident happened.

3. **Adjective clause:** Byron would never forget the awful moment when he lost his swimming trunks after a dive from the high board.

To avoid confusing adverb clauses with noun and adjective clauses, remember that most adverb clauses can be shifted within a sentence; and they tell about a verb: *when, where, why, how,* or *to what degree or extent* something was done.

Using the preceding chart, fill in the blanks in the following sentences with a cue word that makes sense to you; then underline the entire <u>adverb clause.</u>

EXAMPLE: *Because* **the foundation has cracks**, the house floods *when* <u>it rains.</u>

1. _____ we learn from history, we are doomed to repeat it.

2. _____ they have changed the way comprehensive exams are done, the grad students are having much less difficulty in passing them.

3. _____ you are visiting Prince Edward Island, be sure to see the home of *Anne of Green Gables*, _____ it takes you out of your way a bit.

4. _____ money is not showering from the heavens, there are still ways to qualify for scholarships, grants, and low-interest student loans.

5. _____ Jason found nothing to watch on TV, he decided to kayak on Georgian Bay, _____ it was a six-hour drive from his home.

6. _____ Caleb almost passed out, he kept inflating his air mattress _____ Emma just unrolled her Thermarest and let it self-inflate.

7. Write three sentences beginning with an adverb clause. Remember to use commas to separate the introductory non-essential clause from the main clause.

   a. _____

   b. _____

   c. _____

L012.2

Sentence Types

Considering the parts of speech, phrases, and clauses, you know most of the basic sentence grammar you need to write clear, readable, and correct sentences. Now you simply combine this knowledge to work with sentence types.

There are only four grammatical **sentence types** in English. Each is based on the clauses it contains: **simple, compound, complex,** and **compound-complex.**

Simple Sentences

A simple sentence contains *one* main clause with *no* subordinate clauses. It may be short and truly "simple" (as in "uncomplicated"), or it may have several phrases that lengthen it. Here are several examples of simple sentences with the <u>verbs</u> underlined twice and the <u>subjects</u> once:

1. **Darren <u>wants</u> a university education.**

2. **Darren and his <u>friends</u> <u>want</u> a university education.**

3. **Darren and his <u>friends</u> <u>want</u> a university education and a better place to live.**

Sentence 1 has a single subject, *Darren*, and a single verb, *wants*. But we could add another subject, *friends*, as in **sentence 2**. Also, we could add another complement to the sentence completion, *a university education*, and include *a better place to live*, as in **sentence 3**. Simple sentences can be short or long and may contain commas. However, they have only *one* main clause and *no* subordinate clauses.

Compound Sentences

A compound sentence adds *one or more* main clauses to a simple sentence. This creates a sentence with two (or more) sets of subjects and verbs (*main clauses*) that are usually joined with a coordinating conjunction like *and* or *but* and a comma——or a semicolon if the conjunction is omitted. Compound sentences can be short or long, but they do not contain a subordinate clause. Here are several examples with the <u>verbs</u> underlined twice, the <u>subjects</u> underlined once, and the *coordinating conjunction* italicized:

1. **Rowena sleeps deeply, *but* she only gets six hours of rest a night.**

2. **Rowena sleeps deeply, *but* she only gets six hours of rest a night, *and* the lack of sleep leaves her tired.**

Sentence 1 has two main clauses with two sets of subjects and verbs. If we wanted to create two separate sentences, we could put a period after *deeply* and capitalize *but*. **Sentence 2** shows a compound sentence with three main clauses.

HINT

Compound sentences require a comma before a coordinating conjunction linking two main clauses.

Complex Sentences

Complex sentences are not necessarily any more "complex" (as in "complicated") than simple or compound sentences, but they do **contain another kind of clause——the subordinate, or dependent, clause (adverb, adjective, or noun).** This means that a complex sentence has *one* main clause and *one or more* subordinate clauses and often phrases. In the following examples, the <u>verbs</u> are double-underlined, the <u>subjects</u> are underlined, and the *cue words* are italicized:

    MAIN CLAUSE   ADVERB CLAUSE
1. **Ross brings his daughter to class with him *when* her school is closed.**

                             ADJECTIVE CLAUSE
2. **Ross sometimes brings his daughter, *who* is six years old, to class with him.**

                             NOUN CLAUSE
3. **Bringing a child to class in this situation is *what* some students must do.**

       ADJECTIVE CLAUSE   ADVERB CLAUSE
4. **Ross, *who* loves his daughter, brings her to class with him *when* her school is closed.**

Sentence 1 begins with a main clause and attaches a subordinate adverb clause beginning with *when*. **Sentence 2** includes an adjective clause beginning with *who*. **Sentence 3** includes a noun clause, starting with *what*, within the main clause. **Sentence 4** shows a complex sentence with more than one subordinate clause—— in this case, adjective and adverb clauses.

HINT

In most cases, no comma is needed to separate an adverb clause placed *after* a main clause.

Compound-Complex Sentences

The **compound-complex sentence** simply combines the two preceding sentence types, the compound and the complex. This sentence type, then, **must have *two or more* main clauses with *one or more* subordinate clauses.** As with other sentence types, any clause may include phrases. Notice the following examples with the <u>verbs</u> underlined twice, the <u>subjects</u> underlined once, and the *cue words* italicized:

    MAIN CLAUSE   ADJECTIVE CLAUSE
1. **Ashley recently learned about "green roofs," *which* are roofs covered in soil and**

                    MAIN CLAUSE
    vegetation, *and* she was intrigued by the idea.

        ADVERB CLAUSE   MAIN CLAUSE
2. ***Because* she was interested, Ashley searched the Internet, *and* she soon**

    MAIN CLAUSE
    found out more about green roofs.

3. **MAIN CLAUSE**   **NOUN CLAUSE**

   3. <u>Ashley</u> <u>discovered</u> *that* <u>green roofs</u> <u>reduce</u> carbon dioxide, <u>provide</u> wildlife habitat,

                                      MAIN CLAUSE   **NOUN CLAUSE**

      and <u>decrease</u> heating and cooling bills, *so* <u>she</u> <u>wondered</u> *what* <u>cities</u> in Canada

      might <u>be building</u> them.

       MAIN CLAUSE   **ADVERB CLAUSE**   **NOUN CLAUSE**

   4. <u>She</u> <u>was</u> pleased *when* <u>she</u> <u>learned</u> *that* her home <u>city</u> of Vancouver <u>had</u> the most

                                              MAIN CLAUSE

      green roof area, with 100 000 square metres planted, *and* <u>she</u> soon <u>found out</u> *that*

       NOUN CLAUSE

      <u>Vancouver</u> <u>has</u> 200 000 more square metres planned.

     Sentence 1 adds an adjective clause to two main clauses, while **sentence 2** adds an adverb clause. **Sentence 3** shows that there can easily be more than one subordinate clause of the same type. **Sentence 4** shows that several kinds of subordinate clauses are often used together in a compound-complex sentence.

HINT

Remember that the type of sentence depends on the *kind* (main or subordinate) and *number* of clauses it contains. Reviewing the subordinate clause cue words will help you identify the clauses.

ACTIVITY 12.4   WORKING TOGETHER: Identifying and Writing Sentence Types

Working in pairs or small groups, read each sentence aloud and write the clause name (main, noun, adjective, or adverb) in the blank mid-sentence. At the end of the sentence, name the sentence type: simple, compound, complex, or compound-complex.

   EXAMPLE: **Brenna is studying to be a marine biologist,** *main clause* **but she wonders** *main clause* **if she can survive the math requirement,** *noun clause* **even though she did well in math in high school.** *adverb clause* (*compound-complex*)

1. When writers learn some basic sentence grammar, _____ they become more confident in their writing._____

   _____

2. Wayne looked at the classified ad for telemarketers _____and he wondered whether the $15 an hour would be worth it. _____

   _____

3. Only 9 percent of Canadian farmers are under 35, _____ but 25 percent are over 65. _____

   _____

4. Ultralight backpackers usually know _____ what they carry to the gram, _____ and they may trim weight in imaginative ways, such as cutting most of the handle from their toothbrushes. _____

   _____

5. Will the fighting in North Korea continue indefinitely _____or will the involvement of the international community finally make a difference? _____

   _____

6. Young Canadian cellist David Eggert, who is known for his performance of music by Debussy, _____ will be heard this weekend on CBC Radio 2's "In Concert," _____ so John and I will be listening. _____

   _____

7. Write a compound sentence, a complex sentence, and a compound-complex sentence. Write the name of the clause at the end of it (main, adverb, adjective, or noun). Use punctuation thoughtfully; review punctuation guidelines, if necessary.

   a. Compound: _____

   _____

   b. Complex: _____

   _____

   c. Compound-complex: _____

   _____

   _____

HINT

Remember that clauses can be brief, are often embedded within one another, and are set off by commas when they are non-essential but not when they are essential.

Chapter Summary: A Writer's Basic Sentence Grammar

Having practised the basic sentence parts in chapters 11 and 12, you now know how to control sentences. Words (parts of speech) build phrases; phrases grow into, or are attached to, clauses; and clauses are sentences or are attached to them. Knowing how words work——to express action or state of being, to name, describe, or link—you can now confidently revise your sentences and create variety to best express your meaning.

The following charts summarize key sentence parts and serve as this chapter's summary:

English Review Note

Practise your sentence variety. Make sure you use a mix of simple, compound, complex, and compound-complex sentences.

WORDS (EIGHT KINDS)			
verb	**noun**	**pronoun**	**adverb**
to run, to be	chair, love	she, who, many	silently, very, often
adjective	**preposition**	**conjunction**	**interjection**
green, strong, foolish	to, of, in	and, because	oh my!

Words that begin prepositional phrases include *to, of, on, near, around, beside, at, by, in, during, about, like.*

PHRASES (SIX KINDS)

	Type	Definition	Example
1.	Prepositional	Phrase beginning with a preposition and ending with a noun or pronoun—used as an adjective or adverb	*On* the east side of town, the highway *to* Halifax is backed up *for* two kilometres.
2.	Infinitive	Phrase starting with *to* + a base verb—used as a noun, an adjective, or an adverb	*To prepare* for her final, Jamie studied till 2:00 a.m.
3.	Participial	Phrase beginning with a base verb + an *−ing* or *−d/−ed* or *−n/−t* word—used as an adjective	*Swimming* twenty laps, Carol was just starting her workout.
4.	Gerund	Phrase beginning with an *−ing* word—used as a noun	However, *swimming* twenty laps exhausted Carol's brother.
5.	Absolute	Phrase starting with a noun followed by a participle (see 3. above)—describes the whole sentence	His nostrils burning with the sharp odor of gas, Andrew decided not to light the match.
6.	Appositive	Phrase that renames a noun or pronoun	Pandas, bamboo-eating relatives of bears and raccoons, have become critically endangered due to loss of habitat.

HINT

Words that divide main clauses include *for, and, nor, but, or, yet, so.*

CLAUSES (TWO KINDS)

	Type	Definition	Example
1.	Main clause	Clause with complete thought—stands by itself	*Trailer Park Boys is a Canadian TV show.*
2.	Subordinate clause (three kinds)	Clause without a complete thought—linked to a main clause	(see the three examples below)
a.	Noun	Clause used as subject, object, or complement	*That* many of the actors on *Trailer Park Boys* appear in public without breaking character adds to the non-fiction feel of the show.
b.	Adjective	Clause that follows and describes a noun or pronoun	The show, *which* ran for seven years, was made in a mockumentary style.
c.	Adverb	Clause—usually movable—that describes verbs, adjectives, and adverbs, telling *when, where, why, how,* or *to what extent*	*When* the show ended in 2008, fans lamented worldwide.

HINT

Common words that begin adjective clauses are *who, which,* and *that.*

	Type	Definition	Example
1.	Simple	Sentence with one main clause but no subordinate clause	People save money by conserving energy.
2.	Compound	Sentence with two or more main clauses but no subordinate clause	People save money by conserving energy, *and* they reduce pollution.
3.	Complex	Sentence with one main clause and one or more subordinate clauses	People save money by conserving energy *when* they use their appliances wisely.
4.	Compound-complex	Sentence that combines compound and complex sentences and so must have two or more main clauses and one or more subordinate clauses	*When* people use their appliances wisely, they save money by conserving energy *and* they reduce pollution.

SENTENCES (FOUR KINDS)

HINT

Common words that begin adverb clauses include *because, as, if, although, since, when, while, after, before, until.*

HINT

The type and number of clauses identify a grammatical sentence.

Run-ons, Comma Splices, and Sentence Fragments

Flourless peanut butter cookies require only three ingredients: peanut butter, sugar, and eggs. In a paragraph, describe how to make a recipe you love. Anything goes . . . from heating up frozen pizza to making a soufflé. After working through this chapter, check your paragraph's sentences to be sure that they contain the essential ingredients. Fix any fragments, run-ons, and comma splices.

LEARNING OBJECTIVES

13.1 Run-on sentences and comma splices

13.2 Sentence fragments

What Are We Trying to Achieve and Why?

Like a recipe, a sentence needs certain ingredients—a subject and a verb—to be whole. Think of a **sentence fragment** as a recipe missing vital parts. Peanut butter and sugar need eggs to become a cookie, and a subject needs a verb to function as a sentence. You could compare a **run-on sentence** to two recipes accidentally blended, the peanut butter cookie batter dropped into the same bowl with banana cake batter! A **comma splice** is more like what would happen if the baker tried to separate the two merging batters using only a spoon, an inadequate divider.

Chapter 13 will focus on two common problems in our writing: improperly divided sentences and fragmented (or incomplete) sentences. These errors occur when writers do not show where one sentence ends and another begins. The key to controlling run-ons, comma splices, and fragments is determining sentence boundaries. This means locating *verbs* and *subjects* and understanding the difference between *main clauses* and *subordinate clauses*.

As you work through this chapter, make a habit of looking for the **action** (or state of being) **word**(s) in each sentence—the **verb**—and then asking who or what is performing the action—the **subject**.

HINT

For more on these sentence parts, see Chapters 3–6, 10, and 12. See Chapter 3 especially for more on identifying subjects and verbs.

Run-on Sentences and Comma Splices

L013.1

If two or more main clauses run together without punctuation between them, this is a **run-on** or **fused sentence**; main clauses require punctuation and/or joining words to separate them. If two main clauses are divided with only a comma, this is a **comma splice**; by itself, a comma isn't strong enough to separate main clauses.

Both kinds of errors can present problems for readers, as in the following examples:

English Review Note

Sentence boundaries in English may be different from those in other languages.

RUN-ON

FIRST MAIN CLAUSE   SECOND MAIN CLAUSE
James Lovelock is a well-known scientist he predicts the death of six billion people from climate change by the year 2100.

COMMA SPLICE

FIRST MAIN CLAUSE   SECOND MAIN CLAUSE
James Lovelock is a well-known scientist, he predicts the death of six billion people from climate change by the year 2100.

When we reach the end of the first main thought with the final word, *scientist*, we need to mark the spot with strong enough punctuation so the reader knows that a new main thought is beginning. We cannot do this with a comma alone, but we can use one of the following four methods:

WAYS TO FIX A RUN-ON AND A COMMA SPLICE

1. End punctuation: period, question mark, or exclamation point
2. Comma with a coordinating conjunction (and, but, so, or, yet, for, nor)
3. Semicolon (;)
4. Subordination: achieved with words, phrases, clauses

Fixing Run-ons and Comma Splices with End Punctuation

The easiest fix for run-on and comma splice errors is dividing the sentences with a period or other **end punctuation** (such as a question mark or an exclamation point). Below you can see the climate change sentence corrected in this way:

FIXED

FIRST MAIN CLAUSE   PERIOD   SECOND MAIN CLAUSE

James Lovelock is a well-known scientist. He predicts the death of six billion people from climate change by the year 2100.

To decide where to place the period, we have to know how to identify the subjects and verbs in each part of the sentence above; that is, we have to identify each main clause. In the first sentence, we see the linking verb *is* and then ask who or what *is*: the answer is *James Lovelock*. We have the subject and verb. In the second sentence, the action verb is *predicts*. We ask who or what predicts: the pronoun *he* does. So we then have the next subject and verb. You will usually divide run-on and comma splice sentences after the completion of the subject of a main clause, making sure that there is also a complete verb, as in the following example:

INCORRECT: **Birth order may determine success or failure in life in some ways first-born children are often the most successful.**

CORRECT: **Birth order may determine success or failure in life in some ways. First-born children are often the most successful.**

Remember that fixing run-ons and comma splices depends on your ability to find subjects and verbs. Later in this chapter, we will also review how to tell the difference between main clauses and subordinate clauses.

ACTIVITY 13.1   Identifying Run-ons and Comma Splices

In the following sentences, underline each <u>verb</u> or <u>verb phrase</u> and circle each ⟨subject⟩ Next, separate each sentence with a diagonal line, and write *RO* or *CS* in the blank.

EXAMPLE: *RO* ⟨Stephen Harper⟩ is an eldest brother and leader of the Conservative Party \ ⟨Justin Trudeau⟩ is an eldest brother and leader of the Liberal Party.

1. _____ People often defy birth-order stereotypes a person's life is not necessarily defined by birth order.

2. _____ Federal political leaders Michael Ignatieff, Elizabeth May, Jack Layton, and Gilles Duceppe were all first-born children, Thomas Mulcair was the second-born in his family.

3. _____ Payment is a reward for employees' performance and a reason to work, since business began, employers have been trying to pay efficiently and effectively.

4. _____ The first step is to connect the payment system with the performance modern payment systems are flexible, aggressive, and linked to performance.

5. _____ The third type of interaction in poetry of Feudal society is seen in the courtly lyrics of troubadours written to the lady of the heart, courtly poetry has much more individualistic character.

6. _____ Comparative literature studies the similarities in the inspiration of authors across different literary modes classical scholarly works of comparative literature can be placed within the same literary borders.

Fixing Run-ons and Comma Splices with Coordinating Conjunctions

As useful as end punctuation can be for repairing run-ons and comma splices, it is not always the best choice. If dividing sentences with end punctuation creates four or five sentences of similar length one after the other, your writing will have a choppy feel, as in the following example:

RUN-ON AND COMMA SPLICE

> **Canada has only .5 percent of the world's population Canada produces 2 percent of the world's greenhouse gases, some politicians are working hard to reduce climate change, others in the government say, "What climate change?"**

REVISED, BUT CHOPPY

> **Canada has only .5 percent of the world's population. Canada produces 2 percent of the world's greenhouse gases. Some politicians are working hard to reduce climate change. Others in the government say, "What climate change?"**

To avoid this monotonous pattern of short sentences, you can instead use a **coordinating conjunction** preceded by a comma.

COORDINATING CONJUNCTIONS		
and	so	nor
but/yet	or	for

REVISED USING COORDINATING CONJUNCTIONS

> **Canada has only .5 percent of the world's population, *but* Canada produces 2 percent of the world's greenhouse gases. Some politicians are working hard to reduce climate change, *and* others in the government say, "What climate change?"**

Simply using *but* and *and* creates more interesting sentence variety.

When using coordinating conjunctions between clauses, we should be careful to choose those that best express our meaning. For instance, *and* says that the clauses are roughly equivalent and not dependent on each other. *But* and *yet* point out contrast, and *so* shows cause and effect. Notice how we might use these conjunctions in the example below:

> **Canada has only .5 percent of the world's population, *but* Canada produces 2 percent of the world's greenhouse gases, *so* some politicians are working hard to reduce climate change, *yet* others in the government say, "What climate change?"**

Using *so* shows that some politicians feel obligated to reduce climate change *because* Canada produces such a high percentage of greenhouse gases per capita. Using *yet* (a synonym for *but*) emphasizes the contrast between the politicians' reactions to the climate change issue.

ACTIVITY 13.2 Fixing Run-ons and Comma Splices with Coordinating Conjunctions

In the main clauses of each of the following sentences, underline each <u>verb</u> or <u>verb phrase</u> and circle each ⟨subject⟩ Next, write an appropriate coordinating conjunction (and a comma in the case of run-ons) above where the sentences should be divided, and then write *RO* or *CS* in the blank.

> , and
> EXAMPLE: *RO* ⟨Rachel McAdams⟩ <u>admires</u> the music of Heart ∧⟨she⟩ <u>stars</u> in *The Notebook* with fellow Canadian Ryan Gosling.

1. _____ Some men are stay-at-home dads they are becoming closer to their children as a result.

2. _____ People have practised yoga for 5000 years, there must be some benefit in it.

HINT

For more on sentence variety, see Chapter 18.

HINT

For more on coordination, see Chapter 10.

3. _____ Having a cat or dog spayed or neutered is a good idea many people are reluctant to do it.

4. _____ If laughter is the best medicine why is my doctor such a sourpuss he never smiles?

5. _____ Radio frequency identification chips are showing up in thousands of consumer products, some have suggested implanting them in humans for easier tracking.

6. _____ One pair of common house mice can theoretically produce 5000 descendants in one year, there is a good reason for mice predators.

Fixing Run-ons and Comma Splices with Semicolons

A **semicolon** is a strong form of punctuation that can divide two main clauses without the help of a coordinating conjunction. If the main ideas you want to separate are closely related, a semicolon is a good alternative to a comma plus a coordinating conjunction for fixing run-ons and comma splices. The thought in the second clause should complete, complement, or add very relevant information to the thought in the first clause, as in this example:

RUN-ON:

In South America, more women are becoming world leaders former Chilean President Michelle Bachelet and Argentinian President Cristina Fernandez de Kirchner are excellent examples.

COMMA SPLICE:

In South America, more women are becoming world leaders, former Chilean president Michelle Bachelet and Argentinian President Cristina Fernandez de Kirchner are excellent examples.

FIXED WITH SEMI-COLON:

In South America, more women are becoming world leaders; former Chilean president Michelle Bachelet and Argentinian President Cristina Fernandez de Kirchner are excellent examples.

While we could use a period or a comma plus *and*, a semicolon is a reasonable choice since the second main clause completes the statement made in the first clause. These two sentences work as a single unit of thought.

Another option is using a semicolon before a conjunctive adverb followed by a comma. Here is an example:

The movie *Apollo 13* did a great job of simulating floating astronauts; *however*, many of the scenes were actually filmed inside a KC-135 airplane with the actors in free fall.

Notice that we sometimes use the conjunctive adverb *within* a main clause rather than *between* main clauses, in which case we do not use a semicolon:

The movie *Apollo 13* did a great job of simulating floating astronauts. Many of the scenes, *however*, were actually filmed inside a KC-135 airplane with the actors in free fall.

COMMON CONJUNCTIVE ADVERBS			
consequently	however	meanwhile	therefore
furthermore	in fact	nevertheless	thus

In the main clauses of each of following sentences, underline each <u>verb</u> or <u>verb phrase</u> and circle each (subject) Next, place a semicolon where appropriate in each sentence. If you find a conjunctive adverb dividing two main clauses, use a semicolon in front of it, and follow it with a comma. Last, write *RO* or *CS* in the blank.

> EXAMPLE: *RO* (Scientists) <u>have discovered</u> two interesting facts about vibrations; when shaken gently for a few minutes daily, (people) <u>can gain</u> bone mass and <u>lose</u> weight.

1. _____ CARP (the Canadian Association of Retired Persons) has an aggressive membership-recruitment campaign in fact, the organization begins soliciting people when they turn 50.

2. _____ People are saving energy and helping the planet in many small ways switching to energy-efficient bulbs is just one example.

3. _____ Website design is an area that has kept growing book design has been declining as a career prospect for several years now.

4. _____ The passport office says that it takes only two weeks to process a passport however, it often takes many weeks longer than this.

5. _____ Police officers need to follow procedure when arresting suspects some have gotten into trouble for ignoring regulations.

6. _____ Tea is high in antioxidants therefore, it can reduce the risk of heart disease and cancer.

Fixing Run-ons and Comma Splices with Subordination

Another way to avoid run-on and comma splice errors *and* help cut unneeded words is to use **subordination**. When subordinating one clause to another, the writer focuses on the idea in the main clause, letting the reader know which idea is more important. We most often subordinate by using phrases and clauses.

SUBORDINATING WITH PHRASES

Phrases (word groups that may contain a verb form or a subject, but not both) give writers many options for crafting interesting sentences. If you have not tried most or all of these options, this is a good time to experiment.

Below you can see how we might use phrases to fix a run-on or comma splice error. Note how a comma is used to set off phrases preceding main clauses.

RUN-ON:

> **We are looking forward to summer break school is hard work.**

COMMA SPLICE:

> **We are looking forward to summer break, school is hard work.**

PHRASE FIX

PREPOSITIONAL PHRASES
1. **In the months before summer, we work hard in school and so look forward to the break.**

APPOSITIVE PHRASE
2. **We are looking forward to summer break, a time without hard schoolwork.**

HINT

To review phrases, see Chapter 11.

HINT

Learn about the Big Three comma categories in Chapter 15.

3. **Working hard all year, we are looking forward to summer break.**

ABSOLUTE PHRASE
4. **Students and faculty working hard all year, we are looking forward to summer break.**

GERUND PHRASE
5. **Working hard in school makes us look forward to summer break.**

INFINITIVE PHRASE
6. **To look forward to summer break is natural because school is hard work.**

HINT

See Chapters 11 and 15 for more on using commas with phrases.

As you write, choose the phrases that sound best within the context of your paragraphs. If, for example, a participial phrase (as in the preceding **sentence 3**) flows better in your paragraph than an absolute phrase, choose the participial phrase. However, remember that using any phrase (or other grammatical unit) repeatedly, without variety, can make writing tedious to read.

Commas are used to set off phrases in **sentences 1–4**. No comma is needed with a gerund or infinitive subject, however, as in **sentences 5 and 6**.

ACTIVITY 13.4 Fixing Run-ons and Comma Splices through Phrase Subordination

In the following sentences, underline each <u>verb</u> or <u>verb phrase</u> and circle each (subject), and then write *RO* or *CS* in the blank. Next, on the lines provided, rewrite the sentences, subordinating one main clause to the other using the phrase types modelled above. Write using the phrase type specified in the parentheses.

EXAMPLE: *RO* I want a convertible the hot months of July and August are near. (prepositional phrases) *With the hot months of July and August near, I want a convertible.*

1. _____ Some hockey fans cheer and scream for their favourite teams, these fans go wild watching *Hockey Night in Canada*.

   (participial) _____

   _____

2. _____ Microbes can be beneficial, they can even affect our emotional state.

   (participial) _____

   _____

3. _____ Halloween is a holiday made for kids they love dressing up, being out at night, and getting lots of candy.

   (gerund) _____

   _____

4. _____ Health Canada has issued an advisory on cold and cough medicines, the advisory is to protect children two years of age and under.

   (infinitive) _____

   _____

5. _____ To graduate in the shortest time possible is a goal of many students they will sometimes take six classes per term and four in the summer to achieve this.

(prepositional) _____

_____

6. _____ The airline pilot was trying to be funny, the pilot asked all passengers to turn off their "cellphones, BlackBerries, blueberries, and any other kind of berry."

(absolute) _____

_____

USE TEXTBOOK LINES

In many cases, this text provides space to complete writing exercises right here on its pages. You can save paper and practise annotation by using this text as a workbook.

SUBORDINATING WITH CLAUSES

Subordinate clauses can also solve run-on and comma splice problems. Unlike a phrase, a subordinate clause has both a subject and a verb, but it does *not* contain a complete thought. These incomplete clauses must be attached to a main clause to finish their meaning. There are three types of subordinate clauses, as the following chart shows.

THREE TYPES OF SUBORDINATE CLAUSES	
Adverb Common subordinating conjunctions to signal adverb clauses: *after, although, as, because, if, when, where, while*	*When* Ellen comes, the class can begin.
Adjective Common relative pronouns to signal adjective clauses: *who, which, that*	Jake is the student *who* wouldn't stop talking.
Noun Common cue words to signal noun clauses: *that, what, how*	Victor realized *that* he was failing.

HINT

For help punctuating subordinate clauses, see Comma Categories 1 and 3 in Chapter 15.

RUN-ON

We are looking forward to summer break school is hard work.

COMMA SPLICE

We are looking forward to summer break, school is hard work.

CLAUSE FIXES

ADVERB CLAUSE
1. We are looking forward to summer break because school is hard work.

ADJECTIVE CLAUSE
2. We are looking forward to summer break, which will give us some relief from the hard work of school.

NOUN CLAUSE
3. So much hard schoolwork means that we are looking forward to summer break.

As with phrases, choose the subordinate clause that makes the best sense and sounds best within your paragraph.

An adverb clause following a main clause uses no comma (see **sentence 1**). On the other hand, a non-essential adjective clause should be set off from the rest of the sentence by a comma or commas (see **sentence 2**).

ACTIVITY 13.5 Fixing Run-ons and Comma Splices through Clause Subordination

In the following sentences, underline each <u>verb</u> or <u>verb phrase</u> and circle each subject and then write *RO* or *CS* in the blank. Next, on the lines provided, rewrite the sentences, subordinating one main clause to the other. Note the subordinate clause type you should use as indicated in the parentheses.

EXAMPLE: *CS* **Some provinces can't raise enough money to repair roads, provincial governments are selling the jobs to private contractors.**

(adverb clause) *Because some provinces can't raise enough money to repair roads, provincial governments are selling the jobs to private contractors.*

1. _____ Many inexpensive products are produced by sweatshop labour, some people are refusing to buy them.

   (adverb) _____

   _____

2. _____ Emile was swimming in the waters near Belize, he was stung many times by tiny jellyfish called pica pica.

   (adverb) _____

   _____

3. _____ In Iceland Yoko Ono has built the Imagine Peace Tower as a memorial for John Lennon and to promote world peace the tower projects a column of light visible for miles.

   (adjective) _____

   _____

4. _____ Yesterday Kayla learned some bad news she was losing her supervisor who was moving to another university.

   (noun) _____

   _____

5. _____ Fall is a beautiful season, winter soon closes in on the world.

   (adverb) _____

   _____

6. _____ A textbook can be a wonderful learning tool the textbook must be read cover to cover.

   (adverb) _____

   _____

WORKING TOGETHER: Fixing Run-ons and Comma Splices (Mixed Review)

In the following sentences, underline each <u>verb</u> or <u>verb phrase</u> and circle each ⟨subject⟩ and then write *RO* or *CS* in the blank. Next, work with a partner or partners to correct each of the sentences, using the methods we have discussed: end punctuation, coordination, semicolon, and subordination (phrases or subordinate clauses).

EXAMPLE: *RO* ⟨Flight attendants⟩ <u>spend</u> months each year in jets ⟨many⟩ of them <u>avoid</u> air travel on their weeks off.

Period: *Flight attendants spend months each year in jets. Many of them avoid air travel on their weeks off.*

Coordination: *Flight attendants spend months each year in jets, so many of them avoid air travel on their weeks off.*

Semicolon: *Flight attendants spend months each year in jets; therefore, many of them avoid air travel on their weeks off.*

Subordination: *Because flight attendants spend months each year in jets, many of them avoid air travel on their weeks off.*

1. _____ Some children can't wait to go to preschool others are afraid to leave home.

   Period: _____

   _____

   Coordination: _____

   _____

2. _____ Ashley loves the outdoors her sister Heather loves the library.

   Semicolon: _____

   _____

   Subordination: _____

   _____

3. _____ Sal could reach the bank by 5 o'clock, he could not reach the drug-store by 5 as well.

   Period: _____

   _____

   Subordination: _____

   _____

4. _____ Plumbers are well paid for their labour they have a hard and messy job.

   Semicolon: _____

   _____

   Coordination: _____

   _____

5. _____ Ten-year-old Shun Hwa wanted to be a ballerina, she also wanted to be an astronaut.

Period: _____

_____

Semicolon: _____

_____

6. _____The government of Haiti has accepted international aid for earthquake relief many of its people may now be helped.

Coordination: _____

_____

Subordination: _____

_____

LO13.2 Sentence Fragments

Run-ons and comma splices happen when writers cannot tell where one sentence ends and another begins. For similar reasons, we sometimes have difficulty with **sentence fragments**. For a sentence to stand alone, it must have a *verb* and a *subject*, and it must express a *complete thought*. If a sentence lacks any of these elements, readers usually have trouble understanding it, as in the following examples:

PHRASES	SUBORDINATE CLAUSES
Based on the data	After a few moments had passed
According to the survey	Who was a wildlife specialist
The most effective method	Which Jason watered daily
The Independent Learning Centre	Although background knowledge is the most important factor

None of the above examples can stand alone because they lack a finished thought. The sentence fragments in the left-hand column are **phrases**—they lack a subject, a verb, or both. The examples in the right-hand column are **subordinate clauses**. They come the closest to being freestanding sentences because they *do* have a subject and verb, but they lack a main clause to complete their meaning (and the word beginning each clause makes it subordinate).

One reason sentence fragments appear in your writing is that they can look and sound like complete sentences within the context of a paragraph, as in the following example:

FRAGMENTS:

Based on the data. Informal discussion forums about global issues is the activity most favoured by students. According to the survey. The most effective method to introduce global issues to students in the classroom is watching films and documentaries. Providing more audio-visual materials for both classrooms and the Independent Learning Centre. Audio-visual information helps students to learn "difficult-to-understand concepts." Although background knowledge is the most important factor in facilitating student participation in activities about global issues. Therefore, teachers should prepare extra material to assist students in acquiring additional knowledge about these issues.

FIXED:

> Based on the data, informal discussion forums about global issues is the activity most favoured by students. According to the survey, the most effective method to introduce global issues to students in the classroom is watching films and documentaries. Providing more audio-visual materials for both classrooms and the Independent Learning Centre will help students learn "difficult-to-understand concepts." Background knowledge is the most important factor in facilitating student participation in activities about global issues; therefore, teachers should prepare extra material to assist students in acquiring additional knowledge about these issues.

In most cases, we can fix sentence fragments by attaching them to the sentence that precedes or follows them, often using a comma (as in the corrected global issues example above). When this does not work, any missing words—usually subjects or verbs—must be replaced. The two most common kinds of fragments are phrases and subordinate clauses.

Phrase Fragments

By definition, a **phrase** does not have both a verb and a subject. Phrases standing alone are sentence fragments and must be attached to a main clause to express their full meaning. There are two ways to fix phrase fragments:

WAYS TO FIX A PHRASE FRAGMENT

1. Attach the phrases to a main clause.
2. Add words (subjects, verbs, or both) to turn the phrases into main clauses.

As always, when you change the shape of sentences, be careful with comma use. Here are examples of common phrase fragments and two ways to fix them:

Prepositional phrase fragment: The team's practice was difficult. *In the morning and worse in the afternoon.*

1. **Fix by attaching:** The team's practice was difficult *in* the morning and worse *in* the afternoon.
2. **Fix by adding words:** The team's practice was difficult. It was bad in the morning and worse in the afternoon.

Infinitive phrase fragment: *To volunteer with Habitat for Humanity.* Roselyn took a day off from work.

1. **Fix by attaching:** *To volunteer with Habitat for Humanity,* Roselyn took a day off from work.
2. **Fix by adding words:** Roselyn wanted *to volunteer* with Habitat for Humanity, so she took a day off from work.

Participial phrase fragment (present tense): *Swearing several times.* My uncle dropped the hammer and shook his injured hand.

1. **Fix by attaching:** *Swearing several times,* my uncle dropped the hammer and shook his injured hand.
2. **Fix by adding words:** My uncle swore several times. Then he dropped the hammer and shook his injured hand.

Participial phrase fragment (past tense): *Stunned* by the loss. Adam collapsed onto the bench.

1. **Fix by attaching: Stunned by the loss, Adam collapsed onto the bench.**
2. **Fix by adding words: Adam <u>was</u> stunned by the loss. He collapsed onto the bench.**

Absolute phrase fragment: The orbiting space station leaking oxygen. The astronauts had to evacuate.

1. **Fix by attaching: The orbiting *space station leaking* oxygen, the astronauts had to evacuate.**
2. **Fix by adding words: The orbiting space station <u>was</u> leaking oxygen. The astronauts had to evacuate.**

Appositive phrase fragment: A magnificent but small raptor. The sparrow hawk eats mice but also grasshoppers.

1. **Fix by attaching: A magnificent but small raptor, the sparrow hawk eats mice but also grasshoppers.**
2. **Fix by adding words: The <u>sparrow hawk</u> <u>is</u> a magnificent but small raptor. It eats mice but also grasshoppers.**

HINT

When you combine a phrase with a main clause, be sure to punctuate correctly. To review punctuating phrases, see Chapters 11 and 15.

ACTIVITY 13.7 Recognizing and Fixing Phrase Fragments

Fix the following phrase fragments; turn them into sentences by either attaching a phrase to a main clause or adding words to the fragment.

EXAMPLE: **Clinging with one bloody hand to the cliff face. Frodo almost fell to his death.**

Clinging with one bloody hand to the cliff face, Frodo almost fell to his death.

1. The dinner was ruined. Vegetables turned to mush and pasta covering the stovetop. So Beth and her family decided to order pizza.

   _____

   _____

2. CHEO, the Children's Hospital of Eastern Ontario. Treating thousands of children and teens each year. But once a patient turns 18, he or she has to move on.

   _____

   _____

3. Jack and his son entered the museum. By the north door on the first floor across from the library.

   _____

   _____

4. The car stalling again at the intersection. Dan swore he would take it to the shop the next day.

   _____

   _____

5. Even though the road out of Moose Jaw was awful, the Johnsons promised each other that they would make it. To Wakamow Valley.

_____

_____

6. To keep her book publishing files in order. Amanda had developed a complex filing system. With ten different coloured file folders for each book.

_____

_____

ACTIVITY 13.8 Recognizing and Fixing Phrase Fragments

Underline the <u>phrase fragments</u> in the following passage. Then write a revised paragraph in the space provided. You may fix the fragments either by attaching a phrase to a main clause or by adding words.

> Among the scholars on rural organizations. Toshihiro Yogo is exceptionally conscious of the differences between development and social organizations. Yogo defines the latter as organizations that coordinate the social relationships among local people. Then pass the organizational experience from generation to generation. He argues that the formation of a development organization. Depends on the capability of the social organization. He assumes that organizations emerge to resolve constraints. Between the state, local community, market, and household. The social organization, according to Yogo. Exists as an intermediary between the household and the local community. While the development organizations are formed between the other actors. For example, cooperatives are formed to give households access to the market. Although this model shows the difference between development organizations and social organizations nicely. It does not explain how the two organizations are related to each other.

_____

_____

_____

_____

_____

_____

_____

_____

_____

_____

_____

_____

_____

Subordinate Clause Fragments

While sentence fragments are often phrases, they can also be **subordinate clauses**. A subordinate clause contains a subject and a verb but not a complete thought, so a subordinate clause depends on a main clause to finish the thought that it started.

As you know, subordinate clauses come in three varieties—noun, adjective, and adverb—but the most common fragment problems come from adverb and adjective clauses. To identify **adverb clause fragments**, remember the common subordinating conjunctions:

SUBORDINATING CONJUNCTIONS				
after	because	in order that	though	whenever
although	before	now that	till (less formal than *until*)	where
as	even if	once	unless	whereas
as if	even though	rather than	until	wherever
as long as	if	since	when	while

If a sentence begins with one of these conjunctions and is not attached to a main clause, it is a fragment.

There are two ways to fix adverb clause fragments:

WAYS TO FIX AN ADVERB CLAUSE FRAGMENT

1. Attach the adverb clause to the main clause.
2. Drop the subordinating conjunction to create another main clause.

Adverb clause fragment: *Because* the winds have died down in British Columbia. The forest fires are coming under control.

1. **Fix by attaching:** *Because* the winds have died down in British Columbia, the forest fires are coming under control.
2. **Fix by dropping the subordinator:** The winds have died down in British Columbia. The forest fires are coming under control.

Note that an adverb clause at the start of the sentence requires a comma (see **Sentence 1**).

Adjective clause fragments, on the other hand, can usually be identified by one of these three common relative pronouns: *who, which,* or *that.* They can be fixed in two ways:

WAYS TO FIX AN ADJECTIVE CLAUSE FRAGMENT

1. Attach the adjective clause to the main clause.
2. Drop the relative pronoun and replace it with a noun or pronoun.

Adjective clause fragment: The 2008 Paralympic bronze medal for sailing was won by Canada's 46-year-old John McRoberts. *Who* with his teammate Stacie Louttit finished behind the United States and Australia, who took the gold and silver medals, respectively.

1. **Fix by attaching:** The 2008 Paralympic bronze medal for sailing was won by Canada's 46-year-old John McRoberts, *who* with his teammate Stacie Louttit finished behind the United States and Australia, who took the gold and silver medals, respectively.

2. **Fix by dropping the relative pronoun and adding a noun:** The 2008 Paralympic bronze medal for sailing was won by Canada's 46-year-old John McRoberts. *He* and his teammate Stacie Louttit finished behind the United States and Australia, who took the gold and silver medals, respectively.

Note that non-essential adjective clauses require commas (see **Sentence 1**).

> **HINT**
>
> When you combine a fragment with a main clause, be sure to punctuate correctly. To review punctuating clauses, see Chapters 12, 15, and 16.

ACTIVITY 13.9   Creating Sentences from Clause Fragments

Complete the following subordinate clauses with any main clauses that make sense to you.

EXAMPLE: **Because not enough people spay or neuter their dogs and cats,**

700 000 unwanted pets are euthanized every year in Canada.

1. Whenever visitors came, _____

2. _____ while the woman in the red sweater looked in through the window.

3. _____ when my cousin finally showed up for the wedding.

4. _____ that attaches without much difficulty.

5. _____ because Aaron was there to help.

6. _____ who is the best finish carpenter in the city.

ACTIVITY 13.10   Editing for Run-ons, Comma Splices, and Sentence Fragments

Read through the following paragraph. Using the correction methods discussed in this chapter, make corrections for run-ons, comma splices, and sentence fragments.

A massive oil spill in the Gulf of Mexico in April 2010 set back worldwide ecological efforts. Which have become an urgent issue for the 21st century. The worst-case estimate of oil leakage. Was 60 000 barrels a day. However, that figure, in actuality, underestimated daily damage. BP Oil suspended dividends to shareholders. In order to repay the multi-billion dollar debt to the U.S. government for clean-up. Some citizens referred to this ecological disaster as the crime of the century some thought that if the oil could be recovered and sold the spill would be "mopped up in a jiffy." The real problem was finding equipment. To cap the oil leak at such an ocean depth. A depth that had never before been reached. This event proved that humanity does not recognize either its serious responsibility to respect the Earth. Or the consequences of overreaching our technological knowledge.

Source: Information based on http://www.cbc.ca/world/story/2010/06/17/bp-oil-executives-congress.html

_____

_____

_____

_____

_____

_____

_____

_____

_____

_____

_____

_____

_____

_____

Chapter Summary

1. Writers can identify and correct run-ons, comma splices, and fragments by determining sentence boundaries: locating verbs and subjects and distinguishing main clauses from subordinate clauses.

2. A run-on sentence occurs when two or more main clauses run together without punctuation between them. A comma splice occurs when only a comma connects main clauses; by itself, a comma is not strong enough to join them.

3. The easiest way to fix a comma splice or a run-on is to separate the two main clauses with end punctuation, such as a period.

4. Comma splices and run-ons can also be fixed by using commas with coordinating conjunctions, by using semicolons, or by using subordination (phrases or clauses).

5. A sentence fragment is missing either a subject or a main verb; it is an incomplete sentence and does not express a complete thought. Fragments may be phrases or subordinate clauses.

6. To make a phrase fragment into a sentence, either connect it to a main clause or add words (subjects, verbs, or both) to turn the phrase itself into a main clause.

7. To make an adverb clause fragment into a sentence, either attach it to the main clause or drop the subordinating conjunction to create another main clause.

8. To make an adjective clause fragment into a sentence, either attach it to the main clause or drop the relative pronoun and replace it with a noun or pronoun.

Parallelism

From beginning to end, the rails of this railway track run parallel to one another. The world is full of structures with two or more sides that mirror each other: our cars have wheels on both sides, our pant legs match in length and width, and even our bodies are symmetrical. Write a list of things in your everyday life that match or line up when paired or grouped. How does this help them to function? In writing, parallel elements help to coordinate elements in our work.

LEARNING OBJECTIVES

14.1 Making series parallel

14.2 Making pairs parallel

What Are We Trying to Achieve and Why?

Chapter 10 introduced the concepts of coordination and subordination for ordering ideas in a sentence. Another way writers use structure to help readers understand meaning in a sentence is through **parallelism**, a form of coordination that repeats similar grammatical units or structures for clarity and emphasis. The words may be in a series or a pair. Groupings of three or more items use commas between them and a coordinating conjunction like *and* or *but* before the last item. Words or word groups in a pair are separated by a coordinating conjunction. In this chapter, you will learn to edit your writing for parallelism.

LO14.1 Making Series Parallel

Items in a **series** should be similar grammatical units—nouns following nouns, verbs following verbs, phrases following phrases, and so forth. Here are some examples:

1. **Will you remind me to bring <u>pens, pencils, paper, and coffee</u> to class?** (nouns)
2. **Evan <u>collects, studies, and sells</u> sixties memorabilia.** (verbs)
3. **Janey is <u>thoughtful, responsible, caring, and intelligent.</u>** (adjectives)

Notice that it would be a lapse in parallelism if we wrote in **sentence 3**: "Janey is thoughtful, responsible, caring, and *is* intelligent." Adding the verb throws off the parallelism of the series.

4. **<u>Quilting, gardening, and water skiing</u> are a few of Marc's favourite pastimes.** (gerunds)

In **sentence 4**, *water skiing* is a two-word gerund, parallel with *quilting* and *gardening*. It would be non-parallel to rewrite sentence 4 as "Quilting, gardening, and *to water ski* are a few of Marc's favourite pastimes." Using the gerund *skiing* instead of the infinitive *to ski* solves the structure problem.

We can also write parallel phrases, as in the following examples:

5. **The United States is supposed to have a "<u>government *of* the people, *by* the people, and *for* the people</u>."** (prepositional phrases)
6. **Credit card companies want you <u>*to have* their cards, *to use* their cards, and *to pay* monthly finance fees on unpaid balances.</u>** (infinitive phrases)
7. **<u>*Dumping* nine metres of snow, *choking* the roadways, and *leaving* people without power for days,</u> the blizzard devastated Eastern Ontario.** (participial phrases)

Notice that slight variations in parallel structure are fine, as in **sentences 6 and 7**. For example, the last infinitive phrase in **sentence 6** differs from the others by not using *their*, using modifiers before *fees*, and including an additional prepositional phrase, *on unpaid balances*; but overall, the series is parallel, consisting of three infinitive phrases. Generally, the addition of modifiers or prepositional phrases does not affect the parallel structure of a series of infinitive or participial phrases.

Here is an example of parallel clauses:

English Review Note

8. **Sheila said, "I give to charities <u>*because* I can, *because* it makes me feel good, and *because* it's the right thing to do</u>."**

In a series of infinitives, subsequent *to*s may be omitted because they are implied by the first.

Although slight differences in parallel forms are typical in writing, you should avoid the following kind of non-parallel constructions:

NON-PARALLEL   Dan needs *to go* to the hardware store, *to stop* at the bank, and <u>he thinks he might make it to the library before it closes.</u>

PARALLEL   Dan needs *to go* to the hardware store, *to stop* at the bank, and *to make* it to the library before it closes. (three parallel infinitive phrases)

PARALLEL   Dan needs *to go* to the hardware store *and (to) stop* at the bank, and he thinks he might make it to the library before it closes. (parallel pair and a separate main clause)

ACTIVITY 14.1   Seeing Parallelism in Series

Underline the <u>parallel series</u> in each of the following sentences, and check them for correct parallel form. In each, ~~cross out~~ the faulty word group and write the parallel form above it, where appropriate.

number of

EXAMPLE: Diamonds are judged by <u>cut, colour, clarity, and ~~how many carats there are.~~</u>

1. The Sun's major satellites are now divided into the following categories: terrestrial planets, gas giants, moons, and some are called dwarf planets.

2. Genetic researchers have found a way to weaken cancer cells, to reduce their number, and are keeping them from spreading.

3. In many rainforests, miners, loggers, and those who want to conserve the land continue to compete fiercely over the use of land still inhabited by indigenous peoples.

4. To learn more about its rich biological history, its distinct ecosystems, and how diverse its species are, scientists are trying to catalogue all life in the Pacific Ocean.

5. Becky saw that in order to succeed at university she would have to learn quickly about studying hard, reading daily, and how to write a good essay.

6. Write three sentences that use a parallel series (three or more items). Look to the preceding examples for help.

    a. Single-word series: _____

    _____

    b. Phrase series: _____

    _____

    c. Phrase series: _____

    _____

Making Pairs Parallel

LO14.2

Another common form of parallelism is **pairing**. Rather than listing points in a series, we balance two items, usually with a coordinating conjunction. Single words, phrases, and clauses can all be paired, as in the following examples:

1. **Ben spends his free time <u>jogging</u> *and* <u>biking.</u>** (paired gerunds)

2. **Sal <u>raised his glass</u> *and* <u>took</u> a sip.** (paired verbs)

3. **You will probably find the video game <u>in the top drawer</u> *or* <u>under your bed.</u>** (paired prepositional phrases)

4. **<u>Consumers are shocked at the price of oil,</u> *but* <u>oil companies are overjoyed at the windfall in profits.</u>** (paired main clauses)

Notice that **sentence 4** is a compound sentence linking two main clauses that mirror one another in grammatical structure: subject, linking verb, complement, and two prepositional phrases. When clauses are paired this way, the sentence is said to be *balanced,* the parallelism emphasizing ideas in each clause.

We can also use word groups called **correlative conjunctions** (shown in the chart below) to pair ideas.

HINT

Correlative conjunctions require commas when used between two clauses.

CORRELATIVE CONJUNCTIONS		
both . . . and	just as . . . so	not only . . . but also
either . . . or	neither . . . nor	whether . . . or

These paired conjunctions always appear in the same order; we would not, for example, write "I like *and* cake *both* ice cream." Here are several example sentences:

1. Some voters believe that *neither* the Liberals *nor* the Conservatives care much about fulfilling campaign promises.

2. Airport security inspected *not only* Ryan's carry-on bag *but also* his checked luggage.

3. "Look, sir, *whether* you make the flight, *or* you don't, it's not our problem," said the agent, tearing Ryan's suitcase apart.

4. *Either* we will go to the midterm, *or* we will fail the class.

Sentences 1 and 2 show correlative conjunctions used *within* a clause, and **sentences 3 and 4** show these conjunctions used *between* two clauses.

Correlated pairs require parallel structure just as series and pairs separated by a coordinating conjunction do. Note the following non-parallel examples. **Sentence 1** has an unneeded subject and verb, *it was,* and **Sentence 2** is missing the infinitive *to help.*

1. NON-PARALLEL   The corner drugstore was *both* well stocked, *and* it was inexpensive.

    PARALLEL   The corner drugstore was *both* well stocked *and* ~~it was~~ inexpensive.

2. NON-PARALLEL   She wanted *not only* to live a wealthy lifestyle *but also* her wealth for people living in poverty.

    PARALLEL   She wanted *not only* to live a wealthy lifestyle *but also* to help people living in poverty.

Not every word needs to be included in a grammatical pairing; in fact, leaving words out at the front of phrases and clauses can help with variety and economy, as shown in the following examples:

1. The subprime lending crisis was brought on by property appraisers, (by) local lenders, and (by) mortgage companies buying and selling loans that all of them knew were, at best, risky investments.

2. The people of Sudan, (of) Chad, and (of) Somalia are undergoing incredible hardships that the international community is finally beginning to recognize.

3. Beth wrote a letter of protest to her municipal councillor, (her) MPP, and (her) MP.

4. Ian feels that his voice counts, (that) his life has meaning, and (that) his goals will be realized.

Note that in **sentence 2** above, it would be incorrect to write "of Sudan, of Chad, and Somalia," dropping the final *of*. If you commit to the first two *ofs*, you must finish the series using *of*.

Deciding whether to include the words in parentheses above is a question of style. Repetition often helps emphasize a point, and some people might find, for example, that **sentence 4** above is more forceful with all three *thats* left in.

ACTIVITY 14.2 Seeing Parallelism in Pairs

HINT

Look for paired words, phrases, and clauses; and watch for problems using correlative conjunctions.

Underline the <u>parallel pairs</u> in each of the following sentences, and check them for correct parallel form. If the sentence is correct, put a *C* in the space provided; if not, place the faulty word group in parentheses and write the parallel form above it, adding any other missing words, if needed.

EXAMPLE:

staying
_____ Zach's problems were <u>getting to work on time</u> and (to stay) <u>awake after he got there.</u>

1. _____ The classified ad called for knowledge about political science and bilingualism.

2. _____ Art wanted to land not only a summer job but also looking to find a part-time job for evenings and weekends.

3. _____ David plans to spend the morning working in his garage and then a shower.

4. _____ Vijay was interested in playing finger-style guitar and to flat pick.

5. _____ My friends from Calgary couldn't decide where to turn off the highway or to find their way back on.

6. _____ Rachel had a weakness for getting herself into trouble in class but a talent for getting herself out.

7. Write three sentences that use pairs in parallel form. Look to the preceding examples for help.

   a. Single-word pair: _____

   _____

   b. Phrase pair: _____

   _____

   c. Phrase pair with correlative conjunctions: _____

   _____

After reading the following essay, circle ⟨coordinating and correlative conjunctions.⟩ Then correct the errors in parallel structure by placing parentheses around omitted words and adding words in the space above. The first paragraph has been marked as an example.

Home Sweet Home

Our homes are the places we go to feel secure (and) (for) rest from the stresses of everyday living. We expect to be safe there, (but) are we? All too often people overlook dangers
in their homes that may have been there since the foundations were poured.

Houses that create obvious problems for people—symptoms like itchy eyes, runny
noses, (and) throats—may be suffering from "sick building syndrome." Even when such
effects are not obvious, unnoticed homebound toxins may have dangerous long-term
impact on the health of the occupants. Here are several of the chief hazards to watch
out for in your own home.

Airborne pollutants in the home are a major source of illness and can be clearly
seen or hidden. Cigarette smoke is one obvious toxin. If you smoke, avoid doing so in
the house. Second-hand smoke puts those you love at risk for respiratory infections,
heart, and lung disease. One of the hidden killers is radon. This gas increases the risk
of cancer, but the good news is that it is easily and inexpensively tested for, and there
are many companies that can lower radon levels in the home. Not only radon but also
dealing with asbestos can be a problem for homeowners in homes built before 1978.
You are at higher risk of both cancer and getting lung disease from asbestos when
remodelling projects expose the old insulation to the air. Allergens can grow in house-
holds that are too humid, that have poor air filtration systems, and have had water
problems. For example, black mould grows readily under carpets when basements leak.
It is not enough to dry the carpet. Either the carpet must be removed (an expensive
proposition), or it must be sterilized. Regular strength isopropyl rubbing alcohol will kill
the mould before it gets out of hand. To combat other allergens, buy mattress and pillow
dust mite covers.

Other non-airborne hazards lurk in many homes. If your house was built prior to
1978, it may well still have lead paint on the walls. While most adults are not in the
habit of licking walls or will ingest paint chips, a small percentage of children in Canada
suffer from lead poisoning annually. This is especially true in old or renovated houses
where paint is peeling or scraped off the walls. Household cleaning products can also be
a danger, everything from dishwasher soap to carpet cleaners. Not only house cleaners
but also using lawn-care products like herbicides, pesticides, and fertilizers are risky,
particularly for children and animals.

Finally, many of us neither handle food nor do we store it as safely as we should.
Once food has been prepared or a food container has been opened, bacteria begin the
decaying process immediately. Keep perishables cool, at least four degrees Celsius in
the refrigerator, and store food as soon after use as possible. A carton of milk left sitting
on a counter for an hour will spoil much more quickly than one kept chilled properly. In
general, it is a good idea to wash *all* food, including fruits and vegetables, vigorously.

Cutting boards used for raw meats are a major source of cross-contamination when they are not cleaned thoroughly.

With all the potential problems the world throws at us every day, we deserve a place that we can count on for rest and safety. But without spending a bit of time to assess our living space, we may get neither relaxation nor that we have much security. All homeowners should do their best to make their house truly their own "home sweet home."

ACTIVITY 14.4 Write Your Own Paragraph

Using what you have learned in this chapter about parallel structure for both series and pairs within a sentence, write your own paragraph. Choose a topic that considers two or more similar elements. For example, you might write about one of the following: characteristics of a suitable mate; architectural elements of your dream home; daily activities in the ideal job; ingredients for a perfect meal; or foundational plants in your fantasy garden.

Focus on developing two (a pair to make parallel) to five (a series to make parallel) elements.

Chapter Summary

1. Parallelism is a form of coordination that repeats similar grammatical units for clarity and emphasis.

2. Items in pairs and series should be grammatically parallel.

3. Slight variations in parallel structures will not necessarily violate parallel form.

4. A compound sentence in which two main clauses mirror one another in grammatical form is called *balanced*.

Commas

In order for traffic to keep flowing smoothly, we need lights, signs, road markings, and sometimes police officers to give directions. Commas and other punctuation marks serve a similar purpose in writing. Write a brief paragraph describing your trip to class today. Now remove all the punctuation, and exchange paragraphs with another student. How difficult is it to understand his or her work?

LEARNING OBJECTIVES

15.1 The Big Three comma categories

15.2 Secondary comma categories

What Are We Trying to Achieve and Why?

Getting ideas down on paper in a clear, well-organized way is difficult and time consuming; but once we have finally managed it, we want our readers to be able to follow our points. This is where punctuation——the focus of Chapters 15 and 16——comes in. Periods, commas, semicolons, colons, dashes, parentheses, exclamation marks, question marks, and quotation marks help to separate our ideas into recognizable units of thought so that readers can follow where we are trying to lead them. Without correct punctuation, we end up with paragraphs like the following:

CONFUSING

> **One Sunday afternoon in June members of the Windsor Classic Chorale and I learned how important time can be when visiting New York City forgetting to set the alarm clock the night before our performance at Carnegie Hall we overslept as sunlight burst through the hotel window we woke up to Joan yelling ladies wake up our rehearsal starts in an hour hurrying to get ready we left the room a disaster dressed in our uncomfortable black dresses we rushed downstairs to the hotel lobby to find our leader George and a few choir members who had stayed behind waiting for us.**

However, if we take the time to use punctuation to our advantage, we can make a confusing paragraph clear:

CLEAR

> **One Sunday afternoon in June, members of the Windsor Classic Chorale and I learned how important time can be when visiting New York City. Forgetting to set the alarm clock the night before our rehearsal at Carnegie Hall, we overslept. As sunlight burst through the hotel window, we woke up to Joan yelling, "Ladies, wake up! Our rehearsal starts in an hour!" Hurrying to get ready, we left the room a disaster. Dressed in our uncomfortable black dresses, we rushed downstairs to the hotel lobby to find our leader, George, and a few choir members who had stayed behind, waiting for us.**

The second version uses punctuation (and capitalization) to good advantage, making the paragraph easier to read.

Although comma use can seem complicated, there are really just a handful of "rules" that govern most typical writing situations. The trouble comes when we try to apply these rules without knowing some fundamental sentence grammar, especially the correct use of subjects, verbs, phrases, and clauses. Knowing these sentence parts, a writer can see where one sentence begins and another ends and why one spot in a sentence is a more logical place to pause than another.

Chapter 15 will help you learn the conventions for using commas effectively in your own work. In the next few pages, we will work with three main uses of the comma that will help you with most of your comma questions.

> **HINT**
>
> Chapter 16 focuses on editing for other types of punctuation and mechanics, including capitalization.

The Big Three Comma Categories

LO15.1

Commas are primarily used to *separate* and *enclose*. More specifically, they have three main uses:

THE BIG THREE COMMA CATEGORIES

1. To separate a main clause from an introductory word or words
2. To enclose or separate non-essential words, phrases, or clauses that come within or after a main clause
3. To separate two main clauses along with a coordinating conjunction

---

To use commas effectively, first find the main clause (or clauses) from which the rest of the sentence grows. Remember that you identify a clause by looking for the action or being verb and then asking who or what is doing the action or is the focus of the being verb. With the main clause located, next check three areas where commas might be needed: word groups coming *before*, *within*, and *after* the main clause. The following sentence shows these comma uses:

Wandering through the woods,[1] **Mario,**[2] **a boy fascinated by nature,**[2] **found a box turtle,**[3] ***and* he watched it cross the trail,**[4] **a journey that took the little animal five minutes.**

1. The first comma sets off the introductory participial phrase *Wandering through the woods.* (rule 1)

2. The next two commas enclose the non-essential appositive phrase *a boy fascinated by nature.* (rule 2)

3. The comma before the coordinating conjunction *and* separates the two main clauses. (rule 3)

4. The last comma separates the second main clause, *he watched it cross the trail*, from the non-essential appositive that follows it. (rule 2)

Comma Category 1: Introducing Main Clauses

We often begin sentences with an introductory word, phrase, or subordinate clause, which should be separated from the main clause with a comma. This comma usually falls directly in front of the noun phrase ending with the simple subject, as in these examples:

1. ***However,* the tired old man needed to rest.**

2. ***However,* Stan needed to rest.**

In **sentence 1**, the comma that sets off *however* falls at the beginning of the underlined noun phrase, *the tired old man*, which ends with the simple subject *man*. In **sentence 2**, the comma is directly before the simple subject, *Stan*, with no other words attached to it. Most sentences follow the pattern of number 2, as you can see in the examples that follow.

INTRODUCTORY SINGLE WORDS

1. **Conjunctive adverb**

   Common conjunctive adverbs include *however, nevertheless, therefore, in fact,* and *consequently.*

   However, Sadie wants to visit Leamington in the spring.

2. **Adverb**

   Fortunately, she does have the money for the trip.

   No, I'm not going anywhere with him.

3. **Transitional word**

   Common transitional words include *first, finally, next, last, also,* and *second.*

   First, the band had to set up its amplifiers.

4. **Present participle**

   Wondering, Jan watched as the bull-dozer moved closer.

5. **Past participle**

   Exasperated, John hung up on the telemarketer.

6. **Mild interjection**

   Oh, I see that you already have a date.

In the following sentences, find the main clause, underline the <u>verb</u> or <u>verb phrase</u>, and circle the (subject) Next, set off with a comma single words at the beginning of the sentences. Notice that the comma usually falls directly in front of the subject of the main clause.

EXAMPLE: **Also, (you) <u>should pack</u> a lunch.**

1. Surely no one would be that foolish.

2. Next Graham decided to read his grammar textbook.

3. Yes we are coming to the lecture tonight.

4. Finally the professor showed up.

5. Limping Aileen slowly crossed the classroom to the accessible seating area.

6. Unconcerned Jay left the mess for later.

7. Create three of your own sentences that begin with a single introductory word. Underline the <u>verb</u> or <u>verb phrase</u> of your main clause and circle the (subject)

   a. _____

   b. _____

   c. _____

INTRODUCTORY PHRASES

Phrases also require a comma when used at the beginning of sentences, as you may remember from Chapter 11.

1.	**Prepositional phrase**	*Next to the bookshelf in the family room,* <u>Farah</u> <u>set</u> her umbrella.
2.	**Present participial phrase**	*Leaping from the bank,* <u>William</u> <u>splashed</u> into the river.
3.	**Past participial phrase**	*Exasperated by the outcome,* <u>John</u> <u>hung up</u> on the telemarketer.
4.	**Absolute phrase with present participle**	*The plane flying low,* <u>searchers</u> <u>looked</u> for signs of wreckage.
5.	**Absolute phrase with past participle**	*The boat unprepared for the open ocean,* <u>few</u> of the searchers <u>thought</u> they would find any survivors.
6.	**Infinitive phrase**	*To win the lottery,* <u>Terry</u> <u>thought</u> that he should buy at least ten tickets weekly.
7.	**Appositive phrase**	*An accident waiting to happen,* <u>Tom</u> <u>staggered</u> through the door and into the party.

INTRODUCTORY CLAUSES

Adverb clauses that begin sentences also need to be set off where they join a main clause, as shown in the following examples:

1. **_Because the disposal company would no longer pick up glass_, Burt <u>began</u> carting his bottles to the recycling centre.**

2. **_When robins return in April_, we <u>know</u> that spring is near.**

One way to identify adverb clauses is to memorize a few cue words, such as the subordinating conjunctions *because* and *when* in the previous sentences. Here are some common ones: *if, since, when, after, until, while, as, although, before, so that.*

Notice that the word groups in the previous phrase and clause examples add meaning to the main clause, in effect introducing the main idea of the sentence.

PROBLEMS WITH INTRODUCTORY WORD GROUPS

When other words precede phrases and the adverb clause, we sometimes miss where the comma belongs. The following sentences place commas correctly:

1. *A few days after I met her,* I told Sophie that I would help her study.

2. *With the wind howling outside,* no one wanted to walk the dog.

Sentence 1 begins with a noun phrase, so we might miss the comma needed to mark the end of the adverb clause. **Sentence 2** begins with *with*, but this word is part of the absolute phrase, which should be set off with a comma.

Compound and compound-complex sentences can also make it difficult to see where introductory commas belong. When punctuating a two-part sentence, treat the second part as if it were the start of a new sentence. Therefore, if an introductory word group follows a coordinating conjunction (*and, but, so, or, yet, for, nor*) or a semicolon, use a comma after the introductory phrase, as in the following examples:

1. Nora wants to have her friend over this weekend, *but with both her children sick from the flu,* she knows that she can't.

2. Friday was miserable for everyone; *even though Nora gave her children cough medicine,* they still coughed through the night.

In **sentence 1,** an absolute phrase follows *but* in the second part of this sentence, so the phrase requires a comma. The second half of **sentence 2** follows the semicolon with an adverb clause starting with *even though*, so it also must use a comma.

ACTIVITY 15.2 Comma Category 1 with Introductory Word Groups

In each of the following sentences, find the main clause, underline the <u>verb</u> or <u>verb phrase,</u> and circle the (subject.) Now use a comma where needed to set off the introductory adverb clause or phrase.

EXAMPLE: Sliding down the banister, (Eileen) was careful to stop before she reached the bottom of the stairs.

1. On the hutch of her desk Chiku keeps her library books.

2. Excited about summer break students and teachers alike found it hard to concentrate on their work.

3. His Canadian Forces' army reserve unit returning to Afghanistan for another tour of duty Tyler wondered if the war would ever be over.

4. Before the rim of the sun dropped into the Pacific Ron readied his camera to snap a photo of the green flash.

5. Feeling better than she had for a week the coach had a few kind words for her skaters.

6. When the team from Brazil took the field the World Cup fans knew that they were about to see an exciting game.

7. Create three of your own sentences that begin with the following introductory word groups requiring a comma. Underline the <u>verb</u> or <u>verb phrase</u> of the main clause and circle the (subject)

   a. Participial phrase: _____

      _____

   b. Prepositional phrase(s): _____

      _____

   c. Adverb clause: _____

      _____

Comma Category 2: Setting Off Non-essential Word Groups

The second major reason for using commas is to enclose non-essential words or set them off at the end of main clauses. *Non-essential* means that the words are not needed to complete the meaning of the sentence. If such material is cut, the main idea is still clear. Let's compare non-essential to essential word groups:

ESSENTIAL

1. **Last semester, Robert took a class *that* he barely passed.**

NON-ESSENTIAL

2. **Last semester, Robert took Algebra 121, *which* he barely passed.**

3. **Last semester, Robert took Algebra 121, *which* he barely passed, but he took it because he needed it for his major.**

In **sentence 1**, the clause beginning with *that* identifies the class that Robert took, so the clause is essential in the sentence and does not require a comma. On the other hand, **sentences 2 and 3** use a *which* clause to give additional commentary, but not information essential to complete the meaning of the sentence. Therefore, commas are needed. (We use the relative pronouns *that* and *which* to refer to things, animals, and ideas, with *which* reserved for non-essential clauses.)

ESSENTIAL

4. **A writer of children's books *who* is imaginative and industrious can succeed in the business.**

NON-ESSENTIAL

5. **One fabulously successful writer of children's books is Kenneth Oppel, *who* is imaginative and industrious.**

6. **Kenneth Oppel, *who* is imaginative and industrious, is a fabulously successful writer of children's books.**

Sentence 4 uses the *who* clause to identify what kind of children's writer can succeed: one *who is imaginative and industrious*. So no commas are needed. On the other hand, **sentences 5 and 6** have already identified the writer by using a proper noun, *Kenneth Oppel*; therefore, the *who* clause that follows is non-essential to complete the meaning of the sentence, and commas are required. (When referring to people——even indirectly as, for example, *teachers, police officers, nurses*, and so forth——careful writers usually use the relative pronoun *who* instead of *that*.)

> **HINT**
>
> Use the word *who* (not *that*) to refer to people (individuals and groups, both specific and general).

We often use non-essential word groups to enrich writing. However, when doing so, we should signal with commas that the material is of secondary importance. In the following pages, you will see examples of non-essential single words, phrases, and clauses. Notice that the introductory word groups from the previous comma category still require commas when shifted within or attached to the end of the main clause.

NON-ESSENTIAL SINGLE WORDS

Conjunctive adverb

Common conjunctive adverbs include *however, nevertheless, therefore, in fact,* and *consequently.*

Sadie <u>wants</u> to visit Leamington, *however,* in the spring.

Adverb

She <u>does have</u> the money for the trip, *fortunately.*

Present participle

Jan <u>watched</u>, *wondering,* as the bull-dozer moved closer.

Past participle

John, *exasperated,* <u>hung up</u> on the telemarketer.

ACTIVITY 15.3 Comma Category 2 with Non-essential Words

In the following sentences, find the main clause, underline the <u>verb</u> or <u>verb phrase</u>, and circle the (subject) Next, use commas to set off non-essential words within or at the end of the sentences.

EXAMPLE: (You) <u>should</u>, finally, <u>give</u> everyone on the committee a copy.

1. Skipping the writing of a final exam surely is foolish.
2. Both boys trembling tried to dare each other to go into the haunted house.
3. Professor Broomfield listened to her student's creative explanation for the absence fascinated.
4. We had nevertheless no other option but to pay the library late fee.
5. Sue's team leader in fact announced that they would help with Habitat for Humanity over the weekend.
6. Allen in addition decided that he needed a haircut.
7. Create three of your own sentences that use a non-essential word within them or at the end. Underline the <u>verb</u> or <u>verb phrase</u> of the main clause and circle the (subject) and place the comma(s) carefully.

   a. _____
   b. _____
   c. _____

NON-ESSENTIAL PHRASES

Non-essential phrases can often be shifted from the front of a sentence to within it or attached to the end. You can see examples in the following sentences, most of which we worked with in Comma Category 1:

Present participial phrase William, *leaping from the bank,* splashed into the river.

Past participial phrase John hung up on the telemarketer, *annoyed with the outcome.*

Absolute phrase with present participle	Searchers looked for signs of wreckage, *the plane flying low.*
Absolute phrase with past participle	Few of the searchers thought they would find any survivors, *the boat having been unprepared for the open ocean.*
Infinitive phrase	Terry thought that, *to win the lottery,* he should buy at least ten tickets weekly.
Appositive phrase	Tom, *an accident waiting to happen,* staggered through the door and into the party.

We sometimes misuse commas when we confuse essential with non-essential participial phrases within and at the ends of sentences. Compare the participial phrases that end the following two sentences:

1. **Citizens listened yet again to certain politicians *arguing* against Canadian involvement with the Kyoto Protocol.**

2. **Citizens listened yet again to certain politicians arguing against Canadian involvement with the Kyoto Protocol, *wondering* about Canada's commitment to help slow climate change.**

Sentence 1 tells which politicians the people are paying attention to. We could rewrite the phrase into an essential adjective clause that reads *"politicians who were arguing against Canada's involvement. . ."* Therefore, in both cases, we do not use a comma. **Sentence 2**, on the other hand, ends with a non-essential participial phrase, one that merely adds a comment. So we need a comma.

Notice that we could easily shift the phrase *"wondering about Canada's commitment . . ."* to the beginning of the sentence because the phrase describes the subject, *citizens*. However, the phrase *"arguing against . . ."* is fixed in place next to the word it describes, *politicians*. To shift the "arguing" phrase to the beginning of **sentence 1** would create a dangling modifier.

HINT

For more on dangling modifiers, see Chapter 8.

ACTIVITY 15.4 Comma Category 2 with Non-essential Phrases

In the following sentences, find the main clause, underline the verb or verb phrase, and circle the subject. Now use a comma to set off the non-essential phrases. If a sentence is correct as it is, place a *C* in the space provided.

> EXAMPLE: *C* **Seeing his girlfriend's parents watching from the window, Nathan said goodbye to Tammy quickly, falling over himself in his haste to leave.**

1. _____ Doug decided to buy more organic food when he learned of the organic farming industry's benefits sustaining small farms, limiting environmental damage, producing tastier and healthier food, and raising animals more humanely.

2. _____ Recent reports have shown that, to increase their chances of survival, people are better off in the rear of a jet during a crash.

3. _____ Janet was nervous on her first day of scuba diving lessons concerned about sinking like a stone to the bottom of the pool.

4. _____ Emily feeling optimistic filled out the application for a home equity loan.

5. _____ Engineers at MIT, to design better submarine propellers, have been studying bluegill, fish able to swim without backward drag.

6. _____ Some police departments, issuing traffic tickets for going even five kilometres over the limit, have zero tolerance for speeding.

7. Create three of your own sentences that use a non-essential phrase within each of them or at the end. Underline the <u>verb</u> or <u>verb phrase</u> of the main clause and circle the (subject)

a. _____

_____

b. _____

_____

c. _____

_____

NON-ESSENTIAL CLAUSES

HINT

For more on non-essential versus essential word groups, see Chapters 11 and 12.

Like phrases, clauses can be non-essential. When dealing with **adjective clauses** (clauses most often beginning with the relative pronouns *who, which,* and *that*), we must determine if they are essential or not. If they are non-essential, we set them off with commas. Sometimes we create non-essential adjective clauses with words other than relative pronouns, most commonly the words *when* and *where*, as in the following examples:

1. **Essential:** Mary <u>felt</u> more comfortable in the house *where* she once lived.

2. **Non-essential:** Mary <u>felt</u> more comfortable in her last house, *where* she lived for five years.

3. **Essential:** Chris only vaguely <u>remembers</u> the time in his life *when* he used to stay up and party till 3:00 a.m.

4. **Non-essential:** Chris only vaguely <u>remembers</u> his twenties, *when* he used to stay up and party till 3:00 a.m.

 Sentence 1 uses an essential adjective clause to identify which house Mary felt more comfortable in. Contrast sentence 1 with **sentence 2**, which requires a comma because when we say *her last house*, we have identified which house and so do not need the *where* clause that follows. It is non-essential. The same pattern holds true for sentences 3 and 4. **Sentence 3** needs the *when* clause to identify which time in Chris' life; **sentence 4** names the time (his twenties) and so does not require a comma. The adjective clause in sentence 4 is non-essential.

ACTIVITY 15.5 Comma Category 2 with Non-essential Adjective Clauses

In the following sentences, find the main clause, underline the <u>verb</u> or <u>verb phrase</u> and circle the (subject) Then use a comma to set off the non-essential adjective clause. If a sentence is correct, place a *C* in the space provided.

 EXAMPLE: The Arctic Sea (ice) <u>is continuing</u> to melt, which will mean the eventual end of polar bears and other Arctic species.

1. _____ A service dog is a valuable animal that helps some people lead more productive lives.

2. _____ Women in Canada who have made many social and economic advances are still paid less than their male counterparts.

3. _____ Europeans were the ones who first developed the car, and R. S. McLaughlin who lived in Oshawa first developed the car in Canada.

4. _____ Mayflies which may spend a year or more as nymphs at the bottom of ponds and rivers hatch, take flight, breed, lay eggs, and die within 24 hours.

5. _____ Iceland is a country that gets most of its energy from geothermal power.

6. _____ The Arctic Sea, which provides the solid-ground habitat for polar bears, is continuing to melt.

7. Create three of your own sentences that use commas to mark a non-essential adjective clause within them or at the end. Underline the <u>verb</u> or <u>verb phrase</u> of the main clause and circle the ⟨subject⟩

   a. _____

   _____

   b. _____

   _____

   c. _____

   _____

Comma Category 3: Dividing Main Clauses along with a Coordinating Conjunction

The last major reason for using commas is to separate main clauses within compound and compound-complex sentences—sentences that use a coordinating conjunction (*and, but, or, so, yet, nor, for*) to join two main clauses. Here are examples to illustrate the use of coordinating conjunctions:

1. **The <u>history</u> many of us learn in school <u>is</u> often incomplete, *and* sometimes <u>it</u> <u>is</u> inaccurate.**

2. **For example, <u>Christopher Columbus</u> <u>is thought</u> by many to have discovered America, *but* <u>he</u> never <u>set</u> foot on the mainland.**

3. **However, <u>Columbus</u> <u>did</u> "discover" keys in the Bahamas, Hispaniola, and Cuba, *so* <u>he</u> <u>was</u> able to secure financing for three more voyages.**

4. **<u>Columbus</u> <u>did</u> not <u>discover</u> the passage to China that he was looking for, *nor* <u>did</u> <u>he</u> reach the Indonesian Islands.**

5. **<u>He</u> <u>did</u>, however, <u>name</u> the inhabitants of Hispaniola "indios," *for* <u>Columbus</u> <u>thought</u> that he was in the Indies.**

6. **As we look more critically at other historical "facts," <u>will</u> <u>they</u> <u>be confirmed</u>, *or* <u>will</u> <u>we</u> <u>find</u> similar surprises?**

Notice that each sentence has a <u>subject</u> and <u>verb</u> within main clauses on *both* sides of the coordinating conjunction. As discussed in Chapter 10, we often coordinate words and phrases with conjunctions like *and, but, yet,* and *or.* These coordinations do not require commas because they are not separate clauses, although items in a series will, of course, also use commas (see **sentence 3** above).

It is important, however, not to insert a comma *everywhere* that you see a coordinating conjunction, as the following examples show:

1. Not this: **<u>Hyacinths</u>, *and* <u>daffodils</u> <u>mark</u> the beginning of spring, *and* <u>emerge</u> when the rain, *and* warming earth bring them to life.**

2. But this: **<u>Hyacinths</u> *and* <u>daffodils</u> <u>mark</u> the beginning of spring *and* <u>emerge</u> when the rain *and* warming earth bring them to life.**

HINT

Do not put a comma before every coordinating conjunction.

Sentence 1 uses a compound subject, *hyacinths and daffodils,* which requires no comma. Also, no comma is needed to separate the two-part verb *mark* and *emerge.* *Rain* and *earth* are subjects of the adverb clause, so they, too, should not be divided with a comma. As you can see, conjunctions joining pairs do not need a comma.

3. **Not this:** **The spring weather felt, so good that Cassandra went, for a walk, so (that) she could welcome the season properly.**

4. **But this:** **The spring weather felt so good that Cassandra went for a walk so (that) she could welcome the season properly.**

Sentence 3 requires no commas for these reasons: the first *so* is used as an adverb rather than a coordinating conjunction; *for* is used as a preposition; and the second *so* includes an understood *that* (in parentheses in the example but often left out of a sentence). *So that* is a subordinating conjunction. However, when using *so* as a coordinating conjunction, think of it as meaning "thus" or "therefore." When using *for* as a coordinating conjunction, think of it as meaning "because."

One final point about coordinating conjunctions: when the main clauses are short, some writers omit the comma, as in the following example:

Anna is happy so my job is done.

ACTIVITY 15.6 Comma Category 3 with Commas to Divide Main Clauses

In the following sentences, find the main clauses, underline the <u>verbs</u> or <u>verb phrases,</u> and circle the subjects. Next, divide the clauses using a comma before the coordinating conjunction. If a sentence is correct, place a C in the space provided.

> EXAMPLE: _____ Insurance companies say that they exist to protect those they insure, yet the companies' primary goal is profit.

1. _____ Some insurance companies are more profit driven than others so they try to deny any claim that they can avoid paying.

2. _____ Perhaps many health insurance companies are in this category for claims are often huge.

3. _____ Bailey went to the Nelson Art Gallery so that she could see the Impressionist exhibit.

4. _____ The scientist waited for three days in her rainforest tree perch but finally got the video footage that she was waiting for.

5. _____ The players and management will have to settle the strike or the fans will not have baseball this season.

6. _____ Honeybees are dying by the thousands from pesticide use and as a result the honey business is in danger.

7. Create three of your own compound or compound-complex sentences that use coordinating conjunctions. Underline the <u>verbs</u> or <u>verb phrases</u> of the main clauses and circle the subjects.

    a. _____

    _____

    b. _____

    _____

    c. _____

    _____

Secondary Comma Categories

While the Big Three comma categories account for most necessary commas, there are other comma uses that writers should learn in order to avoid confusion.

Items in a Series

When three or more words or word groups are listed in a row, a comma should follow each. This is often called a "serial comma," as seen in the following examples:

Series of nouns:	Steven will shop for *shampoo, toothpaste,* and *hair spray.*
Series of verbs:	On his way to the Science Centre, Kyle *travelled* north on Warden, *turned* west on Eglinton Avenue, and *wove* his way into the parking lot.
Series of main clauses:	*Rohana brought the green salad, Rajkumar brought naan,* and *Gabriel brought wine for the dinner.*

Using a comma before the *and* in a series is now optional, but you are never wrong to use a comma there. By using the comma, you will avoid the potential confusion in sentences like the following:

If you want to work here, you will be doing laundry, vacuuming, cooking and cleaning windows.

Does the job description really include cooking the windows?

Coordinate Adjectives and Compound Nouns

Coordinate adjectives——two or more equal adjectives in front of a noun—— need a comma between them.

Koalas are *cute, cuddly* mammals.

In this sentence, we could use the word *and* in place of the comma (*cute and cuddly*) or reverse the two adjectives (*cuddly, cute*). Therefore, the adjectives describe the noun equally and should be separated by commas.

Contrast this with the following example, which uses **cumulative adjectives:**

Three beautiful young swans floated on the pond.

The words *three beautiful* describe the noun *swans*, but we could neither insert *and* between the words (*three and beautiful*) nor reverse them (*beautiful, three*) and still make sense. The two adjectives do not describe equally so they should not be separated by commas.

Similarly, do not use a comma directly before or between **compound nouns,** like the following:

Marla is happy to work in an *environmentally friendly* <u>office building</u>.

In this sentence, *office building* is a single unit, so no comma should be used between *friendly* and *office* or between *office* and *building*.

> **English Review Note**
>
> Cumulative adjectives fall into these main categories: number, judgment, size, age, colour, location, and material.

Contrasting Expressions

We often contrast ideas in a sentence by using commas with the word *not*:

Gregor, not Karim, is ahead in the tournament.

Misleading Expressions

If a sentence might be misinterpreted without a comma, either insert a comma or restructure the sentence:

MISLEADING: On the shelf above the photo albums of our vacation are stored.

COMMA ADDED: On the shelf above, the photo albums of our vacation are stored.

RESTRUCTURED: The photo albums of our vacation are stored on the shelf above.

Conventions: Numbers, Addresses, Place Names, Titles, Dates, Direct Address, Quotations

When using numbers, addresses, place names, titles, dates, direct address, and quotations, follow the conventions of standard comma placement, observing SI (Système Internationale) notation——no commas——in large numbers:

Numbers	9 674 630
Addresses *Note:* A comma is used to separate the street address from the city, and the city from the province. No comma is used in postal codes.	Joan lives at 1234 Riverside Drive East, Windsor, ON N8Y 3X7.
Place names	Orangeville, Ontario, is near the Caledon Hills.
Titles (of persons)	Professor Green, Ph.D., knows Jay Antwhistle, Jr.
Dates	On September 28, 1952, Lucille Edna gave birth to a healthy son.
Direct address	"Danny, will you please stop fidgeting?"
Quotations	"Yes," Matt Standingwater replied, "we call it the 'Bambi Effect' when people resist killing cute animals even when it is necessary."

ACTIVITY 15.7 Secondary Comma Categories

Put commas where needed in the following sentences. More than one comma may be needed in each. If a sentence is correct, put a C in the blank provided.

EXAMPLE: _C_ **Mario, not Victor, visited relatives in Purcell's Cove, Nova Scotia.**

1. _____ Two iridescent ruby-throated hummingbirds hovered at the feeder.

2. _____ John Henry a champion racehorse won $6 591 860 between 1977 and 1984.

3. _____ Peter Robison M.D. has discovered an effective inexpensive cure for eczema acne and psoriasis.

4. _____ In the shower by the drain you can see the crack starting to develop.

5. _____ Riley said "Mom if I have to eat any more of those mangoes mandarin oranges or papayas I'm going to be sick!"

6. _____ There were 25 smart mischievous second graders at work on the substitute teacher flying paper airplanes talking and chasing each other around the room.

7. _____ "Jamie" said her mother "will you please address this envelope to The Canadian Wildlife Federation at 350 Michael Cowpland Drive Kanata ON K2M 2W1."

Chapter Summary

1. Punctuation helps readers sort out a writer's ideas.

2. There are three main uses (the Big Three Categories) of the comma:
   a. Commas separate a main clause from an introductory word or words.
   b. Commas enclose or separate non-essential words, phrases, or clauses that come within or after a main clause.
   c. Commas separate two main clauses.

3. There are several secondary comma categories:
   a. Commas separate items in a series.
   b. Commas separate coordinate adjectives.
   c. Commas separate contrasting ideas.
   d. Commas are used in the following conventions: addresses, place names, dates, titles, direct speech, and quotations.

Other Punctuation Marks and Mechanics

If we see our writing world as being in its own galaxy, we can realize how the act of writing is like travelling in uncharted territory. The Canadian and U.S. astronauts must forge their own path in space with their mobile satellite system and leave a trail where there are few guidelines to show them the way. Likewise, when you do your own writing, you must make your own trail for your reader to know the way among your words. Before reading further in the chapter, see if you can find a way to use the following marks of punctuation — colon, dash, semicolon, exclamation mark, and parentheses — in a paragraph about exploring uncharted territory. You might consider the act of writing as this territory, or you might consider a phase of your life, or a physical place you have explored, any of which offered few guidelines. After working through the chapter, check back to see if you have used the punctuation correctly in your paragraph.

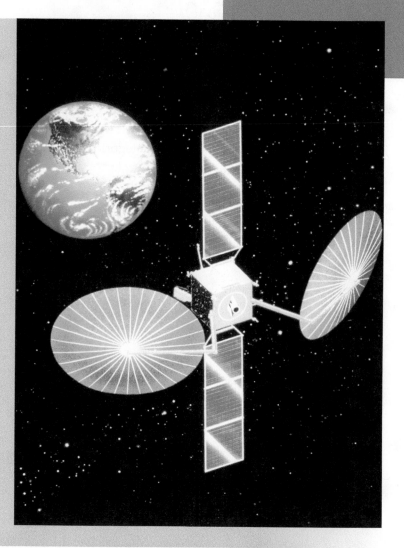

What Are We Trying to Achieve and Why?

In Chapter 15, we learned about the comma as the utility mark of punctuation in writing, but there are other marks and methods useful for grouping and emphasizing ideas. In some cases, these marks are used in similar ways, so the writer has a choice. Here, in Chapter 16, we will see how to work with semicolons and other end marks, colons, dashes, parentheses, and a few other methods for organizing and clarifying our writing.

Semicolons and Other End Marks

L016.1

Semicolons

We know that **periods** are full stops in sentences, bringing the reader to a halt. Semicolons might be thought of as half-stops, marks midway between a comma and a period. We use semicolons for the following two purposes:

1. To divide main clauses without using a coordinating conjunction (such as *and* or *but*)

2. To separate word groups in a lengthy series that contains commas

DIVIDING MAIN CLAUSES

Semicolons have the same power as a period to end a main clause. When you see a semicolon dividing two main clauses, the first complete thought has ended. When it is used, however, the second main clause continues without a capital letter, suggesting that the main clauses on either side of the semicolon are more closely related than two sentences separated by a period. Here are some examples:

> **HINT**
>
> Using semicolons to divide main clauses is one way to fix a comma splice or run-on sentence (see Chapter 13).

1. **It seems as if everyone who loves rock knows "American Woman" by the Guess Who; many people, though, aren't familiar with another classic Guess Who tune, "Rain Dance."**

2. **It seems as if everyone who loves rock knows "American Woman" by the Guess Who; *however*, many people aren't familiar with another classic Guess Who tune, "Rain Dance."**

In **sentences 1 and 2**, periods could replace the semicolons; however, the second main clause in each sentence is so closely related to the first that the semicolon is a good choice. **Sentence 2** shows how to use a conjunctive adverb (in this case *however*) when the relationship between the ideas in the main clauses warrants it. Other common conjunctive adverb connectors are *therefore, nevertheless, then, in fact,* and *consequently.*

A semicolon is also used to replace the comma between main clauses originally joined by a coordinating conjunction if there are commas in either of the main clauses. Here is an example:

> **Even in the days of the early Greeks, dolls were a part of childhood; and since then, they have been objects of great desirability, some being treasured collector's items.**

SEPARATING WORD GROUPS IN A SERIES

The second use of the semicolon is to separate items in a series that have commas within them, as in the following example:

> **Robots have reached the point today where they can interact with people, saying hello, for example, and shaking their hands; interact with their environment, for example, moving away from obstacles in their path and locating objects they are programmed to recognize; and learn from their mistakes.**

In the sentence above, there are three primary word groups in the series, *interact with people, interact with their environment,* and *learn from their mistakes.* However, the first two word groups have other words within them that are separated by commas, so semicolons are used to avoid confusion among the main word groups in the series.

Exclamation Marks

In the same way that a period or a semicolon marks the end of an idea, so, too, does an **exclamation mark**; however, there is emotion indicated by an exclamation mark, such as a strong opinion or a warning.

Feed them *yourself!*

Question Marks

The last end mark that we need to recognize is the **question mark**. It, too, indicates the end of an idea; however, it indicates a different sentence type, specifically, an interrogative sentence, which asks a question. Here is an example:

What would you like for dinner tonight?

L016.2 Colons

The **colon** has three primary uses:

1. It can begin a formal list.
2. It can separate closely related main clauses (as does the semicolon).
3. It can mark a formal appositive (non-essential describing word or phrase) at the end of a main clause.

Two other uses for the colon are **introducing quotations** (Oscar Wilde spoke these words: "I never travel without my diary. One should always have something sensational to read.") and after the **formal salutation** of a business letter (Dear Professor Morris:).

Introducing Formal Lists

When **introducing a list,** the colon should be viewed as end punctuation. Like a period, it ends one grammatical sentence and begins the list:

Margo has three goals this summer: to get in shape, to see her friends more, and to volunteer for service work in her community.

You do not need a colon in a sentence that includes the series of items within it, like this:

Unnecessary colon: This summer Margo plans to: get in shape, see her friends more, and volunteer for service work in her community.

Separating Main Clauses

Similar to a semicolon, a colon can be used to divide closely related main clauses. To use a colon, however, the second clause should explain the meaning of the first:

Some studies show that aspirin is not a good treatment for high blood pressure: the studies say that aspirin can increase heart attacks.

Marking Formal Appositives

The following sentence ends with a **formal appositive,** which describes the noun it follows, *Basra.* A comma or dash could also be used here.

The wealth of Iraq is centred in Basra: the oil producer for the rest of the country.

Dashes

The **dash** is a versatile punctuation mark that can help writers in several ways: to set off a series that begins a sentence, to indicate an abrupt break in thought within a sentence, to enclose items in a series that contain commas, and to emphasize a word or word group at the end of a sentence. Avoid overusing dashes; try to use only one or two per page.

Uses of the Dash

Set off a series that begins a sentence:	The Liberal, Conservative, New Democratic, Green, and Bloc Québécois parties of Canada—they all claim to have the answer for the nation's ills.
Show a break in thought:	Dorothy is going to Vancouver—or so she says—for the weekend. (Commas or parentheses could also be used here. Using dashes provides more emphasis than the other two choices.)
Set off items in a series:	Mwaka checked off the trip gear—clothing, tent, sleeping bag, and food—but did not remember his compass. (Without the dashes, this sentence might mislead readers that *trip gear* is just another item on the list: *Mwaka checked off the trip gear, clothing, tent, sleeping bag, and food. . . .*)
Emphasize final word group:	No one felt as strongly about the issue of climate change as Clarice—unless perhaps it was David Suzuki. (A comma, a colon, or parentheses might also be used here. The dash gives the most emphasis of the three.)

> **HINT**
>
> A dash (—) is longer than a hyphen (-). Use two hyphens on your keyboard to create a dash.

Parentheses

We use **parentheses** primarily to add non-essential material to a main clause, much as we use commas to set off similar unneeded but useful material. Sometimes commas and parentheses are interchangeable in a sentence, but writers usually reserve parentheses for more loosely related material, as in the following example:

> **Himani Bannerji speaks eloquently (and often) about the dehumanizing effects of racial discrimination on both the oppressed and the oppressor.**

If you insert a whole main clause within parentheses, you do not need to capitalize the lead word or end the clause with punctuation:

> **Himani Bannerji speaks eloquently (and she speaks often) about the dehumanizing effects of racial discrimination on both the oppressed and the oppressor.**

> **HINT**
>
> Avoid overusing parentheses; usually once or twice a page is maximum.

ACTIVITY 16.1 Using Punctuation that Separates

In the following sentences, underline the <u>verbs</u> or <u>verb phrases</u> of the main clauses and circle the (subjects). Then locate word groups that should be set off from the rest of the sentence, and use one of the following marks of punctuation to do so: semicolon, period, exclamation mark, question mark, colon, dash, or parentheses.

HINT

There may be more than
one error in a sentence and
more than one way to fix the
problem.

EXAMPLE: (Birds) can breathe so efficiently — three times better than mammals — because they are descended from dinosaurs: creatures that survived during an age of low atmospheric oxygen.

1. Rick Genest also known as Zombie Boy is a Montreal-based artist and model who has toured with Lady Gaga because of his body tattoos.

2. Nine countries now possess nuclear weapons however not all members of the nuclear club advertise their nuclear capability.

3. One urban myth talks about the woman bitten by a venomous snake while trying on a coat shipped from another country Pakistan, India, China, Indonesia, Korea this myth combines fear of snakes with distrust of "foreigners."

4. Upper Canada Village where I worked for three summers is a recreated village representing 1866.

5. Top water lures, spinner baits, and plastic lures David had all he needed for smallmouth bass fishing on the Thames River his favourite bass-fishing location as a teenage boy.

6. After his heart attack, Harold researched how to reduce plaque in his bloodstream, finding this out certain oils such as olive oil raise good cholesterol and other oils dissolve plaque in blood vessels, with only one-half ounce of the oil needed daily.

7. Before leaving for class, Birgit checked all her school supplies pens, pencils, markers, paper, and flash drive so she would be prepared for the day.

LO16.5 Quotation Marks

Quotation marks are used primarily to enclose spoken and written words, either as dialogue or quotations from a text. We also use quotation marks to enclose the titles of short creative works (such as stories, essays, poems, newspaper and magazine articles, songs, and episodes on television), and to show that we question the word's intended meaning. Here are some examples:

Note the following main uses of quotation marks:

Dialogue:	"Let's get the sleds," said Darlene, "before all the snow melts!"
Quotation from text:	In the latest edition of his popular history text, Kenneth Davis remarks: "We like to think of elected officials as leaders, but in fact they often follow where the country is going."
Questioning the word's intended meaning:	The MP declared that she would consider the legislation in a "timely" way, which we took to mean never.

Notice that the comma after *sleds*, the exclamation mark after *melts*, and the period after *going* are placed **inside** the quotation marks; the comma following *Darlene* in the middle of the dialogue sentence is **outside** the quotation marks.

Apostrophes

Apostrophes have two main functions:

1. They mark the omission of letters in contractions.
2. They show ownership—or possession.

Contractions

A **contraction** is a word formed as an abbreviated combination of other words; it uses an apostrophe to stand in for omitted letters. Here are some common contractions: *wouldn't* (would not), *won't* (will not), *let's* (let us), *it's* (it is), *you're* (you are), *who's* (who is/has). Be careful when using contractions not to mistake *it's, you're,* and *who's* for these sound-alike possessive pronouns: *its, your,* and *whose*.

HINT

It's, you're, and *who's* (contractions) are different words from *its, your,* and *whose* (possessive pronouns).

Possession

To show singular ownership, we use the apostrophe like this:

Sarah's exam   **the *storm's* fury**   **the *car's* GPS system**

To indicate plural possession, we put the apostrophe after the *s*:

the *students'* interests   **the *countries'* treaty**   **the *Harrises'* vacation**

We also use *'s* after names ending in *s*:

James's textbook   **Chris's rhubarb pie**   **Mr. Harris's vacation**

Some words that show possession are not obvious; for example, a *week's* delay (the delay *of a week*), last *year's* concert (the concert *of last year*), or a few *dollars'* worth of candy (the worth *of a few dollars*). Restating the possessive word as an "of" phrase usually clarifies the need for the apostrophe.

English Review Note

In English, an apostrophe is used to indicate possession. (This is not the case in all languages.)

Capital Letters

We capitalize **proper names**—specific, unique individuals or things—and words derived from them. Here are several categories of words we capitalize:

People, things, trademarks:	Matthew, Toyota Corolla, Tim Hortons, Kraft Dinner
Professional titles:	Professor Hastings, Doctor Roberts, Reverend Snow
Organizations, institutions, government offices, sports teams, companies:	Alpine Club of Canada, Habitat for Humanity, St. Clair College, Metropolitan Hospital, House of Commons, Ministry of Natural Resources, Toronto Maple Leafs, Cogeco
Nationalities, ethnicities, and races:	Greek, Russian, French, Chinese, Iraqi, Asian, First Nations, Caucasian
Languages:	Italian, Spanish, Mandarin, Swahili, Portuguese, English
Religions, deities, and holy books:	Christian, Buddhist, Muslim, Hindu, Christ, Allah, Yahweh, Bible, Qur'an, Torah
Historical documents, periods, events:	the British North America Act, the Middle Ages, the War of 1812
Geographic names:	the Rocky Mountains, Winnipeg, Pacific Northwest, Middle East, Conception Bay

English Review Note

Review this list. Capitalization rules differ from language to language. For instance, some languages capitalize all nouns, while English capitalizes only *proper* nouns. French uses fewer capitals than English.

Days, months, holidays:	Sunday, June, Thanksgiving
First word in a direct quotation:	Maggie asked, "Will you get the mail?"
Titles of books, stories, films, magazines, newspapers, poems, songs, and works of art:	*The Shack*, "The Moons of Jupiter," *Crash*, *Businessweek*, *The Globe and Mail*, "On Being Asked," "Time after Time," *The Scream*

In titles, capitalize all words except for *prepositions* (*on, in, at,* for example), *coordinating conjunctions* (*and, but, or, so, yet, nor, for*), and *articles* (*a, an, the*)—unless any of these words begins a title or a subtitle (in which case, they will follow a colon—as in the following example):

Sleeper: A Look into the Future

Do *not* capitalize the following:

Seasons:	fall, summer
Plants:	ivy, maple
Animals:	chipmunk, centipede
School subjects:	physics, history
Compass points:	north, south (unless a specific region, such as *Western Canada*)

Also, note that we capitalize a person's professional title but not the general profession:

Doctor Jackson, but Anna Jackson is a doctor

L016.8 Hyphens

Hyphens join words and show where they are divided into syllables.

Prefixes:	ex-politician, anti-government, self-esteem, pro-labour
Compound nouns:	daughter-in-law, go-getter, hand-me-down
Compound adjectives:	middle-class lifestyle, well-behaved son, long-awaited baby, well-known fiddler, first-class tickets

Note that, as a rule, a compound adjective is hyphenated only when it is placed in front of the noun it modifies.

Hyphens can also be used at the end of a line of text to divide a word between syllables:

**She was looking for a clean blouse to wear to the inter-
view when she found her missing scarf.**

Since the use of hyphens reflects changing language trends, it is best to check the dictionary if you are in doubt.

L016.9 Numbers

Often writers prefer to use **numerals** instead of **words** for numbers. However, formal writing calls for spelling out the numbers that are one digit (*two, nine*) and then using numerals for numbers with two digits or more (*55; 101; 3085; 4 896 142*). Here are other formal conventions for number use:

| Ordinals: | We were married on the seventh of March. |
| Fractions (that can be written in one or two words): | Canada supplies almost one-fifth of the crude oil imported into the United States. |

Periods of time:	Almost 40 years ago, John moved to Windsor.
Ages:	Now John is 78 years old.
Sentence beginnings: (Spell out a number at the start of a sentence, or recast the sentence.)	One hundred twelve people escaped from the fire. *or* Escaping from the fire were 112 people.
Percentages/decimals/ fractions:	The mixture was 10.5% (or 10.5 percent) water. She bought 3.5 metres of red velvet. The ladder, 2½ metres high, was too short.
Dates:	March 7, 2007
Addresses:	437 Holly Lane
Series: (Use numerals or words consistently.)	The trench was 116 metres long, 4 metres wide, and 30 centimetres deep.
Abbreviations or symbols:	30°C, 1.3 cm, 9 mm, 407 km, 50 km/h, 25 g, 250 kg, 2 L, p. 36
Amounts of money:	$8.35, 10 cents (or ten cents)
Page numbers:	page 98
Identification numbers:	Room 12, Highway 70, Channel 3
Times:	6:00 p.m. (or six o'clock)

English Review Note

Standard English uses a 12-hour clock, not a 24-hour one.

L016.10

Italics

The following list shows categories of works to italicize:

Books: (Short stories use quotation marks.)	*The Handmaid's Tale,* "The Lost Salt Gift of Blood"
Plays and movies:	*Anne of Green Gables, Bon Cop, Bad Cop*
Pamphlets:	*Training Your Wheaten Terrier*
Musical works:	*Cabaret*
Television and radio programs or podcasts: (Single episodes use quotation marks.)	*The National, Quirks and Quarks,* "Eating Well during the Recession"
Long poems: (Short poems use quotation marks.)	*The Iliad,* "Oh Never More"
Periodicals, such as magazines, newspapers, and journals: (Articles use quotation marks.)	*Businessweek,* "The Lifespan of a Recession"
Published speeches:	*I Have a Dream*
Works of art:	*Mona Lisa*
Websites: (Individual web pages use quotation marks.)	*amazon.com, yorku.ca* "Recommendations for Summer Reading from Indigo.ca"

Other uses of italics include the following:

Names of specific airplanes, trains, ships, and satellites: the *Titanic*, the *Orient-Express*, the *Hubble Space Telescope*

Words and letters specifically referred to: The Newfoundland word *lolly* refers to soft ice beginning to form in a harbour.

Emphasis (use italics sparingly for this purpose): John, you'd best leave *now*!

Note: In the event that a paper is handwritten, or if word-processing programs do not have an italics capability, underlining can be used instead of italics.

ACTIVITY 16.2 WORKING TOGETHER: Practising Mechanics

In the following sentences, correct the errors. Check for quotation marks, apostrophes, capitalization, hyphens, numbers, and italicizing/underlining. In pairs or small groups, compare your corrections with those of other classmates.

EXAMPLE: **The poem our hold on the planet, by robert frost, offers a modestly optimistic view of nature.**

The poem "Our Hold on the Planet," by Robert Frost, offers a modestly optimistic view of nature.

1. As he was reading stopping by woods on a snowy evening, alistair remarked, I wonder how frost really felt about death?

   _____

   _____

2. The movie enchanted is a fun spoof of many fairy tale clichés.

   _____

   _____

3. The Sycamore tree along indian creek in roe park is a beauty, it's bark silver-white and it's main trunk leaning at a 60 degree angle over the jogging path.

   _____

   _____

4. Felicia Abrams, M.d., author of the book the pills that kill you, said, only forty percent of the mice tested survived the New Drug.

   _____

   _____

5. There are many elvis look alikes who keep the kings memory alive through well rehearsed performance and close attention to costuming.

   _____

   _____

6. Nary said, its important to me to raise my kids so that they respect and care for the land, and, she added, that they know its ok to use the land, just not to use it up.

_____

_____

7. The war of 1812 actually went on until 1814 sir isaac brock was killed early on in the war and inspired those fighting on the Canadian side to keep up the struggle to repel the Americans.

_____

_____

Chapter Summary

1. Use a semicolon to divide main clauses without using a coordinating conjunction and to separate items in a series that are subdivided with commas.

2. Exclamation marks are used to indicate a strong opinion or warning.

3. Question marks indicate an interrogative sentence.

4. Use a colon primarily to begin a formal list, to separate closely related main clauses—where the second clause explains the meaning of the first—and to mark a formal appositive.

5. Use a dash to set off a series that begins a sentence, to show an abrupt break in thought, to enclose items in a series that contain commas, and to emphasize a word group at the end of a sentence.

6. Use parentheses to add non-essential material to a main clause.

7. Use quotation marks primarily to enclose the precise repetition of the spoken or written word or to identify the titles of short works, such as poems, stories, and single episodes of television shows.

8. Use the apostrophe to mark contractions and possession.

9. Capitalize proper nouns and words derived from them.

10. Use a hyphen to join words and to show where words are divided into syllables.

11. In general, use numerals for numbers of two or more digits, but spell out numbers of one digit. Formal convention calls for numerals in the following instances: dates; addresses; series of units; percentages, decimals, and fractions of more than two words; scores and statistics; abbreviations and symbols; money amounts; page numbers; identification numbers; and time.

12. Italicize (or underline) to emphasize a word or identify the titles of long works, such as books, plays and movies, pamphlets, musical works, television and radio shows or podcasts, long poems, periodicals, published speeches, works of art, websites, and specific names of vessels and vehicles.

Spelling and Sound-alike Words

Imagine that you are either walking to this school yourself or taking your children there for the first time. How would this huge misspelled word make you feel? Concerned for the quality of education? Amused? Either way, spelling errors, especially in a professional or educational setting, can reflect badly on a single writer or a whole organization. In a paragraph, discuss how and why poor spelling might influence your reader's opinion of you.

What Are We Trying to Achieve and Why?

An argument that might seem convincing in conversation can quickly lose credibility in writing if words are misspelled or used incorrectly. Although spelling should be a low priority in early drafts, careful writers try to catch every misspelling and sound-alike word error during the editing process. It's not just that errors in spelling can affect people's understanding of our ideas; even more often, misspelled words affect people's *perception* of us. Even the brightest, most well-qualified job applicant who submits a resumé littered with mistakes (like using *there* instead of *their* or *are* instead of *our*) or who writes phrases like *exsellent writen communnication skils* will have a hard time getting an interview.

English spelling can be difficult for everyone, especially in the case of words that are not spelled phonetically—words like *knit, knee, gnaw, photograph, xylophone,* and *reign.* But there are patterns we can depend on to answer many spelling questions. Chapter 17 will help you improve your spelling with some basic rules. It also provides lists of commonly misspelled and sound-alike words.

English Review Note

Spelling varies across English-speaking countries. Consult a dictionary—preferably the *Canadian Oxford Dictionary*—for correct Canadian English spellings. Common errors include *realise* (should be *realize*), *color* (should be *colour*), and *meter* (should be *metre*).

Suggestions to Help with Spelling

L017.1

1. **Make a decision to work on your spelling.** If you **want** to improve, you can.

2. **Develop the dictionary habit.** Write with a dictionary nearby. Put a question mark by words you are unsure of as you draft, and then use your dictionary to find the correct spelling. If you try several letter combinations and **still** cannot find the correct spelling, mark the word and ask someone for help—perhaps a fellow student or the professor.

3. **Use an electronic dictionary programmed** to search using approximate spellings.

4. **Take advantage of the spell-check feature** when working on the computer. Understand, however, that even the best spell-checkers cannot distinguish between sound-alike words such as *there* and *their.* Spell-checkers can often help with, but not solve, spelling problems. Be sure to set your word processing program for English (Canadian) as the default. (In Word, this is found under Review—Set Language.) As well, set your spell checker to check for grammar and style as well as spelling. (In Word, this is found under the Office Button—Word Options—Proofing.)

5. **Begin a personal spelling list** of words you are unsure of or have misspelled in your own work. Pay particular attention to the ordinary words you use regularly and to sound-alike words (*it's/its, their/there, then/than*). These words create far more problems than less commonly used words like *photosynthesis* or *encapsulate* that we are more likely to look up. Small, frequently misspelled words are generally more likely to plague writers.

6. **When you begin to edit, look closely at every word in every sentence,** pausing to sound the word out syllable by syllable.

7. **Try to remember pattern words** that have similar consonant/vowel arrangements and the same number of syllables. If, for example, you are unsure of whether to double the *p* in the word *hopped* but are fairly sure about the double *p* in *stopped,* the similarity in syllables and consonant/vowel arrangement will often help you make the right decision.

8. **Test yourself with the lists of commonly misspelled words and sound-alike words in this chapter.** On your spelling chart, list any word that you misspell during the test. It often helps to **pronounce** the word aloud several times, exaggerating the stresses on syllables, such as *REG-is-ter* or *math-e-MA-tics.*

HINT

The Improvement Chart at the back of this book is a good place to record your spelling list.

9. When you discover a misspelled word, look up the correct spelling, and then write the word several times, preferably within a sentence.

10. Study the spelling patterns listed in this chapter.

L017.2 # Review of Vowels and Consonants

English Review Note

Vowels often present a challenge and may need additional practice for mastery.

Much of spelling depends on being able to break words into syllables and to recognize vowels and consonants. **Syllables** are simply units of sound—the way a word is divided in the dictionary, for example, *syl-la-ble* or *foot-ball*. **Vowels** and **consonants** are the names that we give to the two groups of letters into which we divide the twenty-six letters of our alphabet.

> **Vowels:**   *a, e, i, o, u*
>
> **Consonants:**   *b, c, d, f, g, h, j, k, l, m, n, p, q, r, s, t, v, w, x, y, z*

The letter *y* can function as either a vowel or a consonant, depending on the word it is in and its placement in the word.

> **Y as a vowel:**   *pretty* (the *y* sounds like *ee*) and *fly* (the *y* sounds like *i*)
>
> **Y as a consonant:** *yes*

L017.3 # Useful Spelling Patterns

Doubling the Final Consonant

To know when to double the final consonant of a word when adding a suffix (a brief ending like *-ed*, *-ing*, *-er*, or *-est*), ask the three following questions:

1. Is the word one syllable (e.g. *spot*) or accented on the last syllable (e.g. *re-CUR*)?

2. Are the last three letters of the word consonant/vowel/consonant (sp-o-t, rec-u-r)?

3. Does the suffix begin with a vowel (*-ed,-ing,-est*)?

If all three of these conditions are met, double the final consonant, as in the following lists:

SINGLE-SYLLABLE WORDS	WORDS ACCENTED ON THE FINAL SYLLABLE
spin + ing = spi **nn**ing	oc-CUR + ing = occu **rr**ing
drop + ed = dro **pp**ed	be-GIN + ing = begi **nn**ing
tan + er = ta **nn**er	per-MIT + ed = permi **tt**ed
hot + est = ho **tt**est	re-FER + ed = refe **rr**ed

If any of the three conditions are lacking, do *not* double the final consonant.

part + ed = parted	(*part* does not end in consonant/vowel/consonant)
risk + ed = risked	(*risk* does not end in consonant/vowel/consonant)

Notice that the following words fulfill conditions 1 and 3 but not 2. None of the following words ends in consonant/vowel/consonant:

SINGLE-SYLLABLE WORDS	WORDS ACCENTED ON THE FINAL SYLLABLE
brawl + ing = brawling	repair + ing = repairing
loop + ed = looped	suspend + ing = suspending
train + er = trainer	commend + ed = commended
bright + est = brightest	disappear + ed = disappeared

Doubling the Final Consonant (Or Not)

In each of the following sentences, choose a suffix (-ed, -ing, -er, or -est), and spell the word in parentheses correctly in the space provided. Remember to apply the three checkpoints to determine whether to double the final consonant.

> EXAMPLE: **Joseph caused so many problems in school that he was (expel)** _expelled_.

1. Adrienne blew the balloon up one breath too many, and it (pop) _____ in her face.

2. The auto body shop did a great job of (detail) _____ the old Chevy.

3. Periodically, groups consider (ban) _____ books like Margaret Laurence's *The Diviners* from school libraries.

4. The committee chair (permit) _____ discussion for only ten minutes.

5. Randy surprised himself by receiving the (high) _____ grade in the class.

6. The Canadian Wildlife Federation is (commit) _____ to saving animal habitats.

Dropping or Keeping the Final e

As a general rule, when adding a suffix to a word ending in *e*, do the following:

- **Drop the final *e* if the suffix begins with a vowel.** Common suffixes are *-ing, -al, -able, -ence, -ance, -ion, -ous, -ure, -ive*, and *-age.*

move + ing = moving	segregate + ion = segregation
arrive + al = arrival	continue + ous = continuous
rewrite + able = rewritable	foreclose + ure = foreclosure
interfere + ence = interference	operate + ive = operative
insure + ance = insurance	store + age = storage

HINT

Several exceptions to this rule are *manageable, noticeable, courageous, mileage, acreage*, and *dyeing.*

- **Keep the final *e* if the suffix begins with a consonant.** Common suffixes are *-ly, -ment, -ness, -less, -ty*, and *-ful.*

accurate + ly = accurately	care + less = careless
arrange + ment = arrangement	entire + ty = entirety
rude + ness = rudeness	hope + ful = hopeful

HINT

Several exceptions to this rule are *truly, wholly, argument*, and *ninth.*

Dropping or Keeping the Final *e*

In each of the following sentences, choose a suffix from the preceding lists, and spell the word in parentheses correctly in the space provided. Remember to keep the *e* if the suffix begins with a consonant, but drop the *e* if the suffix begins with a vowel.

> EXAMPLE: **One way that private security firms are trying to change their image is by (change)** _changing_ **self-descriptive terms like "mercenaries" to "peacekeepers" and "global stabilization experts."**

1. Ethan thought it might be (advise) _____ to catch up on world events.

2. He was (care) _____ to read and listen to many points of view from several sources before forming an opinion.

3. What he learned through his efforts was (surprise) _____.

4. Among other things, Ethan found out that many national and international issues are more (debate) _____ than he had previously thought.

5. Videotaping of police (interrogate) _____ is now standard practice in many countries.

6. Some pundits propose (privatize) _____ agencies like police forces, fire departments, and emergency response groups.

Changing or Not Changing the Final *y* to *i*

CHANGING *Y* TO *I*

When a word ends with a *y* preceded by a **consonant,** change the *y* to *i* when you add a suffix, as in the following examples:

try + es = tries	lively + ness = liveliness
defy + ance = defiance	wealthy + est = wealthiest
supply + ed = supplied	merry + ment = merriment
mercy + less = merciless	beauty + ful = beautiful

KEEPING THE *Y*

HINT

Here are several exceptions to this rule: *paid, said, laid, daily,* and *gaily.*

1. When a word ends with a *y* preceded by a **vowel,** keep the *y* and add the suffix, as in the following examples:

employ + able = employable	joy + ful = joyful
obey + ed = obeyed	employ + ment = employment
joy + ous = joyous	coy + ly = coyly
gay + est = gayest	essay + ist = essayist

2. When a word ends in *y,* and you want to add the suffix *-ing,* always keep the *y:*

cry + ing = crying	study + ing = studying
enjoy + ing = enjoying	lay + ing = laying
lobby + ing = lobbying	say + ing = saying

ACTIVITY 17.3 Changing or Not Changing the Final *y* to *i*

In the following sentences, choose a suffix from the preceding lists, and spell the word in parentheses correctly in the space provided. Remember to change the *y* to *i* if the *y* is preceded by a consonant but not if it is preceded by a vowel.

EXAMPLE: **April has been the (rainy)** *rainiest* **month this year.**

1. Natalie's composition instructor was (mercy) _____ with the amount of homework assigned.

2. Edward got much (enjoy) _____ from watching *Hockey Night in Canada.*

3. The major (annoy) _____ Teka felt on her trip was that her friend was reluctant to stop for rest breaks.

4. When (sky) _____ are sunny and the weather mild, many people want to be outdoors.

5. After finishing school, most people hope to find (employ) _____.

6. Early in the morning, Morgan's dog was always (play) _____.

Forming Plurals: *s or es*

Most nouns form their plurals by adding *s* (*bills*) or *es* (*brushes*).

English Review Note

Some languages have other markers for number. It may take additional review to understand plural forms in English.

1. **If the word ends in *ch, sh,* ss, *x,* or *z,* add *es*:**

   porch + es = porches   kiss + es = kisses   buzz + es = buzzes
   dish + es = dishes   fox + es = foxes

2. **If the noun ends in *y* preceded by a vowel, add *s*:**

   Monday + s = Mondays   attorney + s = attorneys
   donkey + s = donkeys   buy + s = buys

3. **If the word ends in *y* preceded by a consonant, change the *y* to *i* and add *es*:**

   summary + es = summaries   cherry + es = cherries
   lady + es = ladies   party + es = parties

4. **If the word ends in *o* preceded by a consonant, usually add *es*:**

   tomato + es = tomatoes   potato + es = potatoes
   hero + es = heroes   mosquito + es = mosquitoes

   (Exceptions: piano/pianos, solo/solos, memo/memos, avocado/avocados)

5. **If the word ends in *o* preceded by a vowel, usually add *s*:**

   video + s = videos   patio + s = patios
   pistachio + s = pistachios   portfolio + s = portfolios

ACTIVITY 17.4 Forming Plurals

Review the preceding information on forming plurals, and then write the plural form of each of the following words.

EXAMPLE: church = *churches*

1. wish _____

2. radio _____

3. box _____

4. monkey _____

5. Tuesday _____

6. tomato _____

7. booth _____

8. cloth _____

9. coin _____

10. zoo _____

11. faith _____

12. branch _____

Using *ie* or *ei*

In most instances, the rule is to use *i* before *e*, except after *c*.

> **Use *i* before *e*:**

- **ie:**   friend   relieve   brief   field

   (**Exceptions to the "*i* before *e*" rule:** caffeine, seize, height, leisure, neither, either, weird, foreign)

> **Except after *c*:**

- **ei after c:**   perceive   conceit   deceive   ceiling

   (**Exceptions to the "except after *c*" rule:** science, conscience, efficient, species)

> **BUT use *ei* for the vowel sound *ay*:**

- **ei that sounds like *ay*:**   weigh   freight   sleigh   beige   neighbourhood

---

ACTIVITY 17.5   Choosing *ie* or *ei*

Review the preceding information on how to use the *ie/ei* combinations, and then fill in the needed letters in the words below.

EXAMPLE: fr *ie* nd

1. l____sure
2. gr____vance
3. pat____nce
4. conc____t
5. ____ther
6. c____ling
7. fr____ght

8. dec____t
9. th____f
10. w____rd
11. n____ghbour
12. n____ther
13. hyg____ne
14. sc____nce

LO17.4   # Frequently Misspelled Words

The following is a list of words that writers often misspell. You can quiz yourself (and your classmates) on these words to find out which ones you need to memorize.

accept	believe	completely	curiosity
accommodate	beside	conceive	curious
acquaint	break	conscience	definitely
acquire	breathe	conscientious	dependent
adolescence	business	conscious	desirability
advice	calendar	controlled	despair
advise	cannot	controlling	disappoint
affect	capital	convenience	disastrous
all right	career	council	discipline
a lot	character	counsel	effect
already	choice	counsellor	eighth
argument	choose	criticism	environment
beginning	chose	criticize	equipped

exaggerate	length	practical	than
except	licence	practice	their
experience	license	practise	then
fantasies	likelihood	precede	there
fascinate	liveliest	preferred	therefore
fictitious	loneliness	prejudice	they're
field	lonely	principal	threw
foreign	lose	principle	through
forty	maintenance	privilege	to
fourth	marriage	proceed	too
friendliness	mathematics	professor	transferred
fulfill	mischief	quiet	truly
government	moral	receive	unconscious
governor	morale	referring	unfortunately
grammar	necessary	relieve	until
guarantee	ninety	reminisce	usually
height	noticeable	rhythm	vacuum
heroes	obstacle	sense	vegetable
hypocrite	occasion	separate	weight
immediately	occurred	sergeant	weird
independent	occurrence	shining	where
interest	occurring	similar	whether
interfere	opportunity	since	whole
interrupt	parallel	sophomore	whose
it's	particular	strength	without
its	passed	subtle	woman
jewellery	past	success	written
judgment	perform	suppose	yield
knowledge	personnel	roommate	you're
led	piece	surprise	your
leisure	possess	temperature	

Sound-alike Words

L017.5

1. A, An, And

A is an article used before a noun or noun phrase beginning with a consonant sound:

A violet is a small purple flower.

An is an article used before a noun or noun phrase beginning with a vowel sound:

An owl hunts at night.

And is a coordinating conjunction that links words:

Minks *and* ermines are both members of the weasel family.

2. Accept/Except

Accept means "to receive":

Natasha *accepted* the key to the city.

Except means "excluding," "other than," or "but":

The mayor would have offered Natasha a car *except* he didn't have one to give her.

3. Advice/Advise

Advice (a noun) means "an opinion or suggestion":

Geoff should listen to the *advice* of his friends.

Advise (a verb) means "to counsel or give a suggestion":

They *advised* Geoff to speak respectfully to the officer.

4. Affect/Effect

Affect (as a verb) means "to influence or change":

The ice storm *affected* Kurt's travel plans.

Effect (as a noun) means "the result"—and occasionally means "to cause something":

The *effect* of the storm was that Kurt had to postpone his trip.

5. All Ready/Already

All ready means "prepared":

Are you *all ready* to start gardening?

Already means "before" or "by this time":

We have *already* begun turning over the soil.

6. Are/Our

Are (a verb) is the present tense of *to be*:

Will and Lois *are* on the dance floor.

Our (a pronoun) means "belonging to us":

They are dancing near *our* table.

7. Beside/Besides

Beside means "next to":

Burt drives with his coffee *beside* him.

Besides means "in addition to" or "except for":

Besides his coffee, he also has a box of doughnuts.

8. Brake/Break

Brake means "to stop"; also, it names a device for stopping:

It is good practice to *brake* when nearing an intersection.

Break means "to separate something into pieces or destroy it":

Fine crystal is too easy to *break*.

9. Breath/Breathe

Breath (a noun) means "the air we inhale":

Finishing the 10K run, Tina was still not short of *breath*.

Breathe (a verb) means "the act of filling our lungs with air":

However, she did need to *breathe* a little more deeply.

10. Choose/Chose

Choose means "to select":

"Sheila, which of the lobsters will you *choose*?"

Chose is the past tense of *choose:*

Sheila *chose* the smallest one.

11. Clothes/Cloths

Clothes means "something to wear":

Amy has on her party *clothes.*

Cloths means "pieces of fabric":

Molly always washes and reuses her cleaning *cloths.*

12. Conscience/Conscious

Conscience (a noun) means "an inner sense of ethical behaviour":

Nora's *conscience* was clear.

Conscious (an adjective) means "awake or aware":

She was *conscious* that her conscience was clear.

13. Do/Due

Do (a verb) means "to perform":

We have to *do* the standard maintenance on the car today.

Due (an adjective) means "owing or expected to arrive":

The mortgage payment was *due* on the first of the month.

14. Farther/Further

Farther describes distance:

Calgary is *farther* from us than Sudbury.

Further means "additional":

Heather said that the drawing needed *further* work.

15. Hear/Here

Hear (a verb) means "sensing a sound":

I like to *hear* mockingbirds imitate other birdcalls.

Here (an adverb) refers to a place:

It is common to hear these birds *here* in the country.

16. Its/It's

Its indicates ownership by a thing or animal:

The dragon is shooting flames from *its* mouth.

It's is the contraction for *it is:*

It's beating its wings and rising into the sky.

17. Lead/Led

Lead means "metal" (as a noun) and "to guide" or "to be in front of" (as a verb):

Lead is about as soft as gold.

Milo knows best how to *lead* the choir.

Led is the past tense of the verb *lead:*

Milo has experience as a choirmaster, so he *led* the way.

18. Loose/Lose

Loose (an adjective) means "unrestrained":

> **Roxy, the neighbour's dog, often gets *loose* from her yard.**

Lose (a verb) means "to misplace":

> **One day when she gets loose, she may *lose* her way back home.**

19. Past/Passed

Past means "time before now":

> **Marilyn said, "Let's leave that issue in the *past*."**

Passed is the past tense of the verb *to pass,* meaning "to go by":

> **We *passed* the drugstore at some point in the past.**

20. Quiet/Quite

Quiet (an adjective) means "silent":

> **The crying baby was finally *quiet*.**

Quite (an adverb) means "very":

> **With the baby sleeping, we found the quiet house *quite* restful.**

21. Sit/Set

Sit means "to be seated":

> **He chose to *sit* at the front of the class.**

Set means "to place something":

> **He wanted to sit where he could *set* his coffee on an empty desk.**

22. Suppose/Supposed (to)

Suppose means "to assume or guess":

> **I *suppose* interest rates will rise soon.**

Supposed can be the past tense of *suppose* but, combined with *to,* usually means "ought to":

> **The rates are *supposed* to remain stable for a few months.**

23. Their/There/They're

Their (a possessive adjective) indicates ownership by more than one:

> **The wilderness belongs to the people. It is *their* land.**

There (an adverb) refers to a place:

> **You will find a sign-up sheet over *there*.**

They're is the contraction for *they are:*

> **They're signing up to help with the book fair.**

24. Then/Than

Then means "afterward" or "at that time":

> **Ron will have lunch and *then* have dessert.**

Than indicates that a comparison is being made:

> **However, he would rather have two desserts *than* lunch.**

25. Through/Threw/Thru

Through (a preposition) means "moving from one side to another" or "finished":

Brett drove *through* the Detroit–Windsor Tunnel.

Thru is a commercial shortening of *through* and is used to name a place of business that people briefly pass through. *Thru* should not be used as a synonym for *through*:

For lunch, he decided to drive through the drive-*thru* at Tim Hortons.

Threw (a verb) is the past tense of *throw*:

When Brett passed through the drive-thru, he *threw* some money to the cashier.

26. To/Too/Two

To means "toward" or marks an infinitive (for example, *to* talk):

Naomi rode her bike *to* the soccer field.

Naomi decided *to* ride rather than *to* walk.

Too means "also" or "very":

Naomi was not *too* late to see her brother score a goal; her friend Toby scored, *too*.

Two is a number:

She was too late to see him score the first *two* times.

27. Use/Used

Use means "to operate or work with something" (*used* is the past tense):

Jim wanted to *use* the car that his brother had *used* last evening.

Used, followed by *to*, means "to be accustomed to":

However, Jim's father was not *used* to loaning the family car to either of them.

28. Whose/Who's

Whose shows ownership:

Mark asked *whose* car was parked in the driveway.

Who's is a contraction for *who is* or *who has*:

His sister-in-law is the one *who's* going to have to move it.

29. Were/Where

Were is the past tense of *are*:

People *were* discussing the effectiveness of carbon credits.

Where indicates a place:

People were discussing *where* carbon credits would be most useful.

30. Your/You're

Your shows ownership:

Your plan seems to be working.

You're is a contraction for *you are*:

You're sure that your plan is working?

Gather in a small group; make sure you have at least one copy of this textbook. Assign one person to be the wordmaster. As he or she reads from the list of frequently misspelled words from the list on pages 214 and 215, other group members (with textbooks closed) will spell the words in their journals or on separate paper. (The wordmaster using the word in a sentence should be helpful.) After ten words, the wordmaster should join the spellers and give his or her position to another person in the group. Keep going until everyone in the group has announced ten words. At the end, trade and check each other's work against the list; add the words you've misspelled to your Improvement Chart.

HINT

For Activity 17.6, the wordmaster should also have a Canadian dictionary on hand. Then if spellers want to hear a word's definition or if the wordmaster is having trouble forming a sample sentence, he/she can look up the word.

Chapter Summary

1. Being able to spell according to accepted conventions is an important writing skill.

2. Because many English spellings are not phonetic, knowing a few spelling patterns and memorizing frequently misspelled words will help with spelling conventions.

3. Using a Canadian dictionary is an important habit to develop in spelling correctly.

4. Editing for spelling is best done slowly—word by word, syllable by syllable.

5. Using pattern words, similar in number of syllables and endings, can help you spell words of which you are unsure.

6. Sound-alike words must be memorized to be spelled correctly.

7. To become a better speller, start a chart to track your own misspelled words. Study the words often, and test yourself on them until you can spell them correctly.

18

Varying Sentences

How does variety help attract a reader's interest and intensify his or her sense of focus? Using these two photographs of the prairie as evidence, explain why diversity keeps us engaged.

What Are We Trying to Achieve and Why?

Congratulations! By this point, you have worked through the chapters that were designed to help you master the essentials of good writing. The best part of good writing is the polishing because it allows for so much creativity on your part. Being able to produce well-focused, clearly written, and fully developed paragraphs and essays is a major accomplishment; but we can go one step further. Our ideas can seem more or less interesting depending on how we present them at the sentence level.

In the next chapter, we will focus on our choice of words and the manner in which we arrange them. This can have an enormous impact on the way readers receive our ideas. But first, this chapter will help you overcome monotonous sentence patterns and masterfully emphasize key points.

LO18.1 Varying Lengths of Sentences

LO18.1

HINT

Avoid using more than three or four sentences of the same length in a row.

Sentences that are too similar in length make monotonous paragraphs. The sentences may be short, medium, or long; but too many of approximately the same length in a row can be tedious. What is your reaction to the following paragraph?

DRAFT

> The winter scenery in British Columbia is breathtaking. The mountains frame the skyline with snow-covered, glistening peaks. There are also plunging valleys. There are endless waves of mountain ridges in all directions. The mountains offer a new world to explore. Skiers ride only a few minutes on a lift. Then they reach the summit of a mountain. Here they have a 360-degree view of this magnificent mountain world. Skiers glide to a stop at the top of the ridge. The sun is overhead in a brilliant blue sky. The sun shines down and sparkles off the snow. The sparkles look like thousands of glittering diamonds. Dark-green pines are in rows in the distance. The branches of the pines sag under the previous night's snowfall. Skiers are dressed in multicoloured clothing of blue, red, yellow, and white. The skiers chatter back and forth as they ski. They glide up to the edge of a ridge. They scream in delight as they plunge down the steep chutes. They are earthbound no more!

If this draft feels choppy, one reason is that too many of its nineteen sentences are roughly the same length: around eight to eleven words. Notice how the following revised paragraph offers more variety in sentence length.

REVISION

> The winter scenery in British Columbia is breathtaking. The mountains frame the skyline with snow-covered, glistening peaks and plunging valleys. Endless waves of mountain ridges in all directions offer a whole new world to explore. After only a few minutes riding on a lift, a skier can reach the summit for a 360-degree view of this magnificent mountain world. At the top of the ridge, skiers glide to a stop, the sun shining overhead in a brilliant blue sky, sparkling off the snow like thousands of glittering diamonds. Rows of dark-green pines march into the distance, their branches sagging under the previous night's snowfall. Skiers dressed in multicoloured clothing—bright blues, reds, yellows, pinks, and white— chatter back and forth as they glide to the edge of a ridge, then scream in delight as they plunge down the steep chutes, earthbound no more!

The revised version contains only seven sentences, and they range from seven to forty words. The point in creating variety in sentence length is not to avoid short sentences or to write only long ones, but rather to create a diverse and interesting mix. It is easy to divide or combine sentences to suit your needs.

Increase the readability of the following paragraph by combining some of its sentences. Aim for a mix of sentence lengths, but don't necessarily eliminate all the shorter ones. A short sentence, especially following several longer ones, can be emphatic. Note that this paragraph is sixteen sentences ranging from four to nine words.

By 1800, Europe was captured by revolutionary movements. Literary circles had their own "revolts." These were parallel to the political revolts. A new movement was ripening in world literature. It was the strong, mighty, powerful Romantic Movement. New themes were rising up. There were new styles. There were new types of personalities. There were new social behaviors. Byron was the flag bearer of this movement. He was a leader in high romanticism. This related to the tragedy of his personal life. This literary movement was later called Byronism. It was more than a stage in literary history. Romanticism became a bridge to a newly forming movement. This new movement was realism.

_____

_____

_____

_____

_____

_____

_____

_____

_____

_____

_____

_____

HINT

You may need to drop or add words as you combine sentences for Activity 18.1. For more help with sentence combining, read ahead in this chapter.

Varying Types of Sentences

L018.2

Another way to create sentence variety is by using different **types** of sentences, as we practised in Chapter 12. Here is a reminder of the four sentence types:

1. **Simple** (one main clause):   A snowstorm is moving in.

2. **Compound** (coordination through two main clauses):   A snowstorm is moving in, and <u>it may drop a foot of snow</u>.

3. **Complex** (one main clause and one or more subordinate clauses):   A snowstorm <u>that may drop a foot of snow</u> is moving in.

4. **Compound-complex** (two or more main clauses and one or more subordinate clauses):   A snowstorm <u>that may drop a foot of snow</u> is moving in, so <u>I will have my shovel ready</u>.

As writers use the four sentence types, they coordinate and subordinate. To **coordinate** means to link grammatically equal parts of sentences, usually with a coordinating conjunction (*and, but, or, so, yet, for, nor*), as in **sentence 2** above. **Subordination** de-emphasizes one part of a sentence, as in **sentences 3 and 4**. Both coordination and subordination help us create sentence variety and express our thoughts in more subtle ways.

HINT

Coordinate clauses are equal; subordinate clauses are unequal. See Chapter 10 to review coordination and subordination.

ACTIVITY 18.2 Combining Sentences by Compounding

Combine the following sets of simple sentences into compound sentences separated by a comma and followed by *and* or *but*.

EXAMPLE: Simple sentence: The BMW M5 has a powerful V-10 engine.
Simple sentence: The BMW M5 only gets 5.5 kilometres per litre (kpl).

Compound sentence: *The BMW M5 has a powerful V-10 engine, but it only gets 5.5 kpl.* (Note the comma before *but*.)

1. **Simple sentence:** Joann writes good essays.

   Simple sentence: Janet's essays may be better.

   Compound sentence:_____

   _____

2. **Simple sentence:** Hummingbirds can hover in one place.

   Simple sentence: Hummingbirds can fly backwards.

   Compound sentence:_____

   _____

3. **Simple sentence:** Mike learned that the journey is more important than the destination.

   Simple sentence: Dominic learned that focus is important to reach the destination.

   Compound sentence:_____

   _____

4. **Simple sentence:** Margaret and Cheryl were determined to study rather than party.

   Simple sentence: They planned a few study break treats to help them.

   Compound sentence:_____

   _____

5. Write three **compound sentences** of your own. (Remember to use commas correctly; use a semicolon in place of the comma if either of your main clauses contains commas.)

   a. _____

   _____

   b. _____

   _____

   c. _____

   _____

Using Subordination to Vary Sentences

Aside from coordination, you can also achieve sentence variety through **subordination**: that is, making one part of a sentence less important than another. Subordination helps writers deal with shades of meaning and complex ideas and often involves setting information off with commas, parentheses, and dashes.

A **complex sentence** (a simple sentence plus one or more subordinate clauses), along with **adjective** and **adverb clauses**, provides interesting sentence structure for your readers.

ADJECTIVE CLAUSES—NON-ESSENTIAL

Adjective clauses can usually be identified by the relative pronouns *who, which,* and *that*. Such clauses provide information about the noun or pronoun they follow.

1. **Erin, *who* is a fine soccer player, is a talented musician.**

2. **However, Erin's first love is sports, *which* keep her busy most of the time.**

The sentences above use non-essential adjective clauses. The "who" clause in **sentence 1** adds additional—not essential—information about Erin's soccer ability; but the focus of the sentence is on her musical ability. **Sentence 2** uses the "which" clause to add an end comment, but the focus is on the information in the main clause, Erin's love of sports. Note that commas are used to set off non-essential clauses.

To avoid ambiguity with "which" clauses, it is usually best to position them next to a single noun or pronoun rather than expecting them to refer back to several words or ideas.

> Not this: Erin's first love is soccer, although she is not the best player on her team, *which keeps her busy.* (Is it soccer which keeps Erin busy or the fact that she is not the best player?)
>
> But this: Although she is not the best player on her team, Erin's first love is soccer, which keeps her busy. (It *is* soccer that keeps Erin busy.)

ADJECTIVE CLAUSES—ESSENTIAL

As we have seen, adjective clauses can be non-essential to the meaning of the main part of a sentence. We set off these non-essential clauses with commas. However, adjective clauses can also be **essential**: if we left the clause out, the meaning in the main part of the sentence would be unclear or distorted. Compare the following two sentences:

1. **President Obama, *who* campaigned on a promise of hope and a new direction for the country, was sworn in for four years in January 2009.**

2. **A politician *who* campaigned on a promise of hope and a new direction for the country ran for president in 2008.**

In **sentence 1,** naming President Obama clears up any doubt about who ran for president; therefore, the relative clause beginning "who campaigned on . . ." is non-essential and is set off with commas. However, in the second sentence, we do not know which politician the writer is referring to until we read the adjective clause beginning "who campaigned on. . . ."

Distinguishing between non-essential and essential clauses can sometimes be difficult and often depends on the author's intent. In general, the pronoun *which* introduces a non-essential clause, the pronoun *that* introduces an essential clause, and clauses referring to people, whether essential or non-essential, begin with *who*.

> **HINT**
>
> Common relative pronouns include *who, which,* and *that.* For more on non-essential clauses, see Chapters 10 and 12.

> **English Review Note**
>
> Note that some cultures value writing that is forceful, while others prefer a more subtle approach.

> **HINT**
>
> For more on essential clauses, see Chapters 10 and 12.

Use *who* to refer to people
and *which* and *that* to refer
to animals or things. Use
a comma to set off non-
essential subordinate clauses
but not essential ones.

ACTIVITY 18.3 Combining Sentences with Adjective Clauses

Combine the following sets of sentences by underlining the <u>unneeded noun or pronoun</u> in the second sentence and replacing it with *who, which,* or *that*. You may need to rearrange elements of the sentence.

EXAMPLE: **Joni Mitchell has been making music for more than 40 years. She wrote the classic hit "The Circle Game."**

Combined: *Joni Mitchell, who wrote the classic hit "The Circle Game," has been making music for more than 40 years.*

1. In 2011, Ellen Johnson Sirleaf and Leymah Gbowee of Liberia and Tawakel Karman of Yemen shared the Nobel Peace Prize. They won for their struggle for women's rights to full participation in peace-building work.

    Combined: _____

    _____

2. Genocide still continues in Darfur. Darfur is a region in the sub-Saharan African nation of Sudan.

    Combined: _____

    _____

3. Although most city water is safe to drink, people in North America continue to buy water in plastic bottles. The bottles often end up in landfills—as many as 70 million bottles daily.

    Combined: _____

    _____

4. Jason is a Canadian Rotary-sponsored student visiting Denmark. Jason created a YouTube hit called "Don't Hit Me, I'm Just an Exchange Student." The YouTube hit has been viewed by more than 50 000 people.

    Combined: _____

    _____

5. Write three sentences of your own that contain either an essential or a non-essential adjective clause. Use commas carefully.

    a. _____

    _____

    b. _____

    _____

    c. _____

    _____

ADVERB CLAUSES

Another form of complex sentence you can use for sentence variety combines an adverb clause with a main clause. **Adverb clauses**, like single adverbs, tell *when, where, why, how,* and *to what extent* something was done. They frequently begin with **subordinating conjunctions** like the following:

SUBORDINATING CONJUNCTIONS			
after	before	so that	whenever
although	if	unless	where
as	once	until	whereas
because	since	when	while

HINT

For a more complete list of subordinating conjunctions, see Chapter 10.

COMMA **Because** he forgot to put the garbage out for pickup, Paul was stuck carting three bags to the dump.

NO COMMA Paul was stuck carting three bags to the dump **because** he forgot to put the garbage out for pickup.

We ask the question, "Why did Paul have to take his garbage to the dump?" and answer it with the adverb clause "because he forgot to put the garbage out for pickup." Like adjective clauses, adverb clauses are **subordinate** or dependent on a main clause to complete their meaning. Standing alone, they are fragments; but combined with main clauses, they can add variety to your sentences.

Notice that adverb clauses, like single adverbs and adverb phrases, are flexible sentence parts; usually, they can be repositioned in a sentence to suit the writer's meaning and word flow. When adverb clauses begin a sentence (as in the first sentence above), set them off with a comma. Remember that adverb clauses generally are *not* set off by commas when they come after the main clause unless they follow the conjunctions *although, even though,* and *though.*

HINT

Adverb clauses are generally easy to move around. See Chapters 10 and 12.

ACTIVITY 18.4 Combining Sentences with Adverb Clauses

Combine the following sets of sentences by adding a subordinating conjunction from the list on the preceding page to the beginning of the second sentence in each pair. Write two versions of the combined sentence: the first with the adverb clause beginning the sentence and the second with the adverb clause ending the sentence.

EXAMPLE: **We were astonished by how graceful and fearless green sea turtles are. We first snorkeled with them in the ocean.**

Adverb clause beginning sentence: *When we first snorkeled with great sea turtles in the ocean, we were astonished by how graceful and fearless they are.* (comma needed)

Adverb clause ending sentence: *We were astonished by how graceful and fearless green sea turtles are when we first snorkeled with them in the ocean.* (no comma needed)

1. I feel better now. My final marks are all posted.

   Adverb clause beginning sentence: _____

   _____

   Adverb clause ending sentence: _____

   _____

2. Ask the professor for an extension. The worst that can happen is that she will say no.

   Adverb clause beginning sentence: _____

   _____

   Adverb clause ending sentence: _____

   _____

3. Hundreds of turtles will continue to be killed annually. Anglers abandon their long-line fishing gear.

    Adverb clause beginning sentence:_____

    _____

    Adverb clause ending sentence:_____

    _____

4. Butter, eggs, and nuts are actually healthy choices. People eat too much of them.

    Adverb clause beginning sentence:_____

    _____

    Adverb clause ending sentence:_____

    _____

5. Write three sentences of your own that contain an adverb clause.

    a. _____

    _____

    b. _____

    _____

    c. _____

    _____

L018.3 Varying Beginnings of Sentences

Beyond working with sentences of differing lengths and types, we can also create variety by using different **sentence beginnings**. In English, we often open sentences with a subject; but if we build a pattern of sentences that all begin with subjects, the writing feels monotonous. Let's look back at the paragraph we used in Activity 18.1.

DRAFT

> The <u>mountains</u> offer a new world to explore. <u>Skiers</u> ride only a few minutes on a lift. Then <u>they</u> reach the summit of the mountain. Here <u>they</u> have a 360-degree view of this magnificent mountain world. <u>Skiers</u> glide to a stop at the top of the ridge. The <u>sun</u> is overhead in a brilliant blue sky. The <u>sun</u> shines down and sparkles off the snow.

In the draft, in addition to similar sentence length, all seven sentences begin with subjects. After combining a few sentences and supplying several different openings, the revised paragraph reads like this:

REVISION

> The <u>mountains</u> offer a new world to explore. After only a few minutes riding on a lift, a <u>skier</u> can reach the summit for a 360-degree view of this magnificent mountain world. At the top of the ridge, <u>skiers</u> glide to a stop, the sun shining overhead in a brilliant blue sky, sparkling off the snow like thousands of glittering diamonds.

As a rule, it is best to interrupt the subject-first pattern after three or four sentences in a row. You can do this with single words (such as *however, first, next, additionally,* or *finally*), but you may find phrases and clauses even more helpful in varying your sentence beginnings.

Using Phrases to Vary Sentence Beginnings

Phrases, as we learned in Chapter 11, are groups of related words that do not contain both a subject and a verb. The five types of phrases that follow can be positioned in various spots in a sentence including the beginning. Manipulating phrases is one of the most common methods for creating variety in sentence openings.

- **Prepositional:** Phrases that begin with a preposition (*in, on, of, with, about, during*) and end with a noun or pronoun: <u>At the table down the hall</u>, Jody is waiting patiently.

- **Participial:** Phrases made up of a participle—a verb form ending in the present tense with an *-ing* and in the past tense with a *-d/-ed* for regular verbs and often an *-n/-t* for irregular verbs—and words that together describe a noun or a pronoun:

  Present: <u>Apologizing repeatedly</u>, Denise shook her head as she realized her cellphone had six emergency calls from her boyfriend.

  Past: <u>Thrilled by the news</u>, Quyen called his friends to tell them about his promotion.

- **Absolute:** Phrases that contain a participle (present or past) preceded by a noun or pronoun:

  Present: <u>Her hair standing on end</u>, Wanda announced that a storm must be on the way.

  Past: <u>His car stalled and emptied of oil</u>, Angus was left without a ride.

- **Infinitive:** Phrases that begin with the word *to* in front of a base verb form (*to love, to laugh, to run*): <u>To reach Mosaic Stadium by game time</u>, Sal drove faster than he should have.

- **Appositive:** Phrases that contain a word renaming a noun or pronoun: <u>A strong supporter of renewable energy sources</u>, Caitlin voted for a wind farm outside her hometown of Halifax.

ACTIVITY 18.5 Creating Variety in Sentence Beginnings with Phrases

Underline the <u>introductory phrase</u> in each sentence, and then write the name of the phrase in the parentheses.

> EXAMPLE: **<u>Torn between work and family responsibilities</u>** (*past participial*), **Serge decided not to work Saturdays.**

1. In all of the planet's oceans (_____), plastic drift nets lost from boats are killing fish, turtles, seals, dolphins, and other animals.

2. Photographers snapping pictures from all sides (_____), the kayaker plunged through a spray of water over a two-metre drop.

3. Her thoughts hidden from all but a select few (_____), Jan was quiet and soft-spoken.

4. To treat climate change seriously (_____), the government should fully fund research for renewable energy sources.

5. Write three sentences of your own that each begin with a different type of phrase. Identify the phrase, and be sure to use a comma where appropriate.

   a. _____

   _____

> **HINT**
>
> Remember that participial and absolute phrases are similar, so look for a noun or pronoun in front of the participle to identify absolute phrases.

b. _____

_____

c. _____

_____

Chapter Summary

1. Variety in sentences depends primarily on length, type, and beginnings.

2. Sentences in a paragraph should be a mix of lengths: short, medium, and long. Three or four sentences in a row may be roughly the same length, but the next one should be shorter or longer.

3. Compound sentences have a subject and verb on both sides of a coordinating conjunction (*and, but, so, or, for, nor, yet*).

4. Sentences may subordinate ideas in many ways, including with adjective clauses, which are introduced by *who, which,* or *that. That* and *who* introduce **essential** clauses; *which* and *who* introduce **non-essential** clauses.

5. Sentences may subordinate information through adverb clauses.

6. Sentences may begin with transitional words (*first, second, however, next*) and adverbs (*-ly* words like happi*ly*).

7. Phrases can create sentence variety and can be especially useful in shaping sentence beginnings.

Choosing Effective Words

How do these friends express personal or collective style? Is each person effective in conveying an image?

How are your choices in presentation—wardrobe, hairstyle, accessories, and so on—similar to style choices

in writing? Why do you think style matters in writing?

LEARNING OBJECTIVES

19.1   Using specific and concrete language

19.2   Writing concisely

19.3   Choosing language for tone

What Are We Trying to Achieve and Why?

The polishing phase of the writing process should include attention to **style**—that is, *how* we say what we say. Just as the photo on the preceding page shows a style, or way that people present themselves, so, too, can writing be "clothed" in a variety of words and arranged in ways that best suit the writer's purpose. In Chapter 18, we explored strategies for varying sentences. The purpose of this chapter is to focus more specifically on helping you make word choices and word arrangement choices that present your work in the most effective light.

LO19.1 Using Specific and Concrete Language

Choosing Specific Words

HINT

See Chapter 23 for more on general and specific words.

One of the most important elements of style is the choice of **general** or **specific** words. The more general a word, the larger the category that contains it; conversely, the more specific a word, the smaller the group it belongs to. For example, *food* is general while *a Pizza Hut sausage and pepperoni pizza* is specific.

Imagine that a friend says to you, "Something happened to me today." You reply, "What?" The friend says, "Something scary but exciting." You say, "Well, can you be more specific?" Your friend says, "I asked Amber a question." You are getting a bit annoyed at this point, but you say, "OK, tell me what you asked her." The friend says, "You know, a big question." You say, "Just tell me, or I'll put the headphones on, and you can talk to yourself." Your friend replies, "OK, OK, I asked her if she wants our relationship to be, you know, like more permanent." To try to end the unnecessary suspense, you leap to the conclusion and say it for him: "So, you *proposed* to Amber!"

We can illustrate this movement from general to specific on the following Language Line:

something happened	a scary event happened	a friend asked a personal question	he asked to change a relationship	he proposed marriage

Relatively General   **Relatively Specific**

This process of moving from the general category that contains all the "somethings" out there to a specific category like "marriage proposal" is a procedure that all writers go through when they check their work. If you want to communicate clearly with sharp images, choose specific words.

Avoiding General Verbs

Verbs can also be general or specific:

GENERAL:	The baby <u>is making</u> sounds and <u>moving about</u> over there.
SPECIFIC:	The baby <u>is screaming</u> and <u>thrashing</u> wildly on the changing table.
GENERAL:	The player <u>is making</u> his way down the field.
SPECIFIC:	Rodriguez <u>snatches</u> the pass one-handed and <u>tears off</u> downfield, breaking tackles as he <u>sprints</u> toward the end zone.

HINT

Be, do, have, make, and *get* often are weak verbs.

Specific verbs help make writing more interesting and lively. Try to use them in your own work. As you revise, be especially alert to forms of the verbs *be, do, have, make,* and *get,* all of which can drain the energy from your sentences.

Avoiding General Description Words

Try not to fall into the "very, really, extremely" habit, using general describing words instead of more precise words. In a typical draft, four out of five of these empty intensifiers should be deleted. They can often be replaced with more precise words.

AVOID CONSTRUCTIONS:	**FIX BY SUBSTITUTING MORE SPECIFIC WORDS:**
It's very, very cold outside.	It's frigid outside.
He's really very angry.	He's furious.
She is really thin.	She is emaciated.

OTHER OVERLY GENERAL WORDS			
bad	great	nice	sad
fun	happy	old	thing
good	interesting	pretty	young

SENTENCE USING VAGUE WORDS   A very old person who had done some really interesting things was telling somebody about these great things and about some other fun things he did when growing up.

To improve this sentence in revision, the writer replaced most of the general terms with precise ones:

SENTENCE USING PRECISE WORDS   At 90, Winston Churchill reminisced to one of his biographers on the war years, when he had led England through the Blitz, submarine blockades, and near-defeat in Africa; he also discussed his early education, which he said he disliked, except for English, history, fencing, and marksmanship.

ACTIVITY 19.1   WORKING TOGETHER: Revising for Specific Word Choice

With group members, revise the following sentences to improve interest and clarity by choosing more specific words. Pay particular attention to the subjects and verbs; but also look for other vague words, such as *very*, and either cut or replace them.

> EXAMPLE: **The** <u>animal</u> <u>made</u> some unpleasant noises and <u>moved</u> something around the room.

> **Revised:** *The beagle whined and nudged his food bowl around with his nose.*

1. The children were moving around in the watery area and doing fun things.

   _____

2. The large structure was full of people moving in and out of very interesting stores and doing things in those stores.

   _____

   _____

3. A person threw it a long way, and it was caught by someone else, who moved a long way with it.

_____

_____

4. Some people were doing work on the beginning of a house while across the street other people were doing some things on the top of a house.

_____

_____

5. In a place where very many people were sitting, food items were being moved very quickly by people who took the food to the other people.

_____

_____

L019.2 # Writing Concisely

Another important concept in revising for style is **conciseness**—saying what we mean with no wasted words. In the rush of getting ideas onto paper, writers often include everything that pops into their minds, so first drafts may resemble this example:

DRAFT: WORDY PASSAGE

Well, I think that I can safely say with some degree of certainty that there are many really very good reasons that a student would want to take the time to get himself or herself ready to take an examination in school or any other place of learning where the student or students might find it necessary to take an exam. I can say from my own experience and from the experience of almost everybody I know that when a student studies, he or she will feel less stress before, during, and after the examination. Also, most people would agree that when students take the time to prepare properly for a test or exam or other school academic challenge that they will usually do better on the test and make a higher grade as well.

This revision for conciseness gets to the point, eliminating unneeded repetition, imprecise words, and stalling phrases:

Using concise words may be difficult when translating from your native language, but try to find the clearest way to say what you mean.

REVISION: CONCISE SENTENCE

Being prepared for an exam decreases stress and improves grades.

Shrinking the passage from 136 words to 10 increases economy and clarity. The point is not to cut all repetition—repetition can be used for emphasis—just to write short sentences. We want to remove words that interfere with meaning.

Although repetition, imprecise words, and stalling phrases are common in everyday speech, which tends to be more vague and more verbose than good writing, revising for economy and clarity means removing the following:

- Redundant expressions
- Empty and padded phrases
- Unnecessary detail

Avoiding Redundant Expressions

Some unnecessary words creep into sentences as **redundant expressions**, words that repeat an idea already expressed, as in the following example:

> My wife and I were <u>looking and searching</u> for some <u>old antique</u> candle-holders that were <u>small in size</u> and <u>dark in colour</u>, but we found that there were <u>few in number</u> at the flea market, where we <u>shopped and hunted</u> for bargains.

Eliminating the redundant phrases, we have a clearer, more concise sentence:

> My wife and I were searching for some small, dark, antique candleholders, but we found that there were few at the flea market, where we shopped for bargains.

REDUNDANT PAIRS, MODIFIERS, AND CATEGORIES			
adequate enough	few in number	intentionally try	return again
circle around	final conclusion	link together	safe and sound
climb up	first and foremost	null and void	small in size
continue on	gather together	old antiques	square in shape
cooperate together	heavy in weight	past history	sum total
each and every one	hopes and wishes	proceeded to go	terrible tragedy
end result	if and when	red in colour	true facts
equally as good	important essentials	refer back	very unique

Omitting Empty and Padded Phrases

Writers can be cumbersome when writing with empty and padded phrases. **Empty phrases**, which add no meaning to a sentence, are best if simply cut. Usually, they can be dropped from a sentence without altering the meaning:

EMPTY WORDS AND PHRASES			
absolutely	certain	in kind	really
actually	character of	in terms of	situation of
area of	definitely	kind of	sort of
aspect of	element of	manner	thing
awfully	extremely	nature of	type of
basically	factor	quite	very

Padded phrases are stock expressions that use more words than needed to make their point—for example, *due to the fact that*, meaning *because*:

> <u>Due to the fact that</u> Robert is broke, he's staying home tonight.

> <u>Because</u> Robert is broke, he's staying home tonight.

The word *because* is a better choice.

COMMON PADDED PHRASES AND CONCISE SUBSTITUTES	
Padded Phrases	**Concise Substitutes**
at the present time, at this point in time, at the present moment, in this day and age	now, today
during that time, in the time when, in those days	then, when
at all times	always
despite (regardless of) the fact that	although
due to the fact that, the reason is because, for the reason that, considering the fact that	because
located close by	near
in the event that	if
by means of	by
form a consensus of opinion	agree
a large number of	many
few in number	few
aware of the fact that	know
refer back	refer
in the final analysis	finally
sufficient amount of	enough
make contact with	contact, meet
for the purpose of	for
in a situation in which, in the event that	when, if
is in a position to, has the opportunity to	can
it is important (crucial/critical) that	must
there is a chance that	may
during the time that	while
all of a sudden	suddenly

ACTIVITY 19.2 WORKING TOGETHER: Revising for Conciseness

Discuss the following sentences with a partner, and then cut redundancies and empty/padded phrases. You may need to add words or restructure a sentence, but keep the main ideas intact.

EXAMPLE: **As anyone can plainly see, year-round schooling is a critical issue that certainly requires action, and it is vitally important that we give our undivided support to change the school system in this respect, or students' academic performance will inevitably continue to decline and sink.**

Revised: *People should support year-round schooling, or students' academic performance will continue to decline.*

1. I think there is a chance that researchers, scientists, and engineers from around the world may have gathered together recently in Istanbul, Turkey, to frame a new and current plan and to form a consensus of opinion for the purpose of helping combat and reduce climate change,

which many people think may be a bit of a problem for some people at some point in time, based on its past history.

_____

_____

_____

2. It seems to me that it was some time in November, like maybe on the 11th, that what's his name, oh, yes, David Johnston, who is a new leader in Ottawa, possibly the Governor General of Canada, presented an award and honour (it might have been the Order of Canada) to World War II veteran soldiers, who served bravely and with great courage in World War II.

_____

_____

_____

3. Obviously, we should all be aware of the fact that the parking problem on campus is without a doubt the most crucially pressing problem facing a large number of the students at this college, and, clearly, in the final analysis, the administration should take steps to solve this critical and vital problem, or students' education will inevitably suffer.

_____

_____

_____

Cutting Unnecessary Examples, Details, and Explanations

The overuse of **examples, details,** and **explanations** can also make your sentences wordy. Often in first drafts, writers lose sight of their audience, forgetting what readers already know or want to know about a subject.

Consider the following paragraph, which reminds a driver how to enter a highway:

DRAFT   Accelerate by putting your foot on the gas pedal, that pedal on the floor of your car next to the brake. But don't confuse the brake with the gas pedal. The brake is more rectangular and is to the left of the gas pedal, which is skinnier and longer and to the right of the brake. Now accelerate by going faster along the on-ramp, which is like a part of the highway but really is not because it is more off to the side and often actually slopes like it is the side of a small hill because you may be entering from an overpass, which is like a bridge that lets cars run over and above the highway. As you go fast along the ramp, you will move into what is called the "acceleration lane," which is really just a continuation of the on-ramp, but you should pay close attention to the white or yellow solid painted line that divides the acceleration lane from the rest of the highway because you should not cross over this line until it is safe to do so, meaning that you have checked for traffic and have reached a safe entering speed. Now is a good time to activate your turn signal, which is the little metal arm that usually projects from the left side of your steering column, which is the metal post that your steering wheel attaches to . . .

If reading this paragraph of instructions wears you out, that is understandable. When writers forget whom they are writing for—what that audience really needs or wants to know—this sort of tedious overwriting often results. If we strip away the unneeded examples, details, and explanations from the above paragraph, we can provide clearer and more concise instructions without losing our main point.

REVISION
As you accelerate along the on-ramp, bringing your car up to highway speed, use your turn signal and check your mirrors—both rear and side-view—for traffic. Also, glance to your left to check the blind spot near your bumper. Midway along the acceleration lane, being careful not to prematurely cross the solid dividing line, find a gap in the traffic, be sure your speed is sufficient, and carefully merge into the gap. Caution: It is extremely dangerous to stop on entry ramps!

ACTIVITY 19.3 Removing Unneeded Examples, Details, and Explanations

HINT

As you read each sentence in Activity 19.3, ask yourself, "How much of this information would I need?"

Read the following sentences about careful driving, and revise them to remove unneeded examples, details, and explanations.

1. When driving, one good way to avoid accidents is to limit distractions inside the car.

   _____

2. Before you take off, adjust those mechanical conveniences inside the car, like the seat, steering wheel, mirrors, and music.

   _____

3. The seat can be adjusted forward or backward and often up or down, and sometimes there is a lumbar support to work with.

   _____

4. Of course, the steering wheel often can be pulled forward somewhat or raised or lowered (which you do usually by pulling on this little knob on the steering column, which is the metal post with the steering wheel attached to it).

   _____

   _____

5. The mirrors should be self-explanatory, but just as a reminder sometimes you have to adjust them manually, and sometimes they are electronic.

   _____

   _____

6. Remember that objects often appear farther away than they really are in the right side-view mirror (which always seems weird to me, how tiny cars look, I mean).

   _____

   _____

7. For your music, you might as well preset some radio stations and have iPod playlists ready.

_____

8. Parents, make sure the kids are belted in and can't squirm free—that is, of course, unless they are teenagers, in which case they may not listen to you anyway (ha-ha).

_____

_____

9. Another problem for many drivers is food and drink. If you must eat in the car, lay out the food where you can reach it and have those napkins ready for the spills.

_____

_____

10. About half of the accidents people have while driving occur from outside problems, which are hard to control, but we can do something about the other half, the inside distractions.

_____

_____

Choosing Language for Tone

LO19.3

Beyond eliminating non-essential words, writers should consider other elements of language that affect the **tone** of their work—that is, the *attitude* they reveal toward the subject and their audience. Which of the following sentences would be more appropriate for casual conversation and which for an academic paper?

1. **Hitler was a guy in Nazi Germany. But he was a wacko with a dorky-looking moustache who was bad because he had the power to blow away so many people.**

2. **Adolf Hitler was the leader of Nazi Germany from 1933 to 1945, before and during World War II. He was an unstable psychopath who orchestrated the murder of six million Jews and was responsible for the deaths of countless other civilians and soldiers.**

In casual contexts, people often use the idioms and slang terms with which their group is familiar. Clearly, **sentence 1** is geared to this sort of casual exchange. However, in academic settings, where a more formal tone is required, **sentence 2** would be much more appropriate.

Avoiding Slang and Colloquial Expressions

Slang terms are typically short-lived, invented words that are understood by specific peer groups but are often considered vague or unacceptable by those outside the group. Slang can be colourful and often expresses strong emotions, as in the following expressions: *dissed, wired,* and *psyched out.* Text messaging abbreviations like *LOL, G2G,* and *TTYL* also fall into this informal category.

Colloquial terms are similar to slang—but are typically understood by a wider audience. Examples include words like *a hit,* meaning "a success," or *sweet,* meaning "a good thing."

Slang and colloquialisms are appropriate for informal gatherings but are usually avoided in more formal writing. Writing for academic courses requires formal language usage. Slang almost never appears in academic writing, and colloquial terms are used only occasionally to vary the tone deliberately.

SOME COMMONLY USED SLANG EXPRESSIONS

airhead	(to) diss	hot
awesome	dude	laid back
bad	duh	LOL
bling	(to) dump on	old school
blown away	(to) flame	(to) rip off
bummed	freaked out	suck it up
(to) chill	geek	sweet
(to) chill out	gig	TTYL
cool	(to) go postal	uber
couch potato	(to) hang out	wasted
	(to) hit on	

HINT

You may find that your interpretation of a slang word varies from that of others in your group.

ACTIVITY 19.4 WORKING TOGETHER: Translating Slang

Choose any five of the terms in the preceding chart, and discuss their meaning with members of your group. Next, write a sentence using each slang term, followed by another sentence replacing the term with more formal language; underline the term and its replacement.

EXAMPLE:

Slang version: *It blew me away to learn that my insurance had risen to $3000 a year.*

Revision: *I was shocked to learn that my insurance had risen to $3000 a year.*

1. **Slang version:** _____

   Revision: _____

2. **Slang version:** _____

   Revision: _____

3. **Slang version:** _____

   Revision: _____

4. **Slang version:** _____

   Revision: _____

5. **Slang version:** _____

   Revision: _____

Chapter Summary

1. Style in writing largely consists of strategic word choices and arrangement.
2. Specific words create sharper images than general ones.
3. Conciseness in writing means cutting words that serve no purpose.
4. Writers can achieve conciseness by controlling the following points: redundant expressions, empty and padded phrases, and unnecessary details.
5. Tone can be defined as the attitude a writer reveals toward his or her subject and audience.
6. Slang and colloquial expressions are best kept to a minimum or eliminated altogether from formal or academic writing.

Building
Paragraphs

Introducing the Paragraph

Finding your way through a writing assignment may sometimes feel like wandering through a maze. However, you can find your path if (like the man on the ladder) you seek out a useful perspective. Write a brief paragraph telling of a challenging project that you found confusing at first but succeeded in completing. How did you prepare yourself? How did you organize the project?

What Is a Paragraph?

L020.1

Perhaps in the past when faced with a writing project, you have found yourself puzzled and anxious. "What am I supposed to be doing? I don't know where to begin or where this thing's going to lead me." All writing is a bit mysterious in that we have to find our way through a topic, experimenting with and rejecting ideas, learning more about what we want to say as we go. It is helpful to remember that all longer writing structures are built from sentences, the focus of Chapters 3–19 of this text. You already know how to craft a sentence—and you will continue to improve in doing so. In this chapter, you will focus on putting sentences together in a meaningful way to create a sound structure.

Knowing a structure's form makes the writing task less mysterious and gives us an advantage when writing about any topic. Knowing the structure is like having an aerial view of the maze. The **paragraph**—a collection of clearly related sentences that make a point—is one of these forms. There are four types of paragraphs:

- Introductory
- Body
- Concluding
- Transitional

Essays may use all of these "specialty" paragraphs; but our focus in this unit is the **body paragraph**, which has a predictable form that can help you discover and arrange your ideas. As you can see from the diagram below, the body paragraph has three basic parts—**topic sentence, body,** and **concluding sentence**—as well as more detailed components:

Body Paragraph

Topic sentence = topic + limiting statement (often setting out major points to be written about)

Body of paragraph (contains sentences that develop the idea in the topic sentence)

1. Connector (transition)
2. First example, reason, or detail
3. Supporting ideas for first example
1. Connector (transition)
2. Second example, reason, or detail
3. Supporting ideas for second example

Additional examples, reasons, or details as needed to develop the paragraph

Concluding sentence

1. Connector (transition)
2. Link to topic sentence
3. Expanded thought

> **HINT**
>
> Transitions, also known as connectors, are discussed in detail later in this chapter.

Writing a Topic Sentence

To focus a paragraph, writers start with a single idea, often expressed in a single sentence called a **topic sentence**, which is frequently the opening sentence of the paragraph. This guiding sentence names a topic and then makes a statement about it. Here is an example:

About.com is a terrific source of information.

The topic, About.com, is underlined once, and the statement twice. From this sentence, we expect a paragraph that discusses some terrific information. The topic sentence *limits* the topic to something that can be discussed in a paragraph, and so it is a useful sentence.

However, how much direction would we get from a topic sentence like the following?

About.com hasn't always been around.

This sentence doesn't tell us clearly what the writer plans to say about About.com, so it fails to limit the topic and is, therefore, not very useful.

English Review Note

English paragraphs often start with a topic sentence. This may differ in other languages where a topic sentence might be considered rude because it expresses a strong and direct point.

HOW TO WRITE A STRONG TOPIC SENTENCE

1. **Limit the topic and make a clear statement about it.** Choose a small enough part of a larger topic so that you can cover it fully in a paragraph.

   NOT THIS: Competitive sports in Canada have strong fan support.
   BUT THIS: Fans of the Toronto Maple Leafs are some of the most loyal in professional sports.

   The topic is Toronto Maple Leafs' fans, and the limiting statement is about their loyalty.

   You might further limit your topic with a **forecasting statement**, which names specifically what will be discussed:

   Fans of the Toronto Maple Leafs are so loyal that they buy large amounts of Leafs memorabilia, follow the team on its road trips, and support the players win or lose.

2. **Use specific words.** One way to make a topic sentence more interesting is by adding specific words.

   LESS SPECIFIC: Renfrew is alive with tourists in the summer.
   MORE SPECIFIC: Renfrew, once a *ghost town* in *Nova Scotia*, is alive with tourists in the summer.

ACTIVITY 20.1 Topic Sentences: Finding the Parts

For the following group of topic sentences, underline the topic once and the limiting statement twice.

EXAMPLE: The reality TV shows *Take This House and Sell It* and *Love It or List It* have much in common.

1. Learning to ski at Whistler was a painful experience for me.

2. One cool autumn morning, Brian Strickland found himself in an awful predicament.

3. Powell River, B.C., is one of my favourite places to vacation, for several good reasons.

4. Finding your way around a big city is not hard if you have the right tools.

5. The rising cost of gas has affected people in several unpleasant ways.

Focusing Topic Sentences

Effective topic sentences strike a balance between being too broad and being too limited. The goal is to write a sentence just roomy enough for the detailed examples and explanations in the body of the paragraph to develop. Notice how the following broad topic sentence can be narrowed:

Unfocused: Biting <u>insects</u> <u>bother</u> people.

Focused: In the summer, <u>mosquitoes</u> <u>make my backyard unbearable.</u>

ACTIVITY 20.2 Focusing Topic Sentences

Rewrite the following sentences to narrow their focus. In your revised sentences, underline the <u>topic</u> once and the <u>limiting statement</u> twice.

EXAMPLE:

Unfocused: Animals can be a nuisance.

Focused: *My dog, <u>Bear</u>, <u>causes problems with his digging, barking,</u> and tearing up the trash.*

1. **Unfocused:** People's pets can take up much of their owners' time.

    Focused: _____

    _____

2. **Unfocused:** Vacations can be memorable experiences.

    Focused: _____

    _____

    _____

3. **Unfocused:** There are huge creatures living in the ocean.

    Focused: _____

    _____

    _____

4. **Unfocused:** Some politicians do seem to care about their country.

    Focused: _____

    _____

    _____

5. **Unfocused:** I like some holidays better than others.

    Focused: _____

    _____

To help you focus topic sentences, first read the following groups of sentences from body paragraphs. Next, list the topic discussed in each group. Then write a suitable topic sentence, underlining the <u>topic</u> once and the <u>limiting statement</u> twice.

> EXAMPLE: **Not all Canadian sports fans are as devoted to their teams as those of the Saskatchewan Roughriders. Many people only cheer for the team that is winning. They buy the jersey because that team won the Grey Cup, even though they didn't watch a regular game all season. However, Roughriders' fans wear green and white proudly no matter what the season's outcome because there's always next year.**
>
> **Topic:** *Loyalty of sports fans to their teams*
>
> **Possible topic sentence:** *Saskatchewan Roughriders fans are some of the most loyal in the country.*

1. Students required to do volunteer service in order to graduate from high school aren't always grateful for the opportunity. It just feels like a little bit of slavery; like 40 hours more chores. That's what I thought anyway before I started. But then I started delivering Meals on Wheels with my grandparents and realized how many old people would be eating nothing but tea and toast three times a day, or would be putting the stove on and forgetting to turn it off if they were still cooking. I wanted my 40 hours to really count for something and guess what? I'm still volunteering; I now have my own Meals on Wheels bike route.

   Topic: _____

   Possible topic sentence: _____

   _____

2. When you're on the top of a snow-covered hill looking down, just about to kick off on your snowboard, you feel as free as you've ever been. Then WHOOSH, down the hill you go with the wind trying to push you back up, but nothing can stop you. The adrenaline rush when you fly off a jump is the most amazing feeling of all – a few minutes of soaring like a bird before you touch down again. And when you land your first 720, the rush of accomplishment is like ten Christmases rolled into one.

   Topic: _____

   Possible topic sentence: _____

   _____

3. We got Pongo the same year that *101 Dalmatians* came out on DVD. My older sister is real Disney fan and staunchly refused to name our new dog anything but Pongo. She owns every animated Disney film ever made and dreams of going to Disneyland or on a Disney cruise. Some people say that the Disneyfication of culture is a bad thing – all the real drama and diversity are removed in favour of homogenization and commercialization. All I can say to that is, stay away from my sister! She did everything she could to Disneyfy our family. She even wanted to name me Nala!

   Topic: _____

   Possible topic sentence: _____

   _____

Revising Topic Sentences

As a paragraph grows, a writer may drift from the focusing statement in the topic sentence. Reconsidering the topic sentence within the context of the paragraph may lead to a revision of the topic sentence. For example, to make a rough topic sentence more interesting, you can add specific words. "Specific" describes a word that belongs in a smaller group than another similar but more general word. In the example for Activity 20.4 below, *party* is a general word that could refer to many occasions. *Labour Day celebration* is more specific. General words are necessary and useful, but specific words create sharper images and can make your topic sentence more readable.

ACTIVITY 20.4 Revising Topic Sentences with Specific Words

Rewrite the following rough topic sentences by adding more specific words to make the sentences more interesting. Also, underline the topic once and circle the limiting statement.

EXAMPLE:

Rough topic sentence: I went to a really good party that didn't stay so good.

Revised topic sentence: *The Labour Day celebration at Alfredo's was great until the police knocked on the door.*

1. **Rough topic sentence:** A friend of mine won a prize recently.

    Revised topic sentence: _____

    _____

2. **Rough topic sentence:** I made a difficult decision after I graduated from high school.

    Revised topic sentence: _____

    _____

3. **Rough topic sentence:** My family life was disrupted when our pet died.

    Revised topic sentence: _____

    _____

4. **Rough topic sentence:** In some areas, winter is rougher than others.

    Revised topic sentence: _____

    _____

5. **Rough topic sentence:** Most people look forward to the heat of summer.

    Revised topic sentence: _____

    _____

Developing the Body of a Paragraph   LO20.3

After you have written an effective topic sentence, it is time to work on **support sentences**. To develop these sentences, you will use examples, details, and explanations.

Examples, Details, and Explanations

EXAMPLES

Examples are specific instances that clarify statements. For instance, if a friend says that fall is her favourite season, you might ask why. When she tells you that she likes the changing colour of the leaves, the cooler weather, and the end of that obnoxious shrieking of cicadas, she has just given you three examples. You might offer personal examples based on your own experiences or give examples outside of your immediate experience, as in the categories listed below:

TYPES OF EXAMPLES

1. **Facts or commonly accepted truths:** Whales and dolphins are mammals.
2. **Statistics or numerical facts:** A healthy human body temperature is 37 degrees Celsius.
3. **Information from print sources** (books, newspapers, magazines), **electronic sources** (Internet, TV, radio), **and interviews**
4. **Second-hand anecdotes or stories** that have happened to people other than you
5. **Comparisons:** An agouti is like a giant guinea pig with long legs.
6. **"What-if" situations or speculations about what could happen:** What might happen if car manufacturers took electric cars seriously?
7. **Dialogue** reported or created to express a point

DETAILS

Details are the specific words we use to clarify and add interest to examples. For instance, to make the fall changing of leaves more vivid, we could add the colour words *scarlet* and *gold*. Further, we could attach those sight details to specific trees: scarlet *maples* and gold *poplar*. Mentioning other **sensory** details, like the *cool* fall weather or the *shrieking* cicadas, help to build memorable images.

EXPLANATIONS

Explanations work with detailed examples to develop your paragraphs. Explaining puts examples into a context so that the reader understands them. For instance, you might better understand why the cool of fall weather is important to your friend if she explained that in the summer she no longer uses her air conditioning (to save energy and money) but instead relies on her attic fan to cool the house. The fan doesn't do such a great job when it's 40 degrees Celsius outside, so the cool fall weather is a welcome relief.

Notice how the following student paragraph (in which the <u>topic</u> is underlined once and the <u>limiting statement</u> is underlined twice) is developed with detailed examples and explanation:

<u>My dog, Perry,</u> a Cairn terrier who looks like Toto, the dog from *The Wizard of Oz*, <u>is too hyperactive.</u> Whenever people walk through the front door, Perry gets excited and starts jumping on them. He also runs around in circles and expects me to chase

after him as if it's a game. When I don't feel like getting up from the comfortable sofa, he will continue to run back and forth for 5 to 10 minutes, even when I yell, "Perry, stop!" Eventually, he does stop, looks at me for a second, and then goes back to his hyperactive ways.

—*Phonepraseut Mounivong*

When the writer tells us his dog is "too hyperactive," we ask, "What do you mean by that? Can you give us some detailed examples?" Phonepraseut does this by telling about Perry's habits of jumping on people, running in circles, and running back and forth. Within the more detailed examples, we see specific words like *circles, sofa,* and *5 to 10 minutes*; the breed, *Cairn terrier*; and the clear comparison to Toto from *The Wizard of Oz.* The writer also explains why Perry's hyperactive behaviour irritates him when he "doesn't feel like getting up from the comfortable sofa."

Specific examples and detailed examples with explanations help a reader understand a writer's points.

ACTIVITY 20.5 Developing the Body of a Paragraph

The groups of sentences below begin with a topic sentence (topic underlined once, limiting statement twice) and are followed by a main example to develop the topic. To make the example in each group more clear and interesting, add further details, examples, and explanations.

EXAMPLE:

Topic sentence: There are some rules that I hate to follow.

Example: One rule I can't stand is the law that keeps me stopped at a long red light when there is no traffic anywhere.

Details, examples, explanation: *There I am in the middle of nowhere, a country T intersection at 3:00 a.m., with no traffic for miles around. The light has been red for two minutes, and I feel like a fool just burning gas. I look east down one deserted stretch of road and then west. Nope, nobody there—not even a police officer. I think to myself, "Why don't I just turn left?"*

1. **Topic sentence:** My brother and I were very competitive as boys.

   Example: When we played baseball, the competition really heated up.

   Details, examples, explanation: _____

   _____

   _____

   _____

   _____

   _____

   _____

   _____

2. **Topic sentence:** <u>Learning to ride a bicycle</u>, <u>I had some spectacular crashes.</u>

   Example: I remember my first painful accident happened in the alley alongside our backyard.

   Details, examples, explanation: _____

   _____

   _____

   _____

   _____

   _____

3. **Topic sentence:** If I could time travel, there are <u>three moments in my life I would love to visit.</u>

   Example: The first place I would travel back to is Sackville, New Brunswick, where my brother and I played on the Tantramar Marshes all summer long.

   Details, examples, explanation: _____

   _____

   _____

   _____

   _____

   _____

Unity in Paragraphs: Ideas Working Together

A developed paragraph with a strong topic sentence may still have problems with **unity**, that is, with all ideas and details adding to the topic sentence (or main point). Information or explanations that drift from the main point should be cut, even if they are interesting. Consider the example of the hyperactive dog, Perry. How unified would the paragraph be if these two points (highlighted below) were added to the example?

My dog, <u>Perry,</u> a Cairn terrier who looks like Toto, the dog from *The Wizard of Oz*, is too hyperactive. Although I don't care much for old-time movies, I still think The Wizard is a classic. Whenever people walk through the front door, Perry gets excited and starts jumping on them. However, most of these people don't realize the front door is made of fibreglass. He also runs around in circles and expects me to chase after him as if it's a game. When I don't feel like getting up from the comfortable sofa, he will continue to run back and forth for 5 to 10 minutes, even when I yell, "Perry, stop!" Eventually, he does stop, look at me for a second, and then go back to his hyperactive ways.

These highlighted statements detract from the paragraph's unity. Rough drafts often contain information that digresses a bit or even a lot from the main point, in part because drafting is a process of exploration. But our job as writers (particularly when we revise) is to catch this loosely related material and cut it.

ACTIVITY 20.6 Unity in Paragraphs

Write a first draft of your own paragraph about the profession you hope to enter after college or university. Then reread your paragraph and underline any sentence that drifts from the main point. Next, explain why it doesn't belong.

_____

_____

_____

_____

_____

_____

_____

_____

_____

Explain why the drifting sentence doesn't belong:

_____

_____

_____

HINT

Be on the lookout for unity as you revise your work. See Chapter 21 for more on revising paragraphs.

HINT

You can learn more about definition in Chapter 30.

Clarity in Paragraphs: Defining Terms

Another point to watch for in your writing is **clarity**, or ensuring that your reader understands your words and ideas. In the preceding paragraphs about Perry, the writer uses terms like _Cairn terrier_ and _Toto_, expecting his audience to know what he is talking about. To help them understand what a Cairn terrier looks like, the writer links the dog to _The Wizard of Oz_, expecting his audience to be familiar with the movie. If Phonepraseut has misjudged what his audience knows about dogs or movies, he will leave them puzzled.

When you write, you are trying to connect with your audience, so it is best to define any terms that might be unfamiliar to your readers and to explain ideas that they might not understand.

ACTIVITY 20.7 Clarity in Paragraphs

In this paragraph, underline any <u>word</u> or <u>phrase</u> that you think the stated audience might not be familiar with. Use the example as a model.

Avoid using literal translations, which can be confusing to the audience.

For example, lines 5 and 6 of Émile Nelligan's most famous poem, "Le Vaisseau D'Or," read as follows in the original:

Mais vint une nuit frapper le grand écueil

Dans l'Océan trompeur où chantait la Sirène

Google Translate gives the following translation into English:

But then came one night to hit the big pitfall

Ocean misleading when singing the Mermaid

But a human translation of the poem reads as follows:

Then one night it struck the great reef

In that treacherous ocean where the Siren sang

Translation, like poetry, is an art that cannot be replaced by software.

Source: http://www.ballinagree.freeservers.com/enelligan.html

EXAMPLE:

Audience: First-year college students

In a study by the Wyoming Academy of Science, video games have been shown to improve people's coordination. After playing *Beatmania* for 20 minutes, players' motor skills showed improvement. Also, the APA conducted a study of 86 men who improved their skill acquisition after learning a difficult video game. Finally, experiments have proven that playing games like *Tetris* improves children's mental rotation. As you can see, these studies support the positive psychological effects of some video games.

NOW YOU TRY:

Audience: Middle-aged adults who are only semi–computer literate and don't know much about online buying but who want to learn how to purchase music from the Internet.

The most popular source for music downloads is the iTunes store. This online retailer offers millions of songs and albums, complete with album art and sometimes bonus tracks. It also sells videos, such as episodes of popular programs, so that you can see last night's *The Daily Show* or *Gossip Girl* right after downloading a "Clap Your Hands Say Yeah" song. iTunes software used to be for Mac people only, but now PC users can get access, too. All that is required to start buying music is iTunes software, which is now dual platform. When you visit the iTunes store, you'll be able to search by artist, album, or type of music. Once you've found what you're looking for, you can listen to a sample for free. Usually, you can buy a single MP3 for $1 or an album for about $10. iTunes does limit the number of times you can transfer music files to other media (such as MP3 players and CDs), so you can't make unlimited copies or mixes for your friends. But ultimately, buying music online is a great deal; you'll save on money, time, and space.

LO20.4

Organizing the Body of a Paragraph

Topic sentences are important for focusing your paragraph but arranging the supporting sentences demands equal consideration.

Methods of Organization

If you are writing a **description** (setting out details about a person, place, animal, or something else), you would most likely choose a **spatial order**, that is, giving details from top to bottom, side to side, back to front, and so forth. You will practise this method of arrangement in Chapter 23.

Another organization method, used for narrative (storytelling) and process description (telling how things work), is called **chronological order**, or arranging events as they happen in time. We will work with chronological order in Chapters 24 and 26.

The last, and perhaps most useful, method for most of your college writing is called **order of importance**, arranging examples and ideas from least important or

Chapter 23 focuses on writing descriptions; Chapter 24 focuses on writing personal narratives; Chapter 26 focuses on writing about processes.

least dramatic to most important or most dramatic. This method is discussed in depth in Chapter 25, which focuses on illustrating effectively with examples.

When writing essays, you may find yourself mixing these organizational methods, detailing a place within a paragraph using spatial order, narrating a story in another paragraph using chronological order, and arranging examples within another paragraph by importance.

ORGANIZING PARAGRAPHS ON-SCREEN

Reorganizing body paragraphs is much easier to do in a word-processing program (which allows you to cut and paste easily) than it is on paper (which requires you to scratch out or erase words and rewrite text by hand). Save paper and unnecessary headaches—and avoid squinting at your own handwriting—by writing and revising paragraphs on the computer.

HINT

Organizational methods can be mixed and matched to fit the writing situation.

Coherence in Paragraphs: Connecting Sentences

As we have discussed in this chapter, paragraphs are **unified** when all details, examples, and explanations help support a single idea (set out in the topic sentence). However, sentences within paragraphs must also be well connected or **coherent**, meaning that they should flow smoothly one into the next to move the reader along easily. Here are several common methods for doing this, most of which we use without much thought.

METHODS FOR CREATING COHERENCE

1. Transitions
2. Repetition
3. Synonyms
4. Pronouns

HINT

Transitions are also called **connectors** in this book. The tables on the following pages list and group common transitions by use.

Using Transitions

Transitions are the most common method of linking sentences. They can be single words or phrases and are used to show location, passage through time, addition of material, provision of examples, and so forth.

COMMON TRANSITIONS BY USE

TRANSITIONS FOR LOCATING OR MOVING IN SPACE (Particularly useful for descriptive writing)			
above	below	in	on
against	elsewhere	in the distance	over
alongside	far off (away)	into	through
around	farther on	near	to
at the side (end)	forward	next to	under
behind	from	off	up

English Review Note

Take the time to review these charts. When writing in English, being familiar with common transitions is valuable.

TRANSITIONS FOR MOVING IN TIME			
(Particularly useful in narrative writing)			
after	finally	next	soon
afterward	first (second)	now	suddenly
at last	immediately	often	then
awhile	later	once	until
before	long ago	previously	when
earlier	meanwhile	recently	while

- **All references to calendar time and calendar events:**

  ago (days, weeks, months, years)

  one day (days of the week, months of the year, seasons, holidays)

  that morning (afternoon, evening)

  today (tonight, yesterday, tomorrow)

- **All references to clock time:** clock numbers used with a.m./p.m. (12:00 a.m., 1:00 p.m.); a few minutes (seconds, hours)

- **All references to regular meals:** during breakfast (brunch, lunch, dinner)

TRANSITIONS FOR ADDING MATERIAL			
(Particularly useful in writing that explains how something works)			
again	as well as	furthermore	likewise
also	besides	in addition	moreover
and	further	last	next

TRANSITIONS FOR USING EXAMPLES AND EMPHASIS			
(Particularly useful in explanatory and persuasive writing)			
above all	especially	in fact	specifically
after all	for example	in particular	surely
another	for instance	of course	that is

TRANSITIONS FOR COMPARING			
(Particularly useful in writing that focuses on similarities and differences)			
alike	both	like	resembling
also	in the same way	likewise	similarly

TRANSITIONS FOR CONTRASTING			
(Particularly useful in writing that focuses on similarities and differences)			
after all	even though	nevertheless	otherwise
although	however	on the contrary	though
but	in contrast	on the other hand	whereas

TRANSITIONS FOR SHOWING CAUSE AND EFFECT			
(Particularly useful in explanatory and persuasive writing)			
accordingly	because	hence	then
and so	consequently	since	therefore
as a result	for this reason	so	thus

TRANSITIONS FOR SUMMARIZING AND CONCLUDING			
(Particularly useful at the end of body paragraphs and at the beginning of concluding paragraphs)			
finally	in conclusion	in short	that is
in brief	in other words	largely	to summarize

ACTIVITY 20.8   Coherence through Transitions

Using the preceding transitions tables, locate and underline all the transitional words in the following paragraph. The first sentence is marked as an example.

Another reason for the popularity of the arowana is that it resembles the mystical Asian dragon. For instance, the colourful, reflective scales are similar. Also, the arowana has whiskers not unlike the dragon's moustache. Besides the scales and whiskers, they both have slender bodies and move in much the same way. In Asian culture, the dragon represents good luck, strength, and power. Especially in southern China, many people believe that a dragon can ward off evil. In addition, many businesspeople keep arowanas to maintain a prosperous business.

USING REPETITION

Repeating a word or phrase is another common method of linking sentences effectively. However, be careful not to repeat a word excessively, or the word will become tedious.

Not this: My good friend **Niki** worked hard, and **Niki** cared for **Niki's** family. **Niki** completed her SSGD in three years at a local high school, and then **Niki** went to Queen's for her undergraduate and graduate degrees.

But this: My good friend **Niki** worked hard and cared for her family. She completed her SSGD in three years at a local high school, and then went to Queen's for her undergraduate and graduate degrees.

USING SYNONYMS

Similar words or phrases, which we call **synonyms**, are used frequently to link sentences and avoid tedious repetition.

ACTIVITY 20.9 WORKING TOGETHER: Coherence through Repetition and Synonyms

Working with a partner, cross out unneeded repetition in the paragraph that follows; then write in replacement words above the line. However, do not replace every repeated word because artful repetition can be useful. With your partner, come up with an explanation of why at least one example of repetition used here works and why at least one example does not.

Education can change people's lives in positive ways. One example of education changing a life is a man named Kaka, whom I knew in Kashmir. In his forties, he used to do odd jobs in our neighbourhood. After long days of unchanging hard work, he would often say, "I realize now that education is the key to success." Continuing his hard work, he managed to change his life by educating himself, changing where he lived when he moved to Mumbai to go to college, and then graduating in three years with honours. Not only did his earnings change, but also he was able to bring change to the community, which he did by establishing a high school in his old neighbourhood, a positive change that remains today after Kaka's death.

HINT

Turn to Chapter 7 for more on pronouns and pronoun references.

USING PRONOUNS

Pronouns—words like *I, he, she, they, us, those, each, some, their*—by their nature stand in the place of nouns (and other pronouns) and so can help with coherence. For instance, notice how the noun *Niki* was replaced by the pronouns *she* and *her* in the example under Using Repetition. However, pronouns can be misleading, attaching themselves grammatically to the nearest available noun (or pronoun); so use them with care. Notice the confusing pronoun reference in the following example:

> Tyler and Ethan went to the Razor concert, and they were friendly to everyone at the concert, talking to the fans even when they went up on stage to play some head-banging metal.

The question is who was being friendly, and who played the music? It was probably Razor, but the reference is unclear.

English Review Note

Be careful not to confuse *he* and *she.*

ACTIVITY 20.10 Coherence through Pronouns

In the following paragraph, cross out unneeded or confusing pronouns, and write in the replacement words above the line.

A Paid Vacation

Playing in the snow is always fun for kids, but it's done a little differently in Fredericton, especially when there is no school. First, we would put on our snow clothes and then grab a shovel, planning on making a killing shovelling all of it. After maybe shovelling one of them, though, my pals and I would get bored and soon start pelting each other and innocent bystanders with them. My buddy Mike and I would often have to run for our lives after breaking a car window with it. Other kids would "skitch" their way to safety, holding on to it on the back of a car and sliding along the snow-covered street at 50 km an hour. By late in the afternoon, smoke-filled pizzerias would be packed with soaking wet ones from the neighbourhood. Some of the kids would spend the day's wages on video games, pizza, panzerotti, sausage rolls, and gyros. We would happily brag about it and our paid holiday.

Writing a Concluding Sentence

LO20.5

When you have finished the body of your paragraph, instead of just trailing off or saying, "Well, I'm done now," why not end decisively? A strong concluding sentence reminds the reader again of the topic and limiting statement and makes some final point. A well crafted concluding sentence gives your audience one last reason to have confidence in what they have just read. Here are three points to help you write a concluding sentence:

HOW TO WRITE A CONCLUDING SENTENCE

1. **Use a connector:** Transitional words, like *finally, however, despite, on the other hand,* ease your reader into your final point.

2. **Link to the topic sentence:** Mention your topic and limiting statement again, or use synonyms for them.

3. **Expand the thought:** Make a final point about your topic, using any of the following methods:

   a. Express an emotion.

   b. Give a judgment or opinion.

   c. Ask a related question.

   d. Make a reflective statement.

   e. Tell how your topic has affected your behaviour or outlook on life.

> **English Review Note**
>
> In English, final thoughts may express strong emotional conclusions. This may be unfamiliar in other languages.

Here are four things *not* to do in writing a concluding sentence:

1. Don't just repeat a slightly different version of your topic sentence. Instead, make a point.

2. Don't fail to link this final point to your topic clearly.

3. Make sure the final point is interesting; avoid using worn-out phrases or clichés.

4. Don't say, "I'm ending the paragraph now." Your final point should make it clear that the paragraph is complete (the white space following your last sentence will also be a clue).

Strong Conclusions: Learning from a Student Model

For help in understanding the methods just listed for writing an expanded or final thought, read the paragraph below, and then read the five sentences that *might* have been used as a conclusion.

> **HINT**
>
> Note how this paragraph uses examples effectively.

Staying Fit

As in other aerobic team sports, people can get several benefits from playing soccer. First, there is the health benefit. While playing soccer, athletes use many parts of their bodies: head, chest, thighs, and feet, parts that they don't always use in everyday life. Soccer builds muscle mass, especially in the lower body. Also, since the games last 90 minutes, with players in almost constant motion, participants become aerobically fit. Next, soccer helps to improve a person's attitude on life. Practice and game days help with discipline and focus. Athletes must learn plays and be able to perform them well. They must listen closely to their coach and blend their moves with teammates' to complete a play. When playing against another team, athletes must be able to think quickly and adjust to the skill level and moves of the opposing team. In addition, after the game, win or lose, if they have played hard and well, the players feel an enormous sense of achievement and excitement, and they become more self-confident. However, the most important benefit from soccer is social: meeting people and forming lasting friendships. Soccer is a team sport, so teammates run plays together. They share the same emotions: happiness when winning, disappointment when losing. Players often keep in touch with each other off the field, too, so that the team becomes like an extended family. Playing soccer makes friendships strong.

—*Hyuk Sun*

Now see five possible concluding sentences below:

POSSIBLE CONCLUDING SENTENCES

1. **Emotion:** I have played soccer for many years, and it has so many positives that I would not feel whole without it.

2. **Opinion:** Because soccer has so many benefits, it should be part of every young person's life.

3. **Question:** If you feel bored, out of shape, or lonely, why not join a local soccer team?

4. **Reflective statement:** People sometimes talk about life as a game to be played; if that is so, then perhaps another benefit of soccer is that it mirrors life, a game to be played—and won.

5. **Behaviour change:** The benefits of soccer are clear to me; and without it, I would find the couch hard to resist on a Sunday afternoon.

There is no one "right" concluding sentence for a paragraph, only better and worse options. When you write your own last sentence, you will usually have to work with it a bit to find a final point and the wording that feels best for your topic, purpose, and audience.

In each set of sentences below, (circle) the letter of the concluding sentence that best links to the given topic sentence and makes the strongest final point.

1. **Topic sentence:** Choosing to drink and drive was the biggest mistake my friend Austin ever made.

Possible concluding sentences:

  a. The strange thing is, many of my friends still drink and drive and get away with it.

  b. Although not everyone who drives while intoxicated suffers this awful fate, drinking and driving is always the wrong choice.

  c. I don't like the taste of beer, so I don't have to worry about losing points on my driver's licence.

2. **Topic sentence:** The differences between my new and old neighbourhoods in Kiev are the buildings, people, and cultural advantages.

Possible concluding sentences:

  a. Although I see advantages to my new neighbourhood, I feel most at peace in old Kiev, as the culture there from my past fills my soul.

  b. However, the loveliest place is Andrew Street, which is small and closed off from automobile traffic.

  c. The buildings, people, and entertainment are different in the suburbs than in downtown Kiev.

Choosing a Title

LO20.6

The finishing touch to your paragraph is the title. If you consider that these few words are the first your audience will see and can arouse their curiosity (or not), then it might be worth the trouble to create an interesting title. Sometimes, a title will come to you quickly; at other times, it will take work to create a good one.

Of course, a title should reflect the topic, but it can do more than that. For example, let's take another look at the "Staying Fit" paragraph where we looked for a strong conclusion (see page 257). "Staying Fit" is a workable and logical title for the soccer paragraph, but could it be more engaging? If we link it with the fourth concluding sentence, we might come up with "Winning the Game of Life," or we could play off the fifth concluding sentence and end up with "Keeping Me off the Couch." Linking a title to a paragraph's main idea or final point is one way to produce an effective title.

Below you can see several other suggestions for creating effective, engaging titles:

1. Keep titles short (one to eight words).

2. Link the title to your main idea or final point.

3. Create an image: use a metaphor; make a literal comparison; use specific details and action words.

HINT

See Chapter 22 for more on creating effective titles.

4. Try a question.

5. Make a play on words or a pun.

Knowing what *not* to do when creating a title is also important. Avoid these:

1. Clichés and worn-out phrases. Don't use phrases like "Caught between a Rock and a Hard Place" or "Butterflies Really *Were* Fluttering in My Stomach!"

2. Inappropriate tone. Your title should reflect the feeling you want your readers to have as they read your work (happy, sad, angry, serious, and humorous, for example).

FORMATTING A TITLE CORRECTLY

1. Capitalize all words in your title—even short verbs like *do*, *is*, and *can*—except articles (*a, an, the*), prepositions (*in, on, to, of, between*, for example), and coordinating conjunctions (*and, but, or, so, yet, nor, for*). The first and last words of the title and any word following a colon (:) should be capitalized. (Note that these guidelines are for MLA style. See chapter 32 for alternate guidelines for APA style.)

2. Do not enclose the title in quotation marks or underline it.

3. Centre the title on the page.

Chapter Summary

1. A paragraph is a unified, coherent collection of sentences that is usually grouped with other paragraphs.

2. Body paragraphs must have a central point, expressed in a topic sentence, which is most often placed first in the paragraph.

3. A topic sentence consists of the topic plus a limiting statement; it should be as interesting as possible.

4. Paragraphs are developed with examples, details, and explanations.

5. Paragraphs benefit from specific word choices and specific examples.

6. Three types of organizational patterns for paragraphs are spatial, chronological, and by order of importance. These methods often overlap.

7. A paragraph is unified when all examples, details, and explanations relate to a central point, which is expressed in the topic sentence.

8. Paragraphs are coherent when sentences are clearly linked using transitions, repetition, synonyms, and pronouns.

9. Concluding sentences should end a paper decisively. One way to do this is with an expanded thought.

10. A title's main purpose is to capture a reader's attention. Effective titles are brief, linked to the main idea, and engaging.

Revising Paragraphs

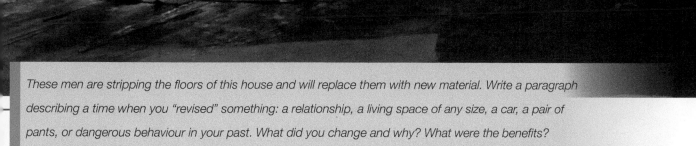

These men are stripping the floors of this house and will replace them with new material. Write a paragraph describing a time when you "revised" something: a relationship, a living space of any size, a car, a pair of pants, or dangerous behaviour in your past. What did you change and why? What were the benefits?

Revising, Editing, and Proofreading

Revising—or re-visioning—a work is one of the hardest yet most necessary parts of the creative act. Whether the task is to paint a wall, design a car, build a bridge, schedule employees, or write a paragraph, it is rarely done the best way the first time or finished in one attempt.

That first collection of ideas—your first draft—provides a foundation, a good starting point. If you believe that you can make your writing stronger, you are more likely to succeed at doing so. However, revision is seldom easy: it requires time, energy, patience, flexibility, and the willingness to learn as you go. The normal procedure is to write several drafts between the first ideas appearing on paper and the final draft where all sentence structure, grammar, and spelling errors have been corrected. If this idea seems overwhelming—to write more than one or two drafts in total—I encourage you to trust the process and do what it takes to get your writing assignment into its final form. Take it from a writer who knows—even Giller Prize–winning authors trust the revision process in order to be pleased by the results.

Just as there are several different words for snow and ice in the Inuktitut language—*qanik* for falling snow, *aniu* for snow used to make water, *qinu* for slushy ice by the sea—professional editors also have several different terms for different types of **editing**, all of which begin *after* the author has revised several drafts on her own to come up with her final, complete, corrected manuscript. **Substantive** or **structural editing** means reorganizing the content and structure of a manuscript; **stylistic editing** means fixing such non-mechanics as eliminating jargon, smoothing language, and clarifying meaning; **fact checking** means making sure that facts and quotes are accurate by going back to the original sources; **proofreading** means correcting page proofs to ensure accuracy before printing. The term **copy editing** is often used by non-editors to refer to all of these different types of editing but to professional editors it means checking and fixing spelling, grammar, punctuation, and other mechanics.

Different types of editing and proofreading need to be done before you hand in an assignment and none of them can be done at the last minute in the middle of the night. When you *revise* your paper, you are doing the fact checking plus substantive and stylistic *editing*—in other words, the "big picture" improvements to your essay. When you *copy edit* your paper, you are checking the spelling, punctuation, and so on, or what some instructors call the GUM (grammar, usage, and mechanics)—the "small picture" improvements. Poor GUM sticks to your paper and clogs up your writing, so working through chapters 3 to 19 of this textbook will help you get the best mark possible on your assignments. *Proofreading* is the final stage—one last check to make sure that you didn't miss anything and that everything is consistent.

For more information about different types of editing, see the Editors' Association of Canada web page "Definitions of editorial skills": http://www.editors.ca/hire/definitions.html.

As you begin revising your draft, review Chapter 2, especially the sections on how to create a productive workspace, break out of writer's block, and revise collaboratively.

> **HINT**
>
> A first draft is not a final draft, and vice versa.

A REVISION PRIORITY LIST

1. **Content (Substantive editing):** detailed examples, explanations, comparisons

2. **Organization (Structural editing):** topic, subtopic, and concluding sentences; arrangement of examples, details, and story elements; and connectors

> **HINT**
>
> Use your revising time more efficiently with this list.

3. **Style (Stylistic Editing):** word choice and arrangement of words into sentences

4. **Mechanics (Copy Editing):** grammar, spelling, and punctuation

The rest of this chapter will give you many specific suggestions for working through the drafts of the paragraph you wrote in response to the question accompanying the picture on page 261. You will also see how another student took her own paragraph through the process—from a first draft that was just OK to a final draft that is excellent.

Revising First Drafts

LO21.2

First drafts are not final drafts; they are often messy, overwritten, or incomplete. This is normal and not a cause for discouragement. Rough drafts give writers an opportunity to move ahead with ideas and see how to present them more effectively. As American writer Joan Didion once said, "I don't know what I think until I write it down." The first draft is all about getting your ideas onto paper; the second, third, and any subsequent drafts are about shaping those ideas.

The following is the first draft of an illustration paragraph by student Crystal Lockner focusing on dangerous childhood activities.

Note: This paragraph is separated into topic and concluding sentences and three main examples only to help illustrate its parts. The final draft should be a single paragraph.

English Review Note

Your instructor can help point out your most common errors. In addition, have a class peer, as well as someone in your campus writing centre, review your work.

Dangers of Being a Kid

Surprisingly, I have survived the crazy dangerous follies of my past. When I was two my mom handed me her car keys so that I could entertain myself with the keys. I looked around the living room for a place to plug them into, and found one—a wall socket, a perfect fit. ZAPP! BANG! THUD! My mom came around the corner to se me half dazed, still holding the keys. I was shaken and scared. I sat there.

Then when I was age eight I played sports with the neighbourhood boys. ~~We got along pretty well and when we were racing they used to say things like, "Watch out! Crystal's gonna smash herself again."~~ There were five of us racing down hill on roler blades. I was in the lead. Suddenly, I was caught off guard and tripped. Head over heals, I won the race with a broken arm.

The scariest and most dangerous time of all. Sledding on an old ski hill in the mountains. My brother an I walked to the top of the hill and then I used my inner tube as a tobbogan as I took off. I picked up speed on my way toward the bottom. Suddenly, I leaned hard to the right to avoid a shed and begun to spin around. Then I went flying and landed in a bank of trees. I don't remember much after I landed on my head, but when I woke up my head hurt, ~~and tears streaked down my cheeks. My mom had already ran helf way up the mountain.~~

I managed to come out of each of these dangerous childhood situations ~~with minor bumps bruises, and a few broken bones.~~ As an adult, I believe my mishaps are in the past. ~~This summer~~ I m going sky diving. ~~Let's just hope my parachute opens.~~

FIRST DRAFT

Notice the ~~unneeded ideas and words~~ that Crystal cuts from this draft.

The writer needs **subtopic sentences** for her examples.

In the next draft, Crystal will add more details to this example to make it more exciting.

First Draft Revision Points

When you begin to look critically at your own first draft, take a few minutes to review the following revision points:

1. **How effective is your topic sentence?** Your topic sentence gives you and your reader direction, so mention the topic and limit it with a statement. In a descriptive paragraph, state the dominant impression; in a narrative, try hinting at the climax or the meaning of the story. To be particularly specific, you can use a **forecasting statement** like this: My favourite comfort foods are Kettle salt and vinegar potato chips, Breyer's French Vanilla ice cream, and Tim Horton's sour cream glazed donuts.

2. **Does your overall method of organization work?** Descriptions are usually best organized spatially, while narratives are arranged chronologically. Informational and persuasive writing often benefit from moving in order of importance.

3. **Does a subtopic sentence introduce each main example? Subtopic sentences** are merely more specific and more limited topic sentences. Neither descriptions nor narratives depend on these sentences to keep readers oriented. However, writing that works with examples and reasons usually benefits from subtopic sentences.

4. **How well developed is your paragraph?** Descriptions require precise details, specific words, and sensory details to help readers "see" the person, place, or object. Narratives must have clearly described action sequences with scene and character details. Most writing benefits from specific, detailed examples, action words, and comparisons.

5. **Are you explaining clearly?** Detailing an example is important, but it's even more important to help your readers understand why you gave that example. Be certain to explain terms carefully and show how the example is linked to those before and after it. Act as a guide to your audience, and you won't lose them.

6. **Are your examples relevant?** Although brainstorming many possible illustrations is a great idea, not all will be equally useful in your paper. Each example should add something significant to the others and to the overall topic.

7. **How well connected are your sentences?** All types of writing profit from clearly linked sentences. Descriptions use transitions of place (*near, by, against*, for example) and time (*when, after, next*, for example), while narratives often employ transitions of time. Writing with examples or reasons may include a variety of transition types. (Consult the lists of connectors on pages 253–255.) Other connectors are repeat words, synonyms, and pronouns.

8. **How effective is your concluding sentence?** The concluding sentence offers the last few words your reader will remember the best. To seize this opportunity, carefully craft a conclusion that links to the topic sentence and makes a final point.

HINT

For more on topic sentences, see Chapter 20.

HINT

For more on organizing by space, time, or importance, see Chapters 23, 24, and 25.

HINT

For more on subtopic sentences, see Chapter 25.

Writing Journal/Blog Entries

Journals and blog entries can help you discover ideas, as well as focus, organize, develop, and edit them. It's worth your time to answer the writing prompts in each chapter as thoroughly as you can.

KEEP A PAPERLESS JOURNAL OR BLOG

Consider reducing paper waste by keeping a paperless journal on your computer or online. If you keep a blog, you can also take advantage of the interactive journaling feature "Feedback" for Journal/Blog Entry 21.1 and 21.3.

To help you focus on the revision process and to alert your instructor to your progress, list three *specific* changes you have made or feel you ought to make in your first draft. Refer to the First Draft Revision Points above, and comment specifically about your own work.

EXAMPLE: *Item 4: I realized that my development was thin, so I added these details*

_____

and this explanation.

_____ .

Next, in a sentence or two, say what you like best about your draft.

_____

_____ .

FEEDBACK   *Trade first drafts with a partner. Note what you think is the strongest part of his or her draft. Then ask one question about it.*

Revising Second Drafts

When you rework your draft, you can save time and avoid some frustration by prioritizing. If you are sure that your topic is well focused, your overall organization makes sense, and your main examples belong, then you can shift your attention to other concerns.

Here is the second draft of Crystal's paragraph. Note these general concerns for re-visioning Crystal's second draft, as well as your own second draft:

- Subtopic sentences (not needed in brief description and narrative)
- Detailed examples
- Complete explanations
- Connectors

HINT

At the start of your writing project, create enough examples and other material so that you can choose the best. It is hard to let go of material if you don't start out with enough.

SECOND DRAFT

Dangers of Being a Kid

Surprisingly, I have survived the crazy dangerous of my childhood. My first dangerous encounter at age 2 was trying to drive a "car." My mom and I had just gotten back from the grocery store. And she handed me her car keys so that I could entertain myself with the keys while she put away the groceries. I looked around the living room for a place to plug them into, and found one—a wall socket, a perfect fit. ZAPP! BANG! THUD! My mom came around the corner to see me half dazed, still holding the keys. I was shaken and scared. I sat there. To this day, my mom says that plugging the keys into the outlet is how I got my curly hair.

HINT

Connectors are especially important in subtopic sentences. For more on connectors, see Chapter 20.

At the age of 8 I ran into my next childhood trauma. I fearlessly played sports with the neighbourhood boys: football, basketball, and ice hockey, and I raced them on roller blades. One day five of us were speeding downhill on roler blades. I was in the lead. Looking back to see how far I was ahead I was caught off guard when I tripped on a pebble in the road. Head over heals, I won the race with a broken arm.

Finally the scariest and most dangerous time of all. Sledding on an abandoned ski hill in the Gatineau Hills, Quebec. My goal was to sled down from where none of the other kids' would go, the top! My brother an I walked, and walked, and walked and finally we were there, with the white mountain spread out below us. My inner tube was my tobbogan. 1, 2, 3, GO!!!! Swishing gently from side to side, I increased my speed. Faster and faster I bounced toward the bottom. Suddenly, out of nowhere came a tin shed, I leaned hard to the right, and begun to spin around. One last hard bump and I went flipping and flying through the air, and landed in a bank of trees. I don't remember much after being knocked unconscious. When I woke up people were standing in a big circle around me. I was woozy and crying and my head hurt, but I was still alive.

Having survived my crazy childhood, I am more cautious these days, but I still love adventure—anyone up for a little skydiving?

HINT

For more on concluding sentences, see Chapter 20.

Second Draft Revision Points

When you begin to look critically at your own second draft, take a few minutes to review these revision points. They will help you write a stronger draft.

1. **How well have you used specific language?** All writing uses both general and specific words, but specific words sharpen an image. Which of these sentences creates a more vivid picture?

   a. A person was doing something there.

   b. Mike Weir was driving the golf ball 75 metres down the fairway.

2. **How thoroughly have you developed sensory details?** Descriptive and narrative writing in particular need details of sight, sound, touch, smell, taste; information-based and persuasive writing can benefit from these details, too. Which of these sentences creates a stronger image?

   a. As I near the arcade, I see the change machine, stuffed animals, and food.

   b. As I near the arcade, I hear the jingling of tokens falling from the change machine, see the colourful stuffed animals—pink poodles, purple bears, orange-and-black striped tigers—and smell the sweet aroma of warm, sugar-coated cinnamon buns.

3. **Are you choosing active verbs to describe action?** Interesting writing uses verbs that show specific action rather than more general verbs (such as *be, do, have, make*). Which of the following sentences seems more interesting?

   a. The giant black bull made his way across the field as I moved away from him toward the white board fence.

b. The giant black bull <u>galloped</u> toward me as I <u>raced</u> across the field, struggling to reach the white board fence 20 metres away.

4. **Are you using any *-ing* words?** Present participles (a verb form with an *-ing* ending) can also convey action well. Which of the following sentences creates the sharper image?

   a. My foot got caught on the pedal, and the ATV flipped over on me in the creek.

   b. My foot got caught on the pedal, and the ATV flipped, <u>slamming</u> me to the bottom of the creek and <u>landing</u> on top of me.

5. **Are the sentences in your paragraph varied in length?** The structure of your sentences alone can make your writing more or less interesting. If you find more than four sentences in a row that are roughly the same length—for instance, 14, 17, 12, and 15 words—either combine two of them or divide a longer one.

6. **Are the beginnings of your sentences varied?** If even two sentences in a row in your draft begin with the same word or phrase, such as *the,* try changing an opening or combining sentences to break up the pattern. Also, look for too many similar openings, even if the sentences are not next to one another.

7. **Have you repeated a word or phrase so often that it becomes noticeable?** While some repetition is fine, too much of the same word group becomes boring.

8. **Have you included words that serve no purpose?** Everyday speech is full of unneeded words, but writing should not be. Cluttered writing can bore and confuse, while concise writing involves the reader and clarifies ideas. Which of the following sentences seems concise?

   a. Junk email, the kind of email that comes into my account from strangers and without me even wanting it, is one of the many online distractions that causes me to waste all of my valuable time.

   b. Junk email is one of my time-wasters.

JOURNAL / BLOG ENTRY 21.2

List three *specific* changes you have made or feel you ought to make in your second draft. Refer to the Second Draft Revision Points above, and comment specifically about your work. Next, in a sentence or two, say what you like best about your draft so far.

Editing Final Drafts

LO21.4

After your major organizational and material concerns are dealt with, you can begin to polish your draft, fine-tuning it for style and editing for correctness.

Your draft should be in good shape now, with important details in place, words carefully chosen, and sentences flowing well. Slowly edit your paper—syllable by syllable, word by word, line by line, stopping often. Write down at least three errors from your draft, and then show the corrections. What steps are you taking to avoid repeating these errors?

FEEDBACK *Trade semi-final drafts with at least two classmates. Use the "Final-Draft Revision Points" as a guide to respond to your classmates' drafts. When you get your own draft back, consider the feedback offered, and then note one suggestion that you found particularly helpful.*

LO21.5 Proofreading

Proofreading is the last step in preparing your paper. After you have finished editing, print the final draft, or give it close on-screen attention. Read through it carefully; there are likely still a few errors to catch.

HINT

Check the spelling of your professor's name!

HINT

Most instructors don't want to fish around in a plastic sleeve and then have to stuff the paper back in after evaluating it.

GUIDELINES FOR PROOFREADING AND PREPARING YOUR FINAL MANUSCRIPT

1. **Check for typographical errors** such as misspelled, run-together, and omitted words. Often when fixing errors in the editing stage, we slip up in small ways on the keyboard. **Be sure to spell-check once again.**
2. **Check the font size** (12 point), **line spacing** (double space), **margins** (3 cm), **title capitalization,** and **headings** (upper left corner, double space).
3. **Spell-check any required material to be handed in,** such as outlines and audience profiles.
4. **Staple your pages in the top left corner.** Avoid putting the paper in a plastic sleeve.

This text highlights two documentation styles for academic papers: APA and MLA. On the following pages, you will find both a title page and a one-paragraph paper formatted in APA style. See Chapter 32 to learn about MLA style. Check with your instructor to see which format he or she prefers. Different disciplines have different requirements; for example, literature papers are usually formatted in MLA style while sociology papers use APA style. Notice that the title in both cases is neither underlined nor enclosed in quotation marks, and all information is double-spaced.

Ouch!   1

On every page, short
title capitalized, at
left-hand margin,
and page number at
right-hand margin

Ouch!

Title centred

12-point font

No underline

No quotation marks

All information
double-spaced

Crystal Lockner

English 107, Section 12

Professor Finlay-Clark

December 1, 2014

Ouch!

Surprisingly, I have survived the crazy dangers of my childhood. My first dangerous encounter at age two was trying to drive a "car." My mom and I had just gotten back from the grocery store when she handed me her car keys so that I could entertain myself while she put away the groceries. I looked around the living room for an "ignition" and found one—a wall socket, a perfect fit. ZAPP! BANG! THUD! My mom came flying around the corner to see me half dazed, still holding the keys. Shaken and scared, I sat there stunned. To this day, my mom swears that is how I got my curly hair. At the age of eight, I ran into my next childhood trauma. I fearlessly played competitive sports with the neighbourhood boys: football, basketball, and ice hockey, and I raced them on roller blades. One day five of us were speeding downhill on roller blades. I was leading. Looking back to see how far I was ahead, I was caught off guard when I tripped on a pebble in the road. Head over heels, I won the race with a broken arm. Finally, the scariest and most dangerous time of all was sledding on an abandoned ski hill in the Gatineau Hills, Quebec. My goal was to sled down from where none of the other kids would go, the top! My brother and I walked and walked and walked, and finally we were there, with the snow-white mountain spread out below us. My fat black inner tube was my toboggan. One, two, three, GO!!!! Swishing gently from side to side, I increased my speed. Faster and faster, I bounced toward the bottom. Suddenly, out of nowhere came a tin shed. I leaned hard to the right and began to spin out of control. One last hard bump and I went flipping and flying through the air and landed in some pine trees. I don't remember much after being knocked unconscious. When I woke up, people were standing in a big circle and staring down at me. I was woozy and crying, and my head hurt, but I was still alive. Having survived my crazy childhood, I am more cautious these days, but I still love adventure—anyone up for a little skydiving?

Spend a moment reflecting on your work in and out of class as you wrote the paragraph assignment for this chapter. Then take five minutes to write a paragraph about the challenges you had to overcome, how you dealt with them, and the strategies you think might be most important to apply to your upcoming writing assignments this semester.

SAVE PAPER AND PRINTING COSTS

Instead of printing multiple drafts, try revising on the computer. Most word-processing programs, such as Microsoft Word, offer opportunities to "track" your edits. Try saving each draft as a separate file so that you can use the "compare documents" function to see how your draft has developed and changed through revision. If you are peer editing for another student, use the "comment" function to add notes to the author. Your changes are easier to spot this way than if you write them within the author's text. Both "Track Changes" and "New Comment" are found on the "Review" tab of Microsoft Word.

ACTIVITY 21.1 Revise, Edit, and Proofread

For many students, English is a second or third language and their writing suffers from what is called "linguistic interference" from their first language. For example, the Chinese language does not make use of such words as *the, a,* or *an* so these words may be over- or underused in English writing. Students who struggle with linguistic interference also may have difficulties in using plurals and correct verb tenses and this can lead to choppiness in the writing style, despite wonderful ideas and good vocabulary.

Students of all mother tongues also grapple with putting ideas to paper in other ways, either not being able to get the ideas out of their heads and into the assignment, or having ideas rush out in an unorganized flood.

Revise the following paragraph of student writing using several stages of revising, editing, and proofreading. Keep each stage as a separate file and use the track changes and comments functions of your word processor.

While contemporary global issues, particular global warming, Eurozone crisis, wepons of mass destruct and terrorism as well as domestic affairs such as imigration reform, Idle No More protests, real estate bubbles, and tuition hikes protest continue to pose major challenge for goverments and leave lasting impacts on millions middle-class families, the historical rivalry never seemed to be forgottin. As long as the questions of Quebec sovereignty will stay on the top of mainstream political agenda, the French-english dilemma shall continue to excise considerable influence in shapeing our national identity as well as crafting any future public policy of the future. Even until this day, this unique relationship still will server as driving forces that shaped the young countrys' dynamic political landscapes.

Chapter Summary

1. Revising a paragraph is a multi-step process; at each stage of revision, you will address different concerns. The list of first draft revision questions can be found on pages 264.

2. For guidelines on proofreading and preparing your final manuscript, see page 268.

3. For various stages of the draft process, use the checklist of draft revision points that follows:

CHECKLIST OF DRAFT REVISION POINTS

☐ **Specific language:** All writing uses both general and specific words, but specific words sharpen an image.

☐ **Sensory details:** Use in descriptive and narrative writing to develop impressions of sight, sound, touch, smell, taste; information-based and persuasive writing can benefit from these details, too.

☐ **Active verbs:** Use to describe action. Interesting writing uses verbs that show specific action rather than more general verbs (such as *be, do, have, make*).

☐ ***-ing* words:** Present participles (a verb form with an *-ing* ending) can also convey action well.

☐ **Vary sentence length:** The structure of your sentences alone can make your writing more or less interesting. If you find more than four sentences in a row that are roughly the same length, either combine two of them or divide a longer one.

☐ **Vary sentence beginnings:** If two sentences in a row begin with the same word or phrase, change an opening or combine sentences to break up the pattern. Also, look for too many similar openings, even if the sentences are not next to one another.

☐ **Word or phrase repetition:** Have you repeated a word or phrase so often that it becomes noticeable? While some repetition is fine, too much of the same word group becomes boring.

☐ **Words that serve no purpose:** Everyday speech is full of unneeded words, but writing should not be. Cluttered writing can be boring and confusing, while concise writing involves the reader and clarifies ideas.

Designing Essays

UNIT

4

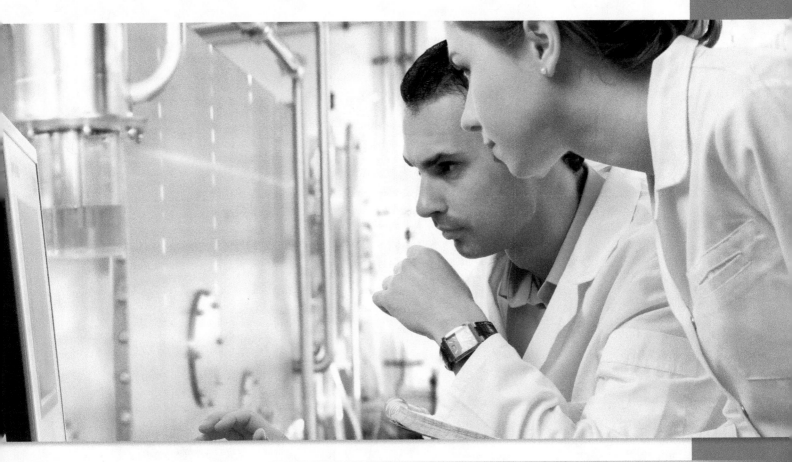

Developing Essays from Paragraphs

22

As many small waterfalls create a large river, so, too, do many small paragraphs merge to create an essay. Write a short paragraph discussing your feelings about moving from paragraph to essay writing. What do you think might be your biggest challenge?

Defining the Essay

In Unit Three, we worked extensively with paragraphs—focusing, organizing, developing, choosing the right wording, and editing closely. As you take the next step, writing essays, you will see that the same principles apply to writing in this longer form; *you already know what you need to do this task well.* This chapter reviews the fundamental principles of effective writing discussed in the previous two units, and it reinforces two specialty paragraphs: the introduction and the conclusion.

Examining Essay Form

Chapter 20 outlined the key parts of a body paragraph. Similar to a paragraph, an essay should also begin with a controlling point, grow through supporting, detailed examples and explanations, and end decisively. The following illustration shows how body paragraphs and essays are related:

> **HINT**
>
> For a review of the four paragraph types, see Chapter 20.

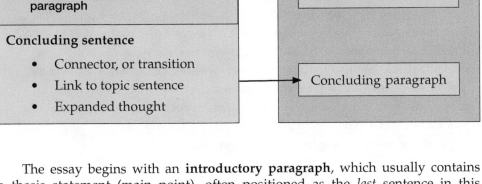

The essay begins with an **introductory paragraph**, which usually contains a thesis statement (main point), often positioned as the *last* sentence in this opening paragraph. The topic sentence in the paragraph and the thesis statement in the essay are comparable; but because essays are more fully developed, the thesis statement often provides expanded or additional points.

Body paragraphs in essays often begin with a **topic sentence** to announce the main point of the paragraph. Both topic and subtopic sentences are then developed with detailed examples and explanations.

Essays end with a **concluding paragraph**. The writer finishes by referring to the paper's main point, which is in the essay's thesis statement. Essays often use a sentence or more to summarize. (The conclusion may occasionally introduce a new point, not previously considered in the body of the essay.)

Of course, not all essays are five paragraphs. If they were, people would have an extremely hard time writing an essay longer than about five pages. A nonfiction book, in fact, is one form of very long essay, and most books are not only more than five paragraphs, they are also more than five chapters. The basic structure of an essay, however, can be expanded to any size by using more points, more details, more examples, and more explanations.

LO22.1 Transitioning from Paragraph to Essay: A Student Model

To see how a paragraph might grow into an essay, let's compare two versions of the student model "Music File-sharing: Right or Wrong?" by Darren Taylor, noting especially the beginnings, endings, and development.

Glancing between the paragraph and essay models, note their chief differences: **length, introduction,** and **conclusion.**

PARAGRAPH MODEL
Length: 217 words

Topic sentence

Subtopic sentence 1

Sentence for development

Subtopic sentence 2

Sentence for development

Subtopic sentence 3

Sentences for development

Concluding sentence

Music File-sharing: Right or Wrong?

Open access to music through computer file-sharing should not be restricted anywhere in the world. In order for music to be bought by consumers, it must be heard. To be heard, music must be accessible through a variety of media such as radio, TV, and the internet. Some people in the music industry claim a large number of sales are lost each time a song is downloaded. However, studies show that music downloads have a limited effect on music sales; and over time, downloads actually lead to increased sales for music that has been made accessible. Furthermore, the music industry's frequent changes in listening technology have caused consumers to embrace music file-sharing. They have paid for the ever-changing technology over the years as it has evolved from vinyl records to eight-tracks to cassette tapes to compact discs to MP3 files and iPods. So after all the money that has been spent, music file-sharing has given consumers a venue to a greater variety of music. In the end, the only way to eliminate file-sharing is for the music industry to find a technology medium that will not allow for reproduction, but this will be difficult to do without alienating consumers and reducing the very market for which the music is being created in the first place.

—Darren Taylor

Music File-sharing: Right or Wrong?

Is music file-sharing a consumer's right to access of information? Or should music file-sharing be considered illegal in order to protect copyright in the music industry? Music is made to be heard; file-sharing does not cause the music industry to lose sales; and the ever-changing technology encourages music file-sharing. Therefore, open access to music through computer file-sharing should not be restricted anywhere in the world.

In order for music to be bought by consumers, it must be heard. To be heard by consumers, music must be accessible. The internet has official websites where musicians offer free samples of their music. Also, with a library card, thousands of compact discs are available to be signed out. Once musicians provide access to their songs by the public, they turn their intellectual property rights into a positive externality for anyone to enjoy. An alternate perspective is represented by the band Metallica. They sued Napster, a software program developed in 1999 by a college student named Shawn Fanning, claiming that the music was their intellectual property only and, therefore, that their band should have full control over access to it. If musicians do not want their music heard by file-sharing, they should only release a compact disc for consumers to buy and allow no other access to it. However, downloading music has enabled me to listen to types of music and artists I would not have been exposed to otherwise. This exposure has broadened my musical tastes so that I now buy music I would not have previously known about.

I am a personal example, therefore, that music file-sharing actually increases sales. In fact, studies indicate that any loss in sales can be attributed to reduced pricing on CDs, and changes in the retail distribution of music. Even though a consumer will not likely purchase a compact disc which contains only one or two songs that he or she is interested in, the music industry has not lost sales if the consumer downloads the music because that consumer did not intend to buy the compact disc in the first place. However, I find that if I am listening to one or two songs I have downloaded, I *am* more likely to purchase the CD, which has a more extensive selection.

The music industry's frequent changes in listening technology have caused consumers to embrace music file sharing. In the 1970s, consumers used eight-tracks and vinyl records to play music. Then the music industry switched the technology to cassette tapes in the 1980s and compact discs in the 1990s. This made consumer music libraries of records, eight-tracks, and even cassettes obsolete. New libraries of compact discs and CD players had to be acquired by consumers, and from this the music industry profited. Today music technology primarily involves personal computers. We have digital technology, compact disc writers, the internet, and several forms of portable storage devices. The music industry has responded by adapting to the technology used for music file-sharing. In fact, it has profited from the conversion.

In conclusion, access to music through computer file-sharing should be open and unrestricted throughout the world. Many musicians readily provide open access to their music; the music file-sharing consumer actually increases sales to the music industry; and evolving technology has continually encouraged consumers to use music file-sharing. Obviously, the artist creating the music must be given some

---

ESSAY MODEL
Length: 669 words

Introductory paragraph:

> Hook: **First two sentences arouse curiosity**
>
> Sentences for development
>
> <u>Thesis statement</u>

Topic sentence 1

Sentences for development

Topic sentence 2

Sentences for development

Topic sentence 3

Sentences for development

Concluding paragraph:

> Essays require a conclusion with <u>a link to the thesis</u>, **transitions**, summary, development, even consideration of another point of view, and **a strong concluding sentence.**

protection for copyright. **Therefore**, legislation, which imposes tariffs on rewritable compact discs and other music-playing storage devices like MP3 players and iPods, has been introduced to compensate the music industry. Finally, the only way to eliminate file-sharing is for the music industry to find a medium that will not allow for reproduction. **But** this will be difficult to do without alienating the consumer. **And after all**, it is the consumer for whom the music is being created in the first place. I know that the quality of my life has been greatly improved by exposure to the variety of music styles and artists provided through music file-sharing.

—*Darren Taylor*

Length

You can increase length in two ways: by adding examples and by developing them. The music file-sharing paragraph of 217 words grew into an essay of 669 words, not by using more main examples, but by developing those already there.

HINT

Refer back to Chapter 20 for a list of transitions.

Introduction

While the music file-sharing paragraph relied on a single topic sentence to focus it, the essay's introductory paragraph is more developed. Even though the essay's main point (thesis statement) is similar to the paragraph's topic sentence, the author added a lead-in sentence to hook the reader, and then used several more sentences to inform and further draw the reader into the thesis.

Conclusion

Rather than ending with a single sentence, the music file-sharing essay uses a concluding paragraph. Here again, much is familiar. The lead sentence begins with a connector, or transition, a restatement of the thesis, and a brief summary of the essay's main points. In addition, the author presents consideration of another point of view and a strong concluding sentence—expanding his thought from the single paragraph.

The remainder of Chapter 22 explains how to transform simple paragraphs into more complex essays.

LO22.2 Writing Introductory Paragraphs

Introductory paragraphs are useful because they can arouse a reader's curiosity, encouraging him or her to read further. Introductory paragraphs usually contain the following three elements:

HINT

Even if your reader would not ordinarily be interested in your topic (or might even be predisposed to dislike it), a well-written introduction can draw him or her into the points you want to make.

1. Hook:	one sentence (the first sentence in the introductory paragraph)
2. Development:	three or four sentences (the middle sentences)
3. Thesis:	one sentence (often the last sentence in the introductory paragraph)

Writing the thesis first can help you focus both your introductory paragraph and your essay.

Crafting the Thesis Statement

The thesis statement is to the essay what the topic sentence is to the paragraph: namely, the focusing sentence. The thesis must be general enough to cover all points in the essay but specific enough to eliminate areas that the writer will not deal with. This balance can sometimes be difficult to achieve. For example, where do you suppose the following thesis statement might take us?

Vague thesis statement: Everyone participates in music file-sharing.

Readers ask, "Who is everyone, what is music file-sharing, and what's the writer's point?" When thesis statements don't name a specific topic or limit the topic, they force readers to guess at the meaning of an essay. Confused readers have little desire to read further.

However, notice how Darren Taylor gives direction to his paragraph and essay:

Topic sentence for paragraph: Open access to music through computer file-sharing should not be restricted anywhere in the world.

Thesis statement essay: Music is made to be heard; file-sharing does not cause the music industry to lose sales; and the ever-changing technology encourages music file-sharing. Therefore, open access to music through computer file-sharing should not be restricted anywhere in the world.

These statements *focus* on music file-sharing and *limit* the topic by stating that music file-sharing leads to advantages for the music industry. Since Darren did not add any further main examples to his essay, he did not change the substance of his topic sentence. Instead, he expanded it by providing specific reasons to support his thesis. He used a reverse form of a **forecasting statement** by telling exactly what points will be discussed and will lead to the thesis statement. If he had followed the forecasting statement pattern, his opening would have looked like this:

Thesis statement + Forecasting = Open access to music through computer file-sharing should not be restricted because music is made to be heard, file-sharing does not cause the music industry to lose sales, and the ever-changing technology encourages music file-sharing.

A thesis can be stretched over more than one sentence, placed in a paragraph other than the introduction, or even left unstated. For example, when trying to persuade a resistant audience — as Jonathan Swift does in his brilliant satire, "A Modest Proposal" written in 1729 (see http://art-bin.com/art/omodest.html#hit) — a writer might delay the thesis until the conclusion. However, to keep yourself and readers oriented in your essay, it helps to locate the thesis somewhere in the first or second paragraph.

FOUR GUIDELINES FOR RECOGNIZING THE THESIS STATEMENT WHEN READING ESSAYS

1. The thesis statement is **the main focus of the essay**. It tells the readers exactly the topic they are going to read about.

   • From "Ambition" by Perri Klass in Chapter 30:

   I've always liked ambitious people, and many of my closest friends have had grandiose dreams.

Note where it is: The first sentence in the third paragraph.

2. Often, the main points of a thesis statement appear as **a stream of detail.**

   - From "Has Canada Got the Cure?" by Holly Dressel in Chapter 28:

   The United States now has the most expensive health care system on earth and, despite remarkable technology, the general health of the U.S. population is lower than in most industrialized countries. Worse, Americans' mortality rates — both general and infant — are shockingly high.

   Note where it is: Second half of the second paragraph. Together, these two sentences make the direction of the essay clear. The many details will be "unpacked" throughout the essay.

3. The thesis statement often answers **W5: Who, What, Where, When, Why — and How.**

   - From "How Not To Be an Energy Superpower" by David Suzuki in Chapter 26:

   Although the federal government demonizes environmentalists as "radicals" bent on derailing exploitation plans for the tar sands and other natural resources, opposition is rising against pipelines to transport Alberta's diluted bitumen to the BC coast via Enbridge's Northern Gateway or to Texas refineries via the Keystone XL. Much of the oil would be exported to countries like China, where the extreme negative effects of fossil fuel pollution are increasing daily.

Who:	federal government
What:	plans for the tar sands and other natural resources
Where:	in Canada, particularly Alberta and British Columbia
When:	now
What:	opposition is rising
Why:	extreme negative effects of fossil fuel pollution
How:	pipelines
Note where it is:	All of paragraph four. The entire paragraph is packed with detail about what Suzuki objects to.

4. The thesis statement sometimes presents **the main points in grammatical parallel** *and* it often **expresses a point of view.** That is, it is **a statement that can be argued.** This format is the most common structure for student research papers.

   - From "Making the Most of Reading" by Esther Cho in Chapter 29:

   By recognizing some common patterns, such as time order, comparison–contrast, cause-and-effect, and listing, readers will be able to understand and remember even complicated information.

Parallel structure:	time order, comparison–contrast, cause-and-effect, and listing
Note where it is:	the last sentence of the first paragraph

HINT

For more information on parallel structure, see Chapter 14.

HINT

For a review of point of view, see Chapter 2.

1. Limit the topic.
2. Make a clear statement about the topic.
3. Refine the statement through clear explanations, specific terms, action words, and sensory details.

ACTIVITY 22.1 Searching for Thesis Statements

Look for the thesis statements in the following text articles and copy them, word for word, in the space provided. Provide a reason for your choice (consider the above four guidelines for recognizing the thesis statement).

1. "Heaven and Earth in Jest" by Annie Dillard, Chapter 23 (page 303):

    Thesis statement: _____

    _____

    _____

    Reason for your choice:_____

    _____

    _____

    _____

    _____

    _____

    Location within essay (sentence? paragraph?): _____

    _____

2. "Elegy in Stone" by Steven Heighton, Chapter 24 (page 319–320):

    Thesis statement: _____

    _____

    _____

    Reason for your choice: _____

    _____

    _____

    _____

    Location within essay: _____

    _____

3. "Daily Shampoo?" by Ruth Bradley-St-Cyr, Chapter 25 (page 336–337):

Thesis statement: _____

_____

_____

Reason for your choice: _____

_____

_____

_____

Location within essay: _____

_____

4. "Baby Bust" by Ted Byfield, Chapter 27 (page 366–367):

Thesis statement: _____

_____

_____

Reason for your choice: _____

_____

_____

_____

Location within essay: _____

_____

ACTIVITY 22.2 Writing Stronger Thesis Statements

The following are weak thesis statements. Using **Four Guidelines for Recognizing the Thesis Statement when Reading Essays** (page 279–280) and **Three Points for Writing an Effective Thesis** (page 281), strengthen the following thesis statements.

1. TV crime shows are intriguing.

_____

_____

_____

2. There are recognizable symptoms for gluten intolerance.

_____

_____

_____

3. The Canadian real estate market is a mess.

4. Admission procedures for Canadian universities are complicated.

Using Hooks

With a well-focused thesis in hand, you will have a good *end* to your introductory paragraph, but how will you move readers toward that thesis? The *first* sentence in your essay can help here. Called the **hook**, this sentence has the special job of arousing curiosity, moving your reader to explore further. Like a trail of bread crumbs, an introduction should lead your audience into the essay.

TWO POINTS FOR WRITING EFFECTIVE HOOKS

1. Avoid stating the obvious.
2. Say something that will interest your reader.

Here is how Darren Taylor hooks his audience in his essay "Music File-sharing: Right or Wrong?"

Hook: Is music file-sharing a consumer's right to access of information? Or should music file-sharing be considered illegal in order to protect copyright in the music industry?

Darren begins with two questions. Readers think, "I wonder why the writer is asking?" Now the author has captured—momentarily—his readers' attention and can begin to draw them forward toward his thesis.

What Darren does *not* do is begin with an obvious statement of fact, such as the following:

Weak hooks:
1. Music file-sharing is fun.
2. The music industry provides a vast store of music.
3. Music file-sharing is legal in some countries, but not legal in others.

Sentence 3 is weak if you don't intend to focus the essay on comparing music copyright laws in different countries; in fact, it is misleading.

METHODS FOR CREATING STRONG HOOKS

1. Ask a question.
2. Begin with a line of dialogue.
3. Begin with a quotation.

4. Make a startling statement.
5. Present an unusual fact.
6. Begin with a vivid image.

Here are hooks that "Music File-sharing" could have used in addition to **asking a question:**

Dialogue:	"Downloaded any good tunes lately?" I asked my friend, Scott, whom I hadn't seen for a month.
Quotation:	"As I was goin' over the Cork and Kerry Mountains I saw Captain Farrell and his money he was countin'."
	These are the familiar opening lines to "Whiskey in the Jar" in a version sung and recorded by Metallica.
	(Source: "Whiskey in the Jar," words and music by Philip Parris Lynott, Brian Michael Downey, and Eric Bell. Copyright (c) 1975 PIPPIN-THE-FRIENDLY-RANGER MUSIC CO. LTD. Copyright renewed. All rights in the U.S. and Canada controlled and administered by UNIVERSAL-POLYGRAM INTERNATIONAL PUBLISHING, INC. All Rights Reserved. Reprinted by permission of Hal Leonard Corporation.)

Avoiding Weak Introductions

Introductions can go wrong in several ways. Try to avoid the following problems:

1. **Beginning with an obvious statement:**

NOT THIS:	I awoke in the morning as I usually do.
BUT THIS:	I awoke with a pounding headache and a feeling that the day was headed for disaster.
NOT THIS:	Some people smoke cigarettes.
BUT THIS:	People who smoke cigarettes are slowly committing suicide.

2. **Stating that you are getting ready to write an essay about something:**

NOT THIS:	In this essay, I will tell you about . . .
OR THIS:	The first part of my essay will discuss . . . and the next paragraph will say . . .

3. **Apologizing for lack of expertise:**

NOT THIS:	I don't know that much about this subject but . . .
OR THIS:	People who really know about this subject might laugh at what I have to say. . . .

Writers ask readers for their time. If a writer begins by telling readers that an essay is not worth reading, why should an audience waste time with the essay?

4. **Needlessly repeating information:**

NOT THIS:	Spanking children is a questionable method of discipline. Parents who spank their children may not be doing the right thing. Children who are spanked may not do well with this form of punishment.

Each sentence in an introduction should *build on* and *add to* the previous one, not just rephrase it.

5. **Using clichés and worn expressions like the following:**

   NOT THIS: I sat in the dentist's chair for what seemed like an eternity.

   BUT THIS: I sat in the dentist's chair for two long, painful hours.

6. **Writing an overly long or too-short introduction:** Introductions should be proportionate to the rest of the work. A book, for instance, might need a chapter-length introduction while an essay of 15 pages might need only a paragraph or two. An introduction for a brief essay like the ones we are writing can be well developed in five to seven sentences, about 100 words.

ACTIVITY 22.3 Recognizing and Revising Weak Introductions

HINT

Explain why the following introduction is ineffective. Then revise it to make it stronger.

> My college campus has students. Some of these students smoke. I don't know much about campus security issues or how hard it would be for security to issue tickets, but I think that they should issue $1 fines to every student they catch throwing cigarette butts on the ground. Well, maybe not $1; maybe that's too much but then again maybe not. That could be just the right amount because students could afford it but wouldn't much like it. I wouldn't want to put security between a rock and a hard place by asking them to issue fines that students couldn't pay. Anyway, like I said, I'm going to write this essay about student smokers who are students on this campus and who throw their cigarette butts on the ground.

Introduction is ineffective because —

_____

_____

_____

_____

_____

Some writers prefer to draft the body of the essay using only a thesis for focus and then creating an introduction after the body is complete.

Writing Body Paragraphs

LO22.3

Introductory paragraphs take the first step of attracting and then focusing a reader, but then the writer must follow through, keeping the essay interesting. We do this in the **body paragraphs**, where we present most of our information.

Like stand-alone paragraphs, essay body paragraphs begin with a topic sentence and end with a summarizing (or concluding) sentence. Also, you will sometimes find subtopic sentences useful, depending on how many points you want to develop in the paragraph. Whereas stand-alone paragraphs are around 200 to 250 words, we reduce body paragraphs in an essay to approximately 150 words each.

Body paragraphs have three main parts:

1. **Topic sentence:** transition + topic + limiting statement (first sentence)
2. **Development:** four to six sentences (middle sentences)
3. **Summary sentence:** restates, or brings to a conclusion, the paragraph's main idea (last sentence)

Topic sentences refine the thesis, offering the *more specific* points or examples from which the essay will grow. Within each topic sentence, it is important to name and focus each example or point and link the sentence to the paragraph preceding it.

Notice how the topic sentence below includes a transition word used to bridge the gap between it and the preceding paragraph, and then more transition words to link the advantage of music file-sharing to the author's own likelihood of purchasing music.

> I am a personal example, therefore, that music file-sharing actually increases sales. In fact, studies indicate that any loss in sales can be attributed to reduced pricing on CDs, and changes in the retail distribution of music. Even though a consumer will not likely purchase a compact disc which contains only one or two songs that he or she is interested in, the music industry has not lost sales if the consumer downloads the music because that consumer did not intend to buy the compact disc in the first place. However, I find that if I am listening to one or two songs I have downloaded, I *am* more likely to purchase the CD which has a more extensive selection.

To conclude longer body paragraphs, writers create a **summary sentence** like the one underlined above. These sentences can be useful because they reinforce an author's message, which was stated in the paragraph's topic sentence.

ACTIVITY 22.4 Revising an Essay

Whether you are revising your own essay or helping a friend or classmate revise theirs by acting as a peer reviewer, editing is an important skill to learn. For example, many instructors prohibit the use of the first person — I, me, mine, myself — in academic essays. The paragraph of Darren Taylor's essay on file-sharing below uses the word "I" five times. If you and Darren Taylor were in the same class and your professor had banned "I" in your assignment, how would you help Darren revise this paragraph of his essay? What other edits would you make? (Hint: Remember the rules about essential and nonessential clauses and the use of *who, which,* and *that* from Chapter 12, p. XXX.) Edit Darren's paragraph in the spaces between the lines below. (Note: The need for the professor to edit is the reason why assignments must be double-spaced when handed in.)

I am a personal example, therefore, that music file-sharing actually increases sales. In fact, studies indicate that any loss in sales can be attributed to reduced pricing on CDs, and changes in the retail distribution of music. Even though a consumer will not likely purchase a compact disc which contains only one or two songs that he or she is interested in, the music industry has not lost sales if the consumer downloads the music because that consumer did not intend to buy the compact disc in the first place. However, I find that if I am listening to one or two songs I have downloaded, I *am* more likely to purchase the CD, which has a more extensive selection.

Arranging Body Paragraphs within Essays

Positioning body paragraphs in essays is much like organizing subtopics within single-paragraph papers. A writer might choose any of these three organizational patterns:

- **Spatial:** describing a person/place/object from front to back, side to side, top to bottom, and so on. You might, for example, describe your dream house as you approach, walk into, and then move through it.

- **Chronological:** relating a series of actions in time order. Personal narrative, fiction, and process descriptions use this method.

- **Order of importance:** arranging points from least to most (or most to least) dramatic. Expository writing and persuasive pieces often use this method. ("Music File-Sharing: Right or Wrong?" in this chapter has been arranged in this way.)

Writers may use one of the preceding overall arrangement methods, and then arrange material by an additional method within a paragraph.

HINT

For more on these patterns of organization, see Chapter 20.

Using Outlines

Another aid in organizing essays is the outline, which can keep even brief essays on track. A formal sentence outline is probably not needed for short essays, but listing primary examples and several supporting points can be useful. An example for Darren Taylor's essay is below:

Thesis	Open access to music through computer file-sharing should not be restricted anywhere in the world.
Topic sentence	I. In order for music to be bought by consumers, it must be heard.
Supporting examples	A. The internet has official websites
	B. Library card to sign out thousands of compact discs
	C. Musicians provide access and their music becomes a positive externality
[Optional: Alternate Viewpoint]	D. Metallica sued Napster
	i. Band should release only compact discs allowing no other access if they don't want music heard through file-sharing
[Optional: Counterpoint]	E. Exposure to music leads to sales
Topic sentence	II. File-sharing actually increases sales.
Supporting examples	A. Studies indicate any loss in sales is due to reduced pricing on CDs
	B. Loss is also due to changes in retail distribution
	C. Listening to one or two songs encourages listener to purchase CD

INFORMAL WORKING OUTLINE FOR "MUSIC FILE-SHARING: RIGHT OR WRONG?"

Topic sentence	III. Frequent changes to listening technology encourages music file-sharing.
Supporting examples	A. History of technology tracked through 1970s to 1990s—vinyl records, eight-tracks, cassette tapes, compact discs
	B. Old technology becomes obsolete and requires new technology purchase
	C. Computers are now main venue and music industry has responded by adapting to evolving technology

Refer to your thesis often. However detailed you decide to make your outline, it can be expanded with supporting examples, illustrations, and statistics.

LO22.4 Writing Concluding Paragraphs

Like introductions, conclusions often pose challenges to essay writers. How can we leave our readers feeling that the promise made in the thesis has been met and that the essay is decisively completed? One solution is to *plan* a concluding paragraph. As you draft the concluding paragraph, be sure to create strong links to the introductory paragraph. Concluding paragraphs should include the following elements:

1. **Lead sentence:**   one sentence (transition + link to thesis)
2. **Summary:**   one sentence or less
3. **Development:**   three or four sentences (often contains an expanded thought)

Crafting Lead and Summary Sentences

Just as introductory and body paragraphs have a **lead sentence** (the "hook" and the topic sentence, respectively), so do concluding paragraphs. Careful writers often begin the first sentence of their conclusion with a connector, touch on the thesis, and then give a brief **summary** of the essay's main points.

Lead sentence introduced by summary:

Since many musicians readily provide open access to their music, the consumer is not denying sales to the music industry, and evolving technology encourages consumers to download music, access to music through computer file-sharing should be open and unrestricted throughout the world.

Alternately, the summary can be placed in the second sentence. Darren Taylor wrote his lead and summary sentences by saving the summary words for a second sentence:

Lead sentence with delayed summary:

In conclusion, access to music through computer file-sharing should be open and unrestricted throughout the world. Many musicians readily provide open access to their music; the music file-sharing consumer actually increases sales to the music industry; and evolving technology has continually encouraged consumers to use music file-sharing.

In these ways, a concluding paragraph eases the reader out of the mainstream of a writer's ideas and into the final comments or observations that finish the essay.

Developing Conclusions

After leading the reader into the concluding paragraph, end the essay decisively, rather than tacking on half a dozen empty, repetitive sentences. The following strategies will help you develop strong conclusions:

1. **Frame:** Return to the image, comparison, story, or other element from the introductory paragraph.

2. **Use an expanded thought:** Ending an essay decisively with an expanded thought takes the audience one step beyond the ideas in the body paragraphs. Many of the ideas below are illustrated with examples from "Music File-sharing: Right or Wrong?" by Darren Taylor.

   a. **Express an emotion:** Let your reader know how you feel about your topic. What emotional response has it created in you?

   > And after all, it is the consumer for whom the music is being created in the first place.

   b. **Give a judgment, opinion, or evaluation:**

   > But this will be difficult to do without alienating the consumer.

   c. **Show how something has affected your behaviour or outlook on life:**

   > I know that the quality of my life has been greatly improved by exposure to the variety of music styles and artists provided through music file-sharing.

   d. **Introduce an alternate point of view:**

   > Obviously, the artist creating the music must be given some protection for copyright. Therefore, legislation, which imposes tariffs on rewritable compact discs and other music-playing storage devices like MP3 players and iPods, has been introduced to compensate the music industry.

   e. **Ask a related question:** Consider an issue or idea that might grow from your topic.

   > Or should music file-sharing be considered illegal in order to protect copyright in the music industry?

   f. **Make a reflective statement:** Tell your reader something that your topic suggests to you beyond the points made in the body paragraphs. Think of some larger or more general application to the world around you.

   > This exposure has broadened my musical tastes so that I now have an awareness of music being created globally in a variety of cultures.

> **HINT**
>
> We used expanded thoughts to end single paragraphs in Chapter 20, but an essay gives writers more room to develop the final point.

g. **Suggest a course of action:** Encourage your reader to act on the information you have presented.

> I encourage you to expand and share your musical appreciation by exploring various styles via file-sharing.

ACTIVITY 22.5 Creating Interesting Conclusions

Using one of your paragraph writing assignments, brainstorm to uncover several main examples for an essay that could grow from it. Next, write a concluding paragraph using any of the seven methods outlined above for expanding the final thought.

Concluding strategy: _____

Lead sentence: _____

_____

_____

Development: _____

_____

_____

_____

_____

_____

_____

Summary sentence: _____

_____

_____

_____

Avoiding Weak Conclusions

Even knowing how to write a strong final paragraph, writers sometimes stumble at the end of an essay, slipping into problems like the following:

1. **Under- or over-summarizing (and repeating):** Most conclusions contain some kind of summary: the longer and more complex the essay, the longer and more detailed the summary might be. However, in a brief essay, the reader does not need much repeating of main points. A single sentence ought to be enough.

2. **Telling readers that you are about to end the essay:** While you should connect the first sentence of your conclusion to the final body paragraph, avoid doing it with statements like these: "OK, that's about it; I've said all I need to" or "I want to end my essay with this thought."

3. **Moving into an unrelated or too loosely related topic:** An expanded thought should grow naturally from the body of the essay. It should be an extension of the thesis, not a different topic altogether.

4. **Over-generalizing:** Expressing opinions and evaluating can be effective concluding strategies. However, it is important to qualify statements, so you don't claim more than you can prove. Avoid assertions like "Canada will always be considered a peacekeeping nation" or "Greenpeace is just a bunch of confused tree huggers." Instead say, "Canada will continue *for some time* as . . ." and "Greenpeace has *some* confused . . ."

HINT

For more on qualifying, see Chapter 31.

5. **Apologizing:** Apologizing is another ineffective concluding strategy. Don't write this: "Well, even if I haven't got all the facts straight, I think you can see why I'm right about this issue." Your conclusion should convey confidence. If you have serious doubts about your essay, get the facts and revise it.

6. **Using clichés and worn expressions:** Beware of clichés like "a slap on the wrist" and "a chill running down my spine." If you can't think of a fresh figure of speech, just use a literal phrase. For example, say "mild discipline" in place of "a slap on the wrist."

7. **Making your conclusion too long or too short:** As already noted for introductions, conclusions should be written in proportion to the rest of the work. A book might require a concluding chapter, but an essay of 15 pages might need only a paragraph or two. Brief essays can support a final paragraph of five to seven sentences—or 100 words.

ACTIVITY 22.6 WORKING TOGETHER: Recognizing and Revising Weak Conclusions

Working in groups, explain why the following conclusion is ineffective, and then revise to make it stronger. Alternately, trade drafts of your own in-progress essays, and respond to classmates' conclusions.

So as I am starting on my conclusion, I just want to summarize the points that I made in the body of my essay when I told you, my readers, that I favour a $1 fine (I think) for students who toss their trashy cigarette butts anywhere but (no pun intended) in a proper waste container. I've already said (in paragraph 3, I think) that campus security could probably, maybe, issue the citations without too much trouble, and most students would pay up if, as a motivator, they weren't allowed in classes or were denied access to their transcripts. No one would object to my proposal because it is sensible. If we could just get the ball rolling, we could make this proposal fly, and all of us who hate smoking with a passion would no longer be caught between a rock and a hard place.

Creating Coherence

LO22.5

Unit Three showed how critical it is to link words within and between sentences, especially between subtopic sentences, to create **coherence**. Essays also require strong transitions, particularly *between* paragraphs.

FOUR WAYS TO CREATE COHERENCE

1. **Transitions:** using categories of linking words like the following:
   - locating or moving in space: *above, against, around, behind, below, on, in*
   - moving in time: *after, at last, awhile, first, next, now, often, then*
   - adding material: *again, also, and, in addition, furthermore, as well as*
   - giving examples: *for example, for instance, another, one reason, in fact*
   - comparing: *alike, also, both, in the same way, similarly*
   - contrasting: *in contrast, although, but, differs from, even though, however*
   - cause/effect: *and so, as a result, because, consequently, since, so, then*
   - summarizing/concluding: *finally, in brief, in other words, in short*
2. **Repetition:** repeating a significant word from a preceding paragraph
3. **Synonyms:** using a word equivalent to one in a preceding paragraph
4. **Pronouns:** using words like *she, they, that, this, those, some, each*

L022.6 ## Selecting a Title

Titles are important because they represent the rest of your work. They are like a first greeting. If someone you meet barely looks at you, mumbles, or walks away after a few moments, how interested will you be in getting to know that person better? Dull, misleading, or missing titles make the same sort of poor impression. Readers are less inclined to give an essay attention when they feel that the author doesn't care much about it either.

The following strategies will help you create an effective title when you are polishing your essay:

1. Keep the title short—one to eight words. Remember that titles are almost never complete sentences and that they follow the capitalization rules outlined in Chapter 16.

2. Link the title to your main idea, point, or dominant impression.

3. Use one or more of the following approaches:

   - Create an image: use a metaphor or simile, specific words, action words, and/or sensory details.
     Slow Love: How I Lost My Job, Put On My Pajamas, and Found Happiness

   - Ask a question.
     Mama, Is It Time To Cut the Broccoli?

   - Make a play on words.
     The Right to Write

   - Refer to something that your reader might know and find interesting.
     The Day Niagara Falls Ran Dry

Chapter Summary

1. An essay is a group of related paragraphs that develops an overall point.

2. Like a single body paragraph, an essay requires an introduction, substantive development, and a conclusion.

3. Introductory paragraphs usually consist of a hook, development, and a thesis statement.

4. A thesis statement is to the essay what a topic sentence is to the body paragraph.

5. Body paragraphs often begin with topic sentences and end with summary sentences.

6. Concluding paragraphs consist of a lead sentence, a summary, and development.

7. Concluding paragraphs may be developed in several ways, including use of an expanded thought.

8. Essays should be both unified (all material is relevant) and coherent (all sentences and paragraphs are clearly linked).

9. A title is an important finishing touch, and there are strategies for creating interesting ones.

Describing a Person, Place, or Object (Description)

Using specific details, describe a celebration or party you recently attended. If there were decorations, what did they look like? How were people dressed? What time of year was it? Was the event held indoors or outside? What kind of food was served? How would you describe the overall mood of the party, and how did it make you feel?

LEARNING OBJECTIVES

23.1 Developing skills in describing

23.2 Writing a descriptive essay

What Are We Trying to Achieve and Why?

If asked to **describe** (or paint a verbal image of) the scene in this photograph, you'd probably offer both a general overview—it's a birthday party—and specific details—colourful balloons and party hats, brightly coloured cups and forks, and the centrepiece: a decorated birthday cake. Details help us describe a scene to someone who isn't there and can't see or experience it. Beyond listing physical details, you could consider the overall theme or mood of the scene. Words like *happiness, family togetherness,* and *joy* help capture the picture's **dominant impression**, the overall feeling that gives it a point, or purpose.

In this chapter, we will focus on **description** in writing. People use words to describe many things—other people, objects, places, even experiences. Vivid descriptions call for **specific words** and **sensory details**, so they challenge writers to use language with particular care. The focus in this chapter will be to describe a place that you know well, or an object that you find interesting, or a person whom you love and want to share with other people (your audience). This organizational pattern of writing is fun to develop; but more importantly, it will sharpen your sense of detail, which will come in handy for both academic and professional writing.

LINKING TO PREVIOUS EXPERIENCE

What You Already Know about Description

We describe every day. When telling a friend about your vacation, you might describe a trip to Daytona Beach, Florida: the golden sand, the warm blue-green ocean water, the air's salty taste, and the bright purple Portuguese man-of-war you swam away from quickly. Or when giving directions, you might describe your house or apartment building so that someone can find it (the beige ranch-style home with the brown shingle roof, or the two-storey red brick with the black-and-white striped awning and potted geraniums on the porch). Perhaps someone wants to know what kind of pet you own, and you respond by describing the ball of chocolate fur you recently adopted—its white eye patches, white-tipped ears, and very sharp puppy teeth. You have been describing since you could first talk. This chapter will help you get better at it. There are many disciplines where being able to describe accurately is essential, such as anthropology, science, engineering, art, and history. In fact, any discipline or career will eventually require you to be able to describe in detail things that cannot be shown, like the atmosphere of a very tense staff meeting or the state of an author's manuscript.

JOURNAL / BLOG ENTRY 23.1

Name three things, people, or places you have described recently (such as a new car, a family member, or a workplace). Choose one and write several sentences of description, being sure to include details. What do you like best about your description? What part would you like to make clearer?

FEEDBACK *Share and comment on each other's descriptions. What do you like best about a classmate's piece of writing? What do you want to know more about?*

Developing Skills in Describing

Think about your favourite novels and what makes them special to you. Perhaps it is the dialogue, the plot, or the character development; however, none of those things would be as meaningful if the author hadn't created a setting in which the story unfolds. What would Harry Potter be, for example, without Hogwarts? The moving staircases, the talking portraits, the secret door to each house's dorm, all of these descriptive details create a whole new world in our imaginations. Novels use descriptive paragraphs worked into the rest of the story in order to create these new worlds. If you look closely at any chapter in a novel, you will seldom find more than a few descriptive paragraphs together. A descriptive paragraph, or perhaps a page of description, is all it takes to set our imaginations flying. In the same way, an essay may include a descriptive paragraph or two to draw in the reader and set the stage for a political event, an art show, or a medical emergency. Learning to write effective descriptions can turn a B+ essay into an A+ essay.

English Review Note

Use a dictionary and a thesaurus to build your vocabulary and help you avoid repeating words.

The following skills will help you create more vivid descriptions:

1. Using specific language
2. Using the five senses
3. Creating a dominant impression
4. Organizing details spatially
5. Using space and time transitions

Using Specific Language

Words can be either relatively **general** or relatively **specific**, belonging to a larger or a smaller grouping, respectively. For example, there are many types of machines (a general grouping): computers, motorcycles, cellphones, and cars (specific groupings). Each time you give a more specific name to something, you further limit the group to which it belongs. Below, you can see this principle illustrated as a bull's eye: the most specific word in the centre belongs to the smallest group:

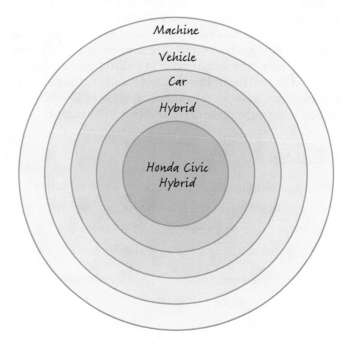

Machine
Vehicle
Car
Hybrid
Honda Civic Hybrid

When writers want to create the clearest picture possible, they choose the most specific word they can find and then add describing words to it: for example, *a sleek silver-gray 2008 Honda Civic Hybrid.*

ACTIVITY 23.1 Narrowing the Group

For each of the words in column A, first think of a more specific word for column B; then add a describing word in column C. Use numbers 1 and 2 as examples.

A	B	C
1. machine	*computer*	*Dell notebook*
2. music	*rock*	*classic*
3. sport		
4. food		
5. vacation		
6. movie		

Using the Five Senses

When we describe, we can create vivid images by using specific words and details, many of which appeal to our five senses. Most writers tend to rely heavily on **sight** and **sound** but may overlook **touch, smell,** and **taste.** Read the two examples below, and decide which of them involves you more as a reader:

1. **The Canadian National Exhibition (CNE) is one of my favourite places. People seem to have fun there on the rides, at the arcades, and at the specialty buildings. I like the food, too.**

2. **The CNE is one of my favourite places to spend a day in the summer. As I listen, I hear the sounds of laughter filling the air. Walking closer to the arcade, I hear the jingling sound of tokens as they fall from the change machine and alarm bells piercing the air as the arcade attendants shout, "We have another winner!" People's faces glow as the tickets dispense. Colourful stuffed animals—pink poodles, purple bears, orange tigers—decorate the ceiling and walls of the arcade. At the concession stand, I smell sweet taffy-coated apples and salty popcorn mixed with exhaust fumes from the hard-working motor that fuels the Ferris wheel. The fizz of strawberry candyfloss tingles on my tongue and makes me forget for a moment that I have to work the next day. In the Better Living Building, I get inspiration for how to reorganize my linen closet with the display of soft sheets and thick towels, and how to mix the latest vibrant colours for my kitchen walls—paprika red and saffron gold. Then I realize it's important to go back to work tomorrow, so I can earn money to pay for these good ideas as well as my escape for a couple of hours to stomach-lifting rides, plush toys, and sweet confections.**

> **HINT**
>
> A good description relies on the quality, not quantity, of details.

In the second example, specific words and sensory details help readers enjoy a good description. Without details, the first example fails to convey a sense of what the experience was like.

ACTIVITY 23.2 Finding Sensory Details

Reread the second paragraph about the CNE and, in the columns below, list all the sensory details. Remember that sight words are often combined with other sense details.

Sight	Sound	Touch	Smell	Taste
___	___	___	___	___
___	___	___	___	___
___	___	___	___	___
___	___	___	___	___

Creating a Dominant Impression

To focus a descriptive paragraph, writers bring specific words, sensory details, thoughts, and feelings together to form a **dominant impression**, or overall feeling. For example, what would you say is the overall feeling the author wanted readers to take from the second CNE description? If you said "fun" or "enjoyment" or "comfortable lifestyle," you have found the dominant impression. Without some way to focus a description, it is difficult to make a point about what you are describing. For instance, can you find a dominant impression or point in the following paragraph?

1. **My bedroom is a place where I spend a lot of time. The walls are pale gold, and the baseboards are white. My closet door has wooden slats to let the air conditioning and heat flow through. I have a desk with two lamps, a computer monitor, and some magazines. There is a poster of a Paris street on a wet, rainy night on the wall next to the entertainment centre, which holds my 27-inch HD TV and stereo.**

Although there are some good specific words and sensory details in **paragraph 1** above, the description does not have a point, so we are not sure what the author is trying to tell us about her room. Contrast the first example with **paragraph 2** below, and try to decide what this author's point is:

2. **My bedroom is my refuge from the world. Standing in the doorway, I can feel the thick gold carpet, warm beneath my bare feet. Across from the doorway is my queen-sized bed, with four medium-firm pillows propped up against the padded headboard. This is my favourite place to read and do homework that doesn't require my computer. On the right side of my bed is a nightstand with a tall flex-arch metal lamp, which makes it easy for me to lose myself in my pillows with the latest *Adbusters* and *Weaving* magazines spread across the comforter. Centred against the opposite wall is my entertainment centre, housing my stereo, DVD player, and 27-inch HD TV. I'm listening to "Blue Ridge Mountains," a Fleet Foxes tune that puts me at ease. Under the window is my grandfather's oak desk, reminding me of his once-comforting presence. This is where I use my Dell desktop and 19-inch LCD monitor. I use my computer more for surfing online and talking to friends than for homework, but it does come in handy for papers like these. All in all, after a day on the job and three classes at the college, I'm happy to get back to my safe, relaxing bedroom.**

If you decided that "refuge from the world," "safety," "security," or "restfulness" is the author's point about her room, you identified the dominant impression.

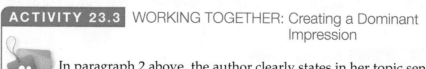

ACTIVITY 23.3 WORKING TOGETHER: Creating a Dominant Impression

In paragraph 2 above, the author clearly states in her topic sentence her dominant impression, "refuge from the world," and repeats it in her concluding sentence with "safe, relaxing bedroom." Discuss with group members what phrases in the paragraph help develop this impression, and list them below. Two are written as examples.

the thick gold carpet, warm beneath my bare feet _____

my favourite place to read _____

_____

_____

_____

Organizing Details Spatially

An effective way to arrange the details of a descriptive essay is **spatially**, or from one point in space to another. This approach helps readers more easily see what is being presented. In describing a place—whether it's a room indoors or an outdoor space—you might begin with close details and then zoom out, or move from one side to another, or from bottom to top, or even describe as you walk through the place.

ACTIVITY 23.4

The following lists of place details are jumbled. Read through them, and then number the details according to the spatial arrangement given in parentheses, with 1 as the first detail in a paragraph and 5 as the last.

EXAMPLE:

Topic sentence: The waiting room in my dentist's office is a place of high anxiety. (*Arrange details from outside to in.*)

   5   On the wall in front of the receptionist's desk, there is a picture of an open mouth full of tooth decay and bleeding gums.

   1   In the parking lot, a mother tugs her resisting 8-year-old from a car.

   2   The windows of the building are darkly tinted so that it is hard to see in or out.

   4   One teenage patient sitting near the entrance is sweating and squirming in his seat.

   3   When I enter the office, I hear the high-pitched whine of a dental drill.

1. **Topic sentence:** My school cafeteria during lunch hour is a busy place. (*Arrange details from your seat at a table some distance from the cashiers and salad bar, and scan the room, beginning with activity at your table and moving beyond.*)

   ___   A 32-inch flat screen TV about nine metres away is blaring out the hockey game.

   ___   Past the cashiers, in the middle of the food line, students and teachers cluster around the salad bar, shovelling lettuce, tomatoes, olives, cheese, and sunflower seeds onto their plates.

___ Every other table is full of people eating.

___ My four friends are laughing, joking with each other, and eating all at once.

___ Three cashiers frantically ring up food as dozens of people push their brown trays up to them.

2. **Topic sentence:** There is often so much wildlife in my backyard that a nature special could be filmed there. (*Arrange details from the ground upward.*)

___ Two metres above the ground hangs a red plastic bird feeder with one chickadee and five sparrows flapping their wings and eating greedily.

___ In the grass, three chipmunks scurry about, snatching seeds spilling from the bird feeder as a baby rabbit looks on.

___ Higher up in the trees, two gray squirrels prepare to descend on the feast.

___ In the branches of an elm tree, a watchful male cardinal and a blue jay consider diving down onto the feeder to snatch some food for themselves.

___ A series of raised tunnels in the grass shows me where the moles are at work again.

Write your own descriptive paragraph of one topic sentence plus five descriptive sentences and the rewrite it in random order as in this activity. Add a suggestion for the proper arrangement. Exchange your scrambled paragraph with a partner and see if you can edit each other's paragraphs into an order that makes sense. If your order and that of your partner differs, discuss why. What different assumptions about order are you using?

Using Space and Time Transitions

HINT

For a more complete list of transitions, see Chapter 20.

As we learned in Chapter 20, linking sentences with connectors, such as repeated words, synonyms, and transitions, is essential if readers are to follow the flow of your ideas. Descriptions especially benefit from **space** and **time** transitions like the following:

English Review Note

Review this chart to master prepositions involving time and space.

SPACE TRANSITIONS				
above	at	in	on	to
against	below	into	over	toward
around	by	near	there	under

TIME TRANSITIONS			
after	now	then	references to clock and calendar time: 1:00, last week, etc.
first (second, etc.)	often	until	
next	once	when	

Fill in the blanks with the time and space transitions from the lists above.

1. The rain pours _____ the awning.

2. Apple tree branches hang _____ the yard, giving welcome shade.

3. Carrie climbed _____ her Hummer, hoping she had enough gas to drive around the block.

4. We looked _____ the bench and everywhere else for the lost cellphone.

5. Water cascades from the fountain and _____ tumbles onto the stones below.

6. Greta and Alex waited at the Taloola Cafe for Katie _____ they could wait no longer.

Learning from a Student Model: A Descriptive Essay

Read the following student model closely. Try to identify the elements of vivid description: **specific words, sensory details,** a clear **dominant impression, spatial organization,** and precise **space and time transitions.**

Back to the Garden

1   Loud rock-and-roll; people swarming through the front door of Houlihan's, impatient to be seated; and late nights with my face stuck in a textbook—my life is jammed. At 23, it seems that I ought to have a little more breathing space than I have managed, but I'm trying to get my life more together. My band may never be the next Radiohead, and I don't think I'm going to get rich waiting tables, so I'm giving college another try. But sometimes I wonder if it's all worth it. Sometimes I need a break from my world of constant rushing and guitar riffs; that's when I head for the tranquility and beauty of the Richardson Park rose garden.

2   I enter the garden from the south and stroll leisurely along the red brick walkway bordered by dark-green bushes labelled burkwood viburnum. Small songbirds and some sparrows flutter about inside the bushes. Some of the birds seem to be nesting, and I imagine new life soon emerging into the spring sunshine. A moment later, the bushes give way to beds of roses: vibrant deep red, yellow, orange, and pink. Some are only knee-high; others climb dark metal trellises higher than I can reach. The brick pathway blends into concrete steps and a wood canopy, beneath which are several stone benches for sitting and admiring the beauty of the garden.

3   As I rest for a moment, I look west toward a marble fountain and see the water arch up, break into glistening drops, and splash down into a pool of lily pads, many of their bright yellow blossoms floating around the pool's edges. I single out individual droplets flashing in the sunlight and follow them on their downward journey. My mind drifts, pleasantly mesmerized.

4   Getting up, I stroll toward the fountain, the heart of the garden, passing from the cool shade of the canopy into the relaxing warmth of the sun. The roses, mostly red and yellow, are waist-high along this section of the brick walk and overhang the path leading to the water. All of the beds are newly mulched in brownish-orange cedar chips, giving a pleasant scent to the air and reminding me of an old cedar chest in the room I always slept in when the family visited Gran on the farm. Bordering the cement circle that surrounds the fountain is a planting of orange and yellow marigolds perhaps 45 centimetres wide and only ankle-high. A butterfly with blue-black wings hovers 10 centimetres above them.

5   Here at the centre of the rose garden, I sit leaning with my back toward the fountain, lulled by the gentle sound of falling water, feeling an occasional mist of spray on my neck, just enough to keep me from falling asleep. With hands clasped around one knee, I follow the brick walkway due west with my eyes 20 metres across a field of spring-green grass to the maple and oak trees that mark the park's boundary. Several squirrels are overturning leaves and digging in the grass for their lunch, no doubt acorns they buried last fall. The animals in this garden are in no more hurry than I am; they know they are safe here in their garden home.

6   However, as much as I would like to stay in my place of ease, I have a dinner shift to work. I drag my wrist upward to see the time: 3:15; my break is over. As I retrace my path toward my car, I find myself once again refreshed by the rose garden, one of the few places I can come to be by myself and collect my thoughts. Waiting tables in a high-volume restaurant, playing in my band, and taking a full course load in college has filled my life to overflowing. I prize the moments I can snatch out of my busy schedule to simply slow down and be.

—*Michael Wolfe*

THINKING ABOUT THE STUDENT MODEL

1. Evaluate the introduction. Comment on the hook, support sentences, and thesis.

2. What is the dominant impression in this essay?

3. How is this essay developed spatially? Trace the movement in this piece.

4. Identify three of the most significant transition words and say how they link the key ideas in the essay. That is, what is the dominant element? (e.g., space, time, examples, comparison)

5. Which of the five senses does the writer appeal to in this essay? Identify the specific words that make these senses vivid.

6. Describe how the elements of description discussed so far would help in your professional writing in your field of study.

Learning from a Professional Model: A Descriptive Excerpt

This next description is an excerpt from Pilgrim at Tinker Creek, *a book by Annie Dillard. The author is well known for her detailed descriptions of nature and her musings on how she and other human beings fit into the natural world. As you read, pay special attention to the images Dillard evokes through simile and her use of action to focus readers on the frog's fate.*

Heaven and Earth in Jest

BY ANNIE DILLARD

1 A couple of summers ago I was walking along the edge of the island to see what I could see in the water, and mainly to scare frogs. Frogs have an inelegant way of taking off from invisible positions on the bank just ahead of your feet, in dire panic, emitting a froggy "Yike!" and splashing into the water. Incredibly, this amused me, and, incredibly, it amuses me still. As I walked along the grassy edge of the island, I got better and better at seeing frogs both in and out of the water. I learned to recognize, slowing down, the difference in texture of the light reflected from mudbank, water, grass, or frog. Frogs were flying all around me. At the end of the island, I noticed a small green frog. He was exactly half in and 2 half out of the water, looking like a schematic diagram of an amphibian, and he didn't jump.

3 He didn't jump; I crept closer. At last, I knelt on the island's winterkilled grass, lost, dumbstruck, staring at the frog in the creek just a metre away. He was a very small frog with wide, dull eyes. And just as I looked at him, he slowly crumpled and began to sag. The spirit vanished from his eyes as if snuffed. His skin emptied and drooped; his very skull seemed to collapse and settle like a kicked tent. He was shrinking before my eyes like a deflating football. I watched the taut, glistening skin on his shoulders ruck, and rumple, and fall. Soon, part of his skin, formless as a pricked balloon, lay in floating folds like bright scum on top of the water: it was a monstrous and terrifying thing. I gaped bewildered, appalled. An oval shadow hung in the water behind the drained frog; then the shadow glided away. The frog skin bag started to sink.

I had read about the giant water bug, but never seen one. "Giant water bug" is really the name of the creature, which is an enormous, heavy-bodied brown bug. It eats insects, tadpoles, fish, and frogs. Its grasping forelegs are mighty and hooked inward. It seizes a victim with these legs, hugs it tight, and paralyzes it with enzymes injected during a vicious bite. That one bite is the only bite it ever takes. Through the puncture shoot the poisons that dissolve the victim's muscles and bones and organs—all but the skin—and through it the giant water bug sucks out the victim's body, reduced to a juice. This event is quite common in warm fresh water. The frog I saw was being sucked by a giant water bug. I had been kneeling on the island grass; when the unrecognizable flap of frog skin settled on the creek bottom, swaying, I stood up and brushed the knees of my pants. I couldn't catch my breath.

dire
dreadful and urgent

schematic diagram
a drawing that details the elements of a system

ruck
to crease or become creased

enzymes
proteins produced by living things

THINKING ABOUT THE MODEL

1. Identify the thesis statement. What is the hook in the first paragraph?

2. What is a simile? Identify examples in this essay (there are several). How does this literary form contribute to the writing?

3. What is the dominant impression in this description? In which sentence is it most clearly stated?

4. Comment on the development of body paragraphs. How does Dillard draw readers into this small spectacle in nature? Why might a reader come to care about the frog's fate?

5. Why do you suppose Dillard uses short sentences like the following: "He didn't jump; I crept closer" (paragraph 2) and "I couldn't catch my breath" (paragraph 3)?

6. Identify an object or situation that you might have to write about descriptively in your field of study.

LO23.2 # Writing a Descriptive Essay

Audience and Purpose

As you draft your essay, knowing who your audience is will help you determine which words or concepts you may need to explain further. In description, your purpose is to inform readers, and to help them see the person, place, or object you're describing as clearly as possible.

If you are choosing a place, here are several suggestions for developing ideas:

1. Choose a limited space within a larger area. Indoors, don't try to describe your whole house: pick one room, or consider an airport terminal, a gym, a daycare centre, a grocery store, a hospital room, or a veterinary clinic. Outdoors, the same applies; for example, choose one section of Vancouver, not the entire city, or consider a stadium, a historic site, an outdoor concert, playground, beach, or cemetery.

2. Go to the place, sit quietly, and take notes. Use all of your senses, and list as many impressions as possible. Be alert to a **dominant impression**: is the place noticeably busy or peaceful, happy or sad, competitive or cooperative? Remember that people—and how they behave—are often part of descriptions.

3. Note the size of the place and the distance of objects from one another.

4. If people are present, write down some of their **dialogue**, or what they say to each other.

5. Try to think of a comparison, maybe a **metaphor** or a **simile** ("the crowd was a multi-headed beast" or "the crowd in the stadium rose like a tsunami").

> **HINT**
>
> Choose a place you can physically visit rather than trying to describe a place from memory.

The Assignment

Write about a local public outdoor space: a park, a wildlife sanctuary, a zoo, or one of the places suggested in the above section, "Audience and Purpose." Before beginning your essay, spend some time in the place. For your dominant impression, focus on (1) the particular beauty and purpose of the place, using details that show why it is important to you or the larger community, or (2) how people treat the space: is it well maintained, strewn with litter, visited frequently, usually deserted, and so on? Write an essay of roughly 500 to 750 words that paints a verbal portrait of the place.

Alternative Assignments

Describing a place is only one way to use description. If you choose one of these alternative assignments, be sure to do the following:

- Create a dominant impression, and state it in your thesis statement.
- Use specific words and sensory details to develop your dominant impression.

- Conclude with a sentence that restates what you are describing, the dominant impression, and a final point about your subject.
- Connect sentences with time and space transitions.

Business in Context:

Place yourself inside the mind of a businessperson you admire. Write a description essay from that person's perspective as he or she is "performing." For example, imagine you are a CEO of a cable company. Position yourself at an Annual Meeting and describe your sensory impressions, thoughts, and feelings as you look out over your key investors and senior administrative staff. You run the most profitable cable network in Canada, even in difficult economic times. What overall feeling might you have today—pride, relief, joy, arrogance? How can you show this dominant impression through your description?

Culture in Context:

Describe an object that impresses you. The object could be small but beautiful, like an intricately carved bowl or figurine; or the object could be huge, a new building, for example, like the addition to the Art Gallery of Ontario. Decide on the feeling you want to project—say, the power of the suspended wing at the AGO—and then choose details that show the dominant impression of the building or object.

Education in Context:

Create a setting for a story (fairy tale, action/adventure, or science fiction, for example). Begin with a thesis statement that names the setting and makes clear the dominant impression. For example, "The woods that Little Red Riding Hood ran into soon became threatening, the knots in tree trunks like large mouths preparing for a dinner of lost little girl." You can create your own character and/or story setting or add to one you have read about or seen in a film.

   Note: You are not writing a story, just creating a setting in which a story is told.

Health Care in Context:

Position yourself as a nurse or paramedic listening to a patient in the hospital Emergency Room. Describe her symptoms. Be aware of the patient's facial expressions, body posture, and tone of voice. Use your essay to describe your dominant impression in detail to the doctor on duty.

Technology in Context:

You have just joined an innovative automobile company and have been asked to describe in detail your specifications for an eco-friendly car that will be fuel-efficient and longwearing. Consider what type of fuel you would propose, what materials the car would be composed of, the car's design, maximum speed, size, passenger and cargo capacity. What is the dominant impression intended for this car? Use details to show how this car will be popular to the public in terms of reliability, economy, design, and ecology, for example.

HINT

Feeling a strong connection to a place will help you focus your description through a dominant impression.

There are probably hundreds of places you could write about, so it might be hard to pick one. Try limiting your choices to places you know well, have been to recently, can go to again, and have strong feelings about. Perhaps you have a peaceful place where you walk, bike, or jog.

JOURNAL / BLOG ENTRY 23.2

Describe the overall feeling of your place in a word or two, and tell why you feel the way you do about it. This dominant impression might fall into any of the assignment categories outlined above.

FEEDBACK *Share your dominant impressions with classmates. What are your own dominant impressions of places others describe (a campus cafeteria, for example, or a dance marathon)?*

Organizing Descriptive Essays

After you have a list of details for your place and have decided on the dominant impression, cut any details that detract from your main point. For example, the descriptive paragraph about the Canadian National Exhibition on page 297 does not include details of people arguing or children crying. Arrange your details in a roughly spatial order. Michael Wolfe's "Back to the Garden" on pages 301–302 organizes details about moving into a garden by entering from the outside, his impressions from one side, and moving toward the centre. Be sure to write a thesis statement that names the place and states the dominant impression.

JOURNAL / BLOG ENTRY 23.3

First, write out your thesis statement, including the specific place name and its dominant impression. Next, explain how you will arrange your essay in spatial order and why this arrangement makes sense to you for this assignment.

Drafting Descriptive Essays

As you begin to draft your description, keep the following points in mind:

1. Describe the place you have chosen, but **do not tell a** story. Use action and dialogue in your essay only to develop your dominant impression.
2. Occasionally, tell your reader what you think and feel about your place.
3. Use many specific words and sensory details in your first draft. In your next draft, you can cut any that seem excessive.
4. Use enough space and time transitions to keep your reader on track.

When you have finished your first draft, write a paragraph of four or five sentences telling what you like most and then least about it. Be specific. For example, you might begin your first response this way: "I like the sight and sound details I have used" (name the details) and your second response like this: "I dislike that my dominant impression seems unclear."

Revising Descriptive Essays

As you begin revising the first draft of your description, use the following checklist as a guide. Then give the draft to your peer reviewer so that he or she can make further comments to help with your revision.

Note to Peer Reviewer: Be sure to reflect on each question in the checklist and provide a thoughtful comment that will help the writer make improvements.

HINT

For detailed suggestions for revising all drafts, turn back to Chapter 21.

PEER REVIEW CHECKLIST FOR REVISING DESCRIPTIVE ESSAYS

☐ Does this essay describe a place/object/person? Or does it accidentally slip into telling a story?

Reviewer Comment: _____

_____

☐ Has the writer used a strong thesis statement, naming the place/object/person and dominant impression?

Reviewer Comment: _____

_____

☐ Has the writer told the reader what he or she thinks and feels about this place/object/person?

Reviewer Comment: _____

_____

☐ Has the writer used plenty of specific words and sensory details? If not, what could he or she add?

Reviewer Comment: _____

_____

☐ Does the writer have a concluding sentence that renames the place/object/person and dominant impression and makes a final point?

Reviewer Comment: _____

_____

☐ Has the writer used sufficient time and space transitions and other connectors?

Reviewer Comment: _____

_____

Description is a necessary ingredient in almost any writing assignment. Whether you want to bring a persuasive essay to life (Chapter 31) or describe a person, place, or object in a narrative (Chapter 24), skill at description will come in handy. Description keeps writing both focused and interesting; it narrows your topic and appeals to your readers' interest through details.

In almost any profession, you will use description daily. People who work in sales or advertising use it to help customers imagine what it would be like to own the company's product. A history teacher makes ancient Greece or the First Nations people in southern Ontario before European settlement come alive for students through description. A headhunter describes positions to job seekers—and potential employees to employers. Seeking treatment, a patient describes his or her own symptoms, and the nurse or doctor also communicates the patient's medical condition through description.

Chapter Summary

1. Describing is the process of using details to build vivid images.
2. Descriptive writing relies on specific words and sensory details.
3. Words can be relatively general or relatively specific—the more specific the word, the clearer the image.
4. Writers often focus descriptions with a dominant impression.
5. A thesis statement in a descriptive essay should include the place/person/object and dominant impression.
6. Descriptions are often organized spatially.
7. Time and space transitions are needed in descriptive writing.
8. Including thoughts and emotions strengthens subjective descriptions.
9. Action is often part of description.
10. Writing is not complete until it has been revised and carefully edited.

Telling a Story (Narration)

24

Think of a movie or television show that you like and know well, one you could watch again and again.

Choose a scene or episode you particularly enjoyed and, in a paragraph, retell that story.

What Are We Trying to Achieve and Why?

The people in the photo sit with eyes turned forward and up, mesmerized, one person eating popcorn, as an audience watches a movie. Films, most TV programs, novels, and short stories are forms of **narrative**, or storytelling. People often tell stories to entertain others, though they also use stories to help present information, or warn or persuade others. Our focus in this chapter is to learn how to tell better stories and incorporate them into our writing.

LINKING TO PREVIOUS EXPERIENCE

What You Already Know about Telling Stories

We tell stories almost every day. Sometimes these tales are long and involved: recapping your two-week vacation to Newfoundland, you might cover the trip there, the places you stayed, your activities, and the great people you met along the way. At other times, we share brief stories to keep others in touch with our lives or to illustrate a larger point; we might tell the tale of a frustrating wait at the post office or tell a story about how the boss has been mistreating us. Sometimes we write stories in letters or emails. And consider how many of our phone conversations begin something like this: "Hi, _____, what are you doing?" (a request for a story) or "You'll never guess what happened . . ." (the promise of one).

JOURNAL / BLOG ENTRY 24.1

Summarize, in a few sentences each, three recent experiences. Who did you tell? What was your purpose in sharing these stories: to entertain, release frustration, give information, or persuade someone of something? Was it perhaps a mix of these? Was your audience unclear about any part of your story? If so, how did you make it clearer?

FEEDBACK   *Respond to a classmate's three stories. Which event would you like to know more about? Ask two or three specific, relevant questions about the event.*

L024.1 ## Developing Skills in Narrating

A good story always contains some form of conflict in order to create drama. Sometimes the conflict is person to person; sometimes it is person to society; sometimes it is person to object; sometimes it is person to fate. Aboriginal people, for example, often use stories in order to teach life lessons. Rather than giving advice directly, a story with a parallel to a real-life problem can make a person rethink and reflect on new ways of dealing with the conflict. For example, the mother of a teenager with a dating issue might choose to tell her daughter a story about a similar incident in her own life. If the lesson is implied rather than explicit, if the mother is not actually telling her daughter what to do, the daughter might be more likely to take her mother's advice. In essay writing as well, an anecdote well told can help emphasize a point, making it more concrete for the reader. The skill of making things concrete rather than abstract, like the use of specific detail, is critical in persuasive essay writing. An anecdote—a short story seldom more than a paragraph long—often makes a great introduction to an essay.

The following skills will help you create more interesting narratives:

1. Emphasizing conflict, suspense, and a climax
2. Finding significance or meaning
3. Telling and showing
4. Using effective dialogue
5. Using space and time transitions

Emphasizing Conflict, Suspense, and a Climax

In a non-writing sense, a conflict is most often seen as an argument between people. In a writing sense, however, the **conflict** is the problem in the narrative or the potential for events to go wrong; a narrative must have a conflict to interest most people. Conflict can be of three basic sorts:

- A person dealing with another person: for example, arguing with a friend
- A person dealing with herself or himself: for example, trying a new exercise plan—or diet
- A person coping with the world around him or her: for example, driving in a blizzard

While presenting the conflict in the story, careful writers also build **suspense**, a state of uncertainty that makes readers wonder what will happen next. You should try to keep your readers in suspense right up until the **climax** (the high point of action) of your story.

Let's look at these elements of conflict, suspense, and climax in the following narrative paragraph, written by student Andrew Lucht.

Close Call

In the summer of 1997, when I was 13, I came the closest I have ever been to death. It was a hot day in the backwoods of Mississippi. My cousin Tommy and I asked my Uncle Jim if he wanted to ride down to the creek on the four-wheelers. Uncle Jim looked doubtful, saying, "I don't know. You boys have a crazy streak. Your parents would kick my butt if anything happened to you." Tommy and I pleaded and joked Uncle Jim into it. "I'll drive reeaall slow. I promise." With Tommy sitting in front and me driving, we headed slowly through the woods and down to the creek, where we had a good time swimming and fishing. Next, we headed upstream where the creek widened into a fast-moving river, driving faster. We began jumping the low sandbars, and then my uncle pulled ahead. I said, "Let's get him," and gunned the engine. We topped the motor out coming off the sandbar, but as we hit the water, the front wheels sank into the river bottom. The four-wheeler nosedived, throwing Tommy through the air. My foot got caught, and the ATV flipped, landing on top of me, pinning

Andrew begins with the topic sentence. Does it make you want to read on?

Notice that the author moves right into the action.

How does the dialogue with Uncle Jim add suspense?

How do the sentences about the ATV landing on top of the author and him being pinned add to the suspense?

me to the bottom of the river. I was stuck underwater. I couldn't get my head up for air. I couldn't move, yell for help, breathe—nothing. I saw my shoe float by on the surface and felt my chest begin to ache. I began to thrash my arms in panic, thinking, "I'm going to die!" But then my uncle arrived and flipped the four-wheeler off, pulling me above the water. I took the biggest, most welcome breath of my life. Although the ATV was smashed, Tommy only had a few scratches, and I didn't have even a bruise. I hadn't thought much about God before then, but that day I felt as if someone was watching over me. I was and still am grateful for how that makes me feel.

The author concludes with the resolution and point of the story.

—*Andrew Lucht*

ACTIVITY 24.1 Conflict, Suspense, and Climax

After reading the narrative paragraph, "Close Call," write on the lines below what the main conflict is and how the writer builds suspense. Next, list the story's key moments in the "action outline" section; the first action is filled in as an example. Finally, tell where the climax occurs.

Main conflict: _____

How the writer builds suspense: _____

_____

_____

Action outline:

1. *asking uncle about riding the ATV* _____

2. _____

3. _____

4. _____

5. _____

6. _____

7. _____

8. _____

Climax: _____

Now that you have analyzed "Close Call," write an outline, as above, about a close call of your own. It doesn't have to be a brush with death; it could be the story of when you were almost late for an exam, a time you forgot an appointment, or even why you were late one night for dinner. The important aspects are conflict, suspense, and climax. Once you have your outline, use it to write a one-paragraph story.

Finding Significance or Meaning

Stories that stick with us usually have a point. They make us pause for a moment and think, "Yes, that makes sense." Or maybe, "I see how that could apply to me." Although the meaning or significance of a story may not be clear to us when we begin to write, if we are interested in telling the story and wonder why we remember it so vividly, we can usually identify why it matters to us.

A narrative's point might show how the story does one of the following:

1. Changes the writer's behaviour, thinking, or emotions
2. Shows something important about who the writer was or has become
3. Affects other people at the time or affects them now
4. Helps the writer learn something about another person or the larger world

In "Close Call," Andrew Lucht tells us the significance of his experience, that he appreciates feeling under God's protection. Andrew implies a change in his thinking and emotions, as in suggestion 1 above. However, there may be more than one possible point to a story, and different people often react differently to similar events.

ACTIVITY 24.2 WORKING TOGETHER: Finding Significance

With group members, discuss how you would have felt in Andrew's place in "Close Call." Having just been saved from drowning, what thoughts or feelings might *you* take from this experience? Review the four points listed above under "Finding Significance or Meaning," and write on the lines below three possible points the story could have explored from the writer's perspective. (Use complete sentences.) One possibility is written out as an example, and other thoughts are begun for you.

Possible Points for "Close Call":

1. **Changed behaviour:** *I learned from that horrible day not to drive any kind*

   of vehicle like a maniac.

   _____

2. **Who the writer was:** *I never realized*

   _____

   _____

3. **Affected other people:** *My Uncle Jim*

   _____

   _____

4. **Learned about another person:** *I learned that*

   _____

   _____

Telling and Showing

In telling stories, we try to bring them to life. The first rule of narrative is "show, don't tell." If we only *tell* and never *show* the reader the action, our story is likely to fall flat. Here are two sentences, one that tells and one that shows. Which do you prefer?

1. I looked back and was terrified.
2. I looked back and saw a gigantic black bull galloping toward me; and for an eternal moment, my legs jellied, unable to move me out of the way of the dark, advancing hulk.

Most people prefer sentence 2, as readers are attracted to a sentence that *shows* action, one that places them in the specific situation. When we *tell*, as in **sentence 1,** the reader must take our word for it; we tell the audience what to believe. When we *show*, however, we give readers enough details that they can decide how to respond. In **sentence 2**, readers can *see*, not just perceive in a broad sense, that the writer was very frightened. Showing is a powerful way to improve a story, though it often takes more words. Good writers mix telling and showing, choosing which moments to sum up and which to spend time with.

ACTIVITY 24.3 Telling and Showing

The following sentences tell a reader what to see in a story. Write a sentence that shows the same incident.

EXAMPLE:

Telling: I was stuck underwater.

Showing: *I couldn't move, yell for help, breathe—nothing.*

HINT

You can *show* with specific words, sensory details, a person's actions, and dialogue.

1. **Telling:** Surely, Carla was a happy graduate.

   Showing: _____

   _____

   _____

2. **Telling:** Driving in the winning run, Brian crossed home plate as his team showed their appreciation.

   Showing: _____

   _____

   _____

3. **Telling:** When Daniel threw a lit string of firecrackers onto the deck, his friends reacted quickly.

   Showing: _____

   _____

   _____

4. **Telling:** Katie had to be the messiest 10-month-old baby ever to eat a bowl of peas.

   Showing: _____

   _____

   _____

Using Effective Dialogue

English Review Note

Practise changing from direct to indirect speech. How does switching affect the word order, pronouns, and tenses?

Most stories use dialogue because readers are interested in hearing what characters have to say. Dialogue helps us get to know the writer and his or her characters. In your personal narrative, you can use three types of "speech":

- **Direct dialogue** uses quotation marks and reproduces what a person has said word for word.

- **Indirect dialogue** does not use quotation marks but reports or summarizes what someone has said.

- **Revealed thought** often uses quotation marks to show what a person is thinking in the midst of action.

In **example 1**, notice both direct and indirect dialogue:

INDIRECT DIALOGUE

1. **It was a hot summer day in the backwoods of Mississippi. My cousin Tommy and I asked my Uncle Jim if he wanted to ride down to the creek on the four-wheelers.**

DIRECT DIALOGUE

Uncle Jim looked doubtful, saying, "I don't know. You boys have a crazy streak. Your parents would kick my butt if anything happened to you."

In **example 2**, notice how the author reveals his thought:

REVEALED THOUGHT

2. **I began to thrash my arms in panic, thinking, "I'm going to die!"**

ACTIVITY 24.4 Using Effective Dialogue

Type or write a paragraph that imagines what the people in this picture might have said to each other during this happy moment at graduation. Call the father "Eric," the mother "Elizabeth," and the daughter "Janine." Try to include all three forms of speech: direct dialogue, indirect dialogue, and revealed thought.

Using Space and Time Transitions

As we learned in Chapter 20, linking sentences with connectors—such as repeated words, synonyms, and transitions—is essential if readers are to follow the flow of your ideas. Narratives especially benefit from **space** and **time transitions** like the following:

SPACE TRANSITIONS				
above	at	in	on	to
across	below	into	over	toward
around	by	near	there	under

TIME TRANSITIONS			
after	now	then	references to clock
first (second, etc.)	often	until	and calendar time:
next	once	when	1:00, last week, etc.

English Review Note

Review this chart to master transitions involving space and time.

ACTIVITY 24.5 Using Space and Time Transitions

Fill in the blanks with the space and time transitions from the preceding lists.

1. Listening _____ the door, Becky fell _____ the room when her sister opened the door.

2. _____ we reached the hospital, no one could find the emergency room.

3. _____, we headed upstream to the huge waterfall.

4. I was following them, so they cut _____ the field.

5. A crowd had gathered _____ the Red Cross van.

6. It was _____ morning and I was falling asleep.

7. My dad parked _____ to a police car.

8. My mom asked me to wait in the lobby _____ she could find the tickets.

Learning from a Student Model: A Narrative Essay

Read the following student model closely, noticing the elements of vivid storytelling that you practised in the skills section of this chapter. Focus on **conflict, suspense,** and **climax; significance; showing** and **telling; dialogue;** and **space and time transitions.**

We Are All Essentially Stardust

1   When I was volunteering in a Special Needs class during high school, I had an experience that humbled me more than any other in my life. I have always been a strong believer in the importance of education and thought that teaching could be a rewarding experience, so when I was a student at John McGregor Secondary School in Chatham, I volunteered in the Special Needs wing twice a week to help the students read. I volunteered with another student, Meghan Morris, who had her co-op placement in the Special Needs wing. As such, she helped the students more with personal living skills than with the academic portion and had a closer relationship with each student. She loved the students so much, and they loved her, that she had more than a couple of individual friendships with them outside the classroom. She would visit them at their homes, or take them on special outings on the weekends. Some students had been with Meghan to a little league baseball game, a county fair, and the movie *Superman 2*. The kids had strong and special affection for her because she liked spending so much time with them.

2   One day, as I was helping Michael, who had Down's syndrome, with understanding astronomy, I told him that many of the elements that the world and animals were made of came from exploding supernovae. He paused for a moment, furrowed his brow, and then a sudden understanding flashed over his face.

3   "So that's why some people are brighter than others!" he exclaimed.

4   Being concerned about his misconception, but wanting to sustain his self-esteem, I said, "No. Some people are born differently than others. It has nothing to do with if the star was bright or not."

5   But Michael was stubborn, and he pressed the point hard. I repeatedly tried to explain to him that intelligence had nothing to do with the stars. After about five minutes of this, I realized that it wasn't him who misunderstood; it was *me*. I had missed the point completely until he protested, "But Meghan shines brighter than all the stars!"

6   Confused, I asked him, "What do you mean, Michael?"

7   He replied, "Some stars aren't very bright and you forget they are there. Some others are pretty bright and always there and you know where they are."

8   "And how is Meghan the brightest?" I asked him.

9   "Because she loves me," he beamed.

10   It was only then that I understood exactly what he meant. He didn't use the word "bright" to mean intellect, but rather how he felt about people and how much they meant to him.

11   What else could I do but stare blankly at him for a moment in the realization that Michael, a supposed mentally deficient teen, had profound insight and a better understanding of what it means to be human than I did. I don't remember the gamut of emotions I felt at that moment, but I do remember the feeling of humbleness. If I were to describe it, I would have to equate it with looking to the night sky, the vastness of the cosmos, knowing full well that it is larger than anyone could ever imagine, and yet knowing that I am in it, insignificant and irrelevant. This made me very truly humble.

12   Later that semester, I was to experience what it would be like if the sun disappeared. Meghan was on a trip to Windsor from Chatham with some friends on a Saturday afternoon. She slept in the back seat of the car with no seat belt on. At the Manning Road overpass, her car swerved to miss another car and it slammed head-on into a pillar. She died instantly.

13   On Monday, the entire school was in mourning. Counsellors were brought in to help the students cope with their loss. But in the Special Needs wing, I saw one of the most terrifying sights ever. Sadness emerged from an unspeakably dark and horrible place, as a couple of the autistic students sat alone, groaning and moaning, rocking back and forth. Others, who were normally outgoing, shut themselves off from the universe, with empty stares that suggested an adamant refusal to suffer their own grief. But the reactions of some, like Michael, were especially unearthly. I have never seen human emotion as raw or as strong from any other human being in my life. Endless tears were streaming and soaking his cheeks. His body trembled, and I heard incomprehensible mumblings in between his choking and sputtering wails. I will never forget those ear-splitting wails. It was like a feral, demonic beast piercing through my eardrums to reach the centre of my brain, and it slowly consumed my body as it ripped and mauled its way down my spine. I don't know where this creature of black sorrow crawled from, but I'm sure I never want to know.

14   One moment in seeing these students' universe tearing apart was more than enough for me to break down. This was different than being in mourning for a

loved one. At best, I was an acquaintance of Meghan and knew the students only slightly more. However, I was saddened more by *their loss of her* than I was for anyone else. Their sun had gone out; the brightest star that Michael and some of the others had was gone. It seemed that they were without a light in their lives, alone in a completely black void.

15   I didn't think that I, or any other "normal" person, could ever have emotions as pure and cutting as these students. It is my belief that in our capacity to think as "normal" human beings, sometimes we are separated from what truly makes us human: our emotions. These adolescents helped me realize that they see the world in a vastly different way.

16   As an end note, our yearbook put a small memorial to Meghan in its pages that was, in part, made by the Special Needs students. And above her picture, her students had placed one bright star.

—Bredt Wells

HINT

For an action outline, see Activity 24.1. For more on telling and showing, see Activity 24.3.

THINKING ABOUT THE STUDENT MODEL

1. What two important points do we learn from the thesis statement?

   _____

   _____

2. Create an action outline that lists eight major actions of the characters in this story.

   1. _____

   2. _____

   3. _____

   4. _____

   5. _____

   6. _____

   7. _____

   8. _____

3. List one example of telling and one of showing.

   _____

   _____

4. How does the dialogue add to the story?

   _____

   _____

5. List at least three time transitions and three space transitions.

   _____

   _____

Learning from a Professional Model:
A Narrative Essay

Elegy in Stone

VIMY RIDGE, APRIL 1992
STEVEN HEIGHTON

1   The park's entrance—a border crossing, really—was modest enough: a small sign you could easily miss if you were driving past. But we were on foot. And though it turned out to be a much longer walk than we'd expected, it was a good place to walk, the fields along the road billowing with mustard, wheat, and poppies, the oaks and maples fragrant with new growth. We could be in Canada, I thought— then remembered that, for official purposes, we were.

2   The wind as we neared the ridge grew chilly, the sky grey.

3   Before long the road passed through a forest of mature growth and entered an old plantation of white pines, thick and towering, a spacious colonnade receding in the gloom. Fences appeared along the road, then signs warning us not to walk among the trees, where sheep foraged above grassed-in trenches, shell holes, unexploded mines. In the blue-green, stained-glass light of the forest, the near-silence was eerie and solemn.

4   Finally we heard voices, saw a file of parked cars ahead through the trees, and came out at the main exhibit site of the park, some distance below the monument that crowns Vimy Ridge. Here, in 1917, from a line of trenches now preserved in concrete and filled daily with French tourists, the Canadian troops had launched their attack. Preserved likewise is the first obstacle they had met: the front-line German trench, barely a grenade's throw away. This whites-of-their-eyes proximity surprised us and made stories of verbal fraternization between the lines—of back and forth banter in broken English and German—all the more plausible, and poignant.

5   At the park's main exhibit site we went into a small, undistinguished brick building to see about a tour of the tunnel system under the trenches. The young guides, in Parks Canada uniforms, explained that we'd just missed the tour and unfortunately would have to wait for the next. But as we turned and went outside to confer, they must have noticed the small Canadian flag sewn onto my back-pack, because one of them came out after us and beckoned us toward the tunnels. "You should have told us you're Canadian," he said with a soft Manitoba-French accent. "We don't get all that many."

6   The low-ceilinged, labyrinthine "subways"—where men ate and slept before the attack and couriers ran with their messages and sappers set charges under the German lines—have been carefully restored, but more or less unembellished. The impression, as above in the trenches, was sobering. I was relieved that this sad, clammy underworld had not been brightened up into some gaudy monument to Our Glorious Past; I was relieved that it still looked, and felt, like a tomb.

7   It was good to get back up into the daylight.

8   We followed the road up the last part of the ridge to the monument, wind blowing over the bare fields in a steady barrage. Seventy-five years before, the

CHAPTER 24 Telling a Story (Narration)   **319**

Canadians had advanced at dawn through driving sleet and snow, and now, nearing the exposed crown of the ridge, we could see how weather of that intensity must be quite common. The monument stands atop Hill 145, the Canadians' final objective and the highest point for miles around—but on the morning of the attack it must have been invisible through the snow and the timed barrage behind which the men were advancing.

9   Before the hilltop and the monument came in sight I'd felt uneasy, recalling the many monuments I had seen that stylized or made-over the true face of war so as to safeguard an ideology, to comply with aesthetic conventions, or to make life easier for the recruiters of future wars. But as we neared the monument—two enormous white limestone pillars that meet at the base to form a kind of elongated U—I was impressed. Here was something magnificent in its simplicity, its solemnity, its understatement. And brilliant in its implication, because the pillars did not quite form a triumphant V, as you might expect, but a shape uncannily resembling the sights mounted on machine guns of the First World War—the kind that claimed tens of thousands of Canadian lives in the war and several thousand on the morning of the attack.

10   We drew closer. Our feeling that this monolith was more a cenotaph, a vast elegy in stone instead of petrified hot air, grew stronger. And with it a feeling of pride. But a kind of pride very different, I think, from the tribal, intolerant swagger so many monuments have been built to inspire. A shy pride in our country's awkwardness at blowing its own horn—because sooner or later every country that does blow its own horn starts looking for somebody else to outblow. A pride in our reluctance—our seeming inability—to canonize brave, scared, betrayed adolescents as bearded heroes of mythic dimension, larger than life. Unreal.

11   And the monument is a cenotaph: we find its base inscribed with the names of the 11,285 Canadians whose final resting place is unknown. Blown to pieces. Lost in the mud, or buried anonymously in the graveyards below the ridge. The parade of names marches on and on, a kind of elegy whose heartbreaking syllables are English- and French-Canadian, Ojibway, Ukrainian, Dutch, German, Italian, Japanese . . . Many are the names of our own distant relations.

12   The figures carved on and around the monument, though dated in style, are not blowing trumpets or beating breasts or drums. They seem instead to grieve. We round the monument and the Douai Plain fans out below us. Another figure, much larger, cloaked, stands apart at the edge of the monument overlooking the plain. Behind her a sparsely worded inscription tells of the ridge's fall. The figure is meant to be an embodiment of Canada, "mourning her lost sons . . ."

13   In the vast graveyards below the ridge, many headstones bear inscriptions echoing that line. IN MEMORY OF OUR DEAR AND ONLY CHILD, reads one. We recite the words aloud, but this time the feeling they inspire has little to do with pride. The huge limestone gunsight looms above us on the ridge as we enter yet another aisle, and read, yet again:

A SOLDIER OF THE GREAT WAR

A Canadian Regiment

Known Unto God

Source: Abridged version of "Elegy in Stone" from The Admen Move on Lhasa. *Copyright © Steve Heighton. Reproduced with permission from the author and House of Anansi Press.*

1. How does the introduction orient readers and draw them into the narrative?

2. Look at paragraph two again. What effect does this one-sentence paragraph have on the reader? What other narrative techniques does Heighton use?

3. How does Heighton incorporate suspense into the narrative? Where is the climax of the narrative?

4. What is the point, or significance, of this narrative to you? What do you think it meant to Heighton?

5. List three examples where Heighton effectively shows, or illustrates, the emotions evoked by the monument and the site itself.

6. Besides essays, Steven Heighton writes poetry, short stories, novels, and reviews. Check out the author's website at http://www.stevenheighton.com/ and read his review of *The Colour of Lightning* by Paulette Jiles. How does Heighton's ability to narrate the plot of another writer's novel work in his book review?

Writing a Narrative Essay

L024.2

Audience and Purpose

Choose an audience who would be interested in reading your narrative. Remember that you may have to explain a situation more thoroughly or define particular words depending on who reads your work. For example, the author of "Close Call" (page 311) assumed his reader would know what *ATV* stands for, so he did not spell out *all-terrain vehicle*.

In a narrative, your purpose may be to inform, persuade, or entertain your reader. Regardless, be sure to make the significance of your narrative clear.

The Assignment

Write an essay of roughly 500 to 750 words (2 to 3 pages) that shows and tells a story about a brief but memorable moment in your life. It could be a special experience in a group: a sports team, band, club, worship service, Girl Guide/Boy Scout troop, or fraternal organization (such as Kiwanis or Rotary), Cadets, or Parent–Teacher Association. Or it could be a moment of special celebration, such as a birthday, first communion, wedding, family reunion, or Mother's Day. Begin with a thesis statement that tells your reader what the narrative is about, move straight into the action, build toward a climax, and finish with a sentence that makes some point that shows the significance or meaning of your narrative.

Alternative Assignments

Here are several additional narrative writing options that might interest you. For any of these assignments, be sure to do the following:

- Create a narrative that has conflict and suspense.

- Choose a story with clear significance.

- Build a narrative that shows as well as tells.
- Use effective dialogue.

Business in Context:

In the business world, every product has a "story." Watching commercials, you'll notice that some tales are taller than others. For example, the story that an iPod is easy to use and transport is both compelling and true; but does ordering pizza make your family happier by freeing up food-preparation time? Consider a product that you can build a story around, concluding by stating its clear significance. Perhaps even write a commercial as a story, including dialogue, suspense, conflict, and a climax.

Culture in Context:

Recall a surprising moment when you were travelling to a new place and something unexpected happened. Write a narrative that places readers into the situation, and has an easily perceived significance. Be sure to describe (briefly) where you are and use dialogue to help the reader "be there" for the experience.

Education in Context:

Write a story for a child. Your story can be real (non-fiction) or imagined (fiction). Decide on an age group (3–5, 6–9, 10–12), and write with those readers in mind. For example, let's say you're writing a story about getting your ears pierced for an 8-year-old girl who wants to wear earrings: you would be careful to use words and dialogue that a young reader would understand (and not be frightened by). You might assume that your reader is concerned about how painful ear piercing is (with her own ears in mind) and address this detail in a reassuring or cautionary way. If you write a fictional story, you could use it to explain something or just to entertain. For example, you could tell how a playground bully was finally stopped when a child stood up to him. Or you could write a fantasy about good fairies that guide lost pets back home. Be sure to begin with a thesis statement that tells what the story is about and conclude with a sentence that reveals the story's point.

Health Care in Context:

Tell the story of someone you know who has a preventable disease. Be sure to describe the situation in detail including the dramatic effects of this disease and the difficulties encountered. Dialogue will place your readers into a situation where the victim considers what s/he could have done to prevent the disease. This narrative could lead to the conclusion that taking care of one's teeth, or limiting sugar consumption, or quitting smoking would have prevented the disease.

Science in Context:

Tell a story about the natural world. To hear a range of interesting stories (and get inspiration for your own), watch David Suzuki's *The Nature of Things* (http://www.cbc.ca/documentaries/natureofthings/video.html), or David Attenborough's *Planet Earth* (http://watchdocumentary.org/all_documentaries/). Consider telling a story about a moment when you felt connected to the natural world or separated from it.

Technology in Context:

Consider an incident in your life where an "aha" experience occurred as you began to learn about a particular mechanical or electronic device. Description will be important but not central to showing your readers the situation. It is important that your readers feel that they are "there." Use dialogue and prepare your essay as a narrative that unfolds with suspense and conflict—and a climax. What is the significance of this incident? Answer this question in the conclusion.

Discovering Ideas: Prewriting for Narration

Finding a good story topic is not always easy, even though (or maybe because) we have lived through hundreds of memorable moments. To help focus your search, you should care about your topic, remember it well, and be able to fit it into an essay. Often, strong stories span only a few minutes' time.

After you have chosen a story to tell, you can use several prewriting methods, such as clustering and listing. For narratives, journalists' questions can be especially useful, as in the following example for the student model "We Are All Essentially Stardust" (pages 316–318):

Who: Bredt, his student Michael, and the co-op student Meghan

What: Meghan was killed in a car accident and the Special Needs students were greatly disturbed

When: Monday following the car accident

Where: the Chatham high school

Why: Meghan died

How: Special needs students were inconsolable, universe tearing apart

What was the result: Special Needs students deeply mourned Meghan, and put a memorial star in the yearbook above her picture

> **HINT**
>
> See the online section for Chapter 2 for more on prewriting methods, including journalists' questions.

As you pre-write, focusing on these points will help give you good material for your narrative:

- **Setting** (where and when): Give your reader enough details to see the story happening.
- **Characters** (people): Give enough details about the characters so that the reader can place them in the story.
- **Dialogue:** Use dialogue unless there is a good reason not to.
- **Action:** Show yourself and others doing something.
- **Thoughts and feelings:** Show and/or tell some of both.
- **Significance:** A story with a point is both memorable and meaningful. Reward your reader at the end.

Organizing Narrative Essays

Narrative essays are most often organized in chronological (time) order. After you have gathered your ideas and sequenced them in chronological order, write a thesis statement that tells what the narrative will be about. Here you can hint at the conflict without giving away the climax, just as Bredt Wells does with his thesis statement for "We Are All Essentially Stardust" on pages 316–318.

Next, move right into the action of your narrative. You might want to prepare an action outline (as in Activity 24.1 on page 310) that lists the major actions of your event as they occur. Limit your main actions to around six to eight per essay, and resist giving several sentences of background explanation.

Also, be sure to limit the time your narrative covers and keep the action in only one or two scenes. Don't skip from place to place.

Drafting Narrative Essays

As you move into drafting, keep the following points in mind:

1. To make the narrative seem more immediate, close your eyes in a quiet place, and try to visualize what happened. Think of specific things and people, sensory details, actions, and dialogue. Try to see the narrative as a movie.

2. Use your "creative memory" to fill in gaps in your narrative. Use details that could have been part of the scene, and dialogue that could have been spoken.

3. Summarize the action to move readers quickly through some parts of your narrative.

4. Describe a scene in detail when you want the reader to slow down and pay attention, especially near the climax.

> ### JOURNAL / BLOG ENTRY 24.2
>
> After finishing your first rough draft, reread it and write about why your narrative is interesting. Where do you build suspense? Does the action reach a climax near the end? Do you wrap up the narrative soon after the climax? If you're using a blog, post the draft of your narrative for feedback.
>
> FEEDBACK   *Read one or two of your classmates' rough drafts, and offer feedback on each narrative's use of suspense and its climax. To you, what seems like each narrative's meaning or significance?*

HINT

For detailed suggestions for revising all drafts, turn to Chapter 21.

Revising Narrative Essays

As you begin revising the first draft of your narrative, both you and your peer reviewer may use the following checklist as a guide:

PEER REVIEW CHECKLIST FOR REVISING NARRATIVE ESSAYS

☐ Does the thesis statement tell what the narrative is about, hinting at the conflict or main point?

Reviewer Comment: ______________________________

____

____

____

____

☐ Has the writer included conflict, suspense, and action that lead to a climax and make a point?

Reviewer Comment: ______________________________

____

____

____

____

☐ Has the writer included details of the setting and people and given the characters some dialogue?

Reviewer Comment: ______________________________

____

____

____

____

☐ As the narrative unfolds, does it show and/or tell the reader what the characters think and feel?

Reviewer Comment: ______________________________

____

____

____

____

☐ Has the writer used sufficient time and space transitions and other connectors?

Reviewer Comment: ______________________________

____

____

____

____

☐ Does the concluding sentence reflect on the event and its meaning?

Reviewer Comment: ______________________________

____

____

____

____

A good story is useful in all types of college and workplace writing. Storytelling is a great way to ground your readers in specific situations and gain their interest and trust. Narratives are commonly used in the introductions of papers or speeches. And in the business world, every product has a "story."

Chapter Summary

1. Narrative essays involve conflict and suspense. They are arranged chronologically, lead to a climax, and have a point.
2. The setting (where and when) is the backdrop for the action of a narrative.
3. Narratives reveal a character's thoughts and feelings and usually use dialogue.
4. Well-organized narrative essays require thesis statements and concluding sentences.
5. Time and space transitions and other connectors are essential in storytelling.
6. Both showing and telling are used to develop narratives.
7. Specific words and sensory details are important for scene building.

Writing with Examples (Illustration)

25

What are some examples of outdoor activities or sports that you enjoy? If you prefer indoor activities, list examples of these instead. Make the list as long as possible.

What Are We Trying to Achieve and Why?

If a friend told you that he or she likes exciting water sports, ones with an edge of danger, what image comes to mind? The picture on page 327 shows us one possibility, whitewater rafting, but there are many other **examples** of "exciting water sports"—waterskiing, surfing, windsurfing, kite surfing, scuba diving, and cliff diving. Whenever you use a specific example to show what you mean, you are **illustrating**, and therefore strengthening, your point. This chapter focuses on using examples effectively in your writing.

As you practise illustrating, you will continue to describe (building images with specific words and sensory details) and narrate (making a point with brief stories). However, in this essay assignment, instead of focusing on *one* place or story, you will choose *several* examples to show what you mean. Also, you will begin each example with a **subtopic sentence** (when writing only one paragraph) or a **topic sentence** (when writing an essay).

HINT

For more on describing, see Chapter 23. For more on narrating, see Chapter 24.

LINKING TO PREVIOUS EXPERIENCE

What You Already Know about Using Examples

Using examples is the most common way we have of telling others what we mean. While we sometimes resort to general statements, more often we need to be specific. When you flop down on the couch at home, exhausted, and say, "I'm beat," you may feel like you've said it all. But if you are looking for sympathy, you will probably add specific examples, like "Shania never showed, so I had to work two stations during the lunch rush!" You have been giving people specific examples all your life. In this chapter, you will get even better at it.

JOURNAL / BLOG ENTRY 25.1

List three recent situations when you have used examples to explain, defend a position, and/or entertain. You may have given examples to explain what you like about a friend, to defend a decision, or to entertain with tales of a quirky co-worker. In each case, how many details did you offer? Did you achieve your purpose? In several sentences, write out the examples and details you used.

FEEDBACK   *Share your examples. Compliment a group member on an example or detail you find particularly interesting in his or her work; then give at least two reasons why you like it.*

LO25.1   Developing Skills in Using Examples

Specific examples are important, as they keep your essay from being vague and abstract. You can make your points much more easily if people can relate to what you are writing about, and specific examples help you do that. Instead of saying,

"University education is more expensive," you might use Statistics Canada data to say, "On average, Canadian university tuition rose from $4747 in 2008 to $5581 in 2012, an increase of 17% in just four years." The second sentence obviously makes a more compelling argument; such illustrations also prove that you know what you are talking about. By using illustrations, you can say more in one paragraph than you could with an entire vague essay.

The following skills will help you use examples more effectively:

1. Introducing examples with topic or subtopic sentences
2. Arranging examples by order of importance
3. Linking topic and subtopic sentences with transitions and other connectors
4. Developing examples with specific words, details, and explanations

Introducing Examples with Subtopic Sentences

A **subtopic sentence** tells about each major example in a paragraph, just as the topic sentence tells about the whole paragraph. Therefore, the subtopic sentence should name its example and make a statement about it. In addition, since subtopic sentences are *within* a paragraph, they should contain a transitional word or other connector.

You can see how subtopic sentences work in the illustration below. The examples are underlined; the statements being made about the examples are circled; and the transitional words are shaded.

Topic sentence: As a child in my bedroom at night, I was often terrified.

Subtopic sentences (introducing each main example):

1. One fear was of the Dust Ball Monster, who I knew lived under my bed.
2. Another creature who frightened me was the Shoe Bug.
3. However, what scared me most of all was the Green Gremlin, who lived in the oak tree by my window.

After you have decided on your main examples and written them out in subtopic sentences, you then continue your paragraph by telling more about each example. For instance, the writer could add these sentences to subtopic **sentence 1** from above:

One fear was of the Dust Ball Monster, who I knew lived under my bed. This monster was covered with gray scales and dust balls and had long, skinny arms with yellow claws. It would grab me and pull me under the bed if I wasn't careful, so I always jumped out of bed and ran for the door.

ACTIVITY 25.1 Recognizing Subtopic Sentences

In the illustration paragraph below, locate the three subtopic sentences. First underline each of the main examples, circle the statement about each example, and highlight the transitional words. Refer to the example above for help in recognizing the pattern.

The Most Essential Digital Tools

Technology—we can't live without it. But all the technology in the world won't work for me if I can't push a button. In order to counteract the symptoms of carpal tunnel syndrome,

I have learned to do three things. First of all, when that tingling begins at the end of my fingers as I type on the keyboard, I put on my hand splints. The splints encourage nerve conduction through my wrists to my fingers. Another helpful remedy is to do exercises. To stretch my fingers, I place the fingertips against the palm of my other hand and gently rotate the palm upward against my fingertips. Finally, if the tingling persists, I stop typing. Reading a book, for example, gives my fingers a rest, and the tingling usually stops. Ultimately, it's important to listen to the body since without it, all the technology in the world will not get a job done.

Arranging Examples by Order of Importance

Examples can be arranged in several ways, but one effective method is **order of importance.** In this arrangement, writers decide which of their examples are more important to them and/or their audience, and then organize from lesser to greater importance, saving the most important or dramatic example for last. People tend to pay the most attention to the last point they read.

ACTIVITY 25.2 Arranging Examples by Importance

The following sets of examples are out of order. Rearrange them from least (1) to most (4) important by numbering them in the spaces provided.

1. **Topic sentence:** My blind dating experiences have been some of the worst in my life.

   __ Even worse than dinner with Sheila was lunch with Jenny, the clone of my mother!

   __ One recent bad date was with Sheila, a vegetarian I cooked steak for.

   __ The worst of them all was Medusa, the snake woman.

   __ Another lapse in judgment was agreeing to meet Roxanne, my brother's boss, who has breath that smells like roadkill.

2. **Topic sentence:** I still can't believe that I survived my dangerous childhood.

   __ My nearest brush with death, however, came when sledding in Fredericton, New Brunswick.

   __ Once again I almost died when I tried to parachute from our roof with a blanket.

   __ Worse than my near-electrocution was the time I broke my arm on roller blades.

   __ My first dangerous experience was putting mom's car keys into a wall outlet.

3. **Topic sentence:** My dog, Perry, is a disaster around the house.

   __ In addition to being hyperactive, Perry damages everything in sight.

   __ One bad habit is his hyperactivity.

   __ But the most obnoxious fact of all is that Perry is still not housebroken.

   __ Further, this animal drives us all crazy with his continuous barking.

Linking Subtopic Sentences with Transitions and Other Connectors

HINT

For more on connectors, see Chapter 20.

Linking sentences within and between paragraphs helps readers follow our ideas more easily. We can make these connections in several ways: using transitions, repetition, synonyms, and pronouns.

Notice the shaded transitions in the following examples. Also, the writer has used a synonym for *monster*—the word *creature*—in the second subtopic. We see the order-of-importance arrangement with the word *most* in subtopic 3.

1. **One fear was of the Dust Ball Monster, who I knew lived under my bed.**

2. **Another creature who frightened me was the Shoe Bug.**

3. **However, what scared me most of all was the Green Gremlin, who lived in the oak tree by my window.**

As you write your own subtopic and concluding sentences, be sure to use solid connectors like the ones in the following lists:

TRANSITIONS FOR ADDING MATERIAL			
again	besides	furthermore	moreover
also	best in	addition	next
and	first	last	one
as well as	further	likewise	worst

TRANSITIONS FOR GIVING EXAMPLES AND EMPHASIS			
above all	especially	in particular	one reason
after all	for example	in truth	surely
another	for instance	most important	that is
certainly	in fact	of course	to illustrate

ACTIVITY 25.3 Linking Sentences

Rewrite each subtopic sentence in the examples below so the sentence clearly connects with the one that precedes it. Use any of the transitional words in the preceding lists and/or any other connectors that work (repeated words, synonyms, or pronouns.) Circle the one you used. Remember to use connectors that indicate an order of increasing importance. The first subtopic sentence is rewritten as an example.

1. **Topic sentence:** Air travel is, for the most part, safe and convenient, but there are several disadvantages to flying.

   Subtopic sentence 1: Weather delays can be a problem.

   EXAMPLE:

   Rewritten with connector: *The first disadvantage is weather delays.*

   Subtopic sentence 2: It can take a long time just to get on the plane.

   Rewritten with connector: _____

   _____

Subtopic sentence 3: A person is trapped in a small space for hours.

Rewritten with connector: _____

_____

2. **Topic sentence:** I love my cat, BW, but he gets into a lot of mischief.

   Subtopic sentence 1: BW likes to raid the garbage.

   Rewritten with connector: _____

   _____

   Subtopic sentence 2: He attacks people for no reason.

   Rewritten with connector: _____

   _____

   Subtopic sentence 3: BW wakes me at 5:00 every morning!

   Rewritten with connector: _____

   _____

Now take the list of favourite sports that you made at the beginning of the chapter and pick the three most different ones. Write a topic sentence that will link them all together and then a subtopic sentence for each sport. Construct a paragraph as you have just done in this exercise, linking your subtopic sentences together using connectors. Keep revising until you have a solid paragraph.

ACTIVITY 25.4 Paragraph Organization

When you are researching, you may find all sorts of fascinating facts about your topic, but you have to remember to keep your work focused. Each paragraph needs to focus on one topic that leads from topic sentence to conclusion. Sometimes you have to omit illustrations, even though you find them fascinating, simply because they don't fit with the rest of the material. Try making one cohesive paragraph from these thirteen sentences about feral cats, deleting the sentences that don't fit and putting the rest in proper paragraph order.

1. A feral cat colony — called a "clowder" — forms when wild cats live and eat in the same area.

2. Erin Hunter is a pseudonym for authors Kate Cary, Cherith Baldry, Gillian Philip, and Tui Sutherland, and editor Victoria Holmes.

3. Many believe that cats are only happy when they can live outdoors, at least part of the time, despite all the dangers, like cars and fishers.

4. My sister's cat is called "Cuddly" even though she's an overweight bully.

5. Responsible pet owners should spay or neuter their cats, keep them indoors, and be prepared to care for them all their lives.

6. Many people confuse outdoor cats and abandoned cats with feral cats.

7. The lifespan of an outdoor cat is about 2 to 5 years, while indoor cats live about 15 years.

8. Cats are one of the most popular pets in North America and some people would do anything for their furry friends.

9. Though they certainly do keep down the rodents, outdoor cats also wreak havoc on songbird populations and are generally harmful to wildlife.

10. If I see a cat dead on the side of the road when I'm driving to work in the morning, I get depressed; I call these "dead cat" days.

11. Abandoned cats may join feral cat colonies but are more likely to be killed by predators, including feral cats.

12. Feral cats, technically, are those born in the wild rather than those abandoned.

13. Erin Hunter writes the "Warrior" book series about feral cats that live in "tribes."

Developing Examples with Specific Words, Details, and Explanations

As we discussed in Chapter 20, writers develop their points through details, examples, and explanations. Below, A and B illustrate two different ways to develop the subtopic sentence in order to explain why the author loves Halloween. Which version do you find more interesting?

Topic sentence: When I was a child, I loved Halloween because of the costumes, the candy, and the adventure of staying up late.

Subtopic sentence 1: The first reason I looked forward to this special night was that everyone dressed up in cool costumes.

A. Kids wore all kinds of costumes. My favourite was of this creepy guy from a slasher movie. I wore a mask and a hat to look like him. It was fun scaring my sister and the kids in the neighbourhood.

B. I liked seeing all the goblins, devils, ghosts, skeletons, and pirates at the school party and on the streets at night. But I also liked being in costume. At various ages I was a ghost, a devil, and a skeleton; I was Superman one year and Batman the next. But my favourite costume was of Freddy Krueger. I wore my black hat down low so people couldn't see at first that I was wearing a rubber mask that faked the melted skin on Freddy's face. I had plastic claws that looked like knives, at least to me. It was fun hearing my sister scream when I jumped out of her bedroom closet. I also enjoyed scaring the little kids while out trick-or-treating.

If you like B more, notice that A is not well developed, whereas B adds specific words, details, and action, as well as more complete explanations: for example, how and why the author wore his Freddy Krueger costume. To involve your reader (and keep yourself interested), develop your examples as in B.

With group members, look at the accompanying photograph, and see if it helps bring back memories of your own Halloween fun. Now, develop each of the two examples below, as the preceding example B was developed. Use specific words and details, action description, and explanation; also, tell your reader your thoughts and emotions.

1. **Subtopic sentence 2:** Besides the costumes, I loved filling my bags with candy.

_____

_____

_____

_____

2. **Subtopic sentence 3:** But the best part of Halloween for me was the adventure of staying out late at night.

_____

_____

_____

_____

_____

_____

ENGLISH REVIEW NOTE

If you are not a fan of Halloween, choose a holiday celebration that you do enjoy, give two examples why, and then develop those examples.

Learning from a Student Model: An Illustration Essay

Illustration means giving an **example** and then connecting it to a point by explaining how the example fits. For instance, in the following student model essay, the author, Clare, tells us in her thesis that she was a fearful child. We ask, "Can you give us an example of your fears?" Clare responds by choosing a few specific instances of childhood fears: a vacuum cleaner, a dog, and a monster. As she develops these examples with details and explanation, we begin to understand why she was a fearful child.

Fear in My Early Years

1   As an adult, I like scary movies because they are not real danger. But I am very cowardly in real life. For example, I have never ridden a roller coaster because I'm afraid I might die on the ride, and I have never gone skiing with my friends because I don't want a broken arm or leg. From where, I wonder, do my fears come? I think that people like me are mostly afraid of physical harm, but if the fear is from an imaginary world, it can be fun. However, as a little girl, real-world dangers and imaginary ones seemed to surround me. When I was young, it seemed that I was afraid of everything!

2   One of my earliest frightening memories was of the vacuum cleaner. When I was 4, I would run from my mother when I saw her getting the evil vacuum out. Sometimes I would hide in my closet or under my bed. By the time she was through cleaning, my mother would often be annoyed that I was hiding from the vacuum instead of doing some small chore, like putting my books in order or putting my crayons in their boxes. She would scold me for my laziness. Although I understand now that she was just trying to improve my work habits, I think her scolding made me fear the vacuum more.

3   Another childhood fear was dogs. I had wanted a dog for as long as I could remember. My friend had a fluffy miniature poodle that did tricks like begging for food and rolling over. But my parents didn't want the mess and responsibility of owning a dog. However, one day while I was playing in my front yard, I saw a small white shaggy dog sniffing around in my neighbour's yard. I observed the dog for a while, and it looked friendly. Then it moved over to the edge of my yard. I wanted to touch that small, messy doggy, so I approached it slowly with my hand out, saying, "good doggy, nice doggy." But when my eyes and its met, it barked at me roughly and pursued me toward my front steps. It leaped up on my back, knocked me down, and ripped my shirt. My mother ran outside and chased the dog away, and it has taken me years to overcome my nervousness around dogs.

4   Worse than dogs for me, though, was my terror at the thought of Gang-xi, a Chinese vampire. In elementary school, I had seen a popular kids' movie that featured Gang-xi as he sucked the blood and the life out of his victims. He discovered his prey by sensing human breathing and even the slightest movement. One autumn night, I awoke in the early morning hours to see a lurid red light shining in my bedroom and a shadow on the shade over my window. I could hear the clock tick-tocking loudly and thought I heard a scratching at the window. I was almost paralyzed with fright. I had just enough strength to creep down under the covers. Sweating and breathing as little as possible, I spent the night awake without changing my position by an inch until the sun rose.

5   As I look back to these frights from my childhood, I think how ludicrous I was. But calming the fears of a child is just as difficult as calming the fears of an adult. Now I am not afraid of a vacuum, a little dog, or a monster movie. Yet, I am still nervous thinking of the many dangers in the real world. However, I want to have lots of experiences as I grow. I want to travel more in the world. I know that if I am to do this, I will have to learn to separate my false fears, my "Gang-xi fears," from my real fears.

—*Yunkyung Clare Bae*

1. Evaluate the introduction. Comment on the hook, thesis, and support sentence.

2. How does the concluding paragraph link to the thesis statement?

3. How are the body paragraphs organized (by space, time, or importance)? What phrase shows you this?

4. Discuss how three of the writer's specific words help you picture her fearful moments.

5. What one point would you add to make any main example more interesting?

Learning from a Professional Model: An Illustration Essay

In the next essay, "Daily Shampoo?" (originally published in the Ottawa Citizen *newspaper), Ruth Bradley-St-Cyr explores the similarities and differences between hair care in 1947 and now. As you read, notice the examples the author uses to clarify her points. Do you think that she makes her point that everything old is new again?*

Daily shampoo? Sixty years ago they would have thought we were nuts

BY RUTH BRADLEY-ST-CYR

1 Everything old is new again. As Sally Beatty reported, originally in the *Wall Street Journal*, many women find dry, brittle hair is healthier and more manageable if they wash it less often than once a day. This statement sent me scurrying back to the notes my mother made for her Grade 8 health class for some good old-fashioned advice about hair care.

2 Miss Good Health of 1947 kept her crowning glory clean, glossy, and free from dandruff by washing it "at least every two weeks, maybe oftener." The signs of need for washing include greasiness, itchiness, stringiness (refuses to curl), odour, dark colour, and dandruff. No thought of washing every day since it was a big production (and a handy excuse to turn down unwelcome male advances — "Oh, sorry, I can't go out tonight. I have to wash my hair!") In 1947 showers and hair dryers were not standard household equipment so your choices for doing it yourself were bathtub, sink, or bucket.

3 Recommended shampoos included any mild cream, liquid, or powder shampoo or even bar soap (my father's shampoo of choice). Brushing 100 strokes a day was recommended to remove dust and dirt, improve circulation in the scalp, and bring out the natural oils to spread them over the hair surface. Strange, isn't it, that today we wash our hair to get rid of the natural oils and then give ourselves a hot oil treatment to repair the dryness? As well, brushing was seen to be a way to "feed" hair, as the improved circulation would bring more vitamins A and D to the hair roots.

For dealing with unwanted straight hair, there were several curling options. A 4
"permanent about once a year is sufficient for hair health" since it tended to dry
out the hair. The nighttime methods of curling included winding locks in rags,
socks, or pipe cleaners. Of course, you should wear a pretty cap over all of that.
And—for maintaining curliness—"avoid the use of water on the hair too much."

Shock, heredity, worry, diet, and sickness could all cause grey hair but hair dye 5
was not recommended, as it was "rather obvious." (How true, how true. Especially
the last time I did mine and they were out of chestnut brown at the drug store.)
However, tinting "does no harm" and "brings out the highlights in the hair."

Also, my mother's notes say that hair grows faster at 10 a.m. and 4 p.m., as 6
well as in summer. I've heard of people just sitting around watching the grass
grow, but who funded the study for someone to watch the hair grow?

Ah, hair! Mine used to be a crowning glory before I found my first grey hair at 7
my brother's wedding (was that shock or worry?) and watched it thin out as I had
children. By then, I was tired of my grandmother's friends running their hands
through it and marvelling at how thick it was. But now it's 10 a.m. and I'm rooting
for it to all grow back, just like it used to be. Maybe I'll help it out by brushing 100
strokes and not washing it for a couple of weeks.

THINKING ABOUT THE MODEL

1. Comment on the introduction: hook, development, and focus. Where does
   the author locate her thesis statement?

2. Since order of importance is significant for examples presented in an illus-
   trative essay, discuss the order of examples presented in this essay. Are
   they effectively organized or would you order them differently?

3. How well does the example in paragraph 3 help explain the author's
   point?

4. What relationship do you have to the past? Do you enjoy old things, living
   history museums, or stories told by old people?

5. With a partner or in groups, make a list of all the things that have NOT
   changed since 1947. Compile all group members' examples. For inspiration, consult the performance of the song "Everything Old is New
   Again" by Anne Murray (and The Muppets): http://www.youtube.com/
   watch?v=7_EdTlGWsdA.

Writing an Illustration Essay

LO25.2

Audience and Purpose

Think about who (besides you) would be interested in your topic. In paragraph
B under "Developing Examples" (page 333), the writer assumes that readers are
familiar with Halloween and with Freddy Krueger from the *Nightmare on Elm
Street* horror movies, so he does not describe the holiday or character in much
detail; he does, however, describe his costume using specific examples. This way,
readers can picture how he looked dressed as Freddy.

Your purpose may be to inform, persuade, or entertain your reader; but be
sure to make some overall point that your examples support.

> **HINT**
>
> For more on audience, see
> Chapter 2.

The Assignment

Write an essay roughly 500 to 750 words (2 to 3 pages) in length. Develop the topic by using three main examples. Be sure to begin each main example with a topic sentence.

Write about forces of nature that have frightened or inspired you (storms, fires, tornadoes, for example).

Alternative Assignments

Here are several additional writing options for illustration essays. With any of the following assignments, be sure to do the following:

- Introduce each major example with a topic sentence.
- Arrange major examples by importance (or occasionally, time).
- Use transition words, especially in topic sentences.
- Develop examples with specific words, details, and explanations.

Business in Context:

Consider and illustrate specific qualities of a good (or bad) boss. You may draw from personal experience or develop your own ideal. You might consider yourself as the ideal boss. Keep in mind the requirements of the assignment as stated above.

Culture in Context:

Tell about your experiences adjusting to another culture—from another country to Canada or vice versa. Choose three differences, list them by importance, and then explain them. For example, many people coming to Canada remark on the number of consumer goods available (think of specific stores) and how Canadians tend to consume those goods constantly. Be sure to conclude your essay with some point or observation about these cultural differences.

Education in Context:

Consider three childhood fears that you might have to deal with in a professional early childhood education setting—a daycare centre or an elementary school. How would you recognize these fears in a child and what would you do to reassure the child? Develop these examples with specific words, details, and explanations. Keep in mind the requirements of the assignment as stated above.

Health Care in Context:

Write about three healthy food groups, with specific examples, that will help patients gain and maintain good health. You might consider contrasting the benefits of these foods, and the health risks if these foods are not eaten. Keep in mind the requirements of the assignment as stated above. Remember to use transition words, especially in the topic sentences.

Science in Context:

Looking at the accompanying picture of the earth and moon, reflect on how small our planet really is in the vastness of space. It is the only place we have. How well are we taking care of it and each other? Choose what you feel are the three greatest problems we face (some possibilities include war, poverty, sickness, famine, slavery, drug trafficking, pollution, species extinction, global warming, and exploitation of natural resources); arrange them by order of importance; and explain why you think each is so serious. Include specific examples and details, and keep in mind the requirements of the assignment as stated above.

Technology in Context:

Write about the advantages or limitations of social networking sites (such as Facebook). Perhaps you can think of two advantages and two limitations. Be sure to include specific examples and details. Use transitions, especially in topic sentences. Refer to the requirements of the assignment as stated above to get organized.

Discovering Ideas: Prewriting for Illustrative Essays

For this assignment, you may want to write from personal experience. Or you may pick a topic that you haven't personally been involved with but know something about.

When you pre-write for your main examples, try to uncover several layers of more specific examples to help your reader see what you mean.

Select a topic for your essay, and follow the prewriting technique of listing. Begin by listing four or five main examples that you could include; then cut the least promising examples, keeping only three. Include several specific examples with details to show your reader what you mean by each of your main examples, and then finally illustrate with the best two. Starting a new paragraph for each example, the body of your essay can be developed into an outline to look something like this:

TOPIC

Example 1 (one of the best)

> *Specific detail (one of the best)*

> *Specific detail (an especially good one)*

Example 2 (one of the best)

> *Specific detail (one of the best)*

> *Specific detail (an especially good one)*

Example 3 (one of the best)

> *Specific detail (one of the best)*

> *Specific detail (an especially good one)*

FEEDBACK *Trade examples with a classmate. Point out your favourite specific example in his or her essay, and ask at least one constructive question. What feedback did you receive for your examples?*

Organizing Illustrative Essays

The "I" approach relies on personal examples and experiences; the "they" approach uses more general knowledge.

With your first round of prewriting completed, you can arrange your three main examples from **least to most** important. If you have not yet written out a thesis statement, now is a good time to do so. Aside from telling what your topic is and limiting it with a focus, your thesis statement will begin with an "I" or "they" approach to the subject. Notice both ways of writing a thesis statement below:

1. **"I" method:** The Internet all too often ruins my day by stealing all of my valuable time.

2. **"They" method:** The Internet all too often ruins people's days by stealing all of their valuable time.

Write out or type your working thesis statement, underlining the topic once and circling the limiting statement. Now list your three main examples. Do these examples fall into a clear order of importance? Why do you think that your last example is the most interesting or dramatic?

FEEDBACK *Respond to a classmate's list of examples. Is it arranged from least to most important? Does the last example seem most important to you? Why or why not?*

Drafting Illustration Essays

Moving into your first draft, keep the following points in mind:

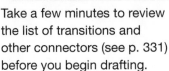

HINT

Take a few minutes to review the list of transitions and other connectors (see p. 331) before you begin drafting.

1. For a quick start, write out your thesis statement followed *directly* by your first topic sentence. Then write out your other topic sentences at spaced intervals on the page. Don't worry about polishing these sentences yet. You may find that it helps to begin writing your last example first since it is the most important one to you.

2. Keep asking the question, "What do I mean by what I have just written?" Develop your topic sentences with specific, detailed examples and explanations.

3. Keep in mind that your examples do not have to be evenly balanced, though they should all be developed. Your first example may need only a sentence or two of explanation, while your last example may be a bit longer than the others.

4. To replace "I" in papers, use the more general-knowledge "they" approach, trying pronouns like *their, they, them,* and *those* and nouns like *people, students, consumers,* and *athletes*.

JOURNAL / BLOG ENTRY 25.4

After finishing your first rough draft, reread it, and highlight with a marker your topic sentences (or use your computer's highlight feature). Now underline the topic of each once and circle the limiting statement. Are the topics arranged by importance? What parts of the draft do you like most and least? Answer in a reflective paragraph.

FEEDBACK *Share this draft with your instructor or select classmates. Write a paragraph about the strengths, weaknesses, and arrangement of topics in a classmate's draft.*

Revising Illustration Essays

As you begin revising the first draft of your illustration essay, both you and your peer reviewer may use the checklist on page 342 as a guide.

HINT

For more detailed suggestions for revising all drafts, turn to Chapter 21.

LINKING TO FUTURE EXPERIENCE

Examples, like descriptions, are used in nearly every piece of good writing in and beyond college. From hard statistics and quotations to case studies and personal observations, they are your evidence; providing them makes your writing more specific, authoritative, and credible. The challenge is to choose the best examples for each purpose and audience—and to articulate them well. For instance, if you were making a case at work for why you should receive a raise, you might mention a few positive contributions you have made to the company, the amount of time you have worked there, and a new skill you have acquired and could put to use; however, you would not want to say that you want the raise because you desperately need a new home computer or a nicer car.

☐ Has the writer used three examples, not just a single long one?

Reviewer Comment: _____

_____

☐ Does the thesis statement name and limit the topic?

Reviewer Comment: _____

_____

☐ Are the examples arranged by importance?

Reviewer Comment: _____

_____

☐ Has the writer included topic sentences that name and limit each main example?

Reviewer Comment: _____

_____

☐ Has the writer used transitions and other connectors, especially in topic sentences?

Reviewer Comment: _____

_____

☐ Does the concluding sentence both rename the topic and make a point?

Reviewer Comment: _____

_____

Chapter Summary

1. Most writing uses examples that become increasingly specific, the next example building on the one that comes before it.

2. Examples can be based on personal experience ("I") or general knowledge ("they").

3. Examples often include elements of description and narration, and explanations may include a person's thoughts and feelings about a situation or idea.

4. Each major example in an illustration essay should be introduced with a topic sentence.

5. Writing with examples is often organized by order of importance.

6. Transitional words and other connectors are especially important in topic sentences.

7. Writing is not complete until it has been revised and carefully edited.

26

Explaining Processes

Break down one of the following processes into a list of steps: going fishing, shopping for groceries, or moving from one home to another.

What Are We Trying to Achieve and Why?

If you were telling a child how to catch a trout, you might describe the following steps: placing bait on the hook, casting the bait, reeling in the line, setting the hook after a strike, landing the fish, and taking the fish off the hook. When we give instructions like these, we are explaining a process in order *to do*.

Or you might find yourself explaining how fish migrate, like the salmon in the picture on this chapter's title page, discussing their life cycle—moving to the ocean, growing up there, and then returning to their birth stream to spawn and die. This explanation would be a process in order *to understand*.

Another way to think about process essays is to make a distinction between "directional" writing (providing instructions) and "informational" writing (explaining or analyzing a sequence). In the first case, you are explaining a process so that, in following your directions, readers can perform the process themselves. In the second case, you are providing information about a process so that readers can understand it, but not perform it. These two ways to explain processes—**to do** (practical) and **to understand** (theoretical)—are the focus of Chapter 26.

LINKING TO PREVIOUS EXPERIENCE

What You Already Know about Process Explanations

Listening to, reading, and giving instructions on how to do things are common human activities. At an early age, we listened as our parents explained how to tie our shoes. A bit later, we began reading and learned how to play Monopoly and bake a cake. A few steps further in life, we began to *give* instructions. Process instructions are a great help in getting a job done, so skills in process explanations are practical knowledge. But beyond doing an immediate task, through personal observations and through the observations of others, we have learned what makes the world work—why electrical storms are dangerous, how our leaders are elected, what the best path is toward an education. In this chapter, we'll practise breaking down processes in a more formal, focused way.

> **HINT**
>
> Process often makes use of other writing patterns, such as description (Chapter 23), illustration (Chapter 25), and cause and effect (Chapter 27).

JOURNAL / BLOG ENTRY 26.1

Write down one activity you can do or one you know about; then list six steps to help someone else do or understand it. "**To-do** activities" include how to parallel park, download music, or get to work on time. "**To-understand** activities" include how a football defence is built, how a car engine works, or how to apply to college or university. For your process, were six steps too few, just enough, or too many? What words might you need to explain further for readers unfamiliar with your process?

FEEDBACK *Trade your list of steps with a classmate's list; comment on the above questions for your partner.*

Developing Skills in Working with Process Explanations

A process paragraph needs to be arranged logically, of course, and in almost all cases, this would mean chronologically. An exception would be if a part of the process is dangerous and you need to place a warning first. Chronology is critical to process. If you are explaining how to write an essay, for example, you can't put the editing before the drafting. If you are explaining a historical event, such as Canadian Confederation, you can't put the Quebec Conference (October 1864) before the Charlottetown Conference (September 1864). Any essay may require a paragraph or two of process explanation in order to help the reader understand your topic. In order to explain why the Ryerson Press was sold to McGraw-Hill in 1970, you will need to explain what led up to the sale, including the history of the Ryerson Press (founded in 1829) and the history of McGraw-Hill (founded in 1909). For an excellent example of chronological organization, see the McGraw-Hill Ryerson website (http://www.mcgrawhill.ca/about-us/history/) for a timeline of their history.

The following activities will help you work with process explanations:

1. Listing all needed steps
2. Explaining steps thoroughly
3. Defining all terms

Listing All Needed Steps

It is important when giving instructions or when helping someone understand a process to include all necessary steps. In this photograph, a young woman is in the process of clearing airport security. If she had not flown since 9/11 and therefore had no experience with current airport security procedures, would the five steps below help her clear security?

1. Have your boarding pass and photo ID ready.
2. Put your luggage into the X-ray scanner.
3. Put all metal objects, bagged cosmetic liquids and creams, and outer clothing into a basket, and put the basket into the X-ray scanner.
4. Walk through the metal detector.
5. Pick up your belongings.

The preceding list is a good start, but to really help the passenger, we should offer a more complete list of steps, like the following:

1.	Be sure not to have any restricted items in your carry-on bags. Follow the airline's guidelines regarding the size of liquid containers, and pack all carry-on liquid products in a clear plastic bag.	**3.**	Have your boarding pass and photo ID in your hand.
2.	Go to the washroom, if necessary, before you pass through security.	**4.**	Make eye contact with the security agent, and behave appropriately.

5.	At the X-ray scanner, remove your shoes, jacket, hat, and gloves; place them in a basket; and put the basket onto the belt of the scanner.	**9.**	Be ready, with boarding pass and ID in hand, to pass through the metal detector; wait for an OK from security.
6.	Put all of your metal objects, including your belt, in a basket; put the basket through the scanner.	**10.**	If the buzzer sounds from the metal detector, stop and follow instructions from security as they pass a metal-sensitive wand around you.
7.	If you have a camera or laptop, open the bag holding the item; put it in a basket; and pass it through the X-ray scanner.	**11.**	If no buzzer sounds when you pass through the metal detector (or when you are cleared by security), move quickly to gather *all* your belongings from the end of the scanner.
8.	Place all carry-on liquids and creams in a plastic baggie, no container larger than 3 ounces or 85 grams; add to the basket so it may pass through the X-ray scanner.	**12.**	Once you have been cleared by security, remember to stay within the secure area of the terminal.

The number of steps and amount of information you give will depend on the complexity of the process, how much you know about it, and how much your audience is likely to know.

ACTIVITY 26.1 WORKING TOGETHER: Listing All Needed Steps

With group members, discuss the topics below, and then list all the steps the specified audience would need to complete each of the three specified processes. Assign one person in the group to take notes.

1. Choose any *one* of these **to-do** processes:
   a. Prepare for a test in school. (*Audience:* a friend your own age who is struggling in school)
   b. Calm an angry friend. (*Audience:* a friend who is shy and non-assertive)
   c. Complete any small project, such as changing guitar strings or baking cookies. (*Audience:* a 15-year-old who is unfamiliar with the project)

2. Choose any *one* of these **to-understand** processes:
   a. Explain how people become alcoholics or become trapped by any addiction. (*Audience:* a person your age who may be falling into addiction)
   b. Explain how home recycling of paper, metal, and glass is done. (*Audience:* young people who have never recycled before)
   c. Explain how some marriages end in divorce. (*Audience:* high school students taking a course on the family)

3. Choose a process of your own—a to-do process or a to-understand process. Specify your audience and list the steps.

Explaining Steps Thoroughly

After you have listed the major steps in a process, you should think them through, considering how best to explain them. For instance, referring back to our example of how to clear airport security, what if a reader wondered why he or she should go to the washroom before passing through the security check? If we tell readers that the clearance procedure sometimes means standing in line for a very long time, they will understand the **reason** for the suggestion and will be more likely to follow it.

Similar to giving reasons, **warnings** are important, especially if they help people avoid serious inconvenience or danger. For example, when you advise readers to "behave appropriately," they may pay more attention if you mention that jokes about bombs or hijacking may subject them to strip searches or worse.

ACTIVITY 26.2 Explaining Steps Completely

In the following student paragraph, which explains how tsunamis occur, the writer has listed three main steps (underlined) in the process. Read this paragraph closely, and then write in the space provided whether the author has explained the step clearly, given reasons for the step, or included a warning to help people escape tsunamis.

Tsunamis, the Killer Waves

How do tsunamis (also called tidal waves) work? <u>The first step is the moving of a huge amount of ocean water.</u> This is usually caused by a big seaquake but can also result from undersea volcanoes, landslides, or even a meteor or asteroid strike. If the earthquake shakes the sea floor sideways, there is no shifting of water, but if the floor drops low or rises high enough, all the water that has been moved will start a series of waves. <u>These waves are the next step in the growth of the tsunami.</u> They spread out in a circle, travelling hundreds of kilometres per hour with a great distance between each one, sometimes 300 to 900 kilometres. These waves are low, between 1 and 1.5 metres high, and ships at sea often don't even notice them. <u>But when the waves near land, they slow down, and another phase of the process occurs as the waves begin to grow.</u> When the crest (top) of the wave is fairly far from land, the water near shore gets sucked into the coming wave. If people see this, they often have several minutes to save themselves from the tsunami by getting far away from the water. As waves move in closer to shore, they begin to grow and can reach a height of more than 30 metres! If the seashore and surrounding land are fairly flat, the wall of water can travel far inland, snapping trees, crushing houses, drowning people, and carrying them out to sea. Fortunately, scientists around the world have been working on an early warning system to detect tsunamis and alert people in the path of these killer waves.

—Aasim Alhussani

Explanation/reason 1: _____

_____

_____

Explanation/reason 2: _____

_____

_____

Explanation/reason 3: _____

_____

_____

HINT

For more on defining terms, see Chapter 30.

Defining All Terms

For people to follow process explanations, they must be familiar with all important terms used. For example, referring back to our airport security process in "Listing All Needed Steps," what are some terms that the inexperienced air traveller might need to know? How about *restricted items*? Should we give examples like scissors, pocket knives, liquids, or aerosol cans over 3 ounces (85 grams)? How about *X-ray scanner* and *metal detector*? Should we distinguish between them, perhaps comparing the metal detector to a device that looks like a doorframe? Is the term *wand* clear enough?

On the other hand, you don't want to burden your reader with unneeded definitions. We can, for example, expect most adult travellers to know terms like *ID, ticket, laptop, video camera,* and *terminal*.

HINT

Knowing your audience will help you choose which terms to define.

ACTIVITY 26.3 Defining All Terms

Choose one of the processes you developed from Activity 26.1; *list* all the terms you think your target audience might need to have explained; and then briefly *define* them. You might use a dictionary, compare or contrast the term with another, explain how the item works, or find a good synonym for it.

_____

_____

_____

ACTIVITY 26.4 Definition, Description, Process Explanation

People who are experts must often explain things to people who are not. The art of breaking down a complex process into simple steps is what makes a good technical writer. Choose a complex subject to explain for general readers. It may be a topic where you already have some expertise, or it may be a topic that you want to understand better yourself. The subject matter may be scientific, technical, historical, musical, or anything not readily understood by the average person. Write two separate paragraphs:

1. description and definition
2. process explanation

In the first paragraph, write a **description** of your subject. Include at least one **definition** of an unfamiliar term. It might be the name of a process or piece of equipment or it might be the subject itself. In the second paragraph, provide the **process explanation** (at least 6 steps). Avoid using point form or num-bered instructions. The challenge is to make your instructions clear in prose (sentence) form. Use the following outline for your two paragraphs:

Paragraph 1 — Description and Definition

  Topic sentence

  Detail

  Detail

  Detail

  Definition

  Conclusion

Paragraph 2 — Process Explanation

  Topic sentence

  Step 1

  Step 2

  Step 3

  Step 4

  Step 5

  Step 6

  Conclusion

LINKING STEPS IN PROCESS EXPLANATION WITH TRANSITIONS

TRANSITIONS FOR LINKING STEPS IN A PROCESS			
at this point	and	then	finally
next	before	after	first (second, etc.)
begin	initially	at the end	immediately

TRANSITIONS FOR DESCRIBING WITHIN A PROCESS			
in	or	when	while
through	by	until	into
as you are	at the same time	during	gradually

ACTIVITY 26.5 Keeping Sentence Patterns Interesting

Rewrite or retype the paragraph below on planting tulips so that the sentences flow more smoothly. Remember to check for chronology.

Now is the time to plant your bulbs. Dig holes 20 centimetres deep. Space the bulbs about 12 centimetres apart. This gives them room to grow. Fill the holes with water. Wait for the water to recede. Place some bulb starter in the holes. Place the bulbs pointy side up. Fill the holes with soil. Press the soil down firmly. This removes the air pockets. Leave a hill over the bulb. Don't leave a depression. Water can sit in a depression. This water can rot the bulb.

_____

_____

Learning from a Student Model: Process Writing

Read the following student model closely, noticing in particular the writer's clear focus in her **topic sentence**; her well-linked **subtopic sentences**; her **chronological** (time order) arrangement of major steps; and her **development** of steps through **specific words, details, explanations, reasons,** and **warnings**. "Sharing with Family" helps readers learn about a **to-do** process rather than a to-understand one.

HINT

See Chapter 25 for more on writing subtopic sentences.

To-do processes often benefit from a preliminary step, in which supplies are brought together and organized.

Sharing with Family

For a long time dumplings have been a "must-have" food for Chinese families at holidays. To make them, first gather the ingredients and other cooking necessities. For the dough, you will need 3 cups of flour, 1¼ cups of cold water, and ¼ tsp. of salt. And for the stuffing, you will need 1 cup of ground beef, pork, or shrimp; 1 tbsp. of soy sauce; 1 tsp. of salt; 3 tbsp. of sesame oil; and 1 green onion, 1½ cups of Chinese cabbage, and 2 slices of ginger, all finely chopped. Also, have on hand, 2 medium-sized mixing bowls, 1 large pot, a mixing spoon, and a rolling pin. The next step is making the dough. Add salt to the flour, mix water in a little at a time (too much will make the dough runny), and knead the dough until it is firm. Cover the bowl, and let the dough sit for about 15 minutes. Now make the stuffing. In a mixing bowl, add and mix evenly the meat, oil, soy sauce, and other ingredients. To prevent the dumplings from falling apart, squeeze out the excess juice. When the dough and stuffing are ready, assemble the dumplings. First, divide the dough into about 50 walnut-sized pieces; then roll them flat to 3 inches, or 7.5 centimetres, across. Wet the dough's edges; add about ½ ounce (or 14 grams) of stuffing; and then fold the dough over into a semicircle, pinching the edges shut. Now 1 dumpling is done; only 49 more to go! To finish, all you have to do is boil them. Add the dumplings to the boiling water (carefully so you don't scald yourself!). When the water returns to a boil, add cold water. Do this 3 times, stirring so dumplings do not stick to the pot. Now your delicious meal is ready to serve. Making dumplings is a lot of work for one person, but it can be fun for the whole family to do the cooking together and then share the meal.

—YanZheng Bai

1. What two important points do we learn from the topic sentence?
2. What point does YanZheng make in her last sentence?
3. List five transitional words that show time arrangement within the steps.
4. What warnings does the author include?
5. Name three ways to develop any major step in this paragraph further. Consider active verbs, specific words, sensory details, revealing thoughts and emotions, and further explanation, including reasons and warnings.

Learning from a Professional Model: A Process Essay

*The following essay is by Canada's most famous environmentalist, David Suzuki. This explanation helps readers **to understand** a process rather than to do one. As you read, notice that Suzuki is explaining what NOT to do rather than what to do and boiling down some very complex issues into a very short article. Watch for specific language, active verbs, sentence variety, and the dash—for emphasis.*

Does Selling off our Resources Make us an Energy Superpower?

Selling off our resources, promoting fossil fuels, destabilizes Canada's economy

BY DAVID SUZUKI

1 Energy is on everyone's minds these days. Prime Minister Stephen Harper is determined to make Canada an energy superpower, fuelled mostly by Alberta's tar sands.

2 Meanwhile, Alberta Premier Alison Redford, elected to lead a province with a strong economy, now finds energy price fluctuations are reducing provincial revenues. Saskatchewan is booming from oil, gas, and uranium revenues, and BC Premier Christy Clark plans to vastly expand exploitation of liquefied natural gas, which requires huge amounts of energy and involves the highly contentious practice of fracking.

3 While Quebec Premier Pauline Marois maintains a moratorium on fracking, New Brunswick Premier David Alward claims it's an energy opportunity for his province. Former Ontario Premier Dalton McGuinty's progressive *Green Energy Act* is under serious attack, and Prime Minister Harper eagerly embraces exploration for oil as Arctic sea ice and tundra melt from the warming climate.

4 Although the federal government demonizes environmentalists as "radicals" bent on derailing exploitation plans for the tar sands and other natural resources,

tar sands
loose sand or sandstone saturated with a thick, sticky form of petroleum

fracking
hydraulic fracturing, a technique used to extract natural gas by changing the pressure in the surrounding rock

bitumen
a sticky, thick, black liquid or
semi-solid form of petroleum

opposition is rising against pipelines to transport Alberta's diluted bitumen to the BC coast via Enbridge's Northern Gateway or to Texas refineries via the Keystone XL. Much of the oil would be exported to countries like China, where the extreme negative effects of fossil fuel pollution are increasing daily.

5   Politicians who want to make significant change must focus primarily on re-election if they are to see their agendas come to fruition. That means they must respond to immediate economic demands while leaving longer-term problems like climate change and water issues on the back burner. Surely the enduring consequences of today's actions or inactions must be a priority. We'll be living with the ramifications of the current crop of politicians' decisions and actions long after they've been relegated to history.

6   Crisis is a powerful motivator, as we saw during the economic crash of 2008. In a matter of weeks, President George W. Bush and his successor, Barack Obama, committed hundreds of billions of dollars to bail out banks and automobile companies—without imposing any conditions that might get them to change their ways. I was astounded at the speed and scale of these actions, compared to the ineffectual snail's pace on ecological issues that threaten the survival of our species and our way of life and society.

7   The science has been in for more than two decades: Human use of fossil fuels creating unprecedented levels of greenhouse gases is altering the chemistry of the atmosphere, leading to climate and weather effects that will be chaotic and devastating. Continued increases in emissions will only exacerbate what is already an out-of-control atmospheric transformation of the biosphere — our only home.

8   We claim brainpower makes us superior to the rest of life on this planet. But what use is intelligence if we don't use it to respond to threats and opportunities? After all, foresight was a great human attribute that brought us to a position of dominance on the planet. We used our knowledge and experiences to look ahead and recognize potential dangers and favourable circumstances so we could take some control over our destiny by acting to avoid hazards and exploit possibilities.

9   This is Canada's moment. We are confronting a crisis with the economy and energy. No economy can grow forever; it is simply impossible on a finite planet. Shouldn't we ask what an economy is for? How much is enough? What are the limits? How do we build a sustainable economy? We have learned from painful experience in single-resource communities that relying primarily on one major component of the economy—logging, fishing, mining—makes for dangerous boom-and-bust cycles.

10   Nations that export fossil fuel too often become over reliant on that sector. That destabilizes the economy (as we're seeing in Alberta), distorts priorities (leading to the so-called "Dutch disease" where other parts of the economy are neglected or ignored), and undermines democracy by holding governments hostage (as we saw in the enormous lobbying power of industry in the last US presidential election).

11   The future of energy in Canada will determine the fate of our society. It must be widely discussed, nationally as well as provincially, beyond the boundaries of politics and economics. This is about the type of country we will leave to our children and grandchildren.

1. Comment on the introduction: hook, development, and thesis. Where is the thesis located?

2. Comment on the development of body paragraphs: what major problems does the author name?

3. In what paragraph does the author describe short-term thinking versus long-term thinking? Why does it happen?

4. Comment on the conclusion. What process to find alternate solutions does the author propose? Would explicit instructions on what to do about the problem be more effective?

5. View the David Suzuki Foundation website at http://www.davidsuzuki.org and find a process description on the blog section. In your journal/blog response, address the issue of whether or not you think how-to instructions make people more likely to follow expert advice.

Writing a Process Explanation Essay

LO26.2

Audience and Purpose

When you explain a process, you will do a better job if you know your audience. If you anticipate how much your reader knows about your topic, you will come closer to explaining enough but not too much. For instance, in "Sharing with Family" (page 350), YanZheng does not define terms like *rolling pin* or *Chinese cabbage*, and she expects readers will know what phrases like *knead the dough* and *finely chopped* mean. If her audience has even a basic knowledge of cooking, explaining these points is unnecessary.

> **HINT**
>
> For more on considering audience, see Chapter 2.

> **HINT**
>
> Remember that after reading your explanation, readers should be able to understand a potentially complicated process or be mentally prepared to complete a task.

The Assignment

Write an essay of roughly 500 to 750 words that explains a process. A *to-do* process might involve instructions for cooking a dish or building a small project; a *to-understand* process might explain a force of nature like a hurricane, a human condition like depression, or a technological process like blogging. It is essential to begin with a clear thesis statement and then break the process down into a series of steps, usually organized chronologically (by time sequence).

Alternative Assignments

For any of the following alternative assignments, be sure to do the following:

- Write instructions for doing a task, or explain how something is done or functions.
- List and explain steps, and, where needed, give warnings.
- Define unfamiliar terms for your audience.
- Develop examples with specific words, details, and explanations.
- Begin with a thesis statement, link sentences, and end with a final point.

Business in Context:

Explain how to lower your car insurance. Include information on whom to contact, the terms and conditions required, specific information the insurance company will require about your driving record and your automobile, and methods of payment. Be sure to define unfamiliar terms for your audience. Don't forget the linking transition words to connect the steps.

Culture in Context:

Explain how to plan a great vacation in a country unfamiliar to the reader. Consider how to choose the best time for travelling, book airline tickets, buy travel insurance, book accommodation, plan what to pack, and decide on the travel itinerary. You could write about an overall plan or focus in detail on any one of the above steps. Be sure to end with a final point.

OR

Write a paragraph that explains how people celebrate some special event in your culture (for example, Cinco de Mayo, Ramadan, Yom Kippur, Christmas, Lantern Festival, Chinese New Year). Treat your explanation as a process, and organize it chronologically. For example, decorating a Christmas tree could be divided into the following major steps: buying a tree, selecting lights and ornaments, draping the tree in tinsel, hanging the ornaments, covering the base, and arranging presents under the tree. You might outline the overall process of celebrating the holiday, or you might prefer to focus on one particular aspect in detail.

Education in Context:

Create a storyboard to explain the process for getting children to bed on time. Use the airline safety card below as a storyboard model. Consider what children need to do before putting on nightwear (e.g., getting a snack, washing, brushing teeth), the process of changing clothes, and how to make the transition from waking to sleeping (e.g., listening to soothing music, reading a book, singing a song, saying prayers). Illustrate a variety of actions. Then write out the storyboard using a variety of verbs and sentence lengths.

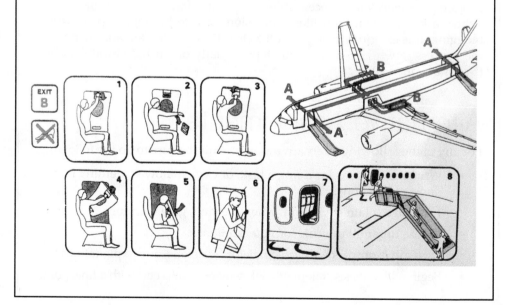

Health Care in Context:

Explain to a teenager how to plan a healthy meal including reference to Canada's Food Guide (http://www.hc-sc.gc.ca/fn-an/food-guide-aliment/index-eng.php) or to "The Politics of Food Guides" (http://www.cbc.ca/news/health/story/2012/07/27/f-food-guide-70.html). Remember the transition words to link the steps. Begin with a thesis statement and end with a final point.

Science in Context:

Explain how to calculate or reduce your carbon footprint by developing a series of steps. Expand examples with specific words, details, and explanations. The following website might provide inspiration and ideas:

"Reduce Your Impact" on *Carbon Footprint*: http://www.carbonfootprint.com/individuals.html.

Technology in Context:

Explain how to create a website or blog (or get started on Facebook or another networking site); **or** explain the steps for operating a digital camera. Make the links from one step to another obvious with transitions. Vary the length of your sentences to make the explanation interesting to read. Define unfamiliar terms for your audience.

Of course, you are writing to communicate information, but you may do so in a way that entertains. The information you give may also move people to think differently about a process or to take some action.

Discovering Ideas: Prewriting for Process Essays

Look to your own life for processes to write about. Think about pastimes that interest you and that you want to discuss, for example, sports. In this one topic, you might know how to throw a curve ball, shoot a perfect layup, grind a rail, or block a soccer goal. There are many possibilities. However, remember to *limit* your process to what can be explained within one essay. For example, it's too much to explain the whole process by which the Blue Jays made it to the World Series, but you could discuss a few important steps the manager took to build that winning team. Your approach could be *to-do* (throw a curve) or *to-understand* (how the team was built).

After choosing several topics, create a list of steps that illustrate them. Choosing the to-do approach in "Sharing with Family" (pages 350), YanZheng started with this list:

1.	Shopping for ingredients	8.	Advising how to deal with torn dumplings
2.	Organizing the ingredients and other cooking necessities in the kitchen	9.	Warning how to keep the pot from boiling over
3.	Preparing the kitchen for cooking	10.	Setting the table for dinner
4.	Making the dumplings	11.	Serving the dumplings
5.	Making the stuffing	12.	Making the dough
6.	Boiling the dumplings	13.	Keeping her family interested while making the dumplings
7.	Warning about runny dough	14.	Warning about scalding

List your topic, approach (to-do or to-understand), audience, and steps. Is the topic limited enough? What further steps might your audience need? Which steps don't they need, and why?

FEEDBACK Ask a partner whether he or she agrees with your choices. Would your partner be able to do or understand your process from the steps you have included?

HINT

Chronologically means in the order that time passes.

Organizing Process Essays

YanZheng began her to-do paragraph with this *rough* topic sentence (<u>topic</u> underlined once and <u><u>limiting statement</u></u> underlined twice):

I am going to tell you <u>how to make delicious dumplings.</u>

With her rough topic sentence in mind, she was able to focus and organize her major steps. First, she arranged them chronologically; then she crossed out several to limit the length of her explanation; and finally, she combined several steps.

Note her prewriting list below:

1.	~~Shopping for ingredients~~	7.	Making the dumplings
2.	Organizing the ingredients and other cooking necessities in the kitchen	8.	Boiling the dumplings: warning about scalding
3.	~~Preparing the kitchen for cooking~~	9.	~~Advising how to deal with torn dumplings~~
4.	~~Setting the table for dinner~~	10.	~~Warning how to keep pot from boiling over~~
5.	Making the dough: warning about runny dough	11.	~~Keeping her family interested while making the dumplings~~
6.	Making the stuffing	12.	~~Serving the dumplings~~

Here is YanZheng's working outline:

1. Organizing the ingredients and other cooking necessities in the kitchen (preliminary)
2. Making the dough: warning about runny dough
3. Making the stuffing
4. Making the dumplings
5. Boiling the dumplings: warning about scalding

Write out your working topic sentence, underlining the <u>topic</u> once and the <u>limiting statement</u> twice. Now, write out your working outline, including a new topic sentence for each major step. What words should you define for your audience, and what warnings should you give, and why?

Drafting Process Essays

Moving into your first draft, keep the following points in mind:

1. Process explanations tend to flow naturally, one step after the other; but you may find that you have begun your process too early or are including non-essential steps. Both of these errors in judgment can create focus problems.

2. Explain the *why* behind steps, and give *warnings* when needed.

3. *Define* any terms that might be puzzling to your reader (try placing your definitions in parentheses).

4. Use specific words, including exact measurements where needed (use numerals).

Revising Process Essays

As you begin revising your process first draft, you and your peer reviewer can use the following checklist as a guide:

HINT

For more detailed suggestions for revising all drafts, turn to Chapter 21.

HINT

See Chapter 18 for help with achieving sentence variety.

PEER REVIEW CHECKLIST FOR REVISING PROCESS ESSAYS

☐ Does the topic sentence name and limit a topic that predicts a process explanation?

Reviewer Comment: _____

_____

☐ Are the steps arranged chronologically (by time), and does each major group begin with a topic sentence?

Reviewer Comment: _____

_____

☐ Has the writer explained the *why* behind steps and given warnings, when needed?

Reviewer Comment: _____

_____

☐ What terms might puzzle the reader? Has the writer defined them?

Reviewer Comment: _____

_____

☐ Has the writer developed the steps with specific words and details, using precise measurements?

Reviewer Comment: _____

_____

☐ Does the concluding sentence rename the topic and make a point?

Reviewer Comment: _____

_____

Process explanations help us satisfy our curiosity and ultimately succeed in life. Being able to break down a process into clear steps is a valuable skill, whether we're giving good directions to a friend, describing a potential plan of action to our boss, or reviewing concepts for an exam. Many academic disciplines and career programs assign process analysis essays and reports: for example, biology, English, history, nursing, firefighter training, law and security, and auto mechanics.

Chapter Summary

1. Process explanations help people get jobs done and understand how the world functions. Process analysis skills are practical life skills.

2. Knowing your audience makes writing process instructions easier and more efficient.

3. Process instructions require a complete list of steps.

4. Each step or suggestion must be explained clearly; provide detailed reasons for the steps and give warnings where needed.

5. Defining terms is an essential part of process instruction; whether a word or concept needs defining depends on the previous knowledge of both you and your audience.

6. The essay should begin with a thesis statement that names the topic and predicts a process explanation.

7. Major step groupings should begin with a topic sentence.

8. Sentences should be smoothly linked with transitions and other connectors.

9. Process writing is organized chronologically.

10. Writing is not complete until it has been revised and carefully edited.

Discovering Cause
and Effect

*What do you think are the main **causes** of global climate change? What **effects** might it have on your life in*

the next 20 years? How might it affect the world you leave to your children and grandchildren?

LEARNING OBJECTIVES

27.1   Developing skills in working with cause and effect

27.2   Writing to develop cause or effect

What Are We Trying to Achieve and Why?

Most scientists believe that our planet is warming dangerously. Looking at the picture of the Earth on the previous page, you can see the bright band of red and orange that spreads across part of North America, a part in which many of us live. Almost everyone agrees that carbon dioxide is the main culprit, trapping heat that would otherwise escape into space. But what causes the increased levels of CO_2? There are many natural sources, such as the decay of vegetation, volcanic eruptions, and forest fires; but there are also many human sources, including the one illustrated in the left-hand photograph below. If global warming is not slowed, what might be the effects: melting glaciers (as shown in the right-hand photo below), rising oceans, more severe droughts, bigger hurricanes? If these effects occur, what might then result: flooding of coastal cities, failing crops, expanding deserts, levelling of cities by killer winds? When we begin to list the reasons, or **causes**, for an event, and then try to predict the results, or **effects**, we are dealing with cause-and-effect reasoning, the focus of this chapter.

LINKING TO PREVIOUS EXPERIENCE

What You Already Know about Cause and Effect

When we have problems, most of us try to solve them. Can you imagine not trying to figure out why your last cheque bounced, or why your significant other is angry with you, or how your team lost the big game? We look hard at these situations, and try to understand what caused them so that we can avoid them in the future. Likewise, when we have important decisions to make—should I go to college? should I take this job? do I really want to marry this person?—we look down the road to see the good and the bad sides, the effects of the decisions. We all have a lot of experience thinking like this—thinking critically. And the better we become at it, the more fulfilling our lives are likely to be.

> ### JOURNAL / BLOG ENTRY 27.1
>
> When have you recently used cause/effect thinking to understand a problem or
>
> make a decision? For example, maybe you are having problems at work, school,
>
> or home: what is causing the problems? how are they affecting you? Or perhaps

you have made an important decision recently—enrolling in evening classes, buying a car, breaking off a relationship? Summarize one of these situations, and list several causes for it and the effects of it.

FEEDBACK *Read a classmate's entry. Which interests you more: the causes or the effects of the decision? In a sentence or two, tell the writer why.*

Developing Skills in Working with Cause and Effect

LO27.1

Cause and effect paragraphs can be important additions to any essay, as they provide explanations for *why* something happened rather than *how* it happened, as a process paragraph would do. For example, to understand *why* Canadian Confederation took place, you would need to understand the political and social situation in the 1860s in Canada. As in post-9/11 times when we have become hyper-aware of security issues, the small British colonies of Upper and Lower Canada, Nova Scotia, and New Brunswick were worried in the 1860s about the American Civil War and the Fenian raids. Similarly, to understand the causes of *why* diseases spread, you might consider how microbes mutate or how few people seem to consider hand washing important. The effects of the disease are obvious to those dealing with its treatment, but when root causes can be addressed, the rate of disease is more likely to decrease.

The following activities will help you write about cause and effect:

1. Exploring cause and effect
2. Developing cause and effect
3. Thinking critically about cause and effect

Exploring Cause and Effect

Cause and effect are not always obvious. In some cases, the outcome of an event is completely unpredictable. For example, in 2012, two Australian radio DJs made a prank call, pretending to be members of the royal family, to a hospital in London, which resulted in the suicide of a nurse (see http://www.guardian.co.uk/uk/2013/apr/29/duchess-cambridge-hoax-call-saldanha). Those making the call certainly did not foresee the tragedy, though they had obviously not anticipated the possible side effects of worldwide humiliation that media can cause.

To help you uncover the most important causes for an event, consider which ones would certainly bring about the event and what cause nearest in time might have produced the event. It is always more difficult to assess what causes might play a role by adding to another cause, might be involved in a lesser way, or might not be readily apparent. Sometimes writers focus their energy on these minor points, missing the opportunity to tell a reader about more significant and interesting reasons. In less obvious causes, experts may be required to explain the interaction of various causes and sub-causes, effects and side effects.

The causes that you will want to focus on in your writing, however, are largely determined by your audience. For example, in thinking about the causes for getting a speeding ticket, the primary reason might be your driving at 150 kph in a 100 kph zone while a hidden one might be thinking about an argument you had with your parents and losing track of your speed. Which causes would be considered important to your audience? The police officer will not be at all interested in hearing about the argument with your parents. But if your main purpose were to encourage people to be conscious of their actions when driving a car, you would be sure to highlight this hidden cause as a significant reason for being ticketed.

When we talk about an effect resulting from a certain cause, we use transitions such as **because, since, as, for, owing to, caused by, due to, thanks to,** and so on. Or as in the following poem, which dates back to the 14th century, the outdated phrase "for want of":

> *For want of a nail the shoe was lost.*
>
> *For want of a shoe the horse was lost.*
>
> *For want of a horse the rider was lost.*
>
> *For want of a rider the message was lost.*
>
> *For want of a message the battle was lost.*
>
> *For want of a battle the kingdom was lost.*
>
> *And all for the want of a horseshoe nail.*

"For want of a nail" is the ultimate cause and effect poem and, as such, has been quoted many times.

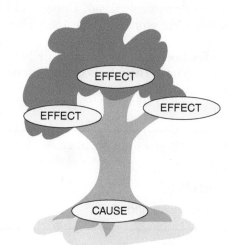

It is often helpful to think of the causes of events as the roots and the effects as the branches that grow out of those roots.

ACTIVITY 27.1 Cause and Effect Paragraphs

Using the transitional phrases **because, since, as, for, owing to, caused by, due to, thanks to,** write the following causes and effects into complete sentences (you can combine them rather than doing seven different sentences). When you have your sentences finished, compose a topic sentence and combine it and your cause-effect sentences into a coherent, chronological paragraph.

Cause	Effect
Sick in bed for a week	missed my essay deadline
Sick in bed for a week	missed my best friend's concert
Fell behind in my school work	had to work all weekend
Shaking hands at church	picked up a flu virus
Sick in bed for a week	missed three shifts at work
Missed my essay deadline	fell behind on all my school work
Sneezed on my best friend	she ended up sick in bed for a week

With group members, discuss the paragraph that follows. Make a list of all the causes for missing the shot. Can you figure out which causes are most important and why?

Missing the Target

Last November, while bow hunting, I had the chance to bag a six-point buck, but I missed two short 5-metre chip shots. The first reason for missing the medium-sized buck was the oak tree I was in. The tree stand was two metres below a huge branch, which was in front of me. When the deer came into range, I drew my bow, but the branch was in the way. After a few minutes, the buck moved behind me, presenting my next problem. To aim, I had to lean around the tree. Trying to stay quiet, I managed to get into a position where I could fire. Unfortunately, then he turned away from me. I decided to wait for a better shot. But even when I got one, I had to deal with a 35-kilometre-an-hour wind blowing in from the east. Shooting to the north, I aimed to the right of where the aim point seemed to be. However, I didn't compensate enough, and my aluminum arrow flew past the whitetail. The buck didn't run off but kept feeding on the grass. When I got a second shot, I struggled with mid-range obstructions, and my arrow was deflected by a small twig only a metre in front of me. Then the buck heard the arrow and ran off, never to be seen again. I realized at that moment that if I had practised shooting in the wind and around obstacles, I could have brought the whitetail home.

—Daniel Hedge

Developing Cause and Effect

To develop causes or effects for your assignment, you will rely on the methods you have practised so far: specific, detailed examples and clear explanations. For a reminder of how to make your writing more interesting, notice how the draft below is improved by adding **details, specific words,** and **explanation** in the revision:

> **HINT**
>
> You might want to make one person in the group the note-taker.

Draft	Revision
While bow hunting one day, I missed a buck. The first reason for missing was my tree stand, which wasn't positioned the right way. When the deer came into range, I drew my bow, but an obstacle was in the way.	<u>Last November,</u> while bow hunting, I had the chance to bag a <u>six-point</u> buck, but I missed <u>two short five-metre chip shots.</u> The first reason for missing the <u>medium-sized buck</u> was the <u>oak</u> tree I was in. The tree stand was <u>two metres below</u> a huge branch, which <u>was in front of me.</u> When the deer came into range, I drew my bow, but <u>the branch</u> was in the way.

ACTIVITY 27.3 Developing Causes

Using the preceding paragraph revision as an example, read through the following excerpt, and then rewrite (or retype) it *leaving out* the specific details and explanations that make the writing so interesting. Now list several details that the author did not use but that might make the description even stronger.

But when I got the better shot, I had to deal with a 35-kilometre-an-hour wind blowing in from the east. Shooting to the north, I aimed to the right of where the aim point seemed to be. However, I didn't compensate enough, and my aluminum arrow flew past the whitetail. The buck didn't run off but instead kept feeding on the grass. When I got a second shot, I struggled with mid-range obstructions, and my arrow was deflected by a small twig only a metre in front of me.

Thinking Critically about Cause and Effect

It is all too easy to jump to conclusions when facing a problem or anticipating an outcome. But we often make poor judgments when we grab for the first reason or result that comes along. Suppose, for instance, that someone claimed Canada could only solve its energy problems by drilling for oil wherever it is available. This claim could lead to drilling in sensitive wildlife areas like the Arctic or off-shore in deep ocean water, where oil spills are more likely. However, perhaps there are other ways to deal with energy concerns, such as funding the development of alternative energy sources, giving tax incentives to car manufacturers to produce more fuel-efficient vehicles, and working with Canadian citizens to reduce their energy consumption voluntarily. The more closely we examine our logic, asking ourselves "Why is this claim right?", the more likely we are to arrive at the truth.

ACTIVITY 27.4 Thinking Critically about Causes and Effects

Read the following oversimplified statements, and list three other likely causes or effects.

1. Liz didn't vote in the last federal election. She must not care about her country.

   Other reasons (causes) for not voting:

   a. _____

   b. _____

   c. _____

2. Jay's boss fired him today. The boss must not have liked him.

   Other reasons (causes) for being fired:

   a. _____

   b. _____

   c. _____

3. Video gamers lose all contact with the real world.

   Other results (effects) of playing video games:

   a. _____

   b. _____

   c. _____

Learning from a Student Model: An Effect Essay

HINT

For more on subtopic sentences, see Chapter 25.

Read the following student model closely, noticing in particular the author's clear focus in her **topic sentence**; her well-linked **subtopic sentences**; her arrangement of major effects by **order of importance**; and her **development** of effects through **specific words**, **details**, and **explanations**.

Driven to Drive in Midlife

1   When I was 36 years old, an accident changed my life forever. My son was 4 years old at the time, and I had been walking him to daycare, but the daycare had relocated, so I needed to begin taking him in a taxi. Unfortunately, one day we rode with a bad driver. When I got out and put my son on the ground, I looked for money in my purse to pay the driver. Suddenly, I heard my son scream because his fingers had been smashed between the taxi's doors. It made me both sad and angry. As I put my arms around him and walked him to the house, I whispered to myself, "This would not have happened if I had driven my own car." This bad experience made me resolve to learn to drive, and that decision has brought many happy consequences.

2   One benefit of being able to drive myself was that I could now do my own errands. Every day I took my son to daycare. Next, I would pick up my mother, who was 75 years old and needed help running her errands. Sometimes we went to friends' or family members' houses and spent time together drinking tea or cool juices. I was glad that I had time to help my mother and time for myself to do my errands and see the people who were important to me.

3   Another good effect that came from my new skill with driving was that when we went out of town, I was able to help my husband with the driving. I remember our first trip to northern Iran with our friends. My husband drove for about four hours on winding mountain roads with steep cliffs on both sides. When we stopped for juice and snacks, all of the women changed position with their husbands. I sat in the driver's seat, adjusted the rear-view mirror, and fastened my seatbelt. When I started the car and began to drive down the mountain road, I was excited because this was the first time that I could see the road from the driver's position. I had to pay attention all the time. I felt proud and independent passing male drivers. One reason I was happy about learning to drive was that I could finally share the task of driving with my husband.

4   The most important result of my decision to learn to drive was that I conquered my fear of driving. When I used to sit in the front seat of my husband's car, I saw old women who drove confidently. I became jealous of them. I wanted to learn, but I was frightened and uncertain. I thought that I was too old to try, yet my husband encouraged me, telling me every day that he knew I could do it. Still, the traffic noise, the narrow streets, and the fatal accidents made me nervous. In the beginning, I decided to drive only to places near our house, such as my son's daycare; but as I became more experienced, I began driving farther from home. After a few weeks of this, I realized that many of my fears about driving were foolish.

5   The sad event with my son has caused many positive effects in my life: I have become independent in my daily work, I help my husband, and I have overcome my fear of driving. Though sometimes I still walk to the market so that I can talk to people in the street, I feel good about myself because I can now drive. I am more productive and independent. I have also learned an important lesson in life from my decision to drive: people can learn anything, anytime, at any age if they just believe in themselves.

—*Nahid Talebizadeh*

THINKING ABOUT THE STUDENT MODEL

1. What two important points do we learn from the thesis statement?

2. What words in the concluding sentence link to the thesis statement?

3. Copy each of the subtopic sentences, and underline the <u>main effect</u> (<u>example</u>) once and the <u>statement</u> about it twice. Circle the connectors: transitions, repeat words, synonyms, and pronouns.

4. Choose a subtopic in this essay, and tell how several specific words add to Nahid's meaning.

5. Name three ways to develop any subtopic in this essay further. Consider action, active verbs, dialogue, specific words, sensory details, describing a person or setting, revealing thoughts and emotions, and further explanation.

Learning from a Professional Model: A Cause-and-Effect Essay

The cause-and-effect pattern of development tries to determine what makes events happen and what results from those events. In this article from Alberta Report *published in March 2002, Ted Byfield discusses the "baby bust" now occurring fifty years after the "baby boom." When analyzing cause and effect, careful writers try to look past the first or most obvious causes and effects. They often find a chain or pattern developing, one cause or effect leading to the next and then the next, often called a chain of events. Notice the problem of the modern "mindset" that Byfield comments on in his final paragraph.*

Baby Bust

BY TED BYFIELD

1   Canadians, says a recent study, are working too hard—too hard for their health, too hard for their sanity, and above all too hard to have children. The study is the largest of its kind in Canada, involving some 31,000 workers. It found that in the struggle to balance the demands of work and family, work continually wins. Consequently, women put off having children and many young people opt to have none.

The research showed that 40% of women in professional jobs have not **2** started a family because of work; 30% of men said they wanted no children, for the same reason. This has profound implications, of course. If many of the best potential parents of any society won't produce offspring, or perhaps only one child late in life, the intelligence level of the next generation will surely decline. Some achievement.

What is most unusual about this study, however, is not so much what it found **3** as who paid for it, namely Health Canada. For by making note of our failure to have children, the federal government has inadvertently called attention to one of the better-kept secrets of current demographic sociology: The much-ballyhooed "population explosion," which for years we were assured would soon crowd the world with wall-to-wall people, was dead wrong. What actually threatens us instead is serious population decline, a "birth dearth" that will wreak great havoc on the economies of much of the Western world.

"Government officials no doubt realize," writes Tom Bethell in *The American* **4** *Spectator* magazine, "that saying there are too few people, so soon after the hue and cry about there being too many, would destroy their own credibility." Other governments are in a similar case, since pretty well everybody bought into the Erlich "population bomb" expectations. Small wonder few care to acknowledge the alarms were false.

The American Enterprise Institute does, however, and its numbers—all **5** taken from official census and other demographic records—leave the factual case beyond doubt. To maintain zero population growth in developed countries, each woman must have an average 2.1 children. The European average 15 years ago had fallen to 1.7, and is now running at 1.4. In Italy it is 1.2, an impending economic disaster.

The effects of such a decline do not appear immediately; a generation must **6** grow up for them to be fully felt. But even if European fertility rates were to return to 2.1 tomorrow—a virtual impossibility—Europe's current population of 727 million would still drop by 171 million by 2050. Since government welfare programs depend upon a steady inflow of tax money, few countries will have enough people by then to support such programs.

Even more surprising, the drop is not confined to developed countries. **7** India's birth rate has fallen from about 5.6 in 1960 to 3.5 and is still dropping. Egypt, whose rate in 1960 at something over 7.0 was the world's highest, is down to 3.9. Mexico has dropped from 6.8 down to 3, Thailand from 6.5 to 2, less than replacement level. The United Nations has been so successful in its don't-have-kids propaganda that it is rapidly making the absence of kids the world's No. 1 economic problem.

Meanwhile in Europe, where one government after another experiments **8** with costly childbearing incentives, the universal experience is that bribes don't work. Women must want to have children. So why don't they? And why do men readily concur? Because, the Canadian study finds, they both make their work more important. And this, we may discover, is a very difficult mindset to change.

1. Comment on the introduction: hook, development, and focus. Why does the author focus on birth rate rather than any of the other issues raised in paragraph 1?

2. Comment on the development of body paragraphs: How does the author build his argument that overpopulation is no longer a problem? Do you believe that this is no longer a global problem? Why or why not?

3. Write out one causal chain leading to the current low birth rate in Canada. What factors have led people to put work before family?

4. Write an effects chain leading away from the present to predict what Canadian society will look like in another fifty years.

5. What does the author mean by the following sentence: "If many of the best potential parents of any society won't produce offspring, or perhaps only one child late in life, the intelligence level of the next generation will surely decline." Do you think his assessment is correct? Upon what premise is his assertion based?

LO27.2 Writing to Develop Cause or Effect

Audience and Purpose

HINT

For more on describing an audience, see Chapter 2.

Having a clear sense of who might be reading your work will help you to choose and focus a topic. The author of "Missing the Target" (Activity 27.2) was writing primarily for hunters—in particular, archers. They would most likely care about Daniel's difficulties in the hunt and be familiar with terms like "tree stand" and "six-point buck." Of course, the larger audience of non-hunters might also be interested in learning why the deer escaped.

After you have chosen a topic and audience, consider what you want to accomplish with your essay: to inform, entertain, or persuade. Now try to communicate your causes or effects clearly, and be sure to make some overall point.

The Assignment

Write an essay of roughly 500 to 750 words to explain either the causes for helping someone in need (it could be a stranger or someone you know), or the effects. Provide three or four of *either* the causes *or* the effects. Be sure to begin each main example with a topic sentence.

Alternative Assignments

Here are several more cause or effect writing options that may interest you. For any of the alternative assignments, be sure to do the following:

- Introduce each major cause or effect with a topic sentence.
- Arrange causes or effects by importance or time.
- Use connectors, especially in topic sentences.
- Develop examples with specific words, details, and explanations.

Business in Context:

Explain either the causes or effects of staying with a job you don't like. Provide three or four of *either* the causes *or* the effects. Arrange them by importance or time (first, second, third). For example, you might consider the job's influence in terms of further education, perhaps reinforcing your determination either to gain more knowledge in the same field or to change your field of study. You might consider the job in terms of your decision to travel (or not), or to move to your first apartment (or not). Be sure to begin each main point with a topic sentence.

Culture in Context:

Write an essay about the effects that a special place—the Rocky Mountains, the Atlantic coast, the Pacific coast—has had on you. You could illustrate this topic with personal examples and possibly arrange them from least to most important. Be careful not to simply tell about your last vacation; select significant effects, and focus them with a limiting statement.

Education in Context:

Consider the causes or effects of returning to college years after high school graduation. You could develop this topic with personal details and arrange them from least to most important. Remember to use connectors, especially in topic sentences.

Health Care in Context:

Write an essay that helps you understand a particular disease. What causes the illness, and what are its symptoms? Using the "they" voice, write an essay exploring either the causes or effects of this illness. Or if you know someone struggling with this disease, you could write the essay from a personal perspective. Online research could be helpful, at websites such as www.WebMD.com.

Science in Context:

Build a chain of causes or effects for global warming. For example, as the atmosphere heats up, glaciers and snowpacks in the mountains are melting; sea ice is retreating from the Arctic; hurricanes are gaining more force; deserts are expanding; flooding is increasing. Try focusing on just one piece of the larger chain of effects, showing how one effect can lead to another. For example, thinning sea ice shortens the polar bears' seal-hunting season. This reduces the polar bear population. However, because the remaining bears can't reach enough seals, they are more likely to scavenge in and around towns, causing problems for people. What might those problems be?

Consider either the causes or effects of regularly speeding on the highway. You could consider personal causes, such as repeatedly waking up late for school, or responding to stress by driving fast. Or you could consider the effects of fast driving on your car's wear, your own sense of peace, or other drivers' safety. Write an essay building a chain of causes or effects, linking one series of either causes or effects from beginning to end. Instead of using a personal experience, you could use the third-person "they" voice of general knowledge.

Discovering Ideas: Prewriting for Cause or Effect Essays

Remember that you will choose either causes *or* effects to write about. Brainstorming for both will give you a better idea of which will be more interesting to you and your audience. Also, you may choose a more personalized approach to your topic, using the "I" voice (as do both student models in this chapter), or you can use the third-person "they" voice of general knowledge, as in the professional model.

When you have chosen a topic, then, the next step is to explore both causes and effects before deciding which approach to focus on. Prewriting methods (see the online information for Chapter 2) can help you with ideas, and making a list works particularly well for this assignment. Below are lists of causes and effects for Daniel Hedge's paragraph on missing his target:

Causes	Effects
1. Cold weather	1. Disappointment
2. Placement of the tree stand	2. Blaming my bow
3. Movement of the buck	3. Pain from hitting the tree in frustration
4. Wind	4. No trophy or meat
5. Branches in the way	5. Friends razzing me
6. Nervousness spoiled aim	6. Considering using a rifle next time
7. Too little practice	7. Resolving to practise more

After thinking through both lists, Daniel decided that he was more interested in telling about the causes for missing his buck.

JOURNAL / BLOG ENTRY 27.2

Tell why you chose your topic and focus. What is your purpose, who is your audience, and why would readers be interested in your focus? Will you write with the "I" or "they" voice?

FEEDBACK *In small groups or online, discuss the advantages of using an "I" versus a "they" voice. What effects can each have on a piece of writing?*

Organizing Cause or Effect Essays

Having decided on causes as his focus, Daniel Hedge next needed to decide which ones he might not need.

~~1. Cold weather~~

2. Placement of the tree stand

3. Movement of the buck

4. Wind

5. Branches in the way

6. ~~Nervousness spoiled aim~~

7. Too little practice

After deciding that neither nervousness nor the temperature were strong causes, Daniel cut them from his list and arranged his remaining causes **chronologically** (as they occurred in time), saving the overall cause—lack of practice—for the expanded thought in his final sentence.

1. Placement of tree stand

2. Movement of the buck

3. Wind

4. Branches in the way

5. Too little practice: expanded thought in concluding sentence

Your causes or effects may be best arranged **chronologically**, as above, or by **order of importance**, as are the effects in this chapter's other student model, "Driven to Drive in Midlife" (pages 365–366).

Write a clear thesis statement that announces the topic, limits it, and indicates either causes or effects. You can state "causes" or "effects" outright or choose similar words. For causes, try *reasons, explanations, problems, factors,* or phrases like *to bring about* or *to create.* For effects, try *results, outcome, consequences,* or a phrase like *what follows* or *what happens.*

Finally, take a few minutes to review the list of transitions and other connectors (Chapter 20) before you begin drafting.

HINT

Sometimes a chronological arrangement is also organized by order of importance.

HINT

See Chapter 20 for more on transitions and other connectors.

JOURNAL / BLOG ENTRY 27.3

Write out or type your working thesis statement underlining the topic once and the limiting statement twice, and circle or box the causes or effects words. Now, using the model above as an example, list six or seven causes or effects; then cut the less promising ones. Keep only three or four main points. How will you arrange these points: chronologically, by importance, or both?

Drafting Cause or Effect Essays

Moving into your first draft, keep the following points in mind:

1. You may need to pause as you work through your essay to do more prewriting in a separate file or on separate paper. Don't be discouraged when ideas stop flowing—or start flowing in another direction; take action.

2. Refer to your thesis statement frequently. It will keep you on track.

3. When you find one cause or effect leading to another, you are establishing a smooth transition of ideas.

4. Keep asking the question "What do I mean by what I have just written?" Develop your topic points with specific, detailed examples and explanations.

5. Complete all thoughts so that the reader can see the cause/effect relationship. Notice that in "Driven to Drive in Midlife," Nahid tells us in her final effect example that people can learn anything (effect) if they believe in themselves (cause).

JOURNAL / BLOG ENTRY 27.4

After finishing your first rough draft, reread it, and highlight your topic sentences with a marker or your word-processing program's highlighter. Now underline the <u>topic</u> (cause or effect) of each topic sentence once and the <u>limiting statement</u> twice, and circle or box any connecting words. Then copy these marked topic sentences, and submit them to your instructor. What parts of the draft do you like most and least? Answer in a paragraph.

FEEDBACK *Look at one or more classmates' drafts, and respond to the following two questions: Do the topic sentences name and limit each example? Are connecting words used effectively?*

HINT

For more detailed suggestions for revising all drafts, turn to Chapter 21.

Revising Cause or Effect Essays

As you revise your cause or effect first draft, both you and your peer reviewer can use the following checklist as a guide:

PEER REVIEW CHECKLIST FOR REVISING CAUSE OR EFFECT ESSAYS

☐ Has the writer used three or four causes *or* effects and given each one its own paragraph?

Reviewer Comment: _____

_____

☐ Has the writer arranged examples (causes or effects) by importance, or by time?

Reviewer Comment: _____

_____

☐ Has the writer included topic sentences that name and limit each main example?

Reviewer Comment: _____

_____

☐ Are the causes or effects developed with specific words, details, and explanations?

Reviewer Comment: _____

_____

☐ Has the writer used transitions and other connectors, especially in topic sentences, so that the causes or effects lead from one to the next?

Reviewer Comment: _____

_____

☐ Does the concluding sentence rename the topic and make a point?

Reviewer Comment: _____

_____

Being able to identify causes and accurately predict effects are powerful skills. They will help you make good decisions in any context—in the voting booth, behind the wheel of a car, and on the essay exam. You will consider carefully the effects (and chain of effects) of choosing classes and eventually a specific program of study, of exploring possible careers, applying for jobs, and even picking a particular interview outfit. Furthermore, you will find yourself writing about cause and effect in many of your college classes. For example, in chemistry, you will discuss the effects of various experiments in lab reports. And a psychology exam question might ask you to discuss the causes or effects of post-traumatic stress disorder.

Chapter Summary

1. Thinking about causes and effects helps us to understand why things happen and to solve problems.

2. Events are often complex, rarely having only one cause or effect.

3. Writers often decide which causes or effects are most important based on their topic, interest, and knowledge, as well as the interest of readers.

4. Writers should develop points with detailed examples and explanations.

5. A thesis statement for a cause or effect essay should name and focus the topic, predicting either causes or effects.

6. Each major cause or effect should be introduced with a topic sentence.

7. Sentences—especially topic sentences—benefit from transition words and other connectors.

8. Examples can be based on personal experience ("I") or general knowledge ("they").

9. Writing about causes or effects can be organized by time or order of importance.

10. Writing is not complete until it has been revised and carefully edited.

Exploring Similarities and Differences (Comparison and Contrast)

28

In a paragraph, discuss the similarities and differences between playing a game just for fun and playing the same game competitively.

What Are We Trying to Achieve and Why?

What is similar about the two pictures on the previous page? They each show people playing tug-of-war, yes, but what other similarities are there? In both photos, the groups compete outdoors on the grass, and the sun is casting shadows. Everyone is dressed casually.

But what differences can you find? One group consists of male teens, dressed similarly in black shirts and boots, struggling mightily to win their competition. The other group is younger, a mix of male and female children dressed in a variety of colours and wearing sneakers. They look directly at the camera, and they are all smiling. Looking more closely, you can see even more differences.

Whenever we notice similarities or differences between people, places, events, objects, or ideas, we are **comparing** or **contrasting**. This is the focus of Chapter 28.

LINKING TO PREVIOUS EXPERIENCE

What You Already Know about Comparing and Contrasting

Comparing and contrasting are basic acts of communication, and we use them often. When trying to describe a Bichon Frisé to a friend who has never seen one, you might say it looks like an untrimmed Toy Poodle. Or your boyfriend might remind you of Ryan Reynolds; your girlfriend might resemble Scarlett Johansson. Furthermore, when describing a family member, you might say your brother is a slug (lazy and slimy-looking, hiding in a dark room) or your sister is a princess (spoiled, demanding, and self-centred). Comparing and contrasting allow us to communicate better by linking the known to the unknown.

JOURNAL / BLOG ENTRY 28.1

Write about two things you have recently compared or contrasted with each other, such as movies, cars, people, places, or events. What points did you compare or contrast? Why did you make the comparison/contrast: to inform, entertain, or persuade someone? Did you succeed in your purpose?

FEEDBACK *In pairs or small groups, share your writing. Then present the topic for a purpose other than what was originally intended for this work. That is, if your original purpose was to inform, try presenting your piece to entertain or to persuade your listeners. Discuss which approach is more effective, given your specific topic.*

Developing Skills in Comparing and Contrasting

Comparing and contrasting items or subjects is a very common way to understand them better. The process is based on a developmental concept called "scaffolding." When we learn new things, we must build upon what we already know. In this way the things we already know provide a scaffold to help us reach new levels of learning. The technique of comparing and contrasting can be used as the overall structure of an entire essay, but compare and contrast paragraphs can be used in any essay to help explain a new concept by comparing it to a better-known one. In this way, you are providing scaffolding for your readers to help them understand new material.

The following activities will help you work with comparisons and contrasts:

1. Making a meaningful comparison or contrast
2. Making an interesting comparison or contrast
3. Developing topics thoroughly
4. Using transitions and other connectors

Making a Meaningful Comparison or Contrast

All writing that is easy to read has a clear purpose and point. The same holds true for your comparison or contrast essay. Without a clear idea of what you want to say, you risk ending up with a fuzzy outline like the following:

UNFOCUSED TOPIC SENTENCE

• Soccer and North American football are similar sports.
  - Soccer is played with a ball, and so is football.
  - Soccer is usually played outdoors, and so is football.
  - Soccer games are won by scoring points, and so are football games.
  - Soccer has defensive and offensive moves, and so does football.
  - Soccer requires running, and so does football.
  - Soccer players must be fast and agile, and so must football players.

Such a list would likely produce an unfocused essay, one difficult to write and more difficult to read. Here are several more effective approaches:

FOCUSED TOPIC SENTENCES

• Soccer requires more agility than football.
• Football players are more prone to injury than soccer players.
• Soccer has far more fans worldwide than North American football.

In order to compare and contrast two topics, we need to ask questions to help us come up with valid and useful points of comparison. For example, in comparing the Black Death of 1348–1350 to the Spanish flu of 1918–1919, we might ask the following questions about each epidemic:

• How was it caused and spread?
• How many people did it kill?
• What were the lasting effects?

If you are content that the answers to your questions give you the material you need for comparison, then proceed with the essay. If the answers can't be found, or if they lead to more questions, then keep researching until your material is solid.

ACTIVITY 28.1 WORKING TOGETHER: Making a Meaningful Comparison or Contrast

For each topic below, brainstorm with group members to find several similarities and differences. Together, come up with three statements that focus the topic by making a point; write these statements in the space provided. Assign each group member one of the points. Based on your point, each of you will write a focused thesis statement that also indicates your approach—comparison *or* contrast.

EXAMPLE:

TOPIC: iPad versus MacBook

Unfocused topic sentence: iPads have internet access, and so do MacBooks.
Points that could be made:

A. _People who have iPads do not have webcams, but people with MacBooks do._

B. _iPads are more expensive than MacBooks._

C. _iPads have longer lasting batteries than MacBooks._

Possible topic sentence: _Although the iPad is more expensive and less versatile than the MacBook, its portability and endurance could make it more popular._

HINT

For more on topic sentences, see Chapter 20.

1. **TOPIC:** Adults in their thirties versus teenagers

   Unfocused topic sentence: Most adults in their thirties are different from teenagers.

   Points that could be made:

   a. _____

   b. _____

   c. _____

   Possible topic sentence:_____

   _____

2. **TOPIC:** Sharks versus grizzly bears

   Unfocused topic sentence: Sharks and grizzly bears can grow to be huge.

   Points that could be made:

   a. _____

   b. _____

   c. _____

   Possible topic sentence: _____

   _____

Making an Interesting Comparison or Contrast

Once you have found a meaningful topic, be sure to ask which is the more interesting treatment of the topic—comparison or contrast? The answer, of course, depends on your (and your audience's) interest in and knowledge about the subject. When you have a strong point to make, you are more likely to choose the more interesting treatment.

To liven up your topic, do the unexpected: if two points seem similar, contrast them; if they seem different, compare them. Looking at the hurricane/tornado topic below, you might be tempted to focus on the similarities between these two clearly destructive forces of nature. But if you wanted to argue that hurricanes are more dangerous, then your purpose would lead you to contrast them.

DIFFERENCES		SIMILARITIES
HURRICANE	*TORNADO*	*HURRICANES AND TORNADOES*
Wide path of destruction	*Narrow path of destruction*	*Cause destruction, death*
Forms over ocean	*Forms over land*	*High winds*
Lasts for hours	*Lasts for minutes*	*Can be unpredictable*
Fewer occur	*More occur*	*Researched by scientists*
Less powerful winds	*More powerful winds*	*Inspire fear*

TOPIC SENTENCE: *While tornadoes cause much damage and loss of life, hurricanes are far more dangerous.*

HINT

Use the preceding hurricane/tornado example as a model for Activity 28.2.

ACTIVITY 28.2 Making an Interesting Comparison or Contrast

Choose one of the following topic pairs. On separate paper, list their similarities and differences. Choose the more interesting approach, and then write a topic sentence indicating comparison or contrast and your focus.

Topic pairs:

Kwanzaa/Christmas	Tough boss/easy boss	Tar sand pollution/ offshore oil spill
Volcano/forest fire	Spiderman/Batman (or any two superheroes)	VW bug/Toyota Prius (or any two cars)
Your children or siblings: oldest/youngest	Vacation in Hawaii/ the Caribbean (or any two holiday destinations)	Any two popular singers or bands

Once you have your topic sentence ready, use your list to choose your supporting points. Choose the best three ideas and arrange them from weakest to strongest. Now write a paragraph comparing or contrasting your two topics.

Developing Topics Thoroughly

HINT

See Chapters 20 and 25 for more on developing examples.

To make comparisons and contrasts interesting, you should explain them clearly and develop them with detailed, layered examples. For instance, to develop several points of contrast from the hurricane/tornado example on the preceding page, we could list the points below and then add some second-level examples:

HURRICANE:

- Main example: wide path of destruction
- Second-level example (becomes more specific): In 2005, Hurricane Katrina devastated the Gulf Coast of the United States from Louisiana to Florida, leaving almost 1300 kilometres of destruction in its wake. Katrina put 400 000 people out of work and killed 1836.

TORNADO:

- Main example: narrow path of destruction
- Second-level example (becomes more specific): Most tornadoes travel only a few miles before they lose their force and ascend back into the clouds. Their path of destruction is seldom more than two kilometres wide, and tornadoes often leave structures standing, seeming to jump over them. The Regina tornado of 1912 was the worst in Canadian history; it killed 28 people and injured hundreds.

ACTIVITY 28.3 Explaining Points Completely

In the following student paragraph, the author has listed three main points (underlined) to explain some differences between office and railroad work. Read this selection closely, and then (in the space provided) write out several second-level examples that the author has used to develop each of his three main points.

A Way of Life

Office workers have a safe, cushy job compared with railroad workers like me. For one, the "weather" in our work spaces is far different. White-collar employees may have to "brave the elements" in their drive to work, but once there, they enjoy controlled climates: heat in the winter, air conditioning in the summer. In contrast, when I reach my outside "office," I deal with rough conditions. The winter brings snow, sleet, and a sub-zero wind chill that leaves my fingers numb. Then the summer brings 35-degrees Celsius days, rain, humidity, stinging insects, and sweat dripping into my eyes. While the most offensive chemical an office worker may encounter is the aftershave of an elevator companion, I am exposed to dangerous material almost daily. Often while working under a railcar, I've found myself wondering, "What *is* that slimy green goo just inches from my face?" Besides weather and chemicals, the greatest difference between office and railroad jobs is in our equipment. The white-collar employee's equipment hazards might be losing a computer file or pinching a finger in the copier. In contrast, my equipment can be lethal. My bolt cutter can lop off a finger; my arc welder generates thousands of Celsius degrees of heat and throws molten steel everywhere; my hydraulic jacks raise a boxcar off a track; and trains roar by at 110 kilometres per hour—1.5 metres away from me. However, despite the harsher working conditions, I enjoy being outdoors—watching the seasons change, seeing the animals, feeling wind on my face—and would not choose to be trapped for the rest of my life in an office.

—*Shane Smith*

1. Second-level examples for point about weather:

   Office job: _____

   Railroad job: _____

   _____

2. Second-level examples for point about chemicals:

   Office job: _____

   Railroad job: _____

   _____

3. Second-level examples for point about equipment:

   Office job: _____

   Railroad job: _____

   _____

HINT

For more on organizing paragraphs, see Chapters 2 and 20.

Using Transitions and Other Connectors

Transitions (like the ones below) and other connectors are important in a comparison or contrast essay, regardless of its organization. They signal the switches between two or more topics.

TRANSITIONS FOR COMPARING			
also	both	like	resembling
as	in the same way	likewise	similarly

TRANSITIONS FOR CONTRASTING			
after all	even though	nevertheless	still
although	however	on the contrary	though
but	in contrast	on the other hand	unlike
difference	in spite of	otherwise	whereas

ACTIVITY 28.4 Using Transitions and Other Connectors

Complete each sentence with a suitable transitional word or other connector.

1. Hermione Granger, _____ her creator, J. K. Rowling, is strong-willed and independent.

2. There may be as many as a million sperm whales left in the world's oceans, _____ with the humpbacks, which number only 20 000.

3. _____, contestants on the reality show *Survivor* ignore the ocean filled with food and instead chase rats with sticks.

4. MySpace has taken steps to protect young people; _____ , they are still not safe from the predators who use the site.

5. Vincent Van Gogh barely made a living in his own time, _____ not long ago one of his paintings sold for $82.5 million.

6. While insurance rates for teens are expensive, many older adults _____ find themselves forced to pay high rates.

Learning from a Student Model: A Contrast Paragraph

HINT

See explanation and illustration of the **block method** on page 387.

Read the following student model closely, noticing in particular the writer's clear focus in her **topic sentence**, her well-linked **subtopic sentence**, her arrangement of major points by **importance**, her overall arrangement of the paragraph by the **block method**, and her **development** of examples through **specific words** and **detailed explanations**.

Worlds Apart

As a home-schooled student through high school, I am finding college to be a very different experience. While I was home-schooled, the workload was relatively light; I could complete most assignments in four hours a day. My parents chose the curriculum and organized my schedule, but they expected me to do most work on my own. If I had problems, then they would help. Unfortunately, I had no say in my routine. My parents expected me to be in the living room, dressed and ready, by 9:00 every morning, 180 days a year. Another downside to home-schooling was that I saw few people daily. Although I had many friends, it wasn't the same as hurrying through corridors filled with students talking and laughing on their way to classes. Now imagine how different from high school college is for me. First, the workload is greater. I am taking 15 credit hours and studying almost 40 hours a week. At times, it seems overwhelming, but now I have more help than my parents could offer. Professors make difficult subjects easier by meeting one-on-one and encouraging study groups. Also, the Learning Commons offers support with math and writing. I'm still an independent learner, but college provides opportunities to collaborate. In addition, I now control my own schedule. If I don't want classes every day, it's up to me. But the greatest and most enjoyable change from high school is all the new people! This year I have met students from a range of backgrounds with a variety of world views. I am fascinated by this diversity. I loved my home-schooling, and it was right for me at the time; but now I look forward to learning everything my new world has to offer.

—Katherine Priest

THINKING ABOUT THE STUDENT MODEL

1. What two important points do we learn from the topic sentence?

2. What point does Katherine make in her last sentence?

3. What four points does the author discuss in relation to high school and then college?

4. Copy each of the subtopic sentences, and underline the <u>main point (example)</u> once and the <u>statement</u> about it twice. Circle the (connectors) transitions, repeat words, synonyms, and pronouns.

5. Name three ways to further develop any major point in this paragraph. Consider active verbs, specific words, sensory details, revealing thoughts and emotions, comparisons or contrasts, and further explanation.

HINT

See explanation and illustration of the **point-by-point method** on page 387.

Learning from a Professional Model: A Comparison–Contrast Essay

*The article that follows is an example of **point-by-point** arrangement with Holly Dressel comparing Canada's health care system to that of the United States. Note her categories for comparison. This article first appeared in* YES! Magazine *in August 2006 and was adapted from her book* Who Killed the Queen? The Story of a Community Hospital and How to Fix Public Health Care, *published by McGill-Queen's University Press.*

Has Canada Got the Cure?

BY HOLLY DRESSEL

1 Should the United States implement a more inclusive, publicly funded health care system? That's a big debate throughout the country. But even as it rages, most Americans are unaware that the United States is the only country in the developed world that doesn't already have a fundamentally public—that is, tax-supported—health care system.

2 That means that the United States has been the unwitting control subject in a 40-year, worldwide experiment comparing the merits of private versus public health care funding. For the people living in the United States, the results of this experiment with privately funded health care have been grim. The United States now has the most expensive health care system on earth and, despite remarkable technology, the general health of the U.S. population is lower than in most industrialized countries. Worse, Americans' mortality rates—both general and infant—are shockingly high.

DIFFERENT PATHS

3 The United States spends far more per capita on health care than any comparable country. In fact, the gap is so enormous that a recent University of California, San Francisco, study estimates that the United States would save over $161 billion every year in paperwork alone if it switched to a single-payer system like Canada's.[1] These billions of dollars are not abstract amounts deducted from government budgets; they come directly out of the pockets of people who are sick.

4 The year 2000 marked the beginning of a crucial period, when international trade rules, economic theory, and political action had begun to fully reflect the belief in the superiority of private, as opposed to public, management, especially in the United States. By that year the U.S. health care system had undergone what has been called "the health management organization revolution."

[1]Professor James Kahn, UCSF, quoted in *Harper's Magazine,* "Harper's List," Feb. 2006.

U.S. government figures show that medical care costs have spiked since 2000, with total spending on prescriptions nearly doubling.[2]

INFANT MORTALITY

Infant mortality rates, which reflect the health of the mother and her access to pre- 5 natal and postnatal care, are considered one of the most reliable measures of the general health of a population. Today, U.S. government statistics rank Canada's infant mortality rate of 4.7 per thousand 23rd out of 225 countries, in the company of the Netherlands, Luxembourg, Australia, and Denmark. The U.S. is 43rd—in the company of Croatia and Lithuania, below Taiwan and Cuba.

All the countries surrounding Canada or above it in the rankings have tax- 6 supported health care systems. The countries surrounding the United States and below have mixed systems or are, in general, extremely poor in comparison to the United States and the other G8 industrial powerhouses.

There are no major industrialized countries near the United States in the 7 rankings. The closest is Italy, at 5.83 infants dying per thousand, but it is still ranked five places higher.[3]

In the United States, infant mortality rates are 7.1 per 1,000, the highest in 8 the industrialized world—much higher than some of the poorer states in India, for example, which have public health systems in place, at least for mothers and infants. Among the inner-city poor in the United States, more than 8 percent of mothers receive no prenatal care at all before giving birth.

OVERALL U.S. MORTALITY

We would have expected to see steady decreases in deaths per thousand in the mid- 9 twentieth century, because so many new drugs and procedures were becoming available. But neither the Canadian nor the American mortality rate declined much; in fact, Canada's leveled off for an entire decade, throughout the 1960s. This was a period in which private care was increasing in Canadian hospitals, and the steady mortality rates reflect the fact that most people simply couldn't afford the new therapies that were being offered. However, beginning in 1971, the same year that Canada's Medicare was fully applied, official statistics show that death rates suddenly plummeted, maintaining a steep decline to their present rate.

In the United States, during the same period, overall mortality rates also 10 dropped, reflecting medical advances. But they did not drop nearly so precipitously as those in Canada after 1971. But given that the United States is the richest country on earth, today's overall mortality rates are shockingly high, at 8.4 per thousand, compared to Canada's 6.5.

VIVE LA DIFFÉRENCE!

Genetically, Canadians and Americans are quite similar. Our health habits, too, 11 are very much alike—people in both countries eat too much and exercise too little. And, like the United States, there is plenty of inequality in Canada, too. In terms of health care, that inequality falls primarily on Canadians in isolated communities, particularly Native groups, who have poorer access to medical care and are exposed to greater environmental contamination. The only major difference

---

[2]National Health Expenditure Data, www.cms.hhs.gov/NationalHealthExpendData/downloads/tables.pdf

[3]CIA World Fact Book. www.cia.gov/cia/publications/factbook/rankorder/2091rank.html

between the two countries that could account for the remarkable disparity in their infant and adult mortality rates, as well as the amount they spend on health care, is how they manage their health care systems.

12   The facts are clear: Before 1971, when both countries had similar, largely privately funded health care systems, overall survival and mortality rates were almost identical. The divergence appeared with the introduction of the single-payer health system in Canada.

13   The solid statistics amassed since the 1970s point to only one conclusion: like it or not, believe it makes sense or not, publicly funded, universally available health care is simply the most powerful contributing factor to the overall health of the people who live in any country. And in the United States, we have got the bodies to prove it.

THINKING ABOUT THE MODEL

1. Comment on the introduction: hook, development, and focus. Where is the thesis statement located?

2. List the connecting words and phrases used within and between the paragraphs. Would you rate the paragraphs in this essay as smoothly connected? Why or why not?

3. Comment on one specific example that helps you understand some point of contrast.

4. If *you* were comparing and contrasting the Canadian and American health care systems, what other points would you mention—and why?

5. Comment on the conclusion to the essay: Is body count the best measure of the overall health of a nation? Why do you think the Americans are so resistant to publicly funded health care? Do you think they would change their minds if they knew the results of the funding experiment they've been a part of for forty years?

LO28.2 # Writing a Comparison or Contrast Essay

Audience and Purpose

HINT

For more on audience, see Chapter 2.

What point do you want to make about your topic, and who do you want to tell? Shane Smith and Katherine Priest, who wrote this chapter's student models, were both writing to let readers know more about their lives. In writing his paragraph, Shane realized that despite working in conditions many people would not want to face, he still prefers his outdoor job to an office job. While valuing her home-schooled K–12 education, Katherine found that she was ready for a change. The topic you choose can give you, too, a chance to reflect on your life or on the world around you. Identifying your readers will help you choose interesting points and decide how much you need to explain.

Your key purpose is to communicate information, but you may do so in a way that entertains. What you write may also move readers to think differently or even take action.

The Assignment

Write an essay of roughly 500 to 750 words that compares *or* contrasts two people, groups, places, events, objects, or ideas. **People**, for example, could include family members, coaches, teachers, employers, significant others, church leaders, politicians, movie stars, athletes, criminals, or soldiers. **Groups** could include sports teams, hunters, anglers, bands, choirs, youth groups, motorcycle clubs, subcultures (such as Goths, skinheads, punks, skateboarders, gamers), and/or your friends. **Places** might be cities, outdoor locations (such as parks, mountains, beaches, prairies, deserts, wetlands, swamps), space locations (such as the moon, planets, sun), and imaginary places (such as Hogwarts or Middle Earth). While writers often develop their work with both comparison and contrast, for this essay, choose one or the other. Then decide which method of overall organization to use: **block** or **point-by-point**. Be sure to begin with a focused thesis statement that indicates comparison or contrast. Also, conclude with a restatement of the thesis, a summary of the main points of comparison, and possibly introduce a new point not considered in the essay.

HINT

For help choosing a method of organization, see page 387.

Alternative Assignments

Here are several more comparison or contrast writing options that may interest you. For any of these alternative assignments, be sure to do the following:

- Pre-write on both similarities and differences before choosing either.

- Have a reason for your comparison or contrast; make it clear in your introduction and your conclusion.

- Develop each topic equally with specific words, details, and explanations.

- Use transitions and other connectors.

Business in Context:

Compare or contrast two jobs that you have had. They could be part-time, full-time, good, bad, temporary, permanent, household work, garden work, or car maintenance. Use either the block method of organization or work point-by-point. The key is to choose two jobs for meaningful comparison or contrast and develop them thoroughly.

Culture in Context:

In the left-hand photograph on the next page, Faith Marie and Charlie are choosing their pumpkins for Halloween. Although he is not in the picture, their father is preparing a lesson for their Sunday church school. In contrast, their cousin Emma, shown in the right-hand photograph, is celebrating her Bat Mitzvah. They are all part of a multi-cultural family. What do you think the cousins have in common, and what makes them different?

Education in Context:

Compare educational stages that a child goes through, such as preschool and kindergarten, or elementary and high school. Be specific with examples of the different stages in your subtopic sentences.

Health Care in Context:

Compare or contrast hospital care and home care, considering such aspects as nursing care, visitors, meal preparation, noise, and stress.

Science in Context:

Compare or contrast your attitude toward conservation with that of a classmate, friend, parent, teacher, or celebrity. Remember that transitions, or connectors, will help to link the differences or similarities.

Technology in Context:

Compare or contrast two objects, such as cars and bicycles, washers and dryers, DVD players and MP3 players. You could consider how to operate two objects, or their technological complexity, or their functions, for example. Be sure to develop your points thoroughly with details and examples.

HINT

Refer to clustering and listing as prewriting strategies in the online section for Chapter 2.

Discovering Ideas: Prewriting for Comparison or Contrast Essays

After you have settled on a topic, you need to focus it and find something to say about it. A cluster like the one below as a basis for the "Worlds Apart" model on page 381 could help you find your focus and build your list of similarities and differences.

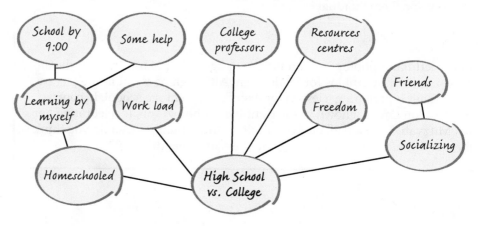

Or you could list both similarities and differences:

DIFFERENCES		SIMILARITIES
HIGH SCHOOL	*COLLEGE*	*HIGH SCHOOL AND COLLEGE*
Working alone	*Working more with others*	*Both offer help with work*
Easy work	*Hard work*	*Both require work*
Less freedom	*More freedom*	*Both have some freedom*
Fewer friends	*More social life*	*Both offer social life*
Fewer activities	*More activities*	*Both have activities*
Living room	*College campus*	*Both have a study area*
Food close by	*Trips to cafeteria*	*Both have food available*
Security with parents	*Uncertainty with strangers*	*Both have people present*

Katherine decided that differences were more interesting than similarities for her topic, so she chose her four most important points, and then moved on to selecting her overall arrangement.

As you think through topic possibilities, be open to less obvious choices. Picking topics that you are familiar with—such as two family members or two cars you have owned—can work well. However, you might surprise yourself and your reader by choosing topics a bit out of the ordinary.

JOURNAL / BLOG ENTRY 28.2

Using the previous prewriting patterns as examples of either clustering or listing, write similarities and differences for the paired topic you have selected. Which will lead to the more interesting paper for you and a target audience: comparing or contrasting the two? Who are you writing for, and why would they want to read your paper? How will you focus your topic enough to cover it in an essay of the required length?

Organizing Comparison or Contrast Essays

Your last major decision before writing a first draft is to pick an overall method of organizing your topics: either block or point-by-point.

- **Block method:** State all your points about one topic in one paragraph, and begin a second paragraph to discuss the same points about the second topic.
- **Point-by-point method:** State one point about your two topics as a pair in one paragraph. Then move to the next paragraph to develop the second point about your two topics as a pair. Finally use this same format for your third and any subsequent points.

HINT

Katherine used the block method in "Worlds Apart" (page 381).

Holly Dressel used the point-by-point method in "Has Canada Got the Cure?" (pages 382–384).

The following outlines show how this chapter's models use each method:

BLOCK: "WORLDS APART"	POINT BY POINT: "HAS CANADA GOT THE CURE?"
High school	**Different Paths**
1. Learning on her own	1. United States
2. Workload	2. Canada
3. Freedom	**Infant Mortality**
4. Meeting people (most important point)	1. United States
	2. Canada
College	**Overall Mortality** (most important point)
1. Learning with others	1. United States
2. Workload	2. Canada
3. Freedom	
4. Meeting people (most important point)	

With both methods of organizing, it is common to arrange major points by **order of importance** (as these models do), though occasionally space and time arrangements can work.

JOURNAL / BLOG ENTRY 28.3

Write out your working thesis statement, underlining the <u>topic</u> once and the <u>limiting statement</u> twice. Now, write out your working outline, using either the block or point-by-point arrangement, including a topic sentence for each major point. Are your main points—within the overall arrangement—listed in order of importance?

FEEDBACK *With a partner, discuss the order and importance of each of your sub-topic sentences. Do both of you agree on the order? If not, where do you differ?*

HINT

After you have outlined your essay, take a few minutes to review the list of transitions and other connectors (see page 380) before you begin drafting.

Drafting Comparison or Contrast Essays

Moving into your first draft, keep the following points in mind:

1. For this assignment, choose either comparison or contrast, not both.
2. Considering all points for each topic, develop each point with at least one detailed example.
3. Use transitions and other connectors with care, especially between major points.
4. In the introduction, write a focused thesis statement and outline the main points for comparison; in the conclusion, restate your thesis, summarize the main points and introduce a new idea.

JOURNAL / BLOG ENTRY 28.4

After finishing your first draft, reread it, highlight your topic sentences with a marker or your computer's highlighting feature, and circle any connecting words.

FEEDBACK *Exchange drafts with at least one classmate. What parts of his or her draft do you like most and least—and why? Answer in a paragraph. What parts of your own draft did your classmate(s) like most and least?*

Revising Comparison or Contrast Essays

As you begin revising your comparison or contrast first draft, you and your peer reviewer could use the following checklist as a guide:

PEER REVIEW CHECKLIST FOR REVISING COMPARISON OR CONTRAST ESSAYS

☐ Does the thesis statement name and limit the topic, predicting a comparison or contrast essay?

Reviewer Comment: _____

_____

☐ Is the writer consistent with overall organization: block or point-by-point?

Reviewer Comment: _____

_____

☐ Has the writer arranged the points by importance?

Reviewer Comment: _____

_____

☐ Has the writer used effective topic sentences?

Reviewer Comment: _____

_____

☐ Has the writer used transitions and other connectors, especially in topic sentences?

Reviewer Comment: _____

_____

☐ Does the conclusion restate the thesis, summarize the main points of comparison or contrast, and introduce a new idea?

Reviewer Comment: _____

_____

HINT

For more detailed suggestions for revising all drafts, turn to Chapter 21.

LINKING TO FUTURE EXPERIENCE

You will find yourself comparing and contrasting within other patterns and in assignments across the curriculum. When writing a definition paragraph, try contrasting various definitions of a word. And when writing persuasively, explore what is similar between two seemingly opposite points of view. In a music history class, you could be asked to identify key differences between Romantic and Classical composers or to note what's similar in two pieces of music written 400 years apart. In a web design class, you might need to name differences among various platforms or browsers. An economics assignment might ask you to compare the likelihoods of various stocks rising under certain circumstances. Writing about similarities and differences will help you better understand relationships between concepts and more effectively express them in upcoming papers and exams.`

HINT

For more on definition, see Chapter 30, and for more on persuasion, see Chapter 31.

Chapter Summary

1. Comparison and contrast involve discovering the similarities and differences between two people, places, events, objects, or ideas.

2. Using comparison and contrast, we explore and evaluate unfamiliar things in the light of those we know.

3. Comparison should be meaningful and interesting and made between two topics that are similar enough to be compared.

4. Block and point-by-point are two overall arrangement patterns for comparison and contrast.

5. Transitional words and other connectors help readers move from one topic to another.

6. Points are frequently arranged by order of importance, but occasionally by time or space.

7. Topic sentences help readers shift from one main point to the next.

8. The thesis statement should name and focus the topic and predict either a comparison or a contrast.

9. The conclusion should begin with a transition word or phrase (such as "In conclusion"), restate the thesis, and summarize the compared or contrasted points.

10. Writing is not complete until it has been revised and carefully edited.

Creating and Explaining Groups (Classification)

Have you ever had to plan a major move? How did you organize your belongings? Consider how your system (or lack thereof) affected the ease of unpacking. How is this process similar to writing?

What Are We Trying to Achieve and Why?

The photo on the previous page is an image that most of us are familiar with—moving day. After much work, the couple rests for a few minutes before plunging into the next phase, the unpacking. Where will they put all their belongings, and what will they do with all those boxes? In preparation for this move, the couple labelled each box according to the room where its contents will go ("Kitchen," "Living Room," and so forth), and each box was then placed in that space. In doing this, they chose a single organizing principle (SOP), classifying (or grouping) by rooms to sort their possessions. This will make unpacking far easier than if they had just jumbled everything into random boxes and stacked them all in one room.

In this chapter, we will practise the same principle: grouping things according to an SOP and then developing our groups with detailed explanations and specific examples.

LINKING TO PREVIOUS EXPERIENCE

What You Already Know about Classifying

We group things every day, seldom paying much attention to the process. When we shop, for example, merchandise is organized into labelled groups, and we find items we need by category: spices and baking goods in one aisle, paper towels and serviettes in another. At home, we group many things: our clothes, music, sports equipment, kitchen utensils, and so forth. To find our way around places, we rely on classifying: in a city, we find sections (downtown or suburbs) and then neighbourhoods (the Danforth or the Annex) and finally individual residences (street and number); in an airport, we find the right terminal and gate; at a college, we find the right building, floor, and classroom. Separating items into groups based on an SOP helps us arrange our lives and solve many problems.

> **HINT**
>
> A single organizing principle, or SOP, is the method used to classify things.

JOURNAL / BLOG ENTRY 29.1

Tell about something in your life that you have classified, and include the SOP. For instance, if you organize your music into categories like classic rock, metal, and hip hop, your SOP would be musical style, not year of release or artist. What is your purpose in using this method of classification, and how does this way of grouping make your life easier?

LO29.1   Developing Skills in Classifying

Developmental psychologists know that classification is part of how we learn. Young children learn quite early the ability to group objects, like animals, together based on common features. As children grow, they learn more advanced forms of classification; for example, that all dogs are animals but not all animals are dogs.

This is called class inclusion. Whereas a process paragraph explains *how* something came to be and a cause and effect paragraph explains *why* something came to be, a classification paragraph explains *what* something is in relation to other things. Many essays can benefit from the inclusion of process paragraphs, as they help to define the topic under discussion.

The following activities will help you work with classifying:

1. Using a single organizing principle
2. Choosing an organizing principle
3. Developing topics
4. Completing the group

Using a Single Organizing Principle

To arrange items logically, we must have a rationale for grouping them, or a single organizing principle (SOP). In the photo of the menu board, how is the food organized? What is the menu's SOP? How do *you* find food items on a menu? To begin with a cup of soup, you would likely look at the appetizer section, and for a piece of pie, you would turn to desserts. The SOP of the usual order of food presentation is important because it helps you find what you want.

ACTIVITY 29.1 Using a Single Organizing Principle

The topics below are grouped by a single organizing principle. Write out the SOP in the space provided, and then place an X by the item in each group that does not belong.

EXAMPLE:

Topic: movies

Groups: __ *The Tale of Despereaux* __ *Ice Age* _X_ *The Bourne Ultimatum* __ *Shrek* __ *Toy Story*

SOP: *animated films* _____

1. **Topic:** weather

   Groups: __ tornadoes __ hurricanes __ blizzards __ thunderstorms __ winter

   SOP: _____

   _____

2. **Topic:** footwear

   Groups: __ running __ hiking __ Reeboks __ dancing __ gardening

   SOP: _____

3. **Topic:** art

   Groups: __ acrylics __ oils __ still life __ watercolours __ clay

   SOP: _____

4. **Topic:** energy sources

    Groups: __ oil __ solar __ geothermal __ hydroelectric __ wind

    SOP: _____

5. **Topic:** animals

    Groups: __ dogs __ cats __ whales __ apes __ Canada geese

    SOP: _____

Choosing a Single Organizing Principle

Sometimes the reason for grouping things is clear to just about everyone. For instance, the system of rating films as G, PG, R, and so on, depends largely on the level of sex, violence, and other "adult" themes. However, films can be classified in many other ways: by genre (comedy, action, romance, sci-fi), how much money they make, how much cultural impact they have, or even how well a person likes them. When you choose a topic, you may find that the SOP you apply to it depends on what you want to say about it and what you think an audience might want to hear.

ACTIVITY 29.2 WORKING TOGETHER: Choosing a Single
Organizing Principle

Discuss with group members what SOPs might be used for the topics below, and then write three possible SOPs for each.

EXAMPLE:

Topic: vacations

Possible organizing principles: a. *expense* _____

    b. _____ *place* _____ c. _____ *level of activity* _____

1. **Topic:** books

    Possible organizing principles: a._____

        b. _____ c. _____

2. **Topic:** parties

    Possible organizing principles: a. _____

        b. _____ c. _____

3. **Topic:** TV commercials

    Possible organizing principles: a. _____

        b. _____ c. _____

4. **Topic:** animals

    Possible organizing principles: a. _____

        b. _____ c. _____

Pick one topic and one SOP and brainstorm ideas for a paragraph on this topic. Use the SOP to create your topic sentence and pick three examples from your brainstorming to illustrate the SOP. Now write the paragraph. Don't forget to compose a concluding sentence.

Developing Topics

After you have chosen a topic and an SOP, you will then list three or four groups, developing them with detailed explanations and specific examples. For instance, choosing the topic of vacations from Activity 29.2, we might take the SOP "level of activity" and then develop three categories for it:

Level-of-Activity Categories for Vacations

1. **Intense action:** ski vacation—racing down the slopes at Whistler Mountain all day, eating out and partying at night, collapsing into bed late, and then hitting the slopes early the next morning.

2. **Moderate action:** beach—lying in the sun on the Yucatan Peninsula with a tray full of beverages at hand, slipping into the water from time to time to cool down, swimming a few strokes, and then rocking with the waves.

3. **Little action:** cruise—resting in a lounge chair on deck 10 of a Norwegian cruise ship, watching the sun set in the north Atlantic, thinking about going for that fourth meal of the day and then later falling into a whirlpool to relax for an early bedtime, planning on sleeping late.

ACTIVITY 29.3 Developing Topics

The following student-model paragraph classifies Ukrainian holidays based on the SOP of time, that is, when the holidays became part of the writer's cultural traditions. Under each major grouping (underlined in a subtopic sentence), note how the author has developed his points, and then write out several specific examples, details, and explanations the author has used.

Ukrainian Holidays

Ukrainian holidays, like those in most nations, did not all appear at the same time; they have come into the culture over many years. One of the oldest festivals in Ukraine is called Ivana Kupala, celebrated on July 7, a holiday for people to enjoy nature and water. People gather to picnic, swim in rivers, and build huge bonfires. Girls make flower garlands for their hair and sometimes float them in rivers to predict their fortunes in the coming year. To cleanse themselves for the year, people jump over the bonfires. The tradition began thousands of years ago when people believed that if they bathed in the river, as the sun god did, they would be purified. As time passed, Ukrainians started celebrating Christian holidays, such as Christmas and Easter. In Ukraine, Christmas is observed according to an older calendar on January 7. Traditionally on Christmas Eve, children would bring food to treat their parents; now the whole family gets together for a cozy dinner. From 1918 to 1991, Ukraine was part of the USSR, which banned religious holidays and made civil holidays more important. For one such holiday, New Year's Eve, people gather for an all-night party. At midnight, everyone greets the new year with fireworks and laughter. <u>The most recent holidays began when Ukraine gained freedom from the Soviet Union</u>. One of the most important of these is Independence Day, celebrated on August 24. The central streets of Kiev are closed to traffic, and bands appear on the square of the capital. This festival ends with colourful fireworks. Holidays, like those in Ukraine, reflect the culture of a people and are an important way to celebrate what matters most in their lives.

—*Sergey Kobzar*

1. Examples, details, and explanation for Ivana Kupala:

   _____

2. Examples, details, and explanation for Christian holidays:

   _____

3. Examples, details, and explanation for civil holidays:

   _____

4. Examples, details, and explanation for most recent holidays:

   _____

Pick your own favourite holiday and then brainstorm about why it is your favourite. From your brainstorming list, look for three examples that share a single organizing principle. For each example, come up with two details and one explanation to elaborate. Once you have your outline, write your own paragraph. Make sure that your organizing principle is clear in your topic sentence.

Completing the Group

There are topics to classify that are so familiar to people that they anticipate the writer's groupings. For instance, most people are aware of the major food groups and would wonder why a writer left out dairy products. If you choose a topic that is clearly "pre-classified," be sure to include all members of the group.

ACTIVITY 29.4 Completing the Group

The following is a list of the forty most famous people in the world, according to http://www.whoismorefamous.com. Using profession as the organizing principle, classify these people into their different professions (what they are famous for) and analyze which profession is most likely to produce famous people (number of famous people in each profession). Make note of any people you find difficult to classify and any SOPs you find difficult to define.

1.	Leonardo Da Vinci	8.	Michelangelo
2.	Michael Jackson	9.	Mother Teresa
3.	Albert Einstein	10.	William Shakespeare
4.	Abraham Lincoln	11.	Christopher Columbus
5.	Martin Luther King	12.	Ludwig van Beethoven
6.	Isaac Newton	13.	Vincent Van Gogh
7.	Walt Disney	14.	George Washington

15. Thomas Edison	28. Elizabeth Taylor
16. Benjamin Franklin	29. John Lennon
17. Napoleon	30. Alexander Graham Bell
18. Princess Diana	31. Mark Twain
19. Pablo Piccaso	32. Elvis Presley
20. John F. Kennedy	33. Aristotle
21. Mozart	34. Marilyn Monroe
22. Neil Armstrong	35. Michael Jordan
23. Charles Dickens	36. Tom Cruise
24. Mohammad Ali	37. Houdini
25. Cleopatra	38. Stephen Hawking
26. Bill Gates	39. Darth Vader
27. Gandhi	40. Clint Eastwood

Once you have classified all forty people, compare your groupings with a classmate. Are the groupings the same for both of you? How do you account for any differences?

Learning from a Student Model: A Classification Essay

The following essay of classification will help you understand how to write your own. Read it closely for organizational points (topic, subtopic, and concluding sentences and connectors) and development (detailed explanations and specific examples). Which group in the author's classification, if any, do you find the most useful for your own reading—and why?

Making the Most of Reading

1   Once people learn to read, they always know how, so why would they need to know more about the subject? The answer to this question is that just being able to read does not make people skilful readers, especially when they are faced with more difficult types of reading like assignments they find in college. Also, if you, like me, are reading in a new language, learning reading techniques can make the process easier. By recognizing some common patterns, such as time order, comparison–contrast, cause and effect, and listing, readers will be able to understand and remember even complicated information.

2   One common pattern in reading is time, or chronological, order. This pattern is used in telling stories but is also often used in giving instructions and in understanding how processes work. Clue words to help recognize this pattern are words like *then, when, next, after, since, later, awhile, earlier, eventually,* and *finally.* Dates and times also show time order. For example, reading, "On September 14, we were gathered in the living room when . . ." or "By 3 o'clock, we knew that something was wrong" is a good sign that you are reading a time order pattern.

3   Another easily recognized pattern of organization in reading is comparing and contrasting. When ideas are compared, the similarities are shown, and when ideas are contrasted, the differences are shown. Sometimes only a comparison or a contrast is made, but there may be both. For instance, a class in government might compare Stephen Harper's time as prime minister to that of Brian Mulroney. Clue words to comparing are *likewise, similarly, also, in the same way,* and *resembling.* Clue words for contrasting are words like *however, even though, on the other hand, yet,* and *in contrast.*

4   In addition to comparison and contrast as an organizational pattern is cause and effect. This pattern tells about what makes things happen. For instance, you might read about Chinese babies being adopted by many Westerners and find explanations for why this is occurring. This would be what is causing the adoptions. On the other hand, the article might instead tell about what happens to the adopted children or how the adoptions affect people in China. This would show the effects of the adoptions. Some clue words to signal causes and effects are *because, since, as a result, thus, so, consequently,* and *accordingly.*

5   Simple listing may be the most common pattern of organization in reading. This pattern is usually used when the author wants to explain a series of reasons or examples or to give supporting details. Sometimes the list has numbers or bullets (also known as acorns), and sometimes not. For example, a college pre-algebra class might list knowing basic skills like addition, subtraction, multiplication, division, fractions, negative numbers, and simple formulae as necessary knowledge before a student can pass on to college algebra. The simple series helps a reader focus on the information and remember the ideas. Some signal words for listing are *and, also, in addition, further, next,* and *last.*

6   The patterns I have listed are just some of the common ones that help people become better readers. Still, you may ask, why bother with learning this knowledge? I will tell you that before I took my reading class, I was struggling in much of my English reading. Even magazines and the newspaper seemed hard for me to understand. Additionally, my college textbooks were very difficult. However, now that I have finished the course and learned the patterns, I read more easily and remember more of what I read. Learning a little bit can help a lot.

—*Esther Cho*

THINKING ABOUT THE STUDENT MODEL

1. What two important points do we learn from the thesis statement? What is the writer's single organizing principle (SOP)?

2. Evaluate the body paragraphs. Comment on the topic sentences (including connecting words) and development (by specific examples).

3. Evaluate the conclusion. Comment on the topic sentence, summary, and expanded thought.

4. How are the body paragraphs sequenced (by time or importance)? What words help you see this method of organization?

5. Discuss how three of the writer's specific phrases or clauses help you picture the main examples discussed in each body paragraph.

Learning from a Professional Model:
A Classification Essay

In the web-exclusive Newsweek *article "A Healthy Drink? Try Plain Water," Temma Ehrenfeld discusses claims made by manufacturers of certain bottled waters. Notice how the author reveals her purpose several times in her introduction and offers evidence to support her position in every paragraph of the article. How do you feel about "enhanced" water? Do you drink it? Do you believe the claims made or implied by its manufacturers? Should water be sold as a commodity, or is it a basic human right, like air?*

A Healthy Drink? Try Plain Water   BY TEMMA EHRENFELD

Bottled water isn't any better for you than tap water in American cities—and even the bottled water industry won't argue the point. But what about the new "enhanced" waters containing vitamins and herbs? Their snappy names and lists of additives do imply health benefits beyond the goal of staying well-hydrated. Unfortunately, the science behind them is weak, according to the American-based Centre for Science in the Public Interest (CSPI), an advocacy group for information on nutrition. So before you load the cooler with pricey vitamin-enhanced waters, consider filling up empties at the tap instead. There are better ways to relax, get refreshed, and boost your immunity than by downing the enhanced waters below:

1. Calming Waters? Coca Cola's VitaminWater B-Relaxed Jackfruit-Guava contains several vitamins B and theanine, a natural ingredient in tea, along with 125 calories' worth of sugar per bottle. According to a Coca-Cola spokesperson, theanine levels of 50 mg to 200 mg have been shown to stimulate the "production of alpha brain waves, which are associated with a relaxed state of mental alertness." A 20-fluid-ounce, or 568 ml, bottle contains 50 mg of theanine, compared to 20 mg in a cup of tea. Coca-Cola also notes that the vitamins B in its product help the body fight stress. However, there is no evidence those vitamins are experienced as calming, says the CSPI. And according to the most recent study of theanine, reported in the journal *Psychopharmacology*, it also does not affect mood. (Theanine does counter temporary rises in blood pressure caused by caffeine.) Buyers note: Despite the name, the product does not contain actual jackfruit or guava, only flavours.

2. Can Water Stave Off Colds? Coca Cola's Dasani Plus Defend + Protect contains zinc and vitamin E, two substances that play a role in immunity. However, according to the CSPI, research suggests that taking vitamin E boosts immunity only if it is consumed in very large amounts by older people who are deficient in the vitamin. Some evidence suggests that zinc lozenges may shorten colds. But that doesn't mean drinking zinc in water will, says the CSPI, and, as Coca-Cola points out, there aren't any studies "using water fortified with zinc to determine the effect on colds."

immunity
being insusceptible to a disease (or similar)

3. Getting Tough on H_2O? Pepsi-Co's Sobe Life Water Challenge Your Life provides taurine, sometimes touted as a muscle strengthener, and ginseng, believed to boost alertness. The science: Participants in one study took 20 grams a day of taurine for seven days, and did a push-up test before and after. Taurine didn't make them any better at push-ups. As for ginseng, the evidence that it boosts alertness is inconsistent, says the CSPI—in fact, it appears to reduce alertness under some circumstances. Dosages count. But the Sobe label doesn't say how much taurine or ginseng is in its product, and Sobe did not provide the information to *Newsweek* when asked. A spokeswoman says, "We allow customers to decide what 'challenge' means to them."

5   **4. Fibre Water?** Pepsi-Co's Aquafina Alive Satisfy does contain maltodextrin, which qualifies under the government definition of fibre. However, it's a soluble fibre, so it won't keep you regular like the fibre in grains and beans.

THINKING ABOUT THE MODEL

1. What single organizing principle (SOP) does Ehrenfeld use to group bottled waters, and into how many major groups is bottled water classified?

2. What evidence in each body paragraph does the author offer to refute claims made by bottled water manufacturers?

3. Has the author persuaded you to accept her thesis? Why or why not?

4. Bottled water is an environmental issue. Read each of the following articles and write a paragraph classifying arguments against and for bottled water:

   • "Five Reasons to Ban Bottled Water": http://www.canadians.org/water/documents/bottledwater-5reasons.pdf

   • "The Case Against Bottled Water": http://www.thestar.com/life/health_wellness/2008/08/11/the_case_against_bottled_water.html

   • "Tide Rising Against Bottled Water": http://www.theglobeandmail.com/report-on-business/industry-news/marketing/tide-rising-against-bottled-water/article4316012/

5. This essay is missing the conclusion. Considering the categories listed up to this point, as well as the SOP, write the conclusion.

LO29.2   Writing a Classification Essay

Audience and Purpose

For your essay, consider who might be interested in your classification. Sergey Kobzar (whose paragraph is shown in Activity 29.3) wanted to explain a bit about his homeland of Ukraine to his classmates. Knowing who he was writing for guided Sergey in defining terms like *Ivana Kupala* and explaining some of the history of Ukraine. Your writing will be easier and more focused if you think about your reader before you begin drafting.

Your main purpose is to communicate information, but you may do so in a way that entertains. Your essay may also move people to think differently about your topic or to take some action.

The Assignment

Write an essay of roughly 500 to 750 words that divides a topic into three or four groups, or divides one classification into three or four subcategories, and then discusses those subgroups. In order to remain focused, you must choose a single organizing principle (SOP), which you will state in your thesis statement. Examples of groups to classify include these:

people: movie stars, athletes, family members, significant others, coaches, teachers, bosses, church leaders, politicians, news reporters;

places: restaurants, homes, gyms, vacation spots, cities, sports arenas, provincial parks, museums, wilderness areas, schools; and

groups: sports teams, nature lovers, bands, choirs, motorcycle clubs, subcultures (Goths, punks, gamers), friends.

Alternative Assignments

Here are several classification writing options that may be of interest. For any of these alternative assignments, be sure to do the following:

- Establish a single organizing principle (SOP) that includes all logical groupings.
- State the SOP in your thesis statement.
- Begin each grouping with a topic sentence.
- End each paragraph with a concluding sentence that makes a point about your topic.
- Use transitions and other connectors.
- Write a conclusion that summarizes the groupings in your body and makes a final point.

Business in Context:

Describe or improve a classifying system at your job. All retail stores group merchandise so that customers can find (and buy) it. Tell how part of your store is arranged. For example, using an SOP of easy customer access, you might describe how part or all of a convenience store is arranged: impulse items like cigarette lighters, LED lights, and candy close to the cash register; soft drinks, coffee, and hot chocolate perhaps grouped toward the middle of the store; and all cold items placed in the coolers against the walls. Perhaps you can tell how to improve the arrangement so that you can work more efficiently (using "efficiency" as the SOP). Your boss might be a good audience for this one.

Culture in Context:

Classify cultural events in terms of one of the following groups, and divide the group into three or four subcategories. Possible groups to be subdivided might include concerts, dances, dates, sports events, weddings, or funerals. State the SOP in your thesis.

Education in Context:

Consider educational stages, such as preschool, kindergarten, elementary, high school, and college. Choose one stage and classify it into three or four subcategories. Establish an SOP that includes all logical groupings, and state the SOP in your thesis. Remember to begin each grouping with a topic sentence.

Health Care in Context:

Consider three or four categories of diets and discuss them in terms of an organizing principle, such as weight loss, energy, or high-fibre. You might consider the Atkins diet, for example, or a vegetarian diet, or a vegan diet, or the South Beach diet. End with a concluding sentence that makes a point about your topic. Use transitions and other connectors.

Science in Context:

How many ways are there for the average person to reduce pollution? Inside a household, we use electric lights, air conditioners, furnaces, washers, dryers, ovens, water heaters, other appliances, and many electronic devices for entertainment. Outside our homes we use lawnmowers, trimmers, leaf blowers, snow blowers, and sometimes fertilizers, herbicides, and pesticides on our lawns. We send massive amounts of waste to landfills. You could classify these pollutants based on how harmful each is or which is easiest to reduce, two possible SOPs. Your goal may be simply to inform your reader, or you may wish to move him or her to take action.

Technology in Context:

Consider a technological device or a computer function that can be subcategorized, and discuss the device/function in terms of three or four categories. You might consider cars, motorcycles, SUVs, video games, search engines, or blogs. Remember to state the single organizing principle (SOP) in the introduction and end with a concluding sentence that makes a point about your topic. Use transitions and other connectors.

HINT

See the online section of Chapter 2 for more on prewriting methods (freewriting, clustering, listing, and so forth).

Discovering Ideas: Prewriting for Classification Essays

Pointless classifications will probably be an awful chore for you to write and for your audience to read. So choose a topic you are interested in and say something about it. If, for instance, you have been job-hunting recently or are working in college toward a career goal, you might choose to classify types of jobs that you would like or perhaps ones that you wish to avoid. Choosing a topic and then prewriting will help you decide on a single organizing principle (SOP), so you will have a focus for your work. The prewriting method of clustering works well for classification essays.

JOURNAL / BLOG ENTRY 29.2

Use clustering (refer back to the online information for Chapter 2 for the model) to discover several possible SOPs for your topic. Choose the one that most interests you, and tell why it does. Next, tell who might be interested in your topic and approach.

FEEDBACK *In pairs or groups, share clusters, and discuss why each topic does or does not interest you. How might each of you make your idea more appealing? Offer and consider advice graciously, and take notes.*

Organizing Classification Essays

When you have chosen your SOP and several subgroups, you should then decide how to organize them. You might choose a chronological arrangement, as Sergey Kobzar does in "Ukrainian Holidays" (page 395–396), or a spatial arrangement, for instance, in describing how merchandise is grouped in a store.

Next, write out your thesis statement, which should include your topic and SOP. You may directly state that you are classifying by using words like *groups*, *types*, *kinds*, *sorts*, and *varieties* or you may simply imply that a classification is about to be announced.

With a thesis statement in hand and your groups arranged, you are almost ready to draft.

JOURNAL / BLOG ENTRY 29.3

Write out your working thesis statement, underlining the topic once and the SOP twice. Next, list your categories in the order you have chosen, and name that order (time, space, or importance). Why do you think this is a good arrangement for your topic?

Drafting Classification Essays

Moving into your first draft, keep the following points in mind:

1. Use your single organizing principle to effectively classify your topic.
2. Be sure your paper makes a point (often made clear in the last sentence).
3. Introduce each group with a topic sentence.
4. Develop each group with detailed examples, specific words, and thorough explanations (which include defining terms where needed).
5. Use transitions and other connectors with care, especially between groups.

HINT

Be sure to introduce each grouping with a topic sentence and end with a concluding sentence that makes a point.

JOURNAL / BLOG ENTRY 29.4

After finishing your first draft, reread it, highlight your topic sentences with a marker or your word-processing software's highlighting feature, and circle or box any connecting words. Now, discuss your marked topic sentences with your instructor, or submit the first draft for his/her comments. What parts of your draft do you like most and least—and why? Answer in a paragraph, which will accompany your first draft.

FEEDBACK *Trade drafts with a partner, and offer feedback on his or her use of topic sentences and connecting words.*

HINT

For more detailed suggestions for revising all drafts, turn to Chapter 21.

Revising Classification Essays

As you begin revising your classification first draft, you and your peer reviewer could use the following checklist as a guide:

PEER REVIEW CHECKLIST FOR REVISING CLASSIFICATION ESSAYS

- ☐ Does the thesis statement name a topic and an SOP? Does it also forecast the main categories?
  Reviewer Comment: _____
  _____

- ☐ Is the essay's organization consistent: by space, time, or importance?
  Reviewer Comment: _____
  _____

- ☐ Does a category drift from the SOP? If so, the writer should drop it.
  Reviewer Comment: _____
  _____

- ☐ What further detail or explanation might the target audience need?
  Reviewer Comment: _____
  _____

- ☐ Has the writer used transitions and other connectors?
  Reviewer Comment: _____
  _____

- ☐ Does the concluding sentence rename the topic and make a point?
  Reviewer Comment: _____
  _____

LINKING TO FUTURE EXPERIENCE

Classifying is a technique that can help you organize ideas in many writing situations. Whether you are discussing chemical elements, works of literature, or traffic violations, dividing a broad subject area into groups makes it easier to understand and manage. In a longer paper, classifying may help you compare or contrast within or among groups. You might use classification to define concepts by showing what fits (and doesn't fit) a description. And you might strengthen your case in a persuasive paper by classifying evidence.

Chapter Summary

1. Classification groups things by a single organizing principle (SOP).

2. We classify information, people, places, events, and objects to simplify our lives, making these things easier to understand and work with.

3. Writers choose an SOP based on the topic, their interest in it, and a reader's potential interest.

4. Classification should include all obvious groups within a topic without overlapping or creating an endless list.

5. Classifications can be organized by time, space, or importance.

6. Each category should be introduced with a topic sentence.

7. Each category should be developed with detailed examples and explanations.

8. Transitional words and other connectors help readers move from one group to another.

9. The conclusion should begin with a connector, restate the thesis, reinforce the SOP, and summarize the categories developed in the essay.

10. Writing is not complete until it has been revised and carefully edited.

Defining Terms (Definition)

30

Do you have a favourite game? Is it a team (or group) activity, a one-on-one competition, or a solitary diversion? What specific qualities distinguish a game from other hobbies or forms of entertainment?

What Are We Trying to Achieve and Why?

Even a simple word like *game* has many different meanings: for example, a game can be an organized sporting event, a leisure activity, something trivial or purely fun, or people's interactions in social situations like dating. If someone asked what you meant by *game*, how might the photos on the previous page—people playing cards and baseball—help you explain the word? If, by *game*, you meant a competitive leisure activity with rules, you might use the card game as an example to help illustrate your meaning. Using examples is one form of definition.

Working through Chapter 30, you will practise various forms of definition. Two key methods in defining what something *is* are to define what it *is not* and to *compare* it to something similar and say how it is yet different. You will have successfully defined a term when you have touched on its essential nature, explaining its meaning fully for a specific purpose.

LINKING TO PREVIOUS EXPERIENCE

What You Already Know about Defining

Defining is such a natural act that we seldom notice we're doing it. Whenever we teach or inform others about something we know about—an idea, object, animal, place, or person—we are **defining** it. We can use many of the patterns of development we have looked at in this text to help us define.

To define a wheaten terrier, for example, you could use **description**, adding details: *size*—13 to 22 kilograms; *fur*—15 centimetres long and golden brown to pale wheat; *face*—terrier chin whiskers; *tail*—cropped short; *personality*—highly energetic, spunky, playful. You might use **narration**, that is, tell a story, about your own wheaten terrier (who follows you around the house, dropping a red ball at your feet), or give a **comparison** (he looks like a taller version of Disney's Benjy), or talk about the **effects** the dog has on your household.

> **HINT**
>
> For more on description, see Chapter 23. For narration techniques, see Chapter 24. Comparison and contrast are covered in Chapter 28, and cause and effect is in Chapter 27.

JOURNAL / BLOG ENTRY 30.1

Choose a term and define it in a brief paragraph. Choose a topic you know well. If you enjoy the video game *Guitar Hero*, try to define it. If you like reptiles, define an *anaconda*. If you are a parent, define what *tantrum* or *fatherhood* means to you. What patterns of development are you using? Is a dictionary definition useful? Do you have to explain any unfamiliar words?

[FEEDBACK] *In groups, share your topics. All members of the group should try, in a few sentences, to define what each word means to them. How do your definitions of the same word differ?*

Developing Skills in Defining

Definition paragraphs are found in many different types of essays, usually near the introduction or thesis. It is often important to define for your readers exactly what your subject is or exactly how you define a particular term that you are using in order to avoid being misinterpreted. People often use a multi-layered word like "postmodernism" or "nationalism" to mean something quite specific without considering that the word may mean something quite different to others. A definition paragraph will help you explain the exact meaning that you are using. Sometimes a dictionary definition will help with this, and sometimes you must elaborate the definition yourself, as Perri Klass does in her essay "Ambition," as she talks about what ambition means to her personally.

The following activities will help you to develop skills in writing definitions:

1. Defining by negation
2. Defining with comparisons
3. Using formal definitions
4. Using extended definitions

Defining by Negation

Our first brief definition is **negation**, which means saying what something is *not* and then telling what it *is* —or what you *mean* it to be. For instance, if you were arguing for the importance of Tim Horton's in the nation's history, you might say, "Tim Horton's is not just another doughnut shop; it is the oasis for coffee, soup, sandwiches, and a vast array of desserts that Canadians have come to expect on every highway and in every neighbourhood." Or you might have had some negative experiences with dating and want to show your attitude with this sentence of negation: "Dating is not so much about finding a best friend or future spouse; it is more about losing self-delusions and finding out more than you want to know about another person." Negation is useful for clarifying your perspective on a topic or issue and may be useful in a topic sentence or thesis statement.

ACTIVITY 30.1 Defining by Negation

Using a dictionary or your own knowledge, write a one- or two-sentence definition by negation for the following terms.

EXAMPLE: **Library:** *Today's big-city libraries are no longer just places to store a lot of books; these institutions are dynamic places of learning and fun that offer music, movies, Internet access, and community programs; libraries are the gateway to another, richer world.*

1. Mother: _____

   _____

2. Coach: _____

   _____

3. Breakfast: _____

   _____

4. Marriage: _____

   _____

5. Tattoos: _____

   _____

Defining with Comparisons

As we learned in Chapter 28, comparisons help people understand ideas. **Literal comparisons** compare two things that are as similar as possible, one which readers don't know and one which they do. For example, we could compare a hiker's backpack to a duffle bag with straps, carried on the back. However, if we were to compare *unlike* images to further a reader's understanding, we would be creating a **metaphor** or **simile**. So we might say that a hiker's backpack is his or her home, containing all the food, shelter, and other supplies a person needs to survive in the wild. Here we have compared the unlike images of a *backpack* and a *home*, trying to help readers see how important the backpack can be.

When we say one thing *is* another (my backpack *is* a home), we have a **metaphor**. Saying one thing is *like* another (my backpack is *like* a home) is a **simile**. In creating a metaphor or a simile, try to avoid phrases and images that you hear often. These common phrases are usually **clichés**, worn-out images that writers should avoid (for example, *piece of cake, by the book,* or *cream of the crop*).

ACTIVITY 30.2 Defining with Comparisons

In a sentence, create a brief metaphor or simile for the following terms.

EXAMPLE: **The glacial lakes were <u>the ice-blue eyes of the mountain.</u>**

1. Zoos are _____

   _____

2. Diving from a high board is like _____

   _____

3. A sexist person is _____

   _____

4. My Canadian pride is _____

   _____

5. Electric cars are _____

   _____

Using Formal Definitions

A dictionary can also help add meaning to a word by showing its **formal definition**. To write a formal definition, we limit our term to one group and then add detailed examples and explanations that further identify the word. Notice the three parts to a formal definition:

TERM	GROUP	DETAILED EXAMPLES/EXPLANATIONS
chinchilla	Rodent	squirrel-like creature native to South America, raised in captivity for its soft, pale-gray fur
baseball	Game	played with a ball and bat by two teams of nine players, each team playing alternately in the field and at bat; to score, the players at bat have to run a course of four bases laid out in a diamond pattern

We have been practising this type of defining since working with description and specific language in Chapter 23. As words become more specific—that is, as the group they belong to shrinks—they become increasingly defined.

Verbs such as *is* or *means* are useful in a formal definition because they link the term with its group and details; for example, "A chinchilla *is* a rodent from South America."

When writing formal definitions, be sure to avoid these two common problems:

1. **Vague, general groups and details:**

   - We could say that a chinchilla is an *animal* or even a *thing*, but these broad words don't help us limit the group the way *rodent* does.

   - If we said that a chinchilla is a *furry rodent* but leave out further descriptions, such as *from South America*, we might be talking about a squirrel.

2. Using *where* and *when* rather than labelling the group:

   - You keep important information from a reader if you replace specific words with *when* or *where*. Instead of writing "Baseball is *where* people form teams of nine players and . . .," try "Baseball is *a game* played with teams of nine players . . ."

English Review Note

When translating definitions from your native language, make sure they make sense in English.

ACTIVITY 30.3 Formal Definitions

Using a dictionary, write out a one-sentence formal definition for each of the following terms. Underline each term's group, and include detailed examples and explanations. Is the dictionary definition enough for you to understand each term? Why or why not?

EXAMPLE: **Carabiner:** *A carabiner is an oblong metal ring with a spring clip, used in mountaineering to attach a running rope to a piton or similar device.*

Term clarified? *Yes, but mostly because I have seen carabiners used and even have one on my backpack. The explanation with the rope helped because I've seen mountain climbers on TV.*

1. Economic recession: _____

   _____

   Term clarified? _____

---

2. Lactose intolerance: _____

_____

Term clarified? _____

3. Meteor: _____

_____

Term clarified? _____

4. Beaufort scale: _____

_____

Term clarified? _____

Now pick one word from above that needs more clarification and write a one-paragraph definition. Start with the dictionary definition but expand it in your own words your own explanation. Make sure that your paragraph has a topic sentence and a conclusion.

Using Extended Definitions

While brief definitions are useful for developing a topic, the patterns of development (description, narration, illustration, cause/effect, process, classification, comparison/contrast) are even more helpful. Because they mirror the way people think, they are a comfortable and natural way of adding meaning to an idea. Notice how the student author Jhonnatan Percca develops his definition paragraph, using several brief definitions and then these patterns in his first major example:

- **effects (of becoming an immigrant):** being frightened; giving up friends, home, and family
- **illustration:** his personal example of leaving Peru; second-level examples to show what he had to give up (soccer games, neighbourhood, friends, family, language)

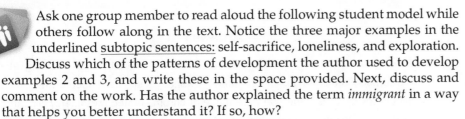 **ACTIVITY 30.4** Working Together: Using Patterns of Development

Ask one group member to read aloud the following student model while others follow along in the text. Notice the three major examples in the underlined subtopic sentences: self-sacrifice, loneliness, and exploration. Discuss which of the patterns of development the author used to develop examples 2 and 3, and write these in the space provided. Next, discuss and comment on the work. Has the author explained the term *immigrant* in a way that helps you better understand it? If so, how?

Explorers: Searching for a Better Life

Dictionary.com says that immigrants are persons "who migrate to another country, usually seeking permanent residence," but this says little about people brave enough to leave their whole world behind. First, to be an immigrant, a person has to be willing to sacrifice much. When I thought about leaving Peru, I was frightened, knowing I would have to give up many things: my familiar neighbourhood, my loved ones, soccer games with friends, even my language. The many letters I write home are not enough to ease the pain inside my heart, and I still struggle to make people understand me in English. Immigrants must also be able to bear the loneliness of their new country. I miss my friends and family. Sometimes I feel as if I have fallen to the bottom of a well. From the darkness and cold at the bottom, I look up to see my grandparents, parents, brothers, and sisters leaning over, calling down to me, "Jhon-natan, come home to us." I have made friends here, like Carlos, from Mexico City, but he is also lonely, missing his wife and son. <u>One of the most important parts of being an immigrant is becoming an explorer.</u> When I arrived in Toronto, I felt as if I was trapped in a forest of cement trees. Finding my way around was confusing because the places I needed to go were far apart, and the stores were so big. Often I got lost but managed to find my way back despite my poor English, asking for directions, read-ing street maps, and learning the subway system. To stay on the path that leads to a better life, immigrants must be ready to sacrifice much, willing to endure loneliness, and courageous enough to explore their new world.

—Jhonnatan Percca

1. Patterns of development for example 2, loneliness: _____

    How effective is the explanation? _____

    _____

2. Patterns of development for example 3, explorer: _____

    How effective is the explanation? _____

    _____

HINT

Choose from the following possible patterns of development: description, narration, illustration, cause/effect, process, classification, comparison/contrast.

Learning from a Student Model: An Extended Definition Essay

The following essay will help you understand how to write an extended defini-tion essay. Read the model closely for organizational points (topic, subtopic, and concluding sentences and connectors) and development (detailed explanations and specific examples). Try to find brief definitions of negation, metaphor/simile, and the dictionary, and look for the mix of patterns of development.

Arowana

1   Although arowana might sound like marijuana, it is actually a fish. Walking into the Jumbo Fish Store, I came upon an arowana. Its scales reflected the sun-light in my eyes as if the fish were made of chrome-plated metal. This elegant 60-centimetre-long animal moved so gracefully that I felt I must have it in my aquarium. Drooling and wondering what the price was, I looked for an employee. "How much for this arowana?" I asked the clerk. "Eleven hundred dollars," he replied, as if that price was nothing. I thought he must be crazy. Who would pay that much for a fish? With a frown, I left the store, determined to find out more about this beautiful creature and why people were willing to pay a small fortune for it.

2   First, I learned a little history of the arowana. They are a primitive freshwater fish whose ancestors were alive over 150 million years ago; arowana are now

found in South America, Australia, and Asia. The people of South America have traditionally harvested the fish for food (although it is called a "bony" fish); but worldwide, the populations of arowana are declining due to destruction of habitat, so they are not eaten as much these days. Instead, they are being raised mostly in Australia and Asia for the aquarium hobbyist market. However, Asia is where the fish is in the highest demand, as I found out, bringing thousands of dollars for the larger and more exotic species. Arowana can be several colours: golden ones are native to Malaysia, golden with red tail and full-red arowanas are found in Indonesia, and green ones swim in rivers in Southeast Asia. These fish can grow to be a metre long and can live for 50 years.

3   Another reason for the arowana's popularity is that it resembles the Asians' mystical dragon (the Asian, not the Western European dragon, which is usually not shown with whiskers and is thicker, like a meat-eating dinosaur with wings). Both the fish and the dragon have colourful scales, and they both have whiskers. Also, the arowana has long, broad pectoral fins (the fins attached to the fish's ribcage, along its sides) that remind many people of a dragon's wings. Dragons in flight are often pictured as snaking through the air, again resembling the graceful swimming movement of the arowana. In Asian culture, the dragon represents good luck, strength, and power. Especially in the southern region of China, people believe that a dragon can ward off evil, and they are attracted to the arowana, calling it the "dragon fish." Many business people keep these fish in their buildings to contribute to successful operations. Arowanas are common in restaurants, as well, not to be eaten but to ensure a prosperous business. Some think that the arowana can even ward off approaching death or give its own life in place of its owner's when death comes for him or her.

4   However, to me, what makes the arowana the most special of fish is its aggressive attitude. I like watching it swim through the water with confidence, not fearing any other fish in its aquarium world. It is at the top of the food chain, a predator seeking prey. In the wild, arowanas feed close to the surface, capturing other fish, snakes, frogs, insects large and small—anything the arowana can get its toothy mouth around. In aquariums, arowanas are also kings. A goldfish is nosing about for food, minding its own business, when suddenly, out of nowhere, wham! The goldfish is gone, and the arowana is spitting out a few scales.

5   Arowanas are thought of by some as simply a "freshwater bony fish of the family Osteoglossidae," but to me this fish represents Asian culture and the power of a major predator. The arowana is no humble goldfish, stupidly drifting about or hiding in fear under a rock. I admire the arowana's way of life and would rather be like it than the goldfish. Thinking these thoughts, I arrive back at the Jumbo Fish Store, having decided to purchase an arowana—not the 60-centimetre one, but a baby, only 8 centimetres long, but still costing $200. I'm crazy for buying an arowana, but this fish reminds me of how I see myself. And when it gets big enough, maybe I'll sell it to some other crazy fish fan—for $1100, or more.

—*Phonepraseut Mounivong*

1. Evaluate the introduction. Comment on the hook, support sentences, and thesis.

2. Evaluate the body paragraphs. Comment on the topic sentences (including connecting words) and development (including specific examples). What is the defining or most special element of the arowana to the author? What essential, defining qualities have you learned about the arowana?

3. Name and discuss how effectively the author uses both formal (brief) and extended definitions.

4. Evaluate the conclusion. Comment on the restatement of thesis, summary, and expanded thought.

5. How are the body paragraphs organized (by time or importance)? What words help you see this method of organization?

Learning from a Professional Model: An Extended Definition Essay

To define is to limit the meaning of something, especially to discover its essential qualities. Dr. Perri Klass does this in the following essay from Self *magazine, exploring the concept of ambition. She lets us see both the positive and negative aspects of the term and clarifies what ambition means to her and why it is important to her. The author uses a mix of patterns of development, leaning especially toward illustration and cause and effect. Notice, as you read, how much the author reveals about her life—she is a pediatrician, mother, writer, dreamer, and hard worker; she is also someone who feels guilt, envy, and confusion. Does this personal approach to writing make you more or less inclined to read Klass's work? Why?*

Ambition

BY PERRI KLASS

1   I've always liked ambitious people, and many of my closest friends have had grandiose dreams. I like such people, not because I am desperate to be buddies with a future secretary of state but because I find ambitious people entertaining, interesting to talk to, fun to watch. And, of course, I like such people because I am ambitious myself, and I would rather not feel apologetic about it.

2   Ambition has gotten bad press. Back in the seventeenth century, Spinoza thought ambition and lust were "nothing but species of madness, although they are not enumerated among diseases." Especially in women, ambition has often been seen as a profoundly dislikeable quality; the word "ambitious" linked to a "career woman" suggested that she was ruthless, hard as nails, clawing her way to success on top of the bleeding bodies of her friends.

profoundly
deeply

3   Then, in the late Seventies and the Eighties, ambition became desirable, as books with titles like *How to Stomp Your Way to Success* became bestsellers. It was still a nasty sort of attribute, but nasty attributes were good because they helped you look out for number one.

attribute
trait

But what I mean by ambition is dreaming big dreams, putting no limits on 4 your expectations and your hopes. I don't really like very specific, attainable ambitions, the kind you learn to set in the career-strategy course taught by the author of *How to Stomp Your Way to Success*. I like big ambitions that suggest that the world could open up at any time, with work and luck and determination. The next book could hit it big. The next research project could lead to something fantastic. The next bright idea could change history.

Of course, eventually you have to stop being a freshman in college. You 5 limit your ambitions and become more realistic, wiser about your potential, your abilities, the number of things your life can hold. Sometimes you get close to something you wanted to do, only to find it looks better from far away. Back when I was a freshman, to tell the truth, I wanted to be Jane Goodall, go into the jungle to study monkeys and learn things no one had ever dreamed of. This ambition was based on an interest in biology and several *National Geographic* television specials; it turned out that wasn't enough of a basis for a life. There were a number of other early ambitions that didn't pan out either. I was not fated to live a wild, adventurous life, to travel alone to all the most exotic parts of the world, to leave behind a string of broken hearts. Oh well, you have to grow up, at least a little.

Jane Goodall
famous chimpanzee expert

Almost all of us have to deal with the tremendous success of friends (or ene- 6 mies), with those who somehow started out where we did but are now way in front. My college-alumni magazine arrives every two months without fail, so I can find out who graduated two years *after* I did but is now running a groundbreaking clinic at a major university hospital (and I'm only just finishing my residency!). Who is restoring a fabulous mansion in a highly desirable town by the sea. Who got promoted yet again, due to natural brilliance and industry.

I read an article recently about how one's twenties are the decade for decid- 7 ing on a career and finishing your training, and the thirties are for consolidating your success and rising within your chosen job (and here I am in my thirties, not even sure what I want to do yet!). With all these external yardsticks, the last thing anyone needs is an internal voice as well, whispering irritably that you were supposed to do it better, get further and that all you've actually accomplished is mush, since you haven't met your own goals.

The world is also full of people so ambitious, so consumed by drive and 8 overdrive that nothing they pass on the way to success has any value at all. Life becomes one long exercise in delayed gratification; everything you do, you're doing only because it will one day get you where you want to be. Medical training is an excellent example of delayed gratification. You spend years in medical school doing things with no obvious relationship to your future as a doctor, and then you spend years in residency, living life on a miserable schedule, staying up all night and slogging through the day, telling yourself that one day all this will be over. It's what you have to do to become a doctor, but it's a lousy model for life in general. There's nothing wrong with a little delayed gratification every now and then, but a job you do only because of where it will get you—and not because you like it—means a life of muttering to yourself, "Someday this will be over." This is bad for the disposition.

slogging
plodding, slow-moving

disposition
general mood or outlook

9   As you grow up, your ambitions may come into conflict. Most prominently nowadays, we have to hear about Women Torn Between Family and Career, about women who make it to the top only to realize they left their ovaries behind. Part of growing up, of course, is realizing that there is only so much room in one life, whether you are male or female. You can do one thing wholeheartedly and single-mindedly and give up some other things. Or you can be greedy and grab for something new without wanting to give up what you already have. This leads to a chaotic and crowded life in which you are always late, always overdue, always behind, but rarely bored. Even so, you have to come to terms with limitations; you cannot crowd your life with occupations and then expect to do each one as well as you might if it were all you had to do. I realize this when I race out of the hospital, offending a senior doctor who had offered to explain something to me, only to arrive late at the daycare centre, annoying the people who have been taking care of my daughter.

10   Of course, I try to be mature about it all. I don't assign my friends Nobel Prizes or top government posts. I don't pretend that there is room in my life for any and every kind of ambition I can imagine. Instead, I say piously that all I want are three things: I want to write as well as I can, I want to have a family, and I want to be a good pediatrician. And then, of course, a voice inside whispers . . . to write a bestseller, to have ten children, to do stunning medical research. Fame and fortune, it whispers, fame and fortune. Even though I'm not a college freshman anymore, I'm glad to find that little voice still there, whispering sweet nothings in my ear.

THINKING ABOUT THE MODEL

1. Comment on the introduction: hook, development, and thesis.

2. Comment on the development of body paragraphs: in particular, what image in paragraph 2 is created through descriptive details?

3. In what paragraph does the author give her personal definition of ambition? How does she use negation to clarify her meaning?

4. What is the topic sentence in paragraph 6? What pattern of development does Klass use to develop it?

5. The author uses understatement (downplaying the serious nature of a statement) at the end of paragraph 8, hyperbole (exaggeration) at the start of paragraph 9, and personification (giving human characteristics to things and animals) at the end of her final paragraph. Comment on what effect she achieves with these figures of speech.

L030.2   # Writing an Extended Definition Essay

HINT

For more on audience, see Chapter 2.

Audience and Purpose

As you think over terms for this assignment, try to choose one that you know and care about, that you want to explain to others. In "Explorers: Searching for a Better Life" (pages 411–412), Jhonnatan Percca wanted to tell his fellow classmates about his experiences as an immigrant. He felt that giving insight into his life might help classmates see immigrants as people with full and challenging lives. Having a purpose and clearly imagining who will read your work will help you find the right words to define your term.

Your main purpose is to explain, to try to capture an essential, defining part of your term, but you may do so in a way that entertains. Your paragraph may also move people to think differently about your topic or to take some action.

The Assignment

Write an essay of roughly 500 to 750 words that defines a term. The word you choose might be a person, place, thing, idea, or emotional state. Possible concepts might be the ideal spouse, your ideal home, your personal interpretation of peace, harmony, chaos, health, credit, freedom, culture, marriage, divorce, political systems, reality TV, or global warming. Begin with a thesis statement that names your term and states or implies that you will define it. As you have practised in the skills section, use brief definitions and the patterns of development to explain your topic; and, as always, include specific, detailed examples.

Alternative Assignments

Here are several definition writing options that may be of interest for your essay. For any of these assignments, be sure to do the following:

- Use several brief definitions and several patterns of development.
- Begin with a thesis statement that names your term and predicts a definition.
- Begin each major point with a subtopic sentence.
- End with a concluding sentence that makes a point about your topic.
- Use transitions and other connectors.

Business in Context:

Write an essay that defines your current job. What are the essential elements in your work that make it what it is? For example, a teacher must interact with students; this is a defining element of the job. Teachers prepare course materials for students, conduct classes (in person or online), evaluate student work, and stay current in their discipline. Auto mechanics must know about the cars they work on, and they must be able to handle tools competently. A server must be able to interact with customers and keep food orders organized. Your purpose in this assignment might be to give a friend some insight into what you have done job-wise or plan to do in the future. Consider opening with the technique of defining by negation (page 408), clearing up myths about what the job involves. Remember, too, that being a student is a job you could write about.

Culture in Context:

Define your concept of the ideal vacation if you could get away for a month. What are the essential elements that would make this a good vacation? Consider the location, your daily activities, the people you would like to be around (or not). Use negation to describe what would not be present in your vacation. You might use several brief definitions and several patterns of development.

Education in Context:

Think of a word used as slang that has a separate formal meaning (for example, *cool, sweet, wicked, jerk*). Write an essay that describes a setting in which you would use the word as slang. Then, use the *Canadian Oxford Dictionary* or visit *Dictionary.com* (http://www.dictionary.com) and find the word's formal meaning. In your essay, explain the difference between the two (or more) meanings. Is one definition the "true" meaning? How do listeners or readers know the difference?

Health Care in Context:

Your own behaviour and the behaviour of people around you are the greatest influences on your emotional well-being. Define yourself according to several characteristic behaviours that others have noticed about you. Or you might consider defining the behaviour of someone close to you. This is a good topic for including several brief definitions since specific examples will make clear your understanding of behaviours—responsible, irresponsible, generous, selfish, charitable, greedy, courageous, cowardly, ethical, loyal, disciplined, sexist, arrogant, industrious, or lazy, for example.

Science in Context:

Consider the following terms: *endangered species, global warming, acid rain, soil erosion, aquifer depletion, pollution*. You might read an article to pin down the main points that you feel define an issue associated with one of these terms. For example, what does it mean to "deplete an aquifer"? You could begin by defining "aquifer" (an underground water source contained in a layer of rock and sand); next, discuss how water accumulates in it; and then, perhaps choose a specific example describing the effects of using up the stored water for irrigation. What will happen to the fertile, irrigated land seen in the accompanying photograph when the remaining 40 percent of the water has been drawn out? The purpose of your essay might be to inform or persuade.

HINT

Slang words are used only in informal settings, and more in speech than in writing. Most are used only by specific groups of people. Most slang goes out of style quickly or changes definition over time.

HINT

As you read articles or consult dictionaries, be careful to put all ideas in your writing into your own words.

Discovering Ideas: Prewriting for Definition Essays

It may seem difficult to find 500 to 750 words to say about a single word, especially when a dictionary definition may be barely a sentence long. However, if you allow your creativity to work for you and pursue several possible terms with the patterns of development in mind, including detailed examples, you may surprise yourself. Think about the two student writings and the professional model, and how each writer chose to detail and explain each term.

Be certain to stick with a *single* meaning for your term (a movie *star* is considerably different from a *star* in the sky, for example). Also, remember that you are trying to determine an essential, defining quality of your term, something without which your term would no longer be itself (for example, a politician has to be able to convince people to vote for him or her, so vote-getting is one defining quality for a politician).

One goal of this extended definition assignment is to use several patterns of development, as most real-world writers do. Thinking about all the patterns of development during your prewriting process will help you uncover useful material.

JOURNAL / BLOG ENTRY 30.2

Use the clustering technique (refer back to the online information for Chapter 2) to discover several defining traits of your essay topic. Which points say the most about your topic? Who are your readers? What might they know about the topic? What words might you need to explain for them?

FEEDBACK   *Prepare a list of words you are planning to use in your definition essay. In small groups, discuss the words that might require further definition and the words with which most people are generally familiar.*

Organizing Definition Essays

The overall organizational pattern of definition essays will often be from least to most important point, although depending on your term, you might organize by time or space. Arranging by time could be useful if, for example, you choose to define an event; arranging by space might work when defining a location. Remember that you will also organize within your main points. One point that discusses how something works or that tells a story might be arranged chronologically. Another point could use order of importance, as Phonepraseut Mounivong did in "Arowana":

> **However, to me, what makes the arowana the most special of fish is its aggressive attitude. (Paragraph 4)**

In your thesis statement, or topic sentence, be sure to <u>name your term</u> and make clear that you intend to define/explain it. You can follow your term with verbs like *is, are,* or *means,* as you can see in Jhonnatan Percca's paragraph "Explorers: Searching for a Better Life":

> **Dictionary.com** says that <u>immigrants</u> are persons "who migrate to another country, usually seeking permanent residence . . ."

JOURNAL / BLOG ENTRY 30.3

Write out your working thesis statement. Have you mentioned your topic? Create a rough outline that lists each pattern of development and the brief definition that you will use. Are your points arranged by order of importance?

Drafting Definition Essays

Moving into your first draft, keep the following points in mind:

1. Brief definitions are a good place to start your essay.
2. Consider adding explanations and briefly defining words using commas, dashes, or parentheses.
3. Consciously try to include several patterns of development.
4. Give your reader details that define your term.
5. Decide on the point to your definition before you draft.

JOURNAL / BLOG ENTRY 30.4

After finishing your first draft, reread it, highlight your topic sentences with a marker or your word-processing software's highlighting feature, and circle or box any connecting words. Now copy your marked topic sentences, and discuss them with or give them to your instructor. What parts of your draft do you like most and least? Why? Answer in a paragraph.

FEEDBACK *Trade papers with a classmate, and use this chapter's peer review checklist below to guide your critique. In your journal or blog, note at least one suggestion from your classmate that you plan to implement during revision.*

HINT

For more detailed suggestions for revising all drafts, turn to Chapter 21.

Revising Definition Essays

As you begin revising your definition first draft, use the following checklist as a guide:

☐ Does the thesis statement name a topic and indicate that a definition is coming?

Reviewer Comment: _____

_____

☐ Is the overall organization consistent in developing the concept of space, time, or order of importance?

Reviewer Comment: _____

_____

☐ Identify the patterns of development (description, narration, illustration, cause/effect, process, classification, comparison/contrast) used by the writer. Has the writer used these patterns effectively?

Reviewer Comment: _____

_____

☐ Has the writer used topic sentences effectively?

Reviewer Comment: _____

_____

☐ What further details or explanations might the target audience need? Has the writer included comparisons and defined unfamiliar terms?

Reviewer Comment: _____

_____

☐ Has the writer used transitions and other connectors?

Reviewer Comment: _____

_____

☐ Does the concluding sentence rename the topic and make a point?

Reviewer Comment: _____

_____

LINKING TO FUTURE EXPERIENCE

Defining is a skill you will practise frequently in college writing. Essays or exams might require you to define "democratic" (political science), "gender" (psychology), or "epiphany" (English). Even more frequently, you will use definitions to help answer questions that don't explicitly say "define this." Whenever you suspect that your audience might be unfamiliar with a term or concept, offer a brief definition. Extended definitions might help you make a persuasive point (Chapter 31), classify information (Chapter 29), or analyze cause and effect (Chapter 27). The writing assignments in preceding chapters focused on specific patterns of development, helping you hone your skills for each. Now, having worked through this chapter, you have learned to combine them. As a result, you are more prepared to tackle complex writing assignments.

Chapter Summary

1. Definition means limiting and clarifying a term, separating it from similar words.

2. We define words with an audience in mind, explaining as much or as little as that audience needs.

3. Definitions can be developed as formal (brief) or extended (using several patterns of development).

4. Definitions depend on detailed, specific examples and thorough explanations.

5. Each main point should be introduced with a topic sentence.

6. All sentences, but especially topic sentences, should be clearly linked by transitions and other connectors.

7. The conclusion should begin with a connector, restate the thesis, and summarize the key elements (points) of the definition.

8. Extended definitions can be organized by time or space, but are more often arranged by importance.

9. Writing is not complete until it has been revised and carefully edited.

Writing Persuasively (Argument)

31

This photo shows a lawyer presenting his argument to a jury. Notice that a couple of the jurors have half-smiles. Write a short monologue from the lawyer's point of view as he attempts to convince the jury with his evidence. Possible topics are wide and various. If you like, consider a recent TV crime show that you have seen—or a crime novel that you have read. Have fun with this assignment. It is not meant to be painful!

LEARNING OBJECTIVES

31.1 Developing skills in persuasive writing

31.2 Writing a persuasive essay

What Are We Trying to Achieve and Why?

Imagine what lawyers want from their audiences. The lawyer in the photo may be arguing to save the defendant from prison. This is just one example of how people try to **persuade** others to change the way they think or act. We might also persuade a friend to see a certain movie, a client to buy an insurance plan, a child to eat salad, or a teacher to reconsider a grade. Persuasion is the focus of Chapter 31.

To persuade people effectively, we need to build an **argument**, that is, a convincing case for our position. Persuasion and argument are not exactly the same thing. There are many forms of persuasion; argument is only one of them. You could persuade, or try to persuade someone by lying, bribery, threats, nagging, tantrums, crying, or all sorts of other methods, but none of these will work in an academic setting or in a writing assignment. An argument is a process of reasoning. Arguments that are persuasive require **reasons** and **evidence** to support those reasons. They should also demonstrate an understanding of any **opposing viewpoint**. In fact, the classic academic thesis is built this way, with thesis, antithesis (opposing viewpoint), and evidence all built into the thesis statement. In this chapter, we will practise building arguments along with appealing to a target audience.

LINKING TO PREVIOUS EXPERIENCE

What You Already Know about Persuasion

Persuasion (along with informing and entertaining) is one of the basic aims of communication. For other assignments in this book, you have already written several essays that try to change a person's mind or behaviour. Certainly, in other classes in college and through grades K–12, we have all tried to persuade. When taking exams, we try to convince the teacher that we know the material. When we are late, or absent, or have missed an assignment, we offer reasons that we hope will persuade the teacher to be "reasonable," meaning to excuse the behaviour. From our early years onward, we have practised persuasion: "Mom and Dad, I want a _____, and I need it because _____" (you fill in the blanks). When our brothers or sisters bothered us, we encouraged them to stop by threatening to tell our parents or by using another motivator. We often persuade our friends to go places and do things (sometimes best not done!).

At school, at home, on the job, and in social situations, people constantly interact and often try to influence one another. Persuasion is a basic part of the human experience.

> **JOURNAL / BLOG ENTRY 31.1**
>
> When was the last time you tried to talk someone into something—going to a movie or ball game, lending you an outfit or a car, or getting along with a co-worker or family member? How did you try to motivate the person? Did you appeal to his or her sense of fun, sympathy, or right and wrong? Did you show how he or she might benefit from your suggestion? In a few sentences, tell how you tried to persuade that person. Did you succeed? Why or why not?

Developing Skills in Persuasive Writing

L031.1

The classic academic introductory paragraph requires a solidly constructed thesis statement. The thesis is the argument of the essay. The introductory paragraph begins generally (but not too generally; avoid overgeneralizations and platitudes) and then narrows down the topic to build to the thesis statement. A classic thesis statement consists of five parts: the thesis (argument), the antithesis (counter argument) and three pieces of evidence. For example:

platitude
a simple-minded remark trying to pass for a profound one

Argument: Love at first sight exists for Romeo and Juliet

Counter argument: many do not believe in it

Evidence #1: meeting

Evidence #2: wedding night

Evidence #3: death

Thesis statement: Although many do not believe in it, love at first sight clearly exists for Romeo and Juliet as is evident from their first meeting, their wedding night, and the fact that they would rather die than not be together.

Of course, your evidence needs to be convincing in order to build your argument, so spending some brainstorming energy on figuring out what evidence you will draw on is critical. The type of evidence used varies from discipline to discipline. Whereas police rely on physical evidence for criminal cases, students of literature rely on quotations from the literary text itself, social scientists rely on population data and statistics, historians rely on primary documents, and so on.

The following activities will help you work with persuasive writing:

1. Defining the issue
2. Giving reasons and support
3. Connecting with the audience
4. Countering opposition

Defining the Issue

Persuasion often backfires from the start when the writer does not present the issue clearly. In this photograph, notice the mood of this discussion and the expression on all three participants' faces. These teenaged sisters have asked their mother to help them buy new outfits, and she has agreed. The three of them just moved to a new town, and both girls have interviews for summer jobs lined up. Last year, they worked jobs after school and made enough money to buy their own clothes, but they quit last month so they could help their mom with moving. Which of the following two presentations do you think most accurately represents the situation, and which would most likely achieve its goal of persuasion?

1. Mom, you need to buy us these outfits. We're broke, and we deserve them. You owe us.

2. Mom, we know things are tight after the move—but think of all the costs we saved by doing it ourselves. We both have job interviews this week, and these new clothes will help us look professional. Also, when we get our first paycheques, we'll take you out to dinner.

If you think version 2 is more persuasive, notice that it clarifies the issue, and shows the young women as being responsible and considerate of their audience's feelings.

ACTIVITY 31.1 Defining the Issue

The following topic sentences present issues that are unclear and so might be misinterpreted by a reader. Rewrite each sentence to clarify the issue and the writer's position on it.

EXAMPLE:

Unfocused issue: Mining is ruining the environment and so should be stopped.

Focused issue/topic sentence: *Deep-rock mining is permanently defacing the Canadian Shield and spewing toxic chemicals into nearby watersheds and so should be stopped.*

1. **Unfocused issue:** Someone should do something about climate change.

   Focused issue/topic sentence: _____

   _____

2. **Unfocused issue:** Cigarette smokers should be more careful about second-hand smoke.

   Focused issue/topic sentence: _____

   _____

3. **Unfocused issue:** Cellphones distract people, so they shouldn't use them.

   Focused issue/topic sentence: _____

   _____

4. **Unfocused issue:** Students should be able to get more money for college.

   Focused issue/topic sentence: _____

   _____

Now take one of these newly focused topic sentences and turn it into a classic five-part thesis statement. In order to do this, you will need to brainstorm for evidence useful in building your argument. Once you are satisfied with the thesis statement, write the introductory paragraph to an essay on this topic.

Giving Reasons and Support

All arguments are developed with **reasons** (the main points made about an issue) and **evidence** (support for those points). Evidence takes several forms with which you are already familiar:

1. **Facts/statistics:** commonly accepted truths in words and numbers

2. **Authorities:** the opinions and ideas of experts in a field

3. **Examples:** specific illustrations

4. **Anecdotes:** brief stories

5. **Scenarios:** "what-if" situations, speculating about causes and effects

6. **Logical interpretation:** explanations of how reasons and evidence support the main point of the argument

If, for example, we wanted to argue that parents should not smoke while their children are in the car, we could give several reasons:

A. **Smoking in the car pollutes the air that your children are breathing.**

B. **Breathing polluted air increases your children's risk of developing respiratory problems.**

C. **You are setting an example of a bad health habit which your children are more likely to adopt than if you did not smoke.**

D. **Smoking in a car is now illegal in Ontario.**

We could then support, say, reason B, developing respiratory problems, with these forms of evidence:

1.	**Fact:**	In a vehicle, children are exposed to up to 27 times more toxins than in a smoker's home.
2.	**Authority:**	Ontario Medical Association president Dr. Elliot Halparin says: "Up to 2600 people in this province die every year as a direct result of second-hand smoke."
3.	**Example:**	In April 2008, Nova Scotia was the first province in Canada to ban smoking in vehicles when children are present. The fine is $394.50.
4.	**Anecdote:**	My best friend, Nick, had problems with asthma as a child and both of his parents were smokers.
5.	**Scenario:**	If you want to make yourself sick and die from smoking, then go ahead; but don't subject anyone else to it, especially your own child.
6.	**Logical interpretation:**	It makes sense that smoking in a car is even a risk on short trips with windows rolled down. The smoke is still clinging to children in the car.

You will be more convincing if you give solid reasons to explain your position on an issue and then back those reasons up with strong evidence.

Source for **Fact, Authority,** *and* **Example** *above:* Jennifer Berube, "Smoking Ban for Ontario Drivers with Children," *Suite 101.com* (Jan. 28, 2009).

ACTIVITY 31.2 WORKING TOGETHER: Giving Reasons and Support

Listed below are four issues with one reason to support each position. With group members, review the forms of evidence above, and invent three kinds of evidence to support each of the reasons. Write these on separate paper.

1. **Topic sentence:** Toronto needs more bicycle paths for its residents.

   Reason: Many people like to cycle in the city, but riding on the streets is unsafe.

2. **Topic sentence:** Our city should build a casino.

   Reason: Casinos bring in a lot of money, and this city needs it.

3. **Topic sentence:** When they move to a new location, convicted child molesters should be required to report their convictions to local authorities.

   Reason: Because pedophiles are seldom "cured," they remain a danger to children.

4. **Topic sentence:** Bartenders should be required by law to stop serving anyone who is clearly intoxicated.

   Reason: Too much alcohol is harmful to the drinker and can be deadly to the public if the person drives drunk.

Connecting with the Audience

In all the writing we have done this semester, we have seen the importance of knowing the reader. A clear sense of audience helps us decide what words to define; how much to explain; and what examples, comparisons, and other references the reader will best respond to. However, being aware of the audience is especially important in persuasive writing because now we are trying not only to present information clearly, but also to present it in a way that is credible and convincing.

Another consideration when connecting with readers is to understand enough about them to meet their needs for information and sense what is important to them. Being aware of three rhetorical appeals, **logos, pathos,** and **ethos,** will help you to connect with your audience.

Logos is the appeal to reason. That is, the writer is logical in presenting facts in an orderly manner. The writer focuses on using the text to appeal to the mind, to present reasons, evidence, and detailed explanations.

Pathos is the appeal to emotion. The writer considers heartfelt ways to influence the reader. The writer relies on the receptiveness of the reader to be open to emotional appeals.

The third appeal is **ethos,** the appeal to morals and values. The writer deliberately chooses words that will affect a reader's sense of right over wrong. In other words, our believability, or credibility, is part of our **persona** in writing, and it can be powerfully persuasive. A persona is the representation of deliberate aspects of a person's character to other people. For example, David Suzuki's persona, or ethos, is as a citizen and professional actively concerned about the sustainability of a healthy and resourceful planet. Think of your own persona in terms of how you want people to think of you, for example, as a good, fun, friendly, intelligent, fair, concerned person. Readers will pay more attention to your writing when they can respect and like you.

When writers, or speakers, succeed in presenting an issue, they achieve the following:

1. they develop the reasons and evidence clearly (logos);
2. they appeal to the reader's emotions (pathos); and
3. they establish and maintain their credibility (ethos).

In this way, writers who appeal to the three areas shown in the Communication Triangle below probably present their argument persuasively.

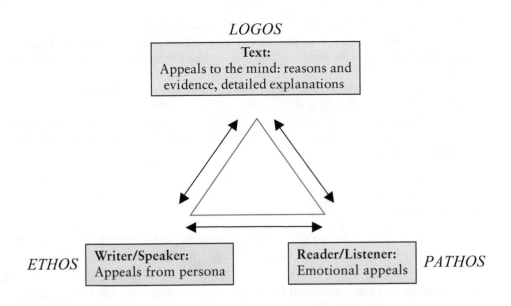

LOGOS

Text:
Appeals to the mind: reasons and
evidence, detailed explanations

ETHOS | **Writer/Speaker:**
Appeals from persona | **Reader/Listener:**
Emotional appeals | PATHOS

Which of the following attempts at persuasion do you think would most effectively connect with an audience of parents with children who watch too much TV?

1. I can't see any good reason for parents to let their kids watch all that junk on TV. If you ask me, these parents are just lazy. They don't want to play with their kids or help them with their homework, so the parents just park the kids in front of the idiot box. Why do you think they call it the idiot box, anyway? Because it turns kids who watch too much TV into idiots—duh. If you let your kids watch as much as the national average of six hours a day, you might as well save some money and take them out of school now because your kids aren't going anywhere—except maybe to a life of minimum-wage work. Go ahead, cave in; let your kids watch all the TV they want to. They'll love you for it . . . till they're older and they realize that you let them flush their lives down the TV toilet.

OR

2. What most disturbs me about excessive television for children is the negative effect it has on their learning. Of course, there is a lot of good programming—on TVOntario, the Discovery Channel, CBC, the History Channel, PBS, and so on—that exposes children to new ideas. But the truth is that most kids are more attracted to the action/role-playing programs than to a History Channel documentary on the life of Tecumseh. When children are unsupervised, they can easily spend four to six hours a day—the national average—watching junk, which leaves little time for homework or other learning activities, or for healthy physical activity. Schools practically beg parents to spend time with their children reading and helping with math and other course work. How can this happen when TV has captured the audience? And schoolwork is not all that teaches. Don't we, as parents, want to involve our children in other learning activities like music, dance, and sports?

—*Marisa Youmbi*

If you chose **example 2**, you can probably see that the writer shows herself as a reasonable, concerned *fellow* parent ("don't *we* as parents"). The author admits that TV can be good and softens, or **qualifies**, her statements, saying "most kids" rather than "all," "can spend" rather than "will," and "little time" rather than "no time." Being careful not to overstate the case—that is, qualifying statements where needed—is an important part of maintaining a reasonable persona. Writers can enhance their **ethical appeal** simply by using pronouns of accommodation (e.g., *we, us, our*).

Also, notice how the writer in example 1 seems to be attacking the audience, calling them "lazy" and telling them that their "kids aren't going anywhere." She uses the pronoun "you", criticizing the readers, thereby cutting herself off from her audience, unlike the writer in version 2, who wisely includes herself with the reader, saying "we."

ACTIVITY 31.3 Connecting with the Audience

On separate paper, revise the following paragraph to make it more persuasive. Refer to the preceding example paragraphs for reminders about how to soften the tone and build credibility (persona).

Issue + your position: Lindsay Lohan should take her rehabilitation seriously, finally leaving behind the drugs and alcohol.

Audience: Lindsay Lohan

Lindsay, let me say this in a way plain enough for you to understand: "You are crashing and burning!" What's with this boozing and drug thing? Here you have a great life—talent, fame, money—and all you can think about is throwing it away. You have ongoing DUIs; you skip probation appointments; and rehab programs are obviously not working for you. So what else can the judge do but give you more jail time? Don't you think that rules and laws apply to you—just like the rest of us? Look at all the people you're disappointing: fans, friends, family. Lindsay, your Disney days are over, so start acting like the adult you are. Save your career; save your life. Do your time in jail; keep your probation appointments; and co-operate with the rehab councillors. It's time to start taking your life seriously.

HINT

When rewriting this paragraph, show the audience that you understand her; use the pronouns *we, us,* and *our* where appropriate; and try to appeal to Lohan's emotions.

DUIs
Legal charges for driving under the influence of alcohol

Countering Opposition

Successful arguments give solid reasons plus support, but they go further: they meet objections to their reasons and overcome reasons given by those on the opposite side of the issue. For example, in this excerpt from the paragraph on too much TV, notice that the author anticipates a reason that some parents might give to justify letting their children watch a lot of TV—good programming:

Of course, there is a lot of good programming—on TVOntario, the Discovery Channel, CBC, the History Channel, PBS, and so on—that exposes children to new ideas.

Another approach to countering opposition is to take sides on an issue, create a pro/con list, and then argue your position in a moderated point/counterpoint exchange. Notice in the example below how, after giving the "opposition's" reason, the author overcomes, or counters, it by telling that most children prefer the fun, lightweight shows:

But the truth is that most kids are more attracted to the action/role-playing programs than to a History Channel documentary on the life of Tecumseh.

Writers often overcome opposing reasons by showing how the reason is incomplete, irrelevant, or illogical. Questioning the evidence that the opposition gives to support the opposing reason is another way of countering.

ACTIVITY 31.4 Countering Opposition

Read through the student model below, noticing the three major reasons in the underlined <u>subtopic sentences:</u> quality time, skills, and career. Write out or type the opposing reasons that the author includes under her final reason, being a housewife as a legitimate career. Now tell in a few sentences whether you think the author has overcome the opposing reasons. Do you think this argument would persuade its intended audience, women who "disapprove" of being a housewife as a career occupation for women? Why or why not?

Wanted: Housewives and Other Career Professionals

Today women have the right to be whoever they want to be, and this choice should include being a housewife without having to deal with disapproval from other women. <u>One advantage for a woman who maintains the home is that she can spend quality time with her children.</u> Most women I know in the workforce feel that they don't have enough time for their kids, and they feel a great deal of stress (and some guilt) over it. However, a stay-at-home mom can be there to help the toddler learn her ABCs, walk her 7-year-old home from school, and review those tough math problems with her middle-schooler. A child's youth flows by so quickly that if a parent isn't close by, she misses much of it. <u>Besides being there for the children, housewives also have to develop a complex skill set—one that any professional might envy—that includes the ability to multi-task, micromanage, and organize her home.</u> A typical day might require her to walk and feed the dog, clean house, wash clothes, drop off the dry cleaning, drop off the kids at practice, shop for groceries, make sure Melanie takes her allergy medicine, help Michael with his algebra, make dinner, wash the dishes, put the kids to bed, and make time for her husband. If a woman does not quickly learn how to organize her time, prioritize, and multi-task, she will not be a successful housewife, and her family will suffer. <u>The main reason women shouldn't feel pressured to avoid being a housewife is that this position is a legitimate career, a life work that deserves the best people and demands the highest level of commitment.</u> If a woman wants to pursue her dream of becoming a doctor, engineer, architect, or lawyer, terrific. Women are every bit men's equals and should have these opportunities. Also, women can and do manage to juggle a professional career and motherhood—but we know that the stress factor is high. The career of *housewife* demands as much hard work and self-sacrifice as any other profession, and the goal of the professional housewife is a worthy one: to raise healthy, happy, productive children and deepen the love and commitment with a spouse as the years pass. As women, in our ongoing efforts to achieve equality with men, we should move past our stereotyping of each other and give those who choose the profession of housewife the respect they deserve.

—Amy Myers

Learning from a Student Model: The Persuasive Essay

The following essay, which argues domestic violence is suffered by men as well as women, will help you understand how to write your persuasive essay. Read the model closely for organizational points (topic, subtopic, and concluding sentences and connectors) and development (detailed explanations and specific examples). Notice how student author Aaron Barash carefully explains his reasons to an audience that includes his classmates who are undecided on the issue. The author develops reasons for why men stay in abusive relationships. Why might this point be persuasive to his readers?

Domestic Violence: The Unheard Voice

1   Consider that domestic violence and abuse against men by women is virtually unheard of in today's society. However, "for every 100 domestic violence situations, approximately 40 cases involve violence by women against men" (www.dvmen.org). There are no absolute rules for understanding the emotional differences between men and women. What will hurt a man mentally and emotionally can be very different from what hurts a woman. Quite often, as a result of psychological abuse by a woman, a man feels like a failure but tends to stay in the relationship for his wife and children. I believe that men are more deeply affected by emotional abuse than physical abuse, and there is more domestic violence against men than is generally recognized in Canadian society.

2   It is a widely held assumption that women are the victims and men are the assailants. Stats Canada shows that "the 5-year trend for police-reported spousal abuse (including physical and sexual assaults) of reported female victims has decreased 8% from 1993 to 1997, while the number of male victims has increased 18%" (www.statcan.gc.ca). There are many reasons why people assume men are never victims. For one thing, women are more organized, supportive, and outspoken about the epidemic of abuse. Very little attention has been paid to the issue of domestic violence and abuse against men, especially because violence against women has been so obvious and was ignored for so long. This has occurred due to the fact that incidents of domestic violence and abuse against men appear to be so low that it is difficult to get reliable estimates. Even when men do report these incidents, most people are so astonished men could possibly be abused that men feel nobody will believe them.

3   While the definition of domestic violence and abuse is the same for women as it is for men, it is commonly thought that there is less violence when carried out on a man rather than on a woman. According to Ellis Cose, "The image of hordes of women wielding guns, knives, broomsticks or brass knuckles to terrorize their husbands is likely a fantasy" (*Newsweek*, November 12, 2008). While it is not likely that a woman would inflict the physical punishment a man would, women administer a very distinct type of abuse. Specifically, domestic

violence and abuse can also be mental or emotional. For some men, being called a coward, impotent, or a failure can have a different psychological impact than it would on a woman. So mental and emotional abuse can be an area where women are more brutal than men. I do acknowledge, however, that men are quicker to resort to physical abuse and they are more capable of physical assaults, sometimes even causing death.

4   Men stay in abusive and violent relationships for many different reasons. Primarily, men stay to protect their children. They are afraid to leave their children alone with an abusive woman. Also, men are afraid that if they leave, they will never be allowed to see their children again. In addition, the man is afraid the woman will tell his children he is a bad person or he doesn't love them. And many abused men believe it is their fault or feel they deserve the treatment they receive. That is, they feel responsible and have an unrealistic belief that they can and should do something to make things better. Lastly, the abused man may be mentally, emotionally, or financially dependent on the abuser. The idea of leaving the relationship causes feelings of anxiety or depression. However, ultimately, it is the man's dreaded feeling of failure towards his children that keeps him hanging on to the hope that one day everything will be better.

5   In conclusion, domestic violence and abuse of men is an inconceivable action for the majority of people. When stated, it has fallen on deaf ears for many years. However, domestic violence and abuse can have many faces. No longer does this epidemic need to be recognized as only physical. Mental and emotional abuse can be just as scarring, even though it is not seen because it is on the inside. So domestic violence and abuse affects both men and women, but ultimately, it is the children who suffer the greatest in this appalling calamity. When all is said and done, we need to consider children's thoughts, emotions, and dreams first, and ensure that they are raised in a loving, caring, and safe environment.

—Aaron Barash

THINKING ABOUT THE STUDENT MODEL

1. What two important points do we learn from the thesis statement? Where is the thesis statement located?

2. What three major reasons does the author give to support his position?

3. What additional point does the author make in his conclusion?

4. What opposing reasons or objections from his audience does the author anticipate and overcome?

5. What rhetorical appeals does the author use (consider logos, pathos, and ethos)? Are they effective? Why?

Learning from a Professional Model:
The Persuasive Essay

Drs. David Suzuki and Faisal Moola write with convincing concern about the role that forests play in the planet's ecological balance. A noticeable trait of Dr. Suzuki's writing style is the presentation of detail—including statistics and examples—to build a case that points to a clearly articulated thesis. In this article, as is characteristic of Dr. Suzuki's style, the thesis statement appears in the final paragraph. Which of the rhetorical appeals presented in the Communication Triangle on page 429—logos, pathos, or ethos—is most obviously at work in this essay?

Forests Are Another Piece of the Global Warming Puzzle

BY DAVID SUZUKI WITH
FAISAL MOOLA

1   We know that global warming is a reality and that we humans are its primary cause. And we know that carbon dioxide emissions, in large part from burning fossil fuels, are one of the biggest contributors to global warming. But we still have much to learn about the Earth's mechanisms when it comes to regulating emissions and warming. Forests are important parts of the equation, and a new report published in the journal *Nature* sheds a bit more light on their role.

2   We've known for a long time that forests are important carbon sinks. That is, they absorb carbon from the atmosphere, thus preventing it from contributing to global warming. But tropical forests absorb more carbon than we realized. Researchers from a number of institutions, including the University of Toronto, analyzed data from 79 intact forests in Africa from 1968–2007, along with similar data from 156 intact forests from 20 non-African countries. They concluded that tropical forests absorb about 4.8 billion tonnes of carbon a year—about 18 percent of the carbon dioxide added to the atmosphere each year by burning fossil fuels.

tonnes
metric tons

3   When trees are cut down, die, and decay naturally, or burn, some of the stored carbon is released back into the atmosphere. Even if carbon remains stored in the form of wood products taken from a logged forest, some is still released when soils in the forest floor are disturbed by logging. And many wood and pulp and paper products are discarded and destroyed in a much shorter time period than the life of an old-growth forest. This means that the carbon is released earlier than it would have been if the forests were left intact.

4   We humans have upset the balance of nature in more ways than we understand. Although the scientists haven't figured out why tropical trees are growing big enough to absorb more carbon than they release, one theory is that global warming and extra carbon in the atmosphere are actually fertilizing the trees. One thing we do know is that we cannot rely on tropical forests to prevent dangerous levels of climate change. But the amount of carbon they store gives us another compelling argument for protecting forests, as they may at least provide a buffer while we work on other solutions, such as reducing our energy consumption and switching to renewable sources of energy.

compelling
arousing strong interest
or admiration

5   Clearly, it's not the only reason to protect forests. Looking at the ability of forests to absorb carbon allows us to see that they have economic value beyond

providing resources such as lumber that we have traditionally considered. Forests are a source of medicine, food, and clean drinking water and are habitat for over half of all land-based plants and animals on the planet. Forests also provide spiritual, aesthetic, and recreational opportunities for millions of people.

6   Everything in nature is interconnected and our planet works to find equilibrium. So we can't confront the problems we have created on a piecemeal basis. We have to look at them together. And conserving the world's forests—which can include sustainable forestry practices—is one obvious place to start dealing with some of the most imminent crises.

piecemeal
done bit by bit

imminent
about to happen

THINKING ABOUT THE MODEL

1. Comment on the introduction: hook, development, and thesis.

2. An important part of writing an argument is defining the issues. What are the issues as outlined by Suzuki and Moola in this essay? Make a list.

3. Argument essays require issues to be supported by reasons. What is the supporting evidence for the issues in this essay? Add them to the list in #2, matching each reason with its issue.

4. Often economists see forests as only valuable for the lumber they produce. What other values do Suzuki and Moola place on forests?

5. Suzuki has been accused of alienating his audience by presenting hopeless situations and blaming the general public for causing them. But how do Suzuki and Moola connect with the audience in this essay? Provide examples of logos, pathos, and ethos.

Writing a Persuasive Essay

LO31.2

Audience and Purpose

Clearly, if writers want to persuade their readers, they should know those readers well. First, it is important to define words and explain ideas for the intended audience. For instance, in "Domestic Violence: The Unheard Voice" (page 432), Aaron Barash expects his readers to be familiar with terms like *assailants, inconceivable,* and *appalling.* Similarly, in "Wanted: Housewives and Other Career Professionals" (page 431), Amy Myers expects her audience to know words like *multi-task, micromanage,* and *stereotype.*

It is also vital to know the audience to anticipate their objections and identify which appeals might work with them. Aaron Barash assumes that his readers value freedom to end suffering, and the rights of children to be loved and cared for in a safe environment, so he appeals to these values. He also responds to objections to his position, such as that men are quicker to resort to physical abuse and they are more capable of physical assaults. Amy Myers reassures her readers that she, like the reader, believes women are equal to men, and that she is not advocating gender stereotyping.

Clarifying your position, explaining thoroughly, and dealing with objections, or opposing reasons, depend on identifying your audience; and all three of these elements will help you build a strong argument.

Your main purpose is to persuade, to change people's thinking and/or move them to action, although you will also communicate information and may entertain your reader while your argument unfolds.

HINT

For more on connecting with your audience, see page 432.

The Assignment

Write an essay of roughly 500 to 750 words that takes a position on an issue. By definition, an **issue** is a topic about which people may disagree, giving reasons for their differing positions and supporting those reasons with evidence (see Activity 31.2). When you try to persuade an audience to accept your position, you must also answer your audience's objections and overcome opposing reasons. You might consider an issue from family life, such as one of the following:

- Families should establish daily "talk time" when everyone discusses daily events.
- Parents should not allow TVs or computers in their children's bedrooms.
- Parents should use other methods besides spanking to discipline their children.
- Families should encourage their elderly family members to live with them instead of in assisted-living situations.

Alternative Assignments

Here are several more persuasive writing options that may be of interest. For any of these alternative assignments, be sure to do the following:

- In your thesis statement, define your issue and position clearly for a specific audience.
- Create a pro/con chart.
- Review the Communication Triangle (page 429).
- Begin each major point with a topic sentence.
- End with a conclusion that makes a point about your issue.
- Use transitions and other connectors.

Business in Context:

Persuade your boss that some part of your job should be changed: for example, how you clock in or leave, some regular clean-up chore or prep for the next shift, how you count out your cash drawer, or the number of customers you have to deal with. List several good reasons for the change, showing your boss how it will improve your performance and so make the business run more efficiently. Consider appealing to your boss's sense of fairness and reminding her or him what a dependable employee you have been. Be willing to compromise, perhaps accepting just a partial change of policy. Anticipate the boss's possible objections, such as that you are simply trying to avoid working hard and that the policy has been in place for years without problems, so why change it now? Other arguments that could be developed from the workplace include these:

- Your company should pay for your college education.
- Your company should allow job-sharing.
- Your company should offer on-site daycare.
- Your company should award merit pay.

Culture in Context:

Go to the *Rotten Tomatoes* website (www.rottentomatoes.com) and read reviews of a movie you saw recently in the theatre, on DVD, or on television. Do you agree or disagree with the general assessment? Include a particular reviewer's name (and newspaper affiliation) from the website, and quote or summarize three of the reviewer's main points. You may refer to more than one reviewer if you like. Write an essay persuading a specific type of audience, such as comedy fans or children, that they would or would not enjoy this film, backing your points up with specific examples from the reviews or your own ideas.

Education in Context:

Develop one of the thesis statements below. Convince the reader of your viewpoint by beginning each major point with a topic sentence. Remember to end with a conclusion that makes a point about your issue; and, as always, use transitions and other connectors.

- Colleges should make used (and therefore less-expensive) textbooks more available.
- Colleges should provide tutors for their athletes.
- Colleges should offer free daycare for students with children.
- Colleges should more strictly enforce attendance policies.

Health Care in Context:

Develop an argument based on one of the following thesis statements. Define your issue and position clearly for a specifically named audience. A useful way to begin your writing is to create a pro/con chart. Review the Communication Triangle on page 429 to consider approaches that would most effectively communicate with your audience.

- You should/shouldn't get a tattoo or piercing.
- You should/shouldn't have cosmetic surgery.
- You should lose/gain weight.
- You should greatly reduce your drinking/smoking/gambling/ drug-taking, or stop doing it completely.

Science in Context:

Write an argument that deals with an environmental issue like global climate change, air or water pollution, species extinction, or habitat destruction. One approach could be to address a small part of the larger issue. For instance, what are ways to cut energy consumption around the house, thereby reducing air pollution and greenhouse gas emissions? Outside the house, inefficient lawnmowers and weed whackers pump carbon into the atmosphere. Inside the home, we often overcool our living spaces in the summer and overheat them in the winter. Electrical devices of all kinds suck up more energy than is needed. Decide on a simple energy-saving measure, and promote it to a friend, family member, or business. For example, you might argue that it makes little sense to leave all the lights on in office buildings overnight (as in the accompanying picture, which shows Toronto's CN Tower and other buildings lit up at night, in contrast to the photo of the Toronto skyline cutting back power during Earth Hour). List reasons that would convince your audience to reduce energy consumption—and anticipate objections.

Technology in Context:

Choose one of the following issues and develop it with strong reasons for your view, being sure to introduce each reason with a topic sentence and develop it with specific examples and evidence. Remember to appeal to the audience through logos, pathos, and ethos. Be aware of the persona you would like to project.

- Our city should create more bike paths and lanes on streets for bicycles.
- The driving age should/should not be raised to 18.
- Our city should/should not provide more direct bus routes.

HINT

Remember, not all topics are issues. Issues are topics on which people can hold opposing viewpoints.

Discovering Ideas: Prewriting for Persuasive Essays

Choose an issue that you feel interested in and passionate about. Your issue does not need to have global consequence (climate change, the turmoil in the Middle East). In fact, some of the best short arguments come from daily life. For instance, maybe you need to persuade your roommate to begin cleaning up after herself. Maybe you deserve a raise and can prove it to your boss. Perhaps you need to end a relationship—gently. We have examples in our student models, which deal with an important Canadian issue, domestic violence, and a personal issue, respect for stay-at-home wives and mothers. Our professional model deals with the universal issue of climate change. If you choose a "larger" issue, be sure to focus it adequately.

After you have chosen an issue, create a pro/con chart listing reasons favouring and opposing your position on the issue. Below is an example of Aaron Barash's prewriting list based on his rough thesis statement: "Men are deeply affected by emotional abuse, and there is more domestic emotional abuse in Canada than is generally recognized":

REASONS FAVOURING MY POSITION	REASONS OPPOSING MY POSITION
Women more outspoken about abuse than men	Men quicker to resort to physical abuse than women
Abuse thought of as physical—but is also emotional	Physical violence against women ignored for so long
Number of male victims up 18%, 1993–97	People are astonished at the idea of men being abused
Men stay in abusive relationships to protect children	Men are stronger than women
Expense of leaving can bankrupt families	Society knows that women need to be protected

Aaron won't use all the reasons he has listed—just as you may not use all of yours—but now he has the material to build his outline and then develop his reasons with appeals, including evidence.

JOURNAL / BLOG ENTRY 31.2

Write a chart like Aaron's, modelled above, to explore reasons favouring and opposing your position. What reasons seem most convincing to you, and what opposing reasons or objections might you have to deal with? Tell in a sentence or two who might be interested in your argument. What words might you need to explain for them?

FEEDBACK *Exchange charts with a classmate and comment on the strength of your partner's reasons. Write in a paragraph which reason is most convincing and which reason is least convincing, and explain why you think so.*

Organizing Persuasive Essays

As you think through your argument, considering what opposing reasons are well known and what objections your audience might have to your reasons, you may cut a few ideas, as Aaron Barash did below:

REASONS FAVOURING MY POSITION	REASONS OPPOSING MY POSITION
Number of male victims up 18%, 1993-97	Men quicker to resort to physical abuse than women
Abuse thought of as physical—but is also emotional	Violence against women ignored for so long
Women more outspoken about abuse	People are astonished at the idea of men being abused
Men stay in abusive relationships to protect children	~~Men are stronger than women~~
~~Expense of leaving can bankrupt families~~	~~Society knows that women need to be protected~~

You can also see from the list above that Aaron rearranged his main reasons by **order of importance**, an effective method for arguments. Notice that he shifted *"number of male victims up 18%"* and *"women more outspoken about abuse than men,"* and he kept *"men stay in abusive relationships to protect children"* as his last, strongest point to better emphasize it.

When you write your thesis statement, which will state your issue and position, you might use words like *should, ought to,* or *must* to let your reader know that you are building an argument.

JOURNAL / BLOG ENTRY 31.3

Write out your working thesis statement, underlining the <u>issue</u> once and your <u>position</u> twice. Next, list your main reasons by importance. What evidence or other appeals (e.g., emotions and ethics) will you use to support your reasons? How do you plan to overcome opposing reasons or objections to your reasons?

Drafting Persuasive Essays

Moving into your first draft, keep the following points in mind:

1. Begin your essay with a focused thesis statement, and clarify your position as you write. For example, Aaron Barash recognizes the importance of acknowledging that domestic violence occurs among men as well as women.

2. Where appropriate, use pronouns like *we, us,* and *our* to help connect with the reader.

3. Avoid making statements that are too broad (e.g., using words such as *always, never, all, none*). Instead, **qualify** your claims with words like *often, many, most, some, few, usually, frequently, seldom, may, maybe,* and *perhaps.* Notice how Aaron qualifies his thesis by saying that there is more domestic violence against men than is *generally* recognized in Canadian society. He develops the statement in this way: "There are *many* reasons why people assume men are never victims." He then goes on to name these reasons.

4. Remember that ethical appeals, as well as emotional and logical appeals, can be powerful.

JOURNAL / BLOG ENTRY 31.4

After finishing your first draft, highlight each main reason with a marker or your computer's highlight function. Then underline each position statement. What parts of the draft do you like most and least—and why? Answer in a paragraph.

FEEDBACK *Exchange drafts with a classmate, and evaluate, in a paragraph, how well his or her essay works to persuade. What elements are most effective? What suggestions can you make?*

Revising Persuasive Essays

As you begin revising your persuasive first draft, you and your peer reviewer can use the following checklist as a guide:

HINT

For more detailed suggestions for revising all drafts, turn to Chapter 21.

PEER REVIEW CHECKLIST FOR REVISING PERSUASIVE ESSAYS

☐ Have you focused and clarified your issue?
Reviewer Comment: _____
_____

☐ Have you used topic sentences to introduce each main reason?
Reviewer Comment: _____
_____

☐ Have you given enough support to make your reasons convincing?
Reviewer Comment: _____
_____

☐ Have you used logical evidence and explained clearly, but also persuaded with ethical and emotional appeals?
Reviewer Comment: _____
_____

☐ Have you overcome major opposing reasons and objections to your position?

Reviewer Comment: _____

_____

☐ Does your conclusion both rename the issue and make a point?

Reviewer Comment: _____

_____

LINKING TO FUTURE EXPERIENCE

Persuasion in writing is one of the most important skills you will learn in college—and its value will only increase as you grow in your academic, personal, and professional lives. Like definition, persuasion is a culmination of other writing patterns: you can use various combinations of descriptions, stories, examples, cause-and-effect analyses, process analyses, classifications, comparisons, contrasts, and definitions to make your case.

In an English class, you might argue for a specific interpretation of a poem, using language or structure as evidence. In political science, you could try to persuade readers that a certain form of government is superior to another for particular reasons. And in almost any type of science class, you would use your own lab results and/or documented research to argue a conclusion about your hypothesis. Beyond the classroom, you might use persuasion for any of the following: keeping your landlord from raising the rent, ending an argument, solving a problem, starting a relationship, defending a friend's choices, or convincing others to share your opinion. In future writing courses, you'll learn even more about reading, developing, and revising sound arguments.

Chapter Summary

1. Persuasion means convincing someone to accept an idea or perform an action.

2. Argument is formal persuasion that tries to convince a target audience, using reasons supported by evidence and overcoming opposing reasons and audience objections.

3. Effective persuasion requires clearly defining an issue and position.

4. It is best to define any term with which your audience may be unfamiliar.

5. Arguments are developed not only by evidence and explanation, but also by emotional appeals and the appeal to ethics.

6. Our believability, an aspect of our writing persona, can be powerfully persuasive.

7. Arguments suffer when writers make too broad a claim. One solution to this problem is to qualify claims where needed.

8. Insulting or trying to intimidate an audience is a poor persuasive strategy.

9. Arguments are often arranged by order of importance.

10. Like all writing, persuasive essays are not complete until they have been revised and carefully edited.

Researching and Documenting

Writing a Research Essay

Writing research essays involves reaching beyond your own knowledge and tapping into the ideas of other people, especially experts in their fields. Just as you need an extension ladder to reach for an object beyond your own arm's length, searching for resources requires you to reach beyond your own knowledge base. Write a paragraph to reflect on when, in your life, you have had to go to sources for information beyond what you already know to solve a problem or find an answer.

What Are We Trying to Achieve and Why?

Writing a research essay is a common academic task, one with which most of us already have some experience. In fact, the research paper is simply an extension of what you have been doing as you worked through the assignments in this textbook: developing a focused idea with detailed examples and clear explanations. However, research requires you to go one step further. Instead of relying entirely on your own personal experience and general knowledge, now you will find out what other people have to say, and you will use their ideas to help explain your own.

Documenting a paper is necessary in order to avoid plagiarism. There is no distinction between whether a student plagiarized intentionally or unintentionally. Often, an inexperienced writer either fails to document words or ideas from his or her source or rewords a passage carelessly. In this chapter, you will learn the important process of how to find, select, use, and document information as you craft a well-developed, source-supported research essay.

LINKING TO PREVIOUS EXPERIENCE

What You Already Know about Writing Research Essays

Most of us have written essays that relied on sources outside our personal experience. For example, many high school students are assigned research essays, as well as short-answer or full essay exams that require them to present information—facts, statistics, names, dates, and so forth. In this textbook, you have already worked on focusing and developing ideas, the basis of all writing. Then you have brought together (synthesized) ideas—a task that research requires—as you combined various patterns of development in essays for different purposes (for example, illustration, cause/effect, definition, and so on).

Determining the Value of Doing Research

Analysis (breaking something into its parts) and **synthesis** (combining ideas) are basic to the ways we think. Without being able to *analyze*, say, a recipe for German chocolate cake to determine its ingredients, you wouldn't be able to *synthesize* the ingredients—put them together—to make a delicious dessert. When you analyze and synthesize the ideas you discover through research, you improve your critical thinking skills, which will help you succeed in and beyond college. Research has the added benefit of increasing your knowledge as you read and analyze the articles you use in your essays. Lastly, being able to cite respected authorities increases your credibility with readers and listeners.

LO32.1 Assessing the Assignment

A research essay assignment asks you to choose a topic and develop an essay that uses information you find in books, in magazines, in newspapers, and on the Internet to support your thesis. You rely on outside sources for most of the information in the research essay, but you may also include personal experience if it helps to develop your ideas. Your professor will tell you how many sources he or she wants you to use, but three to five relevant sources are often adequate for a short research essay. More than any other assignment this semester, the research essay requires careful planning and efficient use of your time.

Establishing Audience and Purpose

Limiting your audience will help you to focus your research. If your readers are knowledgeable, you do not need to explain terms and ideas that are basic to your topic, and you can focus on more specific detail. In other words, you can discuss more about less. For example, in researching the making of the *Lord of the Rings* movies for a group of J.R.R. Tolkien fans, you could assume that they know the story well, so you would not need to provide a plot overview and an in-depth description of the main characters. You might focus your essay on the director's most notable departures from the book, discussing why he did so and what the films may have gained or lost in the process. A less knowledgeable audience might not be able to follow or even be interested in a topic focused on the differences between the books and films. These readers might enjoy a broader discussion of the location, sets, and acting challenges.

Your purpose may be to entertain, persuade, or inform, but supporting your ideas with sources—introducing, rewording, and explaining them correctly and effectively—should be your top priority.

Selecting Appropriate Sources   L032.2

Questions to Ask When Evaluating Sources

1. Is the source **current** enough to be useful? For example, if you are reporting on computer processing speeds, an article from 2000 would not have current information, although it might still give useful background. However, if you were reflecting on the history of DNA, Watson and Crick's discovery, written about in 1953, would be relevant.

2. Is the source **clearly presented**? Do you understand the material well enough to use it in your paper?

3. Is the source **accurate**? Are any claims being made or are facts and statistics presented that seem wrong? If, for instance, you have found a web page that claims astronauts have never landed on the moon, you should suspect the author's credibility—and sanity.

4. Is the source **complete**? Is enough information given to answer questions that you and your audience might have about the topic?

5. Does the source have a **particular point of view**, or bias? Especially if your purpose is persuasive, the opinions and attitudes of your sources will influence how your readers view your work. For instance, if you are arguing to snowmobilers that snowmobiles should be banned from national parks, how likely are they to be convinced by information from a group on either side of the issue? Statistics from a more neutral organization or a government agency, however, might be more convincing.

6. Is the **author** well respected and **qualified** to write the book or article? The author's qualifications can be difficult to determine, but here are some ways to check them out: look for credentials such as M.D. or Ph.D.; check any bibliographic information about the author at the beginning of the book or article; and look for references to the author in other sources.

All Canadian college and university libraries have on-campus access to their own subscribed databases and journals. They are specialized according to fields of study and are accessible to registered students. They provide a wealth of information that is not public. Your librarians will provide helpful instructions for exploring these amazing sources for your research. Usually you require a specific identification number from the library reference desk. Most often, these databases and journals can be accessed from your institution's home page. Your librarian will show you the pathway.

LO32.3 Using Source Material in an Essay
Avoiding Plagiarism

A common problem in research writing is **plagiarism**—the theft of someone else's words or ideas. Sometimes people consciously represent another person's work as their own, deliberately plagiarizing. This is a serious academic offence that can result in a zero for an essay or for the entire course. But more often, inexperienced writers fail to document words or ideas from their sources or reword carelessly. Cut-and-paste is a very easy-to-use computer function. In fact, we all cut and paste almost without thinking about it as we rearrange our own writing. So why not just extend this to dropping someone else's words into a research essay? Doing so is theft of another person's ideas, and as such is dishonest—unless you provide proper documentation of your source. Consider the following example of accidental plagiarism:

ORIGINAL TEXT

Source: Oliver Morton, "Mars Revisited" *National Geographic* (January 2004).

> **Then in the 1970s this Mars too was killed. Orbiting spacecraft—first *Mariner 9* and then the two *Viking* missions—showed there was much more to the Martian surface than craters. *Mariner 9* saw volcanoes twice as tall as any on Earth. There were canyons as deep as the Earth's deepest ocean trenches. (Morton 14)**

ACCIDENTAL PLAGIARISM

> **In the 1970s this Mars too was destroyed. Orbiting spaceships, the first being *Mariner 9* and then two *Viking* ships, were able to show there was a lot more to the surface of Mars than craters. *Mariner 9* showed volcanoes two times as tall as any on Earth. Also, there were canyons as deep as the Earth's trenches (Morton 14).**

Even though the author of the plagiarized paragraph cited Morton, because the author included too many of the source words *in the same order* and *with the same sentence structures*, this paragraph is unacceptable. To avoid accidentally plagiarizing, keep these two suggestions in mind:

1. If you use *more than two or three* of the source's words in a row, use quotation marks.

2. Carefully read the passage you will cite, and then *look away from it* as you "translate" the information into your own words. It is difficult to avoid plagiarizing if you shift your eyes back and forth between your source's words and your own.

To eliminate plagiarism, use **paraphrasing** and **selective quoting** as shown in the example below:

PLAGIARISM ELIMINATED

> The author tells of the changing views scientists have had of Mars, including the shift "in the 1970s when this [image of] Mars too was killed." Whereas scientists had thought that the surface of Mars was largely riddled with craters and little more, they learned otherwise. Several space ventures, *Mariner 9* and *Viking*, discovered volcanoes higher than any on Earth and canyons to match those of our deepest ocean trenches (Morton 14).

Although it is critical to acknowledge your sources—their *ideas* as well as their exact words—some ideas and information are so widely known that they are considered to be everyone's property, or **common knowledge**. You do not need to cite the source of common knowledge. For example, most educated people know that there are seven continents, that Canada became a nation in 1867, that the Holocaust took place in World War II, and that the United States was attacked by terrorists on September 11, 2001.

ACTIVITY 32.1 Avoiding Plagiarism

Read the following original texts. The first one is taken once again from the article on Mars by Oliver Morton. Compare each original text with its plagiarized paraphrase, and then rewrite the paragraph, "translating" the original text, quoting selectively, and changing the word arrangement. Follow this process for each of the three examples.

EXAMPLE 1

Original Text

> Today Mars looks a lot more like a globe of ice than it ever has before. But it also looks like something shucking that ice away, something moving on, something undergoing change. Whatever else Mars turns out to be, it won't be a useless, changeless lump in the universe. (Morton 30)

Plagiarized Version

> Nowadays the planet Mars looks much more like a globe of ice than ever. Yet it also seems like something that is shucking that ice away, something moving along, a thing that is changing. The author says that Mars won't turn out to be a useless, unchanging lump in the universe (Morton 30).

Plagiarism Eliminated

_____

_____

_____

_____

EXAMPLE 2

Original Text

Source: John Langan and Sharon Winstanley, *College Writing Skills with Readings* (5th Canadian Edition), Toronto: McGraw-Hill Ryerson, 2008.

A summary delivers a condensed version of the content of some original work. As such, it is an efficient and useful way to present information and highly valuable in a time when the quantity of information available is expanding so quickly.

Plagiarized Version

A summary presents a shorter version of an original work. In this way, it is an efficient manner of presenting information and valued today when the large amount of information accessible is quickly increasing.

Plagiarism Eliminated

_____

_____

_____

_____

EXAMPLE 3

Original Text
Source: Chapter 31

Our believability, or credibility, is part of our persona in writing, and it can be powerfully persuasive. A persona is the representation of deliberate aspects of a person's character to other people. For example, David Suzuki's persona, or ethos, is as a citizen and professional actively concerned about the sustainability of a healthy and resourceful planet.

Plagiarized Version

Our persona in writing is our believability and this can influence people. A persona, or ethos, represents certain aspects of a person's character. For example, David Suzuki's persona is as someone who is concerned with sustaining the planet.

Plagiarism Eliminated

_____

_____

_____

_____

Paraphrasing and Summarizing Ideas Carefully

What you have been doing in the above exercise as you have found your *own* words to explain the author's ideas is paraphrasing. When you **paraphrase**, you change the author's actual words, but you keep most of the main ideas from your source. A paraphrase is about *the same length as* the original. However, when you **summarize**, you reword the commentary, but reduce it by keeping only the main ideas. Summaries are generally much *shorter* than either the original or the paraphrase.

Three problems commonly occur when writers summarize:

1. Misinterpretation of the source's ideas

2. Omission of an important idea or addition of an idea that should not be there

3. Use of too many of the author's words and a word arrangement that is too similar to the original

Now read how the following example compares the original text with a paraphrase that both misinterprets and leaves ideas out:

ORIGINAL TEXT

Martian ice is not a novelty in itself; for years geologists have expected to find it frozen into the soil at mid and high latitudes. The excitement comes from a growing suspicion that the ice doesn't just sit there but has a dynamic role to play.

MISINTERPRETING AND LEAVING IDEAS OUT

The author says that finding ice on Mars was not a surprise to geologists, who thought it would be <u>all over the place</u>, but now they are interested because <u>they are sure</u> the ice affects the planet's surface.

Notice that the original text says geologists thought the ice would be in a specific location, in the soil and at "mid and high latitudes." Also, the scientists are *suspecting* the dynamic function of ice; they are not "sure," as the distorted paraphrase claims. It is often difficult to report accurately what one of your sources intends, so it is important to read your material several times until you are sure you understand it.

Here is an attempt at an accurate summary of the original text above:

EFFECTIVE SUMMARY

For years, geologists have anticipated finding ice affecting the soil on Mars at the mid and high latitudes.

ACTIVITY 32.2	Summarizing Effectively

Read the original texts below. Then write an effective summary.

EXAMPLE 1

Original Text
Source: Debora Mackenzie, "Insight: Overfishing Is Creating a Jellyfish Plague," *New Scientist* (November 30, 2007).

Overfishing means we need more fish farms and it also boosts populations of jellyfish, which damage fish farms. As the growing human population needs more food, it exacerbates warming, and inedible jellyfish prosper. The final irony is that small plankton-eating fish, which compete most directly with jellyfish and whose decline aids them most, are also being overfished—largely to make fishmeal, the main food for fish farms.

Summary

_____

_____

_____

_____

EXAMPLE 2

Original Text
Source: David Suzuki, "Does Selling off our Resources Make us an Energy Superpower?," *Straight Goods News* (March 27, 2013).

Politicians who want to make significant change must focus primarily on re-election if they are to see their agendas come to fruition. That means they must respond to immediate economic demands while leaving longer-term problems like climate change and water issues on the back burner. Surely the enduring

consequences of today's actions or inactions must be a priority. We'll be living with the ramifications of the current crop of politicians' decisions and actions long after they've been relegated to history.

Summary

_____

_____

_____

_____

Quoting Sources Selectively and Accurately

One useful method for bringing ideas from sources into your essay is quotation. **Quoting** a source means using the author's exact words, placing those words within quotation marks and then acknowledging the author by name, either within the sentence or in parentheses at the end of the quotation. This information in parentheses is referred to as an **in-text citation** or a **parenthetical citation**. (See pages 453–454 for further guidelines on how to include these citations in your essay correctly.)

You should not use quotations merely to fill up space. Rather, you should include quotations when you have good reasons for doing so, as in the following circumstances:

- The author's wording is particularly memorable.
- The material is loaded with statistics, names, dates, and percentages and so is difficult to reword.
- The author of the quotation is significant to the audience.

One other point to remember as you quote a source is that you must do so accurately. You are bound by convention to reproduce each word, punctuation mark, and even error as it appears in your source. If you want to economize by cutting part of a quotation, indicate the missing words with **ellipsis points**—three spaced periods—as in the following example:

"Like much of Mars, the butterscotch plain is . . . pretty dull."

When you need to add a word or two to clarify a point within a quotation or make it fit grammatically within your sentence, use **square brackets [ ]**, as in the following example:

"Like much of Mars, the butterscotch [or yellow] plain is . . . pretty dull."

If you notice an error within a quotation, you can show readers that it is not your mistake by writing the word *sic* within brackets after the error, as in this example:

"Like much of Mars, the butterscotch plane [sic] is . . . pretty dull."

Integrating Quotations from Sources Smoothly

When you quote a source, be sure to include information in your lead-in sentence so that readers are not left to guess at the significance of the quotation. The following examples show how you might either leave readers confused by a quotation or help them understand your meaning by introducing and explaining the idea:

QUOTATION NOT INTRODUCED

Oliver Morton says, "It's dustier than the road to death, drier than Dorothy Parker's martinis, colder than the devil's kiss."

Sic is an editorial term that means "as written," and is "placed after a quoted word that appears odd or erroneous."
Source: Katherine Barber, et al., *Oxford Canadian Dictionary of Current English* (Don Mills: Oxford University Press, 2005).

The author, Oliver Morton, explains how hostile the environment is on Mars with these images: "It's dustier than the road to death, drier than Dorothy Parker's martinis, colder than the devil's kiss" (8).

Writers can vary the verbs they use to introduce quotations by using words such as the following:

VERBS TO INTRODUCE QUOTATIONS					
acknowledges	asserts	continues	explains	offers	reveals
adds	challenges	denies	gives	points out	says
admits	claims	discusses	maintains	presents	states
argues	comments	expands on	mentions	remarks	tells

If you want to use a quotation that is longer than *four* lines when reproduced in your essay, you should put it in **block quotation** form by indenting half an inch from the left margin, single-spacing between lines, and omitting quotation marks around the information. In MS Word, use the ruler to indent your block quotation. Here is an example:

The surface of this part of Mars is barren and arid:

> **It's dustier than the road to death, drier than Dorothy Parker's martinis, colder**
>
> **than the devil's kiss. Like much of Mars, the butterscotch plain is inhospitable,**
>
> **empty, ancient, and, when it comes down to it, pretty dull. But a few hundred**
>
> **metres to the south, over a shoal of low, uneven hummocks, the landscape**
>
> **changes. (Morton 8)**

Note that the author's last name and the page number in parentheses follow the quotation *after* the period rather than before. In contrast, in-text citations for a sentence within a paragraph come *before* the period. Because this long passage is indented, quotation marks are not required, even though the author's exact words are used, and it is a **direct quotation**.

Documenting Sources

LO32.4

Documentation Styles

Research documentation styles have been created by many scholarly organizations, foremost among them being the Modern Languages Association (MLA), the American Psychological Association (APA), the Chicago Manual of Style (CMS), and the College of Science Educators (CSE). Colleges and universities rely primarily on the first two style formats for research papers. If you are studying the humanities and literature, MLA format is preferred. If you are studying the applied and social sciences, APA format is most often required. Since this textbook is intended for use by students of these disciplines, only these two formats will be discussed.

Citing Sources within Your Essay

After choosing information to paraphrase, summarize, or quote, you must credit the author of the information within your essay. You do this to prompt readers to a **Works Cited** or **References** page at the end of your essay where you list all sources used in the essay. If the author of the information you are citing is well known to your audience, or has impressive credentials, you should state his or her name in the sentence that introduces the information, as in "Nelson Mandela once said, . . ." Or you may place the author's last name in parentheses near the source material in your paragraph, usually at the end of the sentence. It is important to cite summaries and paraphrases as well as direct quotations.

The following examples illustrate the MLA (Modern Language Association) format as well as the APA (American Psychological Association) format for in-text citations:

AUTHOR MENTIONED IN YOUR TEXT

When the author's name is mentioned within your sentence, leave the name out of the parenthetical citation:

MLA   **Professor Davis explains, "vampires have left a profound mark on literature" (125).**

APA   **Professor Davis explains, "vampires have left a profound mark on literature" (2003, p. 125).**

Note: APA format includes the year of publication and "p." or "pp." before the page number(s).

AUTHOR NOT NAMED IN YOUR TEXT

Include the name of the author in the parenthetical citation at the end of the sentence if you have not used the name in your own text:

MLA   **Some literary experts maintain that "vampires have left a profound mark on literature" (Davis 125).**

APA   **Some literary experts maintain that "vampires have left a profound mark on literature" (Davis, 2003, p. 125).**

MULTIPLE-AUTHOR SOURCE

Up to three authors, include the names of all the authors:

MLA   **"*The Lord of the Rings* trilogy is the cornerstone of current fantasy fiction" (Senter, Harris, and Hogan 66).**

For more than three authors, include the first author's last name and then use the Latin abbreviation *et al.,* meaning "and others":

To develop fluency in Spanish, you must learn to perform a wide variety of communicative language tasks (Samaniego et al. xi).

Up to five authors, include the names of all the authors:

APA   **Senter, Harris, and Hogan believe, "*The Lord of the Rings* trilogy is the cornerstone of current fantasy fiction" (2006, p. 66).**

Some critics feel that "*The Lord of the Rings* trilogy is the cornerstone of current fantasy fiction" (Senter, Harris, & Hogan, 2006, p. 66).

For more than five authors, include the first author's last name and then use the Latin abbreviation *et al.,* meaning "and others":

According to a study by Lehna et al., "Children with special needs are at a higher risk for the devastating effects caused by a burn injury" though little is known about how to treat this problem (2013, p. 1).

CORPORATE OR INSTITUTIONAL AUTHOR

A work may be attributed to an institution rather than a person:

> **The Nature Conservancy states, "The best way to protect the land is to involve the people who live there" (32).**

> **"The best way to protect the land is to involve the people who live there" (Nature Conservancy, 2008, p. 32).**

UNKNOWN AUTHOR

When the author of an article is unknown, use the whole title of an article if is it short, or the first significant words in the title, within quotation marks:

> **"The best way to protect the land is to involve the people who live there" ("Saving the Land" 32).**

> **"The best way to protect the land is to involve the people who live there" ("Saving the Land", 2009, p. 32).**

If the work you are using is a book, the shortened title should be italicized rather than in quotation marks.

AUTHOR OF SEVERAL WORKS

If you use more than one work by the same author, include the first significant words from the title of each source (not "An" or "The"), use quotation marks or italics as required, and include the author's last name:

> **The Japanese Samurai was akin to the medieval European knight (Halligan, "History" 77).**

> **The Japanese Samurai was akin to the medieval European knight (Halligan, "History," 2004, p. 77).**

DIFFERENT SOURCES GIVING THE SAME INFORMATION

Include both sources (or all), separated by a semicolon, and listing the authors alphabetically:

> **Celtic music has undergone a rebirth in recent years (Broomfield 21; Russell 9).**

> **Celtic music has undergone a rebirth in recent years (Broomfield, 2001, p. 21; Russell, 2004, p. 9).**

INDIRECT SOURCE

Shown below are the forms when using a quotation that your source has taken from someone else:

> **As Jay Antle has remarked, "Storm chasing is not for the faint hearted" (qtd. in Williams 321).**

Note: MLA format uses *qtd. in*, short for "quoted in." In this example, Williams has quoted Antle.

> **Jay Antle has remarked (as cited in Williams, 2006, p. 321), "Storm chasing is not for the faint hearted."**

Note: APA format uses the words *as cited in*, and includes information about the date of the secondary source within the sentence.

Refer back to any of the **Original Texts** for Activities 32.1 (page 448) or 32.2 (page 450). Now, quoting and paraphrasing from these texts, practise setting up the formats requested below. Use MLA or APA style. Wherever possible, include the author's last name(s), the year of publication, and the page number within your answer. Question 1 is done for you.

1. **Author quoted in your text (use direct quotation)**

    Debora Mackenzie says, "Overfishing means we need more fish farms and it also boosts populations of jellyfish, which damage fish farms" (2007).

2. **Author <u>not</u> quoted or mentioned in your text (use paraphrase)**

    _____

    _____

3. **Year of publication referred to in your text (use direct quotation or paraphrase)**

    _____

    _____

4. **Year of publication <u>not</u> referred to in your text (use paraphrase or direct quotation)**

    _____

    _____

GRAMMATICAL GUIDELINES FOR SOURCES CITED IN YOUR RESEARCH ESSAY: COMMAS, COLONS, AND QUOTATION MARKS

Commas

When using quotations, follow the conventions of standard comma placement. Commas are used after a descriptive verb (*replied, said, asked, answered, explained*) introducing a quotation:

Janine Eastwood replied, "We call parents when their children are hurt in the day-care playground."

Add **commas**, where needed, in the following sentences. More than one comma may be needed in each.

EXAMPLE: I said to my cousin, Laura, "Mario, not Victor, visited relatives in Purcell's Cove, Nova Scotia."

1. Graham said excitedly "Come and see the two ruby-throated humming-birds hovering at the feeder."

2. "John Henry" his mother called "the baseball game is starting on TV."

3. Peter Robison M.D. explains "There is an effective inexpensive cure for eczema and acne."

HINT

For a review of all comma rules, see Chapter 15.

4. On his TV show *Holmes on Homes* Mike Holmes explaining the effect of faulty bathtub installation replied "In the shower by the drain you can see the crack starting to develop."

5. The brochure published by Environment Canada states "Children with sensitive nervous systems may be harmed by pesticides found on grocery store produce."

Colons

Like the comma, the **colon** can be used to introduce quotations. It is considered a more formal form of punctuation and follows a complete sentence, which precedes the quotation.

Oscar Wilde spoke these words: "I never travel without my diary. One should always have something sensational to read."

ACTIVITY 32.5 Colons with Quotations

Add **colons**, where needed, in the following sentences.

EXAMPLE: Karen Blixen looked at her empty house before leaving Kenya and said this to Denys Finch-Hatton: "I like it better without the furniture."

1. Chef Riley explains one of the most frequent causes of food poisoning "Leaving unthawed meat in the refrigerator for more than two days will allow bacteria to develop."

2. Martin Luther King Jr's famous speech, "I Have a Dream," is known by these words to people throughout the world "I have a dream that my four little children will one day live in a nation where they will not be judged by the colour of their skin but by the content of their character."

3. In "A Healthy Drink? Try Plain Water," Temma Ehrenfeld makes this claim about expensive vitamin-enhanced bottled waters "There are better ways to relax, get refreshed and boost your immunity than by downing enhanced waters."

4. According to Perri Klass, ambition is a quality that she admires in her friends because of this self-knowledge "I am ambitious myself, and I would rather not feel apologetic about it."

5. In Al Gore's Nobel Prize acceptance speech in 2007, Gore said the following "The future is knocking at our door right now."

Quotation Marks

Quotation marks are used primarily to enclose spoken and written words, either as dialogue or as quotations from a text. We also use quotation marks to enclose the titles of short creative works (such as stories, essays, poems, newspaper and magazine articles, songs, and episodes on television). And occasionally, we use quotation marks to show that we question a word's intended meaning.

The MP declared that she would consider the legislation in a "timely" way, which we took to mean never.

Note the following primary uses of quotation marks:

Dialogue:	"Let's get the chair cushions into the shed," said Denise, "before the storm begins!"
Quotation from text:	In Volume 17, Number 5, of *Adbusters*, Frederick Soddy, the 1921 Nobel laureate in chemistry, is quoted: "We have to stop banks from creating money out of nothing."

Notice that the comma after *shed*, the exclamation mark after *begins*, and the period after *nothing* are placed **inside** the quotation marks; the comma following *Denise* in the middle of the dialogue sentence is placed **outside** the quotation marks.

ACTIVITY 32.6 Using Quotation Marks

Add **quotation marks**, where needed, in the following sentences. Refer to the above information when considering placement in relation to other punctuation marks.

EXAMPLE: **Don Tapscott writes on page 101 in his book *Grown Up Digital*: "Some studies suggest that the teen brain processes, operates, and functions differently than the adult one."**

1. In praise of this book, Eric Schmidt, CEO of Google, writes, Once again, Don Tapscott has captured a piece of the zeitgeist.

2. My phone is an extension of me, says Niki Tapscott. It's an extension of who I am.

3. Jordan Grafman, head of the cognitive neuroscience section at the National Institute of Neurological Disorders and Stroke (NINDS) says, If you're multitasking a lot as a kid, the likelihood is that your brain will develop around your adaptive behaviour.

4. Grafman continues by asking a crucial question: Does optimizing for multitasking result in better functioning—that is, creativity, inventiveness, productiveness?

5. University of Michigan psychologist David Meyer says, You can't think deeply about a subject, analyze it, or develop a creative idea if you're constantly distracted by an e-mail message, a new site, or a cell phone call.

Source: Don Tapscott, *Grown Up Digital* (Toronto: McGraw-Hill Ryerson, 2009).

Preparing a List of Resources

When you are gathering resources from which to glean knowledge so that you can write an informed paper, it is a good idea to organize your resources into a list as you work. Record the author, title, and publishing information for each resource you look at. This suggestion may appear to be working backwards, but it will actually keep your information organized and will save you time as you are developing your essay details. You will need this information to prepare your Works Cited or References page, which will appear at the end of your research paper.

PREPARING A WORKS CITED OR REFERENCES PAGE

To help readers locate sources used in an essay, writers following the MLA format will create a **Works Cited** page, and those using APA format will prepare a **References** page. Both lists are organized in alphabetical order according to an author's last name (or the title of the work if the author's name is not known) for all of the sources quoted, summarized, or paraphrased in the essay. Note that you do not include all sources you have looked at, just the ones you have actually used. The Works Cited or References list appears on a separate page after the conclusion of your essay. Follow these guidelines when creating your Works Cited or References page:

GUIDELINES FOR CREATING A WORKS CITED (MLA) OR REFERENCES (APA) PAGE

1. Centre the words "Works Cited" (for MLA) or "References" (for APA) at the top of the page. Use bold or italics rather than underlining.

2. Alphabetize the authors by last name.

3. Begin the first line at the left margin.

4. The second line of each entry is indented half an inch space. (This is called the hanging indentation style; use the ruler in MS Word to create the indent.)

5. Double-space all lines in and between the entries.

Comparing MLA and APA Style for Various Resource Categories

The following categories will help you build your Works Cited or References page.

MLA Note: For more information, consult the *MLA Handbook for Writers of Research Papers* (7th edition) or the MLA website at http://www.mla.org.

APA Note: For more information, consult the *Publications Manual of the American Psychological Association* (6th edition); or visit or the APA website at http://www.apa.org.

BOOKS

Book By One Author

Author's last name	Title (italicized)	City of publication	Publisher	Date	Medium of Publication	MLA

Langan, John. *Reading and Study Skills*. Toronto: McGraw-Hill, 2007. Print.

Initial only	Date	Title (italicized)	City of publication	Publisher	APA

Langan, J. (2007). *Reading and study skills*. Toronto: McGraw-Hill.

Note: Short forms of the publisher's name are used, so "Corporation" and "Inc." and "Company", for example, are omitted. In MLA, you will see "Cambridge UP" as a publisher; however, in APA format, "University" and "Press" are retained. In APA format, the date comes right after the author, in parentheses. Also, in the APA title, only the first letter of the title is capitalized (upper case), as well as proper names and the first word of a subtitle. MLA also requires the medium of publication: print, web, videocassette, etc.

WEBSITE

"Depression." *Mayo Clinic.com.* Mayo Clinic Health Information. 4 Jan. 1999. Web. 24 Jul. 2009.

Note: 4 Jan. 1999 = date website was created; 24 Jul. 2009 = date information was accessed online.

Mayo Clinic Health Information. (1999, January 4). *Depression.* Retrieved July 24, 2009, from http://pr.quick.SDV2001/02DWK/mayo/depression~risk.

ARTICLES IN ONLINE NEWSPAPERS, MAGAZINES, OR JOURNALS

Goode, Eleanor. "Patient Suicide Brings Therapists Lasting Pain." *The New York Times.* 16 Jan. 2001. Web. 24 Jul. 2009.

Beck, A. T., N. Epstein, G. Brown, and R. A. Steer. "An Inventory for Measuring Clinical Anxiety: Psychometric Properties." *Journal of Consulting and Clinical Psychology,* 56 (1988): 893–397. *Name of Database.* Web. Date of retrieval.

Goode, E. (2001, January 16). Patient suicide brings therapists lasting pain. *The New York Times.* Retrieved July 24, 2009, from http://www.nytimes.com/2001/01/16/health/16SUIC.html?pagewanted = all.

Beck, A. T., Epstein, N., Brown, G., & Steer, R. A. (1988). An inventory for measuring clinical anxiety: Psychometric properties. *Journal of Consulting and Clinical Psychology, 56,* 893–397. doi: 10.1037/0022-006X.56.6.893.

Note: If the article has no Digital Object Identifier (doi), include the URL.

DATABASE

"Crimes by Type of Offense." *Statistics Canada.* n.d. Web. 29 July 2010.

Statistics Canada. (n.d.) *Crimes by type of offense.* Retrieved January 22, 2010, from the CANSIM database: http://www.statcan.ca/english/Pgdb/State/Justice/legal02.htm.

> **HINT**
>
> If there isn't a date available for when a document was created, use n.d. for no date.

Sender	Subject		Medium of Pub.	Receiver	Date
|	|		|	|	|

NCTE Conventions. "Sessions on Assessment at the 2009 Convention." Email to Janet Finlay. 8 July 2009.

EMAIL

Emails are not included in the list of references; instead, parenthetically cite them in your main text: (J. Finlay, personal communication, July 8, 2009).

page. Both lists are organized in alphabetical order according to an author's last name (or the title of the work if the author's name is not known) for all of the sources quoted, summarized, or paraphrased in the essay. Note that you do not include all sources you have looked at, just the ones you have actually used. The Works Cited or References list appears on a separate page after the conclusion of your essay. Follow these guidelines when creating your Works Cited or References page:

GUIDELINES FOR CREATING A WORKS CITED (MLA) OR REFERENCES (APA) PAGE

1. Centre the words "Works Cited" (for MLA) or "References" (for APA) at the top of the page. Use bold or italics rather than underlining.

2. Alphabetize the authors by last name.

3. Begin the first line at the left margin.

4. The second line of each entry is indented half an inch space. (This is called the hanging indentation style; use the ruler in MS Word to create the indent.)

5. Double-space all lines in and between the entries.

Comparing MLA and APA Style for Various Resource Categories

The following categories will help you build your Works Cited or References page.

MLA Note: For more information, consult the *MLA Handbook for Writers of Research Papers* (7th edition) or the MLA website at http://www.mla.org.

APA Note: For more information, consult the *Publications Manual of the American Psychological Association* (6th edition); or visit or the APA website at http://www.apa.org.

BOOKS

Book By One Author

Author's last name	Title (italicized)	City of publication	Publisher	Date	Medium of Publication		MLA

Langan, John. *Reading and Study Skills.* Toronto: McGraw-Hill, 2007. Print.

Initial only	Date	Title (italicized)	City of publication	Publisher		APA

Langan, J. (2007). *Reading and study skills.* Toronto: McGraw-Hill.

Note: Short forms of the publisher's name are used, so "Corporation" and "Inc." and "Company", for example, are omitted. In MLA, you will see "Cambridge UP" as a publisher; however, in APA format, "University" and "Press" are retained. In APA format, the date comes right after the author, in parentheses. Also, in the APA title, only the first letter of the title is capitalized (upper case), as well as proper names and the first word of a subtitle. MLA also requires the medium of publication: print, web, videocassette, etc.

BOOK BY MULTIPLE AUTHORS

MLA Chappelle, Sean, Maria Cox, and Steven Fenton. *As the Last Rain Forest Falls.* New York: McGraw-Hill, 2003. Print.

> **Note:** For more than three authors, use the first author followed by *et al.*:

APA Plag, Ingo, et al. *Introduction to English Linguistics* (New York: Mouton de Gruyter, 2007). Chappelle, S., Cox, M., & Fenton, S. (2003). *As the last rain forest falls.* New York: McGraw-Hill.

> **Note:** APA requires that you list up to seven authors. For *more* than seven authors, use ellipsis to list the authors, in this way:

Rosler, A., Ulrich, C., Billino, J., Sterzer, P., Weidauer, S., Bernhardt, T., . . . Kleinschmidt, A.

MORE THAN ONE BOOK BY THE SAME AUTHOR

MLA Martin, Melanie. *Raising Children the Easy Way.* Fort Worth: Harcourt, 2001. Print.

- - -. *When Time-Out Is No Longer Enough.* Fort Worth: Harcourt, 2002. Print.

> **Note:** In MLA, three hyphens substitute for the author's name when it is repeated in Works Cited. Entries are alphabetized according to title.

APA Martin, M. (2001). *Raising children the easy way.* Fort Worth: Harcourt.

Martin, M. (2002). *When time-out is no longer enough.* Fort Worth: Harcourt.

> **Note:** In APA, use the author's name for all entries, which are listed by year so that the earliest comes first.

BOOK WITH AN EDITOR

MLA Bierhorst, John, ed. *The Sacred Path: Spells, Prayers and Power Songs of the American Indians.* New York: William Morrow, 1983. Print.

APA Bierhorst, J. (Ed.). (1983). *The sacred path: Spells, prayers and power songs of the American Indians.* New York: William Morrow.

WORK IN AN ANTHOLOGY

MLA Dinesen, Isak. "Sorrow-Acre." *The Norton Anthology of Short Fiction.* Ed. R.V. Cassill. New York: Norton, 1990. Print.

APA Dinesen, I. (1990). "Sorrow-Acre." In R.V. Cassill (Ed.), *The Norton anthology of short fiction.* New York: Norton.

ENCYCLOPEDIA ARTICLE

MLA Wyman, Donald. "Lavandula." *Wyman's Gardening Encyclopedia.* Toronto: Collier-Macmillan Canada, 1971. 616. Print.

APA Wyman, D. (1971). Lavandula. In *Wyman's gardening encyclopedia* (p. 616). Toronto: Collier-Macmillan Canada.

PERIODICALS

Magazine Article

MLA

Author's name	Title of article	Publication	Date	Page numbers	Medium of publication

Lamb, Bertrand. "Learning to Talk to Your Teen." *Parenting.* May 2004: 120–23. Print.

APA

Initial	Date	Title of article	Publication	Page numbers

Lamb, B. (2004, May). Learning to talk to your teen. *Parenting,* 120–23.

Note: The date is more specific for periodicals than for book references. Page numbers are included. The title of the article is in quotation marks with all major words capitalized for MLA, but there are no quotation marks and only lower case letters (except for the first word) for APA. Note that a colon precedes the page numbers for MLA, while a comma precedes the page numbers for APA.

MAGAZINE ARTICLE WITH DATE AS WELL AS VOLUME AND ISSUE NUMBER

Leung, Calvin. "Rebuild Your Wealth." *Canadian Business* 82.2 (Jan. 27–Feb. 16, 2009): 63–68. Print.

Leung, C. (2009, January 27–February 16). Rebuild your wealth. *Canadian Business, 82.2,* 63–68.

Note: 82 = volume number 2 = issue number 63–68 = page numbers.

It is acceptable to list only the year when volume and issue numbers are given (i.e., dates for specific weeks are optional).

JOURNAL ARTICLE WITH CONSECUTIVE PAGING OVER SEVERAL ISSUES

Sturbenz, Michael. "Alzheimer's: The Earliest Onset." *Journal of Applied Psychology* 64 (1999): 840–87. Print.

Note: 64 = volume number 840–87 = page numbers.

Sturbenz, M. (1999). Alzheimer's: The earliest onset. *Journal of Applied Psychology, 64,* 840–87.

NEWSPAPER ARTICLE

Yaffe, Barbara. "Aboriginal Policy Changes." *The Windsor Star* 8 Aug. 2009, A7. Print.

Yaffe, B. (2009, August 8). Aboriginal policy changes. *The Windsor Star,* p. A7.

Note: Unlike other periodicals, p. or pp. precedes page numbers for a newspaper reference in APA style. Single pages take *p.*, for example, *p. A7*; multiple pages take *pp.*, for example, *pp. A7, A9* or *pp. A7–A9*.

EDITORIAL

Coleman, Jay. "High-Speed Trains: Their Time Has Come." Editorial. *The Windsor Star* 8 Aug. 2009: A6. Print.

Coleman, J. (2009, August 8). High-speed trains: Their time has come [Editorial]. *The Windsor Star,* p. A6.

ELECTRONIC SOURCES

IMPORTANT NOTE ON THE USE OF URLs IN MLA

Source: "MLA Works Cited: Electronic Sources," *Purdue Online Writing Lab.* Web. 9 Sept 2010.
MLA no longer requires the use of URLs in MLA citations. Because Web addresses are not static (i.e., they change often) and because documents sometimes appear in multiple places on the Web (e.g., on multiple databases), . . .most readers can find electronic sources via title or author searches in Internet Search Engines.

[If your instructor still requires] the use of URLs, MLA suggests that the URL appear in angle brackets after the date of access. For example:
Gray, Henry. *Anatomy of the Human Body.* Philadelphia: Lea & Febiger, 1918; Bartleby.com, 2000. <www.bartleby.com/107/>.

WEBSITE

"Depression." *Mayo Clinic.com.* Mayo Clinic Health Information. 4 Jan. 1999. Web. 24 Jul. 2009.

Note: 4 Jan. 1999 = date website was created; 24 Jul. 2009 = date information was accessed online.

Mayo Clinic Health Information. (1999, January 4). *Depression.* Retrieved July 24, 2009, from http://pr.quick.SDV2001/02DWK/mayo/depression~risk.

ARTICLES IN ONLINE NEWSPAPERS, MAGAZINES, OR JOURNALS

Goode, Eleanor. "Patient Suicide Brings Therapists Lasting Pain." *The New York Times.* 16 Jan. 2001. Web. 24 Jul. 2009.

Beck, A. T., N. Epstein, G. Brown, and R. A. Steer. "An Inventory for Measuring Clinical Anxiety: Psychometric Properties." *Journal of Consulting and Clinical Psychology,* 56 (1988): 893–397. *Name of Database.* Web. Date of retrieval.

Goode, E. (2001, January 16). Patient suicide brings therapists lasting pain. *The New York Times.* Retrieved July 24, 2009, from http://www.nytimes.com/2001/01/16/health/16SUIC.html?pagewanted = all.

Beck, A. T., Epstein, N., Brown, G., & Steer, R. A. (1988). An inventory for measuring clinical anxiety: Psychometric properties. *Journal of Consulting and Clinical Psychology, 56,* 893–397. doi: 10.1037/0022-006X.56.6.893.

Note: If the article has no Digital Object Identifier (doi), include the URL.

HINT

If there isn't a date available for when a document was created, use n.d. for no date.

DATABASE

"Crimes by Type of Offense." *Statistics Canada.* n.d. Web. 29 July 2010.

Statistics Canada. (n.d.) *Crimes by type of offense.* Retrieved January 22, 2010, from the CANSIM database: http://www.statcan.ca/english/Pgdb/State/Justice/legal02.htm.

Sender	Subject		Medium of Pub.	Receiver	Date

NCTE Conventions. "Sessions on Assessment at the 2009 Convention." Email to Janet Finlay. 8 July 2009.

EMAIL

Emails are not included in the list of references; instead, parenthetically cite them in your main text: (J. Finlay, personal communication, July 8, 2009).

Interview

Williams, Janet. Personal interview. 4 Aug. 2010.

An interview is not considered recoverable data, so no reference to this is provided in the reference list. You may, however, cite the interview within the text as
a personal communication. For example:

(J. Williams, personal communication, August 4, 2010) OR

J. Williams (personal communication, August 4, 2010)

FILM OR VIDEO

The Lord of the Rings: The Two Towers. Dir. Peter Jackson. Perf. Elijah Wood, Ian
McKellen, and Viggo Mortensen. Wingnut Films, 2003. DVD.

Jackson, P. (Director). (2003). *The lord of the rings: The two towers* [Motion picture].
Wingnut Films.

TELEVISION PROGRAM

"Living Dinosaurs." Narr. Lance Gunderson. Dir. Maureen Fitzpatrick. The
Learning Channel. 7 Nov. 2004. Television.

Fitzpatrick, M. (Director). (November 7, 2004). *Living dinosaurs* [Television broad-
cast]. The Learning Channel.

MUSIC RECORDING

Groban, Josh. *Noel.* Atlantic Recording, 2008. CD.

Groban, J. (2008). *Noel* [CD]. Atlantic Recording.

ACTIVITY 32.7 WORKING TOGETHER: Constructing a Works Cited
or References list

With a partner or small group, organize the six resources below into a
Works Cited list (MLA) or References list (APA). Determine the category
into which each resource would fit using the models above as guidelines.
Choose the style you are most likely to use in your field of study (i.e., MLA
or APA).

1. The film *Million Dollar Baby* was produced by Warner Brothers Pictures,
   directed by Clint Eastwood and released 28 January 2005. The film starred
   Clint Eastwood, Hilary Swank, and Morgan Freeman.

2. Judith N. Martin and Thomas K. Nakayama wrote *Intercultural Communication in Contexts.* The latest publication was in 2007 by McGraw-Hill in
   New York.

3. Pauline Johnson wrote "As It Was in the Beginning" which appears on
   pages 6 to 16 in the anthology *Pens of Many Colours.* This book was edited
   by Eva C. Karpinski. It was published in 2002 by Thomson Nelson in Scar-
   borough, Ontario.

4. John Metcalf was not writing about Antarctic birds when he wrote
   "Thinking about Penguins" in Volume 74 of *CNQ: Canadian Notes &
   Queries,* which was published in Summer/Fall 2008. The article appears
   on pages 5–7.

5. If you were doing a research essay on North American trade relations, you might be interested in the article "Harper Blames Canada for Visa Furor," which was written by Steven Chase. It was published August 9, 2009, and found on the Internet on September 10, 2009, at the *Globe and Mail* website: http://www.theglobeandmail.com/news/politics/harper-blames-Canada-for-visa-furor/ar

6. If you are interested in teaching English, you might like to read an article called "Hybrid Courses and the Future of Writing Programs" in the March 2009 issue of the journal *College English*. This is Volume 71, Number 4, and the article is written by Catherine Gouge. The article appears on pages 338 to 362.

Student Model: MLA Style

The following student model is presented in an abridged form to illustrate in-text citations and a Works Cited list at the end of the essay. MLA style is required for documentation of a literature essay.

Mary Bowden

Professor Finlay

Communications 3130

9 May 2011

Bowden 1

Grandmother, What Big Lives You Have: Examining the Effects of Generational Relationships on Young Women as Revealed in "Little Red Riding Hood"

Three versions of the fairy tale "Little Red Riding Hood" convey different ideas about generational relationships between women. Through their interpretations of the story, authors Charles Perrault, Angela Carter, and Roald Dahl have altered the narrative discourse surrounding Little Red Riding Hood and her grandmother to depict this relationship. Charles Perrault focuses on a traditional relationship between women of different generations, which allows modern authors Angela Carter and Roald Dahl to develop relationships that intentionally change elements of Perrault's discourse in their newer versions of the tale. By transforming the role of Little Red's cloak and her reaction to the wolf's attack, Perrault, Dahl, and Carter offer different interpretations of the effect that generational relationships have on young women.

As suggested by the story's title, Little Red's riding hood is a significant symbol in the story. It represents the connection between Little Red and Grandmother, who, in turn, represent the younger and older generations of women. Perrault explains Little Red's name as a derivation from the "little red riding hood" that Grandmother "made for her" (51). The gift "suited the girl so extremely well that everyone called her Little Red Riding Hood" (Perrault 51). By beginning his narrative in this way, Perrault suggests that Little Red's character is defined by Grandmother. The physical attributes of the hood connect it to another garment: the mantle. A mantle represents the wearer's definition of life; to "take on someone's mantle" is to take on their ideologies (*King James Bible*, 2 Kings 2:13–14). Little Red, in taking the hood from Grandmother, is seen as taking on Grandmother's life values as her own. This translates as a generational relationship in which ideologies do not change from one generation to the next. Dahl assumes the reader's familiarity with the symbolism of the hood created by Perrault's work and uses that familiarity to transform the generational relationship. In contrast to Perrault, Dahl depicts Little Red rejecting the "silly hood" given to her by Grandmother, much like a generation of women which chooses to shrug off the mantle of the past (36). Little Red's name is altered to "Miss Riding Hood," a transformation that solidifies her abandonment of the past (Dahl 39). She wears, instead, the work of her own hands: a wolf-skin coat gained through an act of violence. In choosing to wear this garment, Little Red symbolizes young women who have created ideologies separate from those of the past. Carter takes a different approach with the defining quality of the cloak, focusing on the red hood as a representation of the prepubescent, virginal state and the passage into womanhood. By choosing a nameless protagonist, Carter defines her heroine by her state and transition. Unlike Perrault and Dahl, who depict Grandmother's action as the sole component of the hood's defining aspect, Carter cites two components. The first is Grandmother, who makes and gifts the cloak. With it she gives the burden of womanhood and the expectation her generation holds regarding virginity. The comparison of the garment to the "ominous if brilliant look of blood on snow" suggests the gravity and power connected to the loss of virginity (Carter 113). Furthermore, Carter denotes her protagonist as representing the second component, her virginal state: "She moves within the invisible pentacle of her own virginity" (113–114). Carter's Little Red is a young woman who is defined both by the expectations of the past and her conscious acceptance of those expectations. This definition is comparable to that of Perrault's Little Red. The effects of conscious and unconscious acceptance, displayed in the works of Carter and Perrault respectively, are determined by how the protagonists face the past's expectations.

The virginity symbolized by the cloak serves a purpose apart from defining Carter's protagonist. Present in all three narratives, it conveys the value that the younger generation puts on female-specific customs and expectations handed down by older women. Perrault transforms the hood's symbolism to represent virginity towards the end of his narrative, as Little Red "[takes] off her clothes and [gets] into bed" (52). Little Red removes her hood without any thought, naively believing Grandmother waits for her in the bed. The loss of her virginity in such a naïve manner suggests that Little Red's connection to the past has blinded her. Being a virgin is simply part of her, but this is never examined for its importance as an entity. She follows an ideology that she did not create or consciously accept and so does not recognize its value. By rejecting a connection with the past, Dahl's Little Red also rejects the past's expectations regarding virginity. She sees innocence as a weight of the past, similar to the burden that Carter's protagonist carries. Little Red compares her two garments, speaking through the voice of the narrator to depict one as a "silly hood upon her head" and herself describing the other as "my lovely furry wolf-skin coat" (Dahl 36, 38). Dahl's Little Red is relieved to abandon her innocence and leaves the reader to judge whether she has lost or gained as she begs the reader to "please note/My lovely furry wolfskin coat" (52). For Carter's protagonist, the dominant expectation handed down is abstinence. Carter depicts a girl who is unfamiliar with sexual experience, who "does not know how to shiver" (114). Later, however, she is awakened: "she shivered in spite of the scarlet shawl" (Carter 117). This suggests that the expectations connected to her hood are not totally binding or controlling; they do not prevent Little Red's sexual awakening. Instead, the past's expectation of abstinence communicates the importance of sexual awakening to the protagonist. She can appease the wolf and save her life by sacrificing the "immaculate flesh" of a virgin. By throwing her cloak into the fire, Little Red offers the wolf her virginity, burning up not only the fabric but also the expectation of abstinence that it represents. Both Dahl's and Carter's protagonists are liberated from the weight of innocence; Carter's protagonist allows innocence to serve its purpose before it is destroyed. Coupled with each protagonist's reaction to the wolf, these differences contrast the effects of blind abandonment versus conscious destruction of the past's expectations.

In each of the three narratives, Little Red's reaction to the wolf's attack is a direct result of her connection to Grandmother. This reflects how the generational relationship between women affects young women's reactions. Numerous meanings are associated with the wolf and can be used to draw conclusions regarding Little Red's reaction; one of the most prominent elements the wolf represents is a threat to life. Carter's protagonist initially reacts to her precarious situation with fear. She thinks of her knife, a symbol of violence, but "did not dare reach for it because his eyes were fixed upon her . . . full of . . . fire, diabolic phosphorescence" (Carter 117). Her knowledge of the wolf, supplied by the past, is what makes her hesitate and keeps her from engaging in violence. Carter inserts several paragraphs of thought between the protagonist's decision against reaching for her knife and her next action. She removes her shawl, simultaneously ending her fear. Her virginity is given up in full confidence of its effect; she laughs when the wolf suggests he will eat her. The protagonist abandons her past with an accurate understanding of the results connected with doing so; thus, she is able to think clearly and face her wolf without fear. She does not kill the wolf, but tames him instead. A bond between them is able to exist because the wisdom of the past not only enables her survival, but also enables her to avoid destroying what threatens her. This is not the case with Dahl's Little Red, who reacts to the wolf's attack with instinct and ignorance. Little Red first speaks to the wolf as one might expect, commenting on his physical features. She mentions his "lovely great big furry coat", the object by which she will redefine herself (Dahl 39). However, at the wolf's threat of eating her, Little Red shoots him point blank. Her reaction speaks of a woman who is defined by the trail of carnage she creates and who responds to threats with carnal instinct. Little Red's actions against the wolf result in her loss of sexual innocence. Unlike Carter's protagonist who also gives up her virginity, Dahl's Little Red reacts with violence as she has no knowledge to suggest that she should act otherwise. Her price for freedom is twice what Carter's protagonist pays; she is identified by the symbol of her bloody victory and by discarding her innocence. Unfortunately for Perrault's Little Red, the wisdom of the past cannot account for all the threats of the present. Little Red is rooted to her Grandmother, who is not able to equip her granddaughter to fully deal with wolves. Incapable of thinking beyond the past, Little Red does not recognize the wolf when she is staring right at him. She is the victim of the wolf's desires and her own ignorance. Carter and Dahl depict a young woman whose choice results in her fate; Perrault's protagonist does not recognize that she can make a choice.

Little Red Riding Hood's reaction to the wolf's attack is a result of her connection to the past, represented by the defining element of her name and her virginity, her hood. Authors Carter and Dahl transform the significance of this element from Perrault's original work to depict distinctly different generational relationships and their corresponding effects on the protagonist. Perrault suggests that a young woman who takes on the ideologies of the women of the past will not recognize the value of the elements that define her and will be unable to cope with the threats of the present. Dahl concludes that a young woman who breaks from the past will have no wisdom to prevent her from functioning based solely on carnal instincts. Finally, Carter's message is that young women who appreciate and respect the past, but are not defined by it, allow themselves to apply past knowledge to issues of the present. Together these works communicate how generational relationships affect young women's choices regarding violence, virginity, ideologies, and expectations.

Works Cited

Carter, Angela. "Company of Wolves." *Bloody Chamber*. Toronto: Penguin, 1981. Print.

Dahl, Roald. "Little Red Riding Hood and the Wolf." *Revolting Rhymes*. New York: Puffin, 1983. Print.

King James Bible. Gospel Communication. *BibleGateway.com*. Web. 4 Oct. 2008.

Perrault, Charles. "Little Red Riding Hood." *The Blue Fairy Book*. Ed. Andrew Lang. London: Longmans, 1889.
Web. 20 Sept. 2008.

Student Model: APA Style

The following student model by Marc Doucett is presented in an abridged form to illustrate in-text citations and a References list at the end of the essay. APA style is required for the majority of college disciplines. The first page of this model essay is labelled page 3 because APA style requires a title page (page 1) as well as an abstract (page 2) before the body of your essay. (There is a sample APA title page on page 270 of this text. See http://flash1r.apa.org/apastyle/basics *for more information.)*

ACUPUNCTURE   3

Acupuncture: Pros and Cons

In the ever-expanding realm of holistic medicine, acupuncture remains one of the most sought-after treatments for many ailments. Developed in China, and dating back more than two thousand years, acupuncture is described as a family of procedures involving the stimulation of anatomical locations on or in the skin by a variety of techniques (www.medterms.com). The use of acupuncture for pain management is its most academically validated and commonly utilized application. Acupuncturist Steven King states, "Several recent studies of large numbers of subjects indicate that acupuncture has beneficial effects for some of the most common pain conditions beyond those that are provided by standard treatments" (2008, p. 28). Although acupuncture has received validation for its applications in pain management, many of its other applied treatments are still being highly scrutinized. One such area is the use of acupuncture to treat drug addiction by causing a release of endorphins thought to aid in the detoxification process (Jordan, 2006, p. 311). The traditional Chinese practice of acupuncture embraces a holistic approach. The goal of acupuncture is not to simply alleviate symptoms of various afflictions, but to restore the delicate balance within the body, and in doing so, correct the root of the problem. In recent years, a new method of acupuncture has emerged in the United States that, as with the Chinese method, is also intended to restore a homeostatic balance to the patient. EFT (emotional freedom technique) was developed by Gary Craig who describes it as "an emotional version of acupuncture wherein we stimulate certain meridian points (acupuncture points) by tapping on them with our fingers" (World Center for EFT, n.d.). EFT is now garnering much attention from the scientific community due to the growing evidence of the technique's effectiveness in treating psychological impairments. The focus of this paper is to determine if acupuncture is an effective course of treatment for pain management, drug addiction, and the release of negative emotions (EFT).

When considering pain management over extended periods of time for common ailments, such as lower back pain, chronic headaches, and arthritis, to name a few, sufferers look to acupuncture for help with easing their discomfort. Doctors are now prescribing acupuncture as part of a patient's long-term pain management plan in an attempt to reduce dependency on pain-suppressing narcotics. Acupuncture received further validation in 2004 when the U.S. National Institutes of Health (NIH) issued a consensus statement saying, "There is sufficient evidence of acupuncture's value to expand its use to conventional medicine" (NIH, 2004). One of the subsequent research papers on daily headache sufferers concluded that, for the most part, patients receiving acupuncture in conjunction with traditional treatments found they suffered less from headaches (Coeytaux, Kaufman, & Kaptchuk, 2005, p. 1114).

Many attempts to prove or disprove the effectiveness of acupuncture in the rehabilitation of drug addicts have been made over the years. A thorough analysis of several research papers was conducted by Dr. James Jordan, who sums up in this way:

> Acupuncture treatment does not demonstrate the type of qualitative and quantitative research needed to validate its efficacy in the treatment of opiate-addicted (or cocaine-addicted) patients. An explanation of past reports on the positive, albeit limited, effects of acupuncture with addicted patients probably was due, in large part, to synergistic placebo effects (2006, p. 312).

Jordan continues to say that additional treatments, such as counselling and support groups that were not methodically controlled, probably contributed to the positive outcomes. I agree with Jordan's idea that there should be a more regimented set of clinical trials and that people should not underestimate "placebo in working towards humans' capacity for recovery" (2006, p. 313).

EFT, recently developed in the United States, is easily dismissed by skeptics as new-age hippie nonsense, yet the positive results garnered from the treatment of psychological distress seem difficult to refute. The emotional freedom technique of acupuncture stems from the idea that "all negative emotions are caused by an imbalance in the body's energy system" (World Center for EFT, n.d.). For example, when a memory is associated with a negative emotion, it is thought that the emotion is only indirectly related to that memory, and instead, the emotion is caused by an imbalance in the body's energy system (World Center for EFT, n.d.). EFT seeks to repair the energy imbalance, thus eliminating the negative emotional reaction to a remembered past event and offering an emotional freedom. In 2005, Dr. Jack Rowe published a paper on the effects of EFT on long-term psychological symptoms and found, "There was a statistically significant decrease in all measures of psychological distress . . ." (2005, p. 104). Therefore, there is evidence to suggest that addressing the energy imbalance can have significant physical benefits, which further validates the theories behind EFT.

In conclusion, many forms of acupuncture have been used to treat a wide variety of problems, ranging from emotional to physical, with varying degrees of success. The consistent goal of all acupuncture techniques is to restore the delicate balance of the body's energy system through stimulation of meridian points, but with the results of clinical trials being inconsistent, there are still more skeptics than believers. I hypothesize that, when using acupuncture for pain management or to treat addiction, the best results would be found by having the patients focus on the problems being treated. I speculate that a state of energy imbalance is not a consistent thing and is probably triggered by the mind. Consider that it's very uncommon for a person to suffer from a non-stop headache, or for an addict to constantly experience cravings, or likewise, a person to constantly experience anxiety related to a phobia. Therefore, if these conditions are indeed caused by an energy imbalance, it must not be a constant state. I think that if the state of energy imbalance can be induced during treatment, more positive results would be seen. Finally, there is a general consensus that more research is required for all methods of acupuncture in an attempt to gain conclusive results to prove or disprove its effectiveness in treating a variety of medical issues.

References

Coeytaux, R.R., Kaufman, J.S., & Kaptchuk, T.J. (2005). A randomized, controlled trial of acupuncture for chronic daily headache. *Headache, 45.9,* 1113–1123.

Jordan, J., Ph.D. (2006). Acupuncture treatment for opiate addiction: A systematic review. *Journal of Substance Abuse Treatment, 30,* 309–314.

King, S. (2008, October). Acupuncture: An update. (Pain management). *Psychiatric Times, 25.11,* 28.

Medterms.com (n.d.). *Medical terms.* Retrieved April 6, 2010, from http://www.medterms.com/script/main/art. asp?articlekey52132

National Institutes of Health (NIH). (2004). *Acupuncture for pain.* Retrieved April 6, 2010, from http://nccam.nih.gov/ health/acupuncture/acupuncture-for-pain.htm

Rowe, J., Dr. (2005). The effects of EFT on long-term psychological symptoms. *Counseling and Clinical Psychology Journal, 2.3,* 104.

World Center for EFT. (n.d.) *Newcomers' information.* Retrieved April 7, 2010, from http://www.emofree.com/ newcomer.htm#Newcomers

LINKING TO FUTURE EXPERIENCE

Learning how to list your resources effectively, according to the style requested by your professors, is a skill that will help you write a well-developed, source-supported essay. It is a skill that will also be helpful when you do research in your chosen field of work. This skill will help you to avoid plagiarism and when you document sources accurately, you are functioning as a scholar.

For more detailed information on research documentation formats, an excellent source is *Writing Intensive: Essentials for College Writers* by Elaine P. Maimon and Janice H. Peritz, published by McGraw-Hill in New York, 2009.

Chapter Summary

1. To avoid accidental plagiarizing, when you use more than two or three words in a row from a source, put them in quotation marks. Also, look away from your source when summarizing or paraphrasing.

2. Information that is common knowledge does not need to be cited.

3. Weave sources into your paper using carefully selected quotations, summaries, and paraphrases.

4. Introduce and explain all sources—especially quotations.

5. Use block quotations when the text would appear in your research essay as more than four lines.

6. When you cite authors within your essay using MLA format, either include the author's name in the introduction to the paraphrase, summary, or quotation, or place the author's last name along with the page number from the work within parentheses at the end of the cited passage. This is called an in-text citation.

7. When you cite authors within your essay using APA format, either include the author's name in the introduction to the paraphrase, summary, or quotation, or place the author's last name, date of publication, and "p." with the page number from the work within parentheses at the end of the cited passage. This is called an in-text citation.

8. Evaluate sources for currency, accuracy, completeness, objectivity, and credibility before you consider using them for your essay.

9. All sources used in a paper must be identified on a separate page at the end of a research essay. This page is called a Works Cited (MLA) or References (APA) page.

10. When creating a resource list, organize alphabetically by the author's last name.

11. For a resource list, use hanging indentation style and double space between lines for each entry.

Text and Essay Credits

pp. 18–19, "The Gift of Music" by Marc Doucett. Reprinted with permission by Marc Doucett.

p. 44, Activity 4.2 , based on www.niagarafrontier/maidmist.html

p. 46, Activity 4.4, based on "Fast Forward: 25 Trends That Will Change The Way You Do Business", at www.workforce.com/section/09/feature/23/45/53

p. 49, Activity 4.7, based on www.tripadvisor.com/ShowUserReviews-g155032-d649517-r34687721-Saute_Moutons_Lachine_Rapids_Jet_Boat_Tours-Montreal_Quebec.html (accessed Apr. 11, 2010).

p. 75, From "Crown to Continent" by Douglas H. Chadwick, *National Geographic*, Sept. 2007, p.66 Douglas H. Chadwick/National Geographic Image Collection. Reprinted with permission.

p. 85, Activity 6.5 "Martial Arts and the Mastery of Body, Mind, and Spirit." Reprinted with permission by Eric Chan.

p. 175, Activity 13.10, information based on http://www.cbc.ca/world/story/2010/06/17/bp-oil-executives-congress.html

p. 276, "Music File-sharing: Right or Wrong?" by Darren Taylor. Reprinted with permission by Darren Taylor.

p. 284, "Whiskey In The Jar," Words and Music by Philip Parris Lynott, Brian Michael Downey and Eric Bell. Copyright © 1975 PIPPIN-THE-FRIENDLY-RANGER MUSIC CO. LTD. Copyright renewed. All rights in the U.S. and Canada controlled and administered by UNIVERSAL-POLYGRAM INTERNATIONAL PUBLISHING, INC. All Rights Reserved. Used by Permission. Reprinted by permission of Hal Leonard Corporation.

p. 303, Excerpt from "Heaven and Earth in Jest" (pp. 7–8) from PILGRIM AT TINKER CREEK by ANNIE DILLARD. Copyright © 1974 by Annie Dillard. Reprinted by permission of HarperCollins Publishers.

p. 316, "We Are All Essentially Stardust" by Bredt Wells. Reprinted with permission by Bredt Wells.

p. 319, Abridged version of "Elegy in Stone" from *The Admen Move on Lhasa*. Copyright © Steven Heighton. Reproduced with permission from the author and House of Anansi Press.

p. 336, "Daily Shampoo? Sixty Years Ago They Would Have Thought we Were Nuts," by Ruth Bradley-St-Cyr. First published as "Dirty Hair Secrets", *The Ottawa Citizen*, Jan. 16, 2003, A7.

p. 351, "Does Selling off our Resources Make us an Energy Superpower?" by David Suzuki. http://www.davidsuzuki.org/blogs/science-matters/2013/03/does-selling-off-our-resources-make-us-an-energy-superpower/. With permission of the David Suzuki Foundation.

p. 366, Originally published in *Report/Newsmagazine* (BC Edition), March 2002, Vol. 29 Issue 5 by Ted Byfield. Reprinted with permission from Link Byfield.

p. 382, Excerpted from Holly Dressel, "Has Canada Got the Cure?," Health & Healing, *YES! Magazine*, August 4, 2006, http://www.yesmagazine.org/issues/health-care-for-all/has-canada-got-the-cure; adapted from Holly Dressel, "Medical Bills" and "The Queen Must Die" in *Who Killed the Queen: The Story of Community Hospital and How to Fix Public Health Care*. Montreal & Kingston: McGill-Queen's University Press, 2008, pp. 180–242 and 243–310.

p. 399, "A Healthy Drink? Try Plain Water" by Temma Ehrenfeld. Reprinted with permission by Temma Ehrenfeld.

p. 414, "Ambition" by Perri Klass, from *Self* Magazine, June 1990. © 1990 Perri Klass. Reprinted by permission of Elaine Markson Literary Agency.

p. 432, "Domestic Violence: The Unheard Voice" by Aaron Barash. Reprinted with permission by Aaron Barash

p. 434, "Forests Are Another Piece of the Global Warming Puzzle" by David Suzuki with Faisal Moola. http://www.davidsuzuki.org/blogs/science-matters/2009/03/forests-are-another-piece-of-the-global-warming-puzzle/. With permission of the David Suzuki Foundation.

p. 447, "Mars Revisited" by Oliver Morton, *National Geographic*, January 2004.

p. 448, Example 2, © 2008 McGraw-Hill Ryerson, *College Writing Skills with Readings* (Fifth Canadian Edition) by John Langan and Sharon Winstanley.

p. 450, Activity 32.2, "Insight: Overfishing is Creating a Jellyfish Plague" by Debora Mackenzie, *New Scientist Magazine*, November 30, 2007.

p. 463, "Grandmother, What Big Lives You Have: Examining the Effects of Generational Relationships on Young Women as Revealed in 'Little Red Riding Hood'" by Mary Bowden. Reprinted with permission by Mary Bowden.

p. 466, "Acupuncture: Pros and Cons" by Marc Doucett. Reprinted with permission by Marc Doucett.

Photo Credits

p. 2, © **Dynamic Graphics/JupiterImages**; **p. 13,** © **Brand X/JupiterImages**; **p. 30,** © Doug Berry/Corbis; **p. 42,** photo by Jake Lacey/© Arizona Daily Wildcat 2006; **p. 65,** © AP/Wide World Photos; **p. 78L,** © Burke/Triolo/Brand X Pictures/Jupiterimages; **p. 78R,** © Library of Congress Prints & Photographs Division [LC-USZ62-96850]; **p. 88,** © AP/Wide World Photos; **p. 104,** © Oliver Benn/Stone/Getty Images; **p. 117,** Monkey Business Images/Shutterstock; **p. 123,** Philip and Karen Smith/Taxi/Getty Images; **p. 135,** Design Pics/Darren Greenwood; **p. 148,** © Javier Pierini/Getty Images; **p. 160TL,** © The McGraw-Hill Companies, INC./Jacques Cornell photographer; **p. 160BL,** Nancy R. Cohen/Getty Images; **p. 160C,** © Royalty-Free/Corbis; **p. 160BR,** © Royalty-Free/Corbis; **p. 177,** Arthur S. Aubrey/Getty Images; **p. 184,** The Canadian Press/Frank Gunn; **p. 198,** © Brand X Pictures/PunchStock; **p. 208,** © **AP/Wide World Photos**; **p. 221L,** © **Lloyd Sutton/Masterfile Corporation**; **p. 221R,** © John Foster/Mastefile Corporation; **p. 231,** © **John Sciulli/WireImage/Getty Images**; **p. 242,** © P. Manner/zefa/Corbis; **p. 261,** © AP/Wide World Photos; **p. 274,** Adalberto Rios Szalay/Sexto Sol/Getty Images; **p. 294,** © Stockbyte/PunchStock; **p. 309,** Ryan McVay/Getty Images; **p. 315,** Comstock Images/JupiterImages; **p. 327,** Photolink/Getty Images; **p. 334,** © Brand X Pictures/PunchStock; **p. 339,** © **Digital Vision/PunchStock**; **p. 343L,** © **Big Cheese Photo/Punchstock**; **p. 343R,** © **Kennan Ward/Corbis**; **p. 345,** © **AP/Wide World Photos**; **p. 354,** © Sébastien Baussais; **p. 359,** © **Digital Vision/PunchStock**; **p. 360L,** Emma Lee/Life File/Getty Images; **p. 360R,** © Carl and Ann Purcell/Corbis; **p. 369,** © **Digital Vision/PunchStock**; **p. 374L,** © Royalty-Free/Corbis; **p. 374R,** © Brand X Pictures/PunchStock; **p. 376T,** U.S. Air Force photo by John Van Winkle; **p. 376B,** © Brand X Pictures/PunchStock; **p. 386L,** © Maura Kenneally Clark; **p. 386R** © Michael L. Spittel; **p. 291,** Rob Melnychuk/Getty Images; **p. 393,** © Yellow Dog Productions/Riser/Getty Images; **p. 406L,** Creatas/PictureQuest; **p. 406R,** © Jan Finlay-Clark; **p. 408,** © **Lee Brown/Alamy**; **p. 418,** © Royalty-Free/Corbis; **p. 423,** © Royalty-Free/Corbis; **p. 425,** © Bob Daemmrich/Stock Boston; **p. 438L,** Jeremy Woodhouse/Getty Images; **p. 438R,** David Cooper/Toronto Star/GetStock.com; **p. 444,** © **Royalty-Free/Corbis**.

Index

titles
capitalization, 204, 268
comma conventions for personal, 196
essay, 292
formatting, 260
page, 269
paragraph, 259-260
punctuation for, 304
"to be," 45, 53, 60
forms of, 34, 53
"to do," 45, 59
"to have," 45, 59
tone, 239, 260
choosing language for, 239-240
inappropriate, 260
topic(s)
development of, 378-379, 395
limiting, 244
topic sentence, 5, 244-247, 264, 276, 285, 286, 376-377
body paragraph, 243, 286
concluding sentence and, 257
essays and, 276, 286
focusing, 245
forecasting statement in, 244
organizing ideas, 16
paragraph, 17
revising, 247
strong, 244
sub-, 262, 264, 285, 291, 329, 331
writing, 244-247
"The Trail of Blood" (Burnett)
first draft of, 21
revised draft, 23-24
rough outline, 17
topic sentence, 16
transition(s), 253-255, 292, 315
for adding material, 254, 331
cause and effect, showing, 255, 362
common, 253-255
comparison/contrast with, 254, 380
concluding sentences, 257
describing within a process, 349
essay coherence using, 292
for giving examples and emphasis, 254, 331
linking steps in process explanation with, 349
paragraph coherence using, 253-255
paragraph to essay, 276-278
space/time, 253-254, 300, 315
subtopic sentence linked with, 331
summarizing/concluding with, 255
transition words, 6, 186, 257
"Tsunamis, the Killer Waves" (Aasim-Alhussani), 347
two-part verbs, 55-57, 62, 64
inseparable, 56
separable, 57
typographical errors, 25, 268

U

"Ukrainian Holidays" (Kobzar), 395-396
underlining, 206
understanding words in context, 9
unity, paragraph, 250-251
URLs, 459

V

vacations, activity level categories for, 395
variety, sentence, 222-230

beginnings, 228-229
length, 222
sentence type, 223-227
subordination for, 225
verb(s), 31, 33-37, 43-64
action, 31, 33, 42
active, 61
agreement between subject and, 66-77
base form of, 44, 46, 47, 50, 53, 55
being, 31, 34, 42
changing order of subjects and, 72-74
compound, 36-37
ESL concerns for, 59-62
forms of, 43-64
future perfect tense, 49, 63
future progressive tense, 52, 63
future tense, 44, 63
general, avoiding, 232
helping, 31, 34-35, 45-46, 63
identifying, 33-37
incomplete, 68-70
inseparable two-part, 57
introducing quotations with, 451
irregular, 47, 53-57, 59-60, 63
linking, 31, 34, 42
modal, 46, 60, 63
order of subjects and changing, 72-75
passive voice subjects and, 74
past perfect, 48, 63
past progressive tense, 51, 63
past tense, 44, 63
perfect tense, 47-49
phrasal, 56-57, 62, 64
plural, 76
present perfect tense, 47-48, 63
present progressive tense, 50-51, 63
present tense, 43, 63
problem, 55
progressive, 50-52
recognizing, 33-37
regular, 47
separable two-part, 56
series, 195
simple past tense, 44, 47, 51
simple present tense, 43
singular, 66, 76
stative, 61, 64
tense, 33, 43-64
two-part, 55-57, 62, 64
unnecessary separation from subject of, 195
word order for, 59
verb phrase, 31, 35-36, 45
word order, 59
verb tense sequences, 57-58
verbals, 33, 68-70, 83-84, 137
gerunds, 69, 83-84
incomplete verbs, 68-70
infinitives, 70, 84, 137
as nouns, 83-84
participles, 68
types, 68
vocabulary, writing, 14
voice
"I" or "they," 370
passive, 74
vowels, 210

W

"Wanted: Housewives And Other Career Professionals" (Myers), 431
warnings, 347
"A Way of Life" (Smith), 379

"We Are All Essentially Stardust" (Wells), 316-318
website, citing, 460
Wells, Bredt, 318
who/whom, 99-100
Wolfe, Michael, 302
word(s). See also cue words
action, 291
adverb clauses' beginning, 153
capitalization of, unnecessary, 204
choosing effective, 232-240
coordinating, 124-125, 136, 162-163, 193-194, 223
describing, 82
developing examples with, 333
eight kinds of, 157
empty, 235
general, avoiding, 233
intervening, 66-67
introductory single, 186
misspelled, frequently, 214-215
non-essential single, 190
pattern, 209
questioning intended meaning of, 202
revising choice of, 263
sound-alike, 215-219
specific, 232, 233, 244, 333
subordinating, 128, 136, 153, 174, 188, 194, 226-227
transition, 6, 186, 257
understanding in context, 9
word groups
essential, 225
final, dash for, 201
non-essential, 189-192
problems with introductory, 188
semicolon for separating, 199-200
word order, verbs in, 59
workspace, preparing, 6
Works Cited page, 456-457
"Worlds Apart" (Priest), 381
writer, reader helping, 3
writer's block, solutions for, 20
writing
concise, 234-238
essay, 14
link between reading and, 3
persona in, 428
throwaway, 20
writing process, 14-25. See also specific processes
beginning, 14
diagnostic writing assignments, 25
drafting step in, 20
editing step in, 24-25
organizing ideas in, 16-19
outline step in, 17-19
prewriting in, 16
project start in, 14-15
proofreading step in, 25
questions to ask when starting, 14-15
revising step in, 21-23
steps in, 15-25
writing project
defining, 15
developing interest in, 15
point of view in, 14-15
purpose of, 14
start of, 14-15
writing vocabulary, 14

Y

"y" endings, 212